MEMORIALS

OF

BARNSTAPLE

BEING AN ATTEMPT TO SUPPLY THE WANT OF

A HISTORY

OF THAT ANCIENT BOROUGH

By JOSEPH BESLY GRIBBLE

THE HISTORY OF A TOWN IS UNITED WITH THAT OF THE
KINGDOM TO WHICH IT BELONGS, AND WITH THAT OF THE AGES
THROUGH WHICH IT HAS STOOD.

Toulmin.

BARNSTAPLE

Originally published in two volumes
by the North Devon Journal Office
1830

This Edition (complete in one volume) 1994
by EDWARD GASKELL
The Lazarus Publishing Co.

i

£15-60

Published and Typeset by
EDWARD GASKELL
The Lazarus Publishing Co.
6 Grenville Street Bideford North Devon EX39 2EA
ISBN 1-898546-03-7

BARNSTAPLE

Print reproduced with the kind permission of Colin Atkins

JOSEPH BESLY GRIBBLE
July 25, 1790 — August 26, 1877

MARGARET JAMES GRIBBLE
September 24, 1793 — September 3, 1881

MARRIED — January 10, 1814

PUBLISHER'S NOTE

In presenting to the reader Joseph Besly Gribble's *Memorials of Barnstaple* I am obliged, in gratitude, to acknowledge the support of the following people :

Jennie Marshall, David Burt, Pauline Isaac, Victor Winstone, Peter Christie, William Dewhurst, and Norma Finn; the U.S.A. descendents of the author, and in particular Ann (Gribble) Barnett of Broken Bow — Texas, for their help in piecing together the life of Joseph Besly Gribble following his emigration. An especial thank you, of course, must go to all the generous subscribers who have made re-publication possible.

The 'mutations of fortune' experienced by our author during the four years he took in compiling this History have now proved to have been very real. That he was 'deprived of all he possessed save a good reputation' is perhaps reason alone to have embarked on this first revised edition of his proud and extensive *Memorials*.

Although the addition of an index was deemed very necessary, I have been careful to ensure that wherever possible original spellings & layout have been strictly adhered to. The only deliberate exceptions to this rule being the application of the author's own errata.

During the time taken to re-set and re-print this work, it became increasingly apparent that the author's love of his home town was only exceeded by his determination never to be led 'by fear, favour or affection', nor to 'deviate from impartiality' . The result has been one of the finest local histories of its type extant. That the subject was *'England's Oldest Borough '* is apt indeed, and makes for fascinating reading.

The portrait of Joseph Besly Gribble and his wife Margaret (kindly supplied by our friends in America; see page iii) on the occasion of their Golden Wedding Anniversary commemorated in Cleveland, Ohio is particularly gratifying in that it was accompanied by an article in the Cleveland Leader which among many glowing tributes, the genuinely happy couple were described as being highly esteemed members of the Plymouth Congregational and Erie Street Baptist churches and that they were "..... two venerable friends, who had walked together, arm in arm, with the fires of youthful affection constantly burning on their family altar, through the varied experiences of half a century, having been the parents of sixteen children...."

I trust with this in mind that the reader will settle back and enjoy every minute of Gribble's *Memorials of Barnstaple* – an account that stretches back over more than one thousand years.

Edward Gaskell

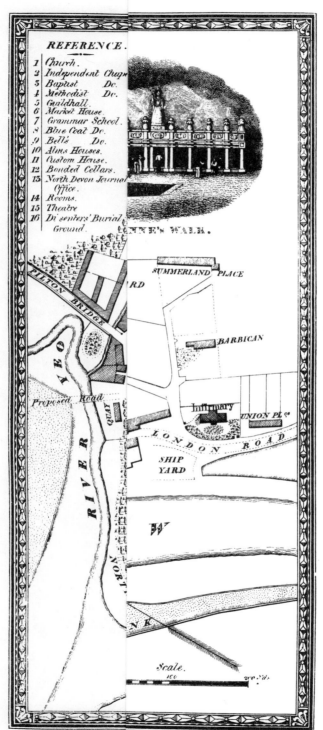

REFERENCE.

1	Church.
2	Independent Chapel.
3	Baptist Do.
4	Methodist Do.
5	Guildhall.
6	Market House.
7	Grammar School.
8	Blue Coat Do.
9	Bell's Do.
10	Alms Houses.
11	Custom House.
12	Bonded Cellars.
13	North Devon Journal Office.
14	Rooms.
15	Theatre
16	Dissenters' Burial Ground.

ANNE'S WALK.

PILTON BRIDGE

YEO

RD

SUMMERLAND PLACE

BARBICAN

Proposed Road

QUAY

Infirmary

UNION PLce

RIVER

LONDON ROAD

SHIP YARD

NORT

NK

Scale.
100   200 Yds.

R.Mortimer delt

ARMS OF HENRY EARL OF WILTSHIRE, K.G.

who died 1523

CARVED ON TWO BLOCKS OF FREESTONE, FOUND IN THE RACKFIELD MAY 1819
(see also page 24)

Subscribers to 1994 Edition

A

The Countess of Arran – Barnstaple
Ian Arnold – Bideford
Colin Atkins – Bideford
Suzanne Atkins – Bideford

B

Noel Beer – Essex (2 Copies)
John Bishop – Westward Ho!
John and Di Bolton (The Portobello Inn) – Bideford
Councillor Catherine Jean Branson – Barnstaple
Stephen Nicholas Braund – Bideford
Christopher, Isobel, Rachel & Catherine Braund – Bideford
Frederick John Brayley – Hadleigh, Essex
Thomas Sussex Brayley – Barnstaple
Rita Iverna Pyne Buckler-Drayton –Barnstaple
Mr. David Brown – Buckland Brewer
Bill & Norma Burns – Arlington, Texas, U.S.A
Edwin David Burt – Bideford

C

Peter Christie – Bideford
Charles Henry Cornish – Clevedon, Avon
James Coulter – Barnstaple
D.J. Cox – Bickington
Mr. Nicholas Crocker – Barnstaple
Miss Frances Mary Curry – Barnstaple

D

Devon County Library – 19 Copies
William Dewhurst – Bideford
Thomas W. Dymond – Barnstaple

E

Michael and Pamela Elliott – Raleigh, Bideford
Tom Evans – Barnstaple
John Davy Eveleigh – Croyde Manor

F

Syd Facey – Ilfracombe
Jill Farwell – Barnstaple
Alexandra Feltham – Barnstaple
Norma Finn – Bideford

G

David W. Gale – Northam
Edward Gaskell (publisher) – Bideford
Stephanie & Natalie Gaskell – Bideford
Glen Risdon Gribble Jr. – Norton, Ohio ,U.S.A.
Doris Grant Gribble – Piping Rock, Houston, Texas, U.S.A.
Madge Gribble Askonas – Winnetka, ILL. U.S.A.
Louise Gribble Maxfield – Carrollton, Texas,U.S.A.
Daisy Mary Gribble Orton – Nacogdoches, Texas, U.S.A.
Ann Taylor Gribble Barnett Broken Bow, Texas, U.S.A.

H

Dennis C. Hain – Barnstaple
A. W. Hawkins – Barnstaple
Mr Gordon R Heard – Frithelstock, Torrington
Mr Robert H. Hicks – Buckland Brewer
Richard and Adrienne Howard – Lee Nr. Ilfracombe
Jane Morrell Hudson – Forth Worth, Texas U.S.A.
Graham, Elizabeth and Sally Hunt – Bideford

I

Dr. Claire L. Isaac – Barnstaple
Mrs E.J.S. Isaac – Barnstaple
Pauline Isaac – Pilton, Barnstaple
William Isaac – Barnstaple

J

Caleb Jarvis, Poet – Bideford
Peter Jewell – Barnstaple

K

Glenda Diana Kirby – Burrington
Robert E King V.R.D. M.D. B.Sc. (Mayor 1956-57) — Instow
Peter and Jan Knight – 'La Gallerie' Combe Martin
Judith Sweeney Kulkarni – Houston Texas U.S.A.

L

Dr. Garland Lang – Midland,Texas,U.S.A.
Peter Laurence – Bideford
J.A.H. Luard – Goodleigh, Barnstaple

M

Jennie & Jemma Marshall – Bideford
Antony James Mullen BSc (Hons) GIBIOL – Bideford

N

Hilda D. Neild – Blackburn
The Nicholas Nickleby Bookshop – Bideford

P

Ruby Gray Peters – Arlington, Texas, U.S.A.
Edward Michael Peters – Arlington, Texas, U.S.A.

R

William H. Redfern – Auckland, New Zealand
Mrs. Ruth M. Regester, LL.B. – Croyde

S

Geoffrey Stuart Shaw – South Molton
Alan W. Slee, F.C.A. – Landkey
Major G. H. T. Sleeman – Bideford
Mrs. H.B.R. Sparks – Chumleigh
Mr. and Mrs. J. M. W. Steer-Fowler – Brynsworthy
Ronald John Stone – Barnstaple

T

Mark J. Taylor B.Sc.(Hon.) – London
Mr. T. W. Thorne – Barnstaple
Bob & Lesley Tulloch – Sukamachi, Tokyo, Japan

W

Dr. Barbara H. Warren – Tucson Arizona, U.S.A.
Stephen Whitehill and Sandra Jane Hadcroft – Bideford
Victor Winstone – Bideford

GAY'S MONUMENT

SUBSCRIBERS.

His Grace the DUKE OF BEDFORD.

The Right Hon. EARL FORTESCUE, Lord Lieutenant of the County of Devon, and High Steward of Barnstaple.

The Right Hon. LORD VISCOUNT EBRINGTON, M. P.

The Right Hon. LORD CLINTON.

The Honorable GEORGE FORTESCUE.

The Honorable and Reverend JOHN FORTESCUE.

Sir BOURCHIER PALK WREY, Bart. High Sheriff of the County of Devon, 4 copies.

Sir GEORGE WARWICK BAMPFYLDE, Bart. Colonel Commandant of the North Devon Regiment of Militia.

Sir THOMAS DYKE ACLAND, Bart. M. P.

STEPHEN LYNE STEPHENS, Esq. M. P. for Barnstaple, 2 copies.

GEORGE TUDOR, Esq. M. P. for Barnstaple, 2 copies.

Acland, T. P. Esq. *Barnstaple.*

Adderly, Mrs. *Bideford.*

Alexander, Henry Esq. late M. P. for Barnstaple, 5 copies.

Arnold, Mr. Robert *Barnstaple.*

Arter, Mr. William ,,

Aveline, Rev. George

Avery, Mr. William *Barnstaple.*

Baker, Mrs. ,,

Baker, Mr. William ,,

Baker, Mr. Frances ,,

Baker, Mr. John *Barnstaple.*

Baker, Mr. John ,,

Barry, Mr. John ,,

Bayley, John Esq. F.R.S., F.S.A., M.R.I.A., His Majesty's Record Office, Tower.

Bencraft, S. Esq. *Barnstaple.*

Berry, Francis, Esq. ,,

Berry, Mr. William *Guernsey.*

Besly, Rev. H. *Ilfracombe.*

Besley, Mr. John *Barnstaple.*

Blakemore, Mr. J. *Birmingham.*
Blackwell, Mr. *Stonehouse.*
Bowen, Mr. John *Barnstaple.*
Bremridge, Philip Esq. *Rusthall.*
Bremridge, R. Esq. *Barnstaple.*
Bremridge, S. Esq. „
Bremridge, Mr. James *London.*
Britton, S. G. M.D. *Newport.*
Bryan, Rev. J. *Barnstaple.*
Brooke, Mr. William *Exeter.*
Brown, Miss *Pilton.*
Buck, Rev. Joseph *Wiveliscombe.*
Budd, Robert Esq. *Barnstaple.*
Burnard, T. Esq. *Bideford.*
Burlton, Mr. *Bristol.*
Carter, C. Esq. *Barnstaple.*
Cartwright, Mr. *Tawstock.*
Chalacombe, Miss *Barnstaple.*
Chappell, Mr. Roger *London.*
Chichester, Miss *Barnstaple.*
Chichester, John Palmer Bruce Esq. High Sheriff of Cardiganshire *Arlington Court.*
Chichester, Robert Esq. *Hall.*
Clarke, Miss *Chudleigh.*
Clay, Mrs. *Barnstaple.*
Colmer, Mr. George *Bideford.*
Coles, Mr. John *London.*
Cornish, Mr. T. *Barnstaple.*
Corrick, Mr. *Bristol.*
Cotton, Mr. John *Barnstaple.*
Cotton, Mr. Gilbert „
Cotton, Mr. William „
Cotton, Mr. Samuel „
Cross, Mrs. *Bristol.*
Culliford, Mrs. *Barnstaple.*
Curtis, Mr. W. „

Cutcliffe, C. Esq. *Barnstaple.*
Davidson, Geo. Esq. *Axminster.*
Davie, Rev. Charles *Heanton.*
Davie, Mr. Edward *Newport.*
Davis, Mr. William *Barnstaple.*
Deane, J. W. Esq. *London.*
Dennis, J. Esq. jun. *Appledore.*
Dennis, Mr. James *Barnstaple.*
Dicker, Mrs. „
Drake, Z. H. Esq. *Springfield.*
Drake, Robert Esq. *Newport.*
Drake, Miss *Barnstaple.*
Eastman, James Esq. *Tordown.*
Evans, Mr. Joseph *Barnstaple.*
Furser, Mrs. *Pilton*
Finch, Mr. Henry *Barnstaple.*
Gamble, Rev. Henry *Newport.*
Gardiner, Rev. H. W. „
Gibbs, Mr. Henry *Barnstaple.*
Gillard, Mr. Humphry „
Glass, Nicholas Esq. Comptroller of Customs.
Glass, Mrs. N. G. *London,* 2 copies.
Glass, Mr. John „
Glass, Mr. Thomas „
Goman, Mr. William *Pilton.*
Grace, R. W. Esq. *Barnstaple.*
Gregory, Mr. R. jun. „
Gribble, John Esq. „
Gribble, C. B. Esq. late.
Gribble, Thomas Esq. *London,* 4 copies.
Gribble, W. Esq. *Barnstaple.*
Gribble, Mr. H. I. „
Gribble, Rev. C. *Topsham.*
Gribble, Mrs. E. *Keswell.*

Gribble, Mr. R. *Bank of England.*

Halls, Mr. T. *Barnstaple.*

Hamlyn, Robert Esq. *Bideford.*

Hammett, James Esq. *Bath.*

Hancock, Mr. J. *Barnstaple.*

Harding, Thomas Esq. late.

Harding, T. W. Esq. *Upcott.*

Harding, Mr. John *Barnstaple.*

Harding, Mr. Philip „

Harding, Robert Esq. „

Harris, Mr. George „

Harris, Mr. Michael „

Harris, Mr. John „

Hawes, Mrs. *Wimborne.*

Hawkins, K. H. Esq. *Torrington,* 2 copies.

Heddon, Miss *Barnstaple.*

Heal, Mr. W. *London.*

Hodgson, F. Esq. late M. P. for Barnstaple, 5 copies.

Hogg, Thomas Esq. *Appledore,* 2 copies.

Honeychurch, Mr. T. *London.*

Hooper, Mr. John „

Hooper, Mr. Joseph „

Hopkins, Mrs. *Barnstaple.*

Huish, Mr. *Landkey.*

Hunt, Mr. J. W. *Barnstaple.*

Huxtable, Mr. A. „

Incledon, R. N. Esq. Recorder of Barnstaple.

Instan, Charles Esq. Collector of Excise.

Johnson, Mr. G. *Barnstaple.*

Jones, Rev. J. P. *North Bovey.*

Kent, Rev. B. *Barnstaple.*

Kingson, Mr. William *London.*

Law, John Esq. *Barnstaple.*

Law, William Esq. „

Lean, John Esq. *Wiveliscombe.*

Leigh, Mr. Charles *Barnstaple.*

Lewis, Mr. Thomas „

Linnington, Mr. S. „

Lowe, Mrs. „

Lovering, Mr. W. „

Luxmoore, Rev. H. M.A. „

Mackrell, Mr. John „

Marsh, James Esq. „

Marshall, John Esq. „

Marshall, Miss „

May, John Esq. „

May, Mr. John *Croyde.*

Metherell, R. Esq. *Barnstaple.*

Miller, John Esq. „

Morgan, J. G. M. D.

Mortimer, Mrs. *Newport*

Moule, Mr. John *Barnstaple.*

Nicholets, J. Esq. *S. Petherton.*

Nicholls, Mr. *London.*

Nicholls, Wm. and Co. Messrs. *Barnstaple.*

Northcote, Mr. G. „

Owen, Thomas Esq. „

Parminter, Mr. J. B. „

Parminter, Miss *A la ronde.*

Partridge, John Esq. *Woodtown.*

Passmore, Mr. *Braunton.*

Patch. —— Esq. *Launceston.*

Pawle, Mr. John *London.*

Prance, W. Esq. *Plymouth.*

Pyke, John Esq. *Barnstaple.*

Pugsley, Mr. T. *Newton Tracey.*

Randall, Mr. J. *Barnstaple,* 2 copies.

Reed, Mr. *London.*
Reed, Charles Esq. *Bristol.*
Rennels, Mr. W. *Barnstaple.*
Rice, Mr. Robert ,,
Richardson, Capt. *Newport.*
Roberts, John Esq. late.
Roberts, Rev. J. R. A. M. Rector
  of *Rotherfield Grays, Oxford.*
Roberts, E. R. Esq. Collector of
  Customs.
Roberts, C. Esq. *Barnstaple.*
Rock, Mr. J. *Birmingham.*
Rodd, Mr. H. *Barnstaple.*
Rook, Mrs. ,,
Rook, Lewis Esq. *Newport.*
Rooker, Rev. Samuel *Bideford.*
Saunders, Mr. E. L. *Barnstaple.*
Searle, Mr. ,,
Shapcott, Mr. A. ,,
Sharland, Miss ,,
Skinner, Mr. *London.*
Snow, Mr. W. *Barnstaple.*
Spurway, Rev. W. ,,
Stribling, Mr. W. ,,
Strong, Mr. W. Bookseller,
  Exeter and Bristol.
Symonds, Mr. Henry *Barnstaple.*
Tamlyn, John Esq. *London.*
Taprell, Mrs. *Bristol.*
Thorne, Richard Esq. *Pilton.*
Thorne, George Esq. *Bristol.*
Thorne, Thomas Esq. ,,

Thorne, John Esq. *Newport.*
Thorne, Mr. W. *Barnstaple,*
  2 copies.
Thorne, Mr. W. H. ,,
Thorne, Mr. John ,,
Thorne, Mr. *Landkey.*
Toller, Richard Esq. late.
Toller, W. Esq. *Barnstaple.*
Trix, Mr. James ,,
Tucker, Mr. E. ,,
Turner, Mr. Joshua ,,
Turner, Mr. William ,,
Vellacott, Mr. *Georgeham.*
Vicary, —— Esq. *Torrington.*
Wavel, William M. D. late.
Webber, General *Buckland.*
Westbrook, R. Esq. *Barnstaple.*
Whitchurch, Mr. S. *Devizes.*
Whitchurch, Mr. C. *Bristol.*
Whitchurch, Mr. T. *London.*
Wildman, Mrs. *Barnstaple.*
Wilkins, Mr. T. ,,
Wilkinson, Mr. J. jun. ,,
Wickey, Admiral ,,
Willis, Miss ,,
Wills, Mr. Joseph ,,
Wills, Mr. H. O. *Bristol.*
Woollacot, Mr. *Barnstaple.*
Wren, Robert Esq. *Bideford.*
Wren, Mrs. *Appledore.*
Wrey, Rev. B. W. *Tawstock.*
Young, Mr. W. *Barnstaple.*

ILLUSTRATIONS & FOLD OUTS

CONTENTS

EDWARD GRIBBLE was married in Pilton Church in 1600 to Mary Pounchard

EDWARD GRIBBLE baptised 1610 at Pilton church • Married in 1634 to Mary Witheridge

EDWARD GRIBBLE baptised 1638 at Pilton Church • Married (2nd marriage) Margaret

EDWARD GRIBBLE baptised 1699 • Married Grace

ROBERT GRIBBLE baptised 1750 • Married (2nd marriage) m Elizabeth Besley in 1786

Robert Gribble — JOSEPH BESLEY GRIBBLE (BORN 1790) — Charles Gribble
married in (1814) — Margaret James
Emigrated to the U.S.A. in 1831

Joseph Besley Jnr. • Charles • Ann Whitchurch • John James • James • Edwin • Risdon Darracott • Eliza •

Alfred • George • Harriet Wilson • Robert Francis • William • Samuel • Risdon Darracott • Harriet Wilson
SOME OF THE SIXTEEN GRIBBLE CHILDREN SHARED THE SAME CHRISTIAN NAME — THE EARLIER NAMED HAVING DIED AT A YOUNG AGE

JOSEPH BESLY GRIBBLE

The Gribble family were well-known in North Devon, many occurrences of the name being found in the area since the sixteenth century. Joseph's family had been settled in Barnstaple for many years when on the 27th of February 1786 at St. Peter's church in the town Robert Gribble, clothier, took as his second wife one Elizabeth Besly.[1]

Robert's first wife, Ancilla, had been buried in March, 1783 leaving a grieving husband and two surviving daughters.[2] Although married in a Church of England building both Robert and his new wife were nonconformists belonging to the Cross Street Congregational Chapel in Barnstaple. At this date however the chapel was not licensed for weddings thus their marriage in St. Peter's.

The new couple soon produced three half-brothers for Robert's two daughters. The second of these sons was our Joseph Besly Gribble who was baptised at the Cross Street chapel on 12th August 1790.[3] The only reference to his early life that I have been able to find occurs in a footnote to his own 'Memorials of Barnstaple'[4] where he speaks of travelling by coach to Taunton in 1805 when he was about fifteen — although why he went there is unexplained. In October 1798 a 'Mr. Robert Gribble' was buried in St. Peter's churchyard which, if he was Joseph's father as I suspect, meant that his widow was left with a very young family to look after.

The first definite mention of the adult author is in the register of St. Peter's where his marriage to Margaret James of Wendton in Cornwall is listed as having taken place on the 10th of January 1814.[5] The couple next appear in the records of Cross Street chapel when, on the 4th of December 1815 they rather unimaginatively baptised their first son with his father's Christian names.[6] This child was the first of six sons and one daughter baptised at the same chapel over the next six years — which was a high rate even by the standards of the time. In the census for 1821 a 'Mr. Gribble' was listed as living in High Street, Barnstaple along with the correct number of children so we can assume that this was his address at the time.[7]

The idea for a history of his home town came about, according to the author, following a dispute concerning the local prison in which Joseph became unwillingly involved.[8] Certainly in August 1824 there was a fierce argument over the gaoler's wages, which rumbled on in the letter columns of the local newspaper for some months.[9] In March 1827 a committee was established from amongst the leading citizens, to investigate the whole question of the gaol and its upkeep.[10] The outcome of all this ferment was an amicable agreement to build a new gaol in 1828.[11]

Joseph's interest in matters of law and order was again shown in March 1828 when, at a public meeting, he asked embarassing questions about an underemployed town official who rejoiced in the title of *Routbeggar*. [12] This officer's job was to ensure beggars were moved out of town whenever they appeared. Joseph suggested scrapping the post and setting up a professional police force instead. The idea was not carried out until 1836 but his was the first voice to raise the possibility of professional policing of Barnstaple.

Joseph's arguments over these matters led him to collect various historical records. He evidently decided not to waste this material, but rather to turn it into ' a Pamphlet'. [13] As he wrote his notes so the manuscript grew in size, until it reached 194 pages in length and was given the grand title 'Memorials of Barnstaple'. We can only marvel at his industry, as when he began there had only been one (failed) attempt at an earlier history.[14]

Publication was advertised in January 1827 and orders were invited via the 'North Devon Journal' office; the Barnstaple and North Devon Bank; and R. Gribble's 'London Warehouse' (a drapery shop) in the High Street.[15] Unfortunately before the volume saw the light of day disaster struck. In December 1827 a small paragraph in the 'Journal' announced that Joseph's ironmongery business had failed .[16]

He was not the only one at this date, but not everyone had a large and growing family to support. In his 'prefatory address' to the book he obliquely notes, ".... it has been my lot since I commenced this undertaking, to experience the mutations of fortune to an extent

that has deprived me of all I possessed, save a good reputation." [17]
From what scanty evidence remains it seems that Joseph became
involved in auctions as records exist of him holding sales of ironmongery, property, and books.[18]

This financial hiccup did not deter him from pushing on with publication of his book, and in February 1828 he announced that the
volume was ready for the press.[19] An imposing list of 'patrons' was
given in this announcement, which included the Duke of Bedford,
Earl Fortescue, Lord Ebrington, and three local Members of
Parliament. The author explained the year's delay by saying that
he had used the extra time gathering more materials which he
trusted "will be found amply to compensate for any disappointment which the subscribers may have felt." In fact his long suffering supporters had to wait another two years before seeing the
book.

There were various reasons for this. In July 1828 Joseph had to
leave his house in Cross Street[20] whilst in June 1829 his draper
brother Robert was declared bankrupt.[21] A month later Joseph had
to sell his furniture and 100 books at his "late residence" in Tawton
Road[22] whilst a few months later he took two local men to court
and successfully reclaimed some of Robert's property.[23]

All of these events held up, but did not prevent, publication of the
'Memorials'. Volume 1 finally saw the light of day on the 22nd of
March 1830 being priced at 7/- (35p).[24] Joseph claimed that "the
remaining volume is in a very forward state, and may be expected
in about four months." The 'Journal' carried a long paragraph
detailing the book's content, adding that it contained "a fund of
pleasing and interesting matter, narrated with a simplicity which,
we anticipate, will recommend itself to the reader."[25]

Even its publication did not see the end to Joseph's troubles. Only
a week later he had to apologise to those subscribers who had not
yet received their copy. This was due to "the inability to get them
fast enough out of the binder's hands, to supplythe demand."[26]

It wasn't until January 1831 that Joseph informed subscribers
that volume two "was nearly completed."[27]

Two months later Joseph had "the satisfaction of announcing the
completion" of volume 2 of his 'Memorials' which was available at

the 'Journal' office.[28] This added another 446 pages so obviously the delay had not been in vain. Within a week he was also announcing the sale of his furniture and various books as he was "about to leave Barnstaple." [29]

His destination was the U.S.A. and a note in a copy of his 'Memorials' now held by the North Devon Athenæum says that he emigrated on the 17th May 1831 and that he died in Cleveland, Ohio on the 26th August 1877.[30]

Various reasons can be suggested for his decision to emigrate. His financial crises were reason enough but one wonders whether the publication of his researches had not created rather too many enemies for comfort. The completed book contains outspoken attacks on the government of the day, Barnstaple corporation, various local people, and the church![31]

At the end of the volume Joseph defends himself against a powerful local man and ex-Mayor Philip Bremridge who charges him with "a false, scandalous and atrocious libel" regarding a Barnstaple charity. Joseph maintained that he had printed the truth, but wished his reply to be placed on record "lest the charge should be revived when I am, as I expect shortly to be, locally, (as I certainly feel I now am *legally*,) beyond the reach of British jurisdiction."[32]

Locally, I have only found two later references to Gribble. In August 1853 he wrote to the 'Journal' to explain where he had obtained various records used in the 'Memorials' and to claim that he was proud that he had "not been led, either by fear, favour or affection to deviate from impartiality."[33]

He wrote again 13 years later giving further details of his sources adding that a Captain May was the first person to suggest he write a book.[34] Whoever first put the idea into Joseph's mind we can only look at his book today and agree with him that " it was no light thing to prepare and carry through the press a work of this multifarious nature."[35] That he did do so, and do it so well, is a tremendous benefit to all interested in the history of Barnstaple. It is a fitting monument to Joseph Besly Gribble .

Peter Christie

References (references to MoB refer to the *original* page nos. in North Devon Athenæum copy)

1	Barnstaple Parish Register — North Devon Record Office
2	Barnstaple Parish Register — North Devon Record Office
3	Cross Street Chapel records — North Devon Record Office
4	J.B. Gribble 'Memorials of Barnstaple' [MoB] (1830) p.596
5	Barnstaple Parish Register — North Devon Record Office
6	Cross Street Chapel records — North Devon Record Office
7	1821 Census – North Devon Athenæum, Barnstaple
8	MoB p. iv
9	North Devon Journal [NDJ] 27.8.1824 4b; 8.10.1824 4c; 22.10.1824 4a; 29.10.1824 4c; 26 11 1824 4e.
10	NDJ 2.3.1827 4b; 23.3.1827 4a; 4.5.1827 4b; 25.5.1827 4c.
11	NDJ 21.2.1828 4b.
12	NDJ 27.3.1828 4b.
13	NDJ 31.3.1831 4e.
14	MoB p.29
15	NDJ 5.1.1827 1b.
16	NDJ 27.12.1827 1a.
17	MoB p.vi
18	NDJ 3.7.1828 4d; 20.11.1828 1d.
19	NDJ 28.2.1828 1a.
20	NDJ 24.7.1828 1b.
21	NDJ 4.6.1829 1c.
22	NDJ 16.7.1829 1a.
23	NDJ 8.10.1829 4a.
24	NDJ 18.3.1830 1a.
25	NDJ 25.3.1830 4b.
26	NDJ 1.4.1830 1d.
27	NDJ 12.1.1831 1d.
28	NDJ 31.3.1831 4e.
29	NDJ 7.4.1831 1d.
30	From Information supplied to the publisher of this edition, by U.S.A. resident descendants of Joseph Besly Gribble; although this date is given as December 9th 1867 in a copy of MoB held at North Devon Athenæum. This copy belonged to R.W. Cotton a noted local historian of Barnstaple. Details of Gribble's life in the U.S.A. are contained in various typescripts supplied by his descendants and now deposited in the North Devon Athenæum.
31	MoB Government – p.230; Corporation – pp. 158, 263, 325, 571; Local people – pp. 309 , 552; Church – p.496
32	MoB p.637
33	NDJ 1.9.1853 6b
34	NDJ 15.11.1866 8e
35	MoB p.599

PREFATORY ADDRESS

"ALBEIT unused to tread *historic* ground;" although but a mere intruder into the ranks of literature; I have ventured to stand forward, as the memorialist of the place, where, some forty years ago, "I first drew vital air."

Whilst Towns of minor importance, and comparitively of no antiquity, have had their " *histories* " sent forth to the world; that a place distinguished above most others in the extensive county in which it is situate – a walled town in the days of the Saxons; one of the most ancient boroughs in the kingdom; a naval port in the reign of Edward the third, and represented as such in a regal council held by that monarch at Westminster ; furnishing on several occasions ships for the navy of Queen Elizabeth, but particularly in aid of the renowned Drake against the Spanish armada; a garrison town in the revolution of 1642, and taking a prominent part in the events of that period; in former years, as at present, the metropolis of the North of Devon! That Barnstaple, thus distinguished, should have so long remained without any public record of the principal events of its history, is to be lamented; inasmuch as many valuable relics of days long past have doubtless been lost beyond recovery. It may also be charged as a reproach on many of her sons, whose talents and resources well fitted them for the execution of such a work.

Only one attempt, that I am aware of, has ever been made towards the accomplishment of this object; and that, as will be seen, was defeated by the death of the individual who had engaged in it.

It is more than probable, that could I in the first instance have viewed this undertaking in all its bearings, with its attendant difficulties, labour, anxiety, and expense, I should have shrunk from the task, and never have commenced it at all; but before I could thus contemplate it ; I had advanced so far as to be unable to make a good retreat. The origin of this work may be thus shortly traced.

In December, 1826, an official document, relative to the insecure state and inefficient government of the town prison, was put into my hands, with a request that I would embody the information it contained, in a Letter to the Editor of the North Devon Journal ; I complied ; the letter was inserted, and a second followed.

The question between the Corporation and the Inhabitants, as to the liability of the respective parties to rebuild the prison, now excited a very lively interest, and of course, a corresponding spirit of inquiry. Documents, which might haply throw light on the subject, were eagerly sought after, and many valuable records were, in consequence, brought under review, which might otherwise never have emerged from the obscurity to which they had been consigned.

Some of these, with the Commissioners' report of the public charities of Barnstaple, it was proposed to publish. Scarcely, however, was the design made known, than a more extended work, which should embrace a History of the Town, was eagerly called for, and numerous offers made for materials, in aid of such an undertaking: the result was, that the original plan became again and again enlarged; until at length, from the quantity and variety of the matter on hand, it was found that Memorials of Barnstaple; instead of being comprised in a pamphlet, as at first intended, could not possibly be done justice to, in any thing short of an octavo volume. Thus was I led on, step by step, until it was impracticable to recede with credit, or without subjecting myself to considerable pecuniary loss.

Let it not then be supposed, that either vanity, or a longing after the sweets of authorship, was the spring that first set this work in motion; on the contrary, should the smallest portion of amusement or information be communicated to the reader through the medium of the following pages, he is desired to bear in mind, that he owes it to the accidental circumstances of the author's having been *solicited* to lend his aid in the discussion of the prison question; but for which, the Memorials would, in all human probability, have never been presented to the public.

It will be expected that I should assign some reason why the publication of this work has been so long delayed; and also, why part of it only now appears, Various adverse circumstances have contributed to the delay. By an ordinance of unerring wisdom, "Man is born to trouble;" and by a providential exercise of this decree, it has been my lot, since I commenced this undertaking, to experience the mutations of fortune to an extent that had deprived me of all I possessed, save a good reputation. Thus situated, and the subject withal of acute feelings, it will not be thought surprising that I for a time abandoned the prosecution of a work like the present.

Another great hindrance to its progress, arose from the length of time (more than twelve months) which was occupied in procuring a copy and translation of one of the charters of the borough, from His Majesty's record office. I ought rather perhaps, to impute the delay to the refusal of the Corporation to permit a copy of the document to be furnished to me at home, by which I was driven to obtain it from the Tower, and that at an expense exceeding twenty pounds – but of this more anon! Altogether, the delay has been considerable, yet it has proved on the whole advantageous; *much additional information, and many curious particulars* have been obtained during the interval, and interwoven with the work, which must otherwise have been wholly excluded from it.

The plan of publishing the accompanying portion of the work, rather than the patience of the subscribers should be longer trespassed upon, has met with the sanction of those to whom it has been mentioned; and it is hoped will give satisfaction generally. The charter, which has been so long waited for, being now in my own keeping, the remainder of the volume will proceed regularly, and with all practicable speed. – It may be looked for in about four months from this time.

In announcing that Memorials of Barnstaple can not possibly be completed within the limits assigned for them, viz. three hundred pages, I trust I shall not be hastily censured; feeling as I do an entire confidence, that I shall be fully exonerated from blame by all who will kindly give the subject their candid and patient consideration. To fix the precise extent of a work of this nature, even when the necessary materials are brought together, is no easy task; but in the present instance, after this had been decided on, (as was thought finally,) a considerable addition of important and interesting matter came to my hands. I could not possibly have anticipated the possession of this; but having obtained it, I should have been guilty, if I may so speak, of a literary misdemeanour, not to have turned it to account. Independent, however, of an accession of materials, I found it requisite to treat some subjects more copiously than I first intended. The Charities, for instance : on attentively perusing the Commissioners' Report, which it was at first proposed to give without comment, the information it afforded, although truly valuable, appeared so incomplete, as to render some further elucidation of the subject really necessary. The "Appendix" to the report (which was attended with no trifling labour,) certainly adds to the bulk of the volume; but surely no one of my subscribers who takes – and who does not take? – an interest in the welfare of the legitimate objects of the various benevolent institutions to which it relates, and whose benefit it is designed to promote, would wish the supplementary matter excluded.

It will be seen in the present publication, that I have expressed my sentiments with freedom: I shall fearlessly pursue the same course to the end of the volume. He who appears in the character of an historian, will often find it needful to assume that of a censor also,* however repugnant to his inclination, and even if contrary to his interest. From this he will not, if he acts from principle, swerve through the influence of "fear, favour, or affection." But he will not, on the other hand, allow himself to indulge any unhallowed feeling which may prompt him to forget, that it is not his province to war with men, but with measures, and with such measures only, as appear to be legitimate subjects for reprehension. Such a standard, it is equally my wish, as it has been my endeavour to act up

---

* Such a course cannot (at least to a man possessed of generous feelings) but be repulsive, under ordinary circumstances; how much more so then, where a writer is a resident of the town of which he essays to give the History; and in the habit of frequent intercourse with persons, of whose conduct as public men (whilst he regards them with sincere respect as individual members of society) he cannot, as a faithful historian, always speak in terms of commendation.

to; "Rather extenuating, than setting down aught in malice." *

The subscribers will be desirous of knowing what the remainder of the volume is to contain. Independent of what may be termed common-place articles in a work like this – a chronological list of occurrences – modern state of the town – trade – public edifices and institutions – population, &c., &c., will be found many possessing an unusual degree of interest, among which may be noticed the following:

An account of the proceedings of the public Authorities of Barnstaple during the Rebellion in the reign of Charles the first, including the minutes of meetings held to provide for the defence of the town, and a minute detail of expenses incurred in various warlike operations. – Curious document relative to the bridge, 1535 – full translations of some, and extracts from other of the numerous characters† granted to the borough – an abstract of the Bye-laws of the Corporation – List of the Mayors from 1304, and the Members of Parliament from the twenty third of Edward the first – Transcripts of the several Inquisitions relative to the customs and privileges of the Borough, made in the reign of Edward the third, and of a similar document of a still earlier date.

Of the execution of the work I hold myself incompetent to form a correct judgement, still less am I qualified to give an opinion on the subject ; but as it respects the matter on which what is now published, and that which is to succeed it, are founded, I may, and can, with the utmost confidence, assure those who may do me the honour to place part the first of Memorials of Barnstaple on their book-shelves, that part the second will be found to exceed it in interest.

My humble work will perhaps be read by some who can look back on the time when, as authors, they first placed themselves at the bar of public opinion ; they will be able to judge correctly of the

---

* "Nothing extenuate, nor set down aught in malice." – *Shakespeare.*

† No apprehension need be entertained that these will prove "a long detail of dry and uninteresting matter;" the early charters are all of them very short; the only one of any length, which will be given in full, is comparatively modern, and will be found to possess a good deal of interest.

feelings of which I am the subject on the present occasion.

I have, however, enlisted, and must now make, at least, one campaign in the Field of Literature, before I can seek discharge ; whether it shall prove successful or unfortunate, – whether I shall come off with whole, or tattered colours, – is, at best, doubtful. My work is before the public; they will be the judges of its merits, and the arbiters of its fate ; to their decision I must submit, and will therefore await it, "with what philosophy I may."

J. B. Gribble

Barum, March, 1830.

MEMORIALS OF BARNSTAPLE,

&c. &c.

CHAPTER I.

Derivation of Name – Situation – Soil – Ancient History – Descent of the Castle Manor – Barnstaple Castle – Priory of St. Mary Magdalen – Manor of Hogg's Fee – Old Town – Chapels and Chauntries – Appendix.

BARNSTAPLE, or Barum*, like most ancient towns, has, during the lapse of ages, and a succession of rulers, been variously named. Leland says, "the olde name of the town was in the Britaine Tunge Abertawe, by cause it stood toward the mouth of Tawe Ryver."

---

* Barnstaple is so well known by this appellation, that a letter sent from any part of England directed to Barum, would reach its destination. I am unable to say more in explanation of the term, than that it is taken as the Latin for Barnstaple. *Query* – Why not the Roman name of the town? Its not having been so recorded, is no positive evidence against the hypothesis. *Yarum* the ancient name of Yare, in Yorkshire, is not in the Roman Itinerary.

Since the above was penned, a clergyman residing near Salisbury, has kindly furnished me with the various etymologies of *Sarum* ; none of them however, throw (as I had hoped they might) any light on the origin of the term we have been discussing. The gentleman referred to suggests the following as

1

This the Saxons changed to Berdenestaple ; corrupted, as Leland supposes, from Abernesse, with the addition of staple, for a market. It may be found in the following public documents, designated thus :–

In the Domesday Book, Barnstaple; – Exon Domesday, Bardestaple, Barnestable; – Records in the Tower, reign of Edward the First, Berdstaple; – Edward the Third, Barnastaple, Barnestaple, Berdstaple; – Richard the Second, Barnastaple; – Henry the Eighth, Barnestapoll, alias Barstaple. Leland writes it Berstaple; – Risdon and Prince, Barnstaple.

SITUATION

Barnstaple stands on the North Bank of the river Taw*, in the Deanery to which it gives name, and in the Hundred of Braunton, Devonshire†. It occupies a central position between the undermentioned towns

SOUTHMOLTON.	11½ Miles
ILFRACOMBE	11½ ”
TORRINGTON	10¼ ”
BIDEFORD	8 ”
APPLEDORE, via Bideford . .	11 ”
” ” Instow Ferry	8 ”

the derivation of *Barum* :–

"Johnson derives the word *Barren*, from the Saxon, *Bare*. Whatever the country about Barnstaple may be *now*, it is easy to imagine that it once sufficiently answered to the meaning of barren, to make the term applicable to it as an etymology."

Another gentleman offers as a definition, "Barum, Heb. Bår. either grain or open country; the market town or town in the vale."

* From Tav, of the same signification as Tavy, Taivy, Teivy; a Water or River. – *Chapple's Add. to Risdon.*

† Anciently called Devonia, Dommonia, Danmonia, Domnonia; and in Exon Domesday, Devenescira, Devrescira.

It is situated in longitude 4° 4' w.; latitude 5° 12' n.;
Distant from:

London, *via* Taunton and Salisbury	192½	miles
London, *via* Bristol and Bath	217½	miles
Bristol, *via* Taunton and Bridgewater	96½	miles
Bristol, *via* *Simonsbath, Dunster & Bridgewater	87	miles
Bristol, *via* Simonsbath, Dunster, Stogursey, Pawlet, and Cross	80	miles
Bath	96¾	miles
Exeter, *via* Chumleigh & Crediton	37½	miles
Exeter, *via* South Molton & Chumleigh	41	miles
Taunton	51	miles
Plymouth	57	miles
Falmouth, *via* Oakhampton & Launceston	100½	miles
Falmouth, *via Holsworthy & Launceston*	95	miles
Swansea, across the Channel from Ilfracombe	35	miles
Linton, (Valley of Rocks)	18	miles
Clovelly	20	miles

The distances of places not printed in italics, are copied from Mogg's edition of Patterson's roads. The remainder have also been procured from authentic sources.

I cannot better describe the situation of the town, with its surrounding scenery, than in the following language, borrowed from a modern tourist. I make the extract more readily, because it is from the pen of a stranger; such a picture, if drawn by a native, might, perhaps, be thought too highly coloured:-

"As we approach Barnstaple, the view from some of the high grounds is very grand; composed on one side of Barnstaple Bay, and on the other

---

* Persons travelling on horseback, will find the ride over Exmoor a very pleasant one in summer. The spirited improvements made by J. Knight, Esq. have quite changed the face of this extensive, and once barren waste. The first effect of this gentleman's liberal outlay of capital, was an excellent road, extending throughout *his* allotment of the forest; (as it is commonly termed, though scarcely a tree is to be found throughout the whole tract.) It is much to be regretted that Mr. Knight's intention of making good the small portion of road that remains, should have been thwarted by the opposition of another proprietor. The worst of it is, however, passable in a carriage. There is a respectable inn at Simonsbath, which is sixteen miles from Barnstaple, and fifteen from Dunster.

"of an extensive vale, the vale of Tawton, carrying the eye far and wide into its rich and ample bosom; although it is one of those views which is too great a subject for painting. The approach to Barnstaple from the low grounds, is as beautiful as from the higher; the river, the bridge, the hills beyond it, and the estuary in the distance, make altogether, a good landscape. The town itself, also situated about nine or ten miles from the sea, stands in a pleasant vale, shut in by hills, forming a semi-lunar cove around it. When the tides are high, it is almost insulated; the flat grounds which lie immediately about it, make an agreeable contrast with the hills. Once these were little better than marshes; but by proper draining, they are now become beautiful meadows. In a word, *Barnstaple is the pleasantest town we have met with in the West of England.*" ——
Gilpin's Observations on the Western parts of England.

SOIL.

The soil of Barnstaple consists chiefly of a stiff yellow clay*, intermixed with small pebbles, and extending from within two feet of the surface, to seven or eight feet in depth, where a stratum of beach is found, usually about four feet in thickness; after which comes a soft (shelfy†) rock. This has been excavated to the extent of forty feet, and found to be the same throughout. Water of an excellent quality is almost invariably met with near the top of this rock, so that wells are scarcely ever required to be sunk to a greater depth than from ten to fifteen feet. These several strata are in one place intersected by two veins of stone, each about twenty feet wide, and running parallel, fifteen or sixteen feet apart, in a southerly direction from Hardaway Head down to the river. One of these is a bastard limestone (Elvin†), excessively hard; the other is of a softer description, and contains mundic and spar. It is also accompanied by a blue clay (Flugen†), which has been cut through to the depth of twenty feet, and contains springs of soft water.

* The town and neighbourhood are supplied with bricks, made from this material.

† So termed by the miners.

ENQUIRY INTO THE ANCIENT HISTORY OF THE TOWN.

Of the history of Barnstaple previous to the Norman conquest, little is known; there is, however, much to be said in favour of its pretensions to high antiquity.

Tradition informs us that Athelstan, after driving the ancient inhabitants of Danmonia* beyond the Tamar, on his return to Cornwall, took up his abode in Barnstaple for a short time. We are told from the same source, that, finding the town walls in a decayed state, he caused them to be repaired, and subsequently built a castle here.

The following remarks are offered on the foregoing statement, as being quite consistant with a desire to give it no more than its due weight in the scale of evidence.

First, – then, we are not called upon in receiving this account as true, to believe a mystery. Tradition, which so delights in romance, here states nothing but what is likely to have occurred in the ordinary course of things. What more probable, than that Athelstan, after having expelled his troublesome foes, the Britons, from the North of Devon, should take measures to secure the district from invasion and plunder, which he might justly fear, both from the enemies he had just expelled, and also from the Danes, both of whom had, by turns, infested and ravaged this part of Wessex†?

Secondly,– Barnstaple was exactly suited for the establishment of a military station, both as to its local situation, and the facilities it possessed for being easily fortified; even supposing it not to have been then walled. If we believe, as with good reason we may, that the Monarch visited the town at this period, we cannot refuse our

---

* *Devon and Cornwall* until the days of King Athelstan, did, from the beginning, continue one province, under the common name of *Danmonia. Athelstan,* coming with a mighty army, after sundry conflicts, at length drives the *Brittains* over the Tamar into *Cornwall* ; upon which the inhabitants of these providences at first obtained the distinction of Eastern and Western Danmonia.

—— Prince's *Worthies of Devon* —— Introduction

† One of the seven kingdoms of the saxon heptarchy. It comprehended the countie of Cornwall, Devon, Dorset, Somerset, Wilts, Hants, and Berks. Was founded A. D. 529, and finally swallowed up all the other states, which were united in 827 into one monarchy.

assent to the remainder of the tradition*.

Lastly, – If there be no direct evidence in favour of the presumption that King Athelstan founded the castle, there is certainly none against it. Except this Monarch, the work has only been attributed to Judhael de Totnes, who is said by some to have built, by others to have rebuilt, and by others to have repaired and beautified the edifice. That he should have improved and made additions to the castle, on being presented with the Manor by his Royal Master, is probable enough; but there does not appear to be any ground for believing that it owed its origin to Judhael de Totnes.

The privileges with which Athelstan is said to have endowed Barnstaple, will come under our consideration in another part of this work.

DOMESDAY.

That interesting and important national register, Domesday Book††, contains several articles relating to Barnstaple, and those persons who had possessions therein, in the reign of William the

---

* The circumstances of Athelstan's having certainly frequented the neighbourhood of Barnstaple, must not be overlooked; it affords fair presumptive evidence in favour of the tradition. Risdon tells us that he had a palace at Umberleigh* ; that he founded a church at Atherington, which he endowed with two hides of land; and another, similarly endowed, at High Bickington. Of the latter, he says, — " *The church of Bickington was founded by King Athelstane, who gave to God and it one hide of land, as appeareth by the donation, a copy whereof, for the antiquity thereof, I here insert. 'Iche Athelstane King, Grome of this home, geve and graunt to the priests of this Church, one Yoke of mye Land frelith to hold, wood in my holt† House to buyld, bitt grass for all hys beasts, fuel for hys Hearth, pannage# for hys sowe and piggs, world without End.'* — "

       * In the parish of Atherington, about six miles from Barnstaple, and three from High Bickington. The house bears evident marks of great antiquity.

       † Saxon term for a wood.

       # The feeding of swine upon mast in woods; also, the money paid for such a license. — *Bailey*

†† An ancient and most valuable record, made by order of William the Conqueror; and containing a register, from which judgement was to be given upon the value, tenure, and services of all lands in England, except the counties of Durham, Cumberland, Northumberland, and Westmoreland, which were not included in the survey. The title by which this book is known, is of uncertain origin. The vulgar notion that it takes its name from *Doomsday*, as being unerring and final in its decisions, is unworthy of being adopted. A more probable supposition is, that which Stow refers to in the Book of Bermondsey, where it is said to have been laid up in the King's Treasury, in a place called *Domus Dei*, whence the corruption of Domesday. — *Ency. Metropol.*

Conqueror. — Transcripts of these, with a translation, will be found in the Appendix [A] to this chapter. Both having been procured from the Keeper of His Majesty's Records, their correctness may be relied on. Extracts are also given from "Exon Domesday." The curious but authentic picture which Domesday Book presents of the degrading state of vassalage in which the great body of our progenitors wore out their existence, cannot but render it interesting to all who feel the value of the privileges, which, as Englishmen, they now enjoy*.

We must now treat of Barnstaple, as forming three distinct properties; — the Castle Manor, comprising the ancient Burgh or Town within the walls; — the Fee of Magdalene, or Priory of Saint Mary Magdalene; — and the Manor of Hog's Fee. The two former, if not the latter (which had probably only a Court Baron), exercised separate jurisdictions, down to the reign of James the First.

---

* During one period of the feudal system, a vassal, though he might be a person of some rank, could not marry without the consent of his Lord, and that permission he was often obliged to purchase. His superior might compel him to marry whom he pleased, or invest with a similar power any one to whom he chose to sell it. When a tenant died, his heir became the Lord's ward; during his minority he was exposed to insult and oppression, and when he became of an age to claim his property, he was made to pay whatever sum might be demanded of him, before he could obtain it. It was not until the thirty-second of Henry the Eighth, that any man could devise his own property; previous to this time, the *privilege* was confined to a few cities and boroughs only.

THE CASTLE MANOR.

This Manor was granted by William the Conqueror, soon after his accession, to one of his favourites :

{1066, William the Conqueror} JUDHAEL DE TOTNES, a distinguished Norman, son of Alured, Earl of Brittany. Judhael retained the barony during the life of his Royal Patron, but was dispossessed of it by his successor, and banished from the kingdom. He had no doubt taken a part in the revolt from William Rufus, in which so many of the Norman barons engaged; and as the penalty of which they paid the forfeiture of their newly-acquired honors.

{1087, William Rufus} WILLIAM RUFUS kept the Manor in his own hands during his reign; as did also :

{1100, Henry the First} HENRY THE FIRST; from whom it passed as crown property to :

{1135, Stephen} STEPHEN; who bestowed it on :

HENRY DE TRACY, by whom it was enjoyed during that King's reign; but on the accession of Henry the Second, the property* was divided, a purparty {1154, Henry the Second} being given to *William de Broase*, great grandson of Judhael de Totnes; in which state it {1189, Richard the First} remained until the seventh year of Richard the First, when de Broase purchased the remainder of the barony from Oliver de Tracy (son and heir of Henry de Tracy); one of the conditions of the sale was an annuity of £20 per annum. He thus became possessed of the whole Manor, but did not long enjoy {1199, John.} it, for soon after, in the reign of King John, ..."being fallen into displeasure upon suspicion, yͤ Kinge tooke against hym, flyeth into France, and there died†; his weif and eldest sonne William were emprisoned, and famished unto death"... The estate again reverted to the crown, but a portion of it was given to HENRY DE TRACY; the other moiety was restored to

---

* The Manor is here termed "The Honour and Castle of Barum." Honour is particularly applied in the English customs to the more noble kind of Seignories or Lordships, whereof other inferior Lordships or Manors depend. As a Manor consists of several Tenements, Services, Customs, &c. so an honour contains divers Manors, Knight's Fees, &c. —— *Enc. Perthen*

† His grandson (son of the Lord Reginald Broase) met a still more ignominious fate; "in the 14 yeere of King H.3, he was hanged by Leolin, Prince of Wales, whoe tooke him in adultery with his wief."

REGINALD DE BROASE, son of William, {1216, Henry the Third*.} in the reign of Henry the Third, this came back to the crown about the end of that reign †.

{1272, Edward the First.} OLIVER DE TRACY (who inherited a moiety of the manor from Henry de Tracy) dying in 1273, his portion came by virtue of a marriage with his only daughter, Eve to :

GUY DE BRIENNE, through whose daughter, Maude, it came by marriage first to :

NICHOLAS, LORD MARTYN, and afterwards to her second husband :

{1307, Edward the Second.} JEFFERY DE CAMVILLE††, who died in 1308; when it descended by inheritance to :

WILLIAM, LORD MARTYN son of Lord Nicholas Martyn, and Lady Maud. His death took place in 1314. He left issue, by Elinor, daughter of Reginald Fitzpiers, and widow of John Lord Mohun, of Dunster, three children — William, Elinor, and Joan. Elinor was married, but died without issue. Joan married Nicholas Lord Audleigh, of Heleigh; she died in 1322. Her brother, WILLIAM LORD MARTYN, of Ceamoys, Dartington, and Barnstaple, succeeded to his father's honours; he married Margaret, daughter of John Lord Hastings, but died in 1325, leaving no issue; and the barony fell, consequently, to his eldest sister :

{1327, Edward the Third.} ELINOR, wife of Phillip de Columbiers; who, leaving no heir, the estate came, in the seventeenth of Edward the Third, to JAMES LORD AUDLEIGH# , of Heleigh and

* The Barony of Barnstaple had, at this period, twenty-eight Knight's Fees attached to it.

† No subsequent distinct notice is taken of this moiety of the property; probably it was given to the possessor of the other portion, without any record of the grant being preserved.

†† A Writ of Quo Warranto was served on Jeffrey, to shew by what right he exercised certain privileges. – See *Chronological Record*, A.D. 1281.

Prince says this nobleman was born either at Dartington or Barnstaple, and "that the Castle at Barnstaple was the place of his principal mansion and inhabitance." The same historian speaks much of the "Heroic Acts of this Right Noble Lord;" particularly of "that immortal action of his at Poictiers, in France, "which of itself is sufficient to eternize his memory. The Knight, with his four esquires, went to the foremost front of all the battle, and there did marvels of arms. This, his noble conduct and valour, so pleased the brave prince (Edward the Third), that as a testimony thereof he settled five hundred marks in land upon him in England, of annual revenue; a considerable estate in those days. The noble-minded Knight divided this gift between his four esquires, saying, they had deserved it as well as he, and had more need of it. The generous prince, highly pleased hereat, praised his bounty as much as his valour, and so doubled his former pension to him to a thousand marks a year. He appointed that there should be about his corpse five great tapers, and five mortars of wax, burning on the day of his funeral; as also £40 sterling then distributed to poor people, to pray for his soul; and to the monks of Hilton Abbey £10, to pray for his soul."
— *Prince's Worthies of Devon*   — See also Baker's *Chronicles*, p.124

9

Rougemont, by virtue of his descent from Joan Martyn. His Lordship was twice married. His first wife was Joan, daughter of Roger Mortimer, by whom he had issue, Nicholas, Roger, and Joan. His second, Isabel, daughter of Lord Strange; by her he had one {1377, Richard the Second} daughter, Margaret. He died in 1385, having made an entail of the barony to his heirs male, with a remainder in the crown, and which now descended to his eldest son:

NICHOLAS LORD AUDLEIGH, who survived his father but four years, and died without issue. His brother, Roger, having been some time deceased, the male line of this noble family became extinct, and the manor, by virtue of the entail, became once more vested in the crown.

RICHARD THE SECOND granted it to :

ROBERT VERE, *Earl of Oxford,* who was to hold it only until the conquest of Ireland should be accomplished; after which, Richard gave it to his brother-in-law :

JOHN HOLLAND, Duke of Exeter, who was executed {1399, Henry the Fourth.} by King Henry the Fourth, in the second year of his reign. It does not clearly appear by whom the Manor was held during this and the two succeeding reigns; but various individuals are supposed to have had grants of it, probably for short periods. In the reign {1461, Edward the Fourth.} of Edward the Fourth, we find it given by that Prince to his Queen; the next grant we {1483, Richard the Third.} find recorded is by Richard the Third, in the first year of his reign, who gave the "Castle and Borough of Barnstaple" to :

THOMAS EVINGHAM, who enjoyed the honour for but {1485, Henry the Seventh.} a short period. In the first of Henry the Seventh it was granted to :

SIR JOHN ST. LEGER, who was also soon deprived of it; the Monarch bestowing the Manor on his own mother, THE COUNTESS OF RICHMOND, for her life. This last grant was made in 1487, subsequent to which no particular account can be given of the Barony, until the reign of:

{1553, Mary.} QUEEN MARY, when it was finally alienated from the crown by that Princess, who granted it by letters patent, to :

THOMAS MARROW, of the county of Warwick, Esq. from whom it came by hereditary descent, to his son:

SAMUEL MARROW, who, in the eighth year of the reign {1558, Elizabeth.} of Elizabeth, sold it to:

SIR JOHN CHICHESTER, KNIGHT,* for the sum of four hundred guineas†; who by a deed of confirmation and release, bearing date August 17th in the same year, conveyed the Manor, with all its Privileges, Rents, Market Tolls, &c. excepting only the site of the Castle, which he reserved, to :

THE MAYOR AND CORPORATION of Barnstaple. The terms of sale were as follows: – A rent in perpetuity of fourteen pounds eighteen shillings, and two fish dinners annually; the Bailiff, on paying the said rent, to receive back one shilling, for the use of the Corporation, for every Court there held in a year, towards the Sheriff's dinner; and also four-pence for proclaiming every such Court, to the use of the Bailiff.

The "Fish Dinners" were compounded for, about the year 1744, in a way highly creditable to the one party, and very beneficial to the other (see Charities, under "Paige's Gift"), as it presumed the cost of such dinners would now more than double the annual rent.

The most remarkable circumstance connected with the descent of the Manor of Barnstaple, to its present proprietors, remains to be recorded; namely, that at the time Sir John Chichester became the purchaser of it, it was *mortgaged to the Corporation, for two*

* The Baronetcy now enjoyed by this family, was not conferred until 1651.

† It is worthy of notice, that the Barony of Barnstaple was, in the reign of Henry the Third, valued at £420 per annum; £15, (or two hundred acres of land) being then the worth of a Knight's Fee. The difference in the relative value of the pound of silver coin *alone* made that sum equal to £1,260 at this period; but if we take into account the proportionate value [*see Appendix*, B] of money and merchandize in the two reigns, we cannot possibly rate a property which, in the time of Henry the Third, was worth £420, at *less* than £4,200 in the reign of Elizabeth. Thus it appears, that the Manor of Old Barum went off at the inglorious sum of one tenth of a single year's purchase of its former value. Whence this enormous depreciation? It is to be accounted for in two ways.

First, — It is *probable*, that in the valuation made of the Borough in the reign of Henry the Third, was included the variously named imposts, by which, in common with other places, it contributed to the public revenue; all of which were either abolished, or merged into a general land tax; but as we cannot in this way account for all the deficiency, we premise,

Secondly, — that most of the tangible property belonging to the Borough must have been alienated from it by successive proprietors. One thing is however, certain; that in whatever way the Manor became thus reduced in value, but little more than *"the honour"* of it fell to Mr. Marrow

hundred pounds.

The question naturally arises — Why did not that body (who, as mortgagees of the property, undoubtedly might have done so) purchase it themselves? We can imagine but one reply to this query; that the state of their funds was such as to make it more desirable to add two hundred pounds to their coffers, than it was then convenient to withdraw a similar amount. Nothing surely but an absolute want of money could have prevented their making so desirable a contract; it will however be seen, that their subsequent speculation was by no means a bad one.

The Castle Court Rental, which probably consists of nominal rents paid on lands virtually sold, at a remote period, produces but a trifling fixed sum. The Tolls, on the contrary, have progressively increased to upwards of ten times their amount in the fifteenth year of the reign of Elizabeth. The whole income derived by the Corporation from the Manor, is as follows:—

	£	s.	d.
Castle Court Rents, in sums of One Penny and upwards, (averaging, on 114 distinct properties, 1s. 17/8d. each)............	6	11	9¾
Penny-Halfpenny*, comprising all tolls received (the Sheep Market and Tollsery excepted) from the Market, and during the Annual Fair......................	107	0	0
Sheep Market (including the Horse Fair)..	46	0	0
Tollsery, or Toll paid on Horned Cattle sold at the Fair.......................	6	10	0
	166	11	9¾

---

* This singular term for a toll, has its origin in a penny being demanded for every pair of panniers pitched in the market, and a half-penny for a basket. I find the impost to have been collected under this name, nearly three centuries back.

Earl Fortescue claims, for the occupiers of certain of his Lordship's estates, comprising the Manors of *Filleigh, North Aller, High Bray, Bremridge, East Buckland, and Challacombe,* Exemption from all Fair and Market Dues. The tenants are furnished with a certificate as follows :—

> "Whereas the Manor of .... is Antient Demesne Lands, and held under his Majesty's Castle and Manor of .... and being so Antient Demesne Lands the tenants and resiants thereof are free from the payment of all sums of money that are or may be demanded for Toll, in any Fair or Market, held within the realm of England, as well for Cattle or Goods by them bought, as for Cattle or Goods which they may sell, according to the Law of this Kingdom.
> These are therefore to Certify" &c. &c.

The following Noblemen and Gentlemen claim similar exemptions for the respective manors and estates named, situate in the neighbourhood of Barnstaple :—

His Grace the Duke of Bedford, for the Manor of *Bishop's Tawton,* comprising the parishes of Bishop's Tawton, Landkey, and Swymbridge.

Lord Rolle, for the Manors of *Landkey,* and *Braunton Gorges.*

Sir Arthur Chichester, Bart. for the Manors of *Sherwill, Bratton Flemming,* and *Stoke Rivers.*

Sir Humphry Davy, Bart. for *Hill Estate.*

Joseph Davie Bassett, Esq. for the Manor of *Heanton Punchardon.*

George Acland Barbor, Esq. for the manor of *Fremington.*

The Tolls are let by auction annually, in the month of November. The sums above stated are what they produced at the last letting; the takers paying all outgoings. Thus, after deducting the rent of the property, and what is paid in lieu of the fish dinners, there remains a clear yearly surplus of £149 11s. 9d. being full nine hundred per cent. on the outlay.

BARNSTAPLE CASTLE

Without good evidence of the fact, we might well doubt that a baronial fortress had ever reared its head on the spot which we know to have been once the site of such an edifice. All that remains of the CASTLE OF BARNSTAPLE, consists of remnants of two or three massive stone walls, now incorporated with the interior of a modern mansion – *The Castle House*.

In the absence of all data by which to direct our enquiries, it would be idle to speculate on the probable extent of the ancient structure; Leland speaks of the ruins of a *"great* Castle;" but this must be here taken as a very indefinite term.

No distinct mention is made of the Castle as a building, from the time of Judhael de Totnes, until the twelfth year of the reign of Henry the Third, when its walls were ordered to be reduced to the height of ten feet*. It does not appear that this edict, which, if strictly obeyed, would have virtually demolished the building, was complied with; as the Castle was certainly habitable more than half a century subsequent to this period. An inquisition was taken in 1282, for the purpose of enquiring into some dispute between the Lord of the Town and the inhabitants, in which the latter maintain as follows:-

" We say that we have synginge in the Chapele of the Castle, the whiche shalle be there put at the wille of the Lord, certyne Rentes being assynged of old Tyme to susteyne the foresaid Chauntry. Sir Walter Chepleyn of Fremyington gave a furlonge of Land in Frelingcote and twenty shillings of annuale Rente."

How much longer it was kept up, we have no means of judging. Leland, whose Itinerary was published in 1542, saw its "Ruins and a Piece of the Dungeon;" and Phillip Wyott tells us that part of the wall was blown down in 1601[†].

* The number of Castles in England amounted, at this time, to 1,115.

† See Chron. Record.

By the summary of disbursements made during the civil wars, 1642-4, we find that a considerable sum was then expended in *fortifying the Castle**. It is very questionable whether this had reference to any thing more than to the Tower or Mount; and perhaps some temporary erections ("platforms") below it, as nothing like a building, or the ruins of one, can be traced on the site of the Castle, on a plan of the town, drawn in 1584[†], whilst the wall[††] and battlements on the mound appear entire; it is therefore to be presumed, that even in Wyott's time, nothing remained of the Castle but a heap of ruins; and that both he and the Chronicler of the Record referred to, applied the term Castle to the tower, as being the only part which retained the semblance of a fortification.

Lord Clarendon speaks of the town as being "well fortified" during the rebellion; but we cannot reconcile the supposition that this was then applicable to the *Castle*, with reference made to it on a public trial[§] in little more than eighty years afterwards, a period much too short to admit of the probability that its having then exhibited "the pomp and circumstance of war" could have been wholly forgotten.

The Castle Green was made the scene of a public execution in 1590.[#]

For more than a hundred and forty years after Sir John Chichester became possessed of the Manor, the Castle grounds lay open to the public; but about the year 1705, Sir Arthur Chichester leased the property to an individual named Gibbs. This person shut out the public by enclosing the premises, on which he built a public house, and a limekiln[†††]. Gibbs's lease expired with himself in about fifteen years from its commencement. During the life time of the lesee, the inhabitants of the town had asserted their right to the free use of the lawn and mount, by breaking down the enclosures, and ranging over the premises; so that for several years

* See Civil Wars
† A description of which, see this chapter
†† A part of the foundation still exists
§ See Appendix
# See Chron. Record
††† This stood on the site of the present walled enclosure, at the East end of the North Walk; it was removed about twenty years since.

15

after Gibbs's death, no one could be found tc take another lease. At length Sir John Chichester's steward had one granted to him for three lives, at the nominal price of ten guineas. The grounds were now more closely fenced, and the inhabitants, being wholly excluded, "murmured against the Corporation," for not interfering on their behalf.

George the Second being proclaimed King, June 20th, 1727, the Mayor, on that occasion, gave directions to have a bonfire made on the Tower, which was done, and a barrel of ale drank. This trespass was made the subject of an action at law, which the Corporation promptly defended. It appeared however on the trial, that the town did not possess the right which they claimed, and thus lost their "supporting place*."

The first important improvement made at the *Castle House*, was effected by William Wavell, M.D. about 1790. At this period, whilst excavating the ground within the space enclosed by the old walls before alluded to, a perfect skeleton was found, lying in a kind of vault†; the area is thought to have been the Castle Chapel. From the depth at which the bones were found, it would appear that the ground has been raised much above it ancient level.

Whilst these alterations were making, chance also brought to light a seal, on which was deeply cut a man robed, standing under a niched canopy, with a sword in his right hand, and a book in his left; at his feet a man was kneeling, and offering a scroll; round these figures was deeply cut, "Gratia Dei sum id quod sum." The seal was very antique in its fashion, and made of a kind of bronze; the letters were Saxon.

The premises, which have been progressively improving for the last thirty years, now present a very inviting aspect. The house is genteel and commodious; the gardens are both usefully and ornamentally stocked; the mount and lawn are tastefully laid out with trees and shrubs, and the residence altogether is a very charming one.

* In the Appendix[c] will be found an extract from the original brief, held by the defendant's counsel on this trial. It is considered to be worth preserving, both as containing a description of the old Castle precincts, and a record of some of the customs of our ancestors.

† The remains it may be, of some renowned warrior, or dignified ecclesiastic still occupy (under a slab in the wine cellar) the same "narrow house" in which they were discovered.

The present occupier is R. W. Grace, Esq. as tenant to Phillip Brembridge, Esq. who holds the property of Sir Arthur Chichester, Bart. under a lease granted by the late Sir John Chichester, in 1784, for ninety-nine years, determinable on the death of three lives, but with a covenant of renewal, on payment of a fine of £50. The premises now produce clear rental of £100 per annum.

BARNSTAPLE PRIORY.

(*Arms*–Gules, a Bend, Or, a Label of three Points Argent)

This was a Priory of cluniac monks, dedicated to St. Mary Magdalene. It was founded in the reign of William the Conquerer, by Joel (or Judhael) de Totnes, and made dependant on St. Martin's in the Fields, near Paris. Joel grants* to the religious, Pilton, with the Wood and Marsh, Pilland, the Mill at Barnstaple, all the Land without the walls between the north and east gates, with all the Waters, Fish, &c.; moreover, the Church of Barnstaple, the Chapel of Sabinus, with their appurtenances, two parts of the Tythe of Fremington, and the whole Tythe of Fish.

The community, it appears from Bishop Bronescombe's Register, consisted of thirteen members. Being an alien Priory, its revenues were frequently seized during the wars between England and France, but was made denizen, probably about the time of Henry the Sixth, and so continued until the general suppression of monastries.

---

* A copy of the deed of foundation may be seen in Dug. Mon. vol. i. p684. Tanner, however says that it "is not that of the Foundation, but a second Grant.". – King William, Henry the First, and William, Bishop of Exon, confirmed Joel's donations, and his descendants, Henry de Tracy, and William de Broase, added their respective Charters; the former dated 1146. The whole of these Grants may be found in the Monast Ang.

The Registers supply the following series of the Priors, from the year 1265* :–

1. – Simon Gurneye, admitted Prior, ... August 1265
2. – Theobald de Curtipalatio, ... 29th June,1275
3. – John 1314
4. – John de Sancta Gemma.– He scandalously neglected
   the duty of residence, and was obliged to tender
   his resignation to Bishop Grandison, in the year . . . 1332
5. – John Soyer, succeeded March18, 1334
6. – Imbertus de Gaumachiis,admitted on the death
   of John Soyer . . . . Dec. 10, 1334
7. – Reginaldus Pirdoc, succeeded . . . . Dec. 9, 1349
   and resigned in the summer of 1351
8. – Roger Hayn, admitted . . . . Nov. 7, 1351
9. – Richard Carre, or Cary, succeeded; he died late in 1376
10. – Ralph Chelfham; he died in 1392
11. – Henry Sutton, succeeded . . . . May 28, 1392
    he died in 1398
12. – Simon Sele, admitted . . . . Sept. 1398
    he died June 15, 1428
13. – Hugh Lyton, succeeded . . . . July 28, 1428
    died Dec. 16, 1461
14. – John Pylton was confirmed as his successor 1461
15. – John Ilfracombe; he resigned in 1502
16. – John Pylton followed, and after governing the
    Priory sixteen years, retired on a Pension of £20.
17. – Robert Thorn, the last Prior, succeeded . . . August 12th 1518

He surrendered his Convent to the King's Commissioners, the 4th of February, in the twenty-seventh year of King Henry the Eighth, 1535, and was allowed a pension of £14 per annum for life†. He was alive in Barnstaple in 1555, having certified, February the 2nd

---

* Richard is mentioned in Prynne's Records as Prior in 1226, and Normanus occurs, but without date, in the Charter of William de Braiosa. – *Tanner's Not. Mon.*

† Roberte Britte was, in 1542, in the enjoyment of a pension of forty shillings per annum, granted him in 1520, by the Augmentation Court.

in that year, that the tenants of the house of Magdalene paid the Quintadecima*.

Risdon says, – "this Prior, for his device, bare a roe-buck leaning to a hawthorn, in an escutcheon, with the word 'Bert' interposed, and this underwritten; – Capram cum spina protegat divina potestas."

Westcote† gives the motto "Capram cum spina protegat potestas divina."

The revenues of the Priory are stated by Dugdale to have been valued at £123 6s. 7d.; by speed at £129 15s. 8d.§

The Taxatio contains the following items:–

	£.	s.	d.
Prior de Barnstapol percipit in capellis de Clifton and Hatheline	0	3	0
In ecclesia de Barnstapol	1	10	0
In ecclesia de Ffremyton	0	8	0
In eccia de Hamme (George)	2	0	0
In Decanatu Barum de terris and redditibus . . .	2	10	0
Apud Waleworthi et Kymelonde tax ad	0	15	0

In the grant to Lord Howard (see Appendix), the undermentioned sums appear to have been paid annually to the Convent of St. Mary Magdalene:–

	£	s.	d.
By the Vicar of Barnstaple	5	0	0
By the Rector of Georgeham	5	0	0
By the Borough of Barnstaple# (or Castle Manor) . .	2	0	0
By the Rector of Fremington	1	10	0

---

* see Chron. Record.

† Manuscript description of Devon in Exeter Cathedral

§ The sum mentioned by Risdon (£223 6s. 7d.) must have been a typographical error.

A deed has, during the past year been discovered at Tawstock House which, there can scarcely be any doubt, has reference to this identical annuity. It is a license under the Great Seal, dated York, 26th January, in the 7th year of the reign of Edward the Third, empowering Sir Philip de Columbers (then Lord of Barum), and Alionora, his wife, to endow their perpetual Chantry Priest with forty shillings annual rent, issuing from lands in Barnstaple. The said Priest was to officiate daily, *singulis diebus celebraturus*. Part of the deed is in such a decayed state, as not to place it *wholly* beyond doubt that the Chantry referred to was in St. Mary Magdalene's Priory; but the fact that both Philip de Columbers and his wife were interred there, may be considered as supplying this chasm in the evidence.

19

Leland tells us that Phillip de Columbers, his wife, and some of the Barons of Slane, in Ireland, were interred in Barnstaple Priory.

"In the garden of this Priory (writes Risdon) was lately the proportion of a knight, lying cross-legged, with his sword and shield, seeming to be one that had vowed a voyage into the Holy Island for that sacred warfare; removed out of the church, doubtless, at the dissolution."

About two years after the surrender of the Priory to Henry the Eighth, that monarch granted it*, with its valuable estates†, to William Lord Howard, of Effingham, and Margaret his wife.

King James the First, by letters patent, dated 12th of February, 1607, granted the reversion *in fee* to William Lord Howard, Earl of Nottingham, Lord High Admiral of England, son and heir of Lord Howard, the first grantee.

William Lord Howard, as appears by indenture, enrolled in Chancery, bearing date the 29th of March, 1613, granted the site of the Priory, with the Rectory, Advowson, and most of the landed property, to :

Reginald Portree, from whom it descended to his two daughters; one of these conveyed it by marriage to ———— Sydenham, Esq.; after which it came into a family named Northmore.

The remaining part or parts of the Priory Estates, Lord Howard disposed of about the same period, some "unto divers people for divers long Terms of Years." One of the sales consisted of "The capital Messuage, Barton, and Farm of Potyngton in Pilton and Barnstaple, late Parcel of St. Mary Magdalene, with Port Mills, and a House and Garden in Boutport Street, belonging to the same." This estate, which is sometimes called the "Manor of Maudlyn," was sold to Henry Rolle, (ancestor of the present Lord Rolle) for the sum of *Two Thousand Four Hundred Pounds*. The proceeds of this comparatively small portion of the Priory property, may give us some idea of the value of its other endowments.

---

* For a copy of this Grant, see appendix [D]

† Not content with these we find Lord Howard in 1538 setting up a claim to the soil of Boutport Street. In the " Mayor's answer," it is set forth that "barnestaple is an anciente Porte, and Bouteporte a Parcelle of the Suburbes belonging to the said Towne Tyme out of Mynde."

How long the Priory might have been preserved as a residence subsequent to the dissolution of the establishment, cannot now be ascertained; but that the building was not suffered immediately to go to decay, is evident; since fifty-five years after the grant to the Howard family, the house was considered a fit habitation for the Sherrif of Devonshire*. This is, I believe, the latest mention made of it. It is not improbable that Lord Howard might have taken up his abode here on becoming possessed of the property; the situation must have been a very inviting one, commanding a fine prospect of the river, as well as a considerable extent of country, and, what would certainly in his Lordship's estimation, add much to the interest of the scenery, he might almost exclaim with Cowper's Selkirk, – " I'm monarch of all I survey†."

The Priory building, and most of the detached offices, have been long since razed to their foundations; only small portions of walls now remain, which probably formed part of some of the numerous out-houses mentioned in the grant.

Amongst the memorandums left by a deceased individual§, I find the following relating to a house built in 1798, on the verge of the Priory site, facing Boutport Street; it is noticed here purposely, as it respects the coins, that the error may be corrected.

"In the building the same they had occasion to dig below the surface of the earth, (no unusual occurrence this!) where they found old Saxon coins, by *pecks*, to a very great value; and also divers bones, which appeared to have lain in beds of lime."

* See Chron. Record

† Besides the long list of Manors and Estates enumerated, all the left hand side of Pilton Street belonged to Barnstaple Priory. (The greater part of the right side belonged to Cleeve Abbey.)

§ The late THOMAS BROOKE KEATE, of Barnstaple, law-writer, whose name deserves honourable mention, he having been the first to enter on the *task* of compiling a History of his native town. If he was not gifted with all the judgement requisite for such an undertaking, he only wanted that which but comparatively few possess, (and what the writer is free to confess *his own deficiency in.*)
With peculiar facilities for procuring materials, Mr. Keate united a persevering industry in the pursuit, and thus brought together a quantity of interesting matter relative to Barnstaple; but having been unfortunately in the habit of lending detached portions of his Manuscript, which no one took the trouble to seek for after his decease, much, and it is to be feared the most valuable part of what he had collected, is irrecoverably lost ; the substance of what has been preserved, is, through the kindness of the individuals into whose hands it fell, incorporated in this work. THOMAS BROOKE KEATE died October 20th 1816, aged twenty-one years.

The writer adds,—

"...enquire about this, as I am very hard in believing it." The gentleman who built the house in question, assures me that two or three coins only were found. I have not been able to meet with more than one of these, which is a shilling of the second year of the reign of Elizabeth.

A more interesting discovery, connected with the Priory, has since been made, which is thus described in the *Gentleman's Magazine*, for January, 1826 –

"In May, 1819, some workmen employed in forming a tan-yard on the site of the Priory, called St. Magdalene, in Barnstaple, laid open the foundations of many extensive walls, thick, and formed of very solid masonry, the mortar cementing the stones being harder than even the stones themselves. They were covered by immense heaps of rubbish, stones, and slates, apparently thrown over them at the demolition of the buildings. Amongst the rubbish were fragments of columns, ribs of groins, paving tiles, glazed with a flower-de-luce on them, and some stones with crosses. Two stones were very perfect, and retained in excellent preservation the arms of which I send you an exact copy.

"The whole of these foundations and rubbish had been covered for ages by a fine green sward, and now being only partly uncovered, and the rubbish again thrown back, as suited the convenience of the workmen; it was not possible to form a correct idea either of the extent or form of these buildings.

"Two skeletons were found, one was very perfect, and a man's. Near this skeleton* lay a small bell, such as is tinkled in the Catholic churches during the celebration of mass; it was of bell-metal, and not in the slightest degree corroded; the clapper, being iron, was destroyed by rust. Several coins were found, and some, as I have heard, of silver; but of the latter I could not obtain a sight.

"A souterrain was laid open, but whether it was an extended passage, or merely the cloaca, it suited neither the purse nor inclination of the tanner

---

* Most probably the remains of the Ostiarius or Doorkeeper, in the form of whose ordination the Bishop says, "Ostiarium oportet perculere cymbalum et *campanum*"

to ascertain. There is a tradition that there once existed a subterranean communication under the river Yeo, from this place to a religious establishment at Bull Hill, near Pilton church, where the Pope's indulgences were sold. I believe, however, there are few places where similar traditions do not exist.

"There is also a tradition that a stone coffin had been found here, containing the body of a man in complete armour."

The letter from which the above is extracted, was accompanied by an engraving, which, by the liberality of the editor of the Gentleman's Magazine, who has kindly granted me the use of the block, I am enabled to copy into this work.

The arms represented in the sketch, are affixed to the back wall of the house, erected in 1822, on the site of the Priory, now the property and residence of Thomas Palmer Acland, Esquire.

From the large quantities of human bones which have been at different times dug up in the Rack Field, (as the Priory site is now called, from the circumstance of its having been long used for the purpose of drying wollen cloths) it would appear to have been made the receptacle of a much greater number of bodies than it is likely were interred there during the period it remained a religious establishment.

Similar discoveries have been made in other fields near the town; the most pobable conjecture with respect to them all, is that they were converted into burying places when the plague raged here A.D. 1646*.

All the houses on the East side of Boutport Street, from Pilton Bridge to Vicarage Lane, as well as the Vicarage House, and the Cottages beyond it, are evidently built on the Priory ground. These have become the property of various individuals. The Rack Field, which still retains the name of Maudlyn (a corruption of Magdalene), is vested jointly in the Reverend Thomas Boyce, Curate of Shirwill, and Miss Dene, of Barnstaple; in proportion to its extent, it is a very valuable property.

* See Chron. Record

MR. URBAN,   *Horwood Nr. Barnstaple*
August 1st 1825

In May 1819 some workmen employed in forming a tan-yard on the site of the Priory called St.
Magdalene in Barnstaple, laid open the foundation s of many extensive walls, thick and formed
of very solid masonry........Amongst the rubbish
were fragments of columns, ribs of groins,
paving tiles glazed with a flower de luce on
them and some stones with crosses. Two stones
were very perfect and retained, in high preservation, the Arms of which I send you an exact
copy...........there is a tradition that a stone coffin
had been found here containing the body of a
man in complete armour.....

** * We consider the arms on the Barnstaple
stone to be that of the Duke of Clarence, second
son of Henry the Fourth..........EDITOR

MR. URBAN,   *February 10th 1826*

In your last number you inserted a very curious
engraving of Arms found on a stone ....which
you considered to be those of Thomas
Plantagenet Duke of Clarence. This statement is
erroneous for they were probably the arms of
John Stafford Earl of Wiltshire......having the
coats of Stafford and Bohun transposed.

*** We have since been favoured with a letter
from an intelligent correspondent, who suggests
that the arms belonged either to John Earl of
Wiltsire or his son Henry Stafford.......the
arrangements of the quarterings precisely agreeing with the Garter plate of the latter in St.
George's Chapel, he is inclined to assign them to
that Earl..........EDITOR

Extracts from Gent. Mag. *January / February* 1826 – A Dispute over the origination
of this coat of arms found in Rackfield, Barnstaple in May 1819, the site of the Priory.

It is erroneously stated in Lyson's Mag. Brit. to belong to R.N. Incledon, Esquire. This gentleman was the proprietor of the site of *Pilton* Priory, which he has lately sold, and is possessed of the Great Tithes of Barnstaple, formerly annexed to the Priory; from one of these circumstances, the mistake made by Messrs. Lyson may have arisen.

A grant was made by Sir James de Audley, in 1348, "of an area in Barnstaple, for poor brethren hermits of the order of St. Augustine." The grant was confirmed by Bishop Grandison, June 9th in that year, and Robert Rowe gave, shortly after, five acres of "land, in Barnstaple, to the said hermits," as appears from the *Inquisitio ad quod damnum, anno,* 27th of Edward the Third.

A house of Friars Austin here, founded by one Robert Bacon, is mentioned in some collections of Mr. Stewart, of pat. 27 Edward the Third*. No further record has been left of these institutions.– Probably the intentions of the Donors were never fully carried into effect.

I cannot allow myself to close this account of the Priory, without acknowledging my obligations to the Reverend George Oliver, a gentleman, of whom it is difficult to say which best deserves our admiration, – his extensive learning, or the liberal and unassuming manner in which he dispenses from his stores of knowledge for the benefit of others.

Not only am I indebted to Mr. Oliver for the List of Priors, which is copied from his "Historic Collections relating to the Monastries in Devon," but for his unrestricted use of notes, taken by him since the publication of that work; and also for valuable information of a more general kind.

---

* Tanner's Nat. Monast. – In the same work and just preceding the paragraph now quoted, occurs the following : – "A Hospital of the Holy Trinity here (in Barum) pat. 9, Henry the Fourth, p.1,m.3,vol.iv." but on referring to the Calen. Rot. Patentium, I find the reference to be as follows : – " De Hospitale seu elemosinario fraternitatis S. Trinitatis in Bristoll per Johannem de Barnstaple perampl." A strange mistake in such a work.

THE MANOR OF HOG'S FEE,

Was anciently in the suburbs, but is now situate nearly in the heart of the town of Barnstaple. Although once thought worthy of being presented by the hands of Royalty, the property now only produces the trifling fixed income of £1 14s. 6½d. in chief rents. The first mention made of it is as follows:–

Temp. Edward the Third.– "Robert Beauple Chevaler has in the said Borough (of Barnstaple) a certain Fee, called Hog's Fee, of which are held twenty-six tenements; he holds his Court once in three weeks*."

The Calen. Inquis. post mortem contains the following reference to this Manor:– " 9 Ric. 2. Nigellus Loringe Chevaler et Margaretta Uxor ejus Barnestaple 10s. reddit' vocat Hogesfee."

It came in to the hands of the crown, in the second year of the reign of Queen Mary, by virtue of the attainder of Henry Duke of Suffolk, and so remained until the eighth of James the First, in which year the Manor was granted, by letters patent, to George Whitemore, and Thomas Whitemore, Esquires; from whom it passed, through Richard and William Bennett, to John Pincombe, of Southmolton, gentleman. Richard Pincombe, son and heir of the last named, left it to his three sisters, Mary, Elizabeth and Gertrude. Mary married John Tuckfield, Esq. whose daughter and heiress devised her portion of the property to John Crew, Esquire, who sold it to the Mayor and Corporation of Barnstaple. Elizabeth Pincombe, dying without issue, her share of the Manor fell to Gertrude, who devised the two-thirds to Roger Tuckfield and John Creyk; they made sale to ———Setler, and others, by whom it was sold to the Mayor and Corporation of Barum, who thus became possessed of the undivided property.

---

* This court was kept up during the lifetime of Mr. Thomas Keate, who officiated as Steward or Bailiffe of the Manor; but has since been discontinued.

The original extent of this estate can not now be correctly ascertained; a bond-stone, projecting from the front of a house on the East side of Boutport (about half way betwixt Back Lane and Silver Street), and the White Horse Inn, in the same street, are *supposed* to mark its extent N. and S. The houses &c. from which the rental is derived, not being in a continuous line, but scattered over different parts of the town, furnish no clue by which to fix the bounds of the Manor.

THE OLD TOWN.

In its primary sense this term is, of course, only appicable to the ancient Burgh; but it may also with propriety be applied, as now intended, to the town and suburbs, as embracing in one community, although under different jurisdictions, the three separate interests (see page 9,) into which Barnstaple was anciently divided.

It is a pleasing feature in the History of Barnstaple, that (as far as my information extends) the town is mentioned by all old writers in terms of commendation.

As we must principally depend on the testimony of Historians, in order to form a jugement of the ancient state of the town, I subjoin extracts from the works of such as I have been enabled to discover have written respecting it.

"The Towne of Berdenestaple hath be waullid and the Waulle was in Compace by estimation half a Myle. It is now almost clene faullen. The names of 4 Gates, by Est, West, North, and South, yet remain, and manifest tokens of them. The suburbes be now more than the Towne. The Houses be of Stone as al Houses in good Townes thereaboute be. There be manifest Ruines of a great Castlle at the North West Side of the Towne. Sum say that one of the Tracys made the right great and sumeptus Bridge of Stone, having 16 high arches, at Berstaple." – Leland's Itinerary 1542

"Barnstaple, a Borough right ancient, bordereth here upon the East Bank of Taw, it is the chief Town of Merchandise next the River's mouth. It was once walled, the foundation of whose Walls, could they be traced out, doubtless the Town would appear nothing so large; which if now walled, so fair built and populous withal, would prove little inferior to some Cities, for it hath Liberties and Privileges as in a City, and is pleasantly and sweetly situate amidst Hills, in form of a semi-circle, upon the River, as it were a Diameter, whose streets in whatsoever weather, are clean and fairly paved. It hath a Friday's Market, for frequency of People, and Choice of all Commodities, the cheapest in this Tract. The inhabitants profess merchandise, and through Traffic have much enriched themselves."— *Risdon's Survey of Devon.*

"Reputed this is a very ancient Towne, and for elegant Buildings and frequencie of People held chiefe in all this Coast. On the South Side it hath a stately Bridge. The inhabitants, for the most Part, are Merchants who in France and Spaine trade and traffique much." — *Camden's Britain*, edition 1637*.

"No place was thought so convenient for his (The Prince of Wales's) Residence, as Barnstaple, a pleasant Town in the North of Devon, well fortified, with a good Garrison in it." *Lord Clarendon's History of the Rebellion.*

"Barnstaple was once walled round, which if it had continued, it would have been little inferior to some Cities for fair Buildings, numerous Inhabitants, and great Liberties and Privileges. It is fairly paved and the Streets are clean in all Weathers."—*Britannia et Hibernia antiqua et nova*, 1714.

"The pleasant Town—the clean and neat Town of Barnstaple"—*Prince's Worthies of Devon.*

---

* This work, which was compiled from an actual Survey, made during the reign of Elizabeth, was first published, in Latin, A.D. 1594

As might be expected of a wall which three centuries ago was "almost clene faullen," there are now no visible remains of the ancient boundary of the town*.

Doctor Johnson somewhere remarks, that "Walls supply materials for building, much more readily than Quarries," and when an increased population required additional dwellings, our ancestors acted but wisely, if, as doubtless was the case, they made the site and materials of a decaying fortification subservient to their convenience, by appropriating both to the erection of houses.

Although "manifest tokens yet remain" of but one of the four gates† mentioned by Leland, there is sufficent evidence to warrant the conclusion that the situation of the other three, as well as the course of the town wall, varied but little from the line described below.

From the ancient northen entrance to the town, the substantial masonry of which is still apparently much in its original state, the wall appears to have passed on in the rear of the present houses on the west side of Boutport Street§, to EAST GATE#, thence to SOUTH GATE, situate at the bottom of High Street††, and (most probably through Maiden Street) along the Beach (now the Quay) to WEST GATE, at the bottom of Cross Street, from whence it ran

---

* Part of the side wall of a house in Boutport Street (about midway between Paternoster Row and Joy Street) is thought by some persons to be a remnant of the Town Wall. The building referred to, certainly stands very near, if not upon the line of the old wall, and this is all that can be said in favour of the supposition.

† It is somewhat extraordinary, that in no one of the many ancient records, &c. that have come into my hands, is there any particular mention made of either of the *Gates* of the town.

§ Two houses are described in 1594, as being " bounded by the Town Wall on the West, and Boutport Street on the East." – See *Charities*, "Appley's Gift."

The situation of this Gate has been fixed (by conjecture) near the spot referred to in a previous note; to admit this would involve the manifest absurdity of supposing an entrance without a street, and at a few yards distance a street without an entrance. I have therefore considered it as having stood, as is certainly most probable, at the top of Joy Street.

on to the Castle, and again joined NORTH GATE. This line describes a circumference of more than four-fifths of a mile*, by actual admeasurement, being nearly double the distance Leland gives "by estimation."

We sit down now-a-day, and discourse coolly enough about walls and castles; it would be well were we sometimes to look back and endeavour to bring home the period when our now peaceable town was a fortress, and its inhabitants clad in mail; when "the confused noise of warriors" was an accustomed sound, and "garments rolled in blood" a familiar sight; when the weak became the prey of the strong, and the strong in his turn was spoiled by "a stronger than he."

The earliest mention that I find made (excepting what is said in Domesday) of the number or state of the houses in the town, occurs in the reign of Henry the Eighth, and is as follows:–

"Whereas there hath been in times past many beautiful houses within the walls and liberties of York, Lincon, Canterbury, Coventry, Bath, Chichester, Salisbury, Winchester, Bristol, Scarborough, Lynn, Hereford, Colchester, Rochester, Portsmouth, Poole, Feversham, Worcester, Stafford, Exeter, Ipswich, Buckingham, Pontefract, Grantham, Southampton, Great Yarmouth, Oxenford, Guildford, Estretfore (quære, if Stafford?) Great Wicomb, Kingston upon Hull, Newcastle upon Tyne, Beverly, Bedford, Leicester, Berwick, Shafton, Sherborn, Bridport, Dorchester, Weymouth, BARNSTABLE, Plymouth, Plympton, Tavistoke, Dartmouth, Lestwithiel, Leskeard, Lanceston, Bodmin, Truro, Helston, Taunton, Bridgwater, Somerton, Alchester, Maldon, Warwick, which houses now are fallen down, decayed, and at this time remain unre-edified, as desolate, and vacant grounds; many of them nigh adjoining to the high streets, replenished with much uncleanness and filth, with pits, cellars, and vaults, lying open and uncovered, to the great peril of the King's subjects; and other houses are in danger of falling. Now if the owners of the waste grounds (on which houses have stood within twenty-five years back), and the decaying houses, do not in three years rebuild them, then the Lord of whom the ground is held, may re-enter and seize the same as in a like law, anno, 1535."— Stat. 32, Henry Eighth, cap. 18, 19.

30

A modern writer*, who appears to have possessed competent means of forming a correct judgement on the subject, considers that the complaint here made, as it respects the *decay* of houses, was frivolous, and had its origin in "the particular humour of Parliament" at this period, since many of the cities and towns mentioned were known to be then in a very thriving condition. Whatever might have been amiss, he considers, was "more owing to careless than actual decay," and that the statement was much exaggerated. Be this, however, as it may, Barnstaple certainly appears in good company, and on the evidence of the Statute referred to, may be fairly considered to have ranked amongst the principal towns of the empire.

I find no reference to this act in any private memorandums, and am therefore unable to afford any information as to what effects might have been produced by it in Barnstaple.

In *"A plotte off that partte off the towne off Barnestaple, neere the ryvere syde before the kaye was buylded Anno D. 1548†,"* the following streets, &c. appear, as described below:–

"Castell hille and Tower."—The Hill appears without a tree or shrub, and surrounded by a ditch. The Tower consists of an embattled wall, with loop holes, in perfect repair.

"Castelle greene" in unenclosed, and nothing like a building appears on the premises, except the Tower already mentioned.

"Castelle poyntte" is represented as a green sward, running nearly out to low-water mark; the whole of the space from the Castle to *"Hollande Streett"* is also a green, enclosed by a low wall.

A building, designated *"William Johnson's housse,"* on *"The Stronde,"* occupies the site of captain Gribble's residence, in the Cattle Market; it is represented as standing on a green, with its front towards the water.

---

* Macpherson – annals of Commerce.

† I have been led to question the accuracy of the date here specified, as having reference to the *State of the Town at that period.* It would appear rather to be "A plotte executed in 1584, shewing what the state of the lower part of the town was before the Quay was built. If we believe that there was no Quay erected at this time, we must also believe that the Corporation, in their petition for the Charter, (see Chap.111.) granted to the town in 1556, practised a deception on the King and his Council, too scandalous to have been attempted, and too palpable to have passed undiscovered. Wyot speaks of a *new* Quay being built in 1600; and we find trhat the Fair was regularly kept on the *Quay* before the 34th year of the reign of Elizabeth. – See *Chron. Record,* 1590, *and* 1600.

No other house or erection of any kind is to be seen on the side of the street next the river, until we reach *"Litsound,"* (Litchdon) except the desecrated Chantry of Saint Thomas, at the corner of the Bridge, and a small house (erected probably for the purpose of collecting money from passengers) on the opposite side. The square, as we now term it, is a beach, with an open sewer running across it from the bottom of Silver Street. The houses on the East, West, and North sides appear however, much as at the present time. Those on the Eastern side have a low wall in front, for the purpose, as it would seem, of securing a dry passage at tide time.

"Litsound" exhibits dwelling houses on the North side of the street, reaching to the *full extent* of Litchdon Terrace*; the buildings on the opposite side are also complete as far as they reach at present.

Part of *"Barbicane Lane"* is shewn, as is also the road passing through *"Portte marish,"* (Port-marsh) and *"Gooze Leaze,"* (now Gooseleigh-marsh) on to *"Cowebrydge."*

The houses in *"Hollande Streett, Crosse Streett,"* Theatre Lane, (not named) and *"Mayden Street,"* and also on the North side of the çattle Market and Quay, on to the Square, occupy, with one exception, the same positions as they now do. The exception regards the site of the Bell Inn, and the Coal Cellars adjoining, which is laid down as a vacant space, having apparently a row of shambles in front. *"The Sande Rudge"* lies close beneath the town, instead of on the Tawstock side as at present.

"The Ryuer Towe" running, at low water, only through the last five arches of *"The Longe Brydge."* The Bridge appears with sixteen arches, as at present.

Such other particulars as I have collected respecting the state of the town and its customs, in " days of yore," will best appear in the Chronological Record, where they will be found under their respective dates.

---

* Probably the houses which appear to have stood at this period on Litchdon Green (now Litchdon Terrace) as well as on the ground occupied by the two adjoining houses (which were built not many years since) were among the number of those " demolished " during the rebellion. – See *Civil Wars*.

CHAPELS AND CHANTRIES*.

Besides a Convent and parish Church, Barnstaple appears to have abounded in religious establishments of a minor order. The following are recorded:—

The Chapel of St. Sabinus has been already noticed, as having formed part of Joel's grant at the foundation of the Priory.

Leland says,

" There hath beene 4 Chapelles yn the Towne, of the which one was at the Est End of the Bridge dedicate to Thomas Becket now profaned; the other 3 yet stande, one of Alhalowes at the North Gate; Another of St. Nicholas at the West Gate, as I remember. One Holman, Vicar of the Paroche Chirch in Berstaple made a fair Chapelle and founded a Chauntrie in it in the Paroche Chirch Yard in Berstaple. "

Brown Willis† mentions three Chantries and a free Chapel, with the pensions paid to the Incumbents of each, in 1553, namely:—

	£	s.	d.
John Hardin Incumbent of St. Ann's Chapel	5	0	0
Robt. Thorne Incument of St. George's Chantry	6	0	0
John Trench of Rowlin's Chantry	1	0	0
Peter Scynthyl incumbent of the Free Chapel there, (and a like sum for the same at Fremington)	2	7	0

---

* Chantry, Chauntry, – A sepulchral Chapel. Such foundations were endowed with revenues arising from landed or other property for the support of priests to chant masses for the souls of the donors and others. – *Britton's Architec. Antiquities.*

† History of Mitred Abbeys, vol.ii.p.66

Of the eight* buildings here mentioned, the situations of four only can be correctly ascertained; but two of these remain, and they were desecrated centuries ago.

THE CHAPEL OF ST. SABINUS,

Was probably annexed to the Church, and enclosed with it when that edifice was rebuilt. This is at once a reasonable supposition, and the best way in which we can account for the omission of the Chapel in the subsequent grant of the Priory, &c. to Lord Howard.

THOMAS-A-BECKET'S CHAPEL,

Was situate at the end of the Bridge, on the precise spot now occupied by the residence of E.R. Roberts, Esq. Leland tells us it was "profaned" in his day. A building (whether the original one or not is uncertain) appears on its site in the old map before referred to. This Chapel was dedicated to Thomas-a-Becket, the canonized Archbishop of Canterbury, and has obtained some celebrity from being said to have been built by Sir William de Tracy, one of the Prelate's assassins, in expiation of his crime. "The Chauntry of St. Thomas," Mr. Oliver informs us, "is frequently mentioned in the Bishop's Registers," but they contain nothing that will warrant a belief that the building was in existence earlier than the reign of Edward the Third.

Historians are much at variance both as to the conduct of de Tracy subsequent to the murder, as well as to the time and place of his death. Giraldus Cambrensis, a contemporary, says that immediately after the murder, Sir William de Tracy hastened to present himself to Bartholomew, Bishop of Exeter, "in cujus Diocesi terras amplas habebat," *in whose Diocese he had large possessions*, to whom he confessed his crime. Some writers state that all the murderers retired to Knaresborough, in Yorkshire, where they remained some time, and then fled to Rome, and were admitted to

---

* Nine are enumerated, but the Chapel in the Church Yard and St. Ann's are the same.

penance by the Pope, Alexander the Third; others again, that some fled for their lives into the North, and some into the West.

One account says that de Tracy died at Cozenza, in Italy, within three years after the death of the Archbishop; another, that he and his companions in guilt ended their days in Jerusalem, and were "buried without the church door belonging to the Templars;" whilst Camden affirms that "Sir William de Traceye, one of the murtherers of Thomas Becket, A.B. of Canterbury, retired twenty-three years subsequent to the occurrence to Mort*, or Morthoe," a village lying on the shore of the Bristol channel, about ten miles West from Barnstaple. There appears certainly but little, if any reason, to conclude that Sir William de Tracy built "The Chantry of St. Thomas," yet it is by no means improbable that the Chapel was founded by some branch of the family†, at a subsequent period.

His relatives would be naturally desirous to do something that might atone for the foul deed by which the name of de Tracy had

---

* In the Church at this place is a handsome momument, said to have been made the depository of the remains of de Tracy, Becket's murderer, but more generally believed to be that of a clergyman named William Tracy, who died at Morte in 1322, and who, as the title of Sir, or "Sire" was commonly applied to the clergy at that period, had it inscribed on his tomb as a customary thing. The following descriptions of this relic of antiquity is copied from the *North Devon Magazine*, for April, 1824 : –

> " It is in length about eight feet, nearly four feet broad, and rises about two feet from the floor of the transept; the figure of it is therefore a long square, or parallelogram, lying across length ways from West to East; but rather broader at one end than the other; the West end being the broadest; the northern side of it is occupied by some armorial bearings consisting of three escutcheons ;– one containing three *lions passant gardant* ; – a second three *bends* ; – a third a *saltire* – and several plain little gothic arches in relief, enclosing under each arch, the remains of a sculptured figure, seemingly intended to represent some female Saint. On the opposite or south side are several small gothic arches also bold in relief, and in various patterns of gothic ornament. At the head, or western end of the tomb, is a defaced sculpture of Christ on the cross between two other figures. The eastern end, or foot of the monument, is now plain; perhaps it once had a sculpture which has been entirely defaced. On the top of all is a larger oblong slab of grey stone, or marble, bordered on the western and southern sides by an inscription, supposed to be in Lombardic letters. Many of these are totally obliterated; but from the remainder the reader may pretty plainly trace something about a *de Tracy* : antiquarians read it :

' SYRE Wm DE TRACY
MAY I FIND MERCY! '

The rest of the slab is covered with an in-sculptured outline (now rather indistinct) of the figure of a man robed, and bearing something in his hand, said to be a chalice; perhaps an hour glass may be as good a supposition."

† Two of the de Tracys were Lords of Barnstaple. – (See descent of Manor.)

been stained; and in no way could they better do this, than by the endowment of a religious edifice; but especially of one consecrated to so popular a saint and martyr as Thomas-a-Becket*.

ALL-HALLOWS CHAPEL.

The Chapel of All-Hallows, or All-Saints, stood immediately over the North Gate. Its place is now occupied by a room built about sixty years since, and appropriated as a school-room for the boys belonging to the *Charity School.*—(See Charities.) I have met with no particulars respecting the ancient building, nor can I state how or when it came into the hands of the Corporation, whose property it appears to have been previous to the erection of the school-room.

ST. MARY AND ST. NICHOLAS CHAPEL.

The earliest mention I have found made of this Chapel, occurs in the ninth year of Henry the Sixth, (1430) when "Henry Piers and Walter Holmore" are noticed as "wardens of St. Mary and St. Nicholas Chapple near the Strande," which shews it to have been then used as a place of worship. The building was purchased from the Crown in December 1550, by the Mayor and Corporation, subject to the payment of 3s. 5d. per annum. It appears to have been almost immediately appropriated to its present use†, that of a warehouse for goods imported, which, from the owners not being residents, or from any other cause, may require to be placed under the custody of the "Quay Master" or wharfinger.

The buildings is of rough stone; but from the solidity of its structure, although perhaps the most ancient, it bids fair to vie in duration with every modern erection in the town.

* One hundred thousand pilgrims have been registered at a time in Canterbury, and £954 6s 3d. was in one year offered at the Archbishop's shrine, whilst at the Virgin Mary's only £4 1s 8d., and at " God's Altar" *nothing* was deposited. Louis the Seventh of France made a pilgrimmage to the tomb, and " bestowed on the shrine a jewel, which was esteemed the richest in all christendom."

† Wyot speaks of it in 1590 under its present designation – the Quay Hall. – (See *Chron. Record.*)

ST. ANN'S CHAPEL.

An account somewhat different from that furnished by Leland (See Chapels and Chantries) is given of this Chapel, but without any authority being quoted, in the periodical work already referred to:—

"The Chapel of our lady, in the church-yard of Barnstaple, in which were two charities (a misprint for Chauntries); one founded by Thomas Holman, Vicar of Barnstaple, valued at seven pounds a year; and the other called *St. James's Charity* (Chauntry), founded by Robert Redmyn, and valued at £10 18*s*. 1*d*. per annum; of which £5 were allowed to a priest, and the remainder appropriated to repairs, and the relief of the poor."

The designation of the Chapel as that "of our lady," or St. Mary, is certainly an error*; how far the rest of the account may be correct, I cannot determine.

The earliest memorandum I have met with relative to this property, occurs in the third year of the reign of Edward the Sixth (1549), May 3rd, in which year "Nicholas and Roger Prideaux granted Chauntry and Lands of St. Ann's Chapel to Henry Cade and others". The 20th of January, in the following year, "St. Ann's Chauntry and Chapel" was sold to the Mayor and Corporation of Barnstaple, who, with becoming liberality, granted the use of it for a place of worship to a number of French protestants, who, having fortunately escaped with their lives from the sanguinary persecution that followed th revocation of the edict of Nantz, in 1685, came to this town†, and took up their abode here. Divine service

* That the quay hall was St. Mary and *St. Nicholas' Chapel*, which we have already seen was "near the Strande" , there can be no doubt; it came into the hands of the Corporation under that title, about the same time that we find them purchasing " St. Ann's *Chantry and Chapel*."

† A friend has furnished me with the following narrative, communicated by an aged gentleman, still living in London :– " his ancestors were amongst those who left Rochelle in a small crowded vessel, in the height of the protestant persecution; they were tossed about in wretched blowing weather for a long time; at length they found themselves in the Bristol Channel. They sailed over the bar, up the river, and landed on the Quay, at Barnstaple, on a Sunday morning, during divine service. In their miserable destitution they ranged themselves in the Market House ; the inhabitants, when they came out of Church, flocked to see the poor refugees ; an old gentlemen" (would his name have been recorded!) " took two of them home with him to dinner, and recommended his fellow townsmen to follow his example; thus, in a few minutes, they were all distributed throughout the town. many of them in a little time received remittances from their

continued to be performed in the French language, as late as the middle of the past century; the last officiating minister was a Dr. Duncan; he died about the year 1760. The building is now used as a *"Grammar School,"* (See Charities, under this head) and is denominated *The High School.* Philip Wyot (Chron. Rec. 1608,) says, "The Town of Barnestaple holdeth the Chantry of St. Ann of the Crown by Soccage, it was bought of Edwd 6, and some other Lands by that Tenure, for wh^ch by Composition the Town paid xx^g." It does not, however, appear that any such payment is now made, except that already noticed.—(See ST. ANN'S CHAPEL)

According to tradition, there was once a Chapel in the narrow passage leading from the Quay, under the Custom House, to the back premises of several houses in High Street. There is also said to have been one behind the residence of Charles Blackmore, Esq. in Cross Street (formerly the *Globe Inn*). That both these accounts have the same local reference, is quite evident, from the relative situations of the passage and house alluded to; two lines drawn from which, at right angles, would cross each other at the distance of eighty or a hundred feet. There are, however, no apparent remains of any religious edifice either on this spot, or elsewhere in the town, except those already pointed out.

correspondents in London, and left the place ; among whom were the ancestors of the individual from whom this account was derived; they were named LE PINE. The following are the names of some of the persons who became residents here, many of whose descendents are still living in the town and neighbourhood, some in affluence, and some in receipt of a stipend paid them by our Government, but which, it is understood, is to cease on the demise of the persons now enjoying it :–

MONS. DE RUE	MONS. SERVANTE
MONS. DE LA TOUR	MONS. L' OISEAU
MONS. DU BARRY	MONS. ROCHE
MONS. MOURNIER	

The inhabitants were no losers by the generous sympathy they exercised towards the refugees, some of whom, introduced an improved mode of drying cloth, and so much did Barnstaple excel in the art, " that the merchants of Exeter, for a long series of years, constantly sent their goods there to be dyed."

* It may appear strange that these individuals should, in their destitute situation, have passed by Appledore and so near to Bideford, and yet have landed at Barnstaple. There is every probability, that this town had long been engaged in commerce with France, either the vessel in which the unfortunate emigrants embarked, had been accustomed to trade to this port, or that some of the individuals had commercial connexions here. We may reasonably suppose that from either of these causes they would be induced to shape their course for Barnstaple, and consequently that their arrival here was not , as would appear from the above recital, the effect of chance. Wyot speaks of "Shipping" to and from *Rochelle.* Chron. *Rec.* 1593

APPENDIX TO CHAPTER I.

[A.]

Containing Extracts relating to Barnstaple (taken from the copies published by the Commissioners of Public Records), from the following national documents:—

DOMESDAY BOOK.— Transcripts from this interesting work are given literally*, and accompanied by a full Latin copy, with an English translation. In order to ensure their correctness, the two latter have been obtained from the Record Office, in the Tower.

EXON' DOMESDAY.—*Literal Copy.*—(from this work, which as a county survey, is unique, the account of Devonshire in the Conqueror's Domesday, was compiled. The original is still preserved in the Cathedral Library, Exeter.)

> CALENDARIUM INQUISITIO POST MORTEM.—*Literal Copy.*
> ROTULI HUNDREDORUM, Vol. 1 . . . . .   ”   ”
> CALENDARIUM ROTOLORUM PATENTIUM . .   ”   ”
> JONES'S INDEX TO THE RECORDS, Vol. I and 2   ”   ”

It will be seen that many of the quotations from these volumes refer to the Manor, Castle, &c. It was not until long since this work had been in progress, that I was aware of the existence of these valuable books of reference; but having, in the course of an anxious and may I add laborious, search after all that could be gathered, either from men or books which might furnish a Memorial of Barnstaple, met with the works, I made the extracts, although more for my own gratification than a view to their publication; since consulting such a number of Records†, and giving extracts from them was of course out of the question, unless the "Memorials" had been to make their appearance in the shape of "a goodly quarto," at least. As however, though merely indices, they possess considerable interest, I conceive it would be doing wrong to suppress them.

---

* As nearly so as was practicable in ordinary type ; the abbreviatory characters only are wanting. the same observation is also applicable to Exon domesday, and in a few instances to the other works.

† I presume it is generally understood that copies of such documents are only to be procured from the TOWER, and that, necessarily, at a *very considerable expense.*

TERRA REGIS—LAND OF THE KING.

"Rex habet burgu Barnestaple—Rex. E. habuit. in dnio. Ibi st intra burgu. xl. burgses. ix st ext burg. Int oms regi. xl. sol ad pensu epo cstantiensi xx solid ad numerum. Ibi st xxiii dom uastatæ postq uenit in Angliam."

Rex habet burgum Barnestaple. Rex Edwardus habuit in dominico. Ibi sunt intra burgum xl burgenses, et ix sunt extra burgum. Inter omnes reddunt regi xl solidos ad pensum, et episcopo Constantiensi xx solidos ad numerum. Ibi sunt xxiii domus vastatæ postquam rex venit in Angliam.

The King has the borough of Barnstaple. King Edward had it in demesne. There are within the borough forty burgesses, and there are nine without the borough. Altogether they render to the King forty shillings in weight, and to the bishop of Constance twenty shillings in number. There are twenty-three houses destroyed since the King came into England.

TERRA EPI CONSTANTIENSIS — LAND OF THE BISHOP CONSTANCE.

"Ipse eps ht in Barnestaple x burgses redd xlv den vii dom uastatas dimid v træ molin redd xx solid xx solid de csutud   burgensui regis."

Ipse episcopus habet in Barnestaple x burgenses, reddentes xlv denarios, et vii domos vastatas, et dimidium virgatæ terræ. Et molendinum reddit xx solidos, et xx solidos de consuetudine burgensium Regis.

The same bishop has in Barnstaple ten burgesses, rendering forty-five pence, and seven houses destroyed, and half a virgate of land. And the mill renders twenty shillings, and twenty shillings of the custom of the King's burgesses.

"Brai teneb Aluuard T.R.E. geldb p dim v træ. Tra e iiii. car. In dnio. e. i. car viii. uilli cu. i. car. Ibi. v. ac. pti. xxx. ac pasturæ. tntd siluœ. In Barnestaple un ortus redd. iiii. denar. Olim. x. sol. modo ual. xx. solid."

Brai tenebatur Aluuard tempore Regis Edwardi, et geldebatur pro dimidio virgatæ terræ. Terra est iiii carucatæ. In dominio est i carucata, et viii villani cum i caruca. Ibi v acræ prati et xxx acræ pasturæ et tantundem silvæ. In Barnestaple unus ortus reddit iv denarios. Olim x solidos. Omodo valet xx solidos.

Brai was holden by Aluuard in the time of King Edward, and was taxed for half a virgate of land. The land is four carucates. In demesne there is one carucate, and eight villeins with one plough. There are five acres of meadow, and thirty acres of pasture, and as much wood. In Barnestaple one garden renders four pence. In time past ten shillings. Now it is worth twenty shillings.

TERRA BALDVINI VICECOMTIS —
LAND OF BALDWIN THE SHERIFF.

"Ide Balduin ht in Barnestaple vii. burgses. vi. dom uastatas. h reddt p annu. vii. solid vi denar."

Idem Balduinus habet in Barnestaple vii burgenses et vi domos vastatas. Hii reddunt per annum vii solidos et vi denarios.

The same Baldwin has in Barnestaple seven burgesses and six houses destroyed. These render by the year seven shillings and six pence.

"Robt. ten. de Balduin in Barnestaple ii. dom. reddt ii. solid."

Robertus tenet de Balduino in Barnestaple ii domos, reddunt ii solidos.

Robert holds of Baldwin in Barnestaple two houses, and they render two shillings.

41

TERRA ROBERTI DE ALBMARIE—
LAND OF ROBERT DE ALBEMARIE.

"Ipse Robt. ht in BARNESTAPLE ii dom uastatas. redd. iiii. denar."

Ipse Robertus habet in BARNESTAPLE duas domos vastatas reddentes iiii denarios.

The same Robert has in BARNESTAPLE two houses destroyed rendering four pence.

EXON' DOMESDAY.

TERRA BALDVINI VICECOMITIS INDEVENESIRA.

" V Balduin ht. i. mansione que uocat Aiscireuuilla. q tenuit brismar ea die qua rex. E. f u m. reddidit Gildu p. i. hida. hanc posst arare. xii. carr. hanc ten & Rotbt de bello monte de Vicecomite. Inde ht. R. i. uirga ii. carr in dnio. uillani hnt iii. uirgas iiii. carr dim. Ibi ht R. ix. uillanos. vi. bord. ii. seruos ii. animalia. viii. porcos. c. oues. xxviii. capras. ii. mansuras. i bardestaplensi burgo q reddunt p annu ii. sol. ccc. agros nem culi. iii. agros pti. i."

DNICAT REGIS AD REGNV PERTINENS I DEVENESIRA.

" V Rex ht. i. burgu q uocat Barnestaple que tenuit, E. rex ea die q ipse fuit. u. &. m. Ibi ht Rex xl. burgenses intra burgn. & foras. xi. & isti reddt. xl. sol ad pensu regi.& xx sol numero epo cstantiensi. & Ibi st. xxiii dom uastate. pq. W. rex habuit anglia."

Under head of "Lideforda."— " Et si expeditio uadit p tra l p mare reddt tantu de seruitio qntu Totenais reddit l Barnestapla."

Under head of "Essecestre."— " Et qn Expeditio ibat p tra aut p mare seruiebat ista ciuitas quantu. v. hide tre & Toteneis. & lideforda. & Barnestabla seruiebant quantu & pdicta ciutas."

42

TERRA EPI CONSTANTIENSIS IN DEVRESCIRA.

" Ibi ht Eps xl uillanos &. xxx. bord. &. vi. serous. i. burgense In barnestapla q reddit xv. den. & xiii porcarios q reddt. xxi porcu & xviii animalia. & c. l. oues. &. x. agros nemoris. & xx.agros pti. &. c. agros pasque. hec mans reddit. xxii. lib. & qu. Eps recepit. reddebat. xii libras"

" V Eps ht. i. mans q uocat Brai. q tenuit Ailuuard ea die q rex. E. f. u. & reddidit gilu p dim uirga. hanc poss arare. iiii. carr. hanc ten & Drogo de epo. Inde ht. D. i. ferlinu. &. i. carr in dnio. & Vill. i. &. i. ortu in barnestapla q reddit. iii. denarios. &xxiii. oues. ferlinu. &. i. carr. Ibi ht. D. viii vill; &. iii. animalia. & iii porc; &. xx. caps. & xxx. agros nemoris. & v. agros prati. & xxx. agros pas que. hec ual &. xx. Sol & qu eps recepit ualebat. v. sol."

" V Eps ht. x. burgenses In barnestapla; q reddit. iii. sol. & ix. denarios & vii. dom uastatas. & dim uirga tre &. i. moledinu q reddit xx. sol. p annu. &. xx sol csuetudine burgensiu. regis."

TERRA BALDUIN VICECOMITS INDEVENESIRA.

" V Balduin ht. vii burgenses In barnestapla. &. vi. dom uastatas. &. isti burgenses &. iste dom uastate reddt p annu. vii. sol & vi. den."

CALENDRIUM

INQUISITIONUM POST MORTEM

SIVE

ESCAETARUM.

VOL. I.

TEMPORIBUS REGUM HEN. III. ED. I. & ED. II

Escaet' & Inquisitiones Anno 2° Edw. I.

100.— "WILL'US FILIUS WILL'I MARTYNE* Barnestaple baron.
—Heselle & Rews unum feod'.— Thelebrugge & Chattemere
unum feod'.—Cloteworthy 4 Pars feod'.—Horton 4 Pars feod'.—
Ralegh & Cahaledecumbe unumfeod'. —Walworthy—Kunemore
—Trendeleshoo—Sevenashe—Pachehole—Northcote—
Cambescote & Bridewike 5 feod'.—Crakeweye 3 Part' feod'—
Cliftracy unum feod'.—Braunford spek dimid' feod'.—Northcote
prioris dimid' feod.—Coriton unum feod'.—Ulneleghey 4 part'
feod'.— Aylerdesford, 20 part' feod'.—Boy Parva dimid' feod'.
—Peddehull dimid' feod—Winmersham unum feod' in com'
Somerset.—Nether Exe unum feod'.—Chaggeford unum
feod'—Milford.—Northrissell.—Thorne.—Roude.—Kymworth
& Newlond 2 feod'.

Barnestaple castrum
advoc' 2 Cantaria'ibm } advoc'ones eccl'iar'."

---

* Including the possessions here enumerated, which all belonged to the Barony of Barnstaple, two hundred and forty
distinct properties, among which are many Manors, are mentioned as being held by this individual.
the first entry (the only one in English) is a curious one : –

" London' un' gardin' & 7 shope in Shoe Lane in warda de } *London* "
' Farindone extent '.

VOL. II.

TEMPORE REGIS EDWARD II.

Escaet' de anno primo Edwardi Tercij.

Num^r.

40.— "NICH'US MARTYN Barnestaple maner'."

82.— "PH'US DE COLUMBARIJS ET ALINORA UXOR EJUS PRO LODOWICO DE KEMEYS P'SONA ECCL' DE COMBEMARTYN Barnestaple Maner'."

Anno Sexto Edwardi III.

14.— "PHILLIPUS DE COLUMBARIJS ET ALINORA UX'EJUS PRO QUODAM CAPPELLANO Barnestaple 40s. redd' exeunt' de quodam furno (*fundo !*) ibm."

Anno Decimo Sexto Edwardi III.

44.— "RICUS DE MERTONE Snitecombe un' carc' terr' &c. ut de honore & Castro de Bernstaple."

50.— "PHILLIPUS DE COLUMBARIJS Barnestaple maner'."

51.— "ALINORA UXOR PHI'. DE COLUMBARIJS Barnstaple maner."

Anno Decimo Octavo Edwardi III.

33.— NICH'US D'AUDELEYE PRO RICO HODY Barnestaple Maner; remanent eidem Nicho."

100.— "BURGENSES DE BARNESTAPLE, Barnestaple burgus diverse liberties et privilegia ibm."

Anno Vicesimo Edwardi III.

58.— "JACOBUS DE AUDELEYE FEOFFAVIT HUGONEM DE
NEWEHALLE CAPELLANUM & AL' Barnestaple Maner';
remanet eidem Jacobo."

Escaet' de anno vicesimo quinto Edwardi III.

30.— "JOH'ES DE STONFORD PRO CERTIS CAPELLANIS.
Bremrigge manner' ut de Baron' de Barnestaple; reman' eidem
Johi."

Escaet' de anno tricesimo tertio Edw. III.

17.— "JACOBUS DE AUDELEYE DE HELEYE FOEFFAVIT
HUGONEM DE NEWEHALL P'SONAM ECCL'IE DE
SOUTHMOLTON Barnestaple Maner'; reman' Jacobo."

Escaet' de anno tricesimo quarto Edw. III.

25.— "JACOBUS D'AUDELEYE FEOFFAVIT HUGONEM DE
NEWEHALL P'SONAM ECC'IE DE SOUTHMOLTON,
Barnestaple baronia reman' eidem Jacobo."

Escaet' de anno quinquagesimo primo Edw. III.
6.— "HUGH DE COURTNEY COMES DEVON'.—Barnestaple
Castrum de."

———

VOL. III.

TEMPORIBUS REGUM RIC. II. & HEN. VI.

Escaet' de anno primo Ricardi Secundi.

63.— " RAD'US DE WILLEMERE Barnestaple 4 Acr'. terr', &c."

Escaet' de anno Quarto Ricardi Secundi.

26.— " THOMAS FILIUS ET HERES SIMONIS FLEMMYNG NUPER
BARO DE SLANE Hautebray maner' ut de honore de
Barnestaple. Barnestaple burgus quedam reddit', &c."

Escaet' de anno Nono Richardi Secundi.

32.— " NIGELLUS LORINGE CH'R ET MARGARETTA UXOR
EJUS—Barnestaple 10s. reddit' vocat Hogesfee."

Escaet' de anno Duodecimo Ricardi Secundi.

183.— " JOH'ES BLAKE DE LODDEFORD *de tenis suis forisfact*—
Barnestaple castrum."

Escaet' de anno Decimo-tertio Ricardi Secundi.

31.— " JOH'ES FILIUS ET HERES WILL'I DE LUSCOTE—
Barnstaple castrum."

Primo Pars escaet' de anno Decimo Quinto Ricardi Secundi.

16.— " MARGARETTA UXOR HUGONIS DE COURTNEY NUPER
COMITIS' DEVON'— Barnestaple castrum."

54.— " JOH'ES PAULET CH'R ET MARGARETTA UXOR EJUS—
Barnestaple castrum."

Escaet' de anno Decimo Octavo Ricardi Secundi.

26.— " THOMAS FILIUS ET HERES JOH'IS KAYLE—
Barnestaple "castrum."

Escaet de anno Vicesimo Ricardi Secundi.

17.— " WILL'US DE COURTNAY NUPER ARCHIEP'US CANTUAR'—
Barnestaple castrum."

Escaet' de anno Vicemo Primo Ricardi Secundi.

23.— " ELIZABETHA UXOR FULCONIS FITS-WARREN CH'R—
Barnestaple castrum."

Escaet' de anno Quinto Henrici Quarti.

36.— " THOMASIA UXOR JOH'IS CHICHESTR'—Barnestaple Maner'
in Com. Devon Somerset, Ralegh maner juxta Barnstaple ut de
manerio de Barnstaple—Barnstaple maner'."

Escaet' de anno Septimo Henrici Quarti.

55.— " ROBERTUS DE HARRINGTON CHIVALER—Barnstaple
reddit' in burgo de brendon maner'."

Escaet' de anno Octavo Henrici Quarti.

66.— " WILL'US BEAMOND Aishwater quarta pars unus feodi
militis ut de castro de Barnstaple—Barnstaple divers' mess', &c."

Anno Nono Regis Henrici Quarti.

36.— " FULCO FITSWARIN' FILUS ET HERES FULCONIS FITZ
WARYN CHIVALER—Barnstaple castr'."

ROTULI HUNDREDORUM

TEMP. HEN. III. & EDW. I.

IN TURR' LOND'

ET

IN CURIA RECEPTÆ SCACCARIJ WESTM. ASSERVATI.

VOL. I.

DEVON, *Edw*. I.

"INQUISITIONES facte p pceptu dni Regis in com' Devon' de' jurin' & libtatib' dni Regis subtractis & excessis vicecom' coron' escaet' & alio' ballivo' dni Regis quo' cumq'alio' ballio' quoquomodo dnm Regem spectantib' anno regni Regis E. t'cio."

VERED 'CM BURGI DE BARNESTABLE.

" Jur' Robtus Horbert, Benedcus de la Pille, Silvestr' de Fursill, Nichus Peytenin, Henr' Wytloc, Robs Rypan, Johs Petyt, consell Ricus de Pilton, Ricus Cissor, Thom' Bylbe, Benedcus le Cuyt, & Alex' le Teynturer, dict sup sacrm suu Quot & que dnica mania &c. nichil."

" Dicut qd Galfrus de Canvill tenet pdem burgum de BARNESTABLE cum castello de dno Rege in captie p decensum Matild ux' pdci Galfri que est hes Henr' de Tracy p sviciu duo' militu vel qa tuo' armigo' cu loric' capell ferreis & lancea qn dns Rex vadit in exccitu p xl dies ad custum pdci Galfri Et istud sviviu fecit p pdco burgo & castello & p membr' ptin' ad dcm burgu scilt FREMYNGTON TAVSTOK NEMET & BOVY Et ita tenuut antec' pdce Matild de Reg' Angl a tempe coquestus Willi le Bastard' Et idem Galfrus ht assiam panis & cvis' furkas & tumbrell & Pillor' a conquestu pdco Et ide Galfrus tenet pdcm burgum cu mbr' pdcis p baron' de dno Rege Et ptinent ad pdcum burg' lij feod milit' Et est pdcs burg cu mbr capd baron' sue."

50

" D' vic capientib' &c."

" Dicut Rogus Pridyas dum fuit vie' cepit de hoibus dei burg' xls. p hidag' faciend cont^a libtatem dci burgi ubi nucq^a hydag' face solebant & anteqa pacem hre possent fine fecunt cu pdco vic' p pdcos xls."

" Dnt & qd idem Rogus dum fuit vic' tenuit trnu suu pluries p annu ubi semel tene debuit p annu & amciavit hoies ad voluntate suam & injuste."

" Dnt & qd prior de Frompton ht wreccum maris & teolon' in manio suo de NORHAM & hoc de novo & cap' teolon' de hoib' pdci burgi injuste ad gave dampnu pdci burgi q° war'ignorant."

" De cetis cap'nichil sciut In cuj rei testimoniu sigilla pdco' jur huic inqi scoi sut appoita."

"In dorso." "Bur de BARNESTABLE."

VERDICTU' HUNDR' DE NORTAUET'.

" Dicut quod NIMET Ta ci tenetr in capite de dno Reg' quasi membru ptines ad baroniam BARNASTAPOL & valet p ann' x libas cu advocacone ecce."

VERDICTU' HUNDR'I DE TEYNGEBRUGG'.

RICUS DE BABECUMBE	ROBERTUS DE WREY
WILLUS HUGHETON	RICUS DE WREY
RICUS GAYER	ANDR' DE HALGHEWAL
RICUS DE GATEPATHE	WILLUS DE HUGHETON JUNIOR
JOHNES DE WYTEWEYE	WILLUS LE MARSCHALL
ROBTUS CRESPIN	MATHS DE CHYTELESBER'.

" Dicut q'Galffr' de Kaunville & Matillux' ejus tenet di feod q'rtam pte & xxm^a' ptem feod uni milit' in SUTHBOVY ptinens ad baron'suam de BARDESTAPLE."

BARON' DE BARNESTAP".

" Thom' de Chageford ten'villa de CHAGEFORD & de TEYNGCOMB'p homag' & svico de Galfro de Canvile Galfrs de Reg'& sut ij feod."

51

" Wills le Espee ten' villa de BRAMFORD SPEC de Hugon' de Cortenay p homag' & svico & secta cur' & Hug' de Galfro de Canvile Galfrus de Reg' & est di feod Morteyn."

" Johs Pycot ten' villam de REWE de Elena de Gorg' Elena de Johe de Blakeford & idm de Galfro de Ganvile idm G. de Rege & est j feod."

" Wills de Campo Arnulphi ten' villam de COVELEGH de Johe de Blakeford p homag' & svico & idm de Galfro de Canvile Galfris de Reg' & est qarta ps feod."

CALENDARIUM

ROTULORUM PATENTIUM*

IN TURRI LONDINENSI.

Secunda Patent' de Anno 14° Regis Edwardi Tertij.
Membr.
7.—   " Pro Priore de Barnestaple."

Prima Patent' de Anno 17° R.E.T.A Tergo.

20.—   " Dors' pro Burgens' de Barnestable."

Prima Patent' de Anno 18° R.E.T.A Tergo.

21.—   "De inquirendo de libertat' villæ de Barnstable."

Prima Patent' de Anno 12° Regis Ricardi Secundi.

27.—   " Pro Decano Ebor'.

---

* " It may be proper to observe, that as this calendar, though entitled to great merit, is only a section, various entries appear on the Patent Rolls, which are not here described ; and therefore, though this work will be found to yield abundant information, no one is to be deterred from an examination of any record referred to elsewhere, as being on the Patent Roll, because it is not to be discovered there. " – *Preface, by the Commisioners, to Calen. Rot. Pat.*

" Rex concessit Johni de Holland fratri suo Comiti Huntingdon et Elizabethæ uxori ejus et hæred' de corpore Elizabethæ procreat' septigentas marcas annuas exeunt' de certis custumis."

" Rex in volore bis mille marcarum per annum una cum septigent marcis prout supra dedit Joh' Comiti Huntingdon et hæredibus masculis de corpore suo et de corpore sictæ Elizabethæ procreat' manerium de Ardington ac manerium vocat' Filberdscourt in Esthanny quæ nuper fuerunt Aliciæ Perrers et Regi fortisfact' villam de Northwich in com' Cestriæ terr' et dominium de Hope et Hopedale in Wallia et quendam redditum 7l. 6s. 8d. de exit' terr' de Couuimershe maneria de Blakedon Ludford et Staunden juxta Dunsterdon in Somers' maneria de Boveytracey Barnstable Cumbemarlyn Fremyngton Northlien Holdesworthy Langacre Southmolton in com' Devon' maner' de Takebere in Cornubia quæ fuerunt Jacobi D'Andlegh de Helegh maner' de Torington et Cokerington in Devon' nuper Johnis Cary attincti ac manerium de Haselebeare in Somerset per servitia debita."

Secunda Patent' de Anno 17° Ricardi Secundi.

137.— " Quod burgenses villæ de Barnestaple quæ est de antiquo dominco coronæ Regis sint quieti de theoneo &c. per totum regnum."

Secunda Patenr de Anno 17° Rex Edwardi Quarti.

20.— " Arnpl' exempl' libertat' pro burgensibus de Barnestaple e recordis infra turr' London' existen'."

Prima Patent' de Anno 2° Regis Henrici Quarti.

1.— " Ricus Lercedeken tenet de Rege pef servic' milit' ut de castro de Barnestaple. n. l."

Prima Patent' de Anno 17° R.E.T.

27.— " Cantar' infra castrum de Barnastaple."

Secun. Pat. de Anno 13° R.E.T.

15.— " De escambio inter Priores de Pilton et de Barnestaple."

Prima Patent' de Anno 14° R.E.T.-A Tergo.

2.— " Pro burgensibus de Barnestaple in com' Devon' ac de libertatibus suis eis concess' per Athelstanum Regem."

Prima Pars Patent' de Anno 2° Regis Ricardi Secundi.

38.— " Priori de Barnestaple manumisit Petro de Gorewell villanum suum per R. confirmat'."

INDEX TO RECORDS,*

CALLED
THE ORIGINALIA AND MEMORANDA,

ON THE LORD TREASURER'S REMBRANCER'S SIDE OF THE EXCHEQUER

VOL. I.

" ORIGINALIA TEMPORE REGAINÆ ELIZABETHÆ BARNESTAPLE (Burgi) Incorporatio, in Com. Devoniæ. 2 Pars Original. Anno 38, Rot.11."

* The following Extract from the preface to this Vol. deserves particular attention. The observations here made apply with equal force to the whole of the works having reference to Documents preserved in the Record Office :–
" The Records of this country, in their various repositories, in point of antiquity, preservation, correctness, and authority, and extent of information, we may say with confidence, exceed those of any country whatever ; and all persons who have been introduced to a knowledge of their nature and importance, have been astonished that matters of such consequence as well to the public at large as to the individuals, should exist in our public offices, which are always accessible, without being more generally known and understood.

To consider our public Records in their various points of view, we not only find it absolutely necessary that the general historian should glean his information from them, but we find also that to the topographical historian they are the very essence of his work.

These Records are of that vast extent, and contain such necessary and useful information, and such multifarious matter, that we can, with almost moral certainty, find a considerable portion of Record evidence relative to all, even the smallest denomination of landed property, throughout the whole kingdom, and proportionally more relative to towns and places of note " – *Preface to Jones's Index to Public Records, p. p. 3 & 4 .*

" ORIGINALIA TEMPORE REGIS JACOBI 1. BARNESTAPLE Burgensibus, Libertates confirmatæ, in Com. Devon. 3 Pars Original. Anno 9. Rotulo 26."

" BARNESTAPLE Majori & Burgensibus, Concessio Libertatum, in Comitatu Dorset. 3 Pars Original. Anno 8. Rotulo 59."

" Originalia Tempore Regis Jacobi II. BARNSTAPLE Aldermani & Burgenses incorporati, in Com. Devoniæ. 2 Pars Original. Anno 4. Rotulo 15."

VOL. II.

MEMORANDA.

" BARNESTAPLE. Pro parte Baroniâ in Comitatu Devoniæ. Hilarii Fines, 2 Ed. III. Rot. ——— "

" A Grant to Thomas Evingham, of the Castle and Borough of *Barnestaple*, in Com. Devoniæ Original. I Ric. III. Rot. 83."

" Majori & Burgensibus, ibid."

" Finis solutus pro Confirmatione Libertatum. Original. 3 Hen. VIII. Rotulo. 92."

" Burgenses incorporati ac de Libertatibus eis concessis. 1 Pars Original. 3 & 4 Phil. & Mariæ. Rotulo 43."

" Note, *Vide* Originalia *for the Charters of the Queen Eliz. and King James 1. that of* 9 James 1. *being an* Inspeximus, recites Charters as far back as K. John."

Extracts relating to Barnstaple, being literal copies from the following national works, as published by the Commissioners of Public Records:-

PLACITA DE QUO WARRANTO
ROUTLORUM ORIGINALIUM, Vol. I and 2
TESTA DE NEVILL
PLACITUM IN DOMO CAPIT. WESTM. ASSERVATORUM
CALENDARIUM ROTULORUM ET INQUISITIONEM
AD QUOD DAMNUM.

PLACITA DE QUO WARRANTO

TEMPORIBUS EDW. I. II. & III.

IN CURIA RECEPTÆ SCACCARII WESTM. ASSERVATA.

" Galfridus de Caunvle sum' fuit ad respond dno Regi de plito quo war' clam hre visum funci plegii furc' emend assie panis & cvis' facte in BOVY TRACY que ad Coron' dui Reg' ptinent sine lic &c."

" Et Galfridus venit et dicit qd ipe tenet maner de BOVY TRACY p legem Angl de her' Willi Matini sine quo no pot' iude dno Regi respondere qui modo venit p sum' & respond siml cum predco Galfro & dicunt qd maner' de "BOVY Tacy est quoddam membru."

" Barone ipius Willi de BARDESTAPLE ad quod pdce lib ptnet."

" Et dicunt qd omes antec' ipi Willi a tempe quo no exstat memor'usi sunt precis libtatib'. Et eo war' clam' ipe hre libtates predcas. Et quia nllm aliud inde ostend warrantu Io ad judm. Et dat est eis dies coram dno Rege a."

" Ad Jud'm die Pasch in unu mensem ubicumq, &c. de audo judo suo &c. Rto. 41. d."

" Idem Galfrs sum' fuit ad r' dno Regi de plito quo war' clam' hre visu fᵃnci pleg' furc' tumbellu & emend assie panis & cvis fᵃcte in BARDESTAPLE sine lic' &c."

" Et Galfrs sunt cum predco Willo ven' et dicunt qd BARDESTAPLE est apud Baroniam pdci Willi ad quod huj mod ilibtates ptinent. Et qd omes antec pdci Willi a tempe quo no exstat memor' usi sunt predcis libtatib'."

" Et oe war' clam' prodcis lib. Et q nllm aliud ostend war' Io ad judm. Et dat est eis dies coram dno Rege a die Pasch in unu mensem ubicuq &c. de audo judo suo. Ad jud'm Rot. 41 d."

ROTULORUM ORIGINALIUM

IN CURIA SCACCARII ABBREVATIO.
VOL. I.

TEMPORIBUS REGUM HEN. III. ED. I. & ED. II.

In Origin' de anno R. E. fil' R. E. xix.
Extract' Clausar'.

"R. assignavit Pho de Columbariis & Alianore ux' ejus sorori & un' hedum Willi fil' Willi Martyn manium de Coumbe Martyn cum ptin' in com' Devon' qd xxxvj^{ll} xviij^s iij^d q' manium de Bernestaple cum ptin' in eodem com' qd ad xxvj^{ll} xj^s vij^d obq' manium de Holne cum ptin' in eodem com qd ad xix^{ll} ix^d ob' quasdam tras & quedam ten' in civitate Exon' in eodem com' q' xij^s ix^d manium de Haldesworth cum ptin' in eodem com' q ad xxx^{ll} xv^s vj^d ob' manium de Southmolton cum hundredo forinseco de Southmolton et cum redditu de West-Ansti & Yest-Ansti cum Ptin' in eodem cum' q' ad xxviij^{ll} ij^s x^d q' et manium de Fremyngton cum ptin' in eodem com' qd ad cxxxix^{ll} xvj^s iij^d q' extendunt' p ann' hend' p partem ipsius Alianore, &c. Ita tamen qd pdci Plis et Alianora durante minore estatis Jacobi de Audlegh consanguinei & altius heredum pdci Willi infra etatem & in custodia R. existensis solvat R. p ann' vij^s q qui ex cedunt, &c. cepit fidelitatem, &c. Et ideo &c.   Ro.23."

VOL. II.

EDWARDI TERTII.

In Orig' de anno ij^{do} R. E. III.

Grossi Fines.

"Phus de Columbariis finem fecit p centum marcus p lic' hend' feoffandi Lodewycum de Kemmeys psonam ecclie Combe Martyn & Rogm de Bradniche psonam ecclie de Berewyk de maniis de Fremyngton Barnestaple Combe Martyn & Holme ac aliis tris q' &c.   Ro.23."

In Orig' de anno r. r. Edwardi t'cii post conquestum xiiij.

" R. p bono s'vicio, &c. concessis Thome Crosse custodiam prioratuum de Craswell Cowyk Barnestaple Oteryngton Totteneyes Tuardrayth & Moddebury as loco' tra' tenemento' & redditum quo'cumq, ad eosdem prioratus spectancium q' &c. hend q mdiu, &c. reddo inde R. p ann' ad sccm R. vel alibi ad mandatum R. p quolibet prioratuum pdco' videlt p dco priorantu de Craswell sexdecim marcus & p pdco prioratu de Cowyk sexaginta marcas & p pfato prioratu de Bernestaple decem marcas & pdco prioratu de Oteryngton centum libr' & p pfato prioratu de Totteneys quadraginta marcas & p dco prioratu de Tuardrayth quadraginta & quinq libr' necnon p pdco prioratu Moddebury sexdecim marcas, &c. et inveniendo, &c. salvis R. feodis militum, &c. Ro.4."

*Grossi Fines de Anno regni R. Edwardi t' eii post conpuestum videl't
Anglie quartodecimo & Franc' primo.*

Rotul' Vascon' 102, 103, 104, 105, 106.

"E. m. mon' R. Simon fil' Baldewini Flemmyng qd cum ipe in cur' R. apud Westm' recupasset seis' suam v' Thomam atte Barre de duab' acris cum ptin' in Barnestaple p consideracoem, &c. Ro.116."

PLACITORUM IN DOMO

Capitulari Westmonasteriensi Asservatorum Abbrevatio

Temporibus Regum Ric. I. Johann. Henr. III. Edw. I. Edw. II.

REGIS RICARDI PRIMI.

*Anno Sexto Regni Regis Ricardi Primi.
Placita apud Westmonasterium a die Sancti Michaelis in 15m dies*

Devon

" Willus de Brahost ponit loco suo, &c. vsus Olivum de Traci de porcone sua de honore de Barnstaple qm idem Olivus ei deforciat, &c. rot.6."

Pl'ita de Termino Pasche & de Termino S'ce Trinitat'
Anno Regni Rs. Johannis Primo.

" Willus de Breus petit vsus Olivu de Traci qd teneat ei fine fcum int eos in cur Rs de mediatate Honor de Bardestaple sedu cyrographu fcum int eos, &c.   rot.5."

———

TESTA DE NEVILL

SIVE

LIBER FEODURUM

In Curia Scaccarii

TEMP. HEN. III. & EDW. I.

———

" Nomina eo' qui tenet feoda militaria in comitatu DEVON' & de quib' ipi tenent."

" Feoda HENRICI DE TRACY de honore de BARNESTAPOL. Inquisitio dominico' tenemento' & feoffamento' dni Reg' vel antecesso suo' in Devonia."

" Petrus filus Herbti tenet BERDESTAPL' cum feodo xv milit de dono dni Reg' J. que fuit Willi Brause s' nescit' p quod servicium."

CALENDARIUM

ROTULORUM CHARTARUM

ET

INQUISITIONUM AD QUOD DAMNUN.

27° Edw. III.

ROB' TUS BOWE.*

" Dedit fr'ibus heremitis de ordine sci Augustini ad ecclaim at cetas domos in Barnestaple de novo construend' quandam placeam terre in villa predicta continentem quinque acr' &c'. "

[B.]

A Table,† showing at one view, how many Pounds,Shillings, and Pennies, have been coined out of a Pound of Silver, at different times in England.

" Whatever the division of money may have been in England in the Anglo-saxon times, there is no doubt that it has been the same ever since the Reign of William the Conqueror, as at present, viz. twelve pennies in a shilling, which never was a real coin till the year 1504, and twenty shillings in a pound, which, though not a real coin, was a real pound, containing twelve ounces of standard silver, till the Reign of Edward 1.; from which period the weight of the normal pound has gradually been diminished, till it is now about one third of what it originally was.

---

* The same individual as is mentioned earlier, where the name was inadvertently spelt 'Rowe'.

† In a work like the present, a Synopsis of the value of the pound sterling at different periods, cannot, it is presumed, be unacceptable. Without such a Guide, it would be obviously impossible to form any thing like a correct Estimate of the worth of a commodity in former times, by the sum which it may have produced.

		FINE SILVER.		ALLOY.				
		oz.	dwt.	oz.	dwt.	£	s.	d.
Before A.D. 1300, a pound of standard silver contained		11	2	0	18	1	0	0
1300	28 Edw. 1	11	2	0	18	1	0	3
1344	18 Edw. 3	11	2	0	18	1	2	2
1346	20 Edw. 3	11	2	0	18	1	2	6
1353	27 Edw. 3	11	2	0	18	1	5	0
1412	13 Hen. 4	11	2	0	18	1	10	0
1464	4 Edw. 4	11	2	0	18	1	17	6
1527	18 Hen. 8	11	2	0	18	2	5	0
1543	34 Hen. 8	10	0	2	0	2	8	0
1545	36 Hen. 8	6	0	6	0	2	8	0
1549	3 Edw. 6	6	0	6	0	3	12	0
1551	5 Edw. 6	3	0	9	0	3	12	0
1551 end of 1552	6 Edw. 6	11	1	0	19	3	0	0
1553	1 Mary	11	0	1	0	3	0	0
1560	2 Eliz.	11	2	0	18	3	0	0
1601	43 Eliz.	11	2	0	18	3	2	0

" and so the money continues down to the present time. " – *Macpherson's Annals of Commerce.*

" There are three things to be considered wherever a sum of money is mentioned in ancient times: first, The change of denomination, by which a pound has been reduced to the third part of its ancient weight in silver; secondly, The change in value by the greater plenty of money, which has reduced the same weight of silver to ten times less value compared to commodities, and consequently, a pound sterling to the thirtieth part of the ancient value; thirdly, The fewer people and less industry, which were then to be found in every European Kingdom. "

Our author concludes this dissertation by saying, that, " taking all circumstances together, we are to conceive every sum of money mentioned by historians, as if it were multiplied more than a hundred fold above a sum of the same denomination at present. "*—*Hume's History of England Appendix 1st.*

* The pound sterling was thus reduced, in intrinsic value, to about four shillings and eight pence of modern money.

Bishop Fleetwood, whose work preceded Hume's by about fifty years, furnishes a very different statement of the value of money.

" He determined, from a most accurate consideration of every circumstance, that in 1240, £4 13s. 9d. was worth about £50 of our present money, and that £3, in the Reign of Henry 6, was equivalent to £28 or £30 now."—*Ency. Perth. Art. Money.*

Between these very opposite accounts of the comparative value of the circulating medium, (perhaps the extremes to which calculators have gone,) the reader must be left to form his own judgement.

[C.]

Extract (copied from the Original) from the Brief held by Defendant's Counsel in an Action –
WILLIAM HIERN, (*Lessee of the Castle Hill, &c.*) v. PAUL TUCKER, (*Receiver to the Corporation of Barnstaple,*) CHARLES VELLEY, JACOB IRISH, NICHOLAS DYER, JOHN SQUIRE, *and* CHARLES WRIGHT.*

" At the West End of the Town of Barnestaple, adjoining to a navigable River, stands the Mount or Hill, called the Castle Hill, about fifty-four feet in height,† about thirty-eight yards in circumference, and about fifty-four feet in breadth at the Top, whereon anciently a Castle§ stood, but no remains thereof are now left. To ascend to the Top of this Mount, which is very steep, there is a narrow Circular Path, as much trod and beaten as any Highway in England, and where there is a

* The " Order in Common Council " to defend the Action, and the " Corporation Warrant of Atty. " to Lewis Gregory, (Town-Clerk,) to appear for the above named Defendants, " in His Majesty's Court of Common Pleas, at Westminster, the next Michaelmas Term," (both which Documents now lie before me,) bear date respectively, July 3, 1727, and Oct. 10, 1727. The *Brief* is without date.

† This must have been set down at random. The present height of the Mount is sixty-five feet, from the level of the Moat, (which is about twelve feet lower than the Lawn,) making, with eleven feet taken from the Top about ten years ago, by the late Mr. Rothwell, seventy-six feet. Diameter at top, sixty feet. The reduction of so ancient a Mound is perhaps to be regretted; but the Premises, in other respects, owe much of their present attractiveness, to Mr. Rothwell's good taste and liberal expenditure.

§ This is manifestly an error, (such an one, however, as may well be excused in a Lawyer's Brief) : that the *Keep* was on the eminence is probable enough, but we cannot for a moment suppose that an Edifice comprising besides the necessary Fortifications, a suitable Residence, could ever have been erected on such a contracted space.

" full Prospect of all the Town, the River, and Country round. This Mount was cast up by art, and round it is a deep Ditch, called the Castle Ditch, which is enclosed all round, and where time out of mind hath been Gardens, except on the wester side thereof. Adjoining to this Ditch, on the west side, is a common sporting-place, called the Castle Green, containing about half an acre of Ground, which always lay open to the Castle Ditch and Hill, till of late years, and through the said Castle Green, adjoining to the Ditch, is a common Foot-path, leading from one part of the Town to the other. In the Castle Green, Castle Ditch, and on the Castle Hill, all the Inhabitants of the Town have, time out of mind, used all manner of recreations, sports, and diversions, and constantly bowled in the said Castle Green, and an Independent Company of the Militia Foot Soldiers, which belonged to the Town, would upon all occasions exercise in the said Castle Green, as would always the King's Soldiers, when any were quartered in the Town; and in the Castle Ditch, Bulls have been baited,* and Butts set up to shoot at with bows and arrows,† without any manner of denyall; and upon all occasions of public rejoicing, as on the 29th of May, the 5th of November, proclaiming or crowning of Kings and Queens, obtaining of Victorys, and also on the first day of July yearly, which was kept by some ancient inhabitants of the Town in rememberance that the Town was on that day delivered from French & Irish wch came against it, and also on all other days of public Rejoicing, Bonfires have constantly, time out of mind, been made on the Top of the said Hill, and drums beating and Great Gunns fired off without any manner of interruption or denyall; and Boys woᵈ every day play on the said Castle Hill, Castle Ditch, and Castle Green, and the Inhabitants of the Town would constantly walk there; and, in short, it is the only sporting place in the Town, and was more constantly used as such, and by more people, than is the Castle of Exon; and at our great Fair in September, which doth last four days, there would be 200 or 300 people all day playing at bowles, nine pins, wrestlers, and lookers on; and men, women, and children, continually walking up and down, sitting and lying on the Castle Hill, and rolling themselves down from the top to the bottom; and when strangers come to the Town, (particularly Judge —— when at Barnstaple, carried there by Sir Nicholas Hooper,) they were generally shewed up on the Top of the Castle Hill to view the Prospect of the Town, the River, and Country all round; till about 22 years since, Sir Arthur Chichester, who was Lord of the Soyle of the said Hill, Ditch, and Green, and had the Pasture of it, having conceived a pique against the Burgesses of the Town, for not choosing him Member of Parliament, granted a Lease of the said Castle Hill and Green to one James Gibbs, for 99 years, determinable on 3 lives."

In the margin of the brief occurs the following:—"Barnstaple a large Town, more than 6000 inhabitants."

*This inhuman sport has been long discontinued here, it is hoped forever.

† This was an ancient and royal pastime. Henry 7th "Lost to my Lord Morging at Buttes, six shillings and four pence;" and for the same Monarch was " Paid to Sir Edward Boroughe thirteen shillings and four pence which the Kynge lost at Buttes with his cross -bowe." – Strutt's Sports and Pastimes, p. 63.

Grant of Barnstaple Priory, to Lord William Howard,
and Lady Margaret his Wife. March 9. 29 Hen. VIII.*

"THE KING to all whom these presents shall come, greeting. KNOW
YE, that we in consideration of the good, faithful, and acceptable
service which our beloved William Lord Howard heretofore hath
done to us, have given and granted, and by these presents do give
and grant, to the same William Lord Howard, and Lady Margaret,
his wife, the House and Site of the late Priory of the Monks of St.
Mary Magdalene, of Barnestapoll, otherwise Barnstaple, in our
County of Devon, by the authority of Parliament surpressed and
dissolved, and all the Church, Belfrey, and Churchyard, of the
same late Priory. And also, all our Messuages, Houses, Edifaces,
Granges, Barns, Stables, Dovehouses, Gardens, Orchards, Lands,
and Soil, as well within as without the site, inclosure, compass, circuit, and precinct, of the same late Priory, and being parcel thereof.
And also, all those our Manors of aBarnestapoll, Pylton, Strechton,
and Ingestowe, otherwise Instowe, with all their Members and
Appurtenances in the County aforesaid, to the said late Priory
belonging and appertaining. And also, all our Rectory of the Parish
Church of Barnestapoll, with all its Rights and Appurtenances, in
the County aforesaid, to the said late Priory appropriated, belonging, and appertaining, and the Advowson, Donation, and Right of
Patronage of the same Church and Vicarage there; and our two
Water Mills, called Port Mills, with their Appurtenances, in
Barnestapoll aforesaid, to the same late Priory belonging and
appertaining. And also, all that our Wood called Monkewode, with
the Appurtenances in Marwode; and all our Wood, called
Yernewode, with its Appurtences, in Pylton; and all those our
Lands and Tenemants, with the Apurtenances, in Inglestowe, in
the County aforesaid, to the said late Priory belonging and apper-
taining. And also, one Annuity or Yearly Pension of a Hundred
Shillings, issuing out of the aforesaid Vicarage or Church of
Barnestapoll, in the County aforesaid, which the Vicar there for the
time being hath been accustomed to pay annually to the said late

"Priory; and one Annuity or Yearly Pension of a Hundred Shillings, issuing out of the Church or Rectory of Georgeham, otherwise Ham St. George, in the County aforesaid, which the Rector there hath been accustomed to pay annually to the said Priory; and one Annuity or Yearly Pension of Thirty Shillings, issuing out of the Rectory or Church of All Saints, of Fremington, in the County aforesaid, which the Rector there hath been accustomed to pay annually to the said late Priory: and one Annuity or Yearly Rent of Forty Shillings, issuing out of the Castle Demesne or Manor or Borough of Barnestapoll, in the County aforesaid, which hath been accustomed to be paid to the said late Priory of Barnestapoll; to be paid at the Feast of Saint Michael the Archangel, by the hands of the Rector, Bailiff, Farmers, or other Occupiers there, for the time being. And also, all other our Manors, Messuages, Lands, Tenements, Mills, Meadows, Feedings, Pastures,Woods, Underwoods, Rents, Reversions, Services, Annuities, Farms, Fee-Farms, Wards, Marriages, Escheats, Reliefs, Waters, Ponds, Stews, Warrens, Commons, Fisheries, Pensions, Portions, Tithes, Oblations, Courts, Leet, Views of Frankpledge, with all things which belong to Views of Frankpledge, and our other Rights, Jurisdictions, Liberties, Possessions, and Hereditaments, whatsoever, as well temporal as spiritual, of what kind, nature, or species soever they may be, or by whatsoever names they may be taken or known; with all their Rights, Members, Appurtenances, and Commodities whatsoever; situate, lying, and being, in the Towns, Fields, Parishes, or Hamlets, of Barnestapoll, Pylton, Bradford Strechton, Wethrige, Delbrige, Fullyngote, Nethercote, Instowe, Collecote, Marwode, Cride, Georgeham, otherwise Ham Saint George, West ansty, Wolley Down, Shyrewell, Heawnton Poncherdon, East Hankenden, Berrynarber, Chalacombe, Langtre, Kyntesbury, Keymelond, Stoke Ryvers, Potyngton, and Fremyngton, in the County aforesaid, or elsewhere wheresoever, to the said late Priory in any manner appertaining or belonging, as fully and entirely, and in as ample a manner and form, as Robert Thorne, late Prior of the said late Priory of Barnestapoll, or his Predecessors, or the Priors of the same place, in right of that Priory, on the 4th day of February, in the 27th year of our reign, or "ever before all and singular the Premises, with the Appurtenances, have been held or enjoyed, or ought to have; and as fully and entirely, and in as ample a manner and form, as all and singular those Premises came to our hands, or ought to come, and now are, or ought to be in our hands, by reason and pretext of a certain Act, for the dissolving certain Monasteries, Abbies, Priories, and Religious Houses, and in our Parliament at London, begun on the 3rd day of November, in the 21st year of our Reign, and thence adjourned to Westminster, and by divers prorogations continued unto, and on the 4th February, in the 27th year of our Reign, and then there held amongst other things is enacted and provided. AND FURTHER, we give and by these presents grant, to the aforesaid, William Lord Howard, and Lady Margaret his Wife, the Rectory of the Parish Church of Tottenham, with the Appurtenances, in our County of Middlesex, to the late Priory of the Holy Trinity, London, lately dissolved, belonging, and appertaining; and the Advowson, Donation, and Right of Patronage of the same Church and Vicarage there; and all our Manors, Messuages, Houses, Edifaces, Barns, Lands, Tenements, Woods, Rents, Reservations, Services, Tithes, Oblations, Obventions, Pensions, Portions, Courts, and other Rights, Jurisdictions, Liberties, Possessions, and Hereditments whatsoever, as well spiritual as temporal, of what kind, nature, or species soever, or by whatsoever names the same may be taken or known; with all their Rights, Members, Appurtenances, Commodities whatsoever, situate, lying, and being in the Towns, Places, Fields, Parishes, and Hamlets of Tottenham aforesaid, and Edelmeton, in the County of Middlesex aforesaid, to the said late Priory of the Holy Trinity of London, in any manner appertaining or belonging, as fully and entirely, and in as ample a manner and form as Nicholas Hancock, late Prior of the said late Priory of the Holy Trinity, or his Predecessors or Priors of the same late Priory, in right of that Priory, at the time of the dissolution of the same late Priory, or theretofore have been held or enjoyed, or ought to have done. WE ALSO give, and by these presents grant to the aforesaid William Lord Howard, and Lady Margaret his Wife, View of Frankpledge, and all things which belong to Frankpledge, Goods of Felons,

"Fugitives, Outlaws, Condemned persons, Felons, of themselves, and Deodands, in all and singular the aforesaid Manors, Lands, Tenements, and other Premises, and in every part thereof; all and singular which said Premises above granted by these presents, with the Appurtenances, are of the clear value of £155 4s. 6d. a year, and not beyond. TO HAVE AND TO HOLD the House and Site aforesaid, and the Manors, Messuages, Lands, and all and singular other the Premises above specified, with the Appurtenances, to the aforesaid William Lord Howard, and Lady Margaret his Wife, and the Heirs of their Bodies between them lawfully begotten, and for default of such issue, then to remain to the Heirs of the body of the said William Lord Howard, lawfully begotten. TO BE HOLDEN of us, our Heirs, and Successors, in Capite by Knight's Service, to wit by the Tenth Part of a Knight's Fee, and by the Rent of £21 yearly, to our Heirs and Successors, to be paid at the Court of Augmentation of the Revenues of our Crown, and the Feast of Saint Michael the Archangel, for all Services, Exactions, and Demands whatsoever, of, in or for the Premises, in any manner to be done, performed, yielded, or paid. AND FURTHER, we give, and by these presents grant to the aforesaid William Lord Howard, the Issues, Revenues, and Profits of the Premises, from the Feast of the Annunciation of the blessed Virgin Mary, in the 27th year of our Reign, hitherto arising or accruing, TO HOLD the same to the same William Lord Howard, of our gift, without yielding, paying, or performing any Account, or any thing else to us, our Heirs, or Successors, so that express mention, &c. IN WITNESS whereof, &c. Witness the King at Westminster, on the 9th day of March."

"By the King himself, and the date of the aforesaid, &c."

[The signature, which is given for its singularity, is a close copy of a Fac-simile, appended to a Document printed in an old Work on Godstow Abbey, Oxfordshire.]

CHAPTER 11

PUBLIC CHARITIES OF BARNSTAPLE.

The following Statement is taken from "The Report of the Commissioners concerning Charities."—

PENROSE'S, OR LITCHDON ALMHOUSE.

PENROSE'S GIFT.

John Penrose, of Barnstaple, merchant, by his will, bearing date the 14th June, 1642, and proved in the Prerogative Court of Canterbury, reciting that he had assigned to William Palmer and others, all his estate in certain lands in the parish of Hartland, which his father-in-law, Richard Beaple, and himself, had in mortgage, jointly, from Nicholas Luttrel, Esq. directed that if the said Nicholas Luttrel should not pay the mortgage money, the said William Palmer and others should sell his moiety of the said lands, and all his term therein; the money made thereof to be employed towards the performance of his will. And, after various devices and bequests, he directed that his executors should convert all the rest of his goods, chattels, and estate whatsoever, not before given, into money, and with part thereof should purchase to them and their heirs, some convenient room or place within the borough and parish of Barnstaple, fit to erect an almshouse upon, and the same being so purchased, should, with part of the said money, erect thereupon such and so many several rooms for an almshouse, as they in their discretion should think fit, and that his said executors, with the money left in their hands after the said charges, should purchase such and so much lands, rents, and hereditaments, to them and their heirs, as the same money should be equal to pay for; and that such lands, and the issues and profits thereof, should be for ever employed for the maintenance of the said almshouse, and for and towards the relief and maintenance of the poor people from time to time placed in the same. And he also directed, that his executors, and the survivors of them, should have the sole ordering and government of the said almshouse, as long as any three of them should be living; and that when they, by death, should come to the number of two, the mayor, aldermen, and capital burgesses, and common council of Barnstaple, for the time being, should from thenceforth have the ordering, government, and disposing of the said almshouse, and the placing and displacing of the poor people therein, and should improve such lands so purchased for the purposes aforesaid, at the best yearly profits they might, and should not lease any part thereof for any fine, but at a yearly rack-rent, for the better maintenance of the said almshouse, and poor people therein. He also directed, that after his executors should, by death, come to the number of two, they should enfeoff six others of the common council of the said borough, of the said lands, and so from time to time, for ever, as often as the feoffees should come to the number of two; and he also directed that the poor people, to be placed in the almshouse, should be inhabitants within the said borough or parish, and none of any other place. And he appointed Richard Beaple, William Palmer, James Bulteel, Gilbert Page, and Richard Medford, to be executors of his said will.

The said testator, by a codicil to his will, bearing date 21st June, 1642, reciting that he had by his said will, given to his brother,

George Penrose, all his estate, term, and interest in his messuage, wherein he dwelt in Barnstaple, and in his tenement and stable in Paige Lane, the inheritance of the heirs of Appley, and in his garden adjoining to the Castle Lane of the said borough, reputed to be belonging to the Corporation of Barnstaple, and in a close of land called Newcombe's Close, another close called Fardeliscombe Meadow, and another close called Slade, in the said parish, thereby revoked the said devise to his brother of those premises, and gave the same to his said brother George, from the time of his (the testator's) death, for fifty years, if his said brother should so long continue respectively. And he gave to the said mayor, aldermen, and burgesses of Barnstaple, after the death of his said brother, his estate and interest in the said premises, and directed that when they should come into their hands, they should demise the said messuage wherein he dwelt, the said tenement and stable in Paige Lane, and the said garden, to some of the capital burgesses and common council of the said borough, for the time being, who would give most for the same; and the said three closes of land, to any persons who would give most for the same, at a yearly rack-rent, and should bestow the rents and yearly profits arising out of the same, when they should amount to a competent sum, in some lands for an estate of inheritance, and should employ the rents and profits of the land so to be purchased, yearly, from time to time, for ever, towards the relief and maintenance of the poor people to be placed in the almshouse mentioned in his will, to be erected; and that the said lands so to be purchased, should be let for a yearly rack-rent; provided that if his said brother, George, should have issue male of his body, such issue should, after the death of his brother, hold and enjoy the said premises, as long as any issue male should continue, to his and their own use.

The premises devised by this codicil are not, at this time, nor can we find any trace of their ever having been, in the possession of this almshouse. It does not appear what term or interest the testator had in this property, nor is it known whether the contigency happened of the failure of issue male of the body of the testator's brother, George Penrose, without which the charity was not entitled to any benefit under the codicil.

A part of the property now belonging to the almshouse, consists of an undivided moiety of lands in the parish of Hartland, (Nos. 3, and 4, in the rental, stated in a subsequent part of this Report,) the possession of which is only accounted for by supposing these lands to be the same as are mentioned in Penrose's will, as held in mortgage, jointly, by his father-in-law, Richard Beaple, and himself.

We have not been able to find any account of the produce of the residue of the testator's personal estate, or of the manner in which it was applied; but an unexecuted deed, bearing sate 18th December, 1670, found amongst the documents of the corporation of Barnstaple, was produced to us, purporting to be a conveyance from John Downe, as the surviving feoffee of the lands of Litchdon almshouse, with the gardens thereunto belonging, of a messuage and garden in Anchor Lane, and a close, containing by estimation two acres, adjoining Barbican Lane, which messuage and close are there stated to have been purchased of William Warman, for an endowment of the said almshouse. It seems probable, therefore, that the money arising from Penrose's gift, was applied in the purchase of the property comprised in this deed. The close adjoining Barbican Lane, and the house and garden in Anchor Lane, now form a part of the Almshouse Lands, Nos. 1 and 2, in the rental. We have not been able to find any other deeds for the purpose of preserving the trust in the manner directed by the founder of this almshouse.

BEAPLE'S GIFT.

Richard Beaple, by his will, bearing date 13th April, 1641, gave to his executors £420. to the intent that they should therewith purchase so much land of inheritance as should be of the yearly value of £20, the yearly profits thereof to be bestowed upon four poor people of the new almshouse erected by Mr. John Penrose, deceased, such of them as he should nominate in his life-time, and in defult thereof, such as should be nominated by his executors, by £5 apiece, to be paid quarterly; and the same annuity of £20 to continue for ever to four poor people of the said almshouse, to be nominated, after the death of all his executors, by the mayor, aldermen, and common council of Barnstaple, or the major part of them. And he directed, that until the said lands should be purchased, the said £420 should be put forth at interest at six per cent, the profits thereof to be bestowed upon the said four poor people.

It is supposed that the tenement called Darracott, in the parish of Georgeham, now belonging to this charity, (No. 6 in the rental,) was purchased with the money thus given by Richard Beaple; but we have not been able to find the purchase-deeds of that tenement.

In the returns made to Parliament in 1786, it is stated, that the said Richard Beaple gave a third part of the residue of his effects to his almshouse, with which a house was purchased, let, at the time of making those returns, at the rent of £8 8s. per annum. As there is a house in High-street, Barnstaple, now in possession of the charity, let at £8 8s. per annum, (no.7 in the rental,) it is probably the house alluded to in the returns; but upon an inspection of this donor's will, which was proved in the Perogative Court of Canterbury, it is not found to contain any such bequest of a part of the residue of his effects to this almshouse.

PALMER'S GIFT

In an old book, found amongst the documents of the corporation of Barnstaple, containing the mayor's accounts for various years, at different periods, and also containing statements of some of the charitable donations to this town, it is mentioned, that William Palmer, of Barnstaple, merchant, by his will gave for the use of the poor in Penrose's almshouse, certain lands in East Heyland, within the parish of Fremington, after one life, for ever. It also appears, from an account in the same book, that in 1657, the then mayor and aldermen received from Anthony Palmer, one of the executors of the said William Palmer, £100, for the use of the poor, of which the sum of £88, was then paid to Richard Gay, esquire, for his estate in a tenement called East Heyland, for the use of the poor in Penrose's almshouse, devised by the said William Palmer, after the determination of the estate of the said Richard Gay. The charity is now in possession of lands in East Heyland, or Yelland. (No. 8 in the rental.)

The will of this William Palmer was proved in the Perogative Court of Canterbury in 1653; but the only charitable gift contained in it is a bequest of £10 to the poor of Barnstaple, to be distributed within three months after his decease. The returns made to Parliament in 1786, state his donation to the almshouse to have been made by deed in 1651, but we have not been able to find any such document.

HARRIS'S GIFT.
An inscription, on one of the tablets in the church, states, that Richard Harris, in 1655, gave £50 to this almshouse; but we have not been able to find any further trace of this donation.

ROLLE'S GIFT.
Denys Rolle, esquire, who represented this borough on Parliament, gave, in 1763, £100 for the support of this almshouse.

STANBURY'S GIFT.
Joan Stanbury, by her will, in 1772, gave £20 to the poor of this almshouse.

It has been customary for the two oldest members of the corporation, who have passed the chair, to have the management of this charity during their lives, to receive the rents, make the payments, and keep the accounts, the senior of whom acts as treasurer.

The accounts have been produced to us from 1744 to the present time, being those of Messrs. Roch and Colley from 1774 to 1797, of Messrs. Roch and Shepherd from 1797 to 1804, of Messrs. Greek and Moule from 1804 to 1815, and of Messrs. Nicholas Glass and John Roberts from 1815 to 1822. The balances in hand have been carried forward to each succeeding account, but there does not appear to have been any regular audit of the accounts, except in 1797 and 1804, when they were examined by a committee of the corporation. We suggest to the corporation the propriety of appointing a fixed day for an annual audit of the accounts of this and other charities of which they are trustees.

The following rental contains a statement of the property held in trust by the corporation, for the benefit of this charity:-

No	Donor	Parish	Premises	Quantity A. R. P.	Lessees	Term	Rent L. S. D.	Estimated clear yearly value L. S. D.	Observations
1	Penrose	Barnstaple	A field in Barbican lane, called Fox's Field.	1 3 34	Harry Leworthy	14yrs from Lady-day 1819	15 15 0	good rent	Let by auction
					Ditto		15 0 0 additional rent for clay for bricks in the same field.		The tenant has agreed to pay this additional rent as long as the clay in the field lasts, and to lay down the land for pasture at end of his term.
2	Ditto	Ditto	A public house in Anchor Lane, called the Seven Stars	0 0 0	Charles Dart	11yrs from Lady-day 1822. Determinable at the end of seven years.	47 0 0	good rent	Let by auction; the former rent was 21l. More than 40l has lately been expended from the fund of the charity in the improvement of these premises; they are now in good repair. The trustees covenent to do the external repairs.
3	Ditto	Hartland	An undivided moiety of a messuage and lands in West Tichbury containing, in the whole...... And an undivided moiety of three fields, called Hedges Parks & Gawlish in East Tichbury containing in the whole....	131 0 18 5 3 2	James Haynes	14 yrs from Lady-day 1810	60 0 0	good rent	Let by auction; the lessee is the owner of the other moiety of this estate.
4	Ditto	Ditto	An undivided moiety of two fields called Roosdon Plots, part of West Tichbury............	about 4 0 0	Rev. T. Hooper Morrison	21 yrs from Lady-day 1817	3 0 0	good rent	The lessee of No.3 is the owner of the other moiety of these fields. They now form a part of the pleasure grounds of the Rev. T.H. Morrison, and are marked by boundary stones.
5	Ditto	Ditto	An undivided moiety of a tenement called Mansley, containing in the whole............	61 1 29 of which 21 1 8 are downland	Thomas Prust	21 yrs from Lady-day 1806	17 10 0	good rent	Let by private contract after an auction had been held; the trustees covenant to repair the walls of the buildings, and a small sum is usually allowed to the tenant out of the rent for this purpose
6	Beaple	Georgeham	A tenement called Darracott.	22 2 38	Peter Smith	21 yrs from Lady-day 1809	31 0 0	good rent	Let by auction
7	Ditto, supposed	Barnstaple	A house in High Street	0 0 0	John Loosemore now Miss Elizabeth Langdon	60 yrs from 25th Dec. 1773	8 8 0	20 0 0	This house was in a dilapidated state when the present repairing lease was granted. it is now in good repair.
8	Palmer	Fremington	Six closes of land in Yelland	23 1 3	Henry Moule	Yearly tenant	17 11 0	20 0 0	The rent appears to have been of the same amount in 1786. It is proposed to re-let these closes by auction, but they are stated to consist of indifferent land, and it is not expected that the rent will be much increased; 12s 3d. has been annually allowed to the tenant of these lands for land-tax.
9	Rolle		100l. invested in two deeds poll of 50l. each, one of the Barnstaple and the other of the Southmolton Turnpike, bearing interest at 4 per cent. .				4 0 0		[A]*
10	Stanbury		20l. invested in 24! Old South Sea Annuities				0 14 10		
11			131l 2s 11d Old South Sea Annuities, purchased by the treasurer in 1788, with 100l arising from surplus income.				4 0 0		* The letters refer to the Appendix at the end of the Chapter
							£223 18 10		

75

The almshouse is a large building, in good repair, situate in Litchdon-street, Barnstaple, and consists of twenty dwelling-houses, each containing two alms people, with a large Garden behind, divided into portions amongst the inhabitants. In one of the wings is a chapel, in which prayers are read twice in the week by one of the almsmen, and in the other wing is a room, formerly used as a compting house.

The almspeople are appointed from the poor parishioners of Barnstaple, a preference being given to natives, and usually to women. At the time of our investigation, in September, 1822, they consisted of thirty-six women four men. There is no specified age for their appointment, but they are seldom chosen under the age of fifty. Upon the first vacancy that occurs by death, after the mayor for the time being enters upon his office, a successor is nominated by him. The others are supplied alternately by the two acting trustees. Each of the almspeople receives six shillings (making in the whole £12,) per lunar month. In 1804, the allowance was £6 per lunar month, from which it has been gradually augmented, as the rents have increased, to its present amount. In part of the winter of 1819-1820, in consequence of the severity of the winter, the monthly allowance was further augmented to £14. On particular occasions a small additional donation has been made to the almspeople from the funds of the charity. Many of the inhabitants, both of this almshouse and of Horwood's and Paige's almshouses, receive parochial relief, in addition to their allowances from the respective charities.

The following is a summary of the average annual expenditure on account of this almshouse:-

	£	s.	d.
Allowance to the almspeople, at £12 per lunar month .	156	0	0
Additional allowance to one of them for reading prayers, at 7s. 6d. per quarter .	1	10	0
Insurance	1	5	0
Chief Rents payable out of parts of the premises to Barnstaple Bridge .	0	10	0
Payment to the poor of Paige's almshouse, in respect of an annuity given by William Canford, understood to be charged upon some part of the almshouse lands .	0	6	8
Land Tax allowed to the tenant of No. 8 in the rental	0	12	3
Repairs of the almshouse on an average of five years, including a small allowance to the tennant of No. 5 for repairs, and a small sum for receipt stamps .	21	0	0
	£181	3	11

No expense whatever is incurred for managing the charity, or keeping the accounts.

It will be seen that the annual income, as stated in the rental, exceeds the expenditure by more than £40; but it should be observed, that the increased rent of No. 2 took place only from Lady-day, 1822, and that the rent paid for digging clay in No. 1 can only be considered as temporary income.

Upon the Treasurer's accounts, as made up to the time of our enquiry, there was a balance of £98 2s. 1d. in favor of the charity, in addition to which arrears of rent were due from some of the tenants; and on the other hand, a part of the expense of the repairs of the Seven Stars public-house, No. 2, amounting to about £30, remained unpaid. We were informed by the acting trustees, that they proposed, with part of the balance in hand, and the temporary income that will arise from digging clay in No. 1, to purchase stock in the public funds, with a view to provide a fund for repairs of the almshouse, the annual expense of which, from the age of the building, may be expected to increase.

The inhabitants of this almshouse, in addition to the above-mentioned allowances, receive £4 per annum, arising from Phillip's gift, mentioned in a subsequent part of the Report, ten shillings of which is paid to the almsman who reads prayers, and the residue is divided equally at Christmas amongst all the almspeople, in sums of one shilling and nine pence to each.

The above-mentioned John Penrose, by his said will, gave to the mayor, aldermen, and burgesses of the borough and parish of Barnstaple, £200, to be by them employed in the keeping to work some of the poor people of the said borough and parish, in the house newly erected near the Castle, for keeping the people to work, called the Bridewell.

It appears, from entries in the old book of mayors' accounts before referred to, that this bridewell was built by the town at an expense of £300; and that in 1633 it was found that, by the carelessness of the keeper of the bridewell, there was not so much good done to the poor as had been expected, and that the town was every year at the expense of repairing the house and other things, and that it was therefore thought good to appoint John Cole to be keeper of the bridewell, who should have the house, and the use of £100 given by John Penrose, for the performance of his office; and that the other £100 should be lent at six per cent. for the reparations of the house, and other charges for diet, &c. We have not found any further trace of this sum of £200. The bridewell described as being near the castle, is supposed to be the present parish workhouse. [B.]

HORWOOD'S ALMSHOUSE.

An inscription on this almshouse states, that it was founded and endowed by Thomas Horwood, merchant, who began it in his life, and was finished by his widow Mrs. Alice Horwood.

By indenture, bearing date 7th September 1674, between the said Alice Horwood, Richard Hooper, mayor elect of the borough of

Barnstaple, William Westcombe, alderman, and Arthur Ackland and two others, capital burgesses of the said borough, of the one part, and Christopher Hunt, mayor of the said borough, and Thomas Harris and three others, capital burgesses of the same, of the other part, reciting, that the said Alice Horwood, by indenture, bearing date 15th August 1665, for settling of the messuages and lands in that indenture mentioned to the issues therein expresses, granted to the said parties of the first part, together with five others since deceased, and their heirs, a plot of land, containing in length, north and south, 70 feet, and in breadth, east and west, 47 feet, and a plot of land next adjoining, called the Little Court, containing in length, 26 feet, and in breadth, 11 feet, and the almshouse thereon erected, situate in or near Whitpit-Lane, in the borough of Barnstaple, between the lands then of Edward Eastmond on the east, the lane called Whitpit-Lane, the old almshouses and the lands belonging to the long bridge of Barnstaple on the west, the lands of Henry Greenwood and Mrs. Paige's new erected almshouse on the north, and the lands of the said Edward Eastmond, and the lands belonging to the long bridge of Barnstaple on the south, and also a garden and garden-house, then in the possession of the said Alice Horwood and the persons then resident in the said new erected almshouse between the church-yard on the north, the lands of Gabriel Sherman on the south, the lands of Barret and part of a garden in the occupation of Nicholas Delbridge on the west, and the lands in the occupation of Robert Fosse and others on the east, and two quillets of land, containing two borough acres, and one piece of a marsh adjoining thereto, in Bishop's Newport, within the parish of Bishop's Tawton, and a messuage and tenement, with the appurtenances, in Newport aforesaid, then in the possession of the said Alice Horwood, and the writings concerning the said premises, which were to be left in the town chest in the Guildhall of the said borough, to the use of the said Alice Horwood, for life, and after her decease, upon trust, that the said trustees should dispose of the rents and profits of the said premises (subject to an annuity payable thereout to certain persons, for their lives) in the reparations of the said almshouses and other premises, and the relief of the poor therein, and upon further trust, that the said trustees or the major part of them should, from time to time, upon the death or removal of any of the poor persons resident and placed in the said almshouse, supply such vacancy, by placing in each room or dwelling two such poor and ancient decayed people as the major part of them should think fit, having always regard to the wants of any poor relations of Thomas Horwood, deceased, the late husband of the said Alice, to prefer them before others, and upon trust, that the walk and garden-house in the said alms-garden should be for the use of the said trustees, for ever, for their general meetings; and reciting, that the said Alice Horwood had, by the said indenture, declared, that when the trustees should be reduced to six, the survivors, to the use of themselves and the said four seniors, upon the like trusts; and reciting, that the said Alice Horwood desired that the six surviving trustees should convey the said premises, upon the trusts aforesaid, to such four of the capital burgesses as the major part of them should think fit; and in case they should not agree in the nomination of such four capital burgesses, such as the mayor and aldermen of the said borough or any two of them should appoint; and that they should not be obliged to grant the same to the seniors of the capital burgesses; it was witnessed, that the said Alice Horwood and the other parties of the first part, by her direction, granted and enfeoffed the before mentioned premises to the parties of the second part and their heirs, to the use of themselves and the surviving trustees, upon the trusts mentioned in the said recited indenture, with such alteration in the mode of appointing the new trustees as before mentioned.

The following rental shows the property belonging to this almshouse:-

No.	Parish	Lessees	Premises	Quantity	Term	Rent	Yearly Value	Observations
				A. R. P.		L. S. D.		
1	Borough of Newport, in the Parish of Bishop's Tawton	John Westacott	House, orchard and garden part of Pudridge	0 3 14	7 yrs. from Lady-day 1820	11 11 0	good rent	Let by auction; the trustees do the repairs; some repairs wanting
2	Ditto	John Bentley & Wm. Hutton	A barn & field, other part of Pudridge	2 1 8	Ditto	22 5 0	Ditto	Let by auction
3	Ditto	William Ackland	Two fields	2 0 2	Ditto	14 0 0	Ditto	Ditto
4	Ditto	William Thorne	Two fields at Rupsham	1 3 19	7yrs.fromMichael-mas 1821	8 0 0	Ditto	Let by private contract after an auction held.
5	Barnstaple	William Cotton	Small stable and Ash-pit in Paige's Lane	—	Yearly tenant	2 2 0	Ditto	
	£100 New South Sea Annuities, which appears to have been puchased in 1759, in consequence of an order of the common council, by the then two acting trustees in the name of the mayor and aldermen of Barnstaple, for 82*l*. 2*s*. 2*d*. (being part of a sum of 102*l*. belonging to this charity, the residue of which sum was directed to be applied for the repairs of the house) producing the yearly dividend of ... It does not appear from whence the sum of 102*l*. arrived					3 0 0	Ditto	
	£10 given by the will of Joan Stanbury in 1772, vested in 14*l*. 4*s*. 11*d*. Old South Sea Annuities, procuring the yearly dividend of					0 8 8	Ditto	
						61 6 8		

The last trust deed of these premises bears date the 1st and 2nd January, 1801, under which six trustees are now living.

It has been customary for the two members of the corporation next in seniority to the two seniors, to have the management of this charity, and to grant the leases of the lands held under it. At the time of our investigation, the acting trustees were Mr. John May and Mr. Richard Rowe Metherell, who are also two of the surviving trustees under the deed of 1801, and the accounts were kept by Mr. John May, junior, for his father.

The almshouse is situate in Church Lane, and consists of eight dwellings, containing two rooms each, inhabited by sixteen poor persons, men and women, with a small garden plot allotted to each dwelling. It is in a fair state of repair. The almspeople are appointed from the poor of Barnstaple, alternately, by the acting trustees, as vacancies occur, and at the time of our investigation, consisted of two men and fourteen women; each of them receives five shillings per lunar month, and the rent of the stable in Paige's lane, being two guineas a year, is divided among them at Christmas. Small additional donations are also made to them out of the funds of the charity, on particular occasions.

The following is a summary of the annual expenditure:-

	£	s.	d.
Sixteen almspeople, at five shillings each per lunar month	52	0	0
Rent of the stable in Barnstaple, divided amongst them at Christmas	2	2	0
Chief rent payable to the Lord of the manor of Newport	0	8	9
Insurance	0	10	0
Repairs, on average of the last three years	4	4	0
	£ 59	4	9

besides small incidental expenses for letting the property.

The balance in favor of the charity at the time of our investigation, was 10s. 11d. and there were then arrears of rent due to Midsummer, 1822, amounting to £8 1s. 6d. There have been hitherto no regular audits of the accounts of this charity, but the book of accounts has been occasionally produced for inspection at the meeting of the corporation.

In 1820, a donation of £3 from Sir Francis Ommaney, and a donation of £5 from Michael Nolan, esquire, to this almshouse, were received by Mr. John May, junior, and carried to the general account thereof.

Each of the poor persons in this almshouse, received one shilling twice in the year, fromPhillip's gift, and sixpence twice in the year, from Tippett's gift, hereinafter mentioned.

PAIGE'S ALMSHOUSE.

The almshouse called Paige's almshouse, is situate in Church Lane, and consists of four dwellings of two rooms each, without garden or courtlage, inhabited by eight poor persons; one of which dwellings, as appears from the will of Elizabeth Paige, hereinafter stated, was built by her in her life-time, and for rebuilding the others of which, on site of a more ancient almshouse, she gave by her said will, £100.

For the support of this ancient establishment, the two following donations of William Canford and Robert Appley, appear to have been previously given.

CANFORD'S GIFT

It appears from the before-mentioned old book of mayor's accounts, that William Canford, by his will, bearing date 28th July, 1553, gave to Roger North, and others, and their heirs, a tenement and meadow, amongst other uses, for the payment of an annuity of 6s. 8d. towards the relief and maintenance of the poor of the almshouse in Barnstaple.

The premises charged with this annuity are supposed to be a part of those now belonging to Penrose's almshouse, and the annuity of 6s. 8d. is paid by the trustees of that charity, and divided amongst the poor inhabitants of Paige's almshouse.

APPLEY'S GIFT.

Robert Appley, alderman, of Barnstaple by his will, bearing date 7th October, 1594, gave to William Collybeare, then mayor of Barnstaple, and ten others, and their heirs, a messuage, orchard, garden, and close of land, situate in the borough of Newton [Newport]* Bishop, upon trust, to permit the mayor and aldermen of the town of Barnstaple to receive the rents and profits thereof, whom he appointed to distribute the same quarterly, unto such twelve poor people as should be, according to the ancient custom of the said borough of Barnstaple, admitted from time to time, into the almshouse of the said town.

* For any interlineations in this report marked thus, [ ] the editor is responsible

These premises (now called Congerham's) are situate within the borough of Newport, in the parish of Bishop's Tawton, and consists of a house, garden, and plot of land, containing in the whole, 1A. 20P. let to William Fairchild, under a lease from the mayor and aldermen of Barnstaple, granted by public auction, for eleven years from Lady-day, 1814, at the yearly rent of £18, which it was found necessary to reduce after the first year of the term, to £14, and this is now considered a good rent. The house is old, and in a decayed state. The tenant covenants to do all repairs except those of the walls of the house. The rent is received from him quarterly, by one of the almswomen, and after payment for the necessary repairs of the almshouse, (which is in an indifferent state of repair,) the residue is divided equally amongst the poor inhabitants thereof. [D.]

PAIGE'S GIFT

Elizabeth Paige, by her will, bearing date 9th March, 1656, gave to the building and erecting of the almshouses, (then in decay,) [situate in the Lane] commonly called Alms Lane, and adjoining to the almshouse built by herself, £100, to be bestowed therein at the discretion of her executors. She also gave to the mayor and aldermen of Barnstaple for the time being, and their successors, £50, to be lent forth for the benefit of those poor people who should be thereafter placed in those almshouses, when built, and as well as those to be built, and the remaining profit of the said £50 to be yearly distributed equally unto the poor, the week before Christide.

The annual sum of 50s. is paid by the corporation, as the interest of the sum of £50, and divided equally amongst the poor inhabitants of this almshouse on St. Thomas's day.

A further annual sum of 20s. is also divided at the same time, amongst them and the inhabitants of Harris's almshouse, hereinafter mentioned, arising as follows :- The corporation, as holding the Castle-court manor, in Barnstaple, under the late Sir John Chichester, baronet, were bound to provide for him two annual fish dinners, his claim to which he voluntarily relinquished, on payment by the corporation, of two annuities of 20s. each, one amongst the poor of this establishment and of Harris's almshouse, and the

84

other for the support of the charity school of the town, and the same arrangement has been continued by the present Sir Arthur Chichester. [E.]

The almspeople are appointed as vacancies occur, from the poor persons of Barnstaple, by the mayor for the time being. At the time of our investigation, all of them were women, but men have sometimes been appointed.

They receive one shilling each, twice in the year, from Phillip's gift, and six-pence each, twice in the year, from Tippett's gift, hereinafter mentioned.

HARRIS'S ALMSHOUSE.

It appears from an inscription on a tablet in the church of this parish, that Thomas Harris, in 1646, gave £20 to build an almshouse for some poor, in the church-yard.

The house supposed to have been built, in consequence of this bequest, ajoins to the church-yard, and to Paige's almshouse above-mentioned. It is inhabited by poor persons, placed there by the mayor of Barnstaple for the time being, and is repaired by the occupiers. The present inhabitants are the sexton of the parish, and his wife, who receive one shilling each, out of the annuity of twenty shillings mentioned in the account of Paige's almshouse; one shilling each twice in the year, from Phillip's gift; and six-pence each, twice in the year, from Tippett's gift.

BEAPLE'S GIFT.

Richard Beaple, whose gift to Penrose's almshouse has already been mentioned, by a codicil to his said will, bearing date 14th November, 1642, gave to the mayor and aldermen of Barnstaple, and their successors, for ever, to the use of the poor people of the town of Barnstaple, a yearly rent-charge of £20, to be issuing out of his barton and demense of Hedd, in the parishes of Chittlehampton and Chumleigh, upon trust, to distribute the same to the most necessitous, sick, old, and impotent people in the said town.

The lands charged with this rent-charge, are now the property of Lord Rolle, whose steward, after deducting £2 13s. 4d. for land tax, pays annually to the mayor of Barnstaple for the time being

£17 6s. 8d. in respect thereof. [F.]

The sum is united with the rents arising from Skinner's gift and Cornish's gift, and forms one fund, the application of which will be stated in the account hereinafter given of the last mentioned charity.

SKINNER'S GIFT.

By indenture, bearing date 30th April, 1719, between Bartholomew Wakeman, son and heir and also executor of William Wakeman, deceased, of the one part; and Edward Fairchild, mayor, Robert Nicholls and John Marshall, aldermen, and twelve others, capital burgesses of the borough and parish of Barnstaple, of the other part; reciting, that Ephraim Skinner, of London, barber chirurgeon, by his will, bearing date 27th December, 1677, gave in trust, to his brother-in-law, William Wakeman, of Barnstaple, the place of his birth, £200, to be invested by him in land, that so the yearly profits thereof should go to such poor of the said town that should not be already pensioners, as his said brother, whilst alive, should think fit, and after his death, as he should appoint; and reciting, that the said William Wakeman, in purchase of the said trust, had laid out the said £200, in the purchase of the fee-simple of the lands thereinafter mentioned, which were conveyed to him and his heirs, by indenture of feoffment, bearing date 27th November, 1678; and reciting that the said William Wakeman did not, by his last will, or otherwise, appoint how and amongst whom the said yearly profits should be distributed after his death; the said Bartholomew Wakeman, for the better manifestation of the said trust, granted to the parties of the second part, and their heirs, three closes of land, containing by estimation, six acres, or thereabouts, situate in the said parish of Barnstaple, commonly called Dobbings, or Tracy's grounds, being the lands so granted by the said indenture of feoffment, as aforesaid, on trust, for the poor of the said parish of Barnstaple, not being pensioners, the yearly profits thereof, for ever, to be distributed amongst them, as the mayor, aldermen, and capital burgesses of the said borough and parish, for the time being, together with the said Bartholomew Wakeman, should appoint, such distribution to be made in such a manner, that the will of the said benefactor might be with the greatest exactness fulfilled.

We have not found any subsequent trust deed of this property, but the leases of it have of late years been granted by the corporation.

The above mentioned three closes of land, contain, by admeasurement, 7A. 29P. and are now in the occupation of Mr. Harry Leworthy, under a lease granted by public auction for 14 years from Lady-day 1815, determinable at the end of the first seven or eleven years, at a clear yearly rent of £30, which is considered to be the full value of the premises. The application of this rent will be stated in the account of the following gift of Richard Cornish.

CORNISH'S GIFT.

Richard Cornish, by his will, bearing date 5th August, 1709, reciting that he was possessed of a close of land called Withy Close, situate in Barnstaple, for a long term of years, gave the same, after the deaths of his wife and brother, to the mayor and aldermen of the borough and parish of Barnstaple for the time being, for the poor of the said parish, the said close to be yearly set at rent by the mayor and aldermen, and the rent to be by them yearly, on the 25th December, distributed amongst the said poor, in such shares and proportions as by the said mayor and aldermen should be thought fit, they having respect to the most necessitous poor.

Withey Close consists of 2A. 1R. 21P. and is now in the occupation of Dr. Morgan, under a lease from the corporation, granted by public auction, for seven years from Lady-day 1819, at the yearly rent of £16, which is considered to be a very good rent. The previous rent was £7 10s. per annum, subject to deductions for rates and taxes.

The annual income arising from this and the two preceding gifts, is united into one fund; until the year 1817, the amount thereof, either in money or in articles of clothing, was distributed, one moiety by the mayor, and one fourth-part by each of the two aldermen of the borough, at their respective houses, to such objects as they thought proper, and no account of the application of these gifts was preserved; but in that year, during the mayoralty of Mr. Edward Richard Roberts, an improved mode of distribution was introduced. Articles of clothing are now provided and given away, together with small donations of money, proportioned to the numbers in each family, by the mayor and aldermen for the time being, amongst the poor, who attend at a public meeting held shortly after Christmas, of which notice is given by the town crier; and an account is kept under the direction of the mayor, of the receipt and expenditure of these gifts, with lists of the persons receiving them. From the year 1820, a book has been appropriated exclusively to the purpose of recording the application of the charities under management of the corporation.

The income and expenditure of these donations for the year 1821, was as follows:-

	£	s.	d.
From Beaple's gift	17	6	8
Rent of Facey's ground (Skinner's gift)	30	0	0
Produce of a tree cut on Facey's ground	2	10	0
Rent of Withy Close (Cornish's gift).	16	0	0
	£65	16	8

	£	s.	d.
Distributed at the Guildhall in March 1822 (a delay having taken place in such distribution, in consequence of a part of the rents not having been received at the usual time) in articles of clothing; viz. 47 shirts, 58 shifts, 34 petticoats, 19 pair of stockings, 64 aprons, and 59 handkerchiefs	34	15	4
Distributed in money	18	18	6
Receipt stamps	0	1	6
Expense of rebuilding a linhay which had been blown down on Facey's ground	12	1	5
	£65	16	9

This distribution was extended to between four and five hundred persons.

All the poor inhabiting in the town of Barnstaple, whether settled parishioners or not, are allowed to partake of these donations. It is to be observed, that the income arising from Skinner's gift, was directed by the donor to be confined to persons not being pensioners. No part of this fund has been exclusively disposed of to persons not having parochial relief, but it is stated, that about one half of those who partake of the distribution, are not in the receipt of such relief.

JEFFERY'S GIFT.

Roger Jeffery, of Barnstaple, apothecary, by will, dated 19th December 1681, and proved in the Archdeaconry Court, at Barnstaple, gave to twelve poor decayed housekeepers, 5s. a piece, to be paid to them yearly for ever on 25th January, being his birthday, 30s. thereof to be paid to them yearly, as aforesaid, by his son-in-law Richard Matthews, his heirs and assigns, for ever,which said 30s. he had reserved to him, his heirs and assigns, for ever, out of his lands in Bickington, which he had formerly purchased of one Mountjoy, which he desired, ordered and ordained the mayor and aldermen of the borough and parish of Barnstaple, for the time being, after his decease, to receive of the said Richard Matthews, his heirs and assigns, for ever, and the same to distribute and pay over, yearly, to the said poor housekeepers also, by the mayor and aldermen of Barnstaple aforesaid, and their successors, which said 30s. last mentioned should arise out of the interest of £25 which he did thereby give and bequeath to the mayor and aldermen of the said borough, for the time being, and their successors for ever, to be paid to them by his executor, Joseph Fraine, within one year next after his decease, to be put out by them at interest into the hands of three sufficient persons, and to be distributed yearly.

A tablet in Barnstaple church, records the gift of Roger Jeffery, as being 30s. a year (instead of £3 as mentioned in the will) for poor decayed housekeepers. The old book of mayors' accounts, does not contain those of any year between the date of this gift and the year 1706, and we have not been able to find any trace of the receipt of the above-mentioned sum of £25 by the corporation, or of the payment of any interest by that body in respect thereof.

The annuity of 30s. is received from the agent of Mr.—Yeo, of Clifton, as being the owner of the lands charged therewith, in the hamlet of Bickington, which is in the parish of Fremington, and it is distributed by the mayor for the time being, in small sums amongst poor housekeepers.

It appears from the book in which the account of the corporation charities is now kept, that in 1820, it was thus given to two poor men and four widows, in larger sums of 5s. each, and that in 1821, it was given to a larger number of persons, in sums varying from 5s. to 2s.

DELBRIDGE'S GIFT.

John Delbridge, by deed, bearing date 25th December, 1632, (as appears from the before mentioned old book of mayors' accounts,) granted to the mayor, aldermen and burgesses of Barnstaple, and their successors, an annuity of 44s. issuing out of a tenement situate at the higher end of Crock [Cross] street, at the corner of the street next to the High Cross, and he appointed the said annuity to be disposed of as follows:- 20s. thereof to be distributed by the churchwardens and overseers of the poor yearly, on the 14th December, unto twenty such poor families in Barnstaple, to each family, 12d. as the mayor and aldermen, or two of them together, with the churchwardens, should, by writing under their hands nominate; and 20s. more thereof to be distributed in like manner by such proportion and to such persons, upon the 2nd day of May yearly; and 2s. of the said annuity to be yearly bestowed by the churchwardens, in the cleansing and reparation of the tomb of his daughter, Mary Markwell; and the other 2s. residue of the said annuity, to be given to the overseers of the poor, for their pains in distributing the said annuity; which grant contained a proviso, that if the mayor, &c. should neglect to collect the said annuity by the space of two years, or should not distribute the same, nor cause the said tomb to be repaired, nor should tell the overseers to account for the same, the grant of the said annuity should be void.

This annuity is not now received, and we have not been able to obtain any farther information relating to it, except that in the returns made to Parliament in 1786, it is stated that the gift had lapsed by the tenor of the deed. It is probable that at some former period, the owner of the property charged therewith, availed himself of some neglect on the part of the corporation, in the collection or disposal of the annuity, to avoid the deed under the proviso contained in it.

OLIVEAN'S GIFT.

Stephen Olivean, by his will, bearing date 2nd May, 1668, gave to the mayor and aldermen of the town of Barnstaple, and to the mayor and aldermen of the town of Bideford, respectively, and their respective successors, two yearly rent charges of £5 each, to be issuing out of two messuages and tenements, with the appurtenances, in Saint Luce's-lane, in the parish of St. John's Bow, Exeter, then in the possession of John Taylor, and others, with which he had purchased of John Dotton, to be employed by them towards the schooling of poor children, born within the said towns respectively. He also gave to the mayor and aldermen of Plymouth, and to the churchwardens and overseers of the parish of Northam, respectively, two yearly rent-charges of £5 4s. each, for a weekly distribution of 2s. worth of bread in each of those places, to be issuing out of the same premises.

We are informed, that Saint Luce's-lane, Exeter, is now called Friernhay-lane, but we have not met with any evidence tending to identify the property charged with these rent-charges, nor have we been able to find in any of the places to which they were given, any trace of their having been received. The gifts to Barnstaple and Bideford, are mentioned in lists of charities upon tablets, in the respective churches of those towns, the donor being called in the former, Stephen Oliphan, and in the latter, Stephen Oliver. The governors of St. John's hospital in Exeter, are in possession of a house in Fore-street, in that city, and in the parish of St. John's Bow, given to them by the will of the said Stephen Olivean.

MAYNE'S GIFT.

A gift of £200 from John Mayne, in 1680, to each of the towns of Dartmouth, Barnstaple, and Bideford, provided that they should, within four years after his death, raise in each of those places £600 or £700; the sums so given by him, and the sums so to be raised, to be employed in erecting of schools in the said towns respectively, was mentioned in a former Report, in the account of the charities of Dartmouth.

We find no trace of this donation having been received in either of these places, and think it probable, that the condition imposed by the donor, was not complied with.

MONIES GIVEN TO BE LENT.

It appears from the old book of mayor's account that the following sums were given by various donors previously to the year 1633, to be lent out to the poor;—

		£	s.	d.
To be raised out of the houses in Boutport-street, given by				
	Robert Appley	100	0	0
	G. Duke	10	0	0
	R. Beaple	20	0	0
	Dorothy Palmer	6	13	4
	W. Gray	30	0	0
	J. Ayres	100	0	0
	L. Smith	12	0	0
	J. Beaple	20	0	0
	T. Berryman	100	0	0
	N. Teakle	100	0	0
	Hugh Atwell	3	0	0
	T. Wescombe	2	10	0
	Denys Westlade	1	0	0
	Hugh Stevens	6	13	4
	T. Westlake	40	0	0
	J. Stanbury	10	0	0

And that in 1633, the sum of £59 16s. 8d. was paid by the corporation, to make good deficiencies in these monies. [G.]

It also appears from an entry in the same book, in 1634, that the mayor, aldermen, and common council of this town, observing, that the poorer sort were not able to find security for loans out of these monies given to be lent to poor tradesmen, especially poor weavers and tuckers, but by leaving the money in the hands of their sureties, whereby little or no profit grew to the said poor; and being desirous that the poor should have some benefit of the said money, though fit to lend part of the said money to some of the townsmen, such as by their trading helped and relieved the poorer sort, at six per cent, which profit, at the end of the year, should be distributed to such poor weavers and tuckers as could not find security, nor employ the money to their profit. They therefore lent four sums of £50 each, and one sum of £25 to different persons, at 6 per cent; the interest of which was distributed to the poor in 1634, in sums varying from £1 to 2s. 6d.; at the same time a part of the said monies, amounting to £326 appears to have been in the hands of several persons, on bond, in sums of £5 and under.

In 1634, Laurence Gibbons gave £20 to be paid to the common council of this town, and employed by them for the benefit of poor tradesmen, free of the town. In 1635, Richard Castleman gave £50 to be paid to the aldermen, and lent out by them as they should think fit, whereby the revenues thereof might be for ever continued for the use of the poor, once a year to be distributed amongst them that should stand in most need. In 1650, James Walsh gave £20 to be put out and employed for the benefit of the poor of this town, for ever.

It appears from the same book, that as late as the year 1671, interest was received for monies lent, called the Poor's Stock, by the mayor, for the time being, and distributed to the poor, subsequently to which, we have not been able to find any trace of these monies.

APPLEY'S GIFT.

Robert Appley, (whose gift to the almshouse, now called Paige's almshouse, has already been mentioned) by his will, bearing date 7th October, 1594, gave to William Collybere, then mayor of Barnstaple, and ten others, and their heirs, two messuages and two gardens at Barnstaple, bounded by the town wall on the west, and the street called Boutport on the east, upon trust, to permit the mayor and aldermen of the town of Barnstaple, for the time being, to receive the rents and profits of the said premises, which persons should pay an annuity of £4 5s. 2d. to his wife for life; and after her death, should take the rents and profits thereof, until there should be a sum of £100 levied thereof, which he directed should be lent forth without interest, from time to time, for ever, to young householders who would give good survey unto the said mayor and aldermen, for the time being, for the repayment thereof, by such portions and sums, and for such terms, as by the said mayor and aldermen, and by the common council of the said town, for the time being, should be thought meet; and after the said sum of £100 should be levied as aforesaid, he directed that all the rents, fines, and profits, that should from thenceforth arise from the said premises, should be by the said mayor and aldermen received, and by them disposed to the relief, behoof and benefit of poor people inhabiting within the borough of Barnstaple, from time to time, for ever.

One of these houses in Boutport street, is now held by Mary Fisher, under a lease granted by the corporation, bearing date 31st May, 1800, for 60 years from the ensuing Midsummer, to William Fisher, at a clear rent of £5 5s. per annum. It appears, to have been previously let for a similar term, at the rent of £2 per annum. The house had been re-built since the existing lease was granted, and is estimated to be worth about £14 per annum, clear rent.

The other house is now held by the Rev. Henry Nicholls, under lease, bearing date 16th June, 1806, granted by the corporation to Samuel Brembridge, the elder, whose daughter Mr. Nicholls married, for 60 years, from the ensuing Midsummer, at the clear yearly rent of £2 10s. in consideration of a surrender of a lease for a similar term, commencing in 1770, at the rent of £2 per annum. This house was improved and partly re-built by Mr. Brembridge, after the existing lease was granted. It is estimated to be worth about £15 per annum, clear rent. The addition to the rent of 10s. per annum, appears to have been a very small consideration for the extention of the lessee's interest in this house. [H.]

The only reason assigned for the corporation having granted leases for terms of so long duration, is, that this was till lately the usual mode of leasing the premises in Barnstaple belonging to that body.

The sum of £100 directed by Mr. Appley's will to be raised out of these premises, given by him, appears in the before-mentioned list, dated in 1633, of monies given to be lent to the poor of Barnstaple; but we find no subsequent trace of it.

The rents of these houses, together with those of the lands in the parish of Pilton, given by Adam Lygg, and the annuity of 40s. given by Richard Ferris, senior, as hereinafter stated, have been for a great number of years received by the overseers of the poor of this parish, and carried to their general account, in aid of the poor's rates. The earliest overseers' account book produced to us, commences 1725, at which time, the income of these gifts was thus disposed of, and the application of them may probably have been the same at a much earlier period.

As this mode of disposing of the rents, in aid of those who are bound by the law to contribute to the support of the poor, rather than for the benefit of the poor people themselves, appeared to us a complete deviation from the intentions of these benefactors; a meeting of parishioners of Barnstaple was at our suggestion held, on the 7th of October, 1822, for the purpose of taking into consideration the application of these gifts, at which it was resolved :-

1st. That the receipt and distribution of the charities of Robert Appley, and Richard Ferris, senior, should for the future be placed in the hands of the mayor and corporation, according to the wills of the donors; and

2dly, That the receipt and distribution of the charity of Adam Lugg, should for future, be commited to the mayor and corporation, on condition, that the minister and churchwardens should be allowed to be present at such distribution.

It only remains, therefore, for the persons entrusted with the distribution of these gifts, to dispose of them annually for the benefit of the poor, in such manner as shall most fully carry into effect the charitable intentions of the donors.

LUGG'S GIFT.

AdamLugg, by his will, bearing date 3rd January, 1622, and proved in the Prerogative Court of Canterbury, gave to the poor of the town of Barnstaple, £100 to be bestowed by his executors and overseers, to remain for ever to the use of the poor of the said town.

By indenture, bearing date 23rd August, 1632, between William Palmer, of one part, and Richard Medford and Gilbert Paige and George Lugg, executor of the will of the said Adam Lugg, of the other part; reciting, that George Peard esq. being possessed of a messuage or tenement, and 14 acres of land, in the parish of Pilton, whereof the closes thereinafter mentioned were lately parcel, for the term of 80 years commencing from the 10th July, 7th Charles 1st; and being likewise interested in the said tenement and 14 acres of land, for the term of 2,000 years, to commence from the 26th of June, 1710, had, by two several indentures, bearing date 10th August, 8th Charles 1st, assigned to the said William Palmer, then mayor of Barnstaple, his executors, &c. a marsh containing two acres; a close called the Shovell, containing one acre; a close called Eastman's ground, containing three acres; and another close, contaning two acres, parcel of the said premises in the parish of Pilton, for the residue of the said term of 80 years, and for the said term of 2,000 years; the said William Palmer thereby published and declared, that the said two several terms were purchased by the said George Lugg, for the use , benefit and profit of the poor of the inhabitants of the borough and parish of Barnstaple, according to the will of the said Adam Lugg; and that the rents of the before-mentioned premises, ought to be employed for the benefit and relief of the poor of the said borough and parish accordingly.

The said William Palmer, by indenture, bearing date 20th July, 1648, for the continuance of the trusts for the poor of the said borough and parish of Barnstaple, and the performance of the charitable intentions of the said Adam Lugg, assigned the above-mentioned premises to Richard Harris, then mayor of Barnstaple, and five others, merchants, of the same place; and a subsequent trust deed of the premises, was made by the surviving trustee in 1667, to William Westcombe, mayor, Nicholas Denys, deputy recorder, George Rooke, alderman, Thomas Matthews, and nine others, capital burgesses, and John Stevens, town clerk of Barnstaple.

We have not been able to find any trust deeds of these lands subsequent to this period, and leases of them have of late years been granted by the churchwardens and overseers.

The above mentioned property consists of four fields :-

		A.	R.	P.	
1	Beaple's Close	3	1	0	In the occupation of John Andrew, under an agreement for a lease for 14 yrs. from Lady-day 1821, determinable at the end of 7 or 14 yrs, at the yearly rent of 14*l*. 5*s*.
2	Lark Lees	2	3	0	
3	Willow Plot	0	3	26	In the occupation of John Folland, under an agreement for a similar term, from the same period, at the yearly rent of 10*l*. 15*s*.
4	The Marsh	1	2	20	
		8	2	6	[I.]

These lettings were by public auction; but the tenants had not at the time of our investigation executed the leases, and the rents being considered too high, some of the parishioners had been appointed to make an arrangement with the tenants, for lowering them to a fair amount.

An entry in the said old book of mayors' accounts, states, that the £100 given by Adam Lugg, not being sufficient for the purchase of the said lands at Pilton, the town dispersed £13 16s. 6d. towards the purchase, which, in 1634, was wholly repaid; and that from thenceforward the whole profits of the land were to be employed for the use of the poor, by the churchwardens and overseers of the poor, and to be by them, from year to year, accounted for. It is probable, therefore, that the rents may have been ever since that time carried to the overseers' general account.

We have stated in the account of Appley's gift, the resolution which has been adopted by the parishioners, for the future distribution of the rents of this property, by the mayor and corporation, in the presence of the minister and churchwardens; in consequence of which, it is hoped, that the poor people of Barnstaple, the object of this donor's bounty, will henceforth receive the benefits which he intended for them.

RICHARD FERRIS, SENIOR'S, GIFT.

Richard Ferris, senior, by his will, bearing date 27th June, 1622, gave to the mayor, aldermen, and burgesses of Barnstaple, 40s. yearly, for the use and benefit of the poor of that parish, to be paid out of a messuage and garden in Holland street, Barnstaple.

The statement of this will is taken from a recital in a conveyance of this house, dated 31st May, 1654, from William Westcombe and Mary his wife, to Mary Thorne, whereby the said Mary Thorne covenanted to pay the said annuity of 40s. according to the effect of the will of the said Richard Ferris.

The annual sum of 40s. is now paid by Mrs. Dene, as the owner of the house charged therewith.

The manner in which this rent-charge has been hitherto employed, and its intended application for the future, have been already noticed in the above account of Appley's gift.

SIR JOHN ACLAND'S GIFT.

The particulars of Sir John Acland's gift in 1616, to this borough (amongst other places,) of an annuity of 52s. directed to be paid to the mayor for the time being, providing, weekly, 13 penny loaves, to be distributed to 13 of the poorest sort of people of the borough, appointed by the mayor and four of the most ancient masters of the borough, have been already stated in a former Report, in the account of the charities of the city of Exeter. [J.]

The annual sum of £2 12s. is received by the churchwardens and overseers of the poor of Barnstaple, from the chamber of Exeter. No weekly distribution of bread takes place, in the manner prescribed by the donor; but the whole sum, together with 20s. arising from Webber's gift, hereinafter mentioned, is laid out annually, shortly after Christmas, in the purchase of penny and two-penny loaves, which are distributed by the churchwardens and overseers, amongst the poor inhabitants of Barnstaple, whether receiving parochial relief or not.

HORSHAM'S GIFT.

Hugh Horsham, by his will, bearing date 3rd January, 1653, as appears from the before-mentioned old book of mayor's accounts, gave to the poor of the town of Barnstaple, £20, to remain for ever, the interest and benefit thereof to be bestowed in bread, and distributed to the poor of the said town, every Candlemas eve, for ever.

The annual sum of 20s. which is understood to be the interest of this sum of £20, is paid by the corporation of Barnstaple to the churchwardens and overseers, and by them disposed of in the manner above stated, in the account of Sir John Acland's gift.

WEBBER'S GIFT.

Thomas Webber, by his will, bearing date 20th May, 1696, gave to the poor of Barnstaple, 12s. per annum, in bread, to be distributed among them on St. Thomas's day, for ever, and thereby charged three tenements, and a garden thereto adjoining, situate in Pilton, with the payment thereof.

This statement of the will is taken from a recital in a conveyance of these premises, dated in 1728, from Humphry Dene, and Arthur Tucker, to Alexander Beare.

Miss Reed, as the owner of a garden in Pilton, called Yeolands, pays this annuity to the churchwardens and overseers of Barnstaple, by whom it is disposed of, in the manner above stated, in the account of Sir John Acland's gift.

WESTLAKE'S GIFT.

Katherine Westlake, of Barnstaple, widow, by her will, bearing date 19th April, 1636, gave to her executors £300, to the intent that they should put forth the same into some good hands for profit, and that the increase and profit thereof should, yearly, be distributed amongst the poor artificers of the town of Barnstaple, according to the discretion of her said executors; the said gift to continue for ever. And she directed, that when three of her executors should be dead, the two survivors should associate to themselves three others, inhabitants of the said town, and so from time to time for ever, as often as by death they should be reduced to two, having regard to those of the common council of the said town, and likewise to those of her kindred; which persons should have the same powers, as if they had been appointed by her will, to execute all things, as her executors might do. She also gave to the executors £100, to the intent that they should, yearly, distribute the profit thereof amongst such poor men and women, within the said town of Barnstaple, as should be newly come out of their appreniceship, towards the setting up of their trade and better livelihood; and she appointed Richard Beaple, William Purnell, George Peard, Richard Medford, and Richard Ferris, to be her executors.

By a decree of commissioners of charitable uses, bearing date 17th January, 1667, it was (amongst other things) directed, that the two surviving trustees of this gift should, within three weeks after they should be reduced to that number, by writing, under their hands and seals, associate to themselves three other persons to act in the management of the trusts; that no trustee should keep in his hands any of the money belonging to the said trust on interest; that once in every year due distribution should be made of the profit of the said money; and that the trustees, once in every year, should render an account to the mayor and aldermen of Barnstaple, for the time being, of their acting in the said trust. [K.]

It appears, from the accounts of this charity, that the sum of £400 given by Mrs. Westlake, was in 1749 and 1750, (previously to which time it had been lent on bond,) laid out to purchase of £390 old South Sea Annuities, in which stock it now remains, the yearly dividends being £11 14s.

The last deed for appointing new trustees is dated in 1788, of whom Mr. John May, senior, is the only survivor. In 1808, the above mentioned stock was transferred into the names of the said Mr. John May, senior, Mr. John May, junior, Mr. Edward Richard [Richards] Roberts, and Mr. Henry Drake, and is now standing in their names. No appointment of new trustees, under hand and seal, was then made, but at the time of our investigation it was intended that this should be done.

The four trustees of the stock meet annually, when each of them appoints a poor person of Barnstaple, whose apprenticeship has lately expired, to receive 15s. making in the whole £3 as the interest of £100 mentioned in the latter clause of Mrs. Westlake's will. The persons receiving these sums sign receipts for them in the book relating to the charity. The residue of the dividends, being £8

14s. is distributed about Christmas amongst the poor artificers of the town, in small sums, varying from 1s. to 2s. 6d. by two trustees, who go from house to house, selecting those whom they consider the most proper objects of the charity. At Christmas 1821, the sum of £7 1s. only was thus given, £1 13s. being reserved towards the expense of the proposed new trust deed. A list of the persons receiving this part of the gift, with the sum given to each, is entered in the book; but it has not hitherto been usual to render an account to the mayor and aldermen of Barnstaple, as directed by the above-mentioned decree.

BARON'S GIFT.

George Baron, by indenture, bearing date 20th January, 1681, granted and assigned to Joseph Fraine, and three others, and their heirs, a yearly rent-charge of £6 issuing out of an estate lying in or called by the name of Brinsworthy, in the parish of Fremington, upon trust, that they should at all times thereafter, upon receipt of this rent-charge, or within ten days at the farthest, distribute the same amongst the most necessitous persons, baize-makers, and their widows, inhabiting within the town of Barnstaple, or the limits or precincts thereof, in such proportions as the trustees, in their discretion, should think fit, respect being had to the necessities of the receivers thereof. And it was declared, that when the trustees should be reduced to two, the survivors should appoint two others.

This statement is taken from a recital in the last deed, dated in 1788, for appointing new trustees, of whom Mr. John May, senior, is the survivor.

The gentlemen in whose names the stock held under Mrs. Westlake's gift is now invested, also act as trustees of the gift, and at the time of our investigation it was intended that they should be appointed trustees thereof by deed.

The annuity of £6 is received from the Reverend Samuel May, the owner of the property charged therewith, and is distributed publicly in the Guildhall, one or two days before Christmas, amongst poor weavers of coarse woollen cloths, and their widows, appointed by the trustees, in small sums, varying from 1s. to 4s.

according to their necessities. A list is kept of the persons receiving the donation, who usually continue to have benefit of it during their lives, if they conduct themselves well, and reside in the town of Barnstaple. The manufacture of baize has nearly ceased in this town, and this charity has for many years been extended to the description of persons to whom it is now given.

At Christmas 1820, the distribution was made to 62 persons, and at Christmas 1821, to 56 persons, the sum of £1 7s. having been in the latter year reserved towards the expense of the proposed new trust deed.

RICHARD FERRIS'S GIFT.

Richard Ferris, of Barnstaple, by his will, bearing date 19th June, 1646, gave to John Downe, Nicholas Dennys, and three others, whom he appointed his executors, and their heirs, his manor, messuages, lands and tenements, called Middleton, situate in the parish of Parracombe, upon trust, to take the rents and profits thereof, and pay them to his brother, John Ferris, for his life; and after his brother's decease, the testator directed that there should be yearly, for ever, raised out of the issues and profits of the said manor and premises, the sum of £10 which should be paid by his executors, yearly, to such able schoolmaster as should be appointed by the mayor and aldermen, to teach children in the town of Barnstaple. And he further directed, that £20 more of the yearly rents and profits of the said manor and premises, after the death of his said brother, should be, from time to time, yearly raised by his executors, and by them employed, for ever, towards the binding forth of such poor children of the said town of Barnstaple, apprentices, as the parents of them should not be of ability to prefer. And he gave the rents and profits of the said manor and premises (the said two annuities excepted) to his wife and her heirs, for ever.

The manor and estate, called Middleton, have been conveyed, from time to time, to trustees, upon the trusts of Mr. Ferris's will. The last trust deed is dated in 1815, under which seven trustees are now living. The two annuities of £10 and £20 are received by Mr. Henry Drake, town clerk of Barnstaple, as the agent of the trustees, from Mr. William Dovell, who is at present in the receipt of the rents and profits of the premises.

The application of the former annuity will be stated in the account of the grammar-school, in a subsequent part of this Report. The latter is applied in apprenticeing poor children of parishioners of Barnestaple, a preference being given to the natives of the town. The rent is usually received about Midsummer, and shortly afterwards notice is given of a day on which persons are to make applications, who wish to have their children apprenticed. On that day, after an investigation of the claims of the applicants, and the fitness of the proposed masters or mistresses, by the Reverend William Spurway, one of the trustees, who has had of late years the principal management of the charity, such children as are considered by him proper objects are ordered to be apprenticed, a premium of £4 being given with each boy, and of £2 with each girl. A book is kept, containing an account of the receipt and expenditure of the charity, in which are entered the names of the children, and of the persons to whom they are apprenticed.

In 1812, the above-mentioned annuities were exonerated from land tax, which had been previously deducted out of them. In the same year, a sum of £6 was given by James Hammett, esquire, in aid of this charity, which was carried to the general account.

If there are not a sufficient number of applicants for the benefit of the charity, the balance is carried to the next year's account. On the account, as settled for the year 1821, the balance remaining in Mr. H. Drake's hands was £1 15s. 2d. No charge is made by that gentleman, for keeping the accounts.

PHILLIP'S GIFT.

It is stated in an inscription upon a tablet in the church, that John Phillips, who died in 1734, gave £100 to be laid out in the [some] purchase, for the use of the poor in Litchdon almshouse, the profits thereof to be paid at Christmas, 10s. thereof to the reader; £200 more to be laid out in some purchase, for the use of the charity school; and 40s. a year, for ever, to the poor in the almshouses in the alms-lane and the court thereof, equally; and directed that his executor, Mr. Henry Beavis, and his assigns, should be trustees of his said legacies and purchases.

103

The application of the said £100 and £200 will be found in other parts of this report.

It is further stated, in the said inscription, that £40 the computed value of the said legacy of 40s. a year, together with £24 the produce thereof, was laid out in the purchase of the clear rent-charge of 50s. to be issuing out of three closes of land at Maidenford, in the parish of Barnstaple, called Fox's Park, by half-yearly payments at Midsummer and Christmas.

The present owner of Fox's Park, Mr. —Pomeroy, pays 25s. at Midsummer, and 25s. at Christmas, to one of the poor women in Paige's almshouse, who distributes the same, together with 1s. added to each half year payment, by Colonel Beavis, the son of Mr. Henry Beavis, and the present trustee of this gift, amongst 26 poor almspeople; viz. 16 in Horwood's almshouse, 8 in Paige's almshouse, and 2 in Harris's almshouse, 1s. to each.

DRAKE'S GIFT.

Elizabeth Drake, by her will, bearing date 18th March, 1755, and proved in the Prerogative Court of Canterbury, devised a dwelling-house, in Joy-Street, Barnstaple, with the brewing furnace, utensils, and household furniture, let therewith to John Scott, Philip Furze, John Rogers, and James Hiern, for all the term and estate she should have therein at her death, upon trust, after the decease of her husband, Henry Drake, to let the premises at a yearly rent, and to pay out of the yearly rent to the churchwardens of Barnstaple, 2s.6d. and to the sexton thereof, 2s. 6d. until her sepulchre should be opened, and to distribute the residue of the rents and profits, one half amongst such of the poor of the parish of Barnstaple, and the other half amongst such of the poor of the parish of Pilton, as they should think fit, preferring such poor persons of each parish as might be related to her then husband, or her former husband, Walter Tucker, deceased, on the 28th of February in every year, during her said term and interest in the premises, with a power from time to time, when any one of the trustees should die, for the survivors to add to themselves others, not exceeding three at one time.

The gift of this house by will for charitable purposes, was void by the statute of mortmain, 9 Geo.2. and no claim to it can be established by the objects of the bounty of the testatrix. Mr. Philip Welsh Hiern, of Barnstaple, is now in the receipt of the rents and profits of it, and informs us that he makes certain charitable payments in respect thereof, but considers them to be altogether voluntary on his part. [L.]

TIPPETTS'S GIFT.

Henry Gardner Tippetts, by his will, bearing date 14th June, 1795, and proved in the prerogative Court of Canterbury, charged a field called Hole Ground, in the parish of Barnstaple, which he thereby gave to Elizabeth Symes Warmington, and her heirs, with the payment of 40s. a year, for ever, to be paid to the poor of Litchdon almshouse, at Christmas, in equal proportions; and with further payment of 26s. a year, for ever, to be paid in like manner among the poor of the Alms-lane, in Barnstaple; and with the further payment of 40s. a year, for ever, to be distributed at Christmas in bread, among the poor inhabitants of the borough of Newport, near Barnstaple; and he directed, that the said charities should be publicly distributed by the officiating clergyman of Barnstaple, and by the officiating clergyman of Bishop's Tawton, for the time being.

The field called Hole Ground, is now the property of the Rev. George Tucker, whose tenant, Mr. William Slocombe, pays £1 13s. at Michaelmas, and the same sum at Christmas, in each year, to the parish clerk of Barnstaple, who at each of these times distributes the said sums amongst the 60 almspeople, to each 6d. – viz 40 in Penrose's almshouse, 16 in Horwood's almshouse, 8 in Paige's almshouse, and 2 in Harris's almshouse. The distribution used to be made by the vicar of Barnstaple, but has been latterly entrusted to the parish clerk. Mr. Slocombe also transmits to the vicar of Bishop's Tawton, £2 at Christmas, for the poor of the borough of Newport, in that parish, the distribution of which will be stated in the account of the charities of that parish.

CORDWAINER'S LANDS.

Various old accounts were produced to us, dated in the early part of the reign of Queen Elizabeth, which tend to show, that there existed at that time a company or fellowship of Cordwainer's, in the town of Barnstaple, governed by a master and wardens, in some instances stiled the master and wardens of the occupation of Cordwainer's, and in others the master and wardens "of the Trynitie," but no such company is now in existence.

The earliest deed that we have found relating to these lands, bears date 1st April, 1633, whereby, after reciting that Paul Worth, and Thomas Clarke, deceased, by their indenture, bearing date 29th March, 39th Elizabeth, had granted and enfeoffed to George Baker, and Richard Jeffery, together with others deceased, all those messuages, lands, tenements, rents, reversions, and services in Barnstaple, Bideford, Hartland, Newport Bishop, and Pilton, which premises lying in Barnstaple aforesaid, then or lately before, were in the several tenures of Adam Wyatt, John Rowe, and Nicholas Budd; and also, all those messuages, lands, tenements, rents, &c. situate in Barnstaple, Bideford, Hartland, Newport Bishop, and Pilton, which the said Paul Worth, and Thomas Clarke had, by the grant of John Manning, and others, to hold the said premises to the said George Baker, Richard Jeffery and others, and their heirs for ever; the said George Baker and Richard Jeffery, in performance of the trust by the said Paul Worth and Thomas Clarke, in them reposed, granted and enfeoffed Richard Ferris, then mayor of Barnstaple, and nineteen others, and their heirs, all the said messuages, lands, tenements, rents, &c.; and also all the messuages, lands, tenements, rents, &c. lying in Barnstaple, Bideford, Hartland, Newport Bishop, and Pilton, which the said George Baker and Richard Jeffery had, by the grant of the said Paul Worth and Thomas Clarke, to the intent and purpose, that the said Richard Ferris and others, should, yearly, on 25th October, out of issues and profits of the said premises, distribute or cause to be distributed, amongst the poor people of the said town of Barnstaple, 3s. 4d.

Although this deed professes to convey lands, &c. in the several parishes enumerated therein, it is to be observed, that the only property specified by the names of the lessees thereof, is described as situate in the parish of Barnstaple, and then tenure of Adam Wyatt, John Rowe, and Nicholas Budd. The same names occur in the above-mentioned old accounts of tenants, as paying rent, of whom there never appear to have been more than three at any one time.

The Cordwainer's lands in Barnstaple are most particularly described in the following, being the latest trust deed; and from the commencement of the old accounts to the present time, we find no trace of the trustees being in possession of the property in any other parish, whatever may have been the case at a still earlier period.

By indenture, bearing date, 4th April, 1787, Simon Moule, as the surviving feoffee of the lands and tenements belonging to the fellowship of Cordwainers, granted enfeoffes to Mounier Roch and nineteen others, and their heirs, a tenement, curtilage, and garden, situate in Anchor-lane, Barnstaple, between the lands of the feoffees of the Long Bridge of Barnstaple, together with the lands of John Dart, and of the heirs of Bear, on the north; the lands theretofore of John Coffin, on the south, the lands theretofore of Harry Jeffery, together with the lands of the heirs of Bear, on the west; and the lane called Anchor lane, on the east; which said tenement, curtilage and garden, were theretofore in the occupation of John Jeffery, since of James Kimpand, afterwards of Catherine Paddon, late of John Baker, and then of Nicholas Glass, and which said premises were formerly known by the sign of the King and Queen; and also a messuage of dwelling-house, situate in High-Street, Barnstaple, formerly in the occupation of Daniel Marriott, afterwards, of Richard Thorn, and then of Nicholas Glass; and also a tenement, with a curtilage thereunto adjoining, in Barnstaple, between the tenement appertaining to the late charity of St. Nicholas, of Barnstaple, on the north; a tenement, then in the occupation of Robert Gribble, on the south; a lane called Paige-lane, on the west; and the High street, on the east; and also a garden, then converted into two gardens, near adjoining to the Castle of Barnstaple, between the lands appertaining to the late chantry of the Blessed Virgin Mary, of Barnstaple, on the north; the lands appertaining to the late priory of Pilton, on the south and east; and the lands of the mayor, aldermen and burgesses of Barnstaple, on the west; which said tenement, curtilage and garden, were some time in the occupation of Elizabeth Vaughan, late of Elizabeth Bicknell, and John Bicknell, her father, or one of them, and then of James Hiern, apothecary, together with all other houses, &c. in Barnstaple, Bideford, Hartland, Newport Bishop, and Pilton, mentioned in the original deed of feoffment thereof, made to the said Simon Moule, and others; upon trust, that the rents and profits of all the said premises, should be from time to time, by Simon Moule, and the said parties of the second part, and the survivors of them, employed to such uses and purposes as the said premises were first given and enfeoffed, with a proviso for the appointment of sixteen new trustees when the number should be reduced to four. Four of the feoffees appointed by this deed are now living.

The present state of this property is shown by the following Rental:—

No.	PARISH	LESSEE	TENEMENTS	TERM	Date of last Renewal	Fine paid On last Renewal			RENT		
						£	s	d	£	s	d
1	Barnstaple	Nicholas Glass, now George Harris	Two small tenements, with stables and small courtlages in Anchor- lane, let to under tenants, and back kitchen with a laundry over, occupied by the present lessee.	33 yrs. from 6th April, 1821	17th December 1794	13	16	0	0	4	0
2	Ditto	Nicholas Glass, now George Harris	Part of a shop in High Street, with a passage and staircase behind, and the rooms over the same, occupied by an under tenant of the lessee.	40 yrs. from 25th March 1818	29th September 1798	20	0	0	0	8	0
3	Ditto	James Hiern, now Philip Welch Hiern	The southern part of the front of a house in High-street, and all the back part of the same house, together with a garden near the castle, and a shed lately built thereon by the lessee	31 yrs. from Lady-day 1816	13th February 1787	16	0	0	1	0	0
										[M.]	

108

The whole of the premises comprised in No. 1, are estimated to be worth about £14 per annum. The premises, No. 2 and 3, are so united with freehold land belonging to the respective lessees, that it is difficult to give an accurate statement of their value.

In 1731, a lease was granted of No. 1, in consideration of a fine of £70 for 60 years from that time. This lease was renewed in 1761, in consideration of a fine of £12 for 30 years, from 1791, and again renewed in 1794, as stated in the rental. In 1758, a lease was granted of No. 2, in consideration of a fine of £3 3s. for 60 years from that time, which was renewed in 1798, as stated in the rental. In 1744, a lease was granted of No. 3, for 60 years, to commence in 1756, after the expiration of a term of 99 years, which had been granted in reversion of a previous term of 90 years, commencing 36 Elizabeth. The rent of No. 1, appears from old accounts to have been formerly 10s. but in the lease of 1731, the rent reserved was the same as at present. The rents of the other premises have always been the same.

The mode has been adopted of granting leases of these premises for 60 years, and renewing such leases after the expiration of about one half of the term, is stated to have been also customary in letting the houses belonging to the corporation of Barnstaple; but it appears to us to be a disadvantageous mode of leasing the property belonging to a charity, as it is not to be expected that the fines to be obtained for such reversionary leases, will bear an adequate proportion to the actual value of the premises.

This property is subject to two chief rents of 1s. each to the trustees of Barnstaple bridge, and to those of Bideford bridge, and to a rent to the Castle Court of 2³/₄d.

One of the feoffees acting as treasurer, has received the rents and fines, and made occasional distributions of them. We have examined the accounts from 1761 to the present time, and find that a distribution has taken place after the receipt of each fine, and that there have also been occasional distributions of the rents in the treasurer's hands, in small sums, among poor shoemakers of Barnstaple, and their widows. The last distribution was made in 1820, when the sum of £10 8s. 7¹/₂d. arising from the rents for seven years preceding, was thus given away, by Mr. Samuel

Brembridge, then treasurer, but since deceased, in sums varying from 1s. to 3s.; a small balance of 8s. 7d. remained at the time of our inquiry, in the chest, containing the documents relating to these lands, which is now in the possession of John Roberts, esquire, one of the surviving feoffees.

GRAMMAR SCHOOL.

FERRIS'S GIFT.

The will of Richard Ferris, bearing date, 19th June 1646, has already been stated, by which he gave an annuity of £10 to be paid to such able schoolmasters as should be appointed by the mayor and aldermen of Barnstaple, to teach children in that town.

WRIGHT'S GIFT.

By deed, bearing date 23d August 1760, John Wright, Clerk, A. M. master of the grammar school of Barnstaple, being moved with gratitude, after receiving for nearly 20 years the annuity of £10 given by Richard Ferris to that grammar school, for the benefit of the master thereof,and considering that the said school had the smallest foundation of any grammar school in Devon, gave to the mayor and aldermen of Barnstaple and their sucessors £100, then placed in four per cent bank annuities, on trust, to the place out the said sum from time to time on the best securiy that could be got, and to receive the yearly interest, and pay the same unto the said John Wright, as long as he should continue actual master of the said school, and after his resignation or death, to pay the interest to every succeeding master of the said school for the time being, for his better support and maintenance; and as every preceding master of the said school had been of the degree of master of arts, it was his particular desire,that in case any future master should be elected to the said school, not of that degree at the time of A. M. as soon as conveniently might be after his election; and if at any time thereafter, any of his descendants should happen to stand candidate for the mastership of the said grammar school, it was his desire that he should, *cæteris paribus*, have the preference, on his

110

conforming to the rules and conditions in the said deed expressed; provided, that if it should happen that any future master of the said school should neglect to attend and perform the duty thereof as he ought to do, and such neglect should appear to the mayor and aldermen for the time being, to be willfully committed, it should be lawful for them (no prejudice being visable) to withhold such yearly interest from such neglectful master, and to keep the same in arrear in their hands, or to add the same to the said principal sum of £100 as should be most beneficial to the next succeeding master.

The above-mentioned £100 is now invested in two deeds poll of the Barnstaple turnpike trust for £50 each, bearing interest at four per cent; the interest thereof, and the annuity of £10 derived from Richard Ferris's gift are paid to the Rev. Henry Nicholls, A.M. the present master of the grammar school, who was appointed to that situation by the corporation in 1795. An ancient building in the church-yard is used as a school-room, and is kept in repair by the corporation, who have also voluntarily permitted the present master to reside in a house in Barnstaple, belonging to them, which was not previously appropriated to that purpose. The present master, in respect of the above mentioned emoluments, instructs one boy free of expense, admitted as a vacancy occurs, by the recommendation in writing of a majority of the members of the corporation. The boy receives a classical education, in common with the other scholars in the school, about 30 in number, principally day boys of the town of Barnstaple.

BARNSTAPLE FREE GRAMMAR SCHOOL

CHARITY SCHOOL.

This school was established in 1710, and various donations of money and rent-charges have been made to it from time to time, which are recorded in tables in the church.

In 1746, an estate, called Francis and Bowden, in the parish of Ilfracombe, was purchased and conveyed to trustees for the support of this school, subject to a rent charge of £4 per annum, for the poor almspeople in Penrose's almshouse. The purchase money of this estate was £1,150 the whole of which has arisen from gifts to this school, except £100, which was a legacy of John Phillips, to the said almshouse, and in respect whereof the said rent-charge of £4 per annum was, by the purchase deeds, made payable for ever to trustees, for the benefit of the almspeople. A legacy of £200, given by the said John Phillips to this school, was also included in the said purchase money.

We have not found the original purchase deeds of this estate, but they are recited in the earliest trust deeds that we have seen, bearing date 9th and 10th November, 1755.

The last trust deeds are dated 19th and 20th September, 1805, under which eight trustees are now living.

The following statement will show the property now enjoyed by this establishment:—

	£	s.	d.
1.– A messuage and farm, called Francis and Bowden in the parish of Ilfracombe, in the occupation of James Watts, containing by estimation, about 160 acres, under a lease granted by auction by the trustees, for 11 years, from Lady-day, 1815, determinable at the end of seven years, at the yearly rent of £110, reduced 1822, in consequence of the depreciation of the produce of land to . .	90	0	0

	£	s	d

2.–A rent-charge given by the will of
Thomas Harris, in 1712, issuing out of
a house in High-street, in the occupation of Mr. Thomas Scott, near the
school-house   0   8   0

3.– A rent-charge given by the will of
Rebecca Fairchild, in 1714, issuing
out of a garden adjoining the school-
house, the property of John Caddy . . 0 16 0

4.– A rent-charge given by the will of
Elizabeth Watson, in 1715, issuing out
of a house in High-street, the property
of Mr. John Dennis 1 0 0

5.– A rent-charge given by the will of Ann
Carpenter, in 1725, issuing out of the
manor of Stanton Fry, near Minehead,
the property of John Fownes Lutterell,

6.– A rent-charge given by Nicholas Dennis,
(date unknown), issuing out of a house
in High-street, the property of George
Northcott 0 4 0

7.– A rent-charge given by a codicil to the
will of James Colley, in 1809, issuing
out of houses on the Quay, in Barnstaple, called the New Works, during
the term which he had therein from the
corporation of Barnstaple; (about 34
years of this term are now expired.). . 2 0 0

8.– A rent-charge given by Philip Bremridge,
in 1813, payable out of a house in
High-street, the property of Joseph Evans . 0 13 0

9.– An annuity, paid by the corporation in
leiu of an annual fish dinner which that
body was bound to provide for the lord
of the Castle Court manor, the said
annuity having been voluntarily given–

	£	s	d
–to this charity, by the late Sir John Chichester, as stated in the account of Paige's almshouse	1	0	0
10.– £124 Old South Sea Annuities, arising from £100 given by the will of Mrs. Elizabeth Stanbury, after the death of her sister Joan Stanbury, producing dividends amounting annually to . .	3	12	6
11.– £470 Old South Sea Annuities, arising from various donations, producing dividends amounting annually to . . .	14	2	0
12.– £260 2s. 3d. Three per cent Consols, arising in the same manner, and including £50 stock, given by the will of James Sciance, in 1815, and £50 stock given by the will of Thomas Sciance, in 1817, producing dividends amounting annually to	10	16	0
Total annual income . .	£125	11	10

We have not found any copies or extracts of the instruments by which the above-mentioned rent-charges were given, except those given by James Colley and Philip Bremridge. In 1803, Edward Paul Pilcher, esquire, gave to this charity one thirty-fifth share of the Barnstaple assembly rooms, which was afterwards sold by the trustees, with Mr. Pilcher's consent, and the produce thereof, being £40, was invested in three per cent consols, and now forms a part of the above-mentioned £260 2s. 3d. in that stock.

In 1810, timber was cut on the farm at Ilfracombe, and sold for £35 8s. which was carried to the general account of the charity.

In addition to the income arising from the gifts above stated, an annual sermon is preached in Barnstaple church, for the benefit of the charity, which usually produces from £25 to £30.

The school-house is situate in High-street, Barnstaple, near [over] the north gate; it was built about 60 years ago, at the expense of the corporation, and is kept in good repair from the funds of the school.

The trustees hold two annual meetings, one in July or August, for the election of boys into the school, and another in September, when one of the trustees is appointed treasurer for the ensuing year, and the treasuer's accounts for the preceding year are audited. [N.]

Upon this establishment 50 boys, chosen by the trustees from the poor children of Barnstaple, are instructed by a schoolmaster, appointed by them, in reading, writing, and arithmetic. The boys are not admitted into the school until they are eight years of age, or allowed to remain after they are fourteen.

This school is confined to boys only; but the school for girls, here-inafter mentioned, founded by Mrs. Alice Horwood, is under the management of the same trustees; and both boys and girls are completely clothed twice a year, and have shoes and stockings twice in the year, from the funds above stated.

A copy of the annual account, as audited, is printed and distributed amongst the inhabitants of Barnstaple.

The following is an abstract of the account for the year ending in September 1821:—

	£	s.	d.
Schoolmaster's salary	40	0	0
Clothing for boys and girls	81	10	0
Repairs of the school house (less than the usual average)	0	13	4
Writing paper for the boys	2	17	0
Printing the annual account, and hyms for the annual sermon	1	5	6
Rent-charge paid out of Francis and Bowden's to Penrose's almshouse, in respect of Philip's gift .	4	0	0
	£130	5	10

The balance on this year's account was £8 12s. in favour of the charity, which was paid over to the incoming treasurer.

ALICE HORWOOD'S SCHOOL FOR GIRLS.

Adjoining to Horwoood's almshouse, of which an account has already been given, is a house inhabited by a school-mistress. An inscription on the almshouse states, that Alice Horwood, "of her own accord, added the adjoining free-school, and endowed it for 20 poor children for ever, in 1659."

We have not been able to find any document relating to this endowment; it is not mentioned in Mrs. Horwood's deed of 1674, relating to an almshouse, of which an abstract has already been given, nor is it included in the trust deeds relating to the charity school for boys, although the trustees of that establishment have also the management of this charity.

There is a tenement, called Gutterstone, at Newport, in the parish of Bishop's Tawton, the rents of which are received by the mistress of this school. It consists of a house, courtlage, garden, and two closes of land, containing 3A. 30P. now in the occupation of John Davis, under an agreement, made with the trustees of the charity school for boys, for a lease for the term of 11 years, from Lady-day 1720, at the clear yearly rent of £15 10s. which appears to be the full value of the premises. The school-mistress, who is appointed by the said trustees, receives this rent, out of which she keeps in repair the house inhabited by her, and instructs therein, in respect of the emoluments derived from the charity, 20 girls, nominated by the trustees, in reading, sewing and knitting. The girls are admitted into the school at seven years of age, and allowed to remain till fourteen, and are clothed out of the funds of the charity school, as has been already mentioned in the account of that establishment.

NEWCOMMEN'S GIFT.

The particulars of Mrs. Margaret Newcommen's will, dated in 1810, will be stated in the present Report, in the account of the charities of the town of Bideford.

Two annual sums of £4 each are paid by her trustees to two dissenting school-mistress, of Barnstaple, for teaching poor children of this town to read. [O.]

MARTIN'S GIFT.

It appears from a copy of a terrier of the vicarage of Barnstaple, dated in 1726, that Mrs Martin, by will, the date of which is not stated, gave to the minister of Barnstaple the sum of £5 yearly, the better to encourage him to the use and exercise of the necessary duty of catechizing of youth in his parish.

This sum is received by the vicar out of an estate called Great Fisherton, in the parish of Bishop's Tawton, now the property of Mrs. Downe.

The present vicar catechizes the children of the charity school twice a year, in the church; and also, occasionally, catechizes the children in this parish, on the Madras system, supported by voluntary contributions.

STANBURY'S GIFT FOR READING PRAYERS.

Joan Stanbury, by her will, bearing date 10th of October, 1772, and proved in the Prerogative Court of Canterbury, gave to the vicar and mayor for the time being of Barnstaple, and their successors, £500, to be by them placed at interest in the public funds, in their names, on trust, to pay the interest thereof to the minister, who should daily, throughout the year, do the duty of reading prayers, from the liturgy of the church of England, in the parish church of Barnstaple, to the congregation there assembled, by seven o'clock in the morning in the summer, and eight o'clock in the morning in the winter; such minister to be chosen and removed from time to time by a majority of the inhabitants of Barnstaple, of the communion of the church of England, and paying church rates there, at any public meeting held for that purpose, after six days' notice given for such meeting by any ten or more of such inhabitants, in the parish church of Barnstaple; and she directed, that if morning prayers should be neglected to be read, at the stated times aforesaid, or not in a proper manner, for the space of twenty days together, that the interest of the said money, during the time that morning prayers should be neglected to be read as aforesaid, should, for such neglect, be paid and distributed amongst the poor of Barnstaple, not having parish relief, as the said inhabitants or the major part of them, at any public meeting, after such notice given, should think fit.

This sum of £500 is now invested in £624 0s. 6d. old South Sea Annuities, in the names of Samuel Bremridge, esquire, and the Reverend J. M. Wade, late vicar of Barnstaple. The Reverend Henry Luxmoore, the present vicar, upon being instituted to this living, about two years since, was also chosen by the parishioners to be the reader under this gift, and now receives the dividends of this stock; morning prayers have been, for several years, read only once in twenty days, with a view to prevent the forefeiture of the gift. It is evident, therefore, that the intentions of the testarix are not fulfilled. But the Reverend Henry Nicholls, late curate of this parish, and reader, chosen under this gift, at the request of the parishioners, performed divine service, a third time, on the Sunday evenings, during the winter months, which he considered himself as doing in leiu of reading morning prayers, as directed by Mrs. Stanbury's will. The present vicar has also, during his incumbency, performed such third service during the winter months, but states, that he does not consider himself bound to continue it. [P.]

APPENDIX TO CHAPTER II.

"It is absolutely necessary that it should be perfectly understood that charity estates all over the Kingdom, are delt with in a manner most grossly improvident, amounting to the most direct breach of trust."

Lord Chancellor Eldon

Since the Commissioners visited Barnstaple, (in the autumn of 1822,) many new leases have been granted of lands belonging to the Charities; notices of these, with such other information as I have been enabled to procure, and a few observations arising out of the subject-matter of the report, will be found in the following pages.

Wherever the present yearly value of property held on *long leases at low rents,* is given, it is done with fidelity and impartiality, and with the sole view of shewing how much the parties for whose benefit the institutions were set on foot, are suffering by the injudicious "mode" of leasing charity lands, &c. which has prevailed here; and which has had the effect of adding to the superfluities of the rich, that which was *designed to administer to the necessities of the poor.*

A system so decidedly injurious to the interests of those for whose *sole benefit* the various charitable institutions were founded, will not, it is hoped, be again resorted to, since, under *any circumstances*, to lease a property, the yearly proceeds of which appertain to any class of persons, but more especially the poor, at a rate below its present value, is to do an act of injustice to the existing proprietors of such property. Charity pensioners have but a life-interest in the lands or monies by which they are benefited, and being necessarily excluded from any share in the management of their own funds, it behoves those to whom that management is deputed, (next to a scrupulous regard to the directions and INTENTIONS of the Donor,) to have an especial eye to the interest of the *living claimants on his bounty.* Should the question possibly arise how this object can be best effected, a trustee has only to ask himself this question; had I a life-interest in this property, whilst I performed my duty in preserving it uninjured, should I not also look well to my own interest, and reap all possible advantage from it?

No defence, it is presumed, will be attempted in favour of *over-leasing* and *under-letting* lands belonging to the Poor, except in the case of a building lease; but a slight examination will shew even this ground to be untenable. Take as an example the house now held by Mr. Fisher, (see Appley's gift,) which produces £5 5s. per annum to the poor; had the premises been let, when the former lease expired, at their marketable value, they would have *certainly* produced £15, being a surplus of £9 15s. above the present rent. Now taking the period in which Paupers usually receive relief to average fifteen years, four generations will be deprived of an annual income of £9 15s. arising, (or which ought to arise *to them*) out of an estate, their right to *all* the rents and *profits* of which for the time being cannot be disputed! and why? because their successors in the fifth and succeeding generations may *possibly* benefit by it; I have said "*possibly*," because, to say nothing of numerous other contingencies, we have no security that the old system may not again prevail, and the poor continue to be deprived of their just rights to an indefinite period.

It is not intended by the motto affixed to this article, to insinuate that any of the charity property belonging to this town, is at present managed otherwise than it should be; but that this has heretofore been the case, is too palpable either to be concealed or denied.

One remark more is perhaps needful here.

The statements I have made of the present value of the different properties, will be found in several instances to be much at variance with the valuations given in the Report; I may claim exemption from the charge of personality, in having furnished more correct estimates than those previously given, when I say that I am quite ignorant from whom the Commissioners obtained their information. I am aware that the personal examinations taken before these gentlemen are in print, but I have not seen the publication, neither have I been informed of any one individual mentioned in it as having been examined touching the Barnstaple Charities.

[A.] *Litchdon Almshouse.*

3.* This estate, as I am informed by one of the trustees, has been let for a fresh term, at a reduction of more than twenty-five per cent. on the former rent. The brother of the late lessee is the present occupier. It's being an "undivided moiety" is doubtless a great drawback on the value of the property, as fair competition amongst bidders for a lease of premises thus circumstanced, cannot be looked for.

4. It is difficult to conceive how 30*s*.† an acre can be considered a "good rent" for lands forming part of a gentleman's "PLEASURE GROUNDS." How are we to reconcile this statement with the fact, that lands belonging to this and other of the Barnstaple Charities, realize more than £7 per acre?

5. This estate is let for a fresh term at the old rent.

7. This house produces to Mrs. Thomas, the present lessee, £32 per annum, clear of all taxes.

8. These fields still continue at the same rent which they produced forty-three years ago, whilst some of the estates have increased in value three-fold since that period. The rent must have been very high in 1786, or is very *low* now.

[B.] Penrose's Bequest to Bridewell.

Amongst the memorandums of the date 1633-4, I find the following :—

" Of the 200*l*.# (that left by Mr. Penrose) there is lent unto John Cole by his bond wth surities gratis, for keeping at worke the poore and to live in the house the some of 100*l*. 00*s*. 00*d*."

"It appears," say the Commissioners, "that this Bridewell was built by the *town*, at an expense of £300."

Query— At whose cost, that of the Parish or of the Corporation? (for the term used may imply either;) from whichever fund the money was supplied for building the house, the Corporation receives £20 per annum for the premises, which have been long used as the parish workhouse.

---

* The figures refer to the number in the rental.

† Query – 30*s*. or 15*s*. ? See rental

This sum being among those of which there remain "no trace" (see page 101) it may not be amiss to bear in mind that both "bond and sureties" were exacted from John Cole, as security for the portion of it lent to him; it is not therefore likely to have been *thus* lost.

[C.] *Horwood's Almshouse.*

During the past and present year (1828), all the lands belonging to this charity have been re-let; the rental of the whole is now as below :–

	£	s.	d.	£	s.	d.
1. House and Garden	8	0	0			
Part of Orchard leased to Mr. Bryant, for a term of 60 years, from Lady-day, 1827, to which 30 years are added, on payment of a fine, at the expiration of half the term	3	0	0			
Another portion of the Orchard leased to Mrs. Mullins, for a like period	1	1	0			
				12	1	0
2. Field	18	0	0			
Barn	2	2	0			
				20	2	0
3. Field	7	0	0			
Ditto	8	0	0			
				15	0	0
4. Two Fields	10	0	0			
				10	0	0
5. Stable	2	2	0			
				2	2	0
				£59	5	0

A substantial dwelling has been built by Mr. Bryant, on the ground of which he has taken a lease. The plot occupied by Mrs. Mullins, now forms a part of a walled garden.

[D.] *Paige's Almshouse.*

The piece of ground (Congerham's) given by Alderman Appley, is now held by Mr. William Thorne, who took a lease of it in 1825, for sixty years, at £20 per annum; a much higher rent than could have been obtained for the property, for any other purpose than that to which it has been applied, besides the substantial improvements which have been made on it. The premises no longer consist of a field and a ruinous mud-wall cottage, but exhibit six small respectable dwelling houses, and twenty-eight neat stone-built cottages, all with garden ground. These several buildings produce a rental of about £220 per annum.

[E.] *Fish Dinners.*

It was stated earlier in this work, that the corporation had compounded with the late Sir John Chichester, for these dinners. Having since discovered that this statement, which was made on the authority of that furnished by the Commissioners, confirmed, as it seemed to be, by the certain fact, that the dinners had long ceased to be given, was incorrect; it is necessary for truth's sake, although otherwise but of little importance, to set the matter right. The following appears to have been the agreement entered into.

"Whereas the corporation of the borough and parish of Barnstaple, have given unto Sir John Chichester, of Youlstone, Baronet, and his ancestors, annually, two certain dinners, called Fish Dinners, within the borough and parish aforesaid. And whereas it is mutually agreed between the corporation and Sir John Chichester, that for the future, there shall be but one such dinner given to the said Sir John Chichester annually, and that the sum, of 40s. being stipend usually allowed by the corporation for the expenses attending the other of such dinners, shall be applied and disposed in such manner and form, and to such purposes as hereinafter mentioned. And whereas also several of the said fish dinners have not been given; and for settling and adjusting the same, it is ordered and agreed between the corporation and Sir John Chichester, that the sum of £6, being an equivalent for such dinners, shall be paid by the said corporation, and distributed in manner hereinafter mentioned, and that the said fish dinners so to be given in future as aforesaid, shall be given on the third Saturday in October, in every year, and that the said sum of 40s. allowed as aforesaid for the other of such dinners, shall be disposed of on the first day of January in every year, in the following manner, i. e. one moiety thereof to be paid to the trustees for the time being for the charity school, within, and for the borough and parish of Barnstaple aforesaid, as further support of the said school; and the other moiety thereof to the use of such other charity as the said Sir John Chichester shall on the said 1st of January yearly direct and appoint the same; and for want of such direction and appointment, to such other charity as the said corporation shall think fit. And it is also ordered and agreed that the said sum of £6 so to be paid in leiu of such dinners as aforesaid, shall be paid by the said corporation on the 1st of January next, and be applied and disposed of to the use of such charity within the borough and parish, as the said Sir John Chichester shall direct and apply the same. And lastly, it is agreed that either party may vacate this order and agreement, on giving six months' notice in writing to the other of them of such their intention, and that in such case, this order shall cease and determine accordingly."

This relic of feudal customs has now grown wholly into disuse, no such dinner, (as far as I have been enabled to discover) having been given since October, 1790, when the cost of a "fish dinner" was £2 13s. 4d; – a moderate sum, certainly, for the entertainment of a baronet, by a town corporation!

[F.] *Beaple's Gift.*

On reading this statement of land tax deducted out of a rent-charge, we naturally look for some explanation or remark by the commissioners !
On making enquiry if any reason could be assigned, why so extraordinary a claim was made and allowed, I was informed, that the trustees have latterly received the full amount of the bequest.
Query – If an error has been committed, why not receive back the arrears due on account of such error?

[G.] *Monies given to be lent.*

	£	s.	d.
Those several sums make a total of . .	561	16	8
besides which the Commissioners notice the following bequests, of which they find no " trace " :—			
Richard Harris .	50	0	0
John Penrose .	200	0	0
Roger Jeffrey .	25	0	0
Laurence Gibbons	20	0	0
Richard Castleman	50	0	0
James Walsh .	20	0	0
	£926	16	0

"In 1634,*" say the Commissioners, " The Mayor, Aldermen, and Common Council of this town, observing that the poorer sort were not able to find security for loans out of the monies given to be lent to poor tradesmen, especially poor weavers and tuckers, but by leaving the money in the hands of their sureties, whereby little or no profit grew to the said poor; and being desirous that the poor should have some benefit of the said money, thought fit to lend part of the said money to some of the towns- men, such as by their trading helped and relived the poorer sort, at six per cent, which profit at the end of the year, should be distributed to such poor weavers and tuckers as could not find security, nor employ the money to their profit."

It is worthy of notice that especial care had been taken to guard against all risk in lending "the poor's stock" to the *poor*, nor is it alleged that any loss was thereby sustained; yet we find that in less than forty years from the above-mentioned date, it has all disappeared. " It appears that as late as 1671, interest," we are not informed how much, "was received for monies lent, called the poor's stock, by the mayor for the time being, and

* I find that in 1633 the Corporation passed a resolution, that "Artificer's Loan Money be lent at six per cent. per annum."

distributed to the poor; subsequently to which we have not been able to find any trace of these monies."

Here then the Commissioners leave us in the dark. They doubtless never suspected, that the "Townsmen" *might have been* the Common Councilmen themselves! But what if this should turn out to be the case?

In April 1665, only six years previous to all trace of the money being lost, their Worships *"thought fit"* to pass the following resolution :–

"that the monies belonging to the poor be not lent to Common Councilmen, but on good security, but—that COMMON COUNCILMEN BE PREFERRED !!!" It is but reasonable to conclude from the tenure of this resolution, that some of these "monies" had been previously "lent to Common Councilmen" either on bad "security" or on no "security" at all, and thus lost, or in danger of being so; or why make such a provision? Surely had not past experience rendered it necessary, a vote so derogatory to the dignity of a corporate body would never have been passed. Query— How did the "deficiencies" arise in these monies "which the Corporation *made good* in 1633?"

We may fairly conclude from the last or *saving* clause of this resolution, that there was some advantage to be gained by retaining the money in their own hands. Was it nothing beyond the simple benefit which might accrue to the borrower of a sum of money after he had paid the interest, that they looked to? If so, and poor tradesmen could not, as was alleged, borrow the money so as to derive profit from it, we may perhaps say, that the corporation of 1665 were honourable men! But how shall we reconcile such a presumption with the fact, that within seven years from the passing of this notable decree of the corporation of Barnstaple, in common council assembled, the six per cent per annum had ceased to be paid, and no "subsequent trace" either of principal or interest can be found ?

Those who could so degrade themselves, as to enter into such a compact, were not likely to be slow in acting upon it; they could not however have done either, but with a full knowledge that they were acting in direct opposition to the specific directions of the "various donors," with the exception of one or two. Whilst they assumed the *power* of distributing these trust monies amongst the *needy*, they were concious of possessing no *right* to lend them to any but the poor.

It singularly happens, that, even at this distant period, some "trace" is left of one of these sums "called the poor's stock." In 1652, the corporation of Barnstaple, out of (as we are bound to believe) a becoming and praiseworthy regard to their own dignity, not unmixed, perhaps, with a desire to shine on feast days and high holidays, determined on having their *maces* re-modelled and beautified, which was done, and for "new making

127

the maces and new cases to the same," an expense of £22 was incurred. A year had now elapsed, the vanity of these venerable worthies had been fed by the exhibition of the gaudy insignia; some of their townsmen admired their taste, others extolled their liberality, whilst the "poor weavers and tuckers," unconcious that they were to be contributors towards it, gazed on the daw-like display, with wonder and delight.

But the "maces" were not yet paid for. Let us go back in imagination, to a "private hall" in 1653; the corporation with the worshipful Thomas Matthews, mayor, at their head, are assembled; among other important matters for discussion, the silversmith's account is produced; he has given twelve months' credit, and wants his money: for the credit of the body it must be discharged, and payment is ordered; the treasury is opened, but it is empty; what shall be done? One individual makes an appeal to the pockets of his brethren, and seconds it by opening his own; but "the noes have it," and he is left alone in the minority. But to quit the regions of fancy, and come to plain matters of fact, such a meeting was held, in the year mentioned, and the result was, that the corporation passed a resolution, to " borrow twenty pounds, left to the poor by James Walsh, towards new making of the Maces. "*

It does not appear that any interest was ever paid on this sum, none certainly, taking the report of the Commissioners as a guide, subsequent to 1671. Had this comparatively trifling account been " put out, and employed for the benefit of the poor " from the time it was "BORROWED," it would have produced, at simple interest, £187, which, looked at as it

* It is possible with reference to the above, as well as to other anecdotes mentioned in this work, two questions may be asked; – Where did the writer obtain his information from? and – how do we know that what he tells us is true? Anticipating such enquiries, I reply – once and for all ; —
FIRST,— that I have received from different hands a great variety of information, and that in a variety of ways. I have gleaned much in the town, and very much at a considerable distance from it. Verbal communications, letters, original documents, and choice scraps, have been liberally supplied; some have been obtained through solicitation, but the greater part has come as voluntary offerings, in aid of a work, for the successful completion of which considerable interest has been felt. It will not be thought surprising, that amongst a numerous list of contributors, there should be some desirous of being kept in the background; and such being their wish, I must, "as in duty bound" *srictly comply with it*.. Since then "I am forbid to tell the secrets of my *writing desk* , " be it known to all who may hereafter be tempted to seek an acquaintence with its mysteries, that all and every person, of whatsoever rank, degree, or calling, who shall make enquiry relative to any matter or thing contained or recorded in Memorials of Barnstaple, be, with all due respect, referred back (*Abernetney* to wit !) to "my book," this page.
SECONDLY,— A better method could not perhaps be devised for impeaching the veracity of a work of this nature, than for the author to vouch for the authenticity of all it contains; could I, however, be assured, that by hazarding such an assertion, a contrary effect would be produced, a regard for consistency would prevent my resorting to such a fellacious expedient. No man can safely assert that occurrences, recorded to have transpired from one to five centuries ago, really happened in the precise manner and time stated! But while I dare not say that everything contained in this book is true, I *can say* that I have inserted nothing relating either to ancient or modern times, which I do not KNOW, OR WITH GOOD REASON BELIEVE, to be true. Many persons into whose hands the work will fall, can bear testimony to my anxious and persevering endeavours in seeking to elucidate matters ambiguous in their nature, or doubtful as to their authority,

ought to be, with reference to what a poor man might have purchased with a shilling at the beginning of the reign of Charles II. and at subsequent periods, compared with the present, cannot be set down at less than £500.

[H.] *Appley's Gift*

The first house mentioned under this gift was re-built, as stated in the Report, (in 1817,) and now produces, with a garden not belonging to the property, for which a deduction of £2 10s. should be made, £25 per annum, clear rent. A malt house and corn lofts, at the back of the premises, may be fairly estimated at £15 a year, making, with the rent of the dwelling house, £37 10s. instead of £14 as stated in the Report.

For most of the following particulars relating to the other of these houses, I am indebted to a respectable individual, who, about forty years ago, was in possession of the property. The premises were leased in 1770, to Jacob Penbetty, who re-built the house, which about fifty years ago let for £8 a year. My informant applied in 1789 or 1790 for a renewal of his term, and would have readily given £10 per annum, from the expiration of the existing lease; he was, however, after repeated applications, informed, that "*a new lease could not be granted until the old one had expired.*" He subsequently sold his interest in the property for one hundred guineas, to William Thomas, and he for a similar sum to a Capt. Boucher; both these persons endevoured to get an extention of the lease, but failed; when the latter disposed of it to Mr. Bremridge, who, as the Report states, for the trifling sacrifice of 10s. per annum, for twenty-four years, suceeded in procuring an addition of thirty-six years to his lease, at £2 10s. a year, or *one fourth of what another individual would have given for it.* (Mr. Bremridge had at this time a son in the Corporation.)

A gentleman named Russell took the house in 1811, for a term of twenty-one years, at £21 per annum, and made some internal improvements in it, in addition to a trifling alteration previously made by Mr. Bremridge. Mr. Russell, on quitting the town some years since, re-let the house, for which the present occupier pays twenty-six guineas per annum, besides a portion of taxes; but this rent, it must be acknowledged, is high, when compared with that of the generality of similar property in Barnstaple.

It is quite clear, that had the same extention of term which Mr. Bremridge obtained in this property, been granted to the first-mentioned applicant at the price he was willing to pay, £10 a year, the charity would, at the close of the present term, have received as below :—

	£	s.	d.	£	s.	d.
Rent from 1830, when the first Lease would have expired, to 1866, when the present Term will cease, at £10 per annum				360	0	0
Deduct 36 years' rental, to be received under the existing Lease, at £2 10s.	90	0	0			
10s. per annum additional rent, for 24 years of the former term	12	0	0			
				102	0	0
Making a difference to the charity of				£258	0	0

But supposing the Corporation to have acted up to the declaration they made of letting the old lease run out, as unquestionably it would have been most consistent with their obligations as trustees to have done, they would then have possession of the premises in two years from this time, 1828.

Let us imagine this to be the case, and the house let, say at £18 per annum, (*about two-thirds of the present rental,*) and we shall have to add to the sum above stated, £288, making in all £546 absolutely lost, out of a moiety of one charity, by improper management.

It is but justice to say, that several members of the body corporate have openly expressed their dissatisfaction at the terms on which the lease was granted.

It is worthy of remark, that Mr Appley left these two houses chargeable with a life annuity of £4 5s. 2d. from which we may presume that the property was worth this sum at least, annually; but there is no lack of evidence to shew that its yearly value was beyond this amount. The sum of £100 appears to have been raised out of the rents of these premises in 1663. Mrs. Appley, as shewn in the parish register, died in 1612, so that in twenty-one years (if not a less period,) the £100 was made up. It is therefore clear that the annual produce of this property was *less* in 1800 than in 1600, whilst its value was many times *greater*; and that even now, under leases newly granted, when the difference in value, as compared with two hundred years ago, may (without taking into the account by Mr. Fisher's house having been re-built,) be stated as upwards of EIGHT to ONE, the income is not DOUBLED, and must remain as its present rate for more than thirty years to come.

[I.] *Lugg's Gift.*

The lands belonging to this charity have remained at the rent mentioned in the report up to this time; but are now partly in hand, and about to be re-let.

[J.] *Sir J. Acland's Gift.*

The following particulars of this bequest are taken from the Commissioner's Report of the Exeter Charities :–

The donor directed that the sum of £75 8s. should be distributed yearly among twenty-seven parishes named, to be applied in the buying and providing weekly for ever, penny loaves of bread of a middle sort, commonly called cheate bread, to be bestowed and distributed every Sunday, immediately after morning prayer, unto such of the poorest sort of people," as those to whose management the different bequests were intrusted, "should nominate and appoint to receive the same."

That to the poor of Barnstaple is as follows :– "And to the mayor of Barnstaple, for providing thirteen such loaves weekly, to be distributed as aforesaid, to thirteen such people of the said borough as the mayor and four of the most ancient masters of the said borough shall appoint, £2 12s."

In the event that any of the several trustees "should be negligent, or refuse, or omit the performance of any of the trusts, and should not, yearly, within twelve days next after the feast of Easter, deliver to the mayor and recorder of Exeter, a true account in writing, how they had disbursed the said sums for bread, &c., some other parish near adjoining to the borough or parish so making default," was to have benefit of the gift "for one whole year next after such default."

The property left in trust by Sir J. Acland, is, besides the amount already mentioned, charged with the payment of other sums, making altogether £97 2s.

The produce of the estate is stated to have been in 1821, upwards of £320 per annum, besides a balance in hand of about £1300. The Commissioners say, "A question has arisen whether any portion of the considerable balance now in the hands of the trustees, can be applied in augmentation of the annual stipend directed to be paid to the exhibitioners;* but we apprehend that the trustees have no authority thus to increase them, and that the other objects of Sir John Acland's charity have no claim beyond the sums specified in his deeds."

[K.] *Westlake's Gift.*

The Commission here alluded to was a special one, "under the great seale of England, bearing date three and twentieth day of March, in the nineteenth yeare of the reigne of our Lord the Kinge, and directed to ye Reverend Richard Merwin, Doctor in Divinity, Philip Naylor, Rector, Nicholas Dennis, Balshazar Beare, Esq. and Arthur Actland, Marchant; and to divers other P'sons dwelling and inhabiting in the said county, [Devon,] who were to enquire into abuses, breaches of trust, negligences, misemploying, misgoverning, and misapplying, &c. &c. the funds of this charity."

The following additional particulars of the decree are extracted from a copy of that instrument, preserved along with the accounts of the charity, now in possession of John May, Esq.— "Found by the oaths of Paul Trix, John Stone, Richard Tamblyn, Thomas Snow, Robert Combe, John Brayley, John Loveringe, John Actland, George Langdon, John Pope, John Ley, and John Langdon; that [here the bequest is recited] John Greade and John Cooke, ffuller, two of the last associates, and now the survivors, that from the last association which was in October last, fourteen years, the said poor have not received the yearly p'fit according to the said will, which p'fit according to the said will, which p'fit according to calculation, for fifteen years, amounts unto £350; and that of this the poor have had butt two hundred twenty and ffour pounds, and that there is due unto the poor of the p'fitts of the said estate, one hundred thirty ffive pounds, ffourteen shillings, which is detained by them, parte by the surviving associates, and the residue by their neglect; and that the said one hundred thirty ffive pounds, ffourteen shillings, profitts of the said ffour hundred pounds, are by their neglect in not perfforming their trust, in danger of looseing, if not timely prevented, by the inquisition hereunto annexed.

---

* Or in other words – in increasing the patronage of the Chamber of Exeter. (Two "exhibitioners" to be chosen from Exeter Free School were to receive £8 per annum each.) Why not have proposed an augmentation of the sums expended for the benefit of the poor? this would have been laudable, and could not have been met by any *reasonable* objection.

"Now the said Commissioners having called before them the said John Greade and John Cooke, upon full hearing and debating what was said and alledged on their behalf in the p'misses,

"Ffor reformation of the said abuse and breach of trust, do hereby order, adjudge, and decree, in manner and fform ffollowing; (viz.)—

"That the said John Greade and John Cooke be no longer associates and trustees in the said trust, but are hereby displaced and discharged from the same, and that they doe before the ffive and twentieth day of March next comeing, transfer, yield upp, and pay over vnto Gilbert Paige, Marchant, Lewis Rosier, gent. Thomas Harris, Henry Drake, and Richard Parminter, whom the said Com^rs do hereby appoint, ordain, decree, and establish to be ffrom henceforward trustees ffor the managemt of the said ffour hundred pounds, given by the said Katherine, wth the profitts thereof, accordinge to the said will, All the bonds, bills, papers, specialtys, chest, money, and other things whatsoever, wch are in their or either of their hands or custody; And that they doe noe ffurther intermeddle or act in the said trust. Lastly, ffor as much as it appeareth to the said Com^rs That the said John Gread and John Cooke are guilty of ye breach and ill-management of the same, wch hath caused the sueing out the commission, they order and adjudge that the said John Gread and John Cooke shall pay unto the said Gilbert Paige, Lewis Rosier, Thomas Harris, Henry Drake, and Richard Parminter, the sume of eight pounds towards the charges and expenses in sueing out the commission, and in the prosecution of the said inquisition and this decree. IN WITTNESS whereof the Com^rs aforesaid have hereunto sett their hands and seales, even the day and yeare ffirst aboue written, Anno Dom. 1667."

This, certainly, very equitable decree was not very promptly obeyed. Messrs. Gread and Cooke refused to surrender their trust, "upon reffusall whereof the said trustees sued out a writt of execution of the said decree from the said high Co^rt of Chancery," which induced the ex-trustees to submit; the *money*, however, was not forthcoming, and this trust debt could only be discharged in the manner explained in the following curious receipt :–

"Received, by order of a decree of Chancery, of Mr. John Gread and Mr. John Cooke, one bond of two hundred pounds, ffore pay^t of one hundred and seven pounds, by Mr. William Palmer, Mr. Anthony Palmer; and Mr. John Palmer ; and one bond of two hundred pounds, ffor pay^t of one hundred and seven pounds, by Mr. John Downe, and Mr. Richard Harris; and one bond of one hundred pounds, ffor pay^t of one and ffifty pounds and ten shillings, by the said Mr. John Cooke, Mr. Nicholas Cooke, and Mr. Bartholomew Bisse ; and one bond of one hundred pounds, ffor pay^t of

133

one and ffifty pounds and ffifteen shillings, by the said Mr. Bartholemew Bisse, Mr. John Cook, and Humphry Bisse ; and one bond of one hundred pounds, ffor pay^t of three and ffifty pounds, by Henry Smale, Humfry Collender, and Daniel Gagg, [or Gayy] ; more, one bond of sixty pounds, ffor pay^t, of thirty pounds and eighteen shillings, by Peter Rowe, Mr. Thomas Matthews, and Nicholas Sweet; and one bond of fforty pounds ffor pay^t of one and twenty pounds and ffower shillings, by Elizabeth Orchard, and Ffrancis Punchard, which said bonds make vppe the sume of ffower hundred pounds,* being that legacy left, &c. Witness our hands, this seventeenth day of October, in the twentieth yeare of the raigne of our Soverigne Lord Kinge Charles the second, over England, Anno Dno. 1668."

It happened, rather untowardly, that at the very time when Mr. Greade was ousted from his trusteeship, he held the office of chief magistrate for the borough ; (see List of Mayors;†) he had previously filled that of mace-bearer.

[L.] *Drake's Gift* .

The house mentioned as having been bequeathed by Mrs. Drake, (who by the way adopted a novel expedient to prevent her remains from being disturbed,#) is that now known as the "White Hart" public-house, and produces a rent of £25 a year, which is lost to the poor of this town and Pilton, in consequence of the donor's ignorance of the law relative to such bequests.§ It must be acknowledged that this charitable dame would have better fulfilled the *law* of charity by leaving her property amongst the "poor persons related to her," than by disposing of it for the benefit of strangers.

By the returns made to Parliament in 1786, it appears that the poor of Barnstaple then received £3 per annum from this property, which is

---

* The sums enumerated make £421 7*s* . perhaps including interest from the time of making the decree. The "profits" in arrear would appear previously to have been paid up.

† His name appears for 1666. The dates mentioned refer to the time when a mayor enters on his office, in which he continues until the month of October in the ensuing year.

The Sexton still receives his fee of half-a-crown annually.

§ It must doubtless have been often thought strange by those unacquainted with the origin of this law, (as may be the case with some of my readers,) that enactments should be made for the express purpose of preventing benevolently disposed individuals from disposing of their property to such charitable uses as they might desire ; the best things are, however, liable to be abused, and long experience has shewn such restrictions to be needful.

At a period even anterior to the Norman Conquest, it was found necessary to curb the inordinate appetite of spiritual fraternities for temporal possessions, which was partially effected by prohibiting religious houses from purchasing lands without the sanction of the King, by what was termed a license of MORTMAIN, (such a state of possession as makes it unalienable ; "whence it is said to be in a dead hand, a hand that cannot shift away the property," as is the case in " an

described as being vested in James Hiern. It is probable that a similar sum was distributed in Pilton; £6 might have been then nearly the produce of the premises.

[M.] *Cordwainer's Lands.*

The following description of the property belonging to this charity, gives us a more particular account of its situation and extent, than the statement furnished by the Commissioners, and also shews the present rental, or estimated value per annum of the different premises.

	£	s	d
1.– Two brick dwellings, nearly adjoining the back way to the King's Arms, in Anchor Lane, now let for £26	21	0	0
[Between these houses, there is a passage or gateway, forming a back entrance to the dwelling house of the lessee, and the two houses next to it on the north side. Only the centre house of the three had such a communication until very lately, the other two having been made by Mr. Harris] A Stable, let with the "Wellington Arms" public -house ; estimated value. . .	6	0	0
A Kitchen, with Laundry over, built by the lessee, and attached to his residence ;– value calculated as if the ground had not been built on, but had remained as before, for purposes of trade	6	0	0

alienation of lands or tenements to any corporation ecclesiastical or temporal.") But so " difficult was it to set bounds to ecclesiastical ingenuity," that statute after statute was framed, " in deducing the history of which statutes, it is curious to observe the great address and subtle contrivance of the ecclesiastics, in eluding from time to time the laws in being, and the zeal with which successive parliaments have pursued them through all their finesses ; how new remedies were still the parents of new evasions ; until at last the legislature, though with difficulty, obtained a decisive victory." Amongst other inventions of the Monks, in order to evade the forfeiture of their lands, was that of " taking long leases for years, which first introduced those extensive terms for a thousand or more years, now so frequent in conveyances, and it is to these inventions also that our practisers are indebted for the introduction of uses and trusts, the foundation of modern conveyancing." Previous to the passing of the last statute of Mortmain, 9 Geo. 11 cap. 36, it was "held that former enactments did not extend to any thing but superstitious uses ; and that therefore a man may give lands for the maintenance of a school, or A hospital, or any other charitable use. But as it was apprehended from recent experience, that persons on their death-beds might make large and improvident dispositions ; it is therefore enacted, (by the above-named statute,) that no Lands or Tenements, or money to be laid out thereon, shall be given for, or charged with, any charitable uses whatsoever, unless by deed indented, executed in the presence of two witnesses, twelve calendar months before the death of the donor, and enrolled in the Court of Chancery within six months after its execution ; and unless such gift be made to take effect immediately, and without power of revocation." — See *Blackstone* and others.

	£	s.	d.
Brought up	33	0	0

2.– A property designated in the trust deed as
"a messuage or dwelling house," and in the rental,
"part of a shop," &c. but understood to comprise
the front part of a house, late the "Wellington
Arms" ; namely, a shop, small sitting room behind
the same, with a way through it to a staircase, and
two or three rooms above ; now vacant, but *let for
many years at £26* **21 0 0**
[The rent now expected is believed to be more than
it lately produced ; but how much cannot be
ascertained]

3.– A dwelling house, nearly opposite No.2, all
but a small parlour, lately converted into a shop,
and a room over. The premises are now occupied
by Miss Griffiths, as under-tenant to Mr. Jas.
Trix, who holds them of Mr. Hiern, for the
remainder of his term. The yearly value of this
property will not, when I state that it now brings
in a clear rent of forty-five guineas, *not* including
the shop mentioned above, be thought *over-rated*
at **33 0 0**

Two small Dwellings in Paige's Lane, and
lying behind the last-mentioned premises,
let for £15 . . . . .   **12 0 0**

A Garden in Castle Lane, on part of which the
lessee has built a Stable, lately let together
for £5 5*s* **4 4 0**

	£49	4	0

The commissioners notice a trust deed of the date of 1663, but furnish no
particulars, respecting the management of the property earlier than 1731;
the data supplied from this period gives the following result :–

		£	s.	d.
1.– Received by fines, in 1731, 1761, and 1794 .	.	95	16	0
Rent received and to be received, from 1731 to 1854, 123 years, at four shillings per ann.	.	24	12	0
		£120	8	0
Or less than 19s. 7d. a year.				
2.– Fines in 1758 and 1798 . . .	.	23	0	0
Rent from 1758 to 1858, 100 years, at eight shillings per annum . . .	.	40	0	0
		£63	3	0
Being under 12s. 8d. per annum.				
3.– Fines in 1744* and 1787 . .	32	0	0	
Rent from 1744 to 1847, 103 years at twenty shillings per annum . .	.	103	0	0
		£135	0	0
Not quite £1 6s. 3d. per year.				

It is, then, from the foregoing calculations, indisputably clear, that the "Cordwainer's Lands" will, when the existing leases shall have expired, have produced to the charity for upwards of one hundred years, an annual average income, *including both fines and rent*, of but TWO POUNDS, EIGHTEEN SHILLINGS, AND SIX PENCE, although now worth full ONE HUNDRED POUNDS *per annum, clear of rates, taxes, and repairs.* It may, perhaps, be urged, that the property is much increased in value; granted; but the increase has been both visible in its effects, and progressive in its operation, and cannot therefore be pleaded in extenuation of such management as the estate has been subjected to. No one will venture to assert that the consideration given has not been always vastly disproportionate to the current value of the property obtained.

Again, it may be said, that the different premises have been improved. Mr. Trix was at considerable expense (about £200†) in 1821, in re-modelling the lower part of the front of the house mentioned as being

* No mention is made of any fine in 1774, but I have given the *management* the benefit of any doubt that may arise as to one having been paid, by estimating it of equal amount with the sum stated in 1787.

† As this alteration extended to the whole front, not more than two-thirds of this sum can be said to have been expended on the charity property

rented by him; and Mr. Harris has, already stated, built a kitchen on the premises held by him; besides which, I am not aware of any improvement worth naming being made; and these, be it remembered, have not been taken into account, in the present valuation of the lands.

From the following statement, the poor cordwainers may see the actual loss of their property has suffered from having been *thus* "delt with."

I have said that these premises have risen, and it may be fairly expected that, situate as they are, in the best quarter of the town for trade, they will *continue* to *rise*, in value. Not, however, to bear too hard upon the management, let us consider the average annual value of the property as only *one third* the amount I have estimated it at, (which, it should be borne in mind, is far below what it is now paying,) and the account will stand as below:-

	£	s.	d.
1.– Produce to the respective lessees, for 123 years, at £11 per annum . . .	1353	0	0
2.– Produce to the respective lessees, for 100 years, at £7 per annum . . .	700	0	0
3.– Produce to the respective lessees, for 103 years, at £16 8s. per annum . .	1689	4	0
	£3742	4	0

Deduct amount of fines and rents :–

	£	s.	d.
1.– . .	120	8	0
2.– . .	63	3	0
3.– . .	135	0	0

	£	s.	d.
	318	11	0
Loss to the charity	£3423	13	0

Enormous as is the difference between the two amounts here shewn, the statement will not appear to be in the least overcharged, when we consider that if the property had produced *nothing* for the first seventy-two years, being about two-thirds of the average duration of the different terms above stated, the present rental, *after deducting twenty per cent. for casualties*, would realize in the remaining period of about thirty-eight years, more than my calculation amounts to for the whole time.

Well then might the poor cordwainers, (who, it would seem, have never been fully aware of the extent of their wrongs,) complain to the Commissioners, "that they had some property in Barnstaple, which did not yield them as much as they conceived they had a right to expect from it; and request that some enquiry might be made on their behalf concerning it."*

[N.] *Charity School.*

The following is a list of the different donations and bequests, (not including the rent charges, which have been already stated,) bestowed on this benevolent institution from its establishment in 1710 to the present time:-

			£	s.	d.
1712.	Mary Eburn	bequest	5	0	0
1713.	John Smith	ditto	10	0	0
1714.	Rev. Mr. Somers	uncertain	5	0	0
1714.	Renatus Greenslade	bequest	10	0	0
1715.	Elizabeth Ackland	uncertain	50	0	0
1717.	Isabella Charlotte Rolle .	ditto	107	0	0
1717.	George Larkin	bequest	20	0	0
1719.	Rev. W. Bampfield	ditto	40	0	0
1720.	Edmund Burgh .	ditto	10	0	0
1720.	John Stevens	ditto	40	0	0
1720.	Bartholemew Wakeman .	ditto	10	0	0
1720.	Edward Hammond	ditto	10	10	0
1720.	Phillis Barnes	ditto	10	0	0
1721.	John Symons	ditto	100	0	0
1721.	Hugh Lord Clinton	uncertain	10	10	0
1721.	John Rowley	ditto	20	0	0
1722.	Sir H. Ackland, Bart.†	ditto	21	0	0
1722.	Philip Ridgate, Esq.	uncertain	10	10	0
1725.	Agnes Waybard .	bequest	30	0	0
1725.	Margaret Rolle .	ditto	5	0	0
1726.	Alexander Harper	ditto	6	0	0

* Three aged shoemakers, as a deputation from their brethren, waited on the Commissioners, with the (to them) very natural expectation of deriving some benefit from their interference ; but they were deceived. The applicants were received with courtesy, their complaint patiently heard, and an investigation made ; the Commisioners could do no more. Two of the three individuals have since paid the debt of nature, and many more must go down to the grave, before the " poor cordwainers of Barnstaple " can have their rights restored to them.

† This gift is mentioned in the return made to Parliament in 1786, but does not appear on either of the tablets in the church.

			£	s.	d.
1726. John Jenkins	.	uncertain	10	10	0
1730. William Docton	.	ditto	50	0	0
1731. Sir Nicholas Hooper, Knt.		bequest	100	0	0
1731. Edward Fairchild	.	ditto	30	0	0
1732. Rev. W. Burgh	.	ditto	10	0	0
1732. Robert Andrews	.	uncertain	10	0	0
1734. John Phillips	.	bequest	200	0	0
1755. Martin Lautrow	.	ditto	10	0	0
1759. Robert Incledon	.	ditto	10	0	0
1767. Mary Score	.	ditto	10	0	0
1776. Nicholas Shepherd	.	ditto	20	0	0
1776. Joan Stanbury	.	ditto	100	0	0
1776. Barnard Whitrow	.	ditto	10	0	0
1783. Daniel Marriott	.	ditto	10	0	0
1796. Frances Barford	.	ditto	10	10	0
1797. Benjamin Incledon, Esq	.	ditto	10	0	0
1807. Nicholas Shepherd	.	ditto	10	0	0
1812. Sir Christopher Robinson, Knt.		donation	10	0	0
1812. Sir Masseh M. Lopes, Bart.		ditto	20	0	0
1815. James Sciance (3 per cent. Con.)		bequest*	50	0	0
1816. Edward Paul Pilcher, Esq.		ditto	40	0	0
1817. Thos, Sciance (3 per cent. Stock)		bequest	50	0	0
1818. Francis Ommaney, Esq. M.P.		donation	10	10	0
1824. Frederick Hodgson, Esq. M.P.		ditto	10	10	0
1825. John May, Esq	.	bequest	10	0	0
1826. Henry Alexander, Esq M.P.		donation	10	10	0
1826. William Slocombe, Esq	.	bequest	20	0	0

There is a Public Clock fixed on the roof of the School House, the Bell of which bears the following inscription, "DENYS ROLLE, ESQ. 1764."

Dec. 10, 1734, An order was made for transferring the Rents and Profits of Facey's Ground, (see Skinner's Gift) to this institution, "but this order was afterwards declared void by the Corporation, as being contrary to the will of the Donor, and the Deed of Feoffment, made by Mr. Bartholemew Wakeman for declaring and settling the same."

* Mr. Sciance gave £100 to be divided between this school and " Bell's School ; " the whole sum in the event of the discontinuance of either, to be applied for the benefit of " the surviving school for ever. "

The interference of the Corporation in this case was as commendable as their decision was just. The Body would have earned to themselves an unfading reputation had they *always, as in this instance, stood forward to maintain the rights of the poor, by enforcing the legitimate application of all funds designed for their benefit.*

The annual Income available for the purposes of this Charity having been given in detail by the Commissioners, more need not be stated here respecting it, than that Francis and Bowden's Estate remains in the hands of the same occupier, and at the same rent, as stated in the Report.

The last Collection made at the Church Doors, September 1828, amounted to £37 7s. 0d. and that of the previous year to £39 9s. being the largest sums ever received after the annual "Charity Sermon."

The expenditure on behalf of the institution, for the year ending Sept. 16. 1828, was as follows :—

	£.	s.	d.
Salary to Schoolmaster	45	0	0
Ditto to Schoolmistress	5	0	0
Woollen Cloth	29	5	0
Dowlas, &c.	21	4	0
Worsted	8	9	8
Shoes	29	16	0
Thirty Bonnets	2	0	0
Knitting Sockings	4	11	6
Making Boys' Clothes (Tailor)	6	5	0
Ditto Shirts	1	5	6
Ditto Girls' Gowns	1	5	0
Stationary and Printing	5	6	6
Glazier's, Carpenter's, Mason's and Smith's Bills	1	14	3
Felling Trees on Estate	0	15	0
Rent Charge to Almshouse	4	0	0
Receipt Stamp	0	0	6
	£165	17	11

The conduct of the Trustees of this School in publishing an annual statement of its accounts, cannot be too highly commended; such a praiseworthy example will, it is hoped, be soon followed by the managers of all the other charities belonging to the Town. It is freely admitted that most of these are, and have been, well conducted, but it is, nevertheless, notorious, that the inhabitants generally know little or nothing about how they are managed; many are perhaps even ignorant of the existence of some of the minor ones. It is not enough for the conductors of a charitable fund to know that their duties are faithfully discharged; this knowledge should be extended to all within the sphere of the influence of the institution itself. The public mind, ever alive to suspicion respecting the management of charitable institutions, is peculiarly so with regard to such funds or establishments, the expenditure of which is only known to the Trustees or Managers; nor can this feeling be in any way so effectually allayed, as by a periodical publication of their Receipts and Disbursments.

[O.] *Newcommen's Gift.*

The following account of the above is copied from that referred to by the Commissioners in the Charities of Bideford.

"Margaret Newcommen, by her will, bearing date 17th August, 1810, gave to the Rev. Samuel Rooker, of Bideford, the Rev. Henry William Gardiner, of Barnstaple, the Rev. William Rooker, of Tavistock, and the Rev. Richard Evans, of Appledore, dissenting Ministers, 1,000*l.* in trust, to invest the same in the purchase of stock in the funds, in their names, and to apply the dividends and interest arising therefrom towards the relief of the aged and the young, namely, in relieving such objects of age as might appear to them truly deserving, whether as faithful and affectionate members of Christ, or otherwise those of his household, whose cases evidently called for assistance; and with respect to youth, in giving premiums or gratitudes to young persons for perculiar good conduct, or for attainments in religious matters, or for extraordinary application to the study and learning by heart the sacred scriptures, and other good publications, and in paying for the schooling and religious instruction of such poor children, as would otherwise be destitute thereof ; and she directed the said trustees not to touch or break in upon the principal sum, but from the most imperious necessity.

"By a codicil to her will, she gave to the said Samuel Rooker and William Rooker 200*l.* stock in the four per cents. the interest thereof to be laid out yearly for the schooling of poor children that would not be taught to read else; three or four at Westdown, the same at Barnstaple and Bideford; and she appointed the Rev. Samuel Rooker, and Rev. William Rooker, Trustees for the same.

"Mrs. Newcommen was a protestant dissenter, residing at Bideford; she died in January, 1813; all the trustees are living; but the management of the trust has chiefly devolved upon the Rev. Samuel Rooker, who resides at Bideford. The legacy of 1,000*l.* after the deduction of the duty, appears to have been invested in March, 1814, in the purchase of navy five per

142

cent stock, which since the reduction of the interest of that fund, amounts to the sum of 960*l*. 19*s*. 6*d*. in the new four per cents, standing in the names of the trustees, and producing a dividend of about 38*l*. 8*s*. 9*d*. The other legacy of 200*l*. stock in the four per cents. appears also to have been transferred into the navy five per cents. by the trustees, with the view of increasing the income of the charity; and there is now standing in the names of the trustees, stock to the amount of 176*l* 15*s*.7*d*. in the new four per cents, producing the dividend of about 7*l*. 1*s*. 3¹⁄₂*d*. Mr. Samuel Rooker has kept one general account of the two gifts since the year 1814, and has paid annually to two schoolmistresses of Barnstaple 4*l*. each; to a schoolmistress of Bideford, including the cost of some books furnished, 4*l*.; and to another of West Down 2*l*. He has also provided books for schools at several places in the north of Devon; and has given sums of money, varying from 1*l*. to 5*l*., to aged and necessitous females, having regard to such as were friends of the testatrix; he has also transmitted sums to the other trustees for their distribution, in like manner. These occasional donations have been chiefly made to dissenters; and all the schools, except that of West Down, are under the management of persons of that persuasion. Mr. Rooker makes up his account at the end of every year."

The Interest for life of the £1200 here bequeathed, would have been a valuable boon (in additiion to an annuity of £5 per annum each left them by Mrs. N.) to four relatives of the Donor, two of whom were at the time of her death, as at present, receiving parochial relief in this Town.

[P.] *Stanbury's Gift.*

Mrs. Stanbury, it must be acknowledged, exercised a sound discretion in excluding such of the parishioners as might not be "of the communion of the Church of England" from any share in the appropriation of her bequest, as the following characteristic anecdote, which may be implicitly relied on, will shew.

"Good-now, Cousin," said the old lady a short time before her decease, to a respectable female named Reeder, "what sort of a bible d'ye use at the Meeting?" For aught the venerable dame knew, the congregation at the Meeting, instead of using the same bible, and holding, essentially, the same doctrines, as that with which she assembled in the church, might have been readers of the Alcoran, or spiritual subjects of his Holiness the Pope !

Annexed is a Tabular View of all the Lands described in the Commisioners' Report as appertaining to the several charities existing in this town; shewing the Donor's name, date of bequests, produce of the estates at different periods, &c.

No one, it is presumed, after perusing the foregoing account of the state, management, and produce, of the different eleemosynary institutions existing in the Town of Barnstaple, will be at a loss for a reason, why, when so many of the Charities have flourished, and proved increasingly productive, others have withered under the hands that should have fostered and protected them, and thus proved altogether unfruitful.* The cause is obvious enough. The business of letting the estates of these "misgoverned" charities, has been transacted with "closed doors," or in plainer terms, without such publicity being given to the proceedings, as would have produced a fair and honourable competition for leases of the different lands, and, as a certain consequence of such rivalry, an *equitable rent.*

I have already said that the greater part of the Barnstaple Charities have been well conducted, but, had the custom prevailed of publishing annually, as in the case of the Blue School, or even septennially, statements of the affairs of *all*, would not the gross mismanagement which has prevailed in *some*, have been prevented? Unquestionably ! Those twin-destroyers of charity property — *secret lettings*, and *long leases*, would have been unknown amongst us, and the poor Cordwainers might now be in receipt of about One Hundred Pounds per annum, instead of *Thirty-two Shillings;* nay, more ! They might have been in possession of Lands in four other Parishes, which it is quite clear belonged to the Company of Cordwainers within the last two hundred years, but which since 1633, appear to have been lost . Rumour indeed, even now, points at Property over which an individual, many years deceased, used to exercise the rights of ownership, which is supposed to have been "Cordwainer's Land."

---

* It is not of course intended to say that these estates have really yielded no profit, the prededing pages bear ample proof to the contrary ; they too " have proved increasingly productive, " but not to the Charities to which they belong. I am here reminded of an ancedote of our late beloved Monarch – George the Third.
His Majesty observing that an immense sum was annually expended in fruit for the Royal Household, enquired what became of the produce of his own gardens ? The reply was, *not* that the Trees were barren — there was an abundance of fruit — " but that it had been customary to distribute it in presents. " Thus the " Cordwainer's Lands " " Appley's Gift " " Monies to be given, lent, " &c. have produced fruit, and *golden* fruit too, but it has been literally *given away.*

Notice of the appointment of new Trustees to this charity having been omitted in its proper place in the Appendix, their names are here given. The deed of enfeoffment bears date 8th May, 1827.

SAMUEL BREMRIDGE,
WILLIAM CHAPPLE PAWLE,
WILLIAM LAW,
RICHARD BREMRIDGE,
BENJAMIN BALLER, JUN.
JOHN BAKER,
FRANCIS BAKER,
ELLICE LEE SANDERS,
JOHN LEWORTHY DAVIS,

GEORGE PETTER,
WILLIAM WOOLLACOTT,
ALEXANDER SHAPCOTT,
ROBERT RICE,
WILLIAM RENNELS,
THOMAS MAY,
THOMAS BAKER,
WILLIAM PETTER,
JOSHUA TURNER.

Since the appointment of these gentlemen, both the lessees of the property have applied for a renewal of their respective leases, but without success. The new feoffees have, much to their credit, disgarded the old system, and the dawn of a brighter day at last opens on the "poor Cordwainers of Barnstaple."

A misstatement has been made, (see Appendix F.) which it is desirable should be corrected. My information was derived from a source which left me no room to doubt its correctness, but I have since learnt from unquestionable authority, that the deduction on account of land-tax is *still* made; *why*, I cannot learn.

The following benefactions did not come under the notice of the Commissioners.

Vicarage-lane Almshouses.

This building consists of two singularly small dwellings,* each having two rooms, one on the ground floor, and one above.

No certain information respecting either the original designation of the premises, or the period of their erection, can be obtained,† but they are evidently very ancient, and are not known to have been ever applied to any other than their present purpose. The inmates are appointed, and the building kept in repair by the Rev. Thomas Boyce, Curate of Shirwill, from whom I have received the following account. " The premises at Vicarage Corner have been in the possession of my family for some centuries past; the occupation of which has always been given to any indigent persons the proprietor has thought proper to place there."

As this statement tends to raise the question, are the premises *charity*, or *private* property? it becomes incumbent on me to state, that they have been always considered as belonging to the poor. The following is a copy of a memorandum relative to it, made several years ago, by an individual now deceased. " Supposed to be built and the gift of Mrs. Phillis Barnes, to the Poor of Barnstaple, and the predecessors of Mr. (Rev.) Thos. Boyce, to whom she gave her property, were bound to repair it. One Mrs. Askham repaired it about 70 years since; she left a daughter who married Mr. S. Stevens. Mr. Thomas Boyce's mother was called Barnes." The writer adds "search the donations in the Church for this gift." I have done so, but find no mention of it.# The name of "Phillis Barnes" appears in 1720, as a benefactor to the Charity School; this individual was probably a descendant of the supposed founder of the House alluded to.

---

* Both are comprised in a space of 215 feet, walls and chimnies included.

† On a Lead Gutter in front of building is the date in front of the building is the date 1618, but this may only mark the time when the lead was placed there.

I have not thought it necessary to give a copy of the donations and bequests inscribed on the tablets (of which there are six in the South Gallery) in the Church, as it would be to do but little more than repeat what has, in some shape or other, been already stated.

Frances Barford's Gift of £33 6s. 8d. to the inmates of
Horwood's, Paige's, and Litchdon Almshouses, in the Town
of Barnstaple.

The present manager of this Charity, John May, Esq. (son and executor of "John May" hereafter mentioned) with a laudable desire to have it more generally known, as a preventive against any future misapplication of its funds; has furnished me with the original statements made by his father respecting it, copies of which follow:-

"Memorandum to Posterity, 30th June, 1787, – It is Mrs. Barford's request that the annual interest of the £33 6s. 8d. Old South Sea Annuities, should be laid out in Bread and distributed among the poor inhabitants of Horwood's, Paige's, and Litchdon Almshouses, in the Town of Barnstaple.

"John May."

"Memorandum also to Posterity. – That Mrs. Frances Barford, of Sailsbury, widow of Richard Barford, Gent. gave in her life time, Old South Sea Annuities, the interest to be given as mentioned above. The said Annuities Old South Sea, was purchased the 22nd of June 1787 by her friend John May, and transferred to him for the purpose that her aforesaid request might be fulfilled and complied with, and my Executors or Executrix are to do the same.

"John May."

"1809. Memorandum. – It was transferred by me to Richard Marston, Esq and John May, Jun. my son, that as the said Richard Marston was living in London, he was thereby enabled to receive the dividends without the expense of a power of attorney, which would be more than the annual dividend amounted to.

"John May."

"Old South Sea Annuities Office, Ely Place, Holborn,
"19th January, 1809.
I hereby acknowledge to have had transferred to me by Mr. John May, of Barnstaple, the sum of thirty-three pounds six shillings and eight pence, into my name and that of his son Mr. John May, Jun. of the same place, which said money is to be given to the Poor of Barnstaple; that no part of it is my own property, and that it is so transferred for the sloe purpose of my receiving the dividends upon it from time to time, and for paying those dividends to the said poor.
"Witness my hand,   "R. Marston."

The annual produce of the stock is £1, which sum was distributed, according to the directions of the Donor, half-yearly, during the life time of the late John May, Esq. regularly distributed in Bread amongst the inhabitants of the three Almshouses already named; one half on New-Year's-day, and the remainder on the fourteenth of February, the latter day being the anniversary of the death of the Donor, who died in 1789. The same arrangement is continued by his son. A regular and correct account (which I have seen) of the receipts and disbursements of this charity has been kept from the commencement to this present year (1829.)

" Matilda Peverell gave, Oct. 20, A. D. 1482, a tenement to the Mayor and others in trust, to repair St. Peter's Church and the Chancel."

Of this gift there is "no trace."

CHAPTER III.

Antiquity of the Mayoralty of Barnstaple – Ancient Government of the Town–Representative History of the Borough–Number, Qualification, and Privileges of Burgesses–Charters–Origin and Intent of Corporations–Municipal Body of Barnstaple–Appendix.

ANTIQUITY OF THE MAYORALTY OF BARNSTAPLE.

The office of Mayor in Barnstaple is certainly of high antiquity; since, although not mentioned in any existing charter earlier than that of Henry VI, the privilege of choosing a Mayor was confirmed to the Burgesses as the prescriptive right, so far back as the reign of Edw. III.* The custom passed at this period the ordeal of three inquisitions, and the only question raised respecting it, was, whether or no the burgesses were free to make the election of themselves, or if they required the Lord's license to do it; this was left doubtful, but the practice was in each enquiry declared to be good by prescription, and must consequently have been *then* ancient.

Oldfield, in his account of Barnstaple,† says, "King John gave it a Mayor;" upon what authority this statement was made does not appear, but that it is an erroneous one there can be little doubt, otherwise the fact of such a grant having been made must have

---

* A writ of Quo Warranto of the reign of Edward 1., and three inquisitions Temp. Edward 111. form Appendix [A.] to this Chapter. These documents are deserving of an attentive perusal, and will, perhaps, be read to most advantage, if taken before the Chapter itself, the three first heads of which have an especial reference to them.

† Representative History of Great Britain and Ireland, vol. 3, p. 299.

come before the jurors, on the aforementioned inquisitions, who would, of course, have made their return accordingly; it is, however, expressly said. "that they" (the burgesses) "have not the charter of the Lord the King nor of his progenitors, to make the said election." The burgesses pleaded that they "had used and enjoyed" this among other "divers liberties and free customs, by the charter of the Lord Athelstan;" but, although they failed to prove the grant of such charter, (which it was the interest of the Lord of the Town to prevent their doing,) their right, "a Mayor from among themselves to elect," was clearly established, and in a way that affords good grounds for concluding that it existed long prior to the time of King John.

I may mention, that the Corporation, who do not, that I am aware of, possess any charter of earlier date than the reign of Henry II, describe the borough as having had "the customs of London in the time of Henry I. and *then governed by a Mayor and Bailiff.*" Probability is certainly opposed to the belief that Barnstaple could have had a Mayor before the chief Magistrate of the city of London was so named,* but the above is not the only evidence which may be adduced in favour of such a supposition. A document is said, and on no very slight grounds, to have been prepared, and to have borne date August 8, 1 Richard 1. (1189) for the purpose of "shewing the [then] Antiquity of Maior of Barnstaple, with seal of office." The question whether or no such an instrument does, or ever did exist, is one which, I confess my inability to solve. Rejecting all doubtful authority, we may, however, safely decide on the evidence afforded by the inquisitions alone, that the Burgesses of Barnstaple *could plead antiquity in support of their right to elect a Mayor, upwards of five centuries ago.*

---

* " Before and since the Conquest, to the time of Rich. 1. London was governed by a Port - reeve, and afterwards by a Mayor appointed by the King ; but King John, in the tenth of his reign, granted them liberty to choose a Mayor. " — *Tomlin's Law Dictionary, Art' London.*

The subjoined List of Mayors of Barnstaple, is (up to 1793) a copy of that collated by the late Benjamin Incledon, Esq., which is, perhaps, the best guarantee that could be given for its correctness.

A. D.

1303 Ralph Wynemor
4
5
6
7 } [It is by no means improbable that the above named individual filled the office during many of these intervening years]
8
9
1310
1
2
3
4
5 John Pollard
6
7
8
9 John Pollard
20
1
2 John Pollard
3 John de Collacot
4 Thomas de la Bar
5 Bernard de la Bogh
6 Bernard de la Bogh
7 John Collacott
8 Galfridus de Fremington
9 Galfridus Tinctor
30 John Collacott
1 Thomas de la Bar
2 William Webber
3 John Pollard
4 Galfridus de Fremington
5 Thomas de la Bar

A.D.

1336 Ralph Smallcombe
7 Galfridus Tictor
8
9
1340
1
2
3
4 Roger Molland
5
6 John Widger
7 John Boughdon
8 John Smith
9 John Collin
1350 John Bowdon
1 Thomas Widger
2 John Bowdon
3 John Squire
4 Richard Dulverton
5 John Pugsley
6 John Widger
7
8
9 Simon de la Bar
60
1
2 John Webber
3 Walter Yeo
4
5 William Gibb
6
7
8 Symon Bade

151

1369 William Gibb
  70 Richard Dulverton
   1 Richard Dulverton
   2 Richard Dulverton
   3 John Bydewill
   4
   5
   6 John Neel
   7 John Boughdon
  80 Joseph Anthony
  81
   2 John Bydewill
   3 John Bydewill
   4 Thomas Lelye
   5
   6
   7
   8 John Pitman
   9
  90 John Pitman
   1 Thomas Lelye
   2
   3
   4
   5 John Bydewill
   6
   7
   8
   9 John Bydewill
1400
   1
   2
   3

1404
   5
   6 Thomas Holman
   7 Thomas Hooper
   8
   9
  10
   1
   2
   3 Thomas Walsh
   4
   5
   6
   7 Thomas Walsh
   8 Thomas Walsh
   9 Thomas Holman
  20 Thomas Holman
   1 Thomas Walsh
   2 Thomas Hooper
   3 William Hertyscot
   4 Thomas Hertyscot
   5 William Hertyscot
   6 John Goldsmith
   7 Thomas Hooper
   8 John Goldsmith
   9 Thomas Hooper
  30 John Goldsmith
   1 Richard Bowdon
   2 William Hertyscot
   3 William Bedwin
   4 Richard Bowdon
   5 John Hutchen
   6 William Hertyscot

1437 William Bowdon
8 William Rowe
9
40 Richard Bowdon
1 John Mules
2 Richard Norris
3 William Bedwin
4 John Mules
5 Walter Hayman
6 Richard Rowe
7 Walter Hayne
8 William Hertyscot
9 Richard Newcomb
50 John Widon
1 Nicholas Bovey
2 William Upcott
3 Richard Pickard
4 John Widger
5 Walter Gaynock
6 Richard Newcomb
7 Walter Gaynock
8 William Charnier
9 John Widger
60 John Bowdon
1 John Smith
2 John Collins
3 John Widger
4 John Collins
5 John Widger
6 John Bowdon
7 John Widger
8 John Pugsley
9 John Bowdon

1470 John Widger
1 John Squire
2 John Widger
3 Philip Stigan
4 John Pugsley
5 John Collins
6 John Hart
7 Philip Stigan
8 John Branton
9 John Bowdon
80 Thomas White
1 John Hart
2 Richard Crews
3 Robert Symons
4 John Smith
5 Walter Nicholls
6 William Dallinton
7 John Hart
8 Philip Warington
9 Robert Symons
90 John Salisbury
1 William Dallington
2 Roger Colmer
3 John Smith
4 Robert Symons
5 Arthur Merryfield
6 John Salisbury
7 Roger Colmer
8 Richard Parminter
9 William Cosby
1500 John Salisbury
1 Richard Dobyn
2 Robert Symons

A.D.

1503 Philip Warington
   4 Arthur Merryfield
   5 John Upcot
   6 John Smith
   7 William Dobney
   8 Thomas Storey
   9 Robert Colmer
  10 John Godsland
   1 Thomas Story
   2 William Dobney
   3 John Gosland
   4 Thomas Beck
   5 Thomas Ferrye
   6 Thomas Alee
   7 Robert Colmer
   8 Thomas Alee
   9 Thomas Ferrye
  20 Robert Cockram
   1 Paul Smith
   2 John Upcott
   3 John Merryfield
   4 Arthur Merryfield
   5 John Godsland
   6 Philip Colmer
   7 Richard Haydon
   8 Richard Haydon
   9 Thomas Beak
  30 Walter Salisbury
   1 Paul Smith
   2 John Manyng
   3 Richard Gay
   4 David Phillips
   5 John Manyng

A.D.

1536 Philip Colmer
   7 Baldwin Peard
   8 Richard Skinner
   9 Walter Salisbury
  40 Henry Drew
   1 John Manyng
   2 Richard Gay
   3 Thomas Jeffery
   4 John Godsland
   5 John Holland
   6 William Canford
   7 Thomas Davy
   8 Henry Cade
   9 Roger Worth
  50 James Godsland
   1 Richard Skinner
   2 Thomas Davy
   3 John Smith
   4 Robert Apley
   5 Robert Cade
   6 George Stapleton
   7 John Dart
   8 William Sailsbury
   9 John Beaple
  60 Edward Colscot
   1 John Daymond
   2 Nicholas Wichalse
   3 William Dawkins
   4 Hugh Brazier
   5 Oliver Peard
   6 John Daymond
   7 John Arscott
   8 John Dart

154

A.D.
1569 Robert Apley
70 Robert Cade
1 Thomas Beaple
2 Philip Holland
3 Hugh Brazier
4 William Dawkins
5 John Barrett
6 William Collibear
7 Paul Worth
8 John Harris
9 John Dodderidge
80 John Welsh
1 John Daymond
2 Robert Apley
3 Richard Avery
4 William Collibear
5 William Palmer
6 George Pyne
7 Richard Peard
 died, and was succeeded by
 John Harris
8 Robert Prowse
9 Richard Dodderidge
90 Roger Beaple
1 Roger Cade
2 Paul Worth
3 James Beaple
4 William Collibear
5 George Pyne
6 John Harris
7 Robert Apley, jun.
8 Nicholas Downe
9 Roger Beaple

A.D.
1600 John Delbridge
1 George Stanbury
2 Bartholomew Harris
3 Paul Worth
4 James Beaple
5 James Woodrooffe
6 John Peard
7 Richard Beaple
8 Richard Harris
9 James Downe
1610 William Shapleigh
1 Pentecost Dodderidge
2 William Palmer, jun.
3 Nicholas Downe
4 Adam Lugge
5 John Delbridge
6 George Baker
7 James Bulteel
8 Thomas Westlake
9 Nicholas Delbridge
20 John Penrose
1 Richard Beaple
2 John Peard
3 Justinian Westcombe
4 John Hammer
5 Edward Eastmond
6 Richard Harris
7 Pentecost Dodderidge
8 Nicholas Downe
9 Gilbert Paige
30 Richard Medford
1 William Palmer
2 Richard Ferris

A.D.
1633 John Delbridge
4 Alexander Horwood
5 Richard Beaple
6 Henry Mason
7 Pentecost Dodderidge
8 George Ferris,
  died, and was succeeded by
  Anthony Gay
9 Walter Tucker
40 Thomas Horwood
1 Gilbert Paige
2 William Palmer
3 Charles Peard
4 Adam Lugge
5 John Downe
6 Richard Ferris
7 William Nottel
8 Richard Harris
9 Nicholas Cooke
50 Hugh Horsham
1 Thomas Dennys
2 Thomas Matthew
3 Thomas Horwood
4 John Horwood
5 Richard Medford
6 Roger Jeffery
7 Peter Docton
8 Joseph Delbridge
9 William Westcombe
60 Richard Hooper
1 Adam Lugge
2 John Downe
3 Arthur Ackland

A.D.
1664 John Seldon
5 John Palmer
6 John Gread
7 Thomas Matthew
8 Thomas Cox
9 Richard Medford
70 Roger Jeffery
1 George Rooke
2 William Westcombe
3 Christopher Hunt
4 Richard Hooper
5 Thomas Cole
6 Thomas Harris
7 Richard Sailsbury
8 John Fairchild
9 Henry Drake
80 John Stephens
1 Hugh Marshall
2 William Wakeman
3 Edward Rice
4 George Fairchild
5 John Peard
6 John Blake
7 Henry Ravening
8 Richard Barnes
9 Christopher Hunt
90 James Kingsland
1 Nicholas Cooke
2 Thomas Seldon
3 John Hunt
4 Nicholas Ginger
5 William Greenslade
6 Jeffery Bagilhole

A.D.
1697 Charles Standish
  8 Nathaniel Cox,
       died, and was succeeded by
  Hugh Marshall
  9 Richard Cornish
1700 Thomas Harris
  1 John Rowley
  2 John Webber
  3 Philip Greenslade
       died, and was succeeded by
  William Wakeman
  4 Richard Cornish
  5 Benjamin Baller
  6 William Taylor
  7 James Sloley
  8 Richard Melhuish
  9 Richard Gread
 10 John Philipps
  1 John Marshall
  2 Robert Incledon
  3 Giles Randle
  4 William Roberts
  5 John Baker
  6 Christopher Lantrow
  7 Robert Nicholas
  8 Edward Fairchild
  9 John Webber
 20 John Philips
  1 Robert Incledon
  2 Lewis Gregory
  3 James Kimpland
  4 Zachary Chappel
  5 Edward Fairchild

A.D.
  6 John Gaydon
  7 John Marshall
  8 Richard Newell
  9 John Baker
 30 George Score
  1 Samuel Berry
  2 Benjamin Baller
  3 Thomas Harris
  4 Charles Velly
  5 Richard Knight
  6 Paul Tucker
  7 Alexander Webber
  8 Henry Beavis
  9 George Wickey
 40 John Fraine
  1 Matthew Roch
  2 Roger Chappell
  3 John Baker
  4 Charles Wright
  5 Robert King
  6 Marshall Swayne
  7 Mark Slee
  8 Charles Marshall
  9 Charles Velly
 50 Richard Knight
  1 Henry Beavis
  2 John Fraine
  3 Matthew Roch
  4 Benjamin Grant
  5 Richard Thorne
  6 Daniel Marriott
  7 Henry Drake
  8 Paul Tucker

A.D.

9 Thomas Earl
60 Mounier Roch
1 Charles Venn
  died, and was succeeded by
Richard Knight
2 Roger Chappell
3 Charles Marshall
4 John Baker
5 Edward Houndle
6 Nicholas Shepherd
7 Richard Thorne
8 Daniel Marriot
9 Richard Honychurch
  died same day on which he
  was sworn – succeeded by
Simon Moule
70 Samuel Chappell
1 John Robins
2 Henry Colley
3 Nicholas Shepherd, jun.
4 George Greek
5 Francis Tucker
6 James Reed
7 Charles Marshall
8 Mounier Roch
9 Stewkley Stephens
80 John Moule
1 Roger Chappell
2 Edward Houndle
3 John Law

A.D.

4 William Cottle
5 Samuel Chappell
6 John Tucker
7 Nicholas Grass
8 John Roberts
9 John May
90 William Dean
1 George Greek
2 William Law
3 John Servante
  left the town, succeeded by
George Greek*
4 Henry Gardiner Tippett
5 Charles Marshall
6 John Moule
7 Richard Rowe Meth
8 William Slocombe
9 John Gaydon
1800 Nicholas Shepherd
1 Thomas Copner
2 William Servante
3 John Law
4 Nicholas Glass
5 Henry Bellew
  died, and was succeeded by
John Moule
6 John Pyke
7 John Roberts
8 Philip Bremridge
9 Samuel Bremridge

A.D
10 John May
1 William Law
2 Richard Rowe Metherell
3 William Slocombe
4 William Chapple Paw
5 John May, jun.
6 Ed. Richards Roberts
7 Samuel Bremridge
8 William Law, jun.
9 John Law

A.D.
1820 Thomas Copner
1 John Pike
2 Charles Roberts
3 John Cooke
4 John Marshall
1825 Samuel Bembridge
6 Henry Nicholls, Clerk
7 Nicholas Glass
8 Robert Budd
9 Richard Bembridge

ANCIENT GOVERNMENT OF THE TOWN.

The manner in which the Town is at present governed, is so different from what it was in former times that it may not prove uninteresting to enquire, to whom the administration of the laws was committed, and to what extent they were allowed to go in the execution of them.

The Management of civil affairs appears to have been divided betwixt the Mayor and Bailiffs, and the Lord of the Town; but the juristiction in criminal matters to have been wholly vested in the latter. This state of things did not, however, continue longer than till the reign of Henry VI. whose charter enacts, that "all pleas of trespasses or contracts, &c. shall be pleaded before the Mayor and Bailiffs;" and also that "the Burgesses of the same Borough may have Infangenethef and outfangenethef, &c."

The Mayor and Bailiffs may be considered as having acted in unison with some other of the principal Burgesses, (usually termed "Maisters," or "Comonaltie,") in order to prevent their privileges from being encroached upon. Feudal Lords possessed considerable power and influence; either, or both of which, as occasion required, they were ever ready to use for the purpose of extending their authority, and adding to their domains.

Instances are not wanting to shew, that endeavours were sometimes made, to abridge the liberties enjoyed by the Burgesses; and there can be little doubt but that the petition which gave rise to the inquisitious already referred to, had its own origin in some attempt of this kind. There is, indeed, just cause for suspicion, that by the exercise of undue influence, in this case the old damage of " might overcomes right" was verified, as we find many privileges denied the Burgesses, to which we may reasonably suppose they were entitled, of which, at least, they would not have claimed, and sought in so determined a manner to establish, but upon good grounds. It is observable, that all the liberties then prayed for by the Burgesses, have, with many additional ones, been since granted to them by Charter.

The authority vested in the Lord of the Town, particularly as it regarded the execution of the penal laws, was extensive; embracing

First,—*View of Frankpledge.* This is an institution of very ancient origin, the *view* of superintendance of which was commonly entrusted to the sheriffs. Cowell describes it as " a pledge or surety for freemen. For the ancient custom of England for the Preservation of the public peace, was, that every freeborn man at fourteen years of age, religious persons, clerks, knights, and their eldest sons, excepted, should find security for his fidelity to the King, or else be kept in prison; whence it became customary for a certain number of neighbours to be bound for one another, to see each man of their pledge forthcomming at all times, or to answer the transgression of any one absenting himself; this was called *frankpledge,* and commonly consisted of ten households. The Sheriffs were from time to time to take the oaths of youths who had reached the above-mentioned age, and see that they combined in one party or other, and this branch of their authority was called *visus franciplegii,* view of frankpledge,"
– Abridged from *Cowel's Law Dict.*

The following is a modern and more comprehensive definition of the term:– "Court Leet or View of Frankpledge; a court of record said to be the most ancient in the land for criminal matters. Its original intent was to view the Frankpledges, that is, the freemen within the liberty, who were, according to the institution of Alfred, pledges for the good behaviour of each other; besides this, the preservation of the peace, and the correction of minute offences against the public good, were the objects of this court; there also, by immemorial usage, the constables of the hundred are elected and sworn. The business of this court has, however, in a great measure developed upon the Quarter Sessions."– *Ency. Metrop., Art. Court.*

Many antiquarians suppose that Frankpledge was anciently denoted by the word *borge* or *borgh,* a borough. Dr. Johnson brings forward a quotation from Spencer, in support of this opinion.

Second,– The *Pillory.* This instrument of punishment, although not much used in England at present, is sufficiently known to render any description of it here unnecessary.*

Third,– The *Thumbrell;* a definition of which, and the uses to which it was applied, may be new to many of my readers.

The *"Cucking-stool, Ducking-stool, or Thumbrell,"* was " an engine for the punishment of scolds and unquiet women." It was called by the Saxons, " a *Scalfing-stole,"* and in Domesday Book, " *Cathedra Stercoralis,* having been anciently employed to duck fraudulent brewers and bakers in *stercore,* stinking water," (literally dung or filth.)

" A woman," says Sir Edward Coke, (3 Inst. 219, 4 Comm. 169), " indicted for being a common scold, if convicted, shall be sentenced to be placed in a certain Instrument of Correction called the *Trebucket, Thumbrell, Tymborella, Castigatory,* or Cucking-stool, which in the Saxon language signifies the *Scolding-stool,* though now it is frequently corrupted into *Ducking-stool,* because the residue of the judgement is, that when she is so placed therein, she shall be plunged into the water for her punishment."

* In looking at the description of offences formerly visited with the infliction of the Pillory, we cannot but be struck with the contrast presented to us in the administration of the law in modern times. "By the statute of the pilory, 51, Hen. 3. stat. 6, it is appointed for bakers, forstallers and those who use false weights! persons guilty of perjury, forgery, &c." Coke's Inst. vol. 3. p. 219.

Some of the offences here enummerated are, it is well known, now punishable only by trifling fines, whilst another is visited, not with retributive justice, as when "the voice of a brother's blood crieth from the ground," but with the *vengeance* of a sanguinary and unequal law.

In the Homilies of the Church it is said that " because this vice [brawling] is so much hurtful to the society of a commonwealth, in all well ordered cities, these common brawlers and scolders be punished with a notable kind of pain, as to be set on the *Cucking-stole.*" So late as the 6th Charles I. a new " iron tumbrel or ducking stool was made for the use of this Borough and Parish, it cost £3;" we may therefore infer, that up to that period, this mode of punishment was common. It is mentioned in the time of Queen Elizabeth, as standing by the river side, " on Castle Poynt;" it was probably usually kept there. The instrument was of very simple construction, consisting of a long beam or lever, moving up and down on a centre; at one end was fixed a chair or stool, to which the culprit was confined, and forthwith plunged into the pond or stream beneath.

Fourth,– The *Gallows.* The earliest authentic record I have discovered in which mention is made of the right of inflicting capital punishment here is the writ of Quo Warranto noticed at page 149. Of the issue of this writ no account is known to exist, but amongst the chronicles of the Town, I find an extract, apparently taken from a similar document, in which the same liberties are claimed, with the additional ones of a " Fair and Market;" *all which*, it is said, " the Jury presented," [confirmed.] This dated 1281.

In three instances during this and the succeeding reign, (in 1303, 1318, and 1325), a "Guild"* was held here and "Furchyngmen appointed;" the names of these officers in 1303, were Matthew Chyvenor, Rus le Dirna, Bernardus de la Boughe, Symson de la Bar.

The word Furchyngmen is not, I believe, to be met with in any glossary, but it is evidently derived from Furca, a gallows, and may be properly taken here for executioners. In this definition of the term, which otherwise I should not advance with so much confidence, I am borne out by the opinion of an eminent scholar and antiquarian, who says, " Furchyngmen may either signify the executioner and his assistants, or the men who had the charge of keeping the gallows, tumbrell, and other instruments of punishment

---

* This word which must here be taken for a court of assize, was anciently used to denote, not only a "fraternity," but a "compensation or penalty for a fault committed."

used in the Manor, in proper repair."

The grant by Henry VI. of *Infangenethef* * and *Outfnagenethef* † to the burgesses, vested the power which had hitherto been exercised by the Lord of the Town, in the Mayor and Bailiffs. The right of inflicting capital punishment appears to have continued until the time of James I. whose charter enacts that the juristiction of the Magistrates shall not extend to the determination of any betraying " of murder or felony, or any other matter touching the loss of life or member." See Charles 8, James 1. clause U, App. [H.]

REPRESENTATIVE HISTORY OF THE BOROUGH.

However defective the evidence may be considered as to the Castle of Barnstaple having been found by Athelstan, it will hardly be disputed that the Borough was represented in the Witena Gemot, or Anglo Saxon Parliament.# Our forefathers, to their lasting honor, at a time when it would appear an attempt was making to deprive them of the ancient privilege of sending deputies to the great council of the nation, nobly stood forward, and, even in those days of feudal tyranny, petitioned again and again in maintenance of their rights. Not only did they succeed in securing to themselves and their descendants the continuance of so valuable an immunity, but to them are we indebted as a nation for perhaps the best evidence which the archives of the Kingdom afford, that any of the cities and boroughs of England had a voice in the parliamentary assembly of our Saxon Ancestors. I refer to the inquisitions made in the reign of Edward III. in consequence of a petition from the town of Barnstaple, touching their privileges, already mentioned.

I am relieved from the duty of discussing the eviction contained in these interesting documents, this having been so ably done by that distinguished historian, Lord Lyttleton, in his Life of King Henry II.

"Having now, " says the noble author, " considered the claim of the

* *Infangthef, Infangenetheof,* from Sax. *Fang* or *Fangen,* i.e. *capere* and *Theof,* Fur. A privilege or liberty granted unto Lords of certain manors, to judge any thief taken *within* their Fee. – *Temlin's Law Diet,*

† A privilege whereby a Lord was empowered to bring a man, dwelling in his own manor, but *taken for a felony out of it,* to trial in his own court. – *Ibid.*

" This great council (the English Parliament) hath been held immemoriably, under the several names of *michel synoth,* or great council; *michel gemote,* or great meeting; and more frequently WITENA GEMOT or meeting of wise men." It was also styled " *magnum concilium regis,*" &c.

town of St. Alban's, I shall transcribe some records in the Tower of London, concerning a petition* in Parliament to King Edward the Third, from the town of Barnstaple, in Devonshire; wherein they set forth, that, among other privileges granted them by a charter of King Athelstan, they had from that time enjoyed the right of sending two burgesses to serve for them in Parliament. And first, I shall give an extract from the writ of inquisition founded on that petition, which is recited therein:– ' Sciatis, quod, cum nuper ad prosecutionem burgensium villæ de Barnstaple, in com. Devon, per petitonem suam coram nobis supplicantium, ut cum villa prædicta, à tempore cujus contrii memoria non existit, liber burgus fuerit, iidemque burgenses, et eorum antecessores, burgenses villæ prædtctæ diversis libertatibus et liberis consuetudinibus per cartam celebris memoriæ. D. Athelstani, dudum regis Angliæ, progenitoris nostri, quæ ad liberum burgum pertinent à tempore confectionis dictæ cartæ usi fuerunt et gavisi, in hoc, viz. quod tenementa sua in eodem burgo in testamento suo in ultimâ voluntate suâ quibuscunque volurint legare, et majorem de se ipsis, coram quo omnia placita dictum burgum et suburbium ejusdem tangentia placitari et terminari debeant, eligire, ac ad singula parliamenta nostra, et dictorum antecessorum nostrorum, duos burgenses pro communitate ejusdem burgi mittere, nec non in singulis taxationibus, etc. consueverunt: therefore the King ordered an inquest to be made into the truth of the facts therein alleged, and particularly, si carta illa fuerit amissa, as the petitioners had set forth, and whether it would be proper to grant them another, confirming to them the same liberties, as they had desired. In the return to this the jurors say,–' Burgenses dictæ villæ ad singula parliamenta duos burgenses pro communitate dicti burgi mittre solebant; item dicunt, quod nihil eis constabat de carta D. Athelstani, dudum regis Angliæ, prædictis burgensibus, seu eorum prædecessoribus, de diversis libertatibus seu consuetudinibus prædictis ut asserunt, concessis.' This not satisfying the burgesses, they obtained a writ ad quod damnum, to enquire,–' Si prædicta burgenses dictas libertates eis per cartam prædicti Athelstani, ut prædicitur, concessas, à

---

* See No. 2 App. [A.] for a translation both of the petition and inquisition.

tempore prædicto usi fuerunt et gavisi, et si carta illa in formâ prædictâ fuerit amissa; nec non ad quod damnum seu præjudicium nostrum aut alterius cujuscunque cederet, si nos dictas libertates eisdem burgensibus per cartam prædicti Athelstani, ut asserunt, concessas, nec non prædictas libertates per eos de novo petitas, prout superius continentur, per cartum nostram concedamus sibi et hæredibus et successoribus suis in perpetuum possidendas; et ideo vobis mandamus, quod at certos dies et locos, quos vos tres, vel duo vestrum, ad hoc provideritis, inquisitionem illam super ræmissis et ea tangentibus in formâ prædictâ faciatis, etc.'

The return of the writ is as follows:– ' Inquisitio capta apud Barnstaple coram Hamone de Derworthy, et Joan. de Baumfels, justiciariis D. regis ad inquisitionem illam capiendam unâ cum Joanne de de Stonford et Ricard. de Hawkeston, in præsent. Walteri de Horton, Viceomitis Devon. die sabbat. etc. an. regni Edw. regis Angliæ tertii 17, etc. super sacramentum R. de Wolfe, etc. qui dicunt super sacramentum suum, quod villa de Barnstaple est liber burgus, et fuit â tempore quo non extat memoria. Item dicunt quod burgenses villæ prædictæ, et eorum antecessores divrsis libertatibus et liberis consuetud inibus per cartam celebris memoriæ D. Athelstani, dudum regis Angliæ progenitoris D. regis nunc, quæ dictum burgum pertinent â tempore confectionis cartæ prædictæ semper hactenus usi fuerunt et gavisi, et adhuc gaudent et utuntur, videlicet quod tenementa sua, etc. etc. Ac ad singula parliamenta D. regis duos burgenses pro communitate ejusdem burgi mittre, nec non in singulis taxationibus, etc. consueverunt. Dicunt etiam quod prædicta carta, de prædictis libertatibus et consuetudinibus, eisdem burgensibus per prædictum D. Athelstanum facta, casualiter fuerit amissa. Item dicunt quod non est damnum seu prejudicium D. regis aut alterius cujuscunque, licet D rex per cartam suam omnes libertates prædictas eisdem burgensibus et hæredibus, etc. per cartam predict. Athelstani prius concessas cederet in perpetuum possidenas.'

"Nevertheless, another writ of the following year, after reciting the proceedings had upon the two former writs, says, that, upon complaint having been made, that the latter return had been artfully and unduly obtained, * ' Nos advertentes, quod hujusmodi libertates absque gravi præjudicio nostro et damno et prejudicio aliorum non possunt concedi hominibus supradictis, præsertim cum dicta villa de nobis teneatur in capite, ut accepimus et custodia ejusdem, nomine custodiæ ad nos et hæredes nostros devlvi, firmaque comitatus prædicti in parte diminui et alia incommoda tam nobis, quam aliis, evenire possent, volentesque eo prætextu super hiis pleniis informari, assignavimus, ect.' The return to this inquisition finds, that Joannes de Audley held this borough of the king in capite per baroniam, contradicts the finding of the former returns in many points, and particularly says,-' Quod nichil eis constat nec constabat de cartâ D. Athelstani dudum R. Angliæ, per quam prædicti burgenses prætendunt sibi et eorum prædecessoribus quasdam fuisse libertates concessas. But with regard to their right in sending burgesses to serve for them in Parliament from the time immemorial, which the two former returns had acknowledged an comfirmed, it says nothing. And we find that they continued to send them uninterruptedly after this time, without any new charter or franchise granted to them, but purely by prescription.

Now, granting that the pretended charter of Athelstan, the existence of which is admitted by the second of these returns, but left doubtful by the first and last, did never exist, yet still these records are of great importance to the question of which I am treating. For, if no burgesses had been sent to Parliament before the forty ninth year of King Henry the third, how is it possible that the Concilium Regis, within fourscore years after that remarkable epocha, viz. in the seventeenth of Edward the third, should have suffered that prince to order an inquisition to be made into the truth of an allegation so apparently false, as that the Burgesses of Barnstaple had enjoyed a right of sending two members to serve for them in all the parliaments of his royal predecessors from the time of King Athelstan? or what evidence could induce jurors, upon the second inquisition before two of the King's Justices and the Sheriff of Devon, to find a fact which the whole county, and indeed the whole kingdom, must have been able to contradict from publick notoriety?

* See No. 3 App. [A.]

The absurdity would be still greater, if the practice of summoning burgesses to parliamentary meetings be dated from the twenty third of Edward the first, as it is by many writers. But the clear inference from these proceedings appears to be, that the custom of sending members from cities and towns to parliaments, or great councils, was then known to be ancient; and the question was, whether Barnstaple was entitled to that privilege, either by charter or prescription. In the final issue we find, that, with regard to the charter, which the burgesses of that town pretended to have lost, sufficent proof was not given; and therefore the other priveleges, which the claimed in virture thereof, were not confirmed or renewed: but this of sending representatives to serve for them in Parliament, was admitted to be good from long usage and prescription.".- *Life of Henry 2nd, vol. 3, pp. 88–91.*

Subsequent writers have also brought forward these inquisitions in support of the position that the Commons formed a part of the Saxon Parliament. From one of these authors an extract shall be given.

"Although we have no direct evidence from records, that the cities and burghs were represented in the witena-gemote, yet there seems to be sufficent probabilities of evidence, that the fact was so. The claim of the borough of Barnstaple in Devonshire, must have considerable weight on our jugement when we reflect on this subject. In a petition to Parliament, presented in the reign of Edward the third, the borough claimed to have been charteres by Athelstan with several privileges, and to have sent, from time immemorial, Burgesses to Parliament. Its claims were investigated by jurors legally appointed, and though from the loss of the charter the other immunities were not confirmed, its right of sending Burgesses was admitted to continue." – *Turner's Hist. of the Ang. Saxons, vol. 3, p. 235.*

Barnstaple is then, beyond controversy, entitled to rank among the most ancient of represented boroughs.

A List of Members, from the twenty third year of the reign of Edward the First * to the present time follows:-

* This is the oldest date of any such record known to exist.

EDWARD I. (began to reign 1272.)

23 Walter le Barnstaple	Durant le Cordwainer
26 Philip Brideport	John Pinumine
28 William de Urye	Bernard le Boghe
30 Thomas Gemyan	Richard Wegg
33 Matthew de Chimenore	Ralph Wylemere
34 Ralph Wynemere	Walter de Pletyngdon
35 Ralph Wylemer	Philip Scherpe

EDWARD II. (1307.)

1 Ralph Wylemer	Matthew de Chynore
2 William Mabbeton	Thomas Yabbeton
6 Ralph Wynnomere	Robert de Meddon
Ditto	Ditto
8 Bernard le Bogh	Ralph Wynnomere
12 Ralph de Winnermere	Thomas Atte Mylle
15 Bernard Atte Bogh	John Surry
19 Bernard Atte Bogh	Thomas Atte Barre

EDWARD III. (1327.)

2 Thomas de la Barre	Vincent Barnstaple
4 Gefry Flittington	Geffry Pilton
5 Ditto	Ditto
6 Ditto	William Scortore
7 Robert Southray	Adam Hakkam
8 John Collacote	Thomas Atte Barre
9 Robert Luctomb	Walter Hugh
9 (At York) J. Collacote	Thomas Atte Barre
10 Geffry Flittington	Thomas Atte Barre
11 Geffry Fardell	Geffry Flittington
11 Robert Aubell	Geffry Flittington
12 Thomas Atte Barre	Thomas Fardell
12 Ralph Winnock	John Aubell
14 Geffry Flittington	Edmund Penny

14 Thomas Atte Barre	Thomas Pole
14 Bernard Atte Bogh	John Coldcote
15 Thomas de Cramthorne	William Atte Welle
17 Simon de Braysford	John Merewood
21 Roger Moliende	Ralph Axbridge
22 Walter Marshall	William Houncote
24 John Mille	Richard Hacche
25 John Mille	Robert de Hacche
29 John Wineauldon	John Bouroun
31 Robert Hacche	Thomas More
34 Walter Fepp	John Burgess
36 Gregory Hakeworthy	William Cary
36 John Hille	Thomas Moore
37 Walter Fepp	John Mille
38 John Aston	Thomas Moore
42 Robert Hacche	Robert Moore
43 Robert Hacche	John Sadlere
45 (Council at Winchester)	William Torner
46 (Parliament at Westm.)	Jno.Coppleston, T. Raymond
47 John Coppleston	John Cross
50 John Coppleston	Thomas Raymond

RICHARD II. (1337.)

1 John Coppleston	Thomas Raymond
2 John Fouk	Alfred Wicke
3 John Coppleston	John Pouke
4 John Cross	John Bidewell
7 Gilbert Newburgh	Henry Wild
8 John Prous	Elias Brace
9 John Gray	John Heuryes
10 John Bradwell	John Anthony
11 Thomas Norris	William Long
12 John Stampford	Roger Rede
12 Robert Cook	Thomas Norreys
15 John Ashton	Robert Combre

17 John Bydewille	Thomas Norreys
18 Thomas Norreys	John Bridwill
20 Robert Napton	Thomas Holman

HENRY IV. (1399.)

1 Thomas Haupere	Walter Spenser
3 Robert Napton	John Gutt
8 John Bakewill	John Hunt
12 Nicholas Bromford	Alured Wonston

HENRY V. (1413.)

1 Thomas Haslegh	John Bromford
2 John Pyne	John Walwayne
7 John Lutterell	Thomas Pyers
8 William Weld	Walter Prideaux
9 John Burley	Henry Sadler

HENRY VI. (1422.)

1 Richard Wode	Walter Atte Barre
2 John Cockworthy	John Moore
3 Thomas Passaware	William Whitfield
4 Richard Thorne	Walter Harry
6 John Trible	John Strete
8 John Cockworthy	Thomas Hill
9 James Gascoine	John Wydeslade
11 John Woolston	Thomas Giffard
13 John Cokeworthy	John Wolston
15 John Bere	Hugh Champernoun
20 Reginald Bertlet	John Clarke
25 Walter Heyngham	William Davey
27 John Dennys	Henry Redwyne
28 John Greech	Richard Truman
29 Thomas Gill	Henry Redwyne

33 John Radford   Walter Ganecoat

EDWARD IV. (1461.)

7 Thomas Stydolf   Reginald Morton
12 Geroace Horne   George Longville
17 John Culme   John Foke

EDWARD VI. (1547.)

1 . . .   . . .
6 . . .   . . .

MARY, (1553.)

1 Robert Carye   Robert Worthe
1 John Pollard   George Ferrys

PHILIP AND MARY.

1 and 2 Robert Apley William Sailsbury
2 and 3 Robert Apley George Stapleton
4 and 5 Richard Skinner William Sailsbury

ELIZABETH, (1558.)

1 . . . .
5 Arthur Bassett   Robert Apley
13 Peter Wentworth Robert Apley
14 Vincent Skinner   Robert Apley
27 John Periam   Robert Prowse
28 Thomas Hinson   Lewis Darte
31 John Hinson   John Dodderidge

35 George Chipping	Richard Leigh
38 Henry Downe	John Delbridge
39 Thomas Hinson	George Perde
43 Edward Hancocke	Richard Martyn

JAMES I. (1603.)

1 Thomas Hinson	George Peard
12 . . .	. . .
18 John Delbridge	Pentecost Dodderidge
21 John Delbridge	Pentecost Dodderidge

CHARLES I. (1625.)

1 Pentecost Dodderidge	John Delbridge
2 Alex. St. John, Knight	John Delbridge
3 Ditto	Ditto
15 George Peard	Thomas Matthews
16 George Peard	Richard Ferris
Philip Skippon	John Dodderidge

CHARLES II. (1649.)

12 John Rolle	Nicholas Dennis
13 John Chichester, Bart.	Nicholas Dennis
31 Hugh Ackland, Knight.	John Bassett
31 Ditto	Ditto
32 John Bassett	Richard Lee

JAMES II. (1685.)

1 Arthur Chichester, Bart	John Bassett

WILLIAM AND MARY, (1689.)

1 Arthur Chichester   Richard Lee
2 George Hutchings   Arthur Champneys

WILLIAM III.

7	Nicholas Hooper	Arthur Champneys
10	Ditto	Ditto
12	Ditto	Ditto
13	Ditto	Ditto

ANNE, (1702.)

1 Nicholas Hooper   Arthur Champneys
4 Nicholas Hooper   Samuel Rolle, jun.
7 Richard Ackland   N. Hooper, Sergeant at Law
9 Nicholas Hooper, Knight Richard Ackland
12 Arthur Chichester, Bart. Nicholas Hooper, Knight

GEORGE I. (1714.)

2 John Rolle   Sir Arthur Chichester, Bart.
5   John Bassett
        on the death of Sir A. Chichester.
8   Sir Hugh Ackland, Bart.
        on the demise of Mr. Bassett
9 Thomas Wetham   Sir Hugh Ackland, Bart.

GEORGE II. (1727.)

1 Richard Coffin   Theophilus Fortescue
8 Sir John Chichester   Theophilus Fortescue
14 John Bassett
on the death of Sir John Chichester.
15 Henry Rolle   John Harris
22 Thomas Benson
on Mr. Rolle's being created a Peer.

23 Sir Bourchier Wrey, Bart.
29 John Harris   George Amyand

GEORGE III. (1760.)

1 Dennis Rolle	George Amyand
7	John Cleveland
	on the demise of Mr. Amyand.
8 John Cleveland	Dennis Rolle
14 John Cleveland	William Devaynes
20 John Cleveland	Francis Bassett
24 John Cleveland	William Devaynes
30 John Cleveland	William Devaynes
36 John Cleveland	Richard Wilson
42 William Devanyes	Sir Edward Pellew
44	Viscount Ebrington
	in the room of Sir Edward Pellew, who resigned.
46 Viscount Ebrington	William Taylor
47 G. Woodford Thellusson	William Taylor
52 William Busk	
on the decease of Mr. Thellusson	
52 Sir M. M. Lopes, Bart.	Sir Eyre Coote, Knight
58 Sir M. M. Lopes, Bart.	Francis Ommaney

GEORGE IV. (1820.)

1 Sir F. Ommaney, Knight	Michael Nolan
5	Frederic Hodgson
	in room of Mr. Nolan.
7 Frederic Hodgson	Henry Alexander

It is well known that in ancient times the bestowment of names was commonly the result of adventitious circumstances; amongst many others, the birthplace or residence, trade or profession, prowess or mental superiority of an individual. Thus, substituting *de* for *le* which is doubtless the proper reading, we have 'Durant the Cordwainer,' (or shoemaker,) so that the sons of St. Crispin may boast that, at least, one of their fraternity has occupied a seat in the senate. The name of Bastable, a very probable corruption of Barnstaple, still exists here.

I have met with three instances of Members being remunerated for their attendance in Parliament.

26. Eliz. "Paid Mr. Robert Prouse towards his charge, being Burgess of the Parliament this year X. XII. VI."

8. Jas. "Paid Mr George Peard, one of the Burgesses in Parliament for this town towards his expences this year, £30."

12. Jas. "Paid Mr. John Delbridge towards being one of the Burgesses in Parliament, £5."

The earliest Petition recorded to have been presented to the House of Commons against the return of a member is dated the 15th of Charles the first. The decision of the House was, "Resolved that Mr. Perd [Peard] is duly elected, and that the election of Mr. Ferris is void." The ensuing Parliament and following year we find both the above named individuals elected, and Thomas Matthews, (Mr. Peard's late colleague,) petitioning against the return of Richard Ferris, but without success. This curious petition and the answer to it are both given at length in the Appendix[B]; they serve to shew in what an arbitrary manner elections were conducted here in former days.

The charges brought against the Mayor, (who as returning officer ought to have been strictly impartial,) that he, by his own acknowledgement, "not being pleased that the petitioners should stand to be elected," had in consequence "invented a new form of election," was not attempted to be disproved; the only reason assigned by his worship for having so cavalierly treated the ex-member, was, his *"not conceiving him so fit"* as the persons nominated by himself, they being *"all of the twenty-four."* *

That there was no precedent for so strange a mode of electing Members of Parliament, is sufficiently obvious, from the sorry attempt to give a colour to the proceeding by quoting the bye law

---

* At this period, it was very common for one or both of the members to be of the Corporation. This was the case in seventeen out of twenty successive Parliaments, beginning with the second of Queen Mary, and in nine out of the seventeen instances, both were of the Common Council.

for the election of the Mayor and other corporate officers.

This is not, the first, or the only instance on record, of Magistrates having assumed the office of Dictators at an election. On three previous and successive occasions, although things were not carried with quite so high a hand as in the case of Matthews, much undue influence appears to have been used.

"1592, 12th Feb.– Mr. George Chippinge, a gentleman of my Lord of Bath, and Richard Leye, were appointed by *common counsell* to be burgesses for this Parliamt. and so returned by indenture to the sherif." It would appear from this account, that the Corporation actually returned these members; they certainly *chose* them.

"1597.– Thomas Hynson and Bartholomew Harris chosen burgesses in Parliamt.; afterwards there was some *misliking* by the Earl of Bath of the choice of B. Harrys to join with Mr. Hynson for one of the burgesses of Parliament, *a new election was made* by the consent of the whole burgesses, and George Peard, of this town, was made a free burgess of the town, and then elected and returned with Mr. Hynson." The Earl of Bath was at this time recorder of the borough, having been appointed to the office in 1596. The burgesses, and especially Mr. Harris. seem to have been quite passive in his Lordship's hands. A seat in the House of Commons was not in those days, *quite* so valuable as at present.

1601.–Edward Hancock, Esq. and Richard Martyn, born in Exeter, and of the Inner Temple in London, are burgesses of the new Parliament for this town of Barnstaple; the first *appoynted* by the Earl of Bath, and the other by Mr. Robert Chichester, of Youlston, who had at this time had the nomination of them both."

The next petition is of Richard Lee, esq., October 25, 1680.

"Resolved that Richard Lee, Esq. is duly elected." May 24, 1685.–"John Rolls, Esq. presented a petition touching the election of [for] this borough." On this, says Oldfield, there was "no determination." Mr. Rolle, as his name should have been written, probably withdrew his petition; he had previously represented the borough.

In 1790, Richard Wilson, Esq. petitioned against John Clevland Esq.; March 14, 1791. The chairman reported the sitting member to be "duly elected, and the petition frivolous and vexatious."

It is a remarkable fact, that of seventy-six votes polled by Mr. Wilson, only one was what is termed a split vote.

The ensuing Parliament we find Mr. Wilson and Mr. Clevland sitting as colleagues, but in the next following, Mr. Wilson again appears as a petitioner, but without success.

1802, "Richard Wilson, Esq. petitioned; but the commitee found Sir Edward Pellew duly elected, February, 1803."

The poll at this election stood thus;–William Devaynes, Esq. 269; Sir Edward Pellew, 190; Richard Wilson, Esq. 84; John Clevland, Esq. 72. The last named gentleman had sat in the seven preceeding Parliaments. "What a falling of was there!"

The next and only subsequent petition presented to the House of Commons against the return of a member for this borough, arose out of the election of 1818, and was preferred by Sir Henry Clements Thompson, Knight, against Sir Masseh Manasseh Lopes, Bart. on the ground that he had obtained his seat through the influence of bribery, practised on certain of the electors.

The proceedings that ensued, form too important an æra in the representative history of the town, to justify my passing them by, and yet so diffuse are the details , that an outline only can be given in a work of this extent.

The attempt of Sir Henry Thompson to remove Sir Masseh Lopes* form his seat proved abortive; but the result of the inquiry instituted by the commitee appointed by the House to consider the petition, was the bringing in of "A Bill for the preventing of Bribery and Corruption in the Election of Members to serve in Parliament for the Borough of Barnstaple, in the County of Devon."

* It is well known that this gentleman was, a few years ago, sentenced to pay to the King a fine of several thousand pounds, and to be imprisoned (although upwards of seventy years of age) for two years in Exeter gaol, for corrupt practices at Grampound; in plain terms, for having purchased a seat for that borough. In 1829, we find Sir Masseh vacating his seat as a member for Westbury, (a close borough of his own,) which is immediately filled by the Secretary of State. *Query* – Did the worthy Baronet retire from motives of gratitude to the Government, for the favour of being fined and imprisoned? I trow not. He did not *sell* his right surely! if he had done so, Ministers must have bought it; and then we should have asked, where is the difference between buying a seat for Westbury of a Baronet, and purchasing one for Grampound of the electors?

This Bill passed the Commons, but was thrown out by the Lords on the second reading,* after an examination by their Lordships of twenty-nine witnesses, principally from Barnstaple.†

The object of this intended enactment, was to extend the right of voting "at every election of a Burgess or Burgesses to serve in Parliament for the said Borough of *Barnstaple*," to the freeholders of the hundreds of Braunton, Shirwell, Fremington, and Southmolton; which would take in the towns of Torrington, Southmolton, and Ilfracombe. It also went to restrict the privilege to such freemen of Barnstaple, "whose right to be so admitted freemen shall have accured to them by birth or servitude, and who shall be resident within the same" borough.

The following extracts from a pamphlet, entitled, "Remarks upon a Bill for altering the right of voting in the Borough of Barnstaple," by the late Michael Nolan, Esq. K.C., will shew the grounds on which this proceeding was founded, as well as the learned gentleman's opinion on the case:–

"It may be admitted, that many of the Electors seem to have conducted themselves with impropriety. But a little calm consideration may shew, that no ingenuity can deduce from the evidence, such enormity of misconduct, as can alone excuse the disfranchisement even of those individuals to whom the imputed practices are legally brought home by the Report.

"The Electors to whom that evidence applies, may be divided into three classes;

"1st. Four, or at most five, who confess themselves to have voted

---

* It has been stated, and it is believed by many persons, that the fate of this Bill was decided by the casting vote of the Lord Chancellor; but this is an error,as will be presently seen. On the 25th of June, it was proposed to put a question to a witness then under examination, which the Lord Chancellor declared to be "irregular and illegal;" a division took place, and the numbers being "for putting the question, 5–against it, 5;" the Lord Chancellor gave his casting vote against the question, which could not then, of course, be put. The second reading of the Bill did not come on till July 7, when, "the order of the day being read, for the further consideration and second reading of the Bill, intituled, An Act, &c."

"Ordered, that the said order be discharged.

"Ordered, that the said Bill be further proceeded in, on this day sevennight."–*See Printed Extracts from Lord's Journals.*

† The expense of the inquiry in the House of Lords, amounted to 1418*l.* 13*s.* 3*d.*, namely, allowance to twenty-nine witnesses for subsistence, loss of time, and coach hire," 752*l.* ; amount of solicitor's bill, including the fees of the officers of this House," 666*l.* 13*s.* 3*d.*– *Ibid.*

in consequence of a previous stipulation that they should receive money* for their votes.–If those persons are to be believed, they have been guilty of bribery; but it cannot be seriously contended, that the existing laws are insufficent to meet their offence, or that the franchises of any other voter should be endangered through their misconduct.

"The 2nd class consists of thirty-four or thirty-five Electors, resident in Barnstaple or its neighbourhood, who received £5 on the Monday morning after the Election.–It must not be forgotten, that the only witness who deposed to this fact, has at the same time expressly sworn, "That he neither directly nor indirectly, previous to the Election, gave hopes or expectations to any voters in the borough of Barnstaple, that any money would be paid to them at any time subsequent to the Election."

"When all previous corrupt stipulation, consideration, or engagement is thus expressly negatived, it must puzzle the most acute lawyer to determine in what the offence consists, or how the receipt of money, under such circumstances, is legally punishable.–When does the bribery or corrupt practice commence? When and how is it completed? What is the essence of the offence? It does not appear by the evidence that the Elector even expected money as a consequence of his vote. But, if he had, without having contracted for it, how can mere expectation be punishable as a civil crime.

"3d. The third and remaining class, whose alleged misconduct is supposed to justify the Bill, consists of Freemen, who, residing at a distance from the borough, received a certain sum from the Candidate or his Agents. The most prominent of those cases is that of some Electors residing in London, who received £20 when they voted for one Candidate; and if a vote was given to two Candidates, each of them paid £10.

"The avowed object of such advances appear to have been–

"1st. To convey the Voter to the place of Election, and back again.

"2d. To maintain him during the time of his absence.

"3d. To compensate for that time which he would otherwise have employed in the course of his trade, or other daily avocation.

---

* Three of these were prosecuted to conviction for the offence, but no judgment has ever been passed upon them, and they still continue to exercise the right of voting.

"It cannot be contended, that the express of conveying the Voters to and from the place of Election may not be fairly and honestly defrayed by the Candidate, or his friends. The university of the practice justifies its necessity. Indeed, it would be easy to demonstrate, that a departure from this established course, would ultimately narrow the popular privilege, and place the representation of the country at the feet of the opulent and the artful.

"2d. Payment of a Voter's expenses at the place of Election, may and possibly does come within the Treating Act; but it is not bribery. If this were otherwise, the acceptance of a glass of ale or a noght's lodging, would equally disqualify both Candidate and Voter, when given before, as well as when give after the writ issues. But it has not hitherto been decided, (and surely never will,) that it is criminal in a Voter to receive, at any time, these hospitable indications of regard, which are only made culpable in the Candidate to supply, after the time of the election is declared.

"3d. To give a fair and honest equivalent to a voter, in recompence of loss actually sustained by absence from those callings, upon which he and his family depend for daily bread, cannot, when taken abstractly, be considered as illegal or immoral.

"It may be or may not be a wise measure, to prohibit the practice as a matter of municipal regulation. But the act is not in its own nature criminal, because no undue influence is obtained over the voter's mind, by the receipt of the same sum for a journey to Barnstaple, which he would otherwise earn during the time by his accustomed employemnt in London.

"The distance of Barnstaple from London is 195 measured, and about 217 computed miles. The Electors must assemble at the place of Poll on the day appointed for the Election, or their coming will be useless. The accustomed modes of conveyance by stage, or otherwise, are adapted only to the regular intercourse between the borough and the metropolis, and can accommodate but a small number of those who are crowding to the Election.

"Calculating the distance and time usually occupied by a contest, voters must be absent during eight or ten days, at least; and unless the means of an immediate return to their several places of residence are insured, expenses must inevitably increase. Can it be said, that £20 is an extravagant allowance under such circumstances. Let the calculator banish every generous and liberal feeling from his mind, yet still can he say that these expenses could be defrayed for much less by contract?

"The corporation is composed of many gentlemen of integrity and fortune. No one has declared to insinuate anything against their honor or their conduct, either at this or any other Election. The great body of freemen stand equally unimpeached, unless vague and unwarranted suspicion is to be assumed as proof. Can it be said, that the corruption was general, when the great mass of Electors are innocent? Are five hundred honest men to suffer because one hundred of their body stand suspected as criminals?"—*p*.7–14.

That bribery exists and is deeply rooted in the borough-system, it would be folly to deny; and how should it be otherwise? if a body be the subject of an organic disease, can the limbs be in a healthy state? Who can say that the representation of this great country is what it ought to be, or, if the mighty change which is wanting in it, were effected, how great England might not become? But how is this change to be wrought? by a reformation; where must this reform begin—at the extremities? no: in the seat of the disease, at the heart of the system.

Let Members have nothing to expect—nothing to hope for—no interest of their own to seek, in going into Parliament; and we shall soon find that none will go thither, but such as have resolved "to do their best for the common weal." Then shall be raised an altar sacred to freedom and the purity of election, on which this species, at least, of bribery and corruption will expire.

Let it not be thought that by making these observations, I wish in the least degree to advocate the barter of the elective franchise, even in the present state of things; far be it from me: this I leave to those who can do it *feelingly*; they, and they only, who can demean themselves by such an act, are fit persons to defend it.

But while I condem such a disgraceful practice in all, I confess I cannot so severely censure the man who labours for his daily bread, and whose education, if haply he has had any, has been too limited to warrant a supposition that he is really aware of the moral degredation to which he submits by taking money for his vote; as I do him who, both by the possession of property and mental attainments, ought to be above such a temptation. I find no palliative, not the semblance of an excuse, for some of those individuals whose names I see recorded in the Lord's Report, as having received five pounds each, after the election.

This affair proved a most disastrous one to Sir Henry Thompson, who was a mere adventurer, seeking advancement in his profession; had he been returned to Parliament, he was not possessed of property sufficent to qualify him for taking his seat. The expenses he incurred in prosecuting the petition against Sir Masseh Lopes, completely ruined him; and soon after that enquiry ended, he became an inmate of the King's Bench Prison, where he is supposed to have died. Some persons who were induced to advance him money for defraying his expenses while here, became minus several hundred pounds.

The election of 1824, which was occasioned by the resignation of Mr. Nolan, on his being appointed a Welsh Judge, was remarkable as having been the first (and only one) ever known, in which the poll was kept open more than one day. It commenced on Saturday morning, at an early hour, but owing to the party spirit that was manifested, so much delay took place in bringing forward the votes, that it was found impracticable to go through with the business on that day, and the poll was in consequence adjourned to the Monday following.

The warmth of feeling that prevailed on this occasion, arose out of a circumstance quite as novel, and still more singular than the above; namely, the entire absence of Mr. Hodgson, the successful candidate, during the whole proceedings.

This gentleman, who had expressed an intention of offering himself for Barnstaple when a vacancy should occur, was at Brussels at the time Mr. Nolan vacated his seat; Mr. Hodgson's friends here, in conjunction with his solicitor and others from London, proposed him, and succeeded in placing him at the head of the poll. No communication was received from Mr. Hodgson until after his election had been secured. That Mr. Nolan ought, in common fairness, to have been replaced in his seat, and that at as little expense as possible, must be acknowledged; he felt the disappointment greatly, because he expected no opposition to be made to his return. Mr. Nolan did not, however, complain of any ungentlemanly treatment from Mr. Hodgson's friends, who would not have come forward until a general election, had not opposition been offered from any other quarter; when this was found to be the case, the field was, of course, open to all. The numbers at this election stand on the poll book as follows:–

Frederick Hodgson, Esq. .	181
Michael Nolan, Esq. . .	153
Alderman Atkins . .	115
The Mayor . . .	1*
	450

Many of my readers must be acquainted with Oldfield's "Representative History of Great Britain and Ireland;" were I to omit noticing what is said in that work of the conduct pursued by the electors of Barnstaple, it would probably be contrued into an admission of the correctness of the author's assertions.

Such a publication should contain no statement but what is founded in truth, nor be made a vehicle for unmerited censure. Had these rules been observed in the present instance, *no consideration* whatever would have included me to attempt doing away any impression, however unfavourable, that might have been made; but knowing the contrary to be the fact, it would be remiss in me to pass it by. I say, therefore,

First,–It is *not true* that "if any one borough in the country is more corrupt than another, it is this." That it has been "corrupt," I seek not to controvert, the fact is admitted; but let the result of the strict scrutiny which the alledged misconduct of the electors underwent in 1819, be compared with that of other boroughs, where similar inquiries have been instituted,† and the illiberality of the assertion above quoted will be at once seen.

Secondly,–It is *not true* that "the expenses of a candidate at a contested election here are from ten to thirteen thousand pounds;" no

---

* On the usual question, "Who do you vote for?" being put to a freeman, named William Marshall, he replied, "The Mayor."

† One instance (amongst many others) may be given, that of Hindon, in Wilts, where, out of 210 persons who polled, 190 were proved to have been bribed.

such sum as the first mentioned amount was ever expended by, or on behalf of any candidate. Elections, from the great number of outvotes, are necessarily expensive; but Mr. Oldfield's information is very incorrect, on that as well as other heads. The expenses of Sir Masseh Lopes's election in 1818, were shewn to have been under £3,050, although he was the member petitioned against on the ground of bribery.*

Thirdly,–It is *not true* that "those of them" (the freemen) "who reside in London, are continually upon the hunt for candidates, under pretence that one of their members is ill, or about to accept a place, or to be created a peer, so that a vacancy is to be expected." That it has been the practice of *an individual* residing in London, when a vacancy occurs, or is likely to happen, to recommend a new candidate to a *select* portion of his brethren, and to use his influence with those persons in favour of the aspirant to the *honour* of receiving their suffrages, is notorious; nor is it doubted, but that the persuasive eloquence employed on these occasions, was backed by arguments of *sterling* weight. This agent, or middleman, does not, however, confine his practice in this way to Barnstaple, where, indeed, he has not officiated of late, but it is equally true, that he renders the same services in other boroughs. It is well known, that there are seat "seekers," as well as candidate "hunters;" it is quite clear that the latter class could not exist but for the former, but where the two meet and coalesce, can we wonder that they succeed in corrupting men in humble circumstances, by holding out to them incentives, such as would induce hundreds to sport with the criminal law of the land, to do that which they conceive to be no harm, and can be none, if kept to themselves?

Fourthly,–It is *not true*, that "a great number of freemen of this place, have received six guineas each, to bear their charges from London to Barnstaple at an election, and that at the poll, every one of them have voted against him, to get their expenses paid over again by another candidate." Instances of robbery in this way, (*for it is nothing less than robbery*,) have occurred certainly, but not the extent stated; one such case, and one only, has come under my own knowledge. Whilst every elector of character and principle, must

* See Extracts from *Lord's Journals*.

deplore the lamentable disregard of both, in persons who can thus disgrace themselves, it is a satisfaction to know, that amongst the freemen resident in London, there are many persons of the highest respectability and honour.

I have thus noticed the four principal charges brought against the electors of Barnstaple by the author of the work referred to; others might be mentioned, but it may be sufficent to say of them, that they are correct in some points, and incorrect in others. The whole isevidently stated upon hear-say evidence, collected, most probably, from prejudiced persons. I have candidly admitted there are grounds for reprehending the conduct of some of my fellow burgesses, but the fact, that part of an accusation is true, and that a few out of the many have transgressed, has ever been held to be no justification of indiscriminate censure.

It is, I believe, not generally known, and the intelligence, to some, may not be of the most welcome kind, that certain transactions are not, because they are past, *forgotten*. I had once laid open before me a book, which, I was informed, contained a register of the name and characteristic of every freeman, in whom a certain peculiar feature might at any time have developed itself

I will just advert, before I conclude this division of the work, to another thing mentioned by Mr. Oldfield in reference to elections here, namely, that candidates have "suffered losses by impositions." Such cases have occurred certainly, nor is it to be wondered at. Do not hunters go in search of prey?

The following story is not the greatest secret in the world:– A number of accounts, amounting in the total to something between *fifteen hundred and two thousand pounds,* had to be paid. An undertaking having been given by a chosen number of persons, that the sum to be furnished them, should be applied in liquidation of these debts, it was promptly remitted through a London banker. The money soon found its way into the hands of one of the individuals, who – forgot! shall I say? how it was to have been applied.

A circumstance of a singular nature, having some connexion with the representative history of the borough, occurred in the reign of George II.; it is already incorporated with the annals of the country, and in one of two works in which I have found it recorded, it is thus narrated:—

"A new species of villainy was invented about this time (1752), viz. that of insuring ships for more than their real value, and afterwards burning or sinking them, in order to defraud the insurers. For this crime, one Lancy, a ship-builder [ship-master], was executed; and Benson, Member of Parliament for Barnstaple, who had been concerned with him, withdrew from the kingdom."

It will be observed, that Sir Bourchier Wrey succeeded to Mr. Benson's seat in the House of Commons, in 1748.* The scheme of destroying the vessel was so ill-contrived, that it might almost have been imagined, that the persons concerned wished rather to court, than to escape detection, the bark having been actually scuttled in Barnstaple Bay, and consequently within sight of the shore in several directions. Mr. Benson, who was the owner of the vessel, had freighted her with woollen goods of the town manufacture, was said to have been riding on the high grounds above the estuary at the time she went down. The unfortunate man, whose life became forfeited to the law, sailed as captain; he was, however, believed to have engaged in the transaction, more at the instigation of others, than as a principal in the infamous fraud attempted to be practised on the insurers. The chief evidence against this deluded felon, was the father of one of our present corporate body, who happened to be on board the vessel. Mr. Benson had been engaged in smuggling transactions, and was the proprietor of an armed ship, called "the Benson Galley," which rendezvoused at Appledore.

NUMBER, QUALIFICATIONS, ETC. OF FREEMEN.

Domeday Book informs us, that there were in Barnstaple at the time of the conquest, sixty-three burgesses; forty within, and nine without the borough, belonging to the King; ten pertaining to the Bishop of Constance, and seven to Baldwin the Sheriff.†

I find no data by which to form an estimate of their number from this period until 1639, when, at a contested election, one hundred

* A discrepance will be observed in the dates, which it is now difficult to explain, it cannot however, be material; that the account is substantially correct, there can be no doubt.
† See *Domsday Extracts*, page 54–56.

and fifty-six voted.* By a poll which I have inspected,

there appears to have voted in

1713,		315	1818,	voted	446
1802,	voted	360	1824,	"	450
1806,	"	375	1826,	"	500†
1812,	"	389			

This statement furnishes (in round numbers) the following ratio of increase in the number of burgesses:–

1088 to 1639,   93, or 20 in 118 years.
1639 to 1713, 159, or 20 in 43   "
1713 to 1802, 89, or 20 in 10   "
1802 to 1812, 29, or 20 in   7   "
1812 to 1826, 111, or 20 in 2½   "

There were made free from

1745 to 1809, . . .702, or nearly 13 per annum;
1810 to May 1830, 397, more than 19 per annum.

Of the last number mentioned, I am unable to furnish any particulars; but of the 702 first named, the following analysis has been drawn from an authentic source:

476 inherited their freedom by birthright,
176 procured it by servitude,
 38 obtained it by purchase, and
 12 received it as a gift from the Corporation.#

Of the thirty-eight mentioned as having purchased their freedom, six paid £10 10 0, five £20 0 0, and nine £21 0 0 each; what was received from the remaining eighteen is not stated, they are merely

* Whenever the number of persons voting at an election is quoted, it must be understood that there was a *contest* otherwise no criterion can be formed, from the number of burgesses polled, of the amount of the whole.

† Great as is the number here stated compared with that preceding it, it would probably have been still greater, but for the circumstance of its being known that the election of the present members was secure. Mr. Nolan, the third candidate, had resigned and left the town; the poll was kept open by some staunch friends of his, but he was so far in the minority, that there was no necessity for persons who wished to avoid the bustle coming forward to give their votes.

I cannot discover that more than one of this number was thus complimented, in return for any service rendered to the *Corporation of Burgesses*. That individual was my own father; who was presented with his freedom in 1789, in consequence of his having given very important evidence for the plaintiffs on a trial at law – "Mayor, Aldermen, and Burgesses of Barnstaple, *v.* Lathy." A statement of the circumstances connected with the trial will be found in a subsequent part of this chapter.

recorded as having been admitted "by fine."

I have not ascertained the number of burgesses on the roll, because from the great proportion of non-residents, which may be taken at two-thirds of the whole, it is impossible to say how many of those on the list may be living. No names are of course struck out, until it was found, in one instance, that out of fourteen persons, (all of the same christian and sirname,) only four were alive. The sum total of freemen must in all cases be calculated at considerably more than the number of voters, as from illness and various other causes, very many must find it impracticable to be at a distance of one, two, or three hundred miles from their homes, on a particular day. There are besides, several burgesses in the sea service, and not a few residing abroad.* The number of absentees, from the best information I can obtain, generally averages at one-sixth.

A considerable accession is usually made to the list of burgesses a day or two previous to an election; on one occasion, July 6th 1802, the unprecedented number of fifty-five sons of freeman were admitted.

The freedom of the borough is to be obtained in four ways; by birthright, apprenticeship, purchase, or by gift from the corporation. The regulations for the admission of persons entitled to their freedom by birth or servitude, are fully stated in the Bye Laws of the corporation, [see App. c. No.7.]

That burgesship is to be procured by *purchase,* must be taken with some limitation. Such was the practice in former times, [see next article, 1599, 1633, 1655.] But subsequently the policy of the corporation has been to make no freemen in this way, but such as are of their own selection. This mode of creating burgesses is in fact only restored to for the purpose if supplying vacancies in the Common Council, which has been done of late, almost exclusively from among those who are not free, nor even natives of the town. The purchase money, or, as it is termed, fine, on such admissions, is twenty pounds, but this is usually remitted, so that the fine is in

* "They were distributed," says *Mr. Oldfield,* "in the East and West Indies, *Botany Bay,* and all over the world." *One* only, a native of London, was transported some years since, and is, I believe, still in N.S. Wales. If an acknowledgement of this fact will afford the *liberal* author any gratification, he is welcome to it.

reality only nominal.

We have seen that during fifty-five years, only twelve persons had their freedom bestowed upon them as a gift; but latterly the favour has been still sparingly dispensed, only one such instance having occurred for the last twenty years, that of Mr. Lee, the architect who designed the Town Hall and Market House.

The right of the Common Council to make honorary freemen without the consent of the burgesses at large, has long been considered doubtful, and more than once publicly questioned. That they do not claim it by charter as "a branch of their prerogative," may be inferred from the following evidence given by the Town Clerk, Henry Drake, Esq. before the House of Lords, touching the election of 1818.

"Have the corporation a right to make honorary freemen?– They have.

Does that depend upon charter or usage? –Upon usage.

Has that always been the usage of the borough as you know? –As long as I can recollect.

How long have you been Town Clerk? – Thirteen years."

I am not aware of any one instance, where this power had been exercised, occurring in the various documents and records which have come under my inspection, nor can I discover any ground for believing that *antiquity*, which alone can constitute *usage* a legal plea, can be urged in support of such a practice. It is in fact, exceedingly doubtful, whether or no, supposing the custom to have prevailed from the time when the borough was first placed under the government of a Mayor and Common Council, the plea of usage can be maintained. The first charter of such incorporation, notwithstanding the antiquity of the borough, it will be seen was only granted about two hundred and seventy years ago. If the number of burgesses thus admitted hitherto be but few, it is only because the corporation have not seen it their interest to admit more; circumstances may arise in which they may find it convenient to do on a large scale, what they have hitherto only done on a small one. The power of admitting strangers to the elective franchise, and other priveleges enjoyed by a body of six hundred men, is too great and too dangerous a one, to be vested in a perpetual, or self-elected committee, of twenty-five of its members.

The immunities enjoyed by freemen of this borough, in all of which honorary burgesses* fully participate, are so clearly defined in the various documents of which I have given copies, that little more than a bare enumeration of them is here necessary.

1st. The first and most important is, that of electing members to represent the town in Parliament: a right purely prescriptive, and therefore not mentioned in any of the charters.

2d. An exemption from fair and market tolls, quay and other dues, both in Barnstaple and throughout England.

3d. Freedom from service on all juries without the borough.†

4th. The exclusive right of serving on juries (coroner's inquests happily excepted) within the borough.

5th. Not to be arrested under a town process of capias at the suit of a non-freeman, until after three court days; eight days' notice to be given of the first court. (See Bye Law, No. 12.)

Last and Least. A saving of two thirds of the usual fee paid to the town crier; burgesses pay two-pence, other persons six-pence. This privelege is, I believe, not often claimed to its full extent.

---

* The term is here quite misapplied, since such persons cannot be said to enjoy "'honour without gain." I have no better reason to give for using (or more properly misusing the appellation) than that all who are admitted to the freedom of the borough by gift or purchase, are distinguished as "honorary burgesses."
† This exemption, in a town situate forty miles from where the assizes and county sessions are held, is a valuable one; it probably belonged in former times to the burgesses only, but is now common to every inhabitant. It is recorded, that on "December 7th, 1688, an Indenture was executed between the Sheriff of Devon and the Mayor of Barnstaple, shewing the Burgesses of Barnstaple to be exempt from juries, out of the borough and parish." This would seem to have been unnecessary, since the charters are so explicit on the subject. *Query* – Was not the exemption intended for the *inhabitants?*

Any freeman may, on paying ten shillings and six-pence, receive a certificate similar to the following:

BOROUGH AND PARISH OF
BARNSTAPLE,
IN THE COUNTY OF DEVON.
(To Wit.)

TO all to whom these presents shall come, or in any wise concern. Know ye, that Joseph Besly Gribble, of Barnstaple aforesaid, Ironfounder, is one of the free burgesses of Barnstaple, aforesaid; by virtue whereof, he, the said Joseph Besley Gribble, not only by prescription, but also by virtue of several charters granted to the burgesses of the borough and parish of Barnstaple aforesaid, by King Athelstan before the conquest, King Henry the First after the conquest, King Henry the Second, King Richard the First, King John, King James the First, and many more Kings and Queens of the Kingdom of England, hath a right to, and is free of, all toll, passage, pontage, lastage, stallage, murage, pannage, piccage, anchorage, quayage, standage, and seagage, of all his goods, wares, and merchandizes, as well in fairs as markets; and of all secular services and customs by our laws, as well on this side the seas as beyond; and that the burgesses of Barnstaple do enjoy all the customs of the city of London. This, at the request of the said Joseph Besley Gribble, we have thought fit to certify under the seal of our office of mayoralty, this seventeenth day of October, in the sixth year of the reign of our Sovereign Lord George the Fourth, by the grace of God, of the United Kingdom of Great Britain and Ireland, King, Defender of the Faith, and in the year of our Lord one thousand eight hundred and twenty-five.

Samuel Bremridge, Mayor.

It is to be observed, that no exemption can be claimed from the payment of dues imposed under the authority of any modern Act of Parliament, unless where an exception has been made in favour of Barnstaple, as was done not long ago, (1828,) in an Act obtained for improving the quay at Bideford, and regulating the port dues; the thirty-third section of this statute enacts as follows:

"And whereas the mayor, aldermen, and burgesses of the borough of Barnstaple, in the county of Devon, claim to be entitled, by several royal charters, to the right and privilege of exemption from the payment of any toll, rate, or duty whatsoever; be it therefore enacted and declared, that this Act, or any matter or thing therein contained, shall not operate either to the prejudice or advantage of any such right or privelege in any manner howsoever."

Every burgess is required on his admission to take the following oath:

" I shall well and truly serve our Sovereign Lord the King, and be buxom and obedient to Mr. Mayor of this borough and parish, and all other his Majesty's Justices of the Peace and Officers in the same, for the time being; and to his and their successors, in all such things as he or they shall lawfully command me to do, or that shall be fitting for me to do. I shall uphold, observe, perform, and keep, the composition, ordinances, orders, and rules, of this borough and parish, to the utmost of my power. I shall give, yeild, pay, and be contributary, with the corporation and fellowship of this borough and parish, in all such matters and things as shall be fit or belongeth for me to do. I shall not by colour of my freedom, colour, bear out, or cover, any foreign person or persons, nor any of their goods, wares, or merchandizes, under me; but justly uphold and maintain the rights, liberties, privileges, and franchises, of this borough and parish, to the uttermost of my power.

"So help me God."

Few, even of the inhabitants, are aware how widely the burgesses of this town are scattered throughout the country. The following statement may amuse some of my readers, and cases may occur wherein the information it contains will prove useful. It is extracted from a poll officially taken at the last election, in 1826.

192

Barnstaple	.	.	168	Devonport	.	.	15
London*	.	.	124	Bristol	.	.	14
Appledore	.	.	12	Falmouth	.	.	1
Bideford	.	.	11	Redruth	.	.	1
Pilton	.	.	9	Weymouth	.	.	1
Torrington	.	.	8	Isle of Sheppey	.	.	1
Braunton	.	.	9	Barnet	.	.	1
Ilfracombe	.	.	7	Newport (Monmouth)	.	.	1
Plymouth	.	.	6	Port Isaac	.	.	1
Combmartin	.	.	6	Lundy Island	.	.	1
Tavistock	.	.	5	Stoke Damarel	.	.	1
Stonehouse	.	.	4	Guildford	.	.	1
Guernsey	.	.	4	Deptford	.	.	1
Swansea	.	.	4	Banbury	.	.	1
Georgeham	.	.	4	Cheltenham	.	.	1
Southmolton	.	.	3	Worcester	.	.	1
Swimbridge	.	.	3	Devizes	.	.	1
Heanton Punchardon	.	.	3	Lyme	.	.	1
Merton	.	.	3	Taunton	.	.	1
Bath	.	.	2	Honiton	.	.	1
Exeter	.	.	2	Glastonbury	.	.	1
Teignmouth	.	.	2	Thorn, Yorkshire	.	.	1
Tooting	.	.	2	Bridgwater	.	.	1
Linton	.	.	2	Ashburton	.	.	1
Fremington	.	.	2	Weare, Somerset	.	.	1
Tawstock	.	.	2	Grinton, Somerset	.	.	1
Newport, Bps.Tawton	.	.	2	Crediton	.	.	1
St. Giles	.	.	2	Cardiff	.	.	1
Shirwell	.	.	2	Exmouth	.	.	1
Berrynarbor	.	.	2	Otterton	.	.	1
Portsmouth	.	.	2	Broadclist	.	.	1
Dublin Castle	.	.	1	Holdsworthy	.	.	1
Sligo	.	.	1	*Chumleigh*	.	.	1
Jersey	.	.	1	*Bradworthy*	.	.	1
Macclesfield	.	.	1	*Clovelly*	.	.	1
Maidstone	.	.	1	*Parkham*	.	.	1
Cambridge	.	.	1	*Warkleigh*	.	.	1
Monkleigh	.	.	1	*Charles.*	.	.	1

* This includes those who reside in the numerous towns and hamlets which surround the Metropolis, such as are usually known as "London votes." To Have mentioned all the places would have lengthened the list greatly.

Highbickington	.	1	*Arlington*	. .	1
Roborough	. .	1	*Stoke Rivers*	. .	1
Chittlehampton	.	1	*Goodleigh*	. .	1
Northmolton .	.	1	*Marwood*	. .	1
Winscot	. .	1			
Abbotsham	. .	1	Total		500
Northam	. .	1			

The places printed in italics, which are principally villages in the neighbourhood of Barnstaple, are distant from it nearly as follow:

Ten	from	1	to	5	miles
Fourteen	.	5	.	10	.
Nine	.	10	.	15	.
Four	.	15	.	20	.

Thus, out of 500 freemen who polled at the last election, only 278, or little more than one-half, appear to have resided in Barnstaple, or within 20 miles of it. The average number of miles which the remaining 222 voters had to travel, will be found on calculation to be about 160; now it cannot be expected that persons should come such a distance to vote at their own cost, it cannot surely be wondered at, that elections here should be expensive to the candidates. That the payment of the travelling expenses of voters is legal, has been decided in the case, amongst others, of our own borough.*

CHARTERS.

The charters which have been granted to the burgesses of Barnstaple, by different Kings and Queens of England, are numerous. It has been shewn, that, at so early a period as in the reign of Edward the Third, the town claimed to have had a charter from Athelstan, the Saxon monarch; but whether or no the claim was a rightful one, must ever remain doubtful.

The first prince, who can be said with certainly, to have conferred immunities on Barnstaple, is Henry the First. No such charter is needed now to be found in the Tower,† nor, as I have reason to believe, among the corporation records; there is, however, ample

---

* Barnstaple case, 1. Peckw, 91.– Nolan.
† I state this on the authority of the Keeper of H. M. Records, John Bayley, Esq. to whose kindness I stand indebted for much useful information.

proof of the former existence of this document.

1158. The charter of Henry the Second, which is given in the Appendix, [D] it will be seen, refers to, and confirms that of Henry the First; as do those also of several other Kings. What were the "right customs" confirmed, or the "bad customs" removed, would now prove an unprofitable enquiry; but to have been privileged, at this period, with "the custom sof London," must be considered as no mean distinction. As the charter of Henry the First to the city of London, which contains and sets forth these "customs" is, in fact, equally descriptive of privileges bestowed on Barnstaple, by the same monarch: and being, besides somewhat curious, I have inserted it at length [E].

Richard the First, confirmed all former privileges, and granted some additional ones; but his having done so, is only evidenced by subsequent charters.

1200. King John, in the second year of his reign, ratified, and extended the benefits conferred on the borough by King Richard and his predessors; see Appendix [F].

1236. Henry the Third, in the twenty-first year of his reign, gave a confirmatory charter.*[G].

Edward the first and Edward the Second granted similar charters, which, as well as the grants before noticed, are all referred to in an inspeximus of Henry

1444. the Sixth, which, independent of its reciting former ones, is more copious and explicit than any which preceded it. [H]

1477. Edward the Fourth, in the seventeenth year of his reign, granted letters patent, in which he recites and confirms the last mentioned charter, but confers nothing additional.

1516. Henry the Eighth, in the eighth year of his reign, and

1547. Edward the Sixth, (supposed in the first year of his reign,) granted similar charters, namely, transcripts of those of their predecessors.

Queen Mary bestowed two charters; one

1554. An inspeximus, dated the second, the other

1556. conferring new and important privileges, in the fourth year of her reign.

* Six years previous (1230). " a subsidy of the 30th part of every man's goods, within Barnstaple, was granted to the King."

This last, which is the first charter of incorporation, and in other respects an interesting document, is given entire in the Appendix. [I]

The following heads comprise the provisions it contains; to which, for the convenience of referring at once to any particular clause, corresponding letters are affixed.

a Preamble, recognizing the government of the town to have been vested in a mayor and bailiffs, "from time, whereof the memory of man is not to the contrary."

b Barnstaple a free borough corporate, of a mayor, aldermen, and burgesses; with perpetual succession.

c Corporation to hold lands in perpetuity.

d To sue, or be sued, at law.

e To have common seal.

f Twenty-four of the "more discreet and honest men," to be capital burgesses; and two of the *"more honest of these,"* to be chosen as aldermen; the whole, with the mayor, to form the common council.

g Corporation to have power to make bye laws.

h Appointment of the first mayor, aldermen, and common council.

i Particular day, and limited hours, for electing the mayor.

j Day on which the mayor is to be sworn into office.

k Provision in the event of the death, or removal from office, of a mayor.

l Nomination, and swearing in of aldermen.

m If aldermen die, or are removed from office, others to be chosen.

n Any capital burgesses dying, being removed from office, or *dwelling out of the borough,* others to be chosen *within eight days* next following.

o Appointment of constables, and other inferior officers; their places also, in case of vacancies, to be filled up in eight days.

p A confirmation of all former immunities.

q Grant of assize and assay, of bread, and wine, and beer.

r To have view of frank-pledge, twice a year.

s A weekly market on Fridays; and an annual fair to continue four days.

t Mayor and corporation to have the custody and government of the persons and property of all orphans within the borough; "the same as in the city of London."*

u "All manner of recognizances, and oblations of malefactors, and transgressors," to be taken by mayor and corporation, to the use of the crown.

Queen Elizabeth also granted two charters; the first dated the second year of her reign (1559), recites that of the fourth of Mary just noticed, which, as well as all preceding ones, it confirms. The last bears date the thirty-eighth year of her reign (1595), and provides for the appointment of a goal, serjeants-at-mace, steward, recorder, clerk of the market, a court of record, aldermen as coroners, &c. As this charter contains nothing material, further than will be found in that which comes next under review, more particular notice of it, is un-necessary.

1610. James the First granted letters patent, in the eighth year of his reign. This charter is a very important and interesting document, a transcript in full† of a translation made at H. M. Record Office, expressly for this work, will be found in Appendix [J], to which the letters appended to the different clauses have reference.

a The preamble; describing Barnstaple as "a very ancient and populuos borough," but with a jurisdiction not extending to the *parish*.

b The town to be "henceforth for ever a free borough and parish of itself;" and the mayor, aldermen, and burgesses, to be a body corporate, &c. "by the name of the mayor, aldermen, and burgesses, of the borough and *parish* of Barnstaple."

c Corporation to have power to hold lands, &c. in perpetuity.

d To sue or be sued at law.

e To have a common seal.

f Capital burgesses to be twenty-five in number, and to be called the common council.

g Corporation to have power to frame bye-laws.

* I am not aware that this benevolently-designed institution has ever acted upon; or indeed, that it is generally known to exist.

† It was my intention, since several heads of this charter have a great similarity to certain parts of the charter of Philip and Mary' to omit printing them; and I had prepared the matter for the press in that form. I cannot however, (with all my anxiety to compress the work,) on re-consideration, see my way clear, in withholding any part of so important an instrument, more especially, as in yielding to a conviction of the propriety of publishing it entire, I do not rely wholly on my own judgement.

h Appointment of first "modern' mayor, aldermen, and capital burgesses.

i Capital burgesses dying, or being removed from office, other to be elected.

j "Mayor, aldermen, and capital burgesses" empowered to "call and hold meetings" of the mayor, aldermen, and capital

burgesses, and to treat, confer, &c. of statutes, articles, &c.

k Particular day and hours when to elect the mayor.

l On what day the new mayor is to enter on his office.

m A mayor dying or being removed from office, another to be chosen.

n Election and appointment to the office of aldermen.

o Aldermen deceasing, or being removed from office, their places to be filled up.

p Appointment of "inferior officers and ministers," with powers to remove them for reasonable causes.

q Any person refusing to take upon himself the office of "mayor, alderman, capital burgess, or other inferior minister," to be liable to imprisonment and fine.

r Two serjeants-at-mace to be appointed to attend on the mayor, &c.

s A chief steward to be elected.

t A recorder to be chosen; "an approved and discreet man, learned in the law – to act by himself, or by his suffcient deputy."

u Mayor, recorder, and aldermen, to be justices of the peace, &c. &c.

v No other "justiciaries" to interfere, but the jurisdiction of the magistrates not to extend to any matter touching the loss of life or member.

w "One approved and discreet man" to be elected, and be clerk of the market.*

x The aldermen for the time being to be coroners within the borough and parish.

y Mayor, aldermen, and burgesses, to elect a "common clerk,

* The standard of weights and measures "was anciently committed to the custody of the Bishop, who appointed some clerk under him to inspect the abuse of them more narrowly; and hence this officer, though now usually a layman, is called *clerk* of the market."

(anglice, the towne clerke, of the boroughe and parishe of Barnestaple)."

z Mayor, aldermen, and burgesses, to "have one prison or gaol," of which the mayor to be the keeper."

aa A court of record to be held every fortnight.

bb Serjeants-at-mace to "execute all pannels of juries, inquisitions, attachments," &c.

cc "Goods and chattels of felons," and all other privileges, jurisdictions, fairs , markets," &c. to be to the use of the mayor, aldermen, and burgesses.

dd None but freemen of the borough to expose goods for sale, &c. &c.

ee Mayor, aldermen, and burgesses, to have, acquire, receive, and posses manors, &c. &c. &c. so that the value of sixty pounds beyond all charges and reprises."

ff Or to dispose of lands, &c. not exceeding the value above mentioned.

gg A confirmation of all former privileges.

hh Nothing contained in these letters patent to prejudice the rights of Howard, Lord Howard, of Effingham, proprietor of the fee of Magdalen.

ii Mayor, aldermen, and burgesses, to use and enjoy all liberties, authorities, &c. without hindrance or impediment. No writ of quo warranto or other process, to issue concerning any matters or claims due before the making of these presents."

1611. King James, in the ninth year of his reign, granted a second charter, which recites many of the clauses contained in the first, and confirms all former immunities.* The only new provision made in it, (as far as I am aware,) is the appointment of "a house of correction for the chastisement of all horlots, Bawds, ****, drunkards, scolds, and other inordinate livers."

In the extracts I have given from Jones's Index to Records," mention is made of a charter having been granted to Barnstaple by

---

* Finding, on enquiry, that the cost of a copy and translation of this document would be twelve pounds; and, after examining the heads of it, seeing no reason to believe that it contained any thing new worth giving to the public, I did not consider that I should be justified in expending such a sum, in addition to the heavy expenses already incurred.

James the Second, [see page 54];* this, of course, became nullity on the abdication of that monarch.

I have thus, with as much brevity as appeared to consist with the importance of the subject, gone through the different patent, by virtue of which the borough of Barnstaple, claims its numerous valuable privileges.† We may reasonably conclude, that most of

* In the extract preceding that above refered to, Barnstaple is mentioned as being in the county of *Dorset*, the copy is a literal one, the error therefore is not *mine*.

At page 55, occurs the following, (also extracted from Jones's Index,) "vide originalia" [see p. 53-54) "for the charters as far as King John." This is also a *correct copy*, but of a very *incorrect* statement. The charter of 2d of Elizabeth, (which Jones makes no mention of,) *is an inspeximus*, reciting as far back as John, but that of 9th James *is not*.

† I must, before I quit the subject of the charters, redeem a pledge which I gave in the preface, relative to the refusal of the corporation to grant me a copy of them. I owe it to my felow freemen, all members of the "body corporate and politic, " designated and known " by the name of the mayor, aldermen, and *"burgesses*, of the borough and parish of Barnstaple."– I owe it to my townsmen in general; and, in truth, to all, whether residents or non-residents, who may be in any way affected by the privileges or exemptions conferred on the Town of Barnstaple by royal charter, to state the circumstances connected with my application for the document in question.

Having engaged in the prospectus of this work, that the privileges granted to Barnstaple by letters patent of King James, should form a part of it: I applied personally, at the summer sessions, 1828, to such of the body corporate as were then present, I believe five in number, requesting to be furnished with a transcript of the charter granted by that monarch. The result of this application will be seen in the following copy of a letter afterwards addressed to their worships, and delivered in the Guildhall, on the day of choosing the mayor.

"Gentlemen,   "August 11th, 1828.

" The purport of this letter is to request that I may be furnished with a copy of the charter granted to the borough of Barnstaple, by King James the First.

It must be in the recollection of some of your worships, that I made a similar application a few weeks since, in which I failed. The decided negative by which my proposal was met, by a part only of the few members of your body to whom it was addressed, ought not in common fairness to be taken as the act of the whole; it is on this ground alone, that I again submit it to the consideration of your worships, and on this day in particular, as one on which it cannot fail to come under the notice of a large majority of the body corporate.

To an observation made by one gentleman, on my former application, that the charter was ' *the private property of the corporation,*' I must, as a free burgess, be allowed to reply, that whilst the custody of the various charters which the borough of Barnstaple has from time to time obtained, is, very properly, committed to the corporation; if there be any ' property' at all in those documents, it is rested equally in the capital and common burgesses; the powers and immunities of the one party, are not more clearly defined than are the rights and privileges of the other.

I am, Gentlemen, most respectfully,
Your Worships' obedient Servant,
J. B. GRIBBLE.
" The Worshipful the Mayor and Corporation of Barnstaple."

On the delivery of the above to the mayor, the court was cleared, and a deliberation took place. The result was, a verbal communication through the bearer of the letter, that *my request could not be complied with.* Why? This question admits but of one answer. The charter contained that, which they were desirous the public should be kept in ignorance of. But ought such an objection to have been allowed to operate? Certainly not. The public have an interest in the charter, (and in all the charters,) and the witholding it from them, savours much more of power than of right. *

200

these were (as the preambles of some signify) petitioned for; and from the number obtained, it would appear, that our forefathers were not backward in preferring their requests.

A copy of one these petitions, had survived the wreck of nearly three centuries. Between the granting of the inspeximus and the charter of incorporation, by Queen Mary, a year and half elapsed; during this time, the mayor and "maisters of the Towne," hit upon a singular, but as it proved, successful expedient, for obtaining the last mentioned document. They petitioned for an extension of privileges, urging as a plea, that *"the towne of Barnstaple is now in greate ruyne and decaye, by reason of the floweing and refloweing of the SEAES comyng unto the saide towne;"* † and that they have there-

---

* It may possibly be said " the corporation knew you could procure it from the Tower;" undoubtedly they did! but they knew also that I must pay for it. If their worships really expected that I should apply to the Tower for the charter, their refusal of it implied a wish to have me incur an *unnecessary expense of* TWENTY POUNDS *and upwars;* but I would willingly acquit them of such an intention, and have besides solid reasons for believing, that they calculated on my not procuring it at such a cost. An individual of the body, not remarkable for taciturnity, almost immediately after the meeting broke up, came to me, and was short-sighted enough to commence a conversation on the subject of my application for the charter, the drift of which might easily be perceived. He took care to inform me, that to have the charter from the Record Office, would cost me the above mentioned sum.

Every *burgess* is interested in the charter;

First, because it confers on him certain privileges, from which others are excluded; it is his title-deed to these immunities, and he had a right to know that he is in possession of all to which he is entitled; but,

Secondly, he is liable also, by the same charter, to pains and penalties, for the non-performance of certain duties therein enjoined upon him; and ought not to be well-informed as to what are his obligations, what the consequences of his failing to fulfil them, and what foundation on which both rest?

There is, however, another class of interested persons, these are *non-freemen*. They find themselves admitted to fewer privileges than their brethren who are burgesses; and at the same time subjected to greater penalties, such too, as they cannot avoid incurring from time to time. And what more natural than that they should know, why they are shut out from the one, and visited with the other!

The refusal of the common council therefore, to grant a copy of the charter for insertion in this work, was unjust – inasmuch as the public are entitled to possess it; it was illiberal – because it was done with a knowledge that I could only procure it elsewhere at an enormous expense; it was impolitic – since it furnished food for suspicion as to the motive for withholding it; and lastly, it availed nothing – since the public are, notwithstanding, in possession of it, and the charter will not be the *less read,* because their worships would fain have prevented its being read at all.

† Due allowance must be made for the hyperbole employed here. We are not to suppose that the town was really in the state mentioned in the petition; with respect to the greater part of it, we know this to have been impossible, (at least from the cause assigned,) nor is there any ground whatever for believing that it was the case in any degree. The only injury of any magnitude recorded to have been done by the tide, occured more than fifty years after this, see "river." the following ludicrous description of the river, penned about the same time, will, I conceive, in the absence of all proof that Barnstaple was then in the condition stated, fully justify the conclusion I have drawn. It occurs in a document referring to the bridge, which is signed, among others, by the mayor and town-clerk, both whose names appear in the list of capital burgesses in the charter which they petitioned for. *"A great, hugy, mighty, perylous, and dreadful water,* named Taw. The foresaid *violente, daungerous,* and *jepardous stream,* wherein salte water doth ebbe and flowe *foure tymes in the day and night."*

fore been enfforced to erecte and make, at their own proper cost and charges, a new wharff or key, conteynynge in length, fyve hundredd yardes and more, whiche dothe ande will stand them at the leaste fyve hundred marks." (£333 6 8)

I shall find occasion to remark on the extent of the quay here stated to have been built, when the present quays come under our notice.

ORIGIN AND INTENT OF CORPORATIONS.

The origin of these political institutions is of very remote antiquity, being ascribed by Plutarch to Numa Pompilius, second King of Rome, who, in order to bring the two factions, into which the city was divided, into peaceable contact, classed the citizens in different communities; granting to each the power of making laws for its internal government.

The term corporation is thus defined by Cowel: " a body politick, authorized by the King's charter to have a common seal, one head officer or more, and members, able, by their common consent, to grant or receive, in law, any thing within the compass of their charter: even as one man may do by law all things that by law he is not forbidden; and bindeth his successors as a single man binds his executors or heirs.

"As all personal rights die with the person, it has been found necessary, when it is for the advantage of the public to have any particular right kept on foot, and continued, to constitute artificial persons, who may maintain a perpetual succession, and enjoy a kind of legal immorality. These artificial persons are called bodies politic, bodies corporate, or corporations: of which there is a great variety subsisting, for the advancement of religion, of learning, and of commerce."– *Blackstone's Com. vol. 1. p. 467.*

"When a corporation is erected, a name must be given to it; and by that name alone it must sue, and be sued, and do all legal acts.

"After a corporation is formed and named, it acquires many powers, rights, capacities, and incapacities. Some of these are necessarily and inseparably incident to every corporation. As, 1. To have perpetual succession. This is the very end of its incorporation: for there cannot be a succession for ever without an incorporation. — 2. To sue or be sued, implead or be impleaded, grant or receive, by its corporate name, and do all the acts as natural persons may. — 3. To purchase lands, and hold them, for the benefit of themselves and their successors; which two are consequential to the former. — 4. To have a common seal. For a Corporation, being an invisible body, cannot manifest its intentions by any personal act or oral discourse; it therefore acts and speaks only by its common seal. For, though the particular members may express their private consents to any act, by words, or signing their names, yet this does not bind the corporation; it is the fixing the seal, and that only, which unites the several assents of the individuals who compose the community, and makes one joint assent of the whole.— 5. To make by-laws or private statutes for the better government of the corporation; which are binding upon themselves, unless contrary to the laws of the land, and then they are void. — *pp* 474 5.

"Any particular member may be disfranchised, or lose his place in the corporation, by acting contrary to the laws of the society, or the laws of the land, or he may resign it by his own voluntary act."

A corporation may be disolved, 1. By Act of Parliment, which is boundless in its operation — 2. By the natural death of all its members, in case of an aggregate corporation. — 3. By surrender of its franchises into the hands of the King, which is a kind of suicide. — 4. By forfeiture of its charter, through negligence or abuse of its franchises;* in which case the law judges that the body politic has broken the condition upon which it was incorporated, and thereupon the incorporation is void. And the regular course is to bring an information in nature of a writ of *quo warranto,* to inquire by what warrant the members now exercise their corporate power, having forfeited it by such and such proceedings." — *pp.* 484-5.

Corporations are divided by the learned author just quoted, into *aggregate* and *sole, ecclesiastical* and *lay;* which last are subdivided into *civil,* (embracing, amongst others, that of *"a mayor and comonality,* bailiff and burgesses, or the like,") and *eleemosynary.*

"Corporate bodies," remarks a modern author, when speaking of

---

* Among other things,"if they neglect to choose officers, or make false elections." — Tomlin's Law Dictionary.

town corporations,* "have not in general proved themselves the most exact and faithful trustees. The reasons of their first constitution, the grounds which recommended them to royal patronage, or to the aids of private generosity, have long since ceased. They arose into existence when the power of the Barons formed a great opposition to that of the crown, and almost overwhelmed the influence of the people. To encourage trade, and to be a check on the barons, were communities incorporated, were strengthened by liberal endowments, and the influence derived from charitable trusts. The advance of commerce, the opulence it has diffused over the country, and the power politically granted by Henry VII. to the barons to alienate their estates, [together with the more enlightened state of society,] have long since superseded the necessity of such an intermediate body between them and the crown. The evils arising from a body of men being separated from the community, united by an independent interest, or divided by mutual jealousies, the abuse of power connected with such constitutions, and the advantages which a corrupt minister may derive from their influence, have been, in many instances, too visable to escape the observations of the most careless."

Having made these preliminary remarks on Corporations in general, I come now to treat of

THE MUNICIPAL BODY OF BARNSTAPLE.

The Burgesses of Barum were first created a body politic by charter of Queen Mary [see Appendix I.] in 1556; which also appoints a select number to be chosen from time to time out of the whole, who are to form a common council, or perpetual committee of management, for conducting the affairs of the community; this association is called in common parlance, THE CORPORATION. In this, its popular sense, the term is of course used throughout this work; but every burgess knows, or ought to know, that, although excluded from any share in the direction of the concerns of the corporation, he is, notwithstanding, as really a member of the body, as any one of the common council.

I am in possession of some voliminous extracts from the Town

* Toulmin.

204

Records, referring, not only to the affairs of the body corporate, from the period of its formation, but to the accounts of the receivers, bailiffs, and mayors, for more than two centuries previous.* The whole is by far too diffuse to be inserted at length, and contains besides, with slight variations, numberless repetitions; a selection is therefore given with the addition of other matter obtained from different sources, partly, as some of my readers will perceive, from Philip Wyot's Register. Such incidents, however, only are transcribed, as have reference to, or are taken from the accounts of, either the corporation or their predecessors, the mayor and bailiffs of the borough.

EDWARD II.

1320. An indenture made at Coventry between the Bishop of Exeter, "Lord of the Manor of Tawton Bishop," and the "Maior and Comonaltie of Barnstaple, for building a Mill upon a River dividing the Bishop's Land and the Land of the Town of Barnstaple, upon their equal charges."

The same or following year, "A grant was made by the Bishop of Exon to Maior and Comonaltie to erect Mills on the Water of Portmore."

The village of "Bishop's Tawton," (distant from Barum two miles,) has a substantial claim to the appellation bestowed on it, having been the first Bishop's see in Devonshire. *Wersanus,* who was consecrated anno 905, "had his see at Tawton, where having sat one year, he died, and was buried in his own church there." Putta, second Bishop of Devon, also resided here, but being slain on his way to Crediton, the episcopal chair was removed to the latter place. The "River" alluded to above is a small stream which divides the Parishes of Tawton and Barnstaple; besides the "Waters of Portmore," it was also called formerly "Forche's Water," it is now known as Cooney Gut.

RICHARD II.

1389. "John Okryg, Receiver.—Received for IX Butcher's Stalls within the Market House,* LXXs. VIIId. and XXXVIIs IVd. for VIII others."

* The transcripts, which bear evident marks of authenticity, I should judge to have been copied from corporation documents, from fifty to seventy years ago; by whom, I have not the least idea.
† The Term used in the Accounts, which are in Latin, in both the above entries is literally *Butcher's House,* the meat market was then under the Guildhall, and was probably enclosed.

"Paid the Bailiff of the Town for the Free Gabel of the Butcher's Market, II¼d. and the Prior of Barnstaple for the same xvIIId."

1394. "Received IVlb. IIIs. for Butcher's Stalls, and no more; there are three stalls empty."

"Paid the Warden of Saint Nicholas, for the Market House, IVd.; and Thomas Rashleigh, for the House aforesaid, IIs."

1397. The King granted "Letters Patent under the Great Seal, to Probi Homines (good men) of Barnestaple, as security for the repayment of forty marks," (£26 13s. 4d)

This, even if reckoned at its value in modern money, which must be taken at not less than £500, was an unroyal sum for a prince to borrow, but Richard accepted many loans at this time of only five marks. A list of the different contributors has been preserved in Fœdera. "Of 193 Subscriptions, there were 78 by the Clergy from £1000 by the Bishop of Winchester, down to £3 6s. 8d.; 40 by Gentlemen, from £400 down to £3 6s. 8d. ; and 70 by "Cities and Towns."* London contributed 10,000 marks; Bristol, 1,200; of the 70 places mentioned only 32 furnished more than 50l.; of the remaining 38, some lent but 6l. 13s. 4d.

HENRY VI.

1437. "Received for Butchers' Stalls CIXs IId. Paid xIIId. for one plank bought of Will. ate Clyff for Butchers' Shambles, (Shamell. Carn.) and VI½d. to Rog. Nychol for 1 day mending Shambles."

1452. A Commission under the great seal was issued 12 November, granting a "general pardon to the Maior and Burgesses of Barnestaple."

Query.—Had they espoused the cause of the Duke of York ? it appears probable that this was the case, and that they obtained forgiveness on promising to return to their allegiance.

1454. "Received VIl. xIVs. VId. for Butchers' Stalls. Received for the same by the day xxxIIIs. VIIId."

"Paid for carrying planks from Pilton to the Butchers' Market, and VId. for mending tressels, and IId. for repairing stalls before the feast of St. Michael."

1458. "Received VIl. VIs. VId. for Butchers' Stalls of different people having fixed places; and VIs. from others who are not constant."

"Paid to the Wardens of the Long Bridge, IIs.; to John Bather for

* *Macpherson, from "Faedera v. 8, p. 9."*

In the *Rot. Pat.* it is recorded of this Monarch, that he borrowed in the first year of his reign, *"infinite thousands of pounds,* from certain merchants."— *Ibid.*

206

11 days' work, x*d*.; and xx*d*. to Thomas Kellygn, for IV days."

This five-pence per day may be reckoned nearly equal to three times the amount of wages earned by an ordinary mechanic in our day; few carpenters in this town get more than two shillings, or two shillings and three pence.

EDWARD IV.

1461. "Received VIII*l*. XIII*d*. for Butchers' Stalls of divers persons this year, and VI*s*. for others not fixed."

1467. The following is an exact copy of an extract taken from the Receiver's Accounts. It is the first entry in which I find any mention made of the Fish Market. "7th William Gybbe R.–Et de VI*l*. VIS. V*d*. recept. de Redd. Stall. Carnific. intrinsec. locat. diversis hominibus ad Cert. per ann. Et de xxi*l*. vs. r. de Reddit. extrinc. Carnific. et Stall. i Pisc. jutstra [juxta] strand de diversis hominibus in cert. hoc Anno cum Sham. Carnific. et Mercer."

1474. "Paid John Hume keeper of the shambles, III*s*. VIII*d*."

1477. In this year's account, there is a charge of VI*d*. paid for wine to the Burgesses of Pilton, to hear the new charter read."

A charter was granted in this year, but what could be meant by the Burgesses of Pilton, I am quite at a loss to conjecture.

RICHARD III.

1483. Allowance to the Mayor for the expenses of his office, V*l*.VI*s*. viiid.

Received for Meat and Fish Stalls, in all IX*l*. IX*s*. ix*d*.

HENRY VII.

1496. "Et de IV*l*. XVII*s*. I*d*. recept. de stall. Carnific. diversis hominibus locat. Et de VI. VII*s*. I*d*. de stall. Pisc. Carnific. ad Mercerorum non locat. per ann. sed Casual. Et de XIII*s*. IV*d*. de exit nunud."

This is the first account of any receipt of tolls, except from butchers, or sellers of fish.

1497. "Et xs. solut. Ball. pro exit nund."

1499. "Paid to the Man of the Clerk of the Market IV*s*. x*d*. Also for making clean of the Shamells against Easter xviid. Also for 3 doz. trussels iis."

HENRY VII.

1528. Total Amount of Tolls xiiil. xs. vd.

This is the last year in which the extracts I am transcribing from, are made in Latin; from which it is to be presumed, that in this reign the practice of keeping the Corporation accounts in that language, was discontinued.

EDWARD VI.

1548. "Received vil. xs. for opening of Shop Wyndows of them who are no Burgesses of this towne, this yeare."

1551. "Received viiil. vs. of all the Butchers and Fishers, for their Standings there this year."

"Paid vis. viiid. in the pension of John Ellis, keeper of the shamells this year; and xvid. to him for making clean of the Flesh and Fish Shambles this year; and iis. for 4 pair of Trussels for the Butchers.

1552. "ixl. iis. vd. Received of all the Butchers and Fishers, for their Standings and Coverage there this year."

"Paid expenses at Mr. Mayor's House, and Mr. Goddesland's, upon the Clerk of the Market, iiis. ; and paving the Market Place xiid."

MARY.

1553. "Received for the Stalls of the Butchers and Fishers, xil. xvs. iid."

"Paid Mr. Uncke, Clerk of the Market, for a reward, vis. viiid."

PHILIP AND MARY.

1554. "Note, the Fish Shambles have Coverings."

[This year was enacted the following strange but ludicrous regulation, in which especial favour was shewn to members of corporate bodies:–

"Whoever shall wear silk in or upon his hat, bonnet, girdle, scabbard, hose, shoes, or spur-leather, shall be imprisoned for three months, and forteit £10, excepting Magistrates of Corporations, and persons of higher rank. And if any person, knowing his servants to offend against this law, do not put him forth of his service within fourteen days, or shall retain him again, he shall forfeit £100."

    – *Stat.* 1. 2. *Philip and Mary, c.* 2.

This prohibition continued in force forty-nine years, when it was repleaded, as being injurious to trade.]

    1555. Mayor's Allowance, VIII *l*.

    1556. In this year, being the first of the existence of the Corporation, the cups and pots at present used for balloting the Mayor and Aldermen appear, by the following inscription on one of them, to have been made, "Potts and Balls, MDLVI."

The cups present nothing remarkable in their appearance; they are of wood, and are furnished with shallow brass pans, in which are holes through which the balls drop.

    1557. "Item to the Bailiffs of the Town, for the Fee-farm Rents of the Market and Fairs, XIIs. VId."

ELIZABETH.

    1558. "Received of the Revenues of the Standings and Coverages of Butchers and Fishers, with others, XIIII*l*. IIs. XId. And of Richard Sweet, for his standing in the Shamells, VIs. VIIId."

    "Paid to John Ellis for his Fee, VIs. VIIId. Item to the same John for making clean of the Shamells, XVId."

    "Paid for the Fee Farm of the Market, VIs. VId."

    1559. "Paid for Sealing Wax for sealing obligations concerning the mortgage of the Manor of the Borough." (No sum.)

    "To the Bailiffs of the Town, for the Fee Farm of the Market, IIs. VId."

    1564. Produce of the Penny-halfpenny, IXl. Vs. Paid to the Clerk of the Market by Mr. Mayor's Commandment, XIIIs. IVd."

    1565. "Paid to the Bailiff of the Lord of the Borough there, for the Fee Farm of the Market, xs."

This year the Corporation purchased the Manor.*

    1567. Produce of penny-halfpenny, VIl. IVs.

    "Paid Clerk of the Market, Xs. Item to his man for a reward, by

---

* Since the publication of the former part of this work, I have been favoured by a gentleman residing in a distant part of the county, with an *office copy* of the deed of conveyance of the Manor from Mr. Marrow to Sir John Chichester, which recites a grant of the lathstedes or Tolls by Henry VIII. and another by Phillip and Mary. This curious and interesting document is given in Appendix [K.]

Mr. Mayor's Commandment, IIs. Item for wine at his being at Mr. Mayor's, xd.'

1568. The Bailiffs "Richard Delbridge and Roger Cade" in their accounts "ask allowance paid to the Lord's Officers of the said Borough, for all the rents due to him, as it was lately agreed between Sir John Chichester, Knight, deceased, Lord of the said Town, and the Mayor, Aldermen, and Burgesses of the same Town, xIvl. xvIIs."

This is the first mention made of payment of the manor rent; the sum subsequently paid varies, but is usually £14 18s. 6d. "The Fee-Farm rents of the town" also continue to be charged 10s. as before.

1569. Mayor's Allowance, XIIIl. VIs. VIIId.

1570. "The Bailiffs do account for XIIIl. XVIIIs. Id. received for toll, custom, and other duties, accustomed to have been paid to the Bailiffs there in the Market Days, commonly called Penny-halfpenny, and for VIl. VIIIs. IVd. received for the rents and free gravel" (called in another entry free gammon) "of the Lands and Tenements there to the use of the Lord of the said Borough, as appeareth by the Rental thereof. and for LIIs. received for the Farm of the Common Oven there this year. And for IIl. VIs. Xd. received for the perquisites of the Castle Courts to the use of the same Lord this year. And for IIs. VId. received for the Farm of the Bridge Pool this year. And for VIs. received for expenses of six Castle Courts holden there this year."

1572. "This year Vl. VIs. VIIId. was allowed towards the charge of Mr Mayor, for the expenses of the Castle Courts."

"Paid for a Bow and Sheafe of Arrows, Ol. Vs. IJd."

Purchased by the Receiver to the Corporation. Query—For their Worships to shoot at butts with on the Castle Green ?*

---

* Such a supposition carries with it nothing in the least derogatory, to a body corporate of the sixteenth century. Stow, in his Survey of London, relates that the Lord Mayor, Sheriffs, and Aldermen, used to go together into the fields, to join in this sport with the citizens. Many of our Kings, down to the time of Charles I, also amused themselves with this pastime; it was written of Henry VII. in an old ballad,—

> "See where he shooteth at the butts,
> And with hym are lordes three;
> He weareth a gowne of velvette blacke,
> And it is coted above the knee."

Various enactments have been made in favour of archery. One act of parliament in the reign of Henry VIII. obliged every man to exercise with the bow, aged or infirm persons, ecclesiastics, and judges, excepted.

Produce of Penny-halfpenny, xv*l*. ix*s*. iv*d*.

1583. Received "of Simon Moungey, for setting his posts by his house, xIId."

1584. Paid "To the Searchers of the Market, for their Fee this year, Iv*s*. and paid to them more, vi*s*. viii*d*.

<small>This is the first notice taken of such an office as searcher of the market.</small>

"Paid to John Blackmore, for keeping a Light in the Shamells, for his Fee, xiii*s*. iv*d*. and paid to the Clerk of the Market, for a reward, xiii*s*. iv*d*."

<small>This "reward" varies in amount, but never exceeds the above sum.</small>

1590. "Paid Philip Francis to gather Toll in the absence of John Knill, one of the Bailiffs, on a Friday, he being at Chumleigh on the Town's Business, vi*d*."

1591. This year the Corporation first enjoyed the luxury of Glass Lights in the Guildhall. "This Month of Maye was the Enterclosure, and the little house downe, the same hall enlarged, and the wyndows of the same glassed."

Mayor's Allowance, xx*l*.

1595. "xI Dec. John Norrys, a Burgess of this Town, brought a new Charter, which I [the Town-clerk] red in English before the Maior and most part of the Comon Council."

"The 2 Aldermen, the 1st Coroners in Town, Thomas Skynner, a common Counsel man, elected clerke of the Market according to new charter, and sworne, &c."

1596. "In the Christmas there was delivered unto his Honor Earl of Bath, by Mr. Maior and the Aldermen, a patent under their common seal of the office of Recorder of this Towne, wche his Honor did willyngly accepte."

"Mr. John Trender, vicar of this Town, inveighed in his sermon [query, on Christmas-day ?] against the Alderman for not coming to Church, whom, he said, were like 2 fat oxen, that they wd not hear when X [Xst for Christ !] call'd unto them, but drew backwards, and drew others from X. The Aldermen were present, but unseen. For this, and his indecent behaviour on being questioned for this abuse, he was committed to warde for want of surties: the E. of Bath next day discharged him.— William Collybear, Senior Alderman, who during his office in a Justice, was bound over by E.

of Bath and Mr. H. Ackland, to appear at the next Sessions for behaviour. The like was never heerd before.'

1598. "18 Aug. Richard Beaple, elected a common Council man in room of Roger Cade, who was put out for that he dwelld out of this Towne above one year."

Up to this time there is a regular salary "paid to the Keeper of the Shamells," but, "beginning of Dec." says one of the Chroniclers of the day, "the old shambles under the Guildhall, the posts, and all were pluck'd down, and the placed pav'd, and a new bench set by the North Wall, and so tis appoynted for a walkying place."

The Receiver also takes credit this year for cash, "Paid for plucking down the flesh shamells, for new benching and paving the same room," &c.

The meat market now held in the street, probably because there was not sufficient room for stalls under the hall.

1599. "Certain inhabitants of this town, which are no burgesses, viz. Pentecost Dodderidge, John Welsh, William Darracot, John Garret, being rated for buying and sellyng and opening the Shopwyndows, to the ancyente custome of this Towne, refused to pay their rates, which the Receyver of this Towne took distress from them for the same, and thereupon the said Dodderidge sent immediately for a writ and arrested the Receyver, who presently put in bail for his appearance at the Michaelmas term.'

The statement is a long one, and given in the prosing style of the writer would prove tedious.

"Recusants" having "combyned together to try the matter with the Towne, two of them, "Dodderidge and Darracot appeared" before the Earl of Bath, who "sat at the Guildhall with Mr. Maior, the Aldermen, and *whole Counsell*." The hearing ended in defendants, who were opposed by "Mr. Thomas Leigh, one of the learned Counsell of this Town," being commyted to Prison," whilst "his Honor" the Earl of Bath and his worshipful colleagues *went to dinner !* "After dinner sentence was gyven against them." Dodderidge to go to prison until he *found sureties for his good behaviour,"* besides being himself bound in cl. [100l.] to appear before the *Lords of her Majesty's Privy Counsell,* the VI of Feb. next following. Darracot to remayne in prison VI days, and be bound to his good behaviour, and to appear at next Assizes for Devon.

Welsh also "appeared, and standing stout he was commyted to prison." Darracot and Welsh were after six days' imprisonment "dismyssed, but by what reason," says the writer, "I knowe not, so that the most part of this mettal in the refyning went off in smoke."

On the twenty-sixth of January, 1600, (in order to be *in time* on the sixth of February,) "Mr. Thomas Leigh and Bartholemew Harris began their journey toward London on Towne's behalf," and on the twentieth of the same month "returned with the order that Dodderidge should pay the xxs. he was sette, and to be made a Burgess of this Towne, paying xl. as others doe." "Recusant" Dodderidge afterwards became Mayor of Barnstaple.

The proceedings in this affair, and that of the unfortunate vicar, [see below,] serve to shew us in what a pompus and arbitrary manner, magisterial proceedings were conducted here at this period.

1600. "Monday, the XIX day of Maye, the new Kaye upon the Strand, almost in the midst of the other Kay, was begun to be buylded."

"XI August.—On this day William Collibeare, who had been Maior IJ tymes of this Towne, for that he had for the space of IJ yeres and above dwelt out of the Towne, and now set out his house in Towne where he dwelt, and so no hope of his returne to Towne agayne, and was dismyssed of his room in the common Council of this Town, and disfranchysed, &c. and immediately thereupon William Shapleigh was elected in his room, and sworne."

"Order in Towne that the Maister and other of the common Counsell shd hang out Candles and Lanterns at their doors in dark nights in the wynter till IX O'clock."

It cannot be disputed then that the Corporation of 1600 were, besides being the "more discreet and honest," the most *enlightened men in the borough.*

"Friday, XIV Nov.—Mr. Maior and Aldermen going upon their search in the evenings as usuall, found the vicar, Mr. Trynder, in John Williams' House, being a Tipler, wh other company, and having amongst them a pipe with a tabor, a little after nyne; and because Mr. Trynder wd not come down to Mr. Maior from the chamber upon commandment, and for other his - - - - - - - - - - - - was commyted to warde, where he abode till Mornynge followyng;

in the mean time he sent a lamentable letter to the B'p of Exeter, advertising his Lordship that he was wrongfully commyted and without any cause; whereupon his Lordship wrote to E. of Bath, who commanded the Maior to come to him, which he did at Tawstock – a day appoynted for hearing – vicar released – Sunday following he preached ıȷ hours, being a cold daye he weryed all his audience. Tuesday following it was heard and determined that there was just cause for his being detayned, and to be bound for his good behavr.; yet Mr. Maior, by his Honour's persuasion, and his own concern, remytted to my Lord of Bath's censure."

"In hillary [term] Mr. Trynder, the vicar, was p: cepted to appear before the high Commissioners in matters ecliastical, to answer Articles exhibited by Richard Ley, [a barrister,} (but by the instance of Mr. Maior and others of this Towne,) so there is no likelihood of good government while such Dissensions last."

Mr. Trinder certainly set his parishioners a sorry example, in associating with such company and for such a purpose; and his conduct would have formed a proper subject for the serious consideration of the Diocesan; but his committal to prison under the circumstances here narrated, presents no very favourable specimen of "good government" in those days.

"Paid to the Lord of the said Borough xıv*l*. xvııı*s*. vı*d*."

It is somewhat extraordinary that up to this date, Sir John Chichester should be so styled in the Corporation Accounts. Thirty years subsequent to this the entry is much the same. "Paid to Robert Chichester, Heir of the Lord of the Manor."

1601. "The Sessions and the Law court of this Towne were kept this yere the ııȷ day of Maye. Mr. John Delbridge, Maior, being absent in Northamptonshire or London, on business;–no Dinner kept at Maior's House for Maisters, Steward, or otherwise; towards expense of Dinner the jury had each vı*d*. and the Towne Clerke vııȷ*d*. This order hath no father to any man's remembrance now living, but sprange up of the infected Ayr, lately amongst us. The Jury, save one, dined at William Clyverdon's, and adding to their allowance spent ıx*d*. apiece, and had good cheer, wine, &c. &c."

The writer (the Towne Clerk) expresses himself very feelingly on the loss of his dinner, but he appears to have "pocketed the affront" and taken 8*d*. as an equivalent for a seat at the Mayor's Table. We learn from the above incident that antiquity may be pleaded for the custom (still practised) of giving dinners to the Corporation, Juries, &c. at the Sessions.

During the long reign of Queen Elizabeth, the Penny-halfpenny varied from 6*l*. 10*s*. 0*d*. to 22*l*. averaging about 13*l*. 8*s*. 0*d*. per annum.

JAMES I.

1603. "6 June.–The Masons began the walls of the New Works, and that day the great Doors of the Gate were sat up."

It is not now, I believe, known, what these "new works"* were, or for what purpose they were intended, when first erected; but they were probably nothing more than a walled enclosure projecting into the river; the warehouse and dwellings have, no doubt, been added since. A powerful oppositiion was raised to this encroachment (as it was then declared to be) on public rights, and kept up (as will be seen) for five years, but availed nothing. The ground of complaint, namely, that an injury had been done to the river, was certainly a most futile one, but it is to be lamented, that instead of being occupied by buildings, it is not avaliable as a wharf, the want of quay-room being at times very much felt."

1604. "Nicholas Gay, Surveyor of Strangers, his fee VI*s*. VIII*d*." This officer is in another place called "Beadle of the Beggars."

1605. "6 June was an Admiralty Court held in this Towne, by the Earl of Bath, Vice Admiral, concerning the new work, because he said Earl doth much envy against it. Mr. Nicholas Wyat, as Judge of the Admiralty, kept the Court. Mr. Bridgman's Son being Notary. Mr. Hugh Ackland and Mr. Hinson sat in the Court in the Morning, and My Lord of Bath in the Afternoon, when the jury gave the verdict, which was, that it was a noysence to the passage of Boats and Barges. Mr. Bar. Harris, [Mayor when the building was begun,] John Norris, James Downe, were all 3 indicted for building the new work, supposing the same to be an annoyance to Boats."

1605. "12 Aug.–James Woodrough was elected Maior. Before the Election he prevailed on 15 to promise that they wd not ballot for him; but they disceived him, and he was chosen. He was *absent*, and had appointed his voice and ball unto Robert Honey."

A precedent for voting at the election of a Mayor, by proxy.

1606. "John Sallisbury elected a common Counsell man in the room of William Shapleigh, who dwelleth at Bideford, and did dwell out of this Town above one yere and a day, and therefore

* The row of buildings called Quay Place, situate nearly opposite the Custom House.

losing his Freedom and Lib'tie that he had in Town, he was likewise dismysed of his Roome."

"Paid to John Darracot for wood to burn stinking Flesh in the Market, vI*d*."

This year action was brought against the Corporation respecting a House claimed by Sir Robert Chichester. "This last Somer Assize came down for Judges, L^d. Chief Baron and Justice Tanfield, at wh^{ch} Assize Sr. Roberte Chichester had a Trial ag^t. the Towne, for Gorton's House by the Castle Green, wch passed wth Sr. Robert C. by reason of three witnesses wch he brought, that did sweare that the house did stand in the dike, altho' it be most apparent that the same is far withoute, and so verefied at the Trial by the Oths of vIJ credible witnesses."

1607. "Last Lent, Mr. Harris and Mr. John Delbridge of the Towne, by order and consent of the Town, exhibited a petition before the Lords in Counsell, contayning a Complaint of the Maior, Aldermen, and Burgesses, against Mr. Hugh Acklande, a Justice of Peace, of divers enormities, injuries, and ill demeanours, by him daily comyted, against the state and government of the Towne, although he had always among them good entertainment. Of which the Lords takying due consideration, wrote Letters to the Judges at Assizes to bind over Mr. Ackland to appear before their Lordships, or end the controversies. The Judge receyving the Letters, Mr. Ackland was called before them, and he told thiose that were present that the Counsell had a great regard for the Town of Barnstaple, that it had done divers services as well to the late grasious Queen as to the present most excellent Majesty, in receyving of souldiers often times sent to Ireland, and therefore their Honours were to uphold the rights [of the Town] then Sir John Ackland desired that he might have the hearing of the causes in difference; which the Judge objected to unless the Townsmen agreed thereto; but by the earnest request of Sr. John Ackland, Mr. Maior and his Brethren commytted the whole cause into Sir John Ackland's hands, upon promises that he and his brother would always hereafter bear good affection to the Towne, and doe any thing for their good, the cause proceeded no farther. Same tyme the new worke was in question, and the Judges havyng receyvd

Letters from Lord of Counsel, were in a milder censure and conceyt therewith there was Mr. Hinson and Mr. Richard Ley, and divers others followed the cause against the Town, and were earnest to [eager for] Judgement, which shewd a plott drawn of the new worke; the Judge being commanded to stop Judgement, and to take a view of the work; Viewers were appoynted by consent of all parties. Sr. John Ackland, Sr. Amais Bampfield, Sr. Thomas Browne, Sr. Henry the elder Knight, Mr. Anthony Monck, Mr. Arthur Harris, and Mr. William Carie, to view and to certify at next Assizes.

"2 July.–The Knights and Gentlemen about the new worke met the greater parte, and did see the Barges pass the bridge with sand, who passed safe except one who struck on purpose. The Gentlemen were Sir William Stroode, Mr. Seymour, Sir Amias Bampfylde, Sir Thomas Browne, Sir Henry Rolle, Mr. Anthony Monck, Mr. A. Harris, and Mr. W. Cary; after view sat in Guildhall and heard the Bargemen; they spoke as they would for they were not sworne. Much ado at this Assize about the new worke, the adverse party procured the Judge to give his verdict against it, but it was not then entered.

1608. "A new Indictmt. against Mr. Bar. Harris, John Norris, James Downe, and others, about the new work."

"At this Assize xxxi day of Julye, the Judges sat at one bench, exceptions argued by Counsel; the Judges went to Launceston, and the Indictees ordered to meet at Sr. John Ackland, the Sheriff's; after conference had about the matter, Mr. Richard Harris, Maior, Mr. Richard Beaple, Mr. Bartholemew Harris, and others, met at Crediton; the Adversaries, Mr. Hinson, Mr. Hugh Ackland, Richard Ley, one Pearse and Attorney, Bar. Berry, Thomas Loverynge, and others, but never a Lawyer, [Barrister] among them, for so the Judge determined. The Affair opened by Riley, but interrupted by the Judge, as he thought he did not tell his tale as *theyse* he shouold, and scarce any sentence that came from the Judge, but was a shock to him and the rest of the company, and little said of Mr. Delbridge's side, savyng that one Pugsley, a poor boteman, was examyned concerning that one Davy of Tawton had sworn before the Jurie at Exon, that by reason of this new worke, he could not pass the Bridge by nyght as well as before; whereas, in truth, Davy passed the Bridge by nyght many times since, and Pugsley in companie, as Pugsley there constantlie affirmed before the Judg, which the Judg did very much consider, and then well thought that the matter was carried against the Town of malice and displeasure; so thare they award that this Busyness should go no farther. Then Richard Ley informed the Judge, that by reason of this new work, the Channel there was become so deep, that Horses could not pass over to fetch sand as they used."

It is, perhaps, necessary to state, that the Quays did not at this time extend so far out into the river as at present. The new work projected, I conceive, wholly beyond them, and must therefore have had, at certain times of the tide, a sensible effect on the current of the river, by causing it to set off in that particular part, which, however, could have little to do with the passage of boats through the Bridge. We find that previous to this period, a sand bank lay abreast of the town, but now Counsel *complains* that the channel is become deep.

1610. "XL*s*. rec^d of Jno Webber, for a fine imposed upon him, for refusing to execute the office of a searcher of the market, he being elected to it."

Charges for wood to burn "corrupt" and "unwholesome" flesh occur frequently about this time.

1612. "Rec of John Venner, of Ilfordcombe, for selling nails in the market, XVIII*d*."

Mayor's Allowance XXX*l*.

1614. "Paid Searchers of the Market their fee VI*s*. VIII*d*., and for their *shoes at Christmas* VI*s*., and paid for watching of Flesh hung up at the High Cross in Time of Lent, II*d*."– Query, why ?

1615. "Paid for a Glove that was put out at the Fair IIIJ*d*."

It is still customary to put a stuffed glove out of the Quay Hall Window on the day preceding the Fair.

1617. "Received for fishing in the Bridge Pool, IV*s*."

About the year 1800, the Corporation received 21*s*. per annum, for this Fishery, but their right to do so was questioned. It has been for many years open to every body, but owing to the scarcity of Fish it is worth nothing to any body.– It was put up at the last Auction for letting the Town Farms, but no one bid for it.

"Paid to John Davy for making a note of the price of corn every market day, II*s*. VI*d*. Besides their Fees and Shoes, a charge is now made for the Searcher's Dinners, IV*s*."

1620. "Paid Mr. Richd Delbridge for the fee-simple of a house and Garden, which is now made to a prison *for the Corporation.*

So wrote their Worship's Receiver; but I do not find that any of the Body Corporate ever became inmates of the building thus stated to have been set apart for their use.

1622. "Mandatory Letter from King James to Mayor and Corporation, to elect Earl of Bath Recorder."

We know the noble Earl to have been Recorder previously, but not having been on good terms with the Corporation, he had, most probably, been dismissed from office in consequence. Disputes must have run high before a Peer could have been thus treated by a Corporate Body. It does not appear whether or no his Lordship was reinstated, but we do not find him again acting as Recorder.

1622. "Paid for Candles to hang by a Bull that was not beaten IId."

The Brutal practice of bull-baiting was not only tolerated here formerly, but enjoyed by the bye-laws of the Corporation. (See Appendix C.) The hapless animal here mentioned appears to have been left for a night in the public streets, preparatory to his being baited.

The penny half-penny toll during this reign in one instance produced but 9*l.* 18*s.* 4*d.*, in another 21*l.* 6*s.* 5*d.*; the average was 18*l.* 7*s.* 6*d.* "

CHARLES I.

1628. "Novr 17. Key, Keyhall, Crane, and Yarn Beam let to Wm. Palmer and Nichs Delbridge, at 86*l.*, with the following stipulation: if plague comes into Town and Markets decay, Payment only to be made to the time of it's entrance."

1629. The same Tolls as above mentioned "taken by Richard Delbridge, at 100*l.* 10*s.* 0*d.* on the same condition as last year."

24 Novr Dr Symes, a learned Physician, engaged by Mayor and Corporation to be resident in Town, and give advice gratis to the Poor at 20*l.* per annum for two years, to be paid out of Town Stock, if not raised by subscription."

1630. About this time, (for I cannot state the precise date,) a fine of 100*l.* was imposed on the Corporation by the Star Chamber, whiuch they were allowed to pay by yearly instalments of 5*l.*

1632. The Market Tolls were first farmed out; Rent 91*l.* In the Receiver's Account this year, credit is given for the extraordinary sum of " XXIV. III. V. recd for Fines and Amerciments at the Court days.

1633, Oct. 19 "Resolved that no stranger be made free, under fine of v*l.* except he marry a Burgess's Daughter, then to pay XL*s.*

It is well known that in Bristol a man becomes free of the city by marrying the daughter of a burgess; but the notice of a custom so nearly approaching to it having existed in Barnstaple will be new to most of my readers. Any person, it appears, might have purchased the Freedom of the Borough for five pounds, but in 1600 the customary sum was ten pounds.

A charge occurs in the Bailiff's Account of "13*s.* 7*d.* disbursed to Watchmen on the Market Days;" and in that the Receiver, of 2*s.* to make stakes, and to those that drove the stakes at the measuring out the Town waste;" also of "35*s.* for surveying the Town and clearing the Shambles."

1644. "Memdm that the . . . day of october in the morning, Charles Peard being Maior, absented himself, and would not appear too yeaid up his office; whereupon he was dismyssed from his Maioralty and fined by the Town, and Henry Mason elected, who within three hours surrendered his Maioralty again unto Adam Lugg, who was sworn Maior then presently for the same year ensuing. 3 Maiors in one day."

1646. Septr Mr. Ferris was elected Maior on the Marsh on the higher side of Konybridge, by Ballets."

This was owing to the plague which raged in the Town. The ground where the ceremony took place is that known as Port Marsh, adjoining the Turnpike House.

1648. "Recd from the Butchers, for Fines from them, I. XVI. O" Average of Market Tolls during this reign, XVIII*l.* II*s.* O*d.*

CHARLES II.

1649. "Paid the pavior for paving the Cawsey without Northgate, 10*s.*"*

"Recd of Butchers for winding [query weighing] their meat, 2*l.* 9*s.* 4*d.*"

* " Precious morcean this to transmit to posterity," exclaimed the writer of a review a few years since, on quoting some trivial record from a topographical work! I am quite conscious how trifling the above and many other extracts given in this work are *in themselves;* they are registered here *only* because they serve to elucidate some subject of interest relating to former times; for example, the ancient state or names of the public ways of the town, situation of particular buildings, customs of the inhabitants, &c.

"Rec^d of John Webber for License to make a Dunghill in Southgate, upon the Town Land, [alias in the street]."

"Licensed" nuisances were formerly very common here; some of these still remain, and others have been either modified or improved, at a considerable expense to the public. The Front of a Public House in Litchdon, (the Golden Anchor,) for the "setting forward" of which 1s. per annum was paid to the Corporation, was, on its being taken down a few years ago to be rebuilt, set back again by the owner, in consideration of 20l. paid out of the Town rates. The opening from Cross Street to the Quay would not, until heightened lately at "Town's Cost," admit of a Carriage being driven under it. For the privilege of "building over this passage, and resting timbers of the Quay Hall," an ancient rent of *sixpence* is paid. "For setting the walls of her (the owner's) House further into the Street near the Cross," (the greatest nuisance in High-Street,) 4d.

Many other instances of a similar kind might be furnished, but the following entry on "a Rent Rolle" of the Corporation Lands crowns the whole:– "Executors of Mr. George Parminter, for erecting a Little House on the Town Waste behind his house, *sixpence.*" This "Town Waste" is an open and constant thoroughfare called the "Drang," and the *Cloaca* stood but a few feet from the *front windows* of the residence of one of the principal inhabitants. It was removed about twenty years ago.

1650. "Maior to have xxl. out of Profits of Quay, and the rest to go towards discharging debts, &c."

1651. Produce of Quay dues 56l. 10s.

This reduction may doubtless be attributed to the plague.

"Mr. Thos Dennys, Maior, was prosecuted and ousted of his Maioalty for being chosen Captain of the Traind Bands, the Town being then for the King when he was chosen Captain."

1652. "Paid for new making of the Maces and new Cases 22l." "Novr 9, Henry Mason admitted a Free Burgess, and excused Fines for using his Trade and opening Shop Windows on the following singular conditions,–that he keep in repair the Windows of the Guildhall and the little windows over the belfry."

1653. "Paid to several Watchmen three Market Days to attend the Market in Budport, 4l. 10s."

"Phillip Wyott chosen Deputy Recorder."

"James Welsh's Bequest borrowed."

"July 30, Paid Chas Hearson for setting up the Tome Stone on the Key, 2l."

A large stone so called, used (prior to this date) to stand on the quay, from the surface of which it was raised to a proper height to be used as a writing table by merchants and others. Why it was called the *Tomb Stone* cannot be discovered; but it has always (as far as known) been so designated. Query,– was the stone thus termed from having been fixed in a similar way to the covering of a sepulchre? or, was it not rather known, originally, as the Town Stone? The substitution of "Tome" for Towne or Toune, (both old ways of writing Town,) is very supposable.

1655. Produce of "Key hall," 52*l*. 10*s*.

Ditto of penny-halfpenny, 16*l*.

"The Sand Ridge lying next above Barnstaple Bridge let for 6*s*. 8*d*. per annum."

This must have been previous to the embankment being made on the opposite side of the river; no such accumulation of sand can now take place in the situation described, which must have been on the Barnstaple side, or the Corporation could not have let the ridge. Query,– had they any right to let it at all?

"27 Feby Sir John Copplestone (Sheriff of Devon) chosen Recorder."

"27 Feby No man shall be hereafter admitted a free Burgess for 40*s*. on the plea of having married a freeman's daughter, his Fine be arbitrary."

The Corporation acted wisely in abolishing the custom of offering a dowry with Freeman's Daughters; the practice existed about twenty-two years. Whence was their authority for making such a provision derived?

1656. "Novr 13, Keyhall, &c. let for 61*l*. The Corporation to maintain the taking of Duties, &c."

This year the Market Tolls, which for the preceding fifteen years had been collected by the Bailiffs, and had considerably fallen off, were again let for 25*l*. 12*s*. with the same Stipulation as above mentioned, which implies that payment of some or all of the dues had been resisted.

"Augt 12, Phillip Wyot, Deputy Recorder, dismissed for imbecility of mind and body, and age."

1657. "Anthony Palmer and John Palmer not to pay interest for 100*l*. on account of good services to Town by William Palmer."

"Penny-halfpenny set for 23*l*. per year."

"Toll of Fair Markets [for cattle] except of quick cattle, which the Town Clerk for the time being hath used to take to his own use in Fair Time, 7*l*. 15*s*."

The present Town Clerk has not been used to exercise such a privilege, nor was he aware, until I mentioned it, that the custom had ever prevailed.

1658. "No Receiver – the Maior chose Daniel Cary; but the Town would not admit of him, he being a turbulent seditious Fellow."

The office of Receiver to the Corporation appears to have been of much greater note formerly than at present. The name and appointment of this Officer is frequently mentioned.

"Thomas Davy, a tallow-chandler, made Town Clerk."

1660. "Recorder Copplestone dismissed from office, he having presumed to appoint several officers, and set at liberty persons from Prison without consent of the Mayor and Aldermen."

1661. "Ordered that the Parish of Fremington do pay Toll for what they buy in the Market."

There had been a lawsuit between this place and Barnstaple, a year or two previous.

"Corporation new modell'd according to act of Parliament. There was removed Mr. Nicholas Cooke, and Mr. Paige placed in his room; Mr. John Cook, and Mr. Xpher Hunt in his room; Mr. Richard Harris, and Mr. Ackland is his room; Mr. Thos Cox, and Mr. Lewis Rosier in his room; Mr. Thos Bipeland, and Mr. Thos Coles in his room; Mr. John Rosier placed in Mr. Cox's office of Town Clerk."

It is well known that Charles II. obtained from his Parliament authority to displace such members of Corporate Bodies as had rendered themselves obnoxious to the Government; but it would appear that two of the above-named individuals refused to submit and lay aside their robes; and also that another member of the Corporation, not mentioned at first, fell under the King's displeasure, since there was issued in the following year—

1622. " 19 Feby – A commission under the great seal for the removal of Nicholas Cook, John Cook, and Bartholemew Biss, for refusing to subscribe to the Act for regulating Corporations."

1664. "– Seldon no Maior by the Act, not having recd the Sacramt in one year before chosen."

1665. April. Resolution passed respecting poor's monies. 1665. " 7 March.– Sr John Chechester, of Rawleigh, was sworren Recorder. Mr. Bassett being put into that place by the Comrs for regulating Corporations, but not approved of by the Corporation, on the 15 May brought a mandamus to shew cause why he should not be admitted Recorder. Mr. Bassett overthrone by a trial at Exon."

"14 Octr–Mr. John Palmer sworn Maior. There was great discution betwixt the Majestrates; Seldon, Ackland, Paige, and others, forsaking the Bench, and refused to sit at the Maior's table, which gave the Maior occasion to keep no Court Dinners that year."

1666. "July .– They warnd a hall to chuse new Majestrates, at which time there was great decsntion began by Mr. Seldon, Ackland, and Paige, concerning their pretended seniority; Ackland, Lewis Rosier, Chr. Hunt, T. Colles, and Gilbert Paige, being put in by the Com^rs would take place before those which had been antient Majestrates, nay, some of them Maior many years before, but the Corporation would not allow it, the new Company protested against it. A deed of insolency, and in former days wd have been punished, either by disfranchisement, or binding them over to answer at the Assizes, for that their contempt of the Power granted by the Charter; but the Maior p'ceeded, and Thomas Harris was elected a Common Councilman, in a room of Mr. John Horwood."

"Mr. John Greade, Maior. Greade was Sergt at mace many years, and now the Serjt sits in the Maior's place. And is not this topsy-turvy."

1667. "Lawrence Gay, inhabiting twelve miles from Barnstaple, requests to be displaced from being a Capital Burgess. Is displaced accordingly."

1670. "Ordered, that the Churchwardens be directed to ripp off two Locks set on two seats in Isle [Aisle], called the Maister's Isle; if any action be brought, to be defended by the Corporation. Ordered also, that the Churchwardens be empowered to set for life or years, any room or place in the backmost three seats on the north-east side, but not more than three in each seat."

1672. " 30 Nov^r —Time out of Mind there hath been three Market days for Flesh, Tuesday, Thursday, and Saturday, which have been constantly used and kept as only days for sale of flesh; but several Butchers, being Burgesses, have of late brought and sold on Fridays, the Market day for selling corn and other sort of victuals, flesh excepted, after being warned by the Maior, two Burgesses were disfranchised."

What could have induced so strange an enactment, and such an arbitrary enforcement of it, conjecture is set at defiance to conceive; particularly as Friday was the day, and the only one appointed by *charter,* on which Market was to be held. If one day of the week was more desirable for the sale of *"Flesh"* than another, surely it was that on which the "seller of corn and other sort of victuals" were here to buy it. It so happened, that four years after this a Butcher filled the office of Mayor. Query,– was there any *rivalship* in the case?

1674. "Jany 18.– Ordered, that a prosecution be commenced against the waterbailiff of Ilfracombe, for making a free burgess pay dues."

1677. "Maior, Aldermen, and Common Council, appoint Christopher, Duke of Albemarle, to raise Trained Bands, to choose their own officers, and receive orders only from the King or his Deputy."

1684. "Aug. 26.– The Corporation served with a Writ of Quo Warranto; they surrendered their Charter in September, but had it restored to them in October."

A heavy fine was doubtless exacted as the price of its restoration by the despotic Charles; but even then Barnstaple fared no worse than others, and much better than some other Corporation Towns. Not even the City of London was exempt from being deprived of its Charter, (in 1683,) "which was only restored," as one of our historians observes, "upon terms of the utmost submission."

Average produce of Market Tolls during this reign, 18*l*. 8*s*.

"Paid the Serchers of the Market, and for a Treat to the Clerk of the Market, 1*l*. 5*s*. 0*d*."

Not the *Mayor* now of course, as is the case now.

In the margin of the "Extracts from the Accounts of the Receivers, Bailiffs, and Mayors, from which I am now culling, is written, under this date, "First Maior's Accot"

JAMES II.

1687. "Jany 29.– An order in Council was made for removing the two Aldermen, the Deputy Recorder, eight of the Common Council, and the Town Clerk, from their offices.{

1688. "May 18.– An order in Council for the removal of all the Corporation," in consequence of their "perverse temper in disputing his Majesties mandate."

"Money for 3 month's assessment for the penny-halfpenny, Key Hall, Crane, and Yarn Beam, 1*l*. 10*s*. Do 2*l*. 5*s*. Money paid John Brock, Junr for half the Pound Rate for the Key Hall, &c. 2*l*. 0*s*. 9*d*."

This is the first mention of Taxes on the Town Dues.

WILLIAM AND MARY.

1689. The following Corporators, being two short of the full number, took the Oath of Allegiance to William and Mary at the Revolution: "Richard Barnes, Mayor; Henry Ravening, Hugh Marshall, Alderman; William Westcombe, Arthur Ackland, John Palmer, Richard Sailsbury, John Stevins, William Wakeman, John Peard, John Blake, John Prideaux, Christopher Hunt, Nicholas Cook, Thomas Seldon, James Kimpland, James Kimpland, Jun., John Hunt, Jeffery Bagelhole, John Law, Thomas Harris, George Fairchaild; Edward Rosier, Town Clerk; William Rayner, Master of the Free Grammar School."

When, after the landing of the Prince of Orange in Torbay, his proclamation was brought to Barnstaple, a number of the inhabitants assembled for the purpose of learning its contents at a house, now the Fortescue Arms; but so great and so general was the dread which the recent executions of Monmouth and his adherents had inspired, that for some time no one could be found bold enough to publish the contents of the instrument to the meeting; at length one of the company took courage, and jumping on a table, read the proclamation aloud.

1689. March 24.– The Bye Laws of the Corporatiion agreed on.

These "statutes and ordinances" have mostly grown into disuse, aome are acted upon, and others might be with good effect, but the code will bear revision, as will be seen by the abstract of it given in the Appendix [C.]

"A fine of 20*l*. imposed of Richard Cole for refusing to take oaths and execute the office of Capital Burgess."

1693. "Paid one year's Tax to the King of 4*s*. in the pound for the Farms of the Town, [Quay Dues, &c.] 6*l*. 10*s*."

1694. "Fearing a Quo Warranto, the Corporation again surrender their Charter."

1696. "Paid Palmer and Pope for the Pound Tax, 4*l*. 10*s*."

1697. "Paid the King' Taxes for the 3 Quarters, 13*l*. 10*s*. 1/2*d*."

1689. The following important "order in council" was made by nineteen of the Corporation, "That no buns be given away by the Maior, nor any allowance be made to him."

"Recd of Mr. James Sloley, Serjt Hawkes, and others, for the Key Hall, Penny-halfpenny, Crane, and Yarn Beam, and laying Dung,

&c. 118*l*. 12*s*."

"Scavenger's Salary, 1l. 8s."

1699. The above dues "and Fishery for one year, 112*l*. 1*s*. 6*d*."

Recd one year's Rent of the Wast Ground at Litchdon, 1*l*. 1*s*., and for the Wast Ground at the Castle, 1*l*."

1701. "Mr. Thos Harris' Mayoralty, building the Mill-end Quay cost 56*l*. 4*s*. 71/2*d*."

On the erection of this Quay, a Stone was fixed on it bearing the following inscription: "This if the Union Quay, Thomas Harris, Mayor, 1701." The stone is now on the Top of the Leaping-stock at the end of the Long Bridge; I have not been able to discover why the Appellation "Union" was applied to it.

Penny-halfpenny, where mentioned separately, averaged about 26l. in this reign.

ANN.

1702. (Mayor's Account.) "To Cash for the whole Farms, 131*l*. 16*s*."

"Paid half a yeare Land Tax for the Farms, 4*l*. 10*s*."

1708. "Jacob Palmer not having taken the sacrament after notice of election to office of Capital Burgess, was fined 40*l*. Present, the Mayor, Aldermen, and most of the Common Council. The said Jacob Palmer was afterwards sworn into office."

The fine here mentioned appears to have been remitted — not so the *Penalty* — that of being compelled to *profane the most holy ordinance ever instituted by God for the use of man, to a secular purpose.* That such unhallowed Laws as the Test and Corporation Acts should have ever existed, will be a disgrace to England as long as the Memory of the statutes shall live.

1711. "Recd for wast Ground at Litchdon, 1*l*. 2*s*. and for the fishery, 1*l*. 6*s*."

1713. "Octr 2.– The Rt Hon. George, Lord Lansdowne, Baron of Bitheford, Treasurer of her Majesty's most Honourable Privy Council, and also one of the Burgesses of the Borough and Parish, was duly elected High Steward thereof, in the room of the Rt Hon. Christopher, Duke of Albermarle, (his Lordship's Kingsman,) deceased."

"Octr 10.–John Bassett, Esq. was elected Recorder and sworn."

Average of penny-halfpenny in this reign, about 34*l*.

GEORGE I.

1715. Scavenger's Salary, 2*l*. 10*s*.

1718. Waste Ground at Litchdon, 1*l*. 13*s*.

1719. "Paid four quarters Pound Tax, 10*l*. 10*s*.; Land Tax, Poor Rates, &c. 4*l*. 15*s*. 10*d*." First mention made of Poor Rates.

"Barnestaple ʃs." ⎫
1724. "Septr ᵉy 26th. ⎭ Ordered by the Mayor, Aldermen, and Capital Burgesses, in the Guildhall, in Common Council assembled, upon Complaint made of the grievous abuse and damage done to the Tables, Forms, Pewter, plate, and other goods of the Corporation, by lending them out to the divers people of the Town. That the said Corporation Goods be not from henceforward lent out by the Mayor for the Time being, or used by any person whatsoever, (other than for the Mayor's use or for the Corporation,) without the consent of the Mayor, Aldermen, and Capital Burgesses, or the major part of them in Common [solemn] Council assembled." Signed by the Mayor and 15 Com. Coun. 1727. "At a Court of Common Councell, held &c. on Wednesday the 19th day of July, anno Dom. 1727. It is ordered and agreed as follows: That the Mayor, Aldermen, and Capital Burgesses, doe now proceed, pursuant to notice given, to an election of a Capital Burgess of this Borough, in the Roome of one Thomas Harris, lately ousted by Judgement of Law, and that the Corporation doe stand by the legality of such election, at the expence of the said Corporation, if any question should arise thereupon."

Signed by the Mayor and 14 Com. Coun.

Thomas Harris was not it seems finally "ousted;" he was Mayor in 1773.

1727. "At a Court &c. held this second day of Octr Anno Dom. 1727, it is ordered as follows: Whereas, a writ of Mandamus issued out of this his Majesty's Court of King's Bench, bearing Teste the 21st day of June last past, directed to the Mayor, Aldermen, and Capitall Burgesses of the Borough of Barnstaple, commanding them to swear and admit Richard Snow into the office of one of the Capitall Burgesses; it is ordered that the suite on such writt of Mandamus be defended with effect at the cost and charges of the Corporation, and that a warrant of Attoruney, under Seal of the Corporation, be given to Mr. Lewis Gregory, Town Clerk of

Barnstaple, their Attorney, to defend such suite."

This year also the Corporation had to defend an action brought against them for a Trespass on the Castle Hill.

Average of Penny-halfpenny in this reign, 31*l*. 3*s*.

GEORGE II.

1730. "Building the Wall across the Gutt from Mr. Tucker's Limekiln to Lichdon, and making the SQUARE, and planting the Trees, and paving the Road, cost 230*l*. 6*s*. 2*d*.; the money was partly paid by the Corporation, and partly by a subscription made by the Inhabitants."

This money was certainly well laid out; but few persons in the present day would have fixed this Improvement at so comparatively recent a date. It surprising that a spot of ground surrounded by Houses as it has been for centuries previous to this time, and of necessity a considerable throughfare, should have been so long suffered to remain *a muddy beach, with an open sewer running through it.*

1738. Portraits of the following individuals were placed in the Guildhall: "Henry Beavis, Mayor; Robt Incledon, James Steed, Clerk, Richard Newell, Thomas Harris, Paul Tucker, John Fraine, Roger Chapple, Charles Wright, Marshall Swayne, William Lantrow, John Swayne, Robt Luck, Clerk, Master of Grammar School, (on South side of Hall) George Wickey, Mayor elect; Richard Merwin, Deputy Recorder; Charles Velley, John Gayton, Samuel Thomson, Clerk, Vicar; Samuel Berry, Richard Knight, Alexander Webber, Matthew Roch, John Baker, Robert King, Mark Slee, Charles Marshall, Nicholas Glass, George Score, Henry Wickey, Henry Drake, Gregory Anthony, (on the North side)."

These were not, of course, all belonging to the Corporation, but the whole, with one exception,* were presented to that body by the sitting Members for the Borough. The likenesses, which were considered good ones, were painted by Hudson, who was supposed to have been assisted in the work by Sir Joshua Reynolds, who studied under Mr. Hudson.

A most ridiculous and utterly unfounded story has gone abroad, that the Corporation had the choice given them of having their portraits taken, or the river

---

* That of the Rev. Samuel Thomson, who died in 1734; this divine had been very highly respected by his parishioners, and his relatives being at this time in possession of his likeness, it was placed in the Town Hall by the Corporation, as a mark of respect to his memory.

Taw made navigable for vessels of larger burden than have ever been able to pass it. I have taken some pains to ascertain if there was any ground for charging them with so monstrous a folly, as that of preferring their own pictures before so great a public benefit, and am perfectly satisfied that there never existed the least. I should be the last one to vindicate such conduct, had the imputation been deserved.* The fiction was given to the world in a *novel*, called the "Curate of Coventry," by a Clergyman named Potter.

1741.   Paid Highway Rates, (first mentioned,) 11s. 8d.

1751.   "Recd of John Perkin clear, 24l. 11s. after the usual allowance (1s. per quarter), and 15s. for the days lost, in all 25l. 10s. for a year's rent of the Penny Halfpenny"

The Right Honourable Matthew, Earl Fortescue, Baron Fortescue of Castle Hill, was elected High Steward of the Borough, in the room of Hugh, Earl Clinton, deceased.

1753.   Paid Church Rates, 3s. 2 1/2d. First mention of this rate.

1755.   Richard Parminter, Esq. chosen Deputy Recorder, in the room of Robert Incledon, Esq. who resigned.

1756.   Robert Incledon, Esq. elected Deputy Recorder, in the room of Richard Parminter, Esq. deceased.

1758.   Benjamin Incledon, Esq. elected Recorder, in the room of John Bassett, Esq. deceased.

1759.   John Short, Esq. sworn into the office of Deputy Recorder, in the room of Robert Incledon, Esq. deceased. Mr. Short was at the same time presented with the Freedom of the Borough.

---

* I would fain record a verdict of 'not guilty' to a charge very similar, but of more recent date, especially as it affects the *Ladies* of Barnstaple.

It is well known to be customary for the successful Candidates at an Election, to give a Ball at the Assembly Rooms; it is always done on a liberal scale, and of course involves considerable expense. After the last Election, (June, 1826,) it was proposed to forgo the Ball, and apply the sum which the enternainment might be expected to cost, in flagging Bouport Street. Mr. Alexander was said to have offered 200l. towards this desirable object, and his collegue, Mr. Hogson, on being informed of what was in contemplation, an equal sum or more, should it be found requisite. A writer in the North Devon Journal gives this statement, and adds, — "A few females, however, exerted, and were unfortunately found to posses sufficient to set aside the intended plan of improvement, and the ephemera of an evening was substituted for the lasting benefit which would have accrued. Can this be a true statement? perhaps your next Journal will inform us." I know nothing of the writer of the Article from which I have been quoting, but can state my own knowledge that the circumstance which is here publicly brought forward, had got abroad even before the Ball in question took place, nor did I ever hear of any attempt being made to contradict it.

I could have wished that *this* "Memorial" had not been left to be recorded; but it is registered in the hope that as atonement may yet be made, the first opportunity of making it will be embraced. Elections are frequent; let but the cost of one Ball be appropriated in the way before proposed, and the reproach will be wiped away. The sacrifice will not be great; for assuredly had Mr. Beresford ever been present at an Election Ball, (especially in the month of June,) he would have classed it among his catalogue of *"Miseries."*

1759. "Wast Ground at Litchdon" let at 10s. "Great Farm, Sheep Market, and Penny-halfpenny, for one year, 139l."
Average of Penny-halfpenny in reign of George II. 27l. 5s.

GEORGE III.

1765. This year was remarkable for the death of four Capital Burgesses, namely, W. H. Drake, Henry Wickey, John Deane, and Richard Knight.
"Received of Edwd Perry, Penny-halfpenny, 33l."
1766. "Cash received for the Rent of the Great Farm, 75l."
1774. This year did not prove a very profitable one to the Corporation, neither did their conduct, in some instances, add lustre to their name.

I am indebted to a venerable relative, (Mr. William Besly, now verging on his eightieth year,) formerly an extensive and highly respected woollen manufacturer in this town, but who has been long resident in a neighbouring county, for an account of the efforts made by the Corporation about this period, to cramp the most flourishing branch of commerce then existing here; I mean not to say that such was their object, but that this was the effect of their policy, whilst their unreasonable and, as it ultimately proved, illegal demand was enforced, is obvious.

As the statement furnishes some interesting information relative to the state of the manufacturing trade of Barnstaple at this time, I give it with scarcely any abridgment in the narrator's own words. I should mention, however, that it was sent me in the form of answers to questions proposed by me.

"About the year 1774, I began to make baize, then the principal manufacture of the town; the trade was also carried on by several of the Corporation, who of course were all free, and bound by their oaths to uphold the rights and privileges of the body. [They were not exempt from yarn-beam dues.]

"When I commenced baize-making, I attended the *Yarn-market* on Friday mornings, at eleven o'clock, where I met all who were concerned in the trade. I soon found that the *Market* was not the place for me to purchase at, as nearly all baize-makers were free, and bought the best yarn before the market began, by sending round to the different public houses. When I found out this, I commenced purchasing yarn at my own house, which stood at the end of Pilton Bridge, where the greatest part of the yarn passed. I went on for a considerable time pretty quietly, but at last I was threatened, and a great stir was made." [No wonder, for it not only lessened the dues of the Corporation, but affected the private interest of several individuals amongst them.] "My being young at that time, and much averse to law, I offered to enter into a bond not to buy any yarn before the market, but they only laughed at me. My Business was now considerable, and I purchased all the yarn I could lay my hands on; they actually sent the Beadle down to my door to order the country people to carry the yarn to the market, yet as soon as the persons had turned the corner into High-street, the servants of " ***** [Corporators and others] "would buy the yarn and weigh it at home.

"Of the quantity of yarn brought to the Town it is difficult for me to judge now; I have bought in an hour and half full 30*l*. worth.

"The charge for weighing used to be, to tradesmen 4*d*., to the country 5*d*. per stone, upwards of a farthing per pound—a vile imposition; at Crediton, where there were large quantities of yarn weighed, and of greater value, a charge of only 1*s*. per pack of 252lbs. was made. I have been given to understand that the yarn-beam brought in 40*l*. per annum."

The consequence of Mr. Besly's perseverance in the same course pursued by members of the corporate body and others, namely, that of weighing their own goods at their own scales, was, that an action was brought against him, which, being decided in his favor, of course did away with the *Yarn Beam*.*

"After this, the Corporation smuggled up a petition, by applying to get it signed by a few persons, who they hoped would keep the secret, for an Act to embody all their dues. With this petition the town-clerk and another person set off in a post-chaise, hoping to get it presented to the House of Commons, before it was known in Barnstaple that such a scheme was in contemplation."

The departure of these gentlemen was quickly known, and by

* It will be seen on references to the Bye Laws, [App, C.] that there was one which imposed a penalty on persons buying yarn without weighing it at the Town Beam; but this availed nothing on the trial. This law was deficient in one very important requisite prescribed by the Charter, it was not "reasonable."

extraordinary activity on the part of two individuals, Mr. Hole a land-surveyor, and Mr. Irwin, a draper, a counter petition was *prepared, signed, carried to London, and presented to the House of Commons before the arrival of the town-clerk and his companion;* who, to their astonishment, were informed by Mr. Cleveland, on whom they waited with their petitiion, that Messers. Hole and Irwin were before them, and had succeeded in getting a petition against the proposed Act "laid on the table" of the House. One party passed through Salisbury, whilst the other was taking a comfortable nap. The Corporation were foiled in their object, no Act was obtained.

A copy of this curious petition was in my hands long before I had any certain clue of its origin. From the execution of the copy, I suspect it to have been *officially* taken; if I am right, there can be no doubt of it's correctness.

"Copy. Petition of the Corporation of Barnestaple to Parliament, on Thursday the 24th Feby 1774.

"The Petition of the Mayor, Aldermen, and Burgesses, of the Borough and Parish of Barnestaple, was presented to the House and read.— Setting forth, that the Town of Barnestaple is a very ancient Borough and Port; and that the Burgesses of the said Borough have been for time immemorial, and still are, a Corporation, and in right thereof, as seized in fee of Lands, and have time immemorilly received the rents, issues, and profits thereof, as also of an Estate called the Town Farms, distinguished by the titles of Great Farms, Penny-halfpenny, Sheep Market, Tolsery, and Bushelage, consisting of small customary dues or payments, and also small fines, which said dues and fines are paid by persons not being free Burgesses, or otherwise customarily exempted. And that the Petitioners and their predecessors have repaired, sustained, and maintained many edifaces and Buildings within the Borough and Parish, made use of by persons trading to or from the Port, or frequenting the Markets and Fairs within the said Borough and Parish. And that the yearly Revenues of the said Corporation, exclusive of the Town Farms, are very inconsiderable, consisting mostly of small highrents for houses, held of them by lease for long terms of years, and the accidental fines arising from "such leases, which are by no means sufficent for the purposes intended. And that in some years the damages done to the Quays and Publick Buildings have been so sudden and great by the Tide and high winds, that moneys have been borrowed from time to time for the support and maintenance thereof, and of other Buildings; that the Quays alone cost them last year much more than all the certain annual income of their revenue, and in all probability will be attended with further considerable expense, it being at this time necessary to enlarge some of the Quays, and build a wall, or make other conveniences for keeping out the tide. And that at present the weekly markets are held in High Street, under large penthouses or sheds fixed to the Houses, which extend so far over the said streets, as to become a great nuisance, and very inconvenient to passengers, and ought to be entirely taken away or reduced considerably; to remedy which the Petitioners are desirous, if their estates and dues shall be sufficient, and are confirmed to them, to build a Market place for the sale of Butcher's meat near the High Street, for the convenience of the Town and Country. And that a considerable sum must now be laid out on the several works and Buildings aforesaid, besides the money already expended thereon. And that it will be necessary for the petitioners to borrow and take up a sum of money on the credit of their estates, farms, tolls, and dues, for the purpose aforesaid. And therefore pray, that for making the tolls and dues an unquestionable security to the lenders, they may be at liberty to bring a bill for confirming to them and their successors, the said Farms, Estate, ancient Tolls and dues, so immemorially received by the Petitioners; and for building a market place in the said Town, and enlarging the said Quays and many other purposes aforesaid. And that they may be at liberty to borrow and take up at Interest a sum of money on the credit of the said Farms, Estates, Tolls, and Dues, in manner before set forth, for the Publick uses and purposes aforesaid."

After all that is here said of the necessity of enlarging the Quays, *keeping out the tide,* &c. &c., it is plain that the principal thing the Corporation had in view, was the "confirming,{ and perhaps increasing,"their tolls and dues." Had the improvement of the town been their object, why go so secretly to work? The folowing extract

234

from a case submitted to counsel in June, 1774, may throw some further light on the subject: "About six years since, one of the Butchers refused payment of his Toll [three pence per week]. About four years after his refusal the Corporation commenced an action for it, but soon withdrew or stopped such action, and discontinued their demand of it from him. In 1774, several other Butchers refused payment of this Toll, whereupon, fresh actions were commenced and are now depending."

Whether or no any trial took place, I cannot learn; but it was certainly a strange proceeding on the part of the Corporation, to endevour privately to procure such an Act of Parliament, at the very time when they were, and had been for six years, hesitating if they should enforce payments of the tolls, they thus sought the aid of the legislature to "*confirm* to them and their successors."

1787. The following presentment was made by the Grand Jury at the Michaelmas Sessions; "We present the Mayor, Aldermen, and Capital Burgesses, of this Borough, for not keeping in repair the ancient Town Hall, the Plaistering of the roof thereof being in so dangerous a condition, that his Majesty's liege subjects [their Worships of course among the rest] are in great danger to enter it."

1789. "The Corporation purchased of the Trustees of Lord and Lady Radnor's Marriage Settlement, a certain fee farm rent of 4s. payable out of certain premises in Barum, for 5l. 12s. 6d. "

This year, in consequence of the refusal of a tradesman of the town, namely Lathy, to pay Quay-dues, the Corporation sued him and gained a verdict; thus establishing their right to impose the dues. Mr. Lathy was supported in his oppositiion to the Corporation by another individual, Mr. Bowhay, the expenses attending the trial were 70l. to each of them.

Mr. Lathy, who had previously purchased the freedom of Newport,* Monmouthshire, now sought to obtain that of London, which occasioned the following letter to be addressed to the Lord Mayor of the city:

"My Lord,– I do myself honour, as Chief Magistrate, to address your Lordship on behalf of the Corporation of the ancient Borough

---

* This Borough, I believe, like Barnstaple and some other Towns, gives to resident burgesses an exemption from Tolls in other places. Mr. L. failed, from his not residing there, to establish his claim to freedom from tolls here, on the ground of his being a freeman of Newport.

of Barnstaple, whose prilileges have been lately attempted to be infringed by an inhabitant of this Town, claiming an exemption from payment of Quay dues, which, by our very ancient records, appear to have been paid for ages. This man, whose name is Nicholas Lathy, was for a trifling sum sworn a Burgess of the little Borough of Newport, in Monmouthshire, on which he founded his exemption; but the verdict of a special Jury before Lord Kenyon, at the last Assizes for the County of Devon, convinced Mr. Lathy, to his cost, that he was in an error.

"I find he is now advised by some friend, to attempt to get the freedom of the City of London, which he says may be obtained for about twenty-five guineas. From your Lordship's known veneration for the Constitution of this Kingdom, and regard for the welfare of all usefull and public bodies, I hope your Lordship will not countenance an application of this sort, which, if made, will be done with a manifest intention of injuring the Revenue of this Corporation, which is at present so small, that it will scarcely support the Quays and Publick Buildings.

"I have the Honour to be, &c."

(Signed by the Mayor.)

"Barnstaple, 29 November, 1789."

The "known veneration" of the Lord Mayor of London "for the Constitution," was a singular plea to urge for his Lordship's acting as he was here called upon to do. If Mr. Lathy, by becoming a freeman of the City, could have been *legally* exempt from dues here or elsewhere, it would have ill-accorded with the spirit of the constitution of England, for two public bodies to have coalesced against him, in order to prevent his doing so.

That our Corporation supposed that such an exemption might be purchased, is evident by their seeking in the way they did to prevent Mr. Lathy's obtaining it; they might however have spared themselves making such an application, residence being necessary to the full participation in the rights of freedom, as well in London as elsewhere.*

The Lord Mayor's reply, dates Dec. 6, 1789, briefly stated his

---

* The borough of Newport is, to a certain extent, an exception to this rule, inasmuch as the Charter grants the same privileges to the inhabitants of several neighbouring Towns therein named, as it gives to the burgesses of Newport.

intention to lay the letter, "before the first Court of Aldermen."

I am not in possession of any further information relative to this business.

Some time subsequent to this, but I do not know the precise year, Mr. Irwin, the individual already mentioned, determined to try the question with the Corporation, if he was bound to pay them a yearly sum (in addition to Quay-dues) by way of license, for carrying on his business in the town, he not being free. He brought his action and succeeded, which put an end to fines "for opening Shop Wyndows of them who are not burgesses of this Towne."

I have already remarked, that the right of the Common Council to elect honorary burgesses has been disputed; I did not however imagine, when the allusions I have made to the subject were penned, that the legality of such elections would be so soon, and in such a decided and persevering manner called in question, as it has since been.

1830. This year will be marked by future generations of Barumites, as an important era in the annals of the Common Council, as well as of the freemen at large, as the question must now be brought to an issue, whether the capital burgesses have or have not the right of creating honorary freemen; whether such a power is henceforward to be exercised by twenty-five individuals, self-elected out of a corporation of six-hundred, or by the whole body in conjunction.

I must now dismiss the subject, as to enter on it at any length, would, in the present state of the proceedings, be useless, and perhaps unfair. That any legal decision of the point in dispute will take place before the publication of this work, is not probable; if however, this should be the case, an impartial statement of the affair shall be given from its commencement to the final issue.

It is enacted by the Charter of Philip and Mary, [see clause n, App.I] that if any Capital Burgess "shall die or *out of the said Borough shall dwell,*" &c. that it shall be unlawful "within eight days next after the death or amotion of the said Burgess," to elect "one other person" &c. The bye-laws also appoint, [see No. 5, App. c.] that "upon the death or moving of any of the chief Burgesses" their places shall be filled up; the time for doing this is however

237

extended to within "fourteen days before the election of the next Mayor."

It is plain that the Corporation is bound to comply with the provision of the Charter, as to making the election, though with respect to the precise time for doing it, the license given by the bye-laws (which cannot, notwithstanding, contravene the Charter,) is an unobjectionable one, and might therefore be allowed, but the filling up vacant places ought certainly no to be dispensed with.

At present, and for many years past, the practice in this Borough, has been to supply the places of such Capital Burgesses as may die, according to the regulations of the bye-laws, (saving that it has not been usual of late to elect *one other of the Burgesses* of the said Borough and Parish.) But it is notorious that vacancies, caused by the removal from the town of members of the body corporate, are not filled up, there being at this time, and having been for many years past, five non-residents, who are still considered as belonging to the Common Council; two reside ten or twelve miles from Barnstaple, two at a less distance, and one in the County of Kent.

Does it ammount to a query whether or no either of these gentlemen is capable of performing a legal act in the Corporation? Let us suppose them not competent to do this, and that one of them takes a part in electing a Mayor, (no very unlikely occurrence,) it follows that the election would be illegal, and as a matter of course that every deed performed by a Magistrate so appointed by virtue of his office, must be void in law. It is certainly both just and necessary that the members of a public body appointed for the government of a town, should inhabit the jurisdiction over which they are placed; not, certainly, to their own injury or inconvenience, but when a removal, from whatever cause, takes place, why appoint a new officer? If it be unlawful to omit filling up vacancies happening in this way, it is equally so as to those caused by death, (the same provision being made for either contingency,) and we know not to what extent the practice might be carried. That the present mode of proceeding would not stand the test of a Quo Warranto, is pretty evident; the Corporation will, perhaps, see it right to return to the regular method in future.

By the Charter of James, [see clause ee. App. J.] the property to be held by the Corporation is limited to "sixty pounds per annum,"[*] beyond all charges and reprises.[†]" Putting the most favorable construction possible on this stipulation, it goes to deprive the Corporation of the power of accumulating property, and, of course, to render it obligatory on them to expend their whole income for the public benefit. It was, however, no doubt intended, by the wording of the clause in question, to restrict the Corporation from becoming possessors of property above the value mentioned.

The following statement will shew pretty nearly the present yearly receipts of the Corporation. I do not pledge myself for its entire correctness, but believe the Amount will not be found *less* than I have fixed it at.

	£	s.	d.
Castle Inn, Rent of	20	0	0
Workhouse	#25	0	0
Barrack Inn	21	0	0
Warehouse in Anchor Lane	6	0	0
Thirty-four Butchers' Shops, at 8l. each	272	0	0
Two Shops under Front of Guildhall	20	0	0
Mill-end Quay (by North Walk)	25	0	0
Castle Quay (lets from 8l. to 12l.) say	††10	0	0
Ground Rent of Litchdon Terrace, Four Houses, at 42s.	8	8	0
Old Chief Rents, &c. on sundry Lands and Tenements, about	##40	0	0
Land Tax redeemed, income from	42	9	10
Produce from Castle Manor	166	1	93/4

* We can only attribute this cavilier treatment of the Corporate Body by King James, to some great dislike or suspicion he entertained towards them. Charles II., incensed as he was against the inhabitants of Taunton, after demolishing the walls of the Town, and depriving the Burgesses of their charter for seventeen years, allowed them in a new Charter which he granted, to hold Lands to the clear annual value of 300*l*, per annum.

† REPRISES (fr. Resumption, a taking back) is used for deductions and payments out of a manor or lands, as Rent Charges, Annuities, &c. And therefore, when we speak of the clear yearly value of a manor or estate of land, we say it is so much per annum *ultra Reprisas,* besides all Reprises.— *Jacob's Law Dict.*

Not 20*l*, as stated at page 122.

†† This Quay is now in hand; but the increased produce of the Castle Manor Tolls this year (III.) may be placed as a set off against it.

This sum may not be relied on as correct; it cannot, however, be much out of the way. About forty years since, the receipts from this source were from 50*l*. to 60*l*.; but many items which were then included under the above term, are not now received.

	£	s.	d.
Ditto of "Great Farm," or Quay Dues .	*140	0	0
Chief Rents, Manor of Hog's Fee .	1	14	1½
†Tonnage duty of vessels lying at the Quay	30	0	0
	£827	14	2¼

I pretend not to be fully acquainted with the manner in which this income is disposed of; but my knowledge of the affairs of the Corporation extends quite far enough to satisfy me that it is *legitimately* applied; and feeling this conviction, I hold it but common justice to express it, particularly as I know that the tide of popular opinion runs counter to such a belief. I speak, however, of things as they are, not as they were; wolves have occasionally got into the flock, and it is acknowledged by members of the present body, that some of the accounts of former, (but not very distant) periods, will not bear inspection.

The lands held by the Corporation are of comparatively trifling value, but their property in houses is very considerable, though they derive at present scarcely any benefit from them, the whole, with the exception of what are mentioned in the foregoing statement, being out on lease. It was customary, until of late, to renew these leases, which are mostly granted for sixty years, every thirty years from the commencement of the term, which was usually done for a very reasonable consideration, but the guardians of the property "now are wiser than of yore;" a resolution was passed a few years since, and has hitherto been pretty closely acted up to, of letting the leases run out; this must be a work of time, and many years must elapse before even a moderate portion of the property can be made avaliable.

The following are the names of the Mayor, Aldermen, Common Council, and principal Officers of the Corporation, at the present time, August, 1830.

---

* This produced last year 157*l.*, the previous year 165*l.* There has been no competion lately for the office of quay-master, as the renter of the dues is termed, or no doubt a greater rent would be obtained.

† The whole produce of this impost, is annually expended in clearing away the soil which constantly accumulates within the river-line of the Quays, to which purpose it is applied by the Clerk of the Customs, without being brought into the corporation accounts.

RIGHT HON. EARL FORTESCUE. *High Steward.*
RICHARD BREMBRIDGE, ESQ. *Mayor.* (22)
ROBERT NEWTON INCLEDON, ESQ.*Recorder.*
THOMAS MOORE STEVENS, ESQ. *Deputy Recorder.*
ROBERT BUDD, ESQ. (21) *Alderman.*
HENRY NICHOLLS, CLERK, (17) *Alderman.*
HENRY DRAKE, ESQ. *Town Clerk.* (18)
NICHOLAS GLASS, (1)
JOHN ROBERTS, (2)
RICHARD ROWE METHERELL, (3)
*THOMAS COPNER, (4)
JOHN PYKE, (5)
*ZACHARY HAMMETT DRAKE, (6)
*PHILIP BREMBRIDGE, (7)
SAMUEL BREMBRIDGE, (8)
WILLIAM CHAPPLE PAWLE, (9)
JOHN MAY, (10)
EDWARD RICHARDS ROBERTS, *Mayor Elect,* (11)
*WILLIAM LAW, (12)
JOHN LAW, (13)
*THOMAS LAW, (14)
CHARLES ROBERTS, (15)
JOHN MARSHALL, (16)
WILLIAM LAW, 2ND. (19)
*THOMAS TARDREW, (20)
HENRY LUXMOORE, VICAR, (23)
CHARLES BESLY GRIBBLE, (24)
ROBERT WELDON GRACE, (25)

---

* The numbers placed against the names denote the seniority of standing. Those marked with an asterisk are non-residents.

APPENDIX TO CHAPTER III.

[A.]

1.–Plea of Quo Warranto	– Edw. 1.
2.–Writ and Inquisition	14 Edw. 3.
3.– *Ditto* *Ditto*	17 Edw.. 3.
4.– *Ditto* *Ditto*	18 Edw. 3.*

No. 1.

Pleas of Quo Warranto tempore Edw. I. Roll 41 dors. Galfrey de Caunvyle was summoned to answer the Lord the King a plea by what warranty he claims to have the view of Frankpledge, gallows, amending of the assize of bread and ale broken in Bovy Tracy, which pertain to the Crown of the Lord the King, without licence, &c.

And Galfrey cometh and saith that he holds the Manor of Bovy Tracy by the law of England, of the heir of William Martin, without he cannot answer to the Lord the King therefore; who now commeth by summons and answers together with the aforesaid Galfrey; and they say that the Manor of Bovy Tracy is a certain member of the same Barony of William de Bardestaple, to which the aforesaid liberties pertain. And they say that all the ancestors of the said William, from time whereof memory is not, have used the aforesaid liberties; and by that warranty they claim to have the liberties aforesaid. And because there is nothing else whereby to shew warranty therefore as to judgement. And a day is given them to be before the Lord the King, from easter day in one month wheresoever &c. to hear their judgement, &c.

The same Galfrey was summoned to answer to the Lord the King, of a plea by what warranty he claims to have view of Frankpledge, gallows, amending of the assize of bread and ale broken in Bardestaple, without licence, &c.

And Galfrey, together with the aforesaid William, come and say that Bardestaple is at the Barony of the aforesaid William, to which such liberties pertain. And that all the ancestors of the aforesaid William, from time of which memory is not, have used the aforesaid liberties. And by that warranty they claim the aforesaid liberties. And because there is nothing else to shew warranty. Therefore as to judgement. And a day is given them to be before the Lord the King from Easter-day in one month, wheresoever &c. to hear their judgement.

* Nos. 1, 2, and 4, are from H. M. Record Office; as a pledge that the translation of No. 3 may be depended on for its correctness, I need only mention that I owe it to Mr. Oliver.

Edward, by the grace of God King of England and France and Lord of Ireland, to his beloved and faithful Hugh de Courteneye the younger, Hamon Dereworth, and Henry Power, Greeting. Know ye, that whereas lately on the prosecution of the Burgesses of the Town of Barnestaple, in the County of Devon, by their petition before us and our Council exhibited, beseeching us, that as the Town aforesaid, from time whereof memory is not the contrary, had been a free Borough, and the same Burgesses and their Ancestors, Burgesses of the Town aforesaid, had used and enjoyed divers liberties and free customs by the Charter of the Lord Athelstan, heretofore King of England, of famous memory, or progenitor, which to a free Borough pertain from the time of the making of the said Charter in this, to wit. that they should bequeath their tenements in the ame Borough, in their testament in their last will, to whomsoever they will, and a Mayor from among themselves to elect, before whom all pleas touching the said Borough and the suburbs of the same, should be pleaded and determined; and to send to every Parliament of us and our said Ancestors, two Burgesses for the Commonalty of the same Borough; and also in all taxations and subsidies to us and our progenitors, formerly Kings of England, by the Citizens and Burgesses of the same Kingdom, heretofore granted to be taxed by themselves, and not with foreigners, and of pontage, passage, murage, pavage, lastage, anchorage, standage, and picage, through our whole Kingdom to be hitherto quit, and the amending of the assize of bread and ale in the same Borough and in the suburbs of the same broken; and the assay of measures and weights: and also tumbrel and pillory as they had been accustomed to have, we would more fully declare the liberties and free customs aforesaid by our Charter, and into a Charter order to be renewed; because the said Charter, as they affirm, is accidentally lost. And further, of our special grace to grant to them, that they and their heirs and successors, may have the full return of all writs of us, our heirs and successors, and summonses touching the Borough aforesaid and suburbs of the same; so that our Sheriff of the County aforesaid, or any other Bailiff or Minister of us, or our Heirs, should in no wise enter that Borough, to do or exercise his office by reason of such writs or summonses in the Borough aforesaid, unless in default of the Mayor and Bailiffs of the same Borough; and that they may elect and create a Coroner from among themselves by the writs of us and our Heirs, to do and exercise the office of Coroner in the Borough aforesaid; and that they, their successors, Burgesses of the Borough aforesaid, may have one Fair in the Borough aforesaid, in every year, for four days to last, that is to say, on the eve, and on the day of the blessed Mary Magdalene, and for two days next following; and that they may not be put with foreigners, or foreigners with them, on any assizes, juries, or inquisitions. And we being willing upon the premises more fully to be certified, and further to incline to the supplication of the same burgesses, as far as can be done without the damage and prejudice of us and others, as shall be meet, have assigned our beloved and faithful Hugh de Courteneye, Earl of Devon, Robert de Horton, John de Stouford, and Matthew de Cranthorn, three and two of them to inquire by the oath of approved and lawful men of the county aforesaid, by whom the truth of the matter may be better known, in the presence of our sheriff of the said county, by the same Earl, Robert, John, and Matthew, three or two of them thereupon to be summoned, if the aforesaid burgesses have used and enjoyed the said liberties to them by the Charter of the aforesaid Athelstan, as is aforesaid granted from the time aforesaid; and whether that Charter had been lost in form aforesaid; and also what damage or prejudice would happen to us or any others whomsoever, if we, by our Charter, should grant the said liberties to the same burgesses, by the Charter of the aforesaid Athelstan, as they assert, granted; and also the aforesaid liberties by them newly besought, as are above contained, to possess to them, their heirs and successors for ever. And now, as we are informed, the aforesaid Earl, Robert, and Matthew, are aiding to expedite divers our affairs in the county aforesaid and elsewhere, which they cannot quit to do and accomplish the premises, in the place of the same Earl, Robert, and Matthew, we have assigned you, and two of you, to take an inquisition upon the premises and touching the same, together with the before named John, in the presence of our said Sheriff, by you and the before named John, or two of you.

And therefore we command you, that at certain days and places which you and the aforesaid John, or two of you, shall provide in this behalf, you diligently make inquisition upon the premises, and in all things touching the same, and the same distinctly and openly made, you send to us without delay into our Chancery, under the seals of you or two of you, and the seals of those by whom it shall be made, and this writ. Also, we have commanded the before named John, that he admit you in the place of the aforesaid Earl, Robert and Matthew, his fellows, as is aforesaid. Also, we have commanded our sheriff of the county aforesaid, that at certain days and places wich you and the aforesaid John, or two of you, of whom we will you the named Hamon to be another, shall make known to him he cause to come before you and the before named John, or two of you, so many and such approved and lawful men of his bailiwick, by whom the truth of the matter in the premises may be better known; and to you or two of you, of whom we will you the before named Hamon to be another, to be assistant in these matters. In witness whereof, we have caused these our letters to be made patent. Witness, Edward, Earl of Chester, our most dear son, Guardian of England, at Shutteleye, the twenty-third day of June, in the year of our reign of England the 14th, but of our reign of France the 1st.

An INQUISITION taken before Hamon de Dryeworth and Henry Power, in the presence of John de Ralegh de Charles, Sheriff of Devon, at Southmolton, on Friday next after the Feast of the Assumption of the blessed Virgin Mary, in the year of the reign of King Edward the 3rd, after the Conquest, the 14th, but of the reign of France the 1st, by the oath of John de Luscote, Richard de Whytefeld, William de Mellecote, Walter de Pillond, Baldewin de Ackelane, Roger de Frensheton, Thomas de Hele, Oliver de Cloteworthy, Richard de Cadebury, Henry atte Wode, William Gyreliston, and Richard de Bellemont, who say, that the town of Barnstaple is a borough, and that the burgesses of the said town, sought not, nor have hitherto used to bequeath their tenements in the same borough in their testaments in their last will. And also, they say that all pleas touching the said borough and suburbs, ought to be pleaded and determined before the Steward of the Lord of the said Town, and not before the Mayor of the said Town, nor have been hitherto so accustomed. Also, they say, that in all taxations and subsidies heretofore granted to the Lord the King and his progenitors, by the citizens and burgesses of the same Kingdom, they have been, and hitherto were used to be taxed by the chief taxers of the county aforesaid and not by themselves. But whether they ought to be quit of pontage, passage, murage, pavage, lastage, anchorage, standage, and picage, throughout the whole kingdom, they know not. Also, they say, that the Lord of the Town aforesaid, hath and ought to have the amending of the assize of bread and ale in the same borough and suburbs broken; and the assay of measures and weights; and also the pillory and tumbrel. And that he and his ancestors have been accustomed to have the same, and not the burgesses. Also, they say, that nothing did appear to them from the Charter of the Lord Athelstan, heretofore King of England, concerning the different liberties or customs aforesaid, as they affirm granted to the said burgesses or their predecessors. Also, they say, that if the said liberties newly prayed, as in the commission to us directed is contained, should be granted to the said burgesses or their sucessors, it will be to the damage of the Lord the King by the year £10; and to the damage of Philip de Columbar and Alianor his wife,

245

and the heirs of the same Alianor by the year, forty marks; and to the damage of the Abbot of Clyve, by the year, forty shillings; and to the damage of the Bishop of Oxford, forty shillings; and to the damage of Randulph de Blanmonster, Lord of Heanton, by the year, forty shillings; and to the damage of Robert Baupel, by the year, six shillings and eight pence; and to the damage of Walter de Ralegh, by the year, six shillings and eight pence. In witness whereof, the Jurors to the aforesaid Inquisition have put their seals.

No. 3.

EDWARD, by the grace of God, King of England and France, and Lord of Ireland, to his beloved and liege men, John de Stouford, Hamo de Derworthy, John de Baumfield, and Richard de Hankeston, send greeting. The burgesses of the town of Barnestaple, in the county of Devon, have been suppliants to us by thier petition presented to us and our Council, that whereas, the town aforesaid, has been from time immemorial, and still is a free borough, and the same burgesses and their predecessors, burgesses of the town aforesaid, in virtue of a Charter of the Lord Athelstan, of famous memory, once King of England, our progenitor, have always hitherto used and enjoyed divers liberties and free customs which belong to a free borough from the time of making the Charter aforesaid, to wit, that they may bequeath by their testament and last will, their tenements in the same borought to whomsoever they will; and that they are accustomed to choose from among themselves a Mayor, before whom all pleas touching the said borough and suburb ought to be pleaded and determined; and to send two burgesses for the commonalty of the same borough to each of our Parliaments and those of our predecessors; and to be taxed by themselves and not with strangers, in every taxation and subsidy hitherto granted to us or our progenitors, once Kings of England, by the citizens and burgesses of the same realm; and to be quit as hitherto from pontage, passage, murage, pavage, lastage, anchorage, standage, and picage, throughout the entire relm, and to have the assize of bread and beer that is made in the same borough and suburb; and the assay of measures and weights; also a tumbril and pillory; and that we would be pleased to declare more fully by our Charter, the liberties and free customs aforesaid, and cause them to be reduced anew into a Charter, because the said Charter, as they assert, is accidentally lost; and that of our special grace we would further grant unto them, that they and their heirs and sucessors may have the full return of all the writs of us and our heirs, and of summonses concerning the borough aforesaid and the suburb thereof, so that our sheriff of the county aforesaid, or any other of our bailiffs or officers, or of our heirs, should by no means enter that borough to do or execute his office, by reason of such writs or summonses in the borough aforesaid; and that they, their heirs and sucessors, burgesses of the borough aforesaid, may have a fair in the borough aforesaid, every year, to last four days, to wit, onthe vigil and on next ensuing; and that they be put not with strangers, nor strangers with them, in any sworn assizes or inquisions. We, willing to be more fully informed by you of the premises, and how far consent as is fitting can be further granted to the petition of those burgesses in this part, without loss or prejudice to us or another, have assigned you three, and two of you, to inquire on the oath of honest and liege men of the county aforesaid, by you three or by two of you therefore to be summoned, if the said burgesses, from the time aforesaid, have used and enjoyed the said liberties granted them by the Charter of the aforesaid Athelstan, as is aforesaid, and if that Charter, in the form aforesaid, has been lost. As also, what loss or prejudice would accrue to us or to any other, if we, by our Charter, should grant to them and their heirs and sucessors, the said liberties granted to the same burgesses, by the Charter of the aforesaid Athelstan, as they assert, as also the liberties aforesaid asked anew by them above set forth, to be possessed for ever. And therefore we command you, that at certain days and places which you three or two of you shall provide for this purpose, you will make such an inquisition upon the premises and what touch the same in the form aforesaid, and that inquisition distinctly and fitly made under your three seals, or under the seals of two of you, and of them by whom it was made, you send to us without delay, and this writ. We have ordered our Sheriff of the County aforesaid, that on the certain days and places which you three or two of you shall notify to him, to cause so many and such honest and liege men of his bailiwick to come before you three or two of you, by whom the truth of the matter in the premises can be better known and inquired into, and that this be and you three, or two of you. In winess whereof we have caused these letters to be made patent. Witness ourselves at Westminster, xviiith day of May, in the seventeenth year of our reign of England, but in the forth year of our reign of France.

By petition in Parliament.

DEVON.— Inquisition taken at Barnstaple, before Hamo de Derworthy and John de Baumfeld, Justices of our Lord the King, for taking such inquisition, with John de Stowford and Richard Hankeston, in the presence of Walter de Horton the Sheriff of Devon, on Saturday next day after the circumcision of our Lord, in the seventeenth year of the reign of Edward,

King of England, the third from the Conquest, and the fourth year of his reign of France, by the oath of Richard le Wolf, John Passelowe, Richard de Lokkesore, John Warde, Richard de Whitefield, William Golde. William de Loriawill, John Noreys, William Tappleigh, Richard de Bradimor, Richard Atte Hill, and William Atte Beare, who say upon their oath, that the town of Barnestaple is a free borough, and has been from time immemorial. Also they say, that the burgesses of the town aforesaid, and their predecessors, have used and enjoyed, and as yet use and enjoy, divers liberties and free customs by the Charter of the Lord Athelstan of famous memory, once King of England, and progenitor of our Lord the now King, which belong to the said borough, from the time of making the Charter aforesaid even until now; to wit, that they can bequeath in their testament and last will their tenements in the same borough and suburb thereof to whomsoever they will, and choose from among themselves a Mayor, before whom and the Steward of the Lord of the borough afore-said, all pleas touching the said borough and the suburb thereof ought to be impleaded and determined; and to send to each Parliament of our Lord the King two burgesses for the commonalty of the same borough; as also in every taxation and subsidy granted to our aforesaid Lord the King or to his progenitors once Kings of England, by the citizens and burgesses of the same realm before the present time, that they should be taxed by themselves and not with strangers; and have hitherto been quit through-out the entire realm of England, of pontage, passage, murage, pavage, lastage, anchorage, standage, and picage, and have been accustomed and still are to have the assize of bread and beer made in the same borough and the suburb thereof, and the assay of measures and weights, as also a tumbril and pillory. They further say, that the said Charter of the afore-said liberties and customs, granted to the same burgesses by the aforesaid Lord Athelstan, has been accidentally lost. They also say, that it is not the loss or prejudice of our Lord the King, or of any one else, though the same Lord the King grant for himself and his heirs, to the same burgesses and their heirs and successors, the full return of all their writs and sum-monses touching the borough aforesaid and the suburb thereof, so that the Sheriff of our Lord the King of the county aforesaid, or any other bailiff or officer of our Lord the King and of his heirs, by no means enter that borough to do and execute his office, by reason of such writs or sum-mons in the borough aforesaid and the suburb thereof, except in default of a mayor and bailiffs of the said borough, nor though they can choose and create a coroner of themselves, by the writs of our Lord the King and of his heirs, to do and execute the office of a coroner in the borough afore-said; nor though the burgesses of the borough aforesaid, have a fair in the borough aforesaid every year, to continue for four days, to wit, on the vigil and the day of blessed Mary Magdalene and the two days ensuing; and though they be not put with foreigners, nor foreigners with them, in sworn assizes or any inquisitions. In Witness whereof, to these presents the seals of the aforesaid jurors to the aforesaid inquisition aforesaid are appended. Given at Barnestaple, on the day and year aforesaid.

No. 4.

EDWARD, by the grace of God King of England and France, and Lord of Ireland, to his beloved Henry Power, Adam le Bret, John de Ralegh de Charles, and Richard de Coumbe, greeting. Although lately by a certain inquisition on the prosecution of the men of Barnstaple in the county of Devon, praying divers liberties to be granted them by us to hold to them and their successors, men of that town, for ever, by our command taken, it hath been found that the burgesses of the said town, ought not, nor have hitherto been accustomed to bequeath their testaments, and that they might elect a Mayor from among themselves, by license of the Lord of the Town aforesaid, and that all pleas touching the said town or borough ought to be pleaded and determined before the Steward of the Lord of the said town, and not before the Mayor of the town, nor have hitherto been so accustomed, and that in all taxations and subsidies to us and our progenitors by the citizens of the Kingdom of England granted, they have been and hitherto were used to be taxed by the chief taxers of the county aforesaid, and not by themselves, and that the Lord of the town hath and ought to have the amending of the assize of bread and ale in the same town or borough and suburbs of the same broken, and the assay of measures and weights, and the pillory and tumbril, as he and his ancestors have hitherto been accustomed to have the same, and not the burgesses aforesaid, and that nothing did appear from the Charter of the Lord Athlestan heretofore King of England, by which the same burgesses pretend certain liberties to have been granted to them, and that if the liberties so newly prayed should be granted to the said burgesses or their successors, it would be to our damage, ten pounds, and to the damage of the Lord of the Town, by the year, forty marks; and also to the damage of the Abbot of Clyve, the Bishop of Exeter, Ranulph de Blanmonster, Robert Baupel, and Thomas de Ralegh, of small sums of money. But, inasmuch as we have understood on the behalf of some men of those parts insisting, as well for our right and profit as for their right and indemnity, that the before-named men of the said town, craftily endeavouring to withdraw those things which are so found to damage and prejudice, and to the damage and disinheriting of the Lord and others aforesaid, by the inquisition aforesaid, will subtilly procure a certain other inquisition to be taken by our commission concerning the first inquisition, or those things which in the same were found, making no mention to those absent and uncalled, whose rights and prejudice the said business specially touches, by which the contrary of those things in the said first inquisitiion contained, are said to be expressly found, affirming thereupon moreover that it is not to the damage or prejudice of us or any other whomsoever, if we should grant to the same burgesses, and their heirs and successors, the full return of all our writs and summonses touching the said borough and suburbs of the same, so that our Sheriff of the County aforesaid, or any other Bailiff or Minister of us and our heirs, to do and exercise his office, by reason of such writs and summonses in the borough aforesaid, and suburbs of the same, should in no wise enter that borough, unless in default of the Mayor and Bailiffs of that borough, nor although they should elect and create a Coroner in the borough aforesaid, nor that although they the burgesses of the borough aforesaid should have one fair in the aforesaid borough in every year for four days to last, that is to say, on the eve and on the day of the blessed Mary magdalene, and for two days next following, and although they be not put with foreigners nor foreigners put with them, on any assizes, juries, or inquisitions. We, considering that such liberties cannot be granted without our great prejudice, and the damage and prejudice of others to the men aforesaid, especially as the said town is holden of us in capite, as we have been informed, and the keeping of the same in the name of the custody may to us and our heirs devolve, and the farm of the county aforesaid may in part be lessened, and other losses may happen as well to us as to others; and, willing on this account to be more fully informed upon these matters, we have assigned you, three and two of you, to enquire by the oath of approved and lawful men of those parts, by whom the truth of the matter may be better known, in the presence of those whose interest and whom the premises may touch, by you three and two of you, when concerning the names of them to be summoned may appear to us, if they will be present, to what damage, prejudice, and inconvenience of others it may tend, and how and in what manner, if the liberties aforesaid should be holden of us in capite as aforesaid, whether of other or by what service, and how and in what manner, and more fully the truth of all othe circumstances touching the same business. And therefore we command you, that at a certain day and place which you three or two of you shal provide in that behalf, you make such inquisition upon the premises, and touching the same in form aforesaid; and the same distinctly and openly made,you send to us under the seals of you three or two of you, and the seals of those whom it shall be made, without delay, and this writ. Also, we have commanded our Sheriff of the county aforesaid, that at a certain day and place which you three or two of you shall make known to him, he shall cause to come before you three or two of you, so many and such approved and lawful men of his bailiwick, by whom the truth of the matter in the premises may be the better known and enquired of. In witness whereof we have caused these our letters to be made patent. Witness myself at Westminster, the twentieth day of February, in the year of our reign of England the 18th, but of our reign of France the 5th.

(Indorsement.)—We, Adam le Bret, John d Ralegh de Charles, and Richard de Coumbe, have diligently enquired of all things concerning the tenor of this writ, which same inquisition we send to you under our seals, and the seals of those by whose oath it was made, sewn to this writ. And Henry Power was elsewhere occupied in the affairs of the Lord the King, so that he could not be present to take such inquisition.

An INQUISITION taken at Chepyngtoriton, before Adam le Bret, John de Ralegh de Charles, and Richar de Coumbe, Justices of the Lord the KIng, assigned to take such inquisition, together with Henry Power, on Friday in Easter week, in the year of the reign of Edward the 3d after the conquest, of England the 18th, but of his reign of France the 5th, by the oath of William de Tottescombe, John Lobbe, Thomas Coffyn, William de Trendelysh, Reginald de Northecote, John de Lockishore, Thomas Gay of Galleworthy, Richard de Colleton, Adam de Steteburg, Humphry Bottler, Richard de Baghedon, and Walter de Lytlwere. Who say by their oath that the town of Barnstaple is a borough, and that James de Audleye holds the said town with the members, of the Lord the King in capite by Barony. And that the burgesses of the town ought not nor have been hitherto used to bequeath their tenements in the same borough in their testements in their last will. And they also say that they may yearly elect a Mayor from among themselves, by licence of the Lord of the Town aforesaid. And they say that they have not the Charter of the Lord the King, nor his progenitors, to make the said election. Also they say that all personal pleas touching the said borough ought have hitherto been accustomed to be pleaded and determined before the Steward of the Lord of the said town, and not before the Mayor of the said town, nor the bailiffs. Also they say that in all taxations and subsidies heretofore granted to the Lord the King and his progenitors by the citizens and burgesses of the kingdom of England, they have been and are accustomed to be taxed by the chief taxers in the county of Devon, and not by themselves. Also they say that the Lord of the same Town hath, and of right ought to have the amending of the assize of bread and ale in the same town or borough and suburbs broken, and the assay of measures and weights, and the tumbrel and pillory, and he and his ancestors have hitherto been accustomed to have the same, and not the burgesses aforesaid. Also they say that nothing appears nor did appear to them from the Charter of the Lord Athelstan heretofore King of England, by which the same burgesses pretend certain liberties to have been granted to them and their predecessors. Also they say that if the Lord the King should grant to the said burgesses the full return of all their writs and summonses touching the aforesaid borough and suburbs of the same, so that the Sheriff of the county aforesaid or any other Bailiff or minister of our Lord the King and his heirs, to do and exercise his office by reason of such writs or summonses in the borough aforesaid and suburbs of the same, should in no wise enter that borough, unless in default of the mayor and Bailiffs of the same borough; and that it will be to the damage of the said Lord, by the year, ten pounds; and that it will be to the damage of the Abbot of Clyve, by the year, forty shillings, who holds of the Lord the King the manor of Braunton with the hundred of Braunton, at fee farm, rendering therfore at the exchequer of the Lord the King, twenty-two pounds and ten shillings. And the said town of Barnstaple is part of the said hundred, and within the precincts of the aforesaid hundred. And they say that the Bailiffs of the aforesaid Abbot of the hundred aforesaid, make and were hitherto accustomed to make in the said borough and suburbs of the same, summonses, attachments, distresses, and executions of the judgments of the court of the Lord the King, and of his writs, and of the county aforesaid. And if the hundred aforesaid shall hereafter fall into the hands of the Lord the King, it will be to the damage of the said Lord the King, by the year, forty shillings. Also they say that it is to the damage of the prior of the blessed Mary Magdalene of Barnestaple, by the year, ten shillings, which prior hath a lordship in the said suburbs of seventeen tenements, which are parcel of the tything of Bradeford, and the same tything is parcel of the hundred aforesaid. And they say that the priory aforesaid is now in the hand of the Lord the King; they say also that it is to the damage of the said Abbot, the farmer of the hundred aforesaid, by the year, six shillings and eight pence. Also they say that Robert Baupel, chiveler, hath in the said suburbs a certain fee which is called Hogge's Fee, and by which is holden there twenty and six tenements, and he hath his court there from three weeks to three weeks. And they say that it will be to the damage of the said Robert, by the year, twenty shillings. Also they say that if the Lord the King should grant to the said burgesses, that they may yearly elect and create from among themselves a Coroner, it will be the damage of the said Lord the King, by the year, forty shillings, and to the damage of the comonalty of that country, one thousand pounds, because they say that in the said town there are many malefactors and disturbers of the peace of the Lord the King, and that it is the common passage of the men of those parts through the middle of the town aforesaid. Also they say that the Lord of the said town hath his market there on Wednesday and Friday in every week; also, that if the said Lord the King should grant unto the same burgesses a fair, as in the commission is contained, it will be to the damage of the said Lord of the Town, by the year, twenty shillings. also they say that the burgesses of the town aforesaid always answer and were hitherto accustomed to answer on assizes, juries, and inquisitions, for a third part of the aforesaid hundred of Braunton. And they say that if the said Lord the King should grant to the same burgesses that they be not put on assizes, juries, or inquisitions, with foreigners, it will be to the damage of the men of the hundred aforesaid, by the year, one hundred shillings. Also they say that the Sheriff of the county aforesaid yearly holds and was accustomed to hold his turn for the aforesaid of Braunton, in the said town of Barnestaple. And they say that the Mayor and twelve men of the said town ought to come before the said Sheriff to present all and singular those matters which pertain and are to be presented at the Sheriff's turn. Also they say that the burgesses of the town aforesaid ought, and were hitherto accustomed to find yearly two men of the same borough to serve the Lord of the said Town there, to collect and receive the rents of the said town and amercements of courts. . . . . the toll and other profits of the fair and market to collect and of all matters aforesaid to render to the said Lord of the Town aforesaid, a faithful account. Also they say that if the said town, through the minority of the heir of the said town, through a minority of the heir of the said James, or by forfeiture of the same or his heirs, or by any other manner, shall hereafter come into the hands of the Lord the King, and the said liberties should be granted to the same burgesses, it will be to the damage of the said Lord the King, by the year, forty marks. Also they say that if the said liberties should be granted to the said burgesses. . . . . it will be to the great damage of many men who have divers tenements and rents in the said town. . . . . and the bailiffs of the said town cannot permit those who have rents in the said town, to levy their rents. . . . . without redemption or fine to be made with the said burgesses, and bailiffs, that is to say, that it will be to the damage of. . . . . .shillings, of Simon le Flemyng, by the year two shillings; of Thomas de Ralegh, by the year, three shillings; of Randulph de. . . . . and Alice his wife, and their heirs of the same Alice, by the year, two shillings; of the Prior of

Pilton, by the year, six shillings and eight pence; of. . . . . two shillings; of John Fank, by the year, twenty shillings; of Robert Fouk, by the year, thirty shillings; of Walter de Merwode,. . . . . ammound, by the year, two shillings; of Baldewin de Ackelane, by the year, four shillings; of John Northe. . . . . hathey, by the year, four shillings; and of Andrew Mathu, by the year, thirteen shillings and four pence. In witness whereof, the jurors aforesaid to this inquisition have put their seals. Dated the day, place, and year aforesaid.

[B.]

Petition against the Return of a Member to the House of Commons. 16 Charles I.

"Richard Fferris, one of the Burgesses of the Parliament for the Towne of Barnestaple, in Devon.

"Thomas Matthews, Petitioner to the howse against the Election of Mr. fferris.

"The Petitioner sheweth that the Maior, Aldermen, and Burgesses of Barnestaple, being 24, and the other free Burgesses being assembled in the Towne Hall thear for the election of Burgesses for this Parliamt. after the Sheriff's warrant was read, the Mayor propoundg to the Burgesses to stand on the election, Mr. George Peard, Mr. Richard Ferris, and Mr. Richard Medford.

"That Mr. Peard and the Petitioner Matthews, by a generall voice of the Electors, weare chosen Burgesses for the said towne, to sende this Parliamt without any opposition, they crying they would have their last Burgesses, to witte, Matthews and Peard, Peard and Matthews, five or six tymes, and not any negative voice dissensioned.

"That the Mayor, notwithstanding having formerly [previously] sent to procure voices for any such of the 24 burgesses as he should nomynate, not being pleased that the Petitioner should stand to be elected, not being one of the 24, as the Mayor hath declared to be the Reason, said he would take another Course in the said Election.

"That the common Burgesses desired that they which had given their Voyces for Mr. Peard and the Petitioner might be sett on the one side of the hall, and those that were against them on the other side, if any wear, that the difference of voices might appear.

"That the Mayor would not yeild thereunto, and thereupon, the

Commons [common burgesses] said they would have noe other burgesses but those they had chosen; that they had done the work they wear called and came for, viz. to chuse two sufficient men for their Burgesses, and would have departed the hall, but could not, in regard the dore was lockt by direction of the Mayor, wch was never before on the like occasion.

"That the Mayor constrayned the Burgesses by shutting the Dore to stay, and invented a new forme of Election of purpose to exclude the Petitioners, which was, by nominating Mr. Peard and Mr. Madford by themselves, and the Mayor and his bretheren having named wch of those two they would have, the rest of the Electors wear comanded to come upp to a barr to give their Voices, wch they having done for Mr. Peard, the Petitioner and the said Mr. fferris wear then putt together on the ellection.

"That the Mayor gave his voice wth Mr. fferris, for whom he and some others of the 24 had much laboured wth Divers of the Comons by threats and other ways, by wch subtile meanes and new invented forme of Election, the Petitioner's former fair Election was quite crossed and altered, for many those that had formerly given their Voices for the Petitioner when they gave it jointly, did when they went single and were distorned;* out of feare and to please the Mayor, gave their voices for Mr. fferris, for whom the Mayor had first given his Voice, and that many of the Comon Burgesses have since declared, that they so gave their voices for feare, against their mynds, and some against their consciences. Whereas, if otherwise the Petitionr had byn putt in competition with Mr. fferris, Mr. Medford, and Mr. Peard jointly, he might have been elected before either of them. By wch meanes in the latter election the said Electors wear much hindered in their . . . . Election, and the Petitioner omitted by the Mayor, who hath unduly returned the said Mr. fferris together with Mr. Peard.

"And therefore prayeth the house of Comons to take the same into Consideration, and if it seem good to declare the retorne of the said Mr. fferris to be voide, and to comand the Mayor in steede of hym to retorne the Petitioner one of the burgesses of the said Towne to serve this Parliamt according to his due election, and to take further order."

"Annsweare to the objections in the Petition.

"First after the Sherriff's warrant read, and the Mayor had named Mr. Peard, Mr. fferris, and Mr. Medford, to stand on the election for Burgesses for this present Parlisament, omitting the Petitioner as not conceiving him so fitt, though he wear formerly in another Parliament by a compact elected and [unable] to discern in the confusion of vioces whome the

* Query, Disturned, — distrained, *obsolete,* constrained.

255

Comons intended to have or chuse for their burgesses, they att first crying Peard and Matthews, some their old burgesses, others nay.

"The Mayor then proposed, that seeing the Petitioner would stand for one of the Burgesses, that he should be put in competition with the other 3, viz. Mr. Peard, Mr. Ferris, and Mr. Medford, and that two of them should be first proposed to the election of the Comon Burgesses, and the other two after, and that the Comons for Distinction sake should severally give their Voyces att the Barr by the poll.

"That petitioner well approved of the manner of Election proposed, but desired that he might not stand on the said Election in competition with Mr. Peard, for then, he said, he should be excluded, but to stand wth any of the other two, Mr. fferris or Mr. Medford, he was well pleased.

"The Mayor then proposed that Mr. Peard and Mr. Metford should first stand in competition in the first Election for the first Burges, And that Mr. fferris and the Petitioner should stand in competition in the Election for the second Burges, wch course the Petitioner well approved off, and gave the Mayor thanks for taking so indifferent and faire course.

"That the Comon Burgesses att the first election choose Mr. Peard, and omitted Mr. Medford, and at the next Election chose Mr. fferris, and omitted the Petitioner, Mr. fferris having 120 Voices for hym, and the Petitioner but 36; Wch being done, the Petitioner came to the Mayor in the view of the Comon Burgesses, gave him thanks for his faire carriage in the business, and likewise came to the said Mr. Peard and Mr. fferris, wished them joy of their places on election, and desired them to do their best in their places for the good of the Comon weale.

"Note:—It is an ancient custome within the towne of Barnestaple used, tyme out of mynd, to elect the Mayor and all other officers by proposing 4 or more, and on the election to sitt 2 first one against another, and the man that is first chosen is to stand for one, and then to sitt the other two in competition, and he that is elected of those two is also to stand, as in the former election of the now burgesses."

[C.]

Bye Laws of the Corporation. *

"BARNESTAPLE fs.

"Ordinances, Statutes, and Bye-Laws, revised, made, constituted,

---

* The preamble, the first "bye law," and all the others commencing with the word "Allso," are given without abbreviation; the rest I have been under the necessity of curtailing of the redundant matter in which they abound. All the "laws" are noticed, and every thing that is material in any of them is copied in full, and marked by inverted commas. The copy I have used is an ancient one, and from *an authentic source.*

ordained, ratified, and confirmed, by Christopher Hunt, Mayor of the Borough and Parish of Barnestaple aforesaid; Richard Barnes and Richard Salisbury, Aldermen; and Capital Burgesses, William Wescombe, Arthur Ackland, Thomas Harris, John Stevins, Hugh Marshall, William Lakeman, George Fairchild, John Peard, John Blake, John Prideaux, Nicholas Cooke, Thomas Seldon, James Kimpland, James Kimpland, jun., John Hunt, Jeffery Bagglehole, John Law, Nicholas Gingar, Richard Ley, and Richard Cole, being of the Common Councell of the same Borough and Parish, for the good government of the Burgesses, Artificers, and Inhabitants of the said Borough and Parish, and for a declaration in what manner and order the aforesaid Mayor, Alldermen, and Burgesses, Articifers, Inhabitants, and Residents, of the said Borough and Parish for the time being, shall use, carry, and behave themselves in their severall Offices and Business within that Borough and Parish and limitts of the same; and also for the further good and publick utility and government of the said Borough and Parish, in victualling of the same Borough and Parish; and likewise for the better government, disposition, setting and letting of Lands, Tennements, and possessions, given, granted, or assigned, or hereafter to be given, granted, or assigned, to the Mayor, Aldermen, and Burgesses, for the time being, on the twenty-fourth day of March, in the year of our Lord God, one thousand six hundred eighty-nine, by virtue of severall letters patents, heretofore granted to the Mayor, Alldermen, and Burgesses of the Borough and Parish of Barnestaple aforesaid, as
follows:–

(1.) "First. For the election of the Mayor of the aforesaid Borough and Parish of Barnestaple, it is ordained, enacted, confirmed, appointed, provided, and established, by the aforesaid Mayor, Alldermen, and Common Councell, that yearly on the Monday next after the Feast of the assumption of the Blessed Virgin Mary, in the Guildhall of the said Borough, when the old Mayor and Alldermen there for the time being come, shall be placed in their rooms, in the presence of the Common Councell or the more part of them, the same Mayor and Aldermen, or two of them, whereof one to be the Mayor, and if they cannot agree, then the more part of the Common Councell shall advisedly and discreetly, without favour or affection, mallice or displeasure, nominate four such men of the Common Councell as be of ability, convenient and meet for the office of Mayoraltie then for the next year following, and the names of two of them incontinently shall be written, separated, and fixed severally on two potts for the same purpose therefore made, then and there as hath been used and accustomed to be sett in a certain place appointed, and every of the said

257

Mayor, Aldermen, and Councell, to have one ball in their hands also provided for the same, holding both their hands close shall put one hand into one pott and the other hand into the other pott at one instant time, and letting his ball fall secretly into which pott he list, shall take his hands out of the same potts showing them forth then openly in such ways as it may not be known for whome he giveth his voyce, nor in what pott he putteth his ball; which being so done and perused particularly from the lowest to the highest, the same potts forthwith to be seen, that it may be known in what pott most balls be; and then the names of two other men of the Common Councell shall be written severally and sett upon the potts, and to be perused by the Mayor, Aldermen, and Common Councell, with balls, in like manner and forme as it was done before removing the two first names; and afterwards those two mens' names having most voices and balls to be again the third the third time sett separately on the said two potts, and to be perused by the Mayor, Aldermen, and Common Councell with balls in the said two potts, in such manner as it was before and as it hath been accustomed; and then at the last he whose name shall be found shall be preferred to the office of the mayorilty of the said Borough and Parish for the year next following, as hath been accustomed.

The form here directed to be used in choosing the Mayor is still punctually observed, but not, it is said, always with the entire absence of those prohibited but subtle intermeddlers, "favour or affection, malice or displeasure." It is customary for Members of the Common Council to be chosen to the office in rotation according to seniority, but there is a regulation which sanctions the making of *"old"* or *"new"* Mayors, (by which is meant those who have, and those who have not, passed the chair,) at their option. Whatever gave rise to this practice, it is evident the Corporation are enabled by it to keep back any member they may have an objection to, from the Mayoralty for several years, without infringing their rules. This system of exclusion is at present in action, and that without any apparent justifiable cause.

Although the ceremony of balloting is kept up, such an occurence as a contest at the election of a Mayor, is, I believe, never known; it is always equally well understood both before and after the ballot, who is to fill the office.

(2.) "Allso, for the election of the Alldermen, it is ordained and established, that the old Mayor shall be the senior Alldeman, of the said Borough and Parish for the next year after he is out of his Mayoralty, if the mayoralty of the Mayor and Comon Councell be not against if; and that at the said time and place before the precedent order order for the election of the Mayor, the said old Mayor and Alldermen for the time being, in like manner to agree upon and nominate two such grave and discreet men of the Common Councell as have been Mayor of the said Borough and Parish, whose names shall be written and fixed separately on the said two potts, and perused by the Mayor, Aldermen, and Common Councell, with balls in the like manneer and forme as it is before declared, and he in whose pott most balls be put, shall be junior Alderman of this Borough and Parish for the next year following.

(3.) "Allso, for the election of the Recorder, Deputy Recorder, and Common Councell, of this Borough and Parish, Clerke of the Market, Receivers, Collectors of the town rents, Bridge Rents, and all other rents belonging to the Corporation, one Serjeant at Mace, and all other Officers, excepting such officers as are otherwayes appointed by Charter to be chosen, or of any of them, when and so often as the case so require. It is ordained that every of them shall be nominated, appointed, tryed, and chosen, in such like manner and forme by balls, as is before ordained for the election of the Mayor of this Borough and Parish, Clerke of the Markett, Receivers, Collectors of the Town Rents, Bridge Rents, and all other rents belonging to the Corporation, one serjeant at Mace, and all other Officers of the said Borough and Parish, shall be chosen by most voices of the Mayor, Alldermen, and Capital Burgesses, for the time being, whereof the Mayor and one of the Alldermen for the time being to be two.

(4.) "At any of the said Elections, or at any other time, should the Mayor be absent by reason of sickness or otherwise, the senior Alldermen to officiate for him, except in matters of Judgement. In the absence of the Aldermen or either of them, such as have or hath been the last former Aldermen or Alderman to act, except in matters of Judgement and for holding of courts. In all and every the aforesaid elections, double balls to be laid aside, and no one shall have two voices or balls, the Mayor excepted, and he only when the number of electors present be equal. Any of the Common Council being absent at any election without a license from the Mayor, or being able to shew such good cause as shall be allowed of, shall forfeit 6s. 8d. to the Mayor, Aldermen, and Burgesses of the Borough and Parish, the same forfeiture to be levied by action of debt or by distress of his or their goods and chattles soe offending.

(5.) "Allso it is further ordained and agreed that upon the death or *moving of any of the aforesaid Chief Burgesses and Common Councell of this Borough and Parish, one other of the Burgesses of the said B. and P. shall be elected and chosen into the same office in his roome* by the said Common Councell or the most part of them, whereof the Mayor and one Alderman for the time being to be two. The said election or elections to be in the Guildhall, at such convenient time or times, between the hours of ten and twelve in the forenoon, as the Mayor for the time being shall think fit, soe it be made fourteen days or more before the election of the next Mayor; but if any of the Councell die or be *removed* from his place within fourteen days of the election of the next Mayor, that then the said election to be made at any time before the election of the next Mayor, and notice of such election to be made is to be given by one of the common serjeants of the Town, *to all the Capital Burgesses residing within the Borough,* at least twenty-four hours before the time of such election."

There appears, at first sight, to be a strange contradiction in those parts of this "ordinance" which are printed in italics; but the latter clause evidently goes to signify, that Capital Burgesses *residing without the borough,* were considered as having virtually vacated their offices, and having consequently no voice in the Common Council, were not to be summoned to its meetings, even whilst their successors remained unappointed.

"Allso, that none be admitted to be a Burgess, and to enjoy the liberty of Burgess of the Borough and Parish of Barnstaple aforesaid, *without the consent and assent of the Mayor and Common Councell* of the same Borough and Parish, or the more part of them, at any time or times of such admission, which shall be in the Guildhall of the said Borough. [This reservation by the Common Council of a power to reject a candidate for admission to burgesship, manifestly involves an acknowledgement of a right being vested in some other persons or body of men, (the freemen, doubtless!) to propose such candidate, and to have a voice in his election. We may, in fact, reasonably infer from it, that such elections had aforetime been decided among the burgesses by a majority of votes, without any distinction of person or office.] "None to be admitted a free Burgess, but those that are comfortable to Church and State, and shall take the oaths of allegiance and supremaice at the time of such their admittance."

This regulation, which, judging by the period in which it was made, was evidently directed against Roman Catholics, has also been made to operate to the exclusion of Protestant Dissenters; no nonconformist having, as far as can be ascertained, been admitted within the pale of the Corporation of Barnstaple, until the year 1828, when Capt. C. B. Gribble, of the H. E. I. C. S. was elected a Common Councilman.

(7.) "First son of a Burgess born after admission, to pay fine of 1*s.* for his burgesship; second son 2*s.*; and every other of his sons, 6*s.* 8*d.* a piece. Any person having served an apprenticeship to any Merchant or Artificer of the Borough and Parish aforesaid, being a free Burgess, here bound to serve for seven years, at least, in the trade of him to whom he is so bound, and accordingly shall so serve, to pay for his freedom 6*s.* 8*d.* so that such freedom be claimed at the next Law court [sessions] of the Borough of Barnstaple aforesaid, to be there holden next after the expiration of such apprenticeship. Any apprentice being beyond the seas, and unable to come to claime his freedom at the time before limitted, must make application within three months next after his return home from the parts beyond the seas. Every fine, certain and uncertain, is to be paid at the same time or times he or they are made freemen of the Borough and Parish of Barnstaple aforesaid, and all other persons not comprized in these Qualifications, shall pay at least 40*s.* for his admittance."

On the death or removal of a master, or by mutual agreement between master and apprentice, the latter may be made over to any other master, being a burgess, for any remaining period of his term; or an apprentice may, should his master die, serve out his time with his mistress, and have an equal claim to his freedom, as if no transfer had been made.

(8.) "Allso, that none other but such as be free Burgesses of the Borough and Parish aforesaid, shall sell any merchandize or wares other wayes then in gross, or other wayes then victual, within the Borough and Parish aforesaid; or keep open his shop window to the intent to sell, except it be at the time of the fair or market to be held within the said Borough: or use any mystery, or occupation, or handycraft within the Borough and Parish aforesaid; without special Lycence under the seals of the Mayor, Aldermen, and Capital Burgesses, of the aforesaid Borough and Parish for the time being, or of the more part of them, whereof the Mayor for the time being to be one, upon paine of such reasonable fine, or amerciment, or yearly sum or sumes of money, to be imposed or inflicted upon him or them soe offending for the same, by the Mayor, Aldermen, and Capital Burgesses of the Borough and Parish aforesaid for thetime being, or fourteen of them, whereof the said Mayor to be one, any custom or usage to the contrary thereof notwithstanding; the said fine or amerciment to be levied by debt or distress on the party so offending.

(9.) The Mayor to appoint such a free burgess "as he pleaseth, to be one of the the two Serjeants at Mace."

(10.) Any person refusing, or who shall, "delay to bear, or be in, or execute any place or office," to which he may have been appointed within the Borough, to be subjected to such "fine or amerciament as shall seem reasonable" by the Mayor, Aldermen, and Capital Burgesses.

(11.) "Allso, it is ordained, that all and every of the officers which be accountable within the said Borough and Parish of Barnstaple, (to witt) the Chamberline, the Receiver, the Bailiffs, Collectors of Rents, Bridgewardens, and all other Accountants, shall make their and every of their Accoumpts truly and fully, yearly on the Tuesday next after the feast of St. Leonard, before the Mayor and Aldermen of the said Borough and Parish for the time being, or to such others as shall be appointed by them in that behalf, in the Guildhall of the said Borough, and then and there to pay the said Mayor and Aldermen for the time being, or to such others as shall be by them appointed in that behalf, to the use of the said Mayor, Aldermen, and *Burgesses* of the Borough and parish aforesaid, all and every such sum and sums of money as each of them shal be respectively found in arrear upon his or their Accoumpt or Accompts, and if they do then and there neglect payment thereof, that then he and they and every of them soe neglecting payment as aforesaid, without reasonable excuse, shall forfeitt and pay to the use of the Mayor, Aldermen, and Burgesses of the said Borough and Parish aforesaid and their successors, twenty shillings for every day afterwards, untill the said Accompt or Accompts be made up, the debt thereupon well and truly levyed."

(12.) It is ordained, that upon any "plaint entered by any foreigner against a Burgess of the said Borough and Parish upon the first process awarded, the defendant is to be warned to appear at the next court following to answer the plaintiff, wherein the said defendant, *being a Burgess,* is to have eight days warning before the Court, and if he then make default, he is then to be amerced six pence," and the same for the second and third courts, then "Process to be awarded against him, either to attach his goods and chattles, or arrest him, by his body to appear at the fourth court to answer the plaintiff in his plaint." If any defendant cannot be found, "on request of the plaintiff another process of Capias may issue. Every defendant being attached by his body, he is forthwith to be brought to the keeper of the Prison of the said Borough and Parish, there to remain." &c.

(13.) Any person so committed to prison, shall, if the action require bail, "find unto the Mayor and Aldermen of the same Borough and Parish for the time being, one or two sufficient *Burgesses and Freemen"* as sureties, "for his continual appearance every Court, soe long as the matter in controversie shall there depend."

(14.) Any burgess summoned on a "Jury for the Tryal of any matter or issue," who shall make default, and "by reason whereof a full jury doth not appear, soe that the matter and case remain for want of jurors, shall be amerced at the first court 3s. 4d., and at the second court 6s. 8d., and so fourth, at every court following, untill a jury do appear.

(15.) "None of the Common Councell shall be at any time hereafter impannelled on any Jury, or become surety for any person in any cause or matter in the said court, on paine of 3l. 6s. 8d. by such person to be forfeited," &c.

(16.) Persons presented by the Grand Jury for petty offences, after notice given of such presentment, shall for every such offence be amerced " *Three Pence,* in every court [sessions] next following, until such offender or offenders doe appear, and submit to the grace of the court, and find surety for his Fine," &c.

(17.) "Aldermen or Commen Councell not attending the Mayor after proper notice to come unto or before him, either in the Guildhall, or at any place within the said borough," to advise with him concerning the service of his Majesty or the affairs of the Town "or shall depart (being come) without leave of the Mayor, until the business in hand be ended or put over," to pay 3s. 4d.

Inferior Burgesses not attending the Mayor on being" legally warned," to forfeit 3s. 4d., or being present, "shall not thence depart without lycence of the Mayor, upon paine of 6s. 8d."

(18.) "Allso, it is ordained, that all they which bring Corn to sell to this Borough and Markett, shall open their Baggs when the Corn Bell doth ring, which shal be at Twelve of the Clock, that the Inhabitants of this Borough and Parish may be served; and that no person haveing Corn of his own, shall buy any Corn in the Markett for change of seed, unless he bring to the Markett the same day so much Corn as he buyeth, and sell the same as the price goeth, upon paine and forfeiture of double the value thereof."

(19.) Any person putting or causing to be put "any Dung, filth, or other unclean thing, upon any of the Keys, Streets, or Lanes, within the Town or Borough," to pay 3s. 4d. "for every Time."

"No one to unload, put, or lie, any Timber, Blocks, Stocks, Milstones, or other Purprestures, upon the said Key or Keys, or Slips or Strands, and suffer the same to remain there above three days next after the landing thereof, without making Composition with the Mayor or Farmers of the Keys or Strands, upon paine of 3s. 4d.

"No one shall suffer any Dung or Soyle, Soap Ashes or Lime Ashes, to lye or continue upon any of the remotest Keys above forty eight hours, upon paine of forfeiture of the said Dung, &c. to the use of the Corporation.

"Every foreigner [non-freeman] which loads any Dung, Soap Ashes, or Lime Ashes, from any Key, shall pay 4d. per boat, and from the Strand 4d. per boat.

"Every one that fetcheth sand from the sand ridge, shall pay for each horse yearly 1d., and for every boat of Crock Sand 1d., according to the ancient custome."

No Lime Stones to be laid on the Town Land, unless compositiion be made, upon paine of forfeiture of the same.

"If any *Inhabitant* of this Borough and Parish shall neglect to cleanse his or their *street* every *week,* [rather a formidable task for an inhabitant of Boutport-street,] shall forfeit 3s. 4d. for every such neglect.

(20,) "Allso, it is ordered and agreed, that the Mayor for the time being, shall have for his pension that year 20l., in part of a recompence for his expences, and charge of his robe and Dinners, as well as at the Law Courts, as other the King's and Queen's Majesty's Courts.

"And also, shall have for the Castle Court's Dinners there yearly as hath been accustomed 5l. 6s. 8d., and for the expence of the Dinner at the Account Day, 2l. 13s. 4d.

"And also the fine of one Burgess at his choice, if there be made during his Mayoraltry.

"The Receiver shall have for his Fee yearly 6s. 8d.

"The Town Clerke for his Fee yearly 20s.

"The first Serjeant at Mace, the benefit of the prison without rent.

"The second Serjeant at Mace, yearly 4l.

"The Bridgewardens, yearly 6s. 8d.

"Each of the Searchers of the Market, 4s. 4d.

"The Mayor for the time being, for fixing the Common Seale to any writing or lease granted by the Corporation of this Borough and Parish, 2s.; and for setting the seale of the office to every writing, certificate, or attestation, 2s., whereof the Aldermen to have one moiety; and the Town Clerke to have for every writing that passeth under, or is sealed, either with the Common Seale, or the Seale of office, 8d., according to the ancient custom of the said Borough."

(21.) Any person "obstinately refusing" payment of any fine levied on him "at any of the Courts Leet, or other Courts of Record," on demand being made by the Receiver, shall forfeit 10s. in addition to the first penalty, the whole to be levied, &c. "If the Mayor be negligent or partial, or forgive thereof in whole above 10s., then he himself to be charged and chargeable to the Corporation of the Borough and Parish for the same, and of him to be had and recovered by such means as any penaltyes forfeited of any Common Burgess.

(22.) No person to "winnow Corn, Malt, or Grain, in any of the open Streets, upon paine of 12d. for every such offence."

(23.) Persons leaving "Dung, &c. before their stables, against their walls or other houses in the Streets, or Lanes," for more than forty-eight hours, to forfeit 12d., and the dung to be taken away by any person to his own use.

(24.) "Allso, it is further ordained, that no inhabitant of this Borough and Parish shall receive any pack or packs of wares into his house, brought hear to be sold by any foreigner or stranger, before the same be brought to the Key Hall, (being the common markett,) upon pain of 5s."

Would even the makers of such a "statute" as this, have ventured to convict under it? What a "reasonable law!"

(25.) Any artificer taking a stranger as a journeyman, without first acquainting the Mayor or Constables thereof, to forfeit 6s. 8d.

(26.) Any inhabitant who shall, without license from the Mayor and Common Council, permit any stranger in his house above the space of twenty days, except in certain cases, to forfeit 10s. for every month to the Churchwardens and Overseers of the Poor. "And allso, it is hereby further ordered, that the Mayor shall yearly make choice of two men in every street, to inform him of all such strangers as come into the Borough and Parish to dwell."

(27.) "Allso, it is ordered and ordained, that all and every such person and persons, as shall bring any Barques, Lifters, [Lighters] Boats, or other Vessels, to the Town and Borough, loaden with any wares or merchandize, here to be unloaden at the Quays or Slips of this Town and Borough, shall within a convenient time unload the same, and then forthwith, or at the next Flood, they shall withdraw their said vessells, and lay off from either of the said Keys or Slips, and that other Vessels that are loaden, may come conveniently to the said Keys or Slips with their Loading, to land the same, upon paine of 10s. for every such default, and the Barque or other such vessell, or the owner thereof, to be attached and stayed for the same penalties.

"All Boats and Barques, and other Vessells, comming to the Quays or Slips, that doth make use of Ballist, to ballist there, or pay 6s.8d.

The sand-ridge, it should be remembered, formerly lay on this side the water; it was of course desirable to reduce it as much as possible near the Quays.

(28.) No person to buy "Herrings or Butter by the Barrell or Pott, and retail the same, or any part thereof, the very same day that he hath bought it, upon forfeiture of the same or the value thereof."

(29.) None but Burgesses to buy any raw Hides, Claves' Skins, or Sheep Skins, except on Fridays, without licence from the Mayor, paying a yearly fine for the same, "upon paine of forfeiture of 3s. 4d. for every Hide, &c. so bought."

(30.) Any "Burgess or Inhabitant forestalling or buying any Coals to sell the same again in any place within the Port of Barnstaple, before the same Coals do come to be "Brought" to the Town, to forfeit 10s. for every wey of Coals so bought.

(31.) "Allso it is ordained that no Butcher or Victualler shall sell in the Markett this Borough, the Flesh of any Bull. or offer the same to sell, except the same Bull immediately before the slaughter be chased or beaten with dogs for the space of one houre, at the Bull Ring and usual place appointed for the same purpose within this Borough, upon paine of forfeiting of 6s. 8d. for every such default.

"And that all Butchers and Victuallers repairing to the Marketts within this Borough with any Victualls, to bring wholsom Victualls and marketable, according to bring their Sheep Skins hanging to the Flesh, according to the custome of this Borough, upon paine of a grievous Amerciament.

(32.) "Allso, it is ordered that no Inhabitant of this Borough and Parish doe receive any strange woman being with child into his House, or any Vagabond or suspected person, without licence and consent of the Mayor and Aldermen, upon paine of 40s.

(33.) "Allso, it is ordained that no Inhabitant of this Town do suffer his Hoggs, Piggs, or Ducks, to goe at large in the Streets, upon paine of loseing 1d. for every foot for every time."

(34.) All "Victualls or Fish" to be brought into the Market for sale, (except Fish sold out of Boats,) under a Penalty of 12d. "And the High Cross is hereby appointed for selling of Fish every week day except Fridays, and the Fish Shambles on the Key is appointed for selling of Fish on Fridays, and every one that buys any Fish privately in his house, shall forfeit 3s. 4d.

(35.) Any person on a market day "tying his Horse in the open Streets or on the Key" for half an hour, to forfeit 4d.

(36.) No Tanner to have any Hides sealed "But by such Sealers of Leather as shall be appointed by the Mayor," under a penalty of "12d. for every dicker of Hides, and 4d. for every dicker of Calves' skins." No Leather to be sealed until it be brought to the Key Hall, "upon paine of forfeiture of 20s. for every dicker of Leather soe sealed," both by the Sealer and the Tanner.

(37.) "Allso, it is ordained and established, according to the ancient custom of this Borough and Parish, that the Mayor of this Borough and Parish for the time being, shall have of every Boat that bringeth Coals to this town for any Foreigner, one bushell of the same Coals; and likewise of every Boat that bringeth Corne to this Town to be sold for any Foreigner, one bushell of the same Corne to his own use and behoofe, provided that if any Freeman shall participate with a Foreigner as a partner in Coals, the Burgess to be excused, and the bushell paid only by the Foreigner, according to the ancient custom of this Borough.

Salt also, although not mentioned here, pays toll to the Mayor in a similar way. 84lbs, (for a "bushell,") is taken on every importation of this article, whether it be a ship-load, or only part of a cargo. This, when salt, in consequence of the enormous duty on it, was retailed at 36s. per cwt., was a perquisite worth enjoying; now it is but trifling.

Query—Why was not this impost noticed in these Bye Laws; can it be of more modern date?

(38.) "Allso, it is further ordained that if any Inhabitant of this Borough and Parish, not being of the Common Councell, upon commanding or warning thereof given to him by the constables or one of them, refuse and do not come before the Mayor of this Borough and Parish, to answer unto such matters as shall be objected against him, having no lawfull impediment or excuse to the contrary, shall forfeit and pay for every such default, 3s. 4d.

(39.) "Allso, it is further ordained and established, that when there is

266

any meeting appointed by the Mayor for the time being, for the Common Councell of this Borough and Parish at the Guildhall, there to consent and treat of causes and matters touching the state and behoof of the Inhabitants of this Borough and Parish, for the establishing of any orders, rules, or provisions, to be observed and kept within this Borough and Parish, or for any other cause or matter whatsoever, that there shall not be spoken or used by the said Common Councell or any of them, any unseemly, irreverent, or reproachful words one to the other of them, but that every of them shall, in decent, comely, and quiet manner, speak and answer unto the matter propounded; and if any of them demean himself otherwise, and be faulty and offend therein, and so found and adjudged by the mayor, and Aldermen, and Common Councell for the time being, there present, or the major part of them, the party so misdemeaning himself and offending to be fined for such his misdemeanor therein, 3s. 4d.

(40.) "Allso, for avoiding of confusion and disorderly and superfluous speeches and talk in the said assemblies and meeting of the said Common Councell as aforesaid; it is also ordered and established, that all and every the said meetings none shall speak or talk while another is speaking, neither talk one with another after silence is command to be kept by Mr. Mayor or the Alldermen for the time being, but that every one shall give attentive ear to him that speaketh untill he hath ended his speech, who shall direct all his speech to the Mayor if present, and if absent, to the Alldermen, and that to the matter propounded and then in question, upon paine of paying for every such offence 12d.

(41.) "Allso, it is agreed that if any of the Common Councell of this Borough shall reveal or disclose any matter communed or treated of in the said meetings and assemblies which is to be kept secret, or that which shall turne to the hurt or displeasure of the whole Common Councell, or ony one or more of them, the parties soe offending shall loose and forfeit for every time 20s. to be levyed by action of debt or distress of the offender's goods.

(42.) "Allso, it is ordained that the Bailiffs of this Borough and Parish or either of them during the time of their office, shall not compound or make composition or bargin with any person or persons repairing to this Borough and Markett for their custome and toll by the year or otherwise, but shal weekly take and receive the same as it ariseth and happeneth to become due; and also that they shall not attach any person or persons upon any plaint in the Castle Court, without they and every of them make use of tipp staves (beyond the memory of man used) by the said Bailiffs within the said Borough, in all attachments used in the said Courts, and that the same Bailiffs for the time being, shall take for serving every attachment 6d., as hath been formerly accustomed to be paid and noe more, and shall be sworn in the Court of Record of the Borough and Parish of Barnestaple, or on the Law-day Court of the said Borough next after their election, upon paine of forfeiture of 40s. to the Corporation of Barnestaple aforesaid.

(43.) "Allso, it is ordained that all the free Burgesses of the Borough and Parish of Barnestaple shall do suit yearly to the two Law-day Courts, holden in the Guildhall of the Borough and Parish aforesaid, before the Mayor and Steward of the said Borough and Parish for the time being, and every one making default and having noe lawfull excuse, shall be amerced at every of the said Courts for such his default, 6d.

(44.) "Allso, it is further ordained and established, to avoid the abuses and cheats in weighing yearn and wooll and private beams, that all those that do buy any yearn or wooll within the liberty of this Borough and Parish of Barnestaple, shall immediately thereupon bring and weigh the same at their Majesty's beam within this Borough, as hath been accustomed, upon paine on the Buyer of 6s. 8d. for every such offence, to be recovered by action of debt or by distress of the offender's goods.

(45.) This excellent, but scarcely known "ordinance," provides, that "for the avoiding of the great inconvenientcy, damage and hurt that may happen to this Borough, or the Inhabitants thereof, by fire, It is ordained, established, and ordered, that no Potter, Brewer, or Baker, within this Town and Borough, or the Liberties of the same, shall from henceforth erect, make, or set up any ffurse Rick or Wood Rick within this Town and Borough of Barnestaple, in any of their Yards or Backsides of their Houses, unless the same can be erected at least Ten Land Yards [165 feet] from any House within the said Town and Borough, upon Paine and Penalty of 5l."

It also enacts, that "no Inhabitant of this Town shall receive or take into their Houses or Yards, any more Furse at any one time, than they or either of them shall burn and consume in twenty-four hours next after bringing in of the same Furse, upon paine of loosing 20s. for every time."

(46.) "Allso, it is further ordained and agreed that the Mayor and Alldermen of the Borough and Parish of Barnestaple aforesaid for the time being, and all the residue of the Common Councell of the same Borough and Parish for the time being, shall yearly from time to time upon the Fair Day to be kept within the same Borough, meet together at the Guildhall there, at one of the clock in the afternoon of the same day, and forthwith from thence go alltogether in comely manner about the same Borough as in times past they have accustomed to do, and that every one of the said Common Councell for the time being that maketh default, and doth not repair to the said Guildhall at the said hour appointed, haveing noe good and lawfull excuse to the contrary, shall forfeit and loose to the use of the Corporation of the Borough and Parish of Barnestaple aforesaid 6s. 8d,

(47.) "Allso, it is agreed and ordained that the Mayor of the Borough and Parish of Barnestaple aforesaid for the time being, shall from henceforth call to his assistance at the Guildhall within the said Borough every Thursday fortnight, the Common Councell of this Borough and Parish for the time being, to meet there and assemble for the treating on, and taking into consideration whatsoever shall be thought fitt, necessary, and convenient for the welfare, reputation, honor, and good government of this Corporation; and that this meeting shall be at nine of the clock in the forenoon of every of the same days, and the first meeting to be the Thursday sennight next after the Mayor for the time being shall be sworne, and thenceforth to continue as aforesaid.

(48.) "Allso, it is agreed and ordained that noe Burgess shall colour the goods of a Foreigner, whereby this Corporation may be defrauded of the receipt and enjoyment of those duties which shall grow due for the same goods, on paine of 5l. to be recovered by action of debt or distress of the offender's goods, or disfranchisement of the offender for acting contrary to his oath, at the choice and discretion of the Mayor, Allderman, and Capitall Burgesses, or the major part of them, for the time being.

(49.) Allso, that within three months next after any person is elected to be one of the Common Councell, he shall provide for himself a comely gown, to be worn by him in conformity to the rest of the Common Councell of this Borough, upon paine of forfeiting 5l. to the use of the Corporation, to be levyed by way of distress of the offender's goods, and for every month after that time that such person shall continue in contempt to forfeit 20s. to be levyed by distress as aforesaid, and weare the same every Sunday at Church with the rest of the brotherhood, onn paine of forfeiting 12d. for every default.

(50.) "Allso, that the Mayor for the time being, and such as have been Mayor of this Town of Barnestaple, shall yearly wear their scarlet robes on the days following viz. the day of the election of the new Mayor, the eighth of September, the fifth of November, Christmas Day, Easter Day, Whitsunday, and the nine and twentieth day of May.

(51.) "Allso, that whereas the land belonging to this Town of Barnestaple and the Long Bridge of the same are by deeds demised and granted unto several persons of this Town as Feoffees in trust for the same, that henceforth no bargin, sale, lease, nor grant of any lands or tenements, garden or rents, belonging to the Corporation of this Towne or

Long Bridge aforesaid, in possession, revertion, remainder, or in use of obligation or acquittance, annuity or pension, to be made to any person or persons for term of life, years, or in fee, by the said Feoffees or their successors, by writing under the common seale, or any other private seales of the said Feoffees, to the prejudice of the Corporation, nor contracted for, but publickly in the Guildhall, and that for all the several fines, monies, profits, and receipts whatsoever resulting from the same, the Feoffees and their successors shall be accountable to the Mayor, Aldermen, and Common Councell of the Town for the time being, and make payment unto them according, for the use of the Corporation, that no person or persons, officer or officers whatsoever, shall presume to do any high or weighty matter touching the Corporation or liberty of the Town, but by publick consent of the Common Councell or the major part of them, upon paine that such offender or offenders shall make satisfaction to the Corporation as shall be answerable to the said prejudice done, to be recovered by action of debt or distress, and further shall suffer and undergoe such other fine for his misdemeanor and breach of this order as shall be suitable to the demeritt of the said offence, to be levyed also by action of debt or distress as aforesaid.

CHRISTOPHER HUNT, MAYOR

RICHARD BARNES, ⎫
RICHARD SALISBURY, ⎭ ALLDERMEN

WILLIAM WESCOMBE	HIGH MARSHALL
JOHN PEARD	WILLIAM WAKEMAN
JOHN BLAKE	JOHN PRIDEAUX
NICHOLAS COOKE	JEFFERY BAGGLEHOLE
JAMES KIMPLAND	JOHN LAW
JAMES KIMPLAND, JUN.	NICHOLAS GINGAR
JOHN HUNT	

"We doe, as much as in us lyeth, ratifye, confirm, and allow of these Bye Laws. Witness our hands and seals the three and twentieth day of September, 1690

—————————— [The first signature is illegible.]

" P. UMBRIS"

[D.]

Charter of King Henry II. (date uncertain.)*

"HENRY, King of England, and Duke of Normandy and Aquitain, and Earl of Anjou, to the Archbishops, Bishops, and Barons, and my faithful man, French and English, greeting. Know ye that I have granted to the Burgesses of the Borough of Banrestaple, all the right customs which they had in the time of King Henry, my Grandfather, having removed all the bad customs after my Grandfather there arisen. Knoe ye that they have the customs of London, and so testify before me that they and the Barons of London so freely, honorably, and justly have the same as ever they better had in the time of my Grandfather. Witness Am. Bishop of Excester, and Reginald Earl of Cornwall, and Thomas Chancellor of London."

[E.]

Charter of King Henry I. to the City of London.

(This Charter, with two others, one by King Henry II., the other by Richard I., both confirmatory of the first Henry's, appear to have been procured at an early period by the Burgesses of Barnstaple, that they might know to what privileges they were entitled in having "The Customs of London.")

"HENRY, by the Grace of God, King of England, To the Archbishop of Canterbury, and the Bishops, and Abbotts, and Earls, and Barons, and Justices, and Sheriffs, and all his faithful men, French and English, of all England, Greeting. Know ye, that I have granted to my citizens of London to hold Middlesex at Farm for 300l. at acc,ount to them and their Heirs, of me and my Heirs, so that the same Citizens may put such Sheriff as they shall chuse of themselves, and any other justice whomsoever they will, from among themselves, to keep the Pleas of my Crown, and to Plead the same; and none other shall be Justice over the same men of London. And the citizens shall be quit of schot and lot, and of danegelt, and of murder;† and none of them shall make war. And if any of the Citizens shall be impleaded of Pleas of the Crown, the man of

---

* This Charter appears never to have been dated. The copy in the Tower is "without date," as is also that (if they possess one) in the Hands of the Corporation.

† This crime was anciently punishable by a fine called Were or Wereguild, "in old customs the price of homicide; paid partly to the King for the loss of a subject, partly to the Lord whose vassal he was, and partly to the next of kin of the person slain." The penalty at this time is said to have been 100s.

London shall justify himself by oath, that he will be ajudged within the City, and no one, neither of my household nor of any other, shall be lodged, nor delivered by foreign force, within the walls of the city; and all the men of London, all of them throughout all England and the seaports, shall be quit and free of toll, and passage, and lastage, and all other customs; and the Churches and Barons, and Citizens, may have and hold, well and in peace, their Stokes with all customs, so that the Guests who shall be lodged in Stokes, give customs to no one but to him whose stoke it shall be, or his Minister whom he shall have placed there. And a man of London shall not be adjudged in amerciament of money, unless the mulct amounts to the sum of 100s. that being the amount of his wear. I speak of a plea which may appertain to money. And further, that there be no miskenning in the hustings, nor in the folksmote, nor in other pleas within the city, and the hustings shall sit once in the week, (that is to say,) on Monday. And I will cause my Citizens to have their Lands, and Recognizances, and Debts, within the City and without. And of the Lands whereof they shall complain to me, I will hold to them right by the Law of the City; and if any one hath taken toll or custom from my citizens of London, the Citizens of London in the City shall take of the Borough or Town, where toll or custom shall have been taken, so much as the man of London gave for the toll, and the damage that he hath received thereupon. And all debtors who owe debts to the Citizens of London, shall pay them in London, or justify themselves that they ought not; but if they will not pay the same, neither come to justify themselves that they ought to pay the same, then the Citizens of London to whom their debts are owing, may take their distresses in the City of London, of the Borough or Town, or of the County, wherein he who owes the debt dwells. And the citizens of London may have their chases to hunt as their ancestors have better and more fully had, (that is to say,) in Cheltre, and in Middlesex, and in Surry. Witness, the Bishop of Winchester, and at Westminster."

[F.]

Charter of King John.–1200.

"JOHN, by the Grace of God, King of England, Lord of Ireland, Duke of Normandy, Aquatain, and Earl of Anjou, to the Archbishops, Bishops, Abbotts, Priors, Earls, Barons, Justices, Sheriffs, Reeves, Ministers, and all his Bailiffs and faithful men, greeting. Know ye that we have granted to our Burgesses of the Borough of Barnstaple, all the right customs which they had in the time of King Henry our Great Grandfather having removed all the bad customs which after our Great Grandfather there arose. And know ye, that they have the customs of London as the Charter of the king our Father reasonably testify. Also we will and firmly command and by this our present Charter have confirmed that the same Burgesses of the Borough aforesaid be quit of toll, passage, pontage, as well in lands as in waters, as well in fairs as in markets, and of all secular service and custom throughout all our lands on this side the sea, and beyond and through all our Dominion which King Richard our brother granted to them, as much as to the King belongs. And we prohibit that any one disturb them hereupon, or do them injury, molestation, or grievance, upon forfeiture to us. Nor that any Burgess of the Borough of Barnstaple aforesaid, when they shall pass through our Land, be disturbed or be permitted to be disturbed for the debt of others, unless they be debtors or the sureties of such debtors. Moreover we grant of our gift thaat thaey may be quit of lastage and stallage throughout all our land as much as to us belongs. Witness, William Marshall Earl of Pembroke, William Brewer, Robert Turnham, John Marshall. Given by the hands of Thomas William Archdeacon, John de Gray Archdeacon of Gloucester, at Sailsbury, on the fifteenth day of June, in the second year of our Reign."

[G.]

Charter of King Henry III.–1236.

"HENRY, by the Grace of God, King of England, Lord of Ireland, and Duke of Normandy and Acquitain, and Earl of Anjou, to the Archbishops, Bishops, Abbots, Priors, Earls, Barons, Justices, Sheriffs, Reeves, Ministers, and all my Bailiffs and faithful men, greeting. Know ye that we have seen the Charter of the Lord John our Father, which he made to our Burgesses of the Borough of Barnstaple, in these words. [Here the Charter of King John is recited.] We, therefore, holding valid the grants of the aforesaid King John our Father, and King Henry our Grandfather, and King Henry our Great Grandfather, and King Richard our Uncle, of which mention is made in the Charter of the aforesaid King, the same for us and our Heirs, do grant, and by this our present Charter have confirmed, as the Charters aforesaid Predecessors of the Kingdom of England, which thereof they have, do reasonably testify. These being Witnesses, Simon de Montford, De Ralejh Treasurer of Excester, John Fitz-Geoffry Almande, Saint Amando, Nicholas De Merlis, Richard de

273

Gray, John de Pleyster, Hammond Fitz-Philip, William Gemoun, Emene de Say, and others. Given by the hand of the venerable Father Robert Bishop of Chichester our Chancellor, at Westminster, the twentieth day of March, in the twenty-first year of our Reign.

[H.]

Inspeximus Charter of King Henry VI.–1444.

"Henry, by the Grace of God, King of Engalnd and France, and Lord of Ireland, to all to whom these present letters shall come, greeting. We have seen a certain transcript of a certain Charter of the Lord Henry, late King of England, after the Conquest the third our progenitor remaining amongst the former records of the Chancery of the Kingdom of England, being within the Tower of London, in these words." (Here follows the Inspeximus of Henry III., of the Charter of John, which it recites at length; also an Inspeximus by Edward II. of the Charter of Edward I. which recccapitulates and confirmes that of Henry II. and takes notice of the abovementioned one of Henry III.)

"And, we holding firm and valid the said grants and confirmations, the same for us and our Heirs as much as in us lies, Do grant unto the afore-said Burgesses and their Successors, as the Charters aforesaid reasonably testify. Willing moreover to do the same Burgesses more ample grace for a fine which they have made with us, we have granted to them for us and their Heirs, that although they or their predecessors have not hitherto used the Liberties above written, or either of them in any case arising, yet they, and their Heirs and Successors, Burgesses of the same Borough, may nevertheless hereafter fully enjoy and use the same liberties and every of them, without the hindrance and impediment of us or our heirs, or our Ministers whomsoever. Moreover, for the fine aforesaid we have granted to them, for us and our Heirs, and by this our Charter have confirmed for the amelioration of the aforesaid Borough of Barnstaple, and the advantage of the Burgesses of the same Borough, that they may so much the more quietly attend to their business, that none of them shall plead or be impleaded before us or our Heirs, or any of the Justices of us and our Heirs, without the Borough of Barnstaple aforesaid, of Lands or Tenements which are within the the bounds and limits of the Borough aforesaid, or in the same suburbs, or of Trespasses or Contracts or other things whatsoever in the same Borough of Barnstaple and the Suburbs made or arising. But all such Pleas which before us or our Heirs, or any of our [Justices] of the Bench or others, shall happen to be summoned or attached without the Borough and Suburbs aforesaid, to be pleaded before the Mayor and Bailiffs for the time being, within the Borough aforesaid, shall be pleaded and determined, unless the same Pleas touch us, or our Heirs, or our Ministers, or the Comonality of the Borough of Barnstaple aforesaid. And that they be not put with foreign men in any Assizes, Juries, or Inquisitions, which by reason of tenement, or trespasses, or other foreign business whatsoever, before the Justices, or other Ministers of us or our Heirs, shall happen to be done, nor that the same foreign men be put with the same Burgesses in any Assizes, Juries, or Inquisitions, which by reason of Land or Tenement being in the same Borough and Suburbs, or of trespasses, or contracts, or other intrinsic businesses, there shall happen to be taken, but by the same assizes, juries, and inquisitions of those things, which in the said Borough and Suburbs shall have arisen, shall be made by the Burgesses of the same Borough in the same Borough only, unless the same business concern us or our Heirs, or the Comonality of the aforesaid Borough of Barnstaple. And that they may have Infangenethef and Outfangenethef, and that of any Pleas within the said Borough and Suburbs aforesaid arising, that they shall not be tried by Foreigners but only by their Burgesses, unless the same business concern us or our Heirs, or our Ministers, or the Comonality of the said Borough of Barnstaple aforesaid, and that the Burgesses of the Borough aforesaid and their Heirs and Successors, Burgesses of the same Borough be for ever quit of murage, pavage, piccage, anchorage, standage, and segiage of all their things, goods, and merchandizes, throughout all our Kingdom and Dominion. These being Witness, &c. Given, &c. and we the tenors of the transcripts aforesaid, at the request of the now Mayor and Burgesses of the Town aforesaid, have commanded to be exemplified by these presents. In testimony whereof we have caused these out letters to be made Patent. Witness ourselves at Westminster, the eighth day of March, in the twenty-third year of our Reign."

[I.]

Charter of Philip and Mary. - 1556

"PHILIP and MARY, by the Grace of God, King and Queen of England,

Spain, France, to the Sicily's, Jerusalem, and Ireland, Defenders of the Faith, Archdukes of Austria, Dukes of Burgundy, Milan, and Brabant, Earls of Strasburgh, Flanders, and Ferol, to all to whom these present letters shall come, Greeting. Whereas our Borough of Barnstaple, in the county of Devon, is a very Ancient Borough, and having in itself one Mayor, two Bailiffs, and other Officers and Ministers, by whom the said Borough, and the Men and Inhabitants of the same, from time whereof the memory of man is not to the contrary, have been governed and hitherto are still governed. And which Men, Burgesses, and Inhabitants of the same Borough, from time whereof the memory of man is not to the contrary, have continually had and enjoyed, as well of the grant and quit of divers of our Progenitors, Kings of England, as by prescription, many acquittances, immunities, rights, jurisdictions, liberties, franchises, and privileges, whereupon and because the said Burgesses and Inhabitants of the said Borough of Barnstaple have humbly besought us for a remedy thereof by them to be had, and that we would vouchsafe sufficiently to incorporate the same Borough and the Inhabitants thereof, and to make thereof a Body Corporate.

b "Know ye therefore, that we, favouring the petition aforesaid, of our special grace and of our certain knowledge and meer motion, have granted, and for us the Heirs and Successors of us the aforesaid Queen, by these presents do grant, to the Burgesses and Inhabitants of the said Borough of Barnstaple, that the said Borough of Barnstaple hereafter be and shall be a free Borough Corporate, in deed, fact, and name of one Mayor, Aldermen, and Burgesses for ever; and the same Borough a body corporate and Politic of itself for ever, of one Mayor, Aldermen, and Burgesses, really and fully, we erect, make, and create by these presents; and that the Inhabitants of the same borough hereafter be and shall be one body Corporate and Politic, and one perpetual Commonalty in deed, fact, and name, by the name of the Mayor, Aldermen, and Burgesses of the Borough of Barnstaple, and that they may have perpetual succession.

c "And that they by the same name be and shall be persons able and capable in the Law to have, acquire, receive, hold, and possess Lands, Tenements, Liberties, Franchises, and Hereditaments, to them and their successors in fee and perpetuity.

d "And by the same name they may and shall be able to plead and be impleaded, answer and be answered, defend and be defended, in any courts and places, and before any Judge or Justices, or other persons whomsoever, in all and singular actions, plaints, causes, matters, and demands of what kind or nature soever they be, in the same manner and form as other our liege subjects, persons able and capable in the Law, may and can plead and be impleaded, answer and be answered, defend and be defended.

e "And that they may and shall have a common seal and for the doing and transacting their causes and businesses whatsoever, and that it may and shall be lawful to them and their successors, at their pleasure, to break, change, and make anew the aforesaid seal.

f "And also we will, and for us and the Heirs and Successors of the aforesaid Queen, by these presents do grant to the Aforesaid Mayor, Aldermen, and Burgesses, and their Successors, that hereafter and for ever there be and shall be in the aforesaid Borough of Barnstaple, twenty-four of the more discreet and honest men of the said Borough, who shall be and shall be called Capital Burgesses of the same Borough, and out of which twenty-four Burgesses from time to time there may and shall be two of the elder and more honest of them, who shall be called Aldermen of the said borough, and which Aldermen and Capital Burgesses shall be assisting and aiding the said Mayor of the same Borough for the time being, in causes and matters touching the same Borough, and shall be the Common Council of the same Borough, for the Statutes, Acts, and Ordinances touching and concerning the public utility and advantage of the same Borough and the Inhabitants thereof, for the time being, by them or the major part of them, with the Mayor of the same Borough for the time being, from time to time to be done and performed, for the better government and rule of the men, and the causes, things, and businesses of the said Borough for the time being.

g "And further we will, and for us and the Heirs and Successors of us the aforesaid Queen, by these presents grant to the aforesaid Mayor, Aldermen, and Burgesses, and their successors, that they and their successors, by their Common Council or the major part of them, may have authority, faculty, and power to frame, constitute, ordain, and make from time to time any reasonable laws, statutes, and ordinances whatsoever, for the government and rule of the Artificers of the borough aforesaid, for the time being, as shall be good and necessary for the Commonwealth of the said Borough and the countries adjoining and for the better government of the same, so that the said laws, statutes, and ordinances be not repugnant nor contrary to the laws and statutes of the Kingdom of England of us and the Heirs of us the aforesaid Queen.

h "And that all and singular the premises may have the better effect, Know ye that we of our more ample grace and of our certain knowledge and meer motion, have assigned, nominated, made, and ordained, and by these presents do assign, nominate, make, and ordain our beloved George Stapleton, an honest man and an Inhabitant of the said Borough of

Barnstaple, to be the first and present Mayor of the Borough of Barnstaple, faithfully to execute the office of Mayor of the same Borough by his Oath, until the Feast of St. Michael the Archangel next coming, and from the same Feast until another person shall be elected, and in due manner sworn faithfully to execute the same office; and the same George Stapleton we do by these presents make, create, constitute and declare to be the Mayor of the borough aforesaid during the time aforesaid. And also we have assigned, nominated made, and ordained, and by these presents do assign, nominate, make and ordain our beloved Thomas Davy the Elder, and Roger Wrothe, to be the first and present Aldermen of the said Borough of Barnstaple. And also we have assigned, nominated, made, and ordained, and by these presents do assign, nominate, make and ordain our beloved Richard Skinner, James Goddesland, Robert Apple, Robert Cade, John Manning, John Smith, William Salisbury, William Pawle, Thomas Gribble, John Bird, Robert Long, Richard Downe, William Dawkins, David Hayne, Richard Waydridge, Edward Colscott, John Holland, John Darte, Nicholas Morcombe, Nicholas Chelenger, Nicholas Wychalls, and Hugh Brangers to be the first and present principal Burgesses of the said borough of Barrnstaple; and the aforesaid Aldermen and principal Burgesses of the Borough aforesaid, upon their Oath corporally taken before the aforesaid George Stapleton, the present Mayor aforesaid, we do by these presents make, create, constitute, and declare to be the Common Council of the same Borough.

i "And also of our more ample grace we will, and of our certain knowledge and meer motion for us the Heirs and Successors of us the aforesaid Queen, by these presents grant to the aforesaid Mayor, Aldermen, and Burgesses of the said Borough of Barnstaple, that they the aforesaid Capital Burgesses and Common Council for the time being, or the major part of them, from time to time every year hereafter for ever, on Monday next before the Feast of the Assumption of the Blessed Virgin Mary, between the hours of nine and twelve in the forenoon of the same day, do assemble, and may and shall be able to assemble within the Guildhall of the aforesaid Borough, or in any other convenient place within the same Borough, and may and shall be able there to nominate and assign one of themselves who shall be the Mayor of the Borough aforesaid, for one whole year then next coming.

j "And that he, after he shall have been so as aforesaid elected to be Mayor of the Borough aforesaid, before he be admitted to execute the same office, shall take his corporal oath, on Monday next following the feast of Saint Faith, after the nomination and election aforesaid, before the Mayor, being his last predecessor, in the Guildhall or in any other convenient place within the Borough aforesaid, in the presence of the Aldermen and ten other Capital Burgesses of the Borough aforesaid for the time being, well and faithfully to execute the said office; and after such oath so taken, he may and shall be able to execute the office of Mayor of the Borough aforesaid, for one whole year then next following.

k "And moreover we will, and for us the Heirs and Successors of us the aforesaid Queen, by those presents grant unto the aforesaid Mayor, Aldermen, and Burgesses of the Borough aforesaid, that if it shall happen that the Mayor of the Borough aforesaid at any time within one year after he shall have been so as aforesaid appointed and sworn to the office of Mayor of the Borough aforesaid, shall die or from his office be amoved, that then and so often it shall and may be lawful to the aforesaid Aldermen and Capital Burgesses of the Common Council of the Borough aforesaid for the time being, or of the major part of them, to elect and appoint another of themselves to be Mayor of the Borough aforesaid, and that he so elected and appointed may have and exercise the same office during the residue of the same year, first taking his corporal oath in form aforesaid, and so as often as the case shall thus happen.

l "And we will, and by these present for us, the Heirs and successors of us the aforesaid Queen, grant to the aforesaid Mayor, Aldermen, and Burgesses of the Borough aforesaid, and their Successors, and the said Aldermen and Burgesses of the Common Council of the Borough aforesaid for the time being, or the major part of them, from time to time and at all times hereafter for ever, may and shall have power and authority yearly and every year, on the said Monday next before the aforesaid Feast of the assumption of the blessed Virgin Mary, to elect and nominate, and they they may and shall be able to elect and nominate, two out of themselves to be the Aldermen of the Borough aforesaid, for one whole year thence next coming, and that they so as aforesaid elected and nominated, before they be admitted to execute the same office of Aldermen, shall take their corporal oath, on Monday next after the Feast of Saint Faith, after the nomination and election aforesaid, before the Mayor and Aldermen so then being their Predecessors, in the presence of ten other Capital Burgesses for the time being, well and faithfully to execute the same office of Aldermen of the Borough aforesaid, and that after such oath so taken they shall and may be able to execute the office of Aldermen of the Borough aforesaid for one whole year then next following.

m "And moreover we will, and for us and the Heirs and Successors of us the aforesaid Queen, by these presents grant to the aforesaid Mayor, Aldermen, and Burgesses of the Borough aforesaid and their Successors, that if it shall happen that the Aldermen of the Borough aforesaid or either of them, at any time within one year after he or they shall have been so as aforesaid appointed and sworn to the office of Aldermen of the Borough aforesaid, shall die, or from his or their office be amove, that then and so often it shall and may be lawful to the aforesaid Capital Burgesses for the time being, or the major apart of them, to elect and appoint one other or others out of themselves to be Alderman or Aldermen of the Borough aforesaid, and that he or they so elected and appointed may have and exercise the same office during the remainder of the same year, first taking his or their Corporal oath in form aforesaid; and so as often as the case shall thus happen.

n "And we will, and by these presents ordain, and for us and the Heirs and Successors of us the aforesaid Queen grant to the aforesaid Mayor, Aldermen, and Burgesses of the Borough aforesaid, and their Successors, that as often as and whensoever it may happen that any of the Capital Burgesses of Barnstaple for the time being, shall die, or out of the said Borough shall dwell, or from his office of Burgess of the same Borough for any cause be amoved, that then and so often it shall and may be lawful to the Mayor, Aldermen, and residue of the Capital Burgesses of the same Borough for the time being, from time to time when and whensoever it shall please and seem expedient to them, within eight days next after the death or amotion of the said Burgesses, in the aforesaid Guildhall or in any other convenient place within the Borough aforesaid, at their pleasure to assemble, and their to nominate and elect one or more of the other persons then Inhabitants of the said Borough of Barnstaple to be the Burgess or Burgesses of the same Borough during his or their life or lives; and that every person so nominated and elected, from the time of such election, shall be a Burgess or Burgesses of the same Borough during his or their life or lives; or otherwise if it shall so seem good and expedient to the Mayor, Aldermen, and other Burgesses of the said Borough of Barnstaple for the time being, and the person so nominated and elected and to be nominated and elected to the office of Capital Burgess of the said Borough, shall take his Corporal oath before the Mayor of the same Borough, well and faithfully to exercise and execute the office of Capital Burgess of the same Borough; and so as often as the case shall thus happen.

p "And further, of our more ample grace, and of our certain knowledge and meer motion, we will, and by these presents for us and the Heirs and Successors of us the aforesaid Queen, grant unto the aforesaid Mayor, Aldermen, and Burgesses of the said Borough of Barnstaple, and their Successors, that they may have and enjoy all the customs, liberties, franchises, immunities, exemptions, acquittances, and jurisdictions, which the

Burgesses of the said Borough of Barnstaple, and which the Mayor and Bailiffs of the Borough aforesaid, and which the Inhabitants of the same Borough, or any or either of them, by any name or names whatsoever, or by any incorporation, or by pretext of any incorporation, have heretofore had, held, or enjoyed, or ought to have had, held, or enjoyed, by reason or pretext of any Charters or Letters patent, by us or by any of the Progenitors of us the aforesaid Queen, Kings of this Kingdom of England, in any wise howsoever, heretofore made, confirmed, and granted, or by any lawful manner, right, custom, use, prescription, or title, heretofore used, had, and accustomed.

q "And further of our more ample grace, and of our certain knowledge and meer motion, we will, and for us and the Heirs and Successors of us the aforesaid Queen, by these presents grant to the aforesaid Mayor, Aldermen, and Burgesses of the said Borough of Barnstaple, and their Successors, that they may and shall have within the said Borough of Barnstaple, and the bounds and limits thereof, assize and assay of bread, wine, and beer.

r "And further, know ye, that we of our more ample grace, and of our certain knowledge and meer motion have given and granted, and by these presents for us, the Heirs and Successors of us, the aforesaid Queen, do give and grant to the aforesaid Mayor, Aldermen, and Burgesses of the Borough aforesaid, and their Successors, View of Frankpledge of all and singular the Inhabitants and Residents, as well entire residents as not entire residents, within the said Borough of Barnstaple, and within the bounds and limits of the same, for the time being, and from time to time for ever, and all things to View of Frankpledge appertaining or belonging, and which shall or ought to belong and appertain, within the aforesaid Borough of Barnstaple, twice by the year, (to wit) once within a month next after the Feast of St. Michael the Archangel, to be held before the aforesaid Mayor and Steward of the borough aforesaid, or before the Steward of the same borough for the time being, every year.

s "And we will, and by these presents for us, the Heirs and Successors of us, the aforesaid Queen, do grant to the aforesaid Mayor, Aldermen, and Burgesses of the said Borough of Barnstaple, and their Successors, that the same Mayor, Aldermen, and Burgesses, and their Successors, may have and hold, and may and shall be able to have and hold for ever, within the Borough aforesaid, one Market every Friday in every week, and one Fair there yearly to be holden and kept on the Feast of the Nativity of the blessed Virgin Mary, and to continue by three days following the same Feast, and on the eve of the same; together with all profits, commodities, and emoluments whatsoever, from such Market or Fair issuing, arising, or happening, and will all the liberties and free customs of such Market and Fair appertaining and belonging, in as ample manner and form as the Inhabitants of the same Borough have, heretofore had and enjoyed. *t* "And further, know ye, that we, the aforesaid King and Queen, design to provide for the protection, defence and government of the Orphans and Infants who hereafter shall and may happen to be in the Borough aforesaid; and that the lands, tenements, goods, and chattels of the same, may hereafter for ever, from time to time, be well, and faithfully, and justly kept, without waste and destruction; and that the same lands, tenements, goods and chattels, may be employed and bestowed to the best use and profit of the same Orphans during their minority, for the more ample advantage and utility of the same Orphans and Infants; of our special Grace, and of our certain knowledge and meer motion, will, by these presents, for us, the Heirs and Successors of us the aforesaid Queen, grant to the aforesaid Mayor, Aldermen, and Burgesses of the Borough aforesaid, and their successors, that the Mayor, Aldermen, and Capital Burgesses of the Borough aforesaid, and their successors, that the Mayor, Aldermen, and Capital Burgesses of the Borough aforesaid, for the time being, and their Successors, may and shall have hereafter for ever the custody and government of all and singular the Orphans, whomsoever of the Burgesses and Inhabitants within the Borough aforesaid, and the liberty of the same. And that they may have and shall have authority, faculty, and power, to receive, levy, collect, sieize, keep, and to cause to be kept in the common treasury of the Borough aforesaid, by the Chamberlain of the Borough aforesaid for the time being, all the goods and chattels and the debts and legacies whatsoever, within the Borough aforesaid, and the precincts of the same, happening, arising, found, or being, of any Orphan whomsoever of any Burgesses and Inhabitants of the Borough aforesaid, hereafter happing to die and to put out, use, bestow, and dispose of the same goods, chattels, debts, and legacies to the better use, advantage, and profit of the same Orphans. And that they shall be charged with the same goods and chattels, debts and legacies, towards the aforesaid Orphans; and that the same goods and chattels, debts and legacies, together with the increase and profit thereof, they shall pay and deliver to the same Orphans, at such age, in the same manner and form in all things as in our City of London, now or hereafter in that behalf is or hath been used and accustomed. And that they may have all and such actions and remedies for the substraction and taking of any Orphans happening to come within the same Borough, and for the recovery of the goods, chattels, debts, and legacies of the same, and all such and the like offices for the better government and preservation of the same Orphans, and of their goods, chattels, debts and legacies of the same, as in the said City of London hath been heretofore used to be done, executed, or performed, and not otherwise, nor in any other manner; all which things we will, and by these presents command to be inviolably observed.

u   "And we will, and by these presents give and grant to the aforesaid Mayor, Aldermen, and Burgesses of the Borough aforesaid, and their Successors, that the Mayor and two Aldermen of the Borough aforesaid, and their Successors for the time being, may have and shall have full power and authority to receive and take to the use of us, the Heirs and Successors of us, the aforesaid Queen, all manner of recognizances and oblations of any malefactors and transgressors whomsoever, who within the liberty aforesaid shall offend and trespass against any statutes and ordinances whatsoever, in our Parliaments [made,] or the laws of us, the Heirs and successors of us, the aforesaid Queen, or of our Progenitors, touching or concerning the good and public tranquillity and government of our Kingdom of England, and of our subjects, although express mention of the true yearly value or of any other value or certainty of the premises or of either of them, or of other gifts and grants by us or by any of the Progenitors and Predecessors of us the aforesaid Queen, heretofore made to the aforesaid Mayor, Aldermen, and Burgesses of the Borough aforesaid, or their predecessors, is not made in these presents, or in any statute, act, ordination, provision, proclamation, or restriction, to the contrary thereof made, passed, ordained, or provided, or any other thing, cause, or matter whatsoever, in any wise notwithstanding.

"In testimony whereof we have caused these our Letters to be made Patent. Witness ourselves at Westminster, the twenty ninth day of May, in the third and fourth years of our reign.

"By writ of Privy Seal, and of the date aforesaid,
by Authority of Parliament."

Charter of King James I.— 1610

"The Fifteenth part of Patents of the eighth year of the reign of King James.

"Concerning a grant for the Mayor, Aldermen,
and Burgesses of Barnstaple, to them and
their Successors.

"The King, to all to whom, &c. greeting.

a "Whereas the Borough of Barnstaple in our County of Devon, is a very ancient and populous Borough, and the Mayor, Aldermen, and Burgesses of the same Borough by divers several names from time whereof the memory of man is not to the contrary, have had, used, and enjoyed divers liberties, customs, franchises, immunities, and preeminences, as well by reason and pretext of divers Charters and letters patent by divers of our Progenitors and Ancestors, late Kings and Queens of England to them heretofore made, granted, or confirmed, as by reason and pretext of divers prescriptions, usages, and customs, in the same Borough anciently used and accustomed. And whereas our beloved subjects, the Mayor, Aldermen, and Burgesses of the Borough aforesaid, have humbly besought us that we, for the better rule, government, and amelioration as well of the Borough aforesaid as of the residue of the whole Parish of Barnstaple, now being without the liberty of the Borough aforesaid, would graciously shew and extend our royal favor and numificence in this behalf, and that we, for the better rule and government of the same Borough, and also of the whole Parish aforesaid, and of all the Inhabitants as well within the land heretofore belonging to the Priory of St. Mary Magdalen, and from the Jurisdiction of the Borough aforesaid, now exempt and wholly distinct, and now parcel of the possessions of the most Honorable William Howard, Knight, Lord Howard of Effingham, as within all and singular other the Lands within the same Parish, the said

Mayor, Aldermen, and Burgesses of the Borough aforesaid, by whatsoever names they now are or heretofore have been incorporated, would make, ordain, constitute, reduce, and newly create into one body corporate and politic, by the name of the Mayor, Aldermen, and Burgesses of the Borough and Parish of Barnstaple, in the county of Devon, with the addition of certain liberties, as it should seem better to us to be and be done.

b "We, therefore, willing that from henceforth for ever, in the same Borough, and in the residue of the Parish aforesaid, may be continually had one certain and indubitable mode of *government,** and for the keeping of our peace, and for the good rule and government of the same Borough and Parish, and of our People there from time to time dwelling, and of others there from time to time resorting, and that the Borough and Parish aforesaid from henceforth for ever may be and remain a Borough and Parish of peace and quiet, to the terror and dread of evil offenders, and in reward of the good. And that our peace and other acts of justice and good rule there, shall and may be able to be better kept; and hoping, that if more amply of our grant, they should enjoy honors, liberties, and privileges, then to the services which they should perform and shew to us our heirs and successors, they may feel themselves specially and strongly bound, of our special grace, and of our certain knowledge and mere motion, have willed, ordained, constituted, and granted, and by these presents, for us our heirs and successors, do will, ordain, constitute, and grant, that the said Borough and Parish of Barnstaple, in the said County of Devon, may and shall be, and remain from henceforth for ever, a free Borough and Parish of itself; and that the Mayor, Aldermen, and Burgesses of the Borough aforesaid and their successors, may and shall be in all times hereafter one body corporate and politic, in deed, fact, and name, by the name of the Mayor, Aldermen, and Burgesses of the Borough and Parish of Barnstaple, in the County of Devon, and them by the name of the Mayor, Aldermen, and Burgesses, of the Borough and Barnstaple, in the County of Devon, into one body corporate and politic, in deed, fact and name, really and fully, for us our heirs and successors, we raise, make, ordain, constitute, create, confirm, ratify, and declare, by these presents. And that by the same name they may have perpetual succession.

c "And that they, by the name of the Mayor, Aldermen, and Burgesses, of the Borough and Parish of Barnstaple, in the county of Devon, may and shall be in all times hereafter, persons able, and in law capable, to have, acquire, receive, and possess, manors, messuages, lands, tenements,

* This word, which appears to be necessary in order to complete the sense of the passage, is wanting both in the translation, and in the Latin copy.

liberties, privileges, jurisdictions, franchises, and other hereditaments whatsoever, of whatever kind, nature, or sort they may be, to them and their successors, in fee and perpetuity, or for term of life, lives, or years or otherwise in whatsoever manner. And also, to give, grant, demise, let, and assign, the same manors, messuages, lands, tenements, and hereditaments, and all and singular other acts and deeds whatsoever, to do and exercise by the name aforesaid.

d "And that by the same name of the Mayor, Aldermen, and Burgesses of the Borough and Parish of Barnstaple, in the county of Devon, they shall and may be able to plead and be impleaded, answer and be answered, defend and be defended, in whatever courts, parts, and places, and before whomsoever the Judges and Justices, and other Officers and Ministers, of us, our Heirs, and Successors, in all and singular actions, pleas, suits, plaints, causes, matters, and demands whatsoever, of whatever kind, name, nature, or sort, they may or shall be, in the same manner and form as other our lieges, within our Kingdom of England, persons able and in law capable, or any other body corporate and politic of this Kingdom of England, can and may have, acquire, receive, possess, enjoy, retain, give, grant, demise, alienate, assign and dispose, plead and be impleaded, answer and be answered, defend and be defended, do permit or execute.

e "And that the Mayor, Aldermen, and Burgesses of the Borough and Parish aforesaid, and their successors from henceforth for ever, may have a common seal, to serve for doing the causes and affairs of them and their successors whatsoever. And that it shall and may be lawful for them and their successors, the same seal, at their pleasure from time to time to break and make anew, as to them shall seem better to be and be done.

f "And further by these presents for us, our Heirs, and Successors, we grant and ordain that from henceforth there may and shall be within the Borough and Parish aforesaid, from time to time, twenty-five of the more discreet and approved Burgesses of the same Borough, who shall be, and be named Capital Burgesses of the Borough and Parish of Barnstaple aforesaid, from which same twenty-five Capital Burgesses of the Borough and Parish aforesaid, for the time being, one shall be annually elected as Mayor of the same Borough and Parish; and also from which twenty-five Capital Burgesses of the Borough and Parish aforesaid, two of the more discreet and elder may and shall be annually from time to time for ever elected and named to the office or offices of Aldermen of the Borough and Parish aforesaid, which same Aldermen and other Capital Burgesses shall be and be called the Common Council of the same Borough and Parish, and shall be from time to time assistant and aiding to the Mayor of the said Borough and Parish of Barnstaple aforesaid, for the time being, in all causes, things, and matters, touching or in any wise concerning the Borough and Parish aforesaid.

g "And further we will and ordain, and by these presents for us, our heirs, and successors grant to the before named Mayor, Aldermen and Burgesses of the Borough and Parish of Barnstaple aforesaid, and their successors, that they and their succesors, by the Mayor of the Borough and Parish aforesaid, who for the time shall be, and the Aldermen and Capital Burgesses being the Common Council of the same Borough and Parish for the time being, or by the major part of the same Mayor, Aldermen, and Capital Burgesses, of whom the Mayor of the same Borough and Parish for the time being, and one of the Aldermen of the same Borough and Parish, and twelve Capital Burgesses of the Common Council of the same Borough and Parish, we will to be fourteen shall and may have full power and authority to frame, constitute, ordain and make from time to time such reasonable statutes and ordinances whatsoever, as to them shall seem to be good wholesome, useful, honest, and necessary, according to their wise discretions, for the good rate and government of the Burgesses, Artificers, and Inhabitants of the Borough and Parish aforesaid, for the time being, and for declaring in what manner and order the aforesaid Mayor, Aldermen, and Burgesses, and Artificers, Inhabitants, and Residents of the same Borough and Parish, in their Offices, Ministerings, and Business within the Borough and Parish aforesaid, and the limits of the same for the time being shall hold, carry, and use themselves and otherwise, for the farther good and public utility of the same Borough and Parish, and the victualling of the same Borough and Parish, and also for the better government, disposition, leasing and demising of lands, tenements, possessions, revenues and heriditaments, to the before named Mayor, Aldermen and Burgesses, and their succcessors, given, granted or assigned, or hereafter to be given, granted, or assigned, and other matters and causes whatsoever, the Borough and Parish aforesaid, or the state, right, and interest of the same Borough and Parish, touching, or in any manner concerning. And that they and their successors by the Mayor, who for the time shall be, and Aldermen and Burgesses being the Common council of the Borough and Parish aforesaid, or the major part of them (as before named) as often as such laws, ordinances, and statues shall be framed, made, ordained, or established in form aforesaid, may impose and assess such and the like reasonable pains, penalties, punishments by imprisonments of bodys, or by fines and amercements, or by either of them, towards and upon all offenders against such laws, statutes, and ordinances, or any or either of them, as and which to the same Mayor, Aldermen, and Burgesses, the Common Council of the Borough and Parish aforesaid, for the time being, or to the major part of them (of whom the Mayor, one Alderman, and twelve Capital Burgesses, of the Borough and Parish aforesaid, we will to be fourteen) shall seem to be reasonable and requisite. And the same fines and amercements shall and may be able to levy and have without impediment of us, our heirs, or successors, to their proper use and benefit, and without any account to us, our heirs or successors to be therefore rendered, all and singular which laws, statutes, and ordinances, so as aforesaid to be made, we will to be observed under the pains in the same to be contained. So nevertheless that such laws, statutes, ordinances, pains, penalties, punishments, imprisonments, fines and amercements, be reasonable, and be not repugnant nor contrary to the laws, statutes, customs, or rights of our Kingdom of England.

h "And for the better execution of the same our gifts, will, and grant in this behalf, we have assigned, named, constituted, and made, and by these presents for us, our heirs and successors, do assign, name, constitute, and make our beloved William Shapleigh, now Mayor of the Borough aforesaid, to become and be first and modern Mayor of the Borough and Parish aforesaid, willing that the same William Shapleigh shall be and continue in the office of Mayor of the same Borough and Parish, from the date of these presents unto the feast or day of the assumption of the blessed Mary the Virgin next coming, and from the same feast until another Burgess of the Borough and Parish aforesaid shall have been preferred and sworn to that office, according to the constitutions and ordinances in these presents herein after expressed and declared, if the same William Shapleigh shall so long live. Also we have assigned, named, and constituted, and by these presents for us, our heirs, and successors, do assign, nominate, constitute and make our beloved James Downe and Bartholomew Harris, Inhabitants of the Borough and Parish aforesaid, to be and become the two first and modern Aldermen of the Borough and Parish aforesaid, to continue in the same office unto the same feast or day of the assumption of the blessed Mary the Virgin next following after the date of these presents and from the same feast until two other Burgesses of the Borough and Parish aforesaid shall have been in due manner elected, preferred, and sworn to the office of Aldermen of the Borough and Parish aforesaid, according to the ordinances and constitutions in these presents below expressed and declared, if the same James Downe and Bartholomew Harris shall so long live. Also we have assigned, nominated and constituted, and by these presents for us, our heirs and successors, do assign, nominate, constitute and make our beloved Paul Worth, Richard

Dodderidge, William Palmer, James Beaple, Nicholas Downe, John Delbridge, John Pearde, Richard Beaple, Richard Harris, John Wichehelfe, John Norris, Henry Downe, George Baker, Thomas Horwood, Henry Cross, Nicholas Takell, Penticost Dodderidge, Adam Lugge, John Sallesburye, John Garrett, Nicholas Deldridge, and John Darracotte, Inhabitants of the Borough and Parish aforesaid, to become and be first and modern Capital Burgesses of the Borough and Parish aforesaid, to continue in the same offices during their natural lives, unless in the mean time for bad government or misdemeaning themselves in this behalf, they shall be removed from their offices.

i "And further we will, and by these presents for us, our heirs and successors grant, that whenever it shall happen the before named Capital Burgesses, so as aforesaid named, or any of them, to die, or to be removed from their offices for bad government on this behalf, that then and so often it shall and may be lawful for the Mayor, Aldermen, and other Burgesses, being Capital Burgesses, the Common Council of the Borough aforesaid, or the major part of them, (of whom the Mayor and one of the Aldermen of the Borough and Parish aforesaid, for the time being, we will be two) one or more others others of the Burgesses of the Borough and Parish aforesaid, in the place or places of the same Capital Burgess or Burgesses, so happening to die or to be removed, to elect, nominate and prefer. And him or them so elected as aforesaid, again for reasonable causes, from the place or office of a Capital Burgess of the Borough and Parish aforesaid, to remove; and that he or they so elected and preferred, or to be elected or preferred, shall be a Capital Burgess or Capital Burgesses of the Borough and Parish aforesaid, in like manner and form as the aforesaid Capital Burgesses before by these presents are and shall be constituted, and this as often as the case shall so happen that by the death or removal of any of the same Capital Burgesses the place of the same Capital Burgesses, or of any or either of them, shall become vacant, another or others of the Burgesses of the Borough and Parish aforesaid, shall be elected or preferred in the place of the same Capital Burgesses so happening to die or to be removed, by the Mayor and residue of the Capital Burgesses or the greater part of them (of whom the Mayor and one of the Aldermen of the same Borough and Parish we will to be two) to be a Capital Burgess or Capital Burgesses of the same Borough and Parish. And that the foresaid Capital Burgesses so from time to time elected and preferred, or to be elected or preferred, shall take, and each of them shall take a corporal oath before the Mayor, Aldermen and other Capital Burgesses of the Borough and Parish aforesaid, or the major part of them, (of whom the Mayor or one of the Aldermen of the Borough and

Parish aforesaid, we will to be one) well and faithfully to execute the same office.

j "And further, we will and by these presents ordain, and of our more abundant special grace, and of our certain knowledge and meer motion, for us, our heirs and successors, do grant to the before named Mayor, Aldermen and Burgesses of the Borough and Parish aforesaid, and their successors, that it shall and may be lawful for them and their successors, as often as it shall seem to them to be meet and necessary in any convenient place within the Borough and Parish aforesaid, to call and hold a meeting of the same Mayor, Aldermen, and Capital Burgesses, or of the greater part of them, at all times hereafter; and in the same meeting shall and may treat, confer, councel, consult and decree, of statutes, articles, and ordinances touching and concerning the Borough and Parish aforesaid, and the good rule, state and government of the same Borough and Parish, according to the tenor of these our Letters Patent.

k "And further we will and by these presents for us our heirs and successors, do grant to the before named Mayor, Aldermen, and Burgesses of the Borough and Parish aforesaid, and their successors, that the foresaid Mayor, Aldermen, and Capital Burgesses, of the Borough and Parish aforesaid, for the time being, or of the major part of them, from time to time, at all times hereafter shall and may have power and authority yearly and every year, on Monday next before the day or feast of the blessed Mary of the Virgin, between the hours of nine and twelve of the forenoon of the same day, to elect and nominate, and that they shall and may be able to elect and nominate one of the Capital Burgesses of the Borough and Parish aforesaid, for the time being, who shall be Mayor of the Borough and Parish aforesaid, for one whole year then next following.

l "And that he, after he shall be so elected and named as Mayor of the Borough and Parish aforesaid, before he is admitted to that office, shall take a Corporal Oath, on the Monday next following the feast or day of St. Faith, then next following the nomination and election aforesaid, before the Mayor, being his last predecessor, in the presence of the Aldermen and ten Capital Burgesses at the least being of the Common Council of the Borough and Parish aforesaid, for the time being, to rightly, well, and faithfully execute that office, in all things touching the same office. And that after such oath so taken, he shall and may be able to execute the office of Mayor of the same Borough and Parish, for one whole year then next following.

m "And moreover we will, and by these presents, for us, our heirs and successors, grant to the before named Mayor, Aldermen, and Burgesses of the Borough and Parish aforesaid, and their successors, that if it shall happen the Mayor of the Borough and Parish aforesaid, for the time being, at any time within one year after he shall be so as aforesaid preferred and sworn to the office of Mayor of the Borough and Parish aforesaid, die, or be removed from his office, that then and so often it shall and may be lawful for the before named Aldermen and Capital Burgesses of the Borough and Parish aforesaid, for the time being, or the major part of them, to elect and prefer another from themselves for Mayor of the Borough and Parish aforesaid. And that he so elected and preferred, may hold and exercise that office, during the residue of the same year, and until another in the office of Mayor of the same Borough and Parish be rightly and lawfully elected, the corporal oath in form aforesaid to be first taken, and so from time to time so often as the case shall so happen.

n "And further of our more abundant grace, we will, and by these presents, for us, our heirs and successors, grant to the before named Mayor, Aldermen, and Burgesses of the Borough and Parish aforesaid, and their successors, that the aforesaid Mayor, Aldermen, and Capital Burgesses of the Borough and Parish aforesaid, for the time being, or the major part of them, from time to time at all times hereafter, may, and shall have power and authority yearly and every year on the said Monday next before the aforesaid feast or day of the assumption of the blessed Mary the Virgin, to elect and name, and they shall and may be able to elect and name two of the Capital Burgesses of the Borough and Parish aforesaid, for the time being, who shall be Aldermen of the Borough and Parish aforesaid, for one whole year then next following. And that they, after they shall be so as foresaid elected and named, as Aldermen of the Borough and Parish aforesaid, before they are admitted to that office, shall take a corporal oath, on the Monday then next following the foresaid feast of St. Faith, then next following the nomination and election aforesaid, in the presence of the Mayor and Aldermen then being, their last predecessors, and ten Capital Burgesses of the same Borough and Parish for the time being, at the least, rightly, well, and faithfully to execute that office, in all things touching and concerning that office. And that after such oath so taken, they shall and may be able to execute the office of Aldermen of the same Borough and Parish, for one whole year then next following.

o "And moreover we will, and by these presents, for us, our heirs and successors, grant to the before named Mayor, Aldermen, and Burgesses of the Borough and Parish aforesaid, and their successors, that if it shall happen the Aldermen of the Borough and Parish aforesaid, for the time being, or either of them, at any time after they shall be preferred and sworn (as aforesaid) to the office of Aldermen of the Borough and Parish aforesaid, die, or be removed from their office of Aldermen of the Borough aforesaid, that then and so often it shall and may be lawful for the before named Mayor, and Capital Burgesses of the Borough and Parish aforesaid, for the time being or the major part of them, to elect and prefer another or others from themselves, for an Alderman or Aldermen of the Borough and Parish aforesaid, and that he or they so elected and preferred, may have and exercise that office during the residue of the same year, and until another or others for an Alderman or Aldermen of the same Borough and Parish, are rightfully and lawfully elected, the corporal oath in form aforesaid to be first taken, and so from time to time, as often as the case shall so happen.

p "And also we will, and by these presents, for us, our heirs, and successors, grant to the before named Mayor, Aldermen, and Burgesses of the Borough and Parish aforesaid, and their successors, that the same Mayor, Aldermen, and Capital Burgesses of the Borough and Parish aforesaid and their successors for the time being, or the major part of them, shall, and may be able to elect nominate, and appoint, from time to time, at all times hereafter, yearly and every year, on Monday next before the feast or day of the assumption of the blessed Mary the Virgin, such and so many inferior officers and ministers within the Borough and Parish aforesaid, as, and which the Mayor, Aldermen, and Capital Burgesses of the Borough aforesaid before the date of these presents, as Mayor or Capital Burgess of the same Borough have had elected or appointed, or have been acustomed to elect or appoint within the same Borough, and the same so elected or preferred, or either of them, from the same office again to remove the reasonable causes, and that the same officers or ministers, so to their offices severally elected, preferred, and named, shall be in due manner sworn, rightly, well and faithfully to execute their offices, in all things touching the same offices, before the Mayor, Aldermen, and Capital Burgesses of the Borough and Parish aforesaid, for the time being, or the major part of them. And that they so elected and preferred, may have and exercise their offices severally, for one whole year, and so from time to time, as often as the case shall so happen.

q "And moreover, we will, and by these presents, for us, our heirs and successors, grant to the before named Mayor, Aldermen, and Burgesses of the Borough and Parish aforesaid, and their successors, that if any who shall hereafter be elected or nominated to the offices of Mayor, Alderman, Capital Burgess, or other inferior Officers or Ministers of the Borough and Parish aforesaid, or to any or either of them, and having notice and knowledge of such election and nomination, shall refuse or deny such office to which he or they so refusing and denying shall be elected or nominated, that then and so often, it shall and may be lawful for the Mayor, Aldermen, and Capital burgesses, being of the Common Council of the Borough and Parish aforesaid for the time being, or the major part of them, him or them so refusing or denying to exercise such office or offices to which he or they shall be so elected and nominated, to commit to the Gaol of the Borough aforesaid, there to remain until or they will exercise such office or offices; and also to put and tax reasonable fines and amercements on such refusing or denying, as to the same Mayor, Aldermen, and Capital Burgesses being of the common Council of the Borough and Parish aforesaid for the time being, or the major part of them for the time being, (of whom the Mayor and one of the Aldermen of the Borough and Parish aforesaid we will to be one,) shall seem to be reasonable, and him or them so refusing to keep in the Gaol of the Borough aforesaid, until he or they shall pay or cause to be paid such fines and amercements, to the use of the Mayor, Aldermen, and Burgesses of the Borough and Parish aforesaid and their successors.

r "And moreover, we will, and by these presents, for us, our heirs and sucessors, grant to the before named Mayor, Aldermen, and Burgesses of the Borough and Parish aforesaid, and their successors, that from henceforth for ever there may and shall be in the Borough and Parish aforesaid, two officers, who shall be and be called Serjeants at Mace, which same Serjeants at Mace shall be attendant, and each of them shall be attendant, from time to time upon the Mayor, Aldermen, and Capital Burgesses of the Borough and Parish aforesaid, for the time being; of which same two Serjeants at Mace, one of them shall at all times hereafter be named by the Mayor so for the time being, and the other of them shall at all times hereafter be named and elected by the Mayor and Aldermen, and Capital Burgesses, being of the Common Council of the Borough and Parish aforesaid for the time being, or by the major part of them, to last for one whole year then next following; and that they so elected and nominated to the office of Serjeants at Mace of the Borough and Parish aforesaid for one whole year, may and shall be in due manner sworn, well and faithfully to execute such office, before the Mayor, Aldermen, and Capital Burgesses, being of the Common Council of the Borough and Parish aforesaid, or the major part of them. And that the aforesaid Serjeants at Mace in the Borough and Parish aforesaid to be deputed, shall bear and carry maces of gold or silver, and the sign of the arms of our Kingdom of England engraven and worked, every where within the Borough and Parish aforesaid, the liberties and precincts of the same, before the Mayor of the Borough and Parish aforesaid for the time being, and his successors. And that the aforesaid Serjeants at Mace be

293

ministers of our court of Record, within the Borough and Parish aforesaid, to execute all processes, precepts, or mandates, of the same Court in due manner, and according to the exigence of right and law.

s "And further we will, and by these presents, for us our heirs and successors, grant to the before named Mayor, Aldermen, and Burgesses of the Borough and Parish of Barnstaple aforesaid, and their successors, that the Mayor, Aldermen, and Capital Burgesses, of the Borough and Parish aforesaid, or the major part of them, (of whom the Mayor for the time being we will to be one,) may and shall have power to name and elect, and that they shall and may name and elect from time to time for ever, one approved and discreet man, to become and be Chief Steward of the Borough and Parish aforesaid; and that he so elected, may hold and exercise the office of Chief Steward of the Borough and Parish aforesaid, at the good pleasure of the same Mayor, Alderman, and Burgesses, or of the major part of them.

t "And further we will, and by these presents, for us, our heirs and successors, grant to the before named Mayor, Aldermen, and Burgesses, of the Borough and Parish aforesaid, and their successors, that the Mayor, Aldermen, and Capital Burgesses, of the Borough and Parish aforesaid, or the major part of them, may have power and authority to elect and name, and that they shall and may elect and name from time to time for ever, one approved and discreet man, learned in the laws of our Kingdom of England, who shall be and be called the Recorder of the Borough and Parish aforesaid; which same Recorder so named and elected, shall take a Corporal Oath before the Mayor, Aldermen, and Capital Burgesses, of the Borough and Parish aforesaid, to execute such office of recorder in all things touching the same office. And that the Recorder of the Borough and Parish aforesaid, so as aforesaid elected, nominated, and sworn, shall exercise and execute the office of Recorder of the Borough and Parish aforesaid, by himself or by his sufficient deputy learned in the laws of England, and the Corporal Oath by such deputy in like manner to be first taken, at the good pleasure of the same Mayor, Aldermen, and Capital Burgesses, or the major part of them. And we will, that the Recorder of the Borough and Parish aforesaid, or his sufficient deputy, so from time to time to be named and elected, shall be from time to time assistant and aiding to the Mayor, Aldermen, and Capital Burgesses of the Borough and Parish aforesaid, and their successors, in all things and causes which in the Court of Record of the Borough and Parish aforesaid, shall be from time to time pleadable and determinable. And shall do and execute all things which to the office of Recorder pertain or belong in as ample manner and form as any other Recorder in any Borough or Town incorporate within this Kingdom of England, by virtue of the office of recorder aforesaid, can and may execute.

v   "Moreover we have granted, and by these presents, for us, our heirs, and successors, do grant, to the before named Mayor, Aldermen, and Burgesses of the Borough and Parish aforesaid, and their successors, that the Mayor, Recorder, and Aldermen of the Borough and Parish aforesaid, during the term in which they shall happen to be in their aforesaid offices, be the Justiciaries of us, and of our heirs and successors, to preserve the peace in the same Borough and Parish, and the precinct and circuit of the same. And to cause the statutes concerning Artificers and Labourers within the Borough and Parish aforesaid, the circuit and precinct of the same, to be preserved and kept. And that the same Mayor, Recorder and Aldermen, for the time being, or three of them (of whom the Mayor and Recorder of the Borough and Parish aforesaid, for the time being, we will to be two) may have full power and authority to enquire concerning whatever felonies, contempts, trespasses, misprisions, and other inferior defaults and articles whatsoever, within the Borough and Parish aforesaid, the liberties and precincts of the same, done, moved, or perpetuated, which before the Keepers and Justiciaries of the peace in any County of our Kingdom of England, by the laws and statutes of the same our Kingdom of England, ought or should be enquired of; so however that the said Mayor, Recorder, and Aldermen, to the determination of any betraying of murder, or felony, or any other matter touching the loss of life, or member, within the Borough and Parish aforesaid, the liberties and precincts of the same, without the special mandate and grant of us, our heirs and successors, in any wise hereafter, shall not proceed. But nevertheless, all and singular other contempts, trespasses, offences, causes, and articles above said, which to the office of Justiciaries of the peace within the Borough and Parish aforesaid, the liberties and precincts of the same pertain, they shall and may be able to do, enquire, hear, perform, and determine, as fully, freely, and wholly, and in as ample manner and form as any other Justiciaries of the peace, of us, and of our heirs and successors in any county of our Kingdom of England (as Justiciaries of the Peace) by the laws and statutes of our Kingdom of England, can or may enquire, hear, or determine.

u   "We will also, and by these presents, for us, our heirs, and successors, grant, that none other of the Justiciaries of us, our heirs or successors, of our County of Devon, the Borough and Parish aforesaid, or in any part thereof, or the liberties and precincts of the same (to do any thing in the same Borough and Parish, the liberties or precincts of the same which the Justiciaries of the Peace of the Borough and Parish aforesaid, by virtue of these our letters patent, can or ought to do and execute) intromit themselves, or presume to enter in any wise.

w "And further we will, and by these presents, for us, our heirs and successors, grant to the before named Mayor, Aldermen, and Burgesses of the Borough and Parish aforesaid, and their successors, that the Mayor and Aldermen of the Borough and Parish aforesaid for the time being, from henceforth for ever, may elect, and from time to time they may and shall be able to elect and name one approved and discreet man, who may and shall be Clerk of the Market of the said Borough and Parish of Barnstaple aforesaid, to do and execute all and singular those things, within the said Borough and Parish, the liberties and precincts of the same, which to the office of Clerk of the Market within other counties of our Kingdom of England pertain; so that no Clerk of the Market of the Household of us, our heirs, or successors, the aforesaid Borough and Parish, liberties, limits, and precincts of the same, (to do or execute any thing which to the office of clerk of the Market pertaineth,) in any wise enter or intromit himself.

x "Also, we have granted, and by these presents, for us, our heirs and successors, of our like special grace, and of our certain knowledge and meer motion, do grant to the before named Mayor, Aldermen, and Burgesses, of the Borough and Parish aforesaid, and their successors, that the Aldermen of the Borough and Parish aforesaid for the time being and their successors, during the time in which they shall be and continue in the office of Aldermen of the Borough and Parish aforesaid, be the coroners of us, our heirs and successors, within the Borough and Parish aforesaid, liberties, and precincts of the same. And that the aforesaid James Downe and Bartholomew Harris, Aldermen of the Borough and Parish aforesaid, be the first and modern Coroners of us, our heirs and successors, of the Borough and Parish aforesaid, in the same office of Coroner, to remain until they go out of their offices of Aldermen of the Borough and Parish aforesaid, and that the Coroners of the Borough and Parish aforesaid, for the time being, may and shall have full power and authority to do and execute within the Borough and Parish aforesaid, the limits and precincts of the same, all and singular those things which to the office of Coroner, by the laws, customs and statutes of our Kingdom of England pertain, or ought to pertain, to do and execute. And that no other Coroner of us, or our heirs or successors, to do any thing which to the officer of Coroner in the Borough and Parish aforesaid, and the limits and precincts of the same pertaineth, shall enter or presume to enter, or in any wise intromit himself.

y "Also we will, and by these presents, for us, our heirs, and successors, grant to the before named Mayor, Aldermen, and Burgesses of the Borough and Parish of Barnstaple aforesaid, and their successors, that they and their successors from henceforth for ever may elect, and that from time to time they shall and may be able to elect, and name one approved and honest man who may and shall be and be called the Common Clerk of the Borough and Parish of Barnstaple aforesaid, (*Anglice the Towne Clarke of the Borough and Parrishe of Barnstaple,*) to do and execute all and singular those things within the Borough and Parish aforesaid, the liberties and precincts of the same, which to the office of Common Clerk within any Borough or Town Incorporate within our Kingdom of England pertain; and that the Clerk of the Market and Common Clerk of the Borough and Parish aforesaid, so as aforesaid to be elected and named, (before they are admitted to execute those offices,) shall take, and each of them respectively shall take a Corporal oath before the Mayor of the Borough and Parish aforesaid for the time being, rightly, well, and faithfully to execute the same offices of Clerk of the Market and Common Clerk of the Borough and Parish aforesaid, according to their knowlege in all things and by all things touching the same offices. And after such oath so as aforesaid taken, the offices of Clerk of the Market and Common Clerk of the Borough and Parish aforesaid, may respectively have, exercise, and use, by themselves, or by their sufficient Deputies by the Mayor of the Borough and Parish aforesaid to be allowed, during the good pleasure of the Mayor, Aldermen, and Burgesses of the Borough and Parish aforesaid for the time being, or the major part of them, (of whom the Mayor for the time being we will to be one.)

z "And further we will, and by these presents, for us, our heirs, and successors, grant to the before named Mayor, Aldermen, and Burgesses of the Borough and Parish of Barnstaple aforesaid, and their successors, that the same Mayor, Aldermen, and Burgesses of the Borough and Parish aforesaid, and their successors for ever, may and shall have within the Borough and Parish aforesaid, and within the liberties and precincts of the same, one prison or gaol, for the preservation and custody of all and singular persons attached and to be attached, or to the prison or gaol of the Borough and Parish aforesaid to be adjudged in what manner soever within the Borough and Parish aforesaid, the liberties and precincts of the same, for whatever cause within the Borough and Parish aforesaid, or the liberties and precincts of the same to be found, there to remain so long and until they shall be delivered in lawful and due manner of right. And that the Mayor of the said Borough and Parish for the time being may and shall be keeper of the same gaol.

aa "And we will, and by these presents, for us, our heirs, and successors, grant to the before named Mayor, Aldermen, and Burgesses of the Borough and Parish aforesaid, and their successors, that they and their successors from henceforth for ever, may have and hold, and shall and may be able to have and hold, within the Borough and Parish aforesaid, one Court of Record on every Monday in every second week throughout the year, before the Mayor, Recorder, and Aldermen of the Borough and Parish aforesaid, or before two of them to be holden; and that in such Court they may hold by plain in the same Court to be levyed, all and all manner, such, the like, and similar pleas, actions, suits, and demands, concerning whatever trespasses with force and arms or otherwise, in contempt of us, our heirs, or successors, done and to be done. And also concerning all and all manner, such, the like, and similar pleas upon the case, debts, accounts, covenants, deceptions, detentions of deeds, writings, and muniments, and chattels, captions and detentions of cattle and chattels, and other contracts, from whatever causes or matters, within the Borough and Parish aforesaid, the limits and precincts of the same arising or happening, such and as at any time heretofore by any lawful charter or grant, or by any lawful custom or prescription in the same Borough have been pleaded. And that such pleas, plaints, and actions, as well real as personal and mixed, shall be heard and determined there before the Mayor, Recorder, and Aldermen of the Borough and Parish aforesaid, or the major part of them, by such and the like processes and methods, according to the law and custom of our Kingdom of England, by which, and as shall be consonant with our laws, and in as ample and similar manner and form, as in any other Court of Record in any other Borough or Town Incorporate within this kingdom of England, is used and accustomed, or can or ought to be done.

bb "And we will moreover, and for us, our heirs, and successors, ordain that the Serjeants at Mace of the Borough and Parish aforesaid, for the time being, or any or either of them, shall do and execute all pannels of juries, inquisitions, attachments, precepts, mandates, warrants, judgments, processes, and other things necessary to be done, concerning the causes aforesaid, within the Borough and Parish aforesaid, the liberties, limits, and precincts of the same, as it shall be commanded them, according to the exigence of law, and according to the custom of the Borough aforesaid, and as in similar cases is used, or ought to be done in any court of Record, in any other Borough or Town Incorporate within this Kingdom of England.

cc "And further, or our more abundant special grace, and of our certain knowledge and mere motion, for us, our heirs, and successors, we have given and granted, and by these presents do give and grant to the before named Mayor, Aldermen, and Burgesses of the Borough and Parish afore-said, and their successors, all and all manner of goods and chattels of felons whomsoever, and also of felons of themselves, for all and singular the Burgesses resident within the Borough and Parish aforesaid, the lib-erties and precincts of the same, from time to time arising, happening, or coming; and also all other privileges, jurisdictions, fairs, markets, exemp-tions from juries without the said Borough and Parish and all and singu-lar hereditaments within the said Borough and Parish from time to time increasing and arising, in as ample manner and form and as fully, freely, and wholly, as the Mayor, Aldermen, and Burgesses of the Borough afore-said, or their predecessors at any time heretofore, by any lawful charter or grant, or by any other lawful manner, have heretofore had receive, or enjoyed. And that it shall and may be lawful to the same Mayor Aldermen, and Burgesses of the Borough and Parish aforesaid, and their successors, to put themselves in seisin and possession of the goods and chattels aforesaid, an other emoluments and advantages aforesaid, and the same to the behoof and use of the same Mayor, Aldermen, and Burgesses of the Borough and Parish aforesaid, and their successors, to receive and retain without the hinderance of us, our heirs or successors, or of any officers or ministers of us, our heirs, or successors whomsoever.

dd "And further we will, and by these presents, for us, our heirs, and successors, grant to the before named Mayor, Aldermen, and Burgesses of the Borough and Parish aforesaid, and their successors, that no stranger or foreigner, unless he be a freeman of the Borough and Parish aforesaid, shall sell or expose to sale any wares or merchandizes within the Borough or Parish aforesaid, otherwise than in gross, or otherwise than all other necessaries for victualling of the Borough and Parish aforesaid, unless it be at the times of the fair and markets, to be holden within the Borough and Parish aforesaid, or the liberties or precincts of the same, without the special licence of the Mayor, Aldermen, and Capital Burgesses of the Borough and Parish aforesaid, or the major part of them, (of whom the Mayor for the time being we will to be one) in writing, under their seal, under our indignation, and under such other pains, penalties and forfei-tures, as by the laws and statutes of our kingdom of England can be inflicted or imposed on such like offenders, for their disobedience and contempt in this behalf.

ee "And further, of our more abundant special grace, and of our certain knowledge and mere motion, we have given and granted, and by these presents, for us, our heirs, and successors, do give and grant to the before named Mayor, Aldermen, and Burgesses of the Borough and Parish of Barnstaple aforesaid, and their successors, special, free, and lawful licence, power, faculty, and authority, to have, acquire, receive, and possess, to them and their successors for ever, manors, messuages, lands, tenements, meadows, feedings, pastures, woods, rectories, tithes, rents, reversions, and other hereditaments whatsoever, as well of us, our heirs, and successors, as of any other person or persons whomsoever, which are not holden of us, our heirs, or successors, immediately in chief, or by military service, so that the same manors, messuages, lands, tenements, and other hereditaments, so hereafter to be acquired, together with the lands, manors, tenements, and other hereditaments by the before named Mayor, Aldermen, and Burgesses or their predecessors heretofore acquired, do not exceed in the whole, the clear yearly value of sixty pounds, beyond all charges and reprisals, the statute concerning lands and tenements not to be but in mortmain, or any other statute, act, ordinance, or perquisition heretofore had, made, ordained, or provided, or any other thing, cause, or matter whatsoever, to the contrary thereof in any wise notwithstanding.

ff "Also we give, and by these presents, for us, our heirs, and successors, grant to all and all manner, and whatsoever and whomsoever the subjects of us, our heirs, and successors, special, free, and lawful licence, power, faculty, and authority, that they or any or either of them, shall and may be able to give, grant, sell, bequeth, or alienate, lawfully and impunitively, any manors, messuages, lands, tenements, or other hereditaments whatsoever, which are not holden of us, our heirs, or successors, immediately in chief nor by military service, to the before named Mayor, Aldermen, and Burgesses of the Borough and Parish of Barnstaple aforesaid, and their successors, so that all the foresaid manors, messuages, lands, tenements, and other hereditaments, so to the same Mayor, Aldermen, and Burgesses of the Borough and Parish aforesaid, as before named, to be given, granted, alienated, or bequeathed, together with the manors, messuages, lands, tenements, and other hereditaments, heretofore to the same Mayor, or Aldermen, and Burgesses, given, granted, alienated, bequeathed, do not exceed in the whole the clear yearly rent value of sixty pounds, beyond all charges and reprisals by the year, the statute concerning lands and tenements not to be put in mortmain, or any other thing, cause, or matter whatsoever, to the contrary thereof inany wise notwithstanding.

gg "And further we will, and by these presents, for us, our heirs, and successors, grant, give confirm, ratify, and approve, to the before named Mayor, Aldermen, and Burgesses of the Borough and Parish aforesaid, and their successors, all and all manner of manors, messuages, mills, lands, meadows, feedings, pastures, markets, fairs, tolls, customs, and so many, so much, such, the same, the like, and similar liberties, franchises, immunities, exemptions, privileges, quittances, jurisdictions, wastes, voids, ground, commons, ways, commodities, profits, emoluments, tenements, and hereditaments whatsoever, as many, as much, such, and which the Mayor, Aldermen, and Burgesses of the Borough aforesaid, or by whatever names or name, or by whatever incorporation or pretext, of whatever name or incorporation they have been heretofore had, holden, used, or enjoyed, or out to have, hold, use, or enjoy, or now have, hold, use, and enjoy, to them and their successors of hereditary estate, by reason or pretext of any charges or letters patent by any of our progenitors or ancestors late Kings or Queens of England in any wise made, granted, or confirmed, or by whatever other legal manner, right, title, custom, use, orprescription, heretofore lawfully used, had, or accustomed, although the same, or any or either of them have or hath been forfeited or lost, and although the same have or hath been badly used or not used, abused, or discontinued.

hh "Provided always, that neither these our letters patent, nor any thing herein contained, in any other manner extended themselves to give and grant to the before named Mayor, Aldermen, and Burgesses, or their successors, any Court Leet, view of Frank Pledge, Court Baron, assize or assay of bread, wine, or ale, treasure, trove, goods and chattels waived, estrays, or goods or chattels of felons or fugitives, within the aforesaid parcel of the Parish aforesaid, formerly belonging to the aforesaid Priory of Saint Mary Magdalene, or within the place or precinct commonly called Magdalene Fee, or any part or parcel of the same part of the Parish, or of the same place or precinct, or to give or grant to the same Mayor, Aldermen, and Burgesses, or their successors, any Court Franchise, liberty, privilege, right, jurisdiction, profit, emolument, or hereditament within the aforesaid parcel of the Parish aforesaid, formerly belonging to the aforesaid Priory, or within the aforesaid place or precinct, called Magdalene Fee, or any part or parcel of the same part of the Parish, or of the same place or precinct, which now belongeth or pertaineth, or ought to belong or pertain, to the before named William Howard, Knight, Lord Howard of Effingham; to have, hold, and enjoy, to the before named Mayor, Aldermen, and Burgesses of the Borough and Parish of Barnstaple aforesaid, and their successors for ever; and yielding and paying therefore yearly to us, our heirs, and successors, so many, so much, such, the same, the like, and similar fee farms, rents, services, sums of money,, and demands whatsoever; as many, as much, such, and which, have been heretofore accustomed to be rendered, or paid, or ought to be rendered for the same.

ii "Wherefore we will, and by these presents, for us, our heirs, and successors, firmly enjoining, we command that the aforesaid Mayor, Aldermen, and Burgesses of the Borough and Parish aforesaid, and their successors, may have, hold, use, and enjoy, and shall and may be able to have, hold, use, and enjoy, for ever, all the liberties, authorities, jurisdictions, franchises, exemptions, and quittances aforesaid, according to the tenor and effect of these our letters patent, without the hinderance or impediment of us, our heirs, or successors, justiciaries, sheriffs, escheators, or other bailiffs or ministers of us, our heirs, or successors, whomsoever. Not willing that the same Mayor, Aldermen, and Burgesses, or any or either of them, by reason of the premises, or any of them, by us, our heirs or successors, justiciaries, sheriffs, escheators, or other bailiffs or ministers of us, our heirs, or successors whomsoever, therefore be hindered, molested, aggrieved, vexed, or in any manner disturbed. Willing, and by these presents commanding and charging as well the treasurer, chancellor, and barons of us, our heirs, and successors, as our attorney and solicitor general for the time being, and every of them, and all other our officers and ministers whomsoever, that neither they, or any or either of them, shall prosecute, or continue, or make, or cause to be prosecuted or continued, any writ or summons of Quo Warranto, or any other our writ, writs, or processes whatsoever, against the before named Mayor, Aldermen, and Burgesses of the Borough and Parish aforesaid, or any or either of them, for any causes, things, matters, offences, claim, or usurpation, or any of them, by them or any of them due, claimed, used, attempted, had, or usurped, before the day of the making of these presents. Willing also that the same Mayor, Aldermen, and Burgesses of the Borough and Parish aforesaid, nor any or either of them, by any or either of the justices, officers, or ministers aforesaid, in or for the due use, claim, or abuse of any other liberties, franchises, or jurisdictions, within the Borough and Parish aforesaid, liberties, limits, or precincts of the same, before the day of the making of these presents, be in no wise molested or impeded, or compelled to answer the same or any of them. Any statute, act, ordinance, provision, or any other thing, cause, or matter whatsoever to the contrary thereof in any wise notwithstanding. So that express mention, &c.

In witness whereof, &c. Witness the King at Westminster, the twenty-third day of January.

"By Writ of Privy Seal, &c."

Literal Transcript of Office Copy "Grant of Lathstedes Tolls, &c. of BARNSTAPLE, SAM^L. MARROWE to SIR JOHN CHECHESTER.—7th Nov. 7th Eliz. Inrolled Michas. Term, 7th and 8th Elizabeth."

"Rotu* de cartis scriptis & protecconitz cognitis & allocatis coram Jacobo Dyer milite & sociis suis justic: dne regine de banco de termino sci Michis anno regni dne Elizabeth dei gra Anglie Franc: & Hibn Regine Fidei Defensor &c. septimo & octavo.

"Rotlis 27 28

"Samuell Marrowe de Barkeswell in Com Warr Armig ven extraa cur t'cio decimo die Novemb isto codem t'mio coram Rico Weston uno Justic: dne regine de Banco apud Serjeaunts June in venella cancett et cogn scriptum subsequ fore fem sun et pet illud irrotulari et irrotulatur in hec v'ba.

" *Thys Indenture* made the vij^th daye of Novembre in the seventh yere of the raygn of or sov'aygn Ladye Elizabeth, by the grace of God, Quene of England, France, and Ireland, defendor of the Fayth, &c. Betwene Samuell Marrowe, of Barkeswell, in the Countye of Warwyck, Esquyer, of the one ptye, and Sr John Chechester, of Raleigh, in the countye of Devon, Knyght, of the other ptye, wytnesseth, that wheras the late Kynge of famosse memorye, Henry the Eyght, by hys graces letters patens, berynge date at Westmynster the xxi^th daye of Februarye, in the xxxvi^th yere of his raygn, dede graunt, demysse, and to ferme let, to hys wel beloved John Golsland, Roger Worth, and Roberte Cade, of Barnestable, in the sayde Countye of Devon, the Lathstedes within Barnestaple aforesayde, and all the yssues, rents, and pfytts therof comynge, and all the yssues and pfytts of the tolle boxe of the marketts ther & hys fayers ther holden in the feaste of the natyvytye of or blyssed Ladye the Vyrgyn, and all yssues & pfytts of the sayde Fayers comynge or growynge, whyche late were pcell of the lands and possessions of Henry Duke of Rychemond & Some's; To have and to hold all & singler the pemysses before expresssed, with all & singuler ther apptennces to the foresayd John Golsland, Roger Worth, & Robte Cade, ther exec: and assign, from the feaste of Saynte Mychell th archaungell, then laste paste, untyll the ende and terme of twentye one yeres then nexte followynge, fullye to e complette and ended; yeldynge therfore yerelye to the sayde late King Henry the eyght, hys heires and

---

* The abbreviatures are necessarily wanting.

successors, to the handes of hys Baylyffs of Barnestable aforesayde, or to the handes of the gen'all receavor of the rents and pfytts of the lands and possessions aforesayde, or to the handes of the tresorer of hys Chamber, & of hys Courts of Survey for the tyme beynge, seventene shyllyngs and foure pence of lawful money of Eglande; vz for the sayd Lathstedes, foure shyllyngs, for the pfytts of the sayd Tolle boxe of the sayd Marketts three shyllyngs four pence, and for the sayde Fayer & pfytts thereof tenne shyllyngs, & thyrtene shyllyngs foure pence starlynge, newly approved, yerelye at the feasts of the Annunscyacon of Saynte Mary the Vyrgyn and of Saynte Mychell the Archanngell, by even percons as by the same letters patents more playnlye appeareth. And wheras also the late Kynge and Quene Philippi and Marye, by ther hyghnes Ires patents, berynge date at Westmynster, the ixth daye of Apryll, in the third & fourth yeres of their Majestyes raynges, resytying the sayd Ires patents, & lesse so made of the pemysses, by the sayd late Kynge Henry the viiith, of their especyall grace, certayne knowledge, & mere mocon, dede amongest other thyngs, geve and graunte for them, and the heires and successors of the sayd late Quene Mary, to one Thomas Marrowe Esquyer, father to the sayd Samuell, the rev'con and rev'cons of all the sayd Lathstedes, and all the yssues, rents, and pfyts therof, comynge and growynge, and of the yssues and pfytts of the tolle boxe of the sayde Marketts & Fayers ther to be holden, and of all other the pemysses in the sayde Ires patents of the sayd late Kynge Henry the viiith before expressed, and all the sayd yerelye rents of seventene shyllyngs fourepence, and thyrtene shyllyngs foure pence, by the sayd Ires patents, as ys aforesayd resved. To have and to hold the sayd rev'con & rev'cons of the sayd Lathstedes & of all the yssues, rents, pfytts, therof comynge & growynge, and of the yssues of the tolle boxe of the Marketts & of the Fayers ther holden and of all yssues & pytts of the same comynge & growynge, & of all & singler other the pemysses in the sayde Ires patents of the sayd late Kynge Henry the Eyghte, expressed and specifyed, and of ev'ye pcell therof, and all the sayd rents of xvij$s$ iiij$d$ & iiij$d$ by the sayd Ires patens resved to the sayd Thomas Marrowe, his heires and assign to hys and ther onlye use for ev. And wherase also the sayd late Kynge & Queen Phillippe & Mary, by their sayd Ires patens berynge date at Westmynster, the ixth daye of Apryll in the sayd third & fourth yeres of theire raygnes, of theire lyke especyall grace, certayne knowledge & mere motion amongeste other thygns dede further geve and graunte to the sayd Thomas Marrowe, all that theire Lordshypes & Mannor of Barnestable als Barnestaple, and all that there Lordshyppes & Mannors of Barnestable als Barnestaple Fee with all & singuler theire rights, members, and apptennces, sett, lyeinge and beynge in the sayd Countye of Devon, pcell of ther lands called Rychemonds landes, and all & singuler messuags, mills, houses, buyldyngs, lofts, barnes, stables, wastgroundes, dovehouses, orchards, gardyns, landes, ten'ts, meadowes, pastures, comons, wayes, wasts, mores, hethes, furres, mayshes, waters, fyshyng, woodes, underwoodes, watercurses, rents, chargs, rents, secte, rev'cons, & servics, resvyd uppon anye demyse and graunte of the pemysses, or of anye pte or pcell hereof, courts & letts, & all pquystyts & pfyts of Courts & letts, vewe of Franckpledge, & all thyngs appteynynge unto a Courte leete or vewe of Franckpledge or that herafter shall appteyne or belonge, assyce of bred, wyne, & ale, and also goods & chattells, weyved, estreyes, fee fermes, annuytyes, knyghts fees, wardes, marryags, escheats, releves, herryots, fynes, amercyaments, advousons, pnages, vyllens, & bondmen, & all fayers, marketts, tolls, tallage, & customes, & all other the jurisdiccons, franchyses, pryveliges, pfytts, comodytyes, emoluments, and hered: whatsoev they be, with ther apptonnces, sett, lyenge, beynge, comynge, growynge, or arrysynge in the Townes, Fyldes, Bourough, pryshe, or hamlett of Barnestaple & Barnestaple Fee, als Barnestable, als Barnestable Fee, in the sayde Com of Devon, or in anie other place whatsoev they be to the sayde lordshipps or mannors belongynge or appteynynge, or before thyse tyme had knowen, accepted, used or taken, as pte, pcell, or member of the same lordshyppes & mannors, or with the same to ferme, letten, dimisssed, or occupyed, suche like & as fullye, holy and frelye, and in as ample mann and forme as anye Duke of Richemond or any other pson or psons havynge, possessynge, or beynge seassed of the sayd mannors, lordshippes, and Boroughe, and other the pemysses, or anye pte or pcell therof, ev hade, held or enjoyed, or oughte to have holden or enjoyed the same, by reason or color of anye ch're, gyfte, graunte or confirmacon, by anye of the pgenytors of the sayd late Quene, before thyse tyme had, made, graunted or confirmyde, or by reason of anye other laufull pescripcon, use, or custome, before thys tyme hade or used or otherwyse, by anye other lawfull meanes ryghte or tytle, and as fullye, whole, & frelye, & in as ample mann & forme, as they the sayd late Kynge and Quene, or anye of the pgenitors of the sayd late Quene, Kyngs of Englande, have helde or enjoyed, or ought to have hade, holden or enjoyed. To have and to hold all the sayd Lordshypps or Mannor, & other the pemysses, with all & singler ther apptennces, to the sayd Thomas Marrowe, hys heires and assigns, to the upper use and behouffe of the sayd Thomas Marrowe, hys heires and assigns for ev, as by the sayd Ires patens amongeste other thyngs more at large, yt dothe and maye appere. *Thys Indenture nowe therfore further wytnesseth* thatthe sayd Samuell Marrowe, sonne & heire of the sayd

Thomas Marrowe, decessed, as well for an in consyderacon of the some of fourtye poundes of lawfull money of England before the date hereof well and trulye contented and payed by the sayd Sr John Chechester Knyght, to the said Sammuel Marrowe, wherof the sayd Sammuel acknowledgeth hymselfe contented & payed, and therof & of ev'ye pte & pcell therof, acquyteth and dyschargeth the sayd Sr John Che[che]ster, hys heires & executors by these presents, as for the some of three hundreth threscore poundes of lawfull money of England, to the sayd Samuell Marrowe or hys assign, well & trulye to be contented or payed by the sayd Sr John Chechester, hys heires or assign, at or in the eyght daye of November nexte ensuynge the date herof, uppon the fontstone of the Temple Chruche within the suburbes of the cyttye of London, between the houres of two & five of the clocke in the afternoone of the same daye, hathe bgayned and solde, and by these pesents doth clerlye and absolutelye bgayne & sell unto the sayd Sr John Chechester, All that hys sayd Lathstedes within Barnestable aforesayd, tolle boxe of the Marketts & Fayers, & all the yssues and pfytts of them and ev'ye of them, comynge & growynge of the rev'con & rev'cons of all & singler hys sayd Lathstedes, tolles boxes & fayers, and of all yssues, rents, and pfytts of them or anye of them comynge & growynge, & all hys sayd rents of seventene shyllyngs foure pence, & thyrtene shyllyngs fourepence, & all othersvices resved uppon the sayd leasse, dimisse & Ires patens of the sayde late Kynge Henr the viijth, *And further* the sayd Samuell for the consyderacon aforesayd hath bgayned and sold, and by these pwessents dothe clerelye and absolutley bgayne and sell unto the sayd Sr John Chechester, Knyght, all those hys Lordshypps & Manor of Barnestaple, als Barnestable & Barnestaple Fee, aforesayd, with all hys messuags, houses, buyldyngs, lofts, barnes, stables, wast groundes, dovehouses, orchards, gardyns, landes, ten'ts, meadowes, pastures, comons, waies, pathes, wasts, mores, fursse, heth, marshes, watrs, fyshynges, woodes, underwoodes, water courses, rents, rev'cons, svics, courts lets, vew of Franckplege, assise of bred, wyne, and ale, weyves, estrees, fefermes, annuytyes, knyghts fees, wards marryages, eschetes, releves, herryotts, fynes, amcyaments, advosons, vyllens, fayres, marketts, tolls, tallags, customes, ryghts, jurysdyccons, franchyses, privileges, pfytts, comodytyes, emoluments, & hereds whatsoev, beynge anye pte, pcell, or member of the sayd lordshyppes or mannor, or anye of them, or knowen, hade, reputed, taken occupyed, or enjoyed as pte, pcell, or member thereof, with all & singuler ther apptennces. And all hys ryght, tytle, intereste, use and possession, whiche he hathe in or to the sayd pemysses, and evye pte & pcell therof, and all & singuler other the landes, ten'ts, reents, rev'cons, svics, and heredyta-

306

ments, with their apptencs in Barnestaple, als Barnestable aforesayd, specyfyed and contained in the sayd Ires patens; & all hys Castell and bouroughe of Barnestable, als Barnestaple, and all other hys lands, ten'ts, rents, rev'cons, svics, & hereds whatsoev, with all & singler theire apptennces, sett, lyenge, and beynge in the towne, fyldes, & pyshe of Barnestable, als Barnestaple aforesayd, wherof the sayd Samuell ys and stondeth seassed of the eney estate of enherytance in fee symple, or fee tayle, together with all evidences, charters, dedes, wrytyngs, & mynuments, rentalls, terrors & courte roulls, concernynge onlye the sayd Lordshyppe & Mannor or other the pemysses by these pesents bgayned and sold & the true copyes of all suche other evydencs, charters, dedes, wrytyngs, & mynyments, as doe consne the pemysses, together with other

Mannors, lands, & ten'ts. To have and to hold all & singler the sayd Lathstedes, Tolle boxe, Marketts, & Fayers, and the yssues and pfytts of them & ev'ye of them comynge and growytnge, & the rev'con & rev'cons of the same & ev'ye of them, & all the sayd Lordshyppes, Mannors, Castell, Bourough, and all other the sayd pemysses, with all & singler their app-tences, & ev'yepte & pcell therof, to the sayde Sr John Chechester, Knyght, hys heires and assign, to the p'per use of the sayde Sr John Chechestser, hys heires, & assign for ev, in as ample mann & forme as he the sayd Samuell hath or ought to have, hold, & enjoye the same, by force of the graunte of the sayde late Kynge & Quene Philippe & Marye, or by anye other wayes, meanes, conveyancs, or assurancs, whatsoev. And the sayde Samuell Marrowe couonteth for hym, hys heyres, executors, & administr, to and with the sayd Sr John Chechester, hys heires, & assign, thaat the sayde Lordeshyppes or Mannor, and all other the pemysses with thapptnncs & ev'ye pte & pcell therof, the day of then sealynge, delyvye, & makynge of these pesents, and from hensfourthe at all tymes, shal be & contynew clerelye acquytede, exon'ated, & dyscharged, or savyed harmeles, of & from all formr bgaynes, sales, tytles, joyntures, dowers, statuts of the staple, statuts, marchaunts recognisannces, judgments, chargs, rents, am'cements, & ev'ye of them; & of & from all other chargs, trubles, & incombranes whatsoev they be, hade, made, or don by the sayd Sameuell Marrowe, or by anye other pson or psons, by hys meanes, pcure-mente, or assente, the chyeffe rente or rents of the ffee therof from hens-forth to be dewe, onlye excepted. And the sayd Samuell Marrow doth further covennte & graunte by these pesents, for hym, hys heires, execu-tors, & adminstr, to & with the sayde Sr John Chychester, hys heires, & assign, that he the sayd Samuell hath nott at anye tyme syns the dethe of the sayd Thomas Marrowe hys father, made anye bargayne, sale, fefment, gyfte, graunte, leasse, or leasses, or any other intereste, estate, assurans, or conveyannce whatsoev, of & in the sayd Lordeshyppe,, mannor, or anye other the pemysses, or anye pte or pcell thereof, by these presents before bgayned and sold, or of & in anye other mannors, messuags, houses, landes, ten'ts, rents, rev'cons, svics, or hereditaments whatsoev, sett, lyenge, and beynge in the sayd towne, fylde, or pyshe of Barnestaple, als Barnestable, whyche the sayd Thomas hys late father, ther hade, & descended from hym to the sayd Samuell, or whyche by redempcon of anye morgage, or by any other wayes or meanes, are come, or at anye tyme hertofore werein the hands, seison, tenure, occupacon, or possession of the sayd Samuell. And further, the sayde Samuell, for hym, hys heires, executors, and administrators, covennteth & graunteth to & with the sd Sir John Chechester, hys heires & assign, that the sayde Samuell Marrowe and Margarett hys wyffe, & ev'ye of them, shall make, doe, or sufer to be made or done, to the sayde Sr John Chechester, hys heires & assign, all such further acte & acts, thynge & thyngs, in the lawe, assurance, and conveyance, for the suer makynge of the sayde pemysses, & ev'ye pte & pcell therof, with warrantye onlye agaynste the sayde Samuell, hys heires & assign, at the costs & chargs in the lawe of the sayd Sr John Chechester, hys heires & assign, as shall be reasonablye devysed or advysed by the sayde Sr John Chechester, hys heires or assign, or by hys or their lerned Councell in the lawe, at all tyme & tymes, at the requeste of the sayd Sr John Chechester, hys heires or assign, within the space of three yeres nexte ensuyng the date herof, so that the sayd Margarett be nott at anye tyme or tymes compelled or requeste for the makynge of the sayd assurance, to travyll or goo further then to the Townes of Coventrye or Warwycke. In wytnes wherof the ptyes aforesayd to these indentures, interchaungeably have sett ther handes and selles, the daye and yere fyrste above wryttyn.

"T. JEFFREYS, Clk. Try.
10th Aug. 1774."

CHAPTER IV.

Barnstaple a Naval Port in the Reign of Edward III. –
Vessels and supplies furnished to Queen Elizabeth –
Reprisal Ships – Ship Tax in the reign of Charles I. –
Civil War.

BARNSTAPLE A NAVAL PORT IN THE REIGN OF EDWARD III

The state of the British Navy in the present day, forms a magnificent contrast with what it was in former times, when the maritime strength of the Kingdom consisted almost entirely in trading vessels, belonging to private individuals. No expedition could be undertaken without the aid of merchant ships, and fishing barks. As a proof of the importance these were considered to be of, and also how subservient they were made to the use of the crown, it may be mentioned that Edward II., on the detention of three English vessels by the Norwegians, wrote to the king of Norway to demand their being given up, urging that he "cannot quietly put up with the vessels belonging to his Kingdom, *which ought at all times to be ready for his service*, being detained in foreign countries."* Edward III. also, (1340, Oct. 11,) wrote to the "Shirefs of the maritime Shires," ordering them, *"as the security of the Kingdom depended upon the vessels being kept in the hands of his own subjects,* to make proclamation forbidding persons having ships to "give or sell them to any Foreigner" †

* Fœd. V. 3, p. 400.

† Ibid. 5, p. 200

I do not find it recorded that Barnstaple furnished either of these Monarchs with any ships, but it is certain that we sent a deputy to a council held by Edward III. in 1344.

Feb. 6. " The King, again desirous to be informed of the states of the navy or shipping in England, sent precepts to the Magistrates of all the Ports, ordering them to return a number of representatives, proportioned to their trade or population, well acquainted with maritime affairs, to a council of shipping, or naval parliament, to be held in the ensuing Lent."

Forty-four places, of which Barnstaple is one, are mentioned, sending in all sixty-four representatives. We have here sufficient evidence that Barnstaple was a port of some importance early in the fourteenth century, with a probability that it then furnished, as occasion required, part of the defensive force of the kingdom.

VESSELS AND SUPPLIES FURNISHED TO QUEEN ELIZABETH

Barnstaple we know had the distinguished honor of lending her aid towards the destruction of a hostile fleet, which, says Camden,* " was the best appointed of men, ammunition, and provisions, of all that the ocean ever saw, [what has ocean seen since!] and called by the arrogant appellation of *invincible armada*; it consisted of 130 ships of all kinds, 19,290 soldiers, 8,530 sailors, 2,080 galley slaves, 2,630 cannon." The whole English fleet sent to oppose this formidable armament " consisted of but 76 ships paid by the Queen,† and 38 by the City of London, besides 83 coasters, &c. sent by several other seaports, in all 197 vessels great and small. "

Towards this fleet, Barnstaple contributed five vessels; their departure from hence in March, 1588, is thus briefly recorded; "five ships went over the bar to join Sir F.D. at Plymo ". No mention is made of the size or equipment of the ships, but they were probably the same as will come under our notice in the next article.

* Ann. Eliz. ad an. 1588

† What was termed the Navy of Queen Elizabeth was stated by Burchet, secretary to the Admiralty in her reign, to consist of " 59 line of battle ships, 1 of 100 guns, 9 of 88 to to 60 guns, and 49 0f 58 to 40 guns ; besides which there were 58 vessels of 30 to 20 guns, and 29 0f 18 to 6 guns ; 146 in all. " *Of this number only 13 were the property of the Crown* ; the remainder were all hired.

310

Numerically taken, the proportion of vessels furnished was considerable, being full one fortieth of the whole number employed on the expedition. This circumstance cannot but impress us with a favorable idea of the means, as well as public spirit of the inhabitants at this period, both which must, in order to accomplish such an undertaking, have been called forth in no ordinary degree.

In 1595, we find " orders from the Councill that intelligence of two or three Spanish ships being into St. George Channel, the Maior was to p'vide a shipp of this harbour to rencounter [encounter] with them, her Majesty wd bear one half of ye Charge, and this Country adjoining to bear the other; the Justices appointed John Barrett, of this Towne, Captayn of a new made shipp of William Morcome, for the service, which Mr. Maior & his Brethren do well leke of.* "

1596. " In March a Commandment from the privy Councel was brought, that this Towne shd sett forth the *prudence*, being about 100 Tons Burthen, presently out of hand in warlike sorte, at the Charge of this Towne, into whiche charge the whole north Division, being x hundred, [hundreds] shd be Contrybutaries. A letter to the like effect came to the Earl of Bath and Mr. H. Fortescue, for the rating the Country, and the Counsel [Corporation] appointed George Pyne, Maior of this towne, Mr. Thomas Leigh and Bartholomew Harrys, for purveyors for the Victals, and other charge of the Ship. By the Earl of Bath's letter and order, there was appoynted to be laid out by this town forthwith, one hundred pounds; by Molton, forty pounds; by Torrington xllb ; and by Bediford, xxlb;† and at a meeting at this time by divers of the said Townes, who agreed and made p'portion of the charge thereof for five months to be nyne hundred pounds and above; this charge was both for the victualling the xl men that shd go in the said Shipp, for their Wag's, and the Wag's [Hire] of the Shipp, and other necessaries."

* Such was the style in which a Town Clerk of Barnstaple wrote two centuries ago. [sic.]

† This may certainly be taken as a fair criterion of the comparative importance of the different towns; but we should rather have expected Bideford to have contributed more, instead of less, than Southmolton

The *Prudence* appears to have joined the expedition sent this year against Cadiz, consisting of 126 ships, (" 17 belonging to the Queen, the others hired,") by which Spain was calculated "to have suffered loss, by captures, and spoilation, to the amount of 20 millions of ducats."

Part of the plunder found its way here, as on " 8th August arrived the *Prudence*, which brought much pillage from takeying of Cades [Cadiz]. "

Soon after this " came to the Custom House a stay for shippyng, with a commandment from the privy Counsellors to adv'tise them of number of marynes [mariners!] and shippynge with their burdens belonging to Barnestaple,*" but I meet with no further account of ships being furnished to the government at this time. Sir Richard Grenville one of Queen Elizabeth's naval commanders, appears to have made Barnstaple his head quarters during the war with Spain.

In 1586, " 16 April, Sir Richard Grenvylle sailed over the bar with his flee [fly] boat and frigett; this Sir Richard Greynville pretended his goinge to Wyngandecora, where he was last year."†

" In December this year (1586) Sir Richard Greynfild# came home, bringing a prise with him lade with sugar, ginger, and hyds."

This enterprising officer was a Justice of the Peace for this division, and in that capacity was present at " a general muster here at Barn,' (24th Feb. 1586,) before my Lord of Bath, Sᵣ Richard Greynfild, Mr. Hugh Ackland, and Mr. George Wyot, Justices, of all the able men, with a shew of their arms and furniture, of the hundreds of Braunton, Sherwell, and Fremington; and on

---

* It is much to be regretted that no record of this official return of the number and tonnage of vessels belong to the Port, has been preserved.

†Sir R. Grenville had the previous year gone out to N. America with seven ships sent by Sir Walter Raleigh; he anchored in Wococon Harbour, Virginia, and left behind him a colony of 108 persons at Roanoke, " most of whom were either destroyed by the natives, or perished for want."

The account above given, must refer to his second voyage to the same place, when he left 50 men; the remnant of the first party had been in the mean time brought away by Sir Francis Drake. This second colony all perished; in July 1987 " not one óf them remained." That these unfortunate emigrants went from this neighbourhood, will not I think be doubted. A third settlement was attempted, but of 115 persons not one survived in 1590; " they had all miserably perished with hunger, or had been massacred by the Indians."

To find the name of an individual spelt in two or more different ways in old documents, is of very frequent occurrence.

312

Wednesday following the Inhabitants of this town and Parish mustered before the s^d Justices *in the Church, with a shewe of their arms and artillery* ". Our chronicler subsequently mentions the capture of Sir R. Grenville by the Spaniards, which is thus spoken by Sir Walter Raleigh:– " But beyond all was that unparalleled resistance made by the gallant Sir Richard Grenville in the Queen's Ship, the Revenge, in which he sustained a cruel engagement for fifteen hours against fifteen great Spanish Galleons, at the Azores, till his ship had neither men nor ammunition for defence any longer, and therefore yielded. "

The victualling system was very differently conducted at this period to what it is at present; orders were frequently received here from Government to collect provisions (butter, cheese, bacon, and grain) for the fleets acting against Spain. The following gloomy picture was drawn of the states of things here, in 1587; part of the evil arose, perhaps, from a temporary scarcity of corn.

" The Dearthe of Corne yet remains; Wheate, viij; and yet this countrye is dailey further charged with ammunition and harness, expecting and p'vidinge for invasions and warrs, which maketh the common sort fall into poverty for want of trade, so that divers fall to robbynge and stealinge; the like hath nevery been seene."

Barnstaple was further serviceable to the crown, both in this, and the following reign, as a shipping port for soldiers on their way to Ireland; considerable numbers embarked here at different times; one one occasion (in 1601) it is mentioned that nearly 800 were staying in the town, which must have been equal to more than one fifth of the inhabitants.

These were but a part of what were sent at this time. " Mr. Maior returning from London, brought letters that ij thousand soldyers would be transported to Ireland. P'vision & shyppyng for them acordingly. "

On another occasion " 1607, orders to the Maior to provide for 200 soldyers for Ireland, 100 whereof were Devonshire men, who had their conduct money & apparel, to wit, a monmouth capp, a coate, a doublet, ij shirts, a paire of breeches, a paire of stockinges, a pair of shoes, and vd in money."

REPRISAL SHIPS.

Several vessels under this specious title, belonged to this port, during the latter part of the reign of Queen Elizabeth. It can hardly be questioned that part if not all of them were the same as joined the fleet sent against the Spanish Armada; in order to engage in this service, they must have been well armed and equipped, and most probably returned from it much in the same trim.

The supposition may be reasonably entertained, that the owners of these vessels, considering that being now fitted out " in warlike sort," they might be profitably employed in hostile operations, resolved to send them " a reprising, " as Peter Wyot terms it. Licences for such a purpose might, of course, be readily obtained, since Elizabeth, by granting letters of reprisals,* would be helping forward what she was most desirous to accomplish, the humiliation of Spain.

" 1586. A Ship† of Sir William Courtenay, who went to sea by force of Letters of Reprysals, and about May Day last, took a French Ship laden with Oyles, and in her dyvers Barrels of Coucheneall, besides xxiiij Baggs of Ryalls of Plate and Mondey, contg in every bagge iiij or v C Ryalls, and arryved at Salcombe."

1589. " Unicorn, a reprisal Ship of this town, sent in a price [prize]."

" John Norrys with his Bark returned, having been a reprising."

1590. " The Prudence, a ship of 100 tons, belonging to Mr. Dodderidge, of this town, with *fourscore men*, sailed over the bar on a reprisal voyage."

" Arrived the Prudence, with a prize taken on the coast of Guiney, [Guinea] having in her iiii Chests of gold, to the value of xvi thousand pounds, and divers chaynes of gold, with civit and other

---

* The origin of reprisal ships is thus states. " In 1295, A merchant of Bayone, having been plundered, whilst at Anchor on the coast of Portugal, of a large quantity of almonds and raisins, which he was bringing to England; had licence granted to him his heirs, to seize the property of the Portuguese, wherever he could find it, during five years, or until he should be reimbursed for his loss and all expenses." Fœd. v. 2, p. 691.

† It is doubtful whether or no this vessel belonged to Barnstaple.

things of great value; such a price as this was never brought into this Port. Price about cxxx ton brought to Key Head, at Barnstaple, chests & baskets of gold, weighed cccxx pound. "

We can readily believe that such a prize was never brought here before; we should scarcely credit the statement, but for the weight of the gold being mentioned, which serves to corroborate the account given of its value; this at four guineas per ounce, would exceed sixteen thousand pounds.

1591. " The Prudence of Barn : sent home 2 prices."

" A bark of this Town wch had been a reprising, called the White Hart, put into Ilfordcombe 12th Octr brought home some Elifants teth."

" A pinnace called the Fortmouth, a reprisal ship of the Harbour, brought in a Price laden with wynes."

1592. " xxv January, the Prudence brought in over the Bar, a price worth x thousand pounds."

1593. " The White Hart is Taken."

" The Gifte, a reprisal ship of this towne, belonging to W. Morcomb of this towne and others, carried a rich price into Ilfordcombe."

These valuable captures must have greatly enriched the town at this time; but I am disposed to look on the property thus obtained, as ill-gotten wealth. The owners of these " reprisal ships " probably never asked themselves what *right* they had to prey on the possessions of individuals, merely because they were of a nation which was at war with their own; the authority of the Queen could not convey such a title as our townsmen ought to have possessed, before they sent vessels "a reprising."

I come now to speak of the exactions drawn from Barnstaple by King Charles, under the appellation of

SHIP MONEY

One of the most obnoxious measures set on by this impolitic and arbitrary Prince, is well known to have been that of issuing " *writs*, commonly called *shipwrits*, under the great seal of England, for the providing and furnishing of certain ships for the King's service, &c." contrary as it was afterwards declared to be, " to the laws and statutes of the realm, the petition of right, and the liberty of the subject." In 1634, " London and other Ports were ordered to provide shipping with ordnance, tackle, &c. for 26 weeks."*

The work just referred to, gives a particular account† of the ships which the different counties were, in 1635, directed to supply for the public service; in which year " King Charles, bent on bringing the Dutch to acknowledge his sea dominion, the better to enable him to fit out a superior fleet, ordered his Chancellor Coventry to issue writs to the Sheriffs and Magistrates for assessing and collecting money for fitting out ships of war, for suppressing pirates, and for the guard of the seas."

Each vessel was to be furnished with " a commander and sailors, with cannon, small arms, spears, darts, ammunition, &c. answerable, and stored with provisions and double equipage, and all other necessaries, for 26 weeks at least; all which to be paid and maintained at their own charge. "

The number of ships was 44; burden of the whole, 11,500 tons; complement of men, 8610.

Only one ship was ordered to be of 900 tons, and that was allotted to Devonshire ; she was to be provided with 360 men. The rest varied form 800 tons and 320 men; to 200 tons, and 80 men; London furnished two of the former, and Bristol one of the latter size. " Duty repeated annually till 1639, and was valued at £200,000 per annum."

We have now to see what Barnstaple contributed towards this impost. Turning to an ancient record, I find the following

" Accot in the year of our Ld 1634."

" An assessment was made on the inhabitants & tenements of the town and parish of Barum towards setting forth a ship of war of 400 tons for His Majesty's service, for their whole estates and abilities, the total amount of which was £601 3s."

1635, 1636, 1637. " There were 3 other assessments made on the inhabitants for ships of 900 tons."

* Foed v. 19, p. 547.

† Vol. 19, p. 686. See also Macpherson's Anuals of Commerce.

The cost of the Essex ship, which was one of 800 tones, is stated, by way of example, to have been 8,000*l*. Taking this as a guide, we have no difficulty in ascertaining the probable amount of the other vessels.

That for which the first assessment was made here, would, of course, cost 4,000*l*. ; of this, if the statement given is correct, and there is no reason to believe it to be otherwise, Barnstaple supplied, say in round numbers, 600*l*., or more than a seventh part. By a parity of calculation, the rate for a 900 ton ship must have amounted to 9,000*l*., or 27,000*l*. for the three years, and the proportion raised by Barnstaple to 4,050*l*. equal to 10, or 12,000 in the present day.

Enormous as this sum appears, I am only surmising the tax to have been paid for the period recognized by our own records, in which, however, it is more probable that an omission may have occurred, than that Barnstaple should have been exempted for two years from an impost which was general throughout the country and levied by a despotic and needy prince. Supposing then, as we must, that Barnstaple was not excused her quota of the tax, she paid 1,350*l*. per annum for *five* successive years in *ship money only*.*

The next subject which presents itself, both in order and in connexion with what we have just noticed, is that of the

CIVIL WAR

which " followed hard upon, " and in which Barnstaple took a conspicious and energetic part, against the ill-fated Charles.

The large sums of which the town had been drained, by means of the ship tax, we may fairly conjecture to have weighed much with the inhabitants in their early and resolute determination to espouse the cause of the Parliament. Fully aware of the consequences that must ensue from the adoption of such a course, their declaration of war against the regal power was followed up by

---

* This is the only one of the many obnoxious taxes imposed in this reign, to which I find any particular allusion made; perhaps it was selected by the writer of the" account " as being more oppressive than the rest.

active measures for the maintenance of their opposition; the town was put into a respectable state of defence, and a martial force provided.

1642. In August this year, " the fortifications of the town," are mentioned as approaching towards a finished state; " a watch provided with musquets," was appointed; and a resolution passed, " that every Maior do allow out of his stipend of £30, &10 towards the fortifications."

In September, four companies of foot, and a troop of horse soldiers were raised and armed, and a considerable quantity of warlike stores provided.

₊ " Oct.15.* Whereas much monie hath been disbursed about the fortifications, and more likely to be, and the town without stock of money; for supply whereof, Mr. Geo. Peard offers to lend £50, Mr. Rich^d. Beaple £50, Mr. Pent. Dodderidge £50, Mr. Richard Ferris £25; for which sums Mr. Wm. Palmer, Maior, Gilbert Paige, and Henry Masson, Aldermen, to give their bonds, for the raising whereof, &c. surveys of town lands to be held to raise, &c.

William Palmer, Maior	William Nottle
Gilbert Paige, ⎫ Aldermen	Roger Peard
Henry Masson, ⎭	Anthony Gay
Richard Beaple	Thomas Horwood
Pentecost Dodderidge	George Baker
Justinian Westcomb	James Gommon
Richard Ferris	Richard Harris
John Down	Adam Lugg

₊ Octr. 17, " Thomas Horwood, William Nottle, Penfound Curry, James Gommon, Roger Peard, Thomas Matthew, John Downe, Nicholas Harris, appointed at a committee or Councell of War, to order business for the fortifications and defence of the towne; who, or the greater number, to meet together at the Guildhall every day,

---

* The several articles which follow, marked thus *₊* are given without abbreviation or alteration, from a conviction that they ought to be preserved entire. They are from a source of unquestionable authenticity.

to order what is to be done about the fortifications, &c. and what is to be then done, and is confirmed by

William Palmer, Maior	Gilbert Paige ⎫ Aldermen
George Peard, Depy. Recr.	Henry Masson ⎭

1643. The projected fortification of the town being still incomplete, and a further supply of money required;

₊ " January 24. Agreed that a general meeting of Common Counsel, Burgesses, and other Inhabitants of Town, meet at Guildhall to propound a Rate to be made for finishing Fortifications of the town, &c. and that six be appointed to make rate and to take oath to make rate indifferently.

W. Palmer, Maior	Mr. Lewis Downe
Geo. Peard, Depy. Recr.	Mr. G. Baker
Gilbert Paige, Alda.	Mr. Lewis Palmer
Richd. Beaple	James Baker
Pent. Dodderidge	Adam Lugg
Justinn. Westcomb	Jno. Downe
Richd. Ferris	W. Nottle
Walter Tucker	R. Peard

R. Harris.

₊ " Jany. 26. At Asssembly of Common Counsell, Burgesses, and Inhabitants, agreed that seven men be appointed to make a rate for moneys, for defrayment of charges disbursed, &c. about the fort, and other defensive provisions for the town. Raters to take oath to rate men without partiality, and none to be rates but such as have been rated to subsidy, and such others as raters think fit. That notice be taken who have already subscribed, and what they have subscribed, and of such as have subscribed and not paid. That they and such as refuse to pay as rated, shall be taken as malignants and enemies to the town, and such as are ill affected to the cause. The raters chozen and agreed upon on all sides are George Peard, John Downe, W. Nottle, Roger Peard, Jos. Bonifant, John Frost, John Sweete.

" What rate they or the greater number shall make, agreed to be paid, which raters have taken their oath, the form of which is as followeth.

" I, George Peard, do voluntarily swere by the contents of the Holy Evangelists, that the rate which I am now entrusted to make, shall be by me done without any favour or affection, hatred or malice, or any other partial respect, and according to my best judgment; the like by the rest. "

I cannot find that any copy of the rate here mentioned, is in existence; had it been preserved to the present time, it would be curious, and might prove a useful document.

₋ " May 30. Agreed at general meeting, that a Counsell of War, chosen for ordering martial affairs within this town, during these troublesome times, and the parties so to be chosen of the town are Mr. William Palmer, Maior, Mr. Geo. Peard, Esq. Recorder, Mr. Henry Masson, Mr. Alexander Horwood, Mr. Richard Harris, Mr. William Nottle; and of strangers, Mr. Hugh Fortescue, Esq. Col. Chudleigh, Col. Rolles, Lieut. Col. Stevenson, and Captn. Bennett; who have power to determine what is necessary for defence of the town; which Counsell of War to meet once a day."

₋ " June 13. Forasmuch as the necessities of the tymes require that great sums of money be raised for the defence of the town against those adversaries who have threatened the ruin thereof; and whereas the Maior and Aldermen, have engaged themselves and are to engage themselves, for great sums of money, employed, and to be employed, about the fortifications and other provisions, for the defence of the town; for which engagements other persons have obliged themselves unto them, for indemnity; therefore, it shall be lawful for the Maior, Aldermen, and Feoffees of Town Lands, or Bridge Lands, to fill up Estates and grant reversionary Leases;* such monies to go towards discharging such debts as the Maior, Aldermen, and other persons, have engaged themselves for on the behalf of the town and its defence; if soe much money shall not be raised as will suffice to discharge the said engagements, to

---

* It would hence appear that the practices of letting the Corporation and Bridge Lands for long terms, had its origin at this period.

such persons as are, or shall be engaged, then so much as shall be raised, to be paid in proportion; that some other course shall be taken for full satisfaction.

William Palmer, Maior	Roger Peard
Gilbert Paige	Walter Tucker
Henry Masson	Charles Peard
Richard Beaple	John Downe
Pentecost Dodderidge	Richard Harris
Richard Ferris	William Nottle

Alexander Horwood "

About this time, i.e. in this year, an Act of Parliament was passed " for protecting and saving harmless all such as should use their best endeavour, for fortifying and preserving the town of Barnstaple, in the county of Devon."*

⁎ " June 27. Whereas divers of the Capitall Burgesses and other inhabitants, have promised to be bound in sums of money, towards payment of greater sums borrowed and employed in fortifications, &c. for the defence and preservation of this town, and inhabitants thereof, against all surprisals and attempts which shall be made against the same ; It is agreed, if any parties who have so promised refuse to enter in bonds, &c. such persons shall be declared to be adversaries to the King [!] and Parliament, the liberties of the subject, and professed enemies to the good and welfare of this Town, and of the inhabitants thereof.

William Palmer, Maior	Richard Harris
Gilbert Paige	Alexander Horwood
Henry Masson	Walter Tucker
Richard Beaple	Charles Peard
Pentecost Dodderidge	John Downe
Richard Ferris	Roger Peard

William Nottle."

* Macauley, Vol. 5, App. vii.

Within a month from the last mentioned date, the city of Bristol surrendered to the King's forces. This event, whilst it damped the spirits of the adherents of the Parliament in the west, rendered it necessary for them to be on the alert, and we soon find the valiant men of Barnstaple and Bideford uniting their forces in order to attack a body of the King's troops, which were stationed at Torrington, under the command of Colonel Digby, for the purpose of preventing a junction between the North Devonians and the Garrison at Plymouth, whose object was to unite, for the purpose of relieving Exeter, then in a state of siege.

They went — but not to victory! Lord Clarendon's account of this luckless expedition sets the courage of our countrymen, whose numbers he states to have amounted to 1,200 foot and 300 horse,* in but a sorry light. On their arrival without Torrington, " a forlorn hope of 50 musqueteers," was sent against a party of the enemy; on being charged by Colonel Digby and five of his officers, this *"forlorn"* party fell back on the main body, who, partaking of their panic, joined them in inglorious flight, and were pursued by the enemy's cavalry " till their swords were blunted with slaughter, and his numbers overburdened with prisoners.

" In this action† there were near 200 killed, and above 200 taken prisoners, and those that fled contributed more to the victory than the prisoners or the slain; for they were scattered and dispersed over all the country, and scarce a man without a cut over the face or head, or some other hurt, that wrought more upon their neighbours towards their conversion, than any sermon [that] could be preached to them. Some of the principal officers and of their horse got into Bediford and Barnstaple, and, not considering the inconvenience of acknowledging that God was extraordinary propitious to

* Query, Are not these numbers greatly overrated? Barnstaple appears by the "Summarie of Disbursements," given in a subsequent part of this chapter, which carries with it every appearance of correctness, to have furnished but 370 foot, and 130 horse, or one third of the number stated. Bideford was evidently inferior in the extent of her resources to Barnstaple, so much so, as even to require succour from her neighbour, how then was she to provide twice as many troops on this occasion as were sent by Barnstaple?

† This disastrous affair took place, according to Clarendon, about August 21, but by our own records (see "Summarie of Disbursements") it happened on the 3rd or 4th of that month.

the cavaliers, told strange stories of the ' horror and fear that seized upon them, and that nobody saw above six of the enemy that charged them,' which proved a greater dismay to their friends than their defeat.*

Hitherto the Barumites, although they had seen something of the " pomp and circumstance of war," in the raising and equipment of soldiers, the erection of fortifications, occasional dispatch of troops to other parts of the country, &c.† had had nothing to do with the enemy at home; they were now to behold a spectacle as yet new to them, – that of a hostile army taking posession of their town. As might have been expected, the defeat at Torrington was followed by the conquest both of Barnstaple and Bideford, and also of " the Fort at Appledore,# which commanded the river to Barnstaple and Bideford. " They, however, submitted quietly, (panic struck, no doubt,) and by this means secured their persons and property from injury. They " yielded upon promise of pardon, and such other articles as were of course; which Colonel Digby saw precisely observed in point of plunder and violence towards the inhabitants. And this success so wrought on the spirits and temper of the people, that all persons of eminent disaffection withdrawing themselves according to the articles, Colonel Digby within a very few days increased his small party§ to the number of 3,000 foot and 800 horse."

Nothing material appears to have happened here until Barnstaple against changed masters. This event occurred in less than a year from the time of its surrender to Colonel Digby, the town in the mean time having been left, it would seem, with scarcely any regular troops for its defence.

" Memdm. That the 1 day of July, 1664, a day never to be forgotten by the inhabitants of Barnestaple for God's mercie and favor shewed in that miraculous deliverance of them from that bloody conspiracy of some of our neighbours, in inviting and bringing in 5 or 600 horse and foot, being French, Irish, and some English, against the said town with purpose to have put all therein to the

* Lord Clarendon's History of the Rebellion, vol. 2, p. 338.

† See " Summarie of Disbursements."

Clarendon's Rebellion, vol. 2, p. 338

§ I do not find it any where stated, of how many this "small party" consisted.

sword, and to have possessed themselves of the whole town, but were repulsed and driven away by the small power our townsmen had; our warning and notice was but two days before.

" On the 9th July, one Howard, a Lieutenant, who was taken prisoner in the fight, was hanged at the High Cross of Barnestaple."

It is difficult to reconcile this statement with the fact that the town came at this precise period into the hands of the parliamentary forces,* many hundreds of whom were stationed here for different periods between July 1st and September 17th, by which the inhabitants were drained of nearly 3,000*l*.† Was the "bloody conspiracy," (so named, probably, in excess of party feeling, (in reality any thing more than a plan concerted by some of the "eminently disaffected," to put the Round Heads again in possession of the town? Which was, in fact, accomplished, notwithstanding the assailants are said to have been repulsed and driven away, and the first of July to have been observed as a day of rejoicing in commemoration of the victory.

An attempt to reconcile the two accounts would be vain; it is not however of importance, since the main point, namely, that the town was in the hands of the Parliament, is sufficiently established without it. Further proof of this, " if proof were wanting," is supplied by the circumstance of Barnstaple having been retaken for the King, on September 17th, the identical day on which it is recorded that " the Lord General Essex, his life guards and servants, " with several hundred soldiers, ceased to be chargeable to the inhabitants. The Garrison surrendered to General Goring, (whether in consequence of a siege, or a battle, or merely a summons, we are not informed) on the following conditions,

" Garrison to march away with a convoy to Portsmouth, with drums beating, colours flying, and their arms; and that the town should not be plundered, nor the inhabitants molested."#

---

* Sir Edward Walker, in his " Historical Discourses," a work which I cannot now refer to, mentions the revolt of Barnstaple from the King, in July, 1644; and also, if I mistake not, of the town being then immediately garrisoned by the Earl of Essex, for the Parliament.
† See "Summarie of Disbursements."
# " Rushworth's Historical Collection," vol. 5, p. 713.

Here, adds the historian, " his Majesty gained fifty pieces of ordnance, and at Ilfar Combe, taken a few days before, near twenty."

1645. Whether our ancestors had now really become good subjects, or only wore the mask of loyalty in the presence of the King's troops, is a question not now to be solved; but however this might be, it was not judged unsafe to permit the Heir Apparent to the throne, to sojourn amongst them; Barnstaple was indeed considered the most eligible place* to which the Prince of Wales could remove from Bristol, which it was deemed advisable he should quit. This occurred just about the time of the battle of Naseby, so disastrous to the royal cause; the first intelligence the Prince received of this engagement, awaited him on his arrival at Barum. During his stay here, which was from one to two months, he transacted business with " the commissioners of Devon and Cornwall " whom he had appointed to meet him. The object of both bodies was, principally, to prefer complaints against Sir Richard Grenvil, for " several exorbitant and strange acts of tyranny " in one county, and " raising what money he pleased, and committing what persons he pleased " in the other.

This officer, who acted in the double capacity of military Commander, and High Sheriff of Devon,† and General Goring were, each in his turn, the scourge of the North of Devon. Of the later, Lord Clarendon says, – " When he was at Barnstaple, he gave himself his usual licence of drinking," at the same time allowing " his army, which was then quartering at Torrington, and all over the North of Devon," to commit " such intolerable insolences and

---

* See chapter one..

† To what diabolical schemes of rapine and injustice does war give rise! Invest an unprincipled man with power, and with what fiend-like ingenuity and eagerness will he proceed to the lawless exercise of it, as opportunity may offer for doing so with impunity. One way in which this notable plunderer amasssed wealth, was by frequently calling out the *posse comitatus*, and that without ocasion. Those who might not obey the call, had " a party of horse presently sent to apprehend their persons, and drive their grounds. If men hid themselves from being apprehended, they durst not send to require their stock; so that he had a greater stock of cattle of all sorts upon his grounds, than any person whatsoever in the West of England. – Clarendon's Hist. Vol. 2. We find this titled marauder subsequently " desiring at Barnstaple a protection for his houses and lands " from the Prince of Wales; but we afterwards see him committed by the Prince, to Launceston Goal, for disobedience of orders; from thence he was removed to Saint Michael's Mount, and, lastly, he had leave granted him to transport himself " beyond the seas."

disorders, as alienated their hearts who were best affected to the King's service."

The Prince of Wales also received a visit here from Prince Maurice of Bohemia, a commander in the royal army.

I find no reference made to the sojourn of the Prince in Barnstaple in any of the private records I have met with; which, though somewhat extraordinary, is not much to be regretted, when we consider the general profligacy of his habits. One circumstance however, characteristic of the man whom history designates " an irreconcileable enemy of the protestant religion, a parliament, and a *virtuous woman*," has been handed down, traditionally, viz. that (to use the words of my informant) " though his visit was short, he left a scion of royalty in the town, and his descendants are still living, numerous and highly respectable, both in Barnstaple and its neighbourhood." The royal bantling was a female. The family alluded to is said to have once enjoyed an hereditary title.

The house in which the Prince is supposed to have resided, is that now numbered 112 in High Street, formerly (that part of it, at least, in which the house in question stands) Southgate Street. Those of my townsmen who may have heard it stated that the royal residence was on or near the Quay, will recollect, that the house already alluded to has now a back way from the Quay, which, two centuries ago, was, doubtless, more commodious than at present. It is very probable, indeed, that this was formerly the principal entrance, and that there was a full view of the river from what is now considered the back part of the house; hence it might very properly be termed "near the Quay."

1646. April. But a year and a half ago, we saw the King's troops supplanting those of the Parliament, the latter marching away with the shew of military honours, leaving their conquerors in possession of the more substantial part of the thing, namely, the town of old Barum, with its lieges, fifty pieces of ordnance &c. &c. But the wheel of fortune has made another revolution, and the Cavaliers must now in their turn file off, with the empty parade of drums and colours, before the victorious Round Heads; whilst the peaceable inhabitants, as if they were so many automatons, are turned over to their new masters, and the town becomes once more a rebel garrison. This was, however, to be the last transfer; already was the power of the unfortunate Charles annihilated, his friends dispirited, his enemies triumphant, himself a captive, and the crisis of his fate hastening rapidly onward.

" Sir Thomas Fairfax advanced to Barnstaple, Friday, April 10th, and summoned that town, who, [which] not being in a capacity to make a long defence, came to a capitulation, which was concluded on Sunday, 12th; the articles being in effect much the same as those of Exeter;" * these were to be allowed to march out of garrison, fully armed and equipped, with drums, colours, &c."†

The following narration (which I judge to be from a private record, but cannot state with certainty) gives a more detailed and, it may be presumed, not less correct account of this capitulation.

" General Fairfax, after taking Exeter for the Parliament, invested Barnstaple, in the year 1646. It was then commanded by Colonel Bassett, who was made Governor for his loyalty and steadiness in the cause of his King. From its defenceless state he could not make much resistance, but he obtained the same terms as Exeter, vis. – That the churches should not be defaced; that the Garrison should march out according to the most honourable custom of war, with arms, and not be compelled to march above ten miles a day; that the composition of persons of quality should not exceed two years' purchase; that all persons comprised within these articles, should quietly and peaceably enjoy all their goods, debts, and moveables; and be free from all oaths, covenants, and protestations."

The taking of the town at this time by the parliamentary troops, who were now everywhere victorious followed their other conquests as a matter of course.

As might be expected, no further historical account is to be met with, relative to proceedings here during the short remaining period of the Civil War; but two or three private records of some importance remain yet to be noticed.

The "Summarie" which follows will be regarded with interest not only by Barumites, but by the lovers of English history in general;

. * Rushworth, vol. 6, p. 226.
† Ibid

it presents us with an excellent epitome, not only of the disbursements, but of the military proceedings in the principal garrison town in the North of Devon, during the height of the revolution.

*** " Summarie of Disbursements made by the Inhabitants of the town of Barnstaple, in Plate and Money, for fortifying the said town, and the payment and quartering of soldiers, faithfully collected from the particulars, which by credible and honest persons, in that behalf entrusted, will appear upon oath.

	£	s.	d.
" Lent in Money and Plate . . .	1191	17	9
For raising and arming 4 foot companies and a troop of horse, upon the first publishing the Commission of Array, which in money and quarters from 15th Septr to 15th Decr 1642 came to . .	1030	0	6
" For nyntie barrels of Powder . . .	450	0	0
a " For foure tonne of Match . . .	112	0	0
" For foure tonne of Shott greate and smale .	72	0	0
b " For setting forth 460 foot, and 40 horse against Torrington, Jany 1643, with			
" Money and Victual, 2 daies . . .	70	0	0
" For setting forth 2 companies to Modbury consisting of 154 Soldiers, under " Captn Benson and Captn Currie, 27 daies with Monie and Victual . . .	50	0	0
" For Bisquet, Bacon, Pease, and Beere, sent to Stratton, by order to the Army, " May 3, 1643	106	0	0
" For setting forth 400 foote and 70 horse, to beat off the enemy in South Molton, with Monie and Victual, 17 July, 1643 .	40	0	0
" For setting 370 Soldiers and 130 Horse against Torrington, with Money and " Victuals, 3 Aug. 1643, 2 daies . .	80	0	0
Carried forward . . .	3201	18	3

		£	s.	d.
Brought forward . . .		3201	18	3

c " In Money and Provisions to furnish 2
Ships, to keep the Port from May to
Sept. 2nd, 1643, and setting forth a
Man of War 190 0 0

d " In Disbursements for Materials and
Wages to build the Fort, in which were
mounted 28 Pieces of Ordnance . . 1120 0 0

e " For entrenching the Town . . . 450 0 0

" In Fortifying the Castle, building 3
defensible Gates, and making 16 Platforms . 660 0 0

" For Money, Corn, and Powder, sent to
Bitheford, to encourage them to hold
out the siege against Col. Digby . . 200 0 0

" For Money and Quartrs, for 640 foot
Souldiers, under Col. Chidley, Capt.
Trevillian, and Capt. Bennet, together
with 70 Horse under Capt. Freeman,
from 16 Decr 1642 to 17 Septr 1643 . . 4900 0 0

" For quartering the Lord Marshall's
Brigade, with his Traine, 10 days,
July 1644 . . . . . 650 0 0

" In Money lent the Lord Marshall to be
repaid in 20 daies, yet unsatisfied . . 465 0 0

f " Raised for his Soldiers upon the Town at
their departure. 314 10 0

" In Money and Quarters of 374 Soldiers
under Col. Lutterell, 11 weeks, from
July 1 to Septr 17, 1644 . . . 708 8 0

" For quartering Captn Deane's, Captn
Needham's, and Captn Spooner's Companies,
for 4 July to 17 Septr 1644 . . . 412 10 0

" For Money which Col. Luttrell raised in
the town 160 0 0

" For quartering of Lord General Essex,
his Life Guards, and Servants, in all
126, from 6 to 17 Septr 1644 . . . 69 6 0

Carried forward . . 13500 14 3

	£	s.	d.
Brought forward . .	13500	14	3

"In Money paid the L^d G^l and his Life
Guards, at their departure   .   .   . 60 0 0

"In Money and 2 Chirurgions, for curing
wounded Soldiers 20 0 0

g "The Repaire of our Bridges, the demolishing
of Houses, and laying Wast of
Land, on which the Fort Lyne and
Intrenchments were made, more than .   . 3000 0 0

Total   .   .   .   . h £16581 12 3

a This appears an enormous quantity of such an article, especially when compared with the shot; of the latter, however, they must doubtless have procured a much larger supply.

b I find no mention elsewhere made of these skirmishing expeditions.

c No other notice occurs of this armament; the sum mentioned can hardly be correct. Should it not rather have been one *thousand* and odd pounds?

d It is a generally received opinion that no building was erected on Fort Hill, because (for I know of no other reason being given) there remains no trace of any; this entry may be fairly allowed to set the question at rest, by deciding that there *was a fort built*. Might it not have been of wood? but whether formed of that material or of stone, there is every probability from the state of the town finances, that what remained at the close of the war was converted into money. Timber would, of course, be quickly cleared away; and stone, so conveniently situated for removal, (since there appears never to have been a good supply near the town,) must have been valuable. The proprietor of the field also would be desirous to see it restored to a proper state of cultivation. The ground was well chosen for the purpose to which it was applied, being an eminence commanding the principal approaches to the town, as well as the river. It was, without doubt, from this spot that the church at Pilton was cannonaded.*

e No trace whatever now remains of these intrenchments.

f The "ten days" sojourn of the Lord Marshall (apparently) "and his Traine," was an honour less highly esteemed than dearly purchased. The expense of the visit to the inhabitants was upwards of 140*l*. per diem.

g No statement has, I believe, been preserved of what houses were demolished or other damage done; but in all probability Litchdon suffered, as indeed might have been expected from its situation. The door of an apartment forming the left wing of the Almshouse in this street, exhibits numerous shot holes, and up to a very recent period musket balls were to been seen in many of them.

h The amount here stated to have been expended was a large one for the inhabitants to have raised in two years, but there is good reason to believe that the whole sum of which the town became minus from the commencement to the close of the Civil War, was nearly double what is here specified. In a fragment of a copy of a petition (from which has been torn, unfortunately, a portion comprising a part of each line of the document) thirty thousand pounds is stated as having been raised by the inhabitants of Barnstaple on behalf of the Parliament. Whatever may have been the actual expenditure during this lamentable and unnatural warfare, the whole is doubtless like the "money lent the Lord Marshall to be repaid in twenty days, yet unsatisfied."

The Parliament having gained their ends, paid but little attention to the claims of their old and staunch friends the Barumites, who appear to have been left to "repent at leisure."

---

* This edifice, which is situated a few furlongs N. of Fort Hill, and at a similar elevation, suffered considerable damage towards the close of the war. Over the porch is the following inscription,
" the Tower of this Parish being by force of arms pul'd down in ye late unhappy Civil Wars, Anno Dom. 1646, was rebuilt 1696." A great part of the body of the church was also destroyed, but has never been replaced; portions of the walls still remain at nearly their original height.
The idea of a massive and lofty stone tower having been pulled down as above expressed, is quite ludicrous, especially as the party to whom the act has always been (and no doubt justly) attributed had a powerful battery at their command, by which they could, without any laborious exertion accomplish their mischievous purpose.
Why this church was so much injured does not appear, but it requires no great stretch of fancy to imagine Fairfax's soldiery, in the sheer wantonness of power, and without any particular motive, levelling their artillery at the tower, merely because it happened to stand a conspicuous mark within range of their shot.

⁎ " 1650. Whereas there have been great sums of money disbursed and lent for the service of the Parliament, by the inhabitants of this town of Barnstaple, of which, hitherto, no restitution hath been made, nor any satisfaction given for the same; it is therefore now ordered by all whose names are here underwritten; that Mr. John Tucker be employed to solicit the Parliament and State, for the obtainment of some restitution and satisfaction to be made of such monies as they have lent and disbursed for the service of the Parliament, which the said John Tucker undertaketh to do at his own charges; for which it is agreed, that he shall have a third part of whatever he shall recover.

"Hugh Horsham, Maior
Nicholas Cooke ⎫ Aldermen
Adam Lugge ⎭
William Palmer
Justinn Westcomb
Charles Peard
John Downe
William Wood

William Nottell
Henry Messon
Walter Tucker
Richard Medford
Thomas Dennis
James Rosyer
Joseph Bonifant
Joseph Delbridge

John Horwood "

Eight more years passed away in fruitless efforts to obtain " restitution. " That it was now almost a desperate case may be inferred from the rate of premium offered to two fresh adventurers on what they might recover.

⁎ " 1658, 7 Augt. Ordered by the Maior, Aldermen, and common councellmen, of this town &c. that whereas Coll George Walters and Captn William Walters, are desired and authorized, in behalf of this Town and Borough, to endeavour the recovery of satisfaction and reparation for such disbursements as this Towne hath been at for the use and service of the Parliament of this common weal in the late wars; in liewe and consideration of the Paines which they shall bee at, and that the whole charge of the said prosecution shall be born by the said Coll Walters and the said Captn Walters, we to enjoy the one fourth or quarter part of what shall be so recovered; at it is desired for the effectual prosecution of the same, that Mr. Richard Medford and Thomas Cox will betake upon them the care

of holding correspondence with the said Captn and Col^l Walters, advising the Maior and Aldermen for the time being with what they shall act, write, or doe in the same. The charge of Postage, &c. to be paid by the Receiver, and a Piece of Plate of the value of 5l. to be conferred on the said Mr. Medford and Thomas Cox, for their Paines, upon the good success of this affair.

" Peter Doctor, Maior
Roger Jeffery } Aldermen
John Downe
Adam Lugge
Richard Harris
John Horwood
Richard Medford
Joseph Bonnivant

J. Delbridge
Richard Hooper
Thomas Cox
Jno. Palmer
Bartholomew Bisse
John Greade
James Cornish
Laurance Gay."

The following curious epistle, which is without date, was sent from Bideford, some time subsequent to conclusion of the war; it serves at least to shew the deference in which the authorities here were held by those of Bideford.

" Mr. Maior and you Gent^n

"We have though it good to acquaint you hereby, that one Francis Achard, a Frenchman, (who hath lately presented a petition to his Majesty at Oxford and thereupon obtained commission for the seizing of any merchants goods *at this harbour in France** to 1008 value) is sent over from Swanzey, by Mr. Walter Thomas, and is now here in town; he hath shewn himself a notorious fellow in the business. Pray afford us your advise what you conceive best to be done with him, and werther we shall send him to you at Barum, or you be pleased to meet here and confer with us touching him; he affirms that when he got his commission at Oxford, your townsmen were there solliciting for their pardon, to whom he shewed his commission, and he saith that they approved of his proceedings. Other things of him we refer till we heare your answer, which we desire you to dispatch to us. And even thus we bid you heartily farewell, and rest

" Your loving friends,
John Heard, Maior
Thos Wadland
John Strange."

---

* This is obscure, but it is correctly transcribed from my copy.

An instance of individual suffering in an inhabitant of this town, arising out of circumstances connected with the Civil War, must not pass unnoticed; – the case of the Rev. Martin Blake, Vicar of the Parish. Of the persecutions this worthy divine was the subject of, a long account is given in " Walker's Sufferings of the Clergy," published in 1714. Making due allowance for the spirit in which that work was written, and the strong bias of the author towards the royal party, there cannot be a doubt that Mr. Blake was treated with great cruelty. His only crime (if a crime it can be called) appears to have been a firm and, no doubt, conscientious attachment to the interests of his Sovereign, Charles the First.

" His sufferings " says Walker, " were chiefly occasioned by his writing a letter to the Mayor and Aldermen of his native town (Plymouth,) when it was besieged; exhorting them to return to their duty, and reconcile themselves to his Majesty; offering withal his own service, as far as he was capable, for that end. To which it must be added, (if any credit can be given to one of the petitions which was presented against him,) that he had been instrumental in getting the town of Barnstaple delivered up to his Majesty, which they called betraying it to the King."

Every possible attempt, if Walker's narrative may be relied on, was made to bring Mr. Blake to absolute ruin. He was repeatedly summoned to answer charges which appear only to have originated in the malice of his enemies, and which his accusers were unable to substantiate;– three times illegally (as it must be judged) dispossessed of his living; – on one occasion " seized by the party of horse and hurried prisoner to Exeter, in a very bitter stormy winter's day, tho' he was then old, and the journey at least 40 miles;" – twice was his residence, " even that very vicarage house which he had at a great charge built new from the ground " broken into " by a party of horse." These and other indignities, all which are fully detailed by the author alluded to was the upright and honest vicar subjected to for loyalty's sake.

After the restoration, Mr. Blake was finally reinstated in his cure, and continued in peaceable possession of it for many years, his enemies no longer " daring to make him afraid." He died in a good old age,* in 1673, having been interred, as appears by the parish register, Sept. 13, in that year.

The good vicar was allowed, during the heat of the persecution against him, to fix a monument in the most conspicuous part of the church, which, although it was erected to the memory of his children, contains pointed allusions to his own sufferings. His having accomplished this is a proof that he had powerful friends; it is therefore the more extraordinary that the parish clerk should have been the brief and only chronicler of his decease. Although it was foreign to my intention to notice any sepulchral design, or give any inscription at length, yet the monument alluded to has so close a reference to Mr. Blake's case, and besides shews his character in such a favorable light, both as a man and a Christian, that I am induced in this particular instance to depart from the plan I had laid down, by describing the devices, and transcribing the different inscriptions on it. It is affixed to the wall on the south side of the Communion Table.

In the centre is the figure of a man robed, his head reclining on his right hand, the elbow resting on a human scull; the left hand grasping a bible. Above, to the right of the figure, the representation of a hand casting corn into the ground, and of wheat ears in a growing state. – *Cum Foenore et Flore reddit.* – It returns it with flower and increase.

To the left, the face of an angel with four stars. – *Splendebunt ut stellae, eryntq; sicut angeli.* – They shall shine like the stars, and be as the angels. In the centre to the right, the figures of two children bearing palm branches; names,WilliamBlake,Mary Blake. – *Sequuntur agnum.* – They follow the Lamb.

To the left, figures of two children bearing palm branches; names Elizabeth Blake, Agness Blake. – *Non esurient amplius, neq sitient.* – They shall neither hunger nor thirst any more.

Below to the right, a hand cutting off a flower which is represented as growing. – *Ut flos simul ac agressus est succiditur.* – As a flower is cut down as soon as it is sprung up.

---

* In evidence of this I transcribe the following entry from the register of burials.

" 1622. Octr. – Mary, daughter of Mr. Martyn Blake, Minister, buried 17th day." He was not of course vicar at this time, but he was certainly in orders.

To the left, a hand throwing bubbles into the air. – *Dies Hominis palmares et homo bulla.* – The days of man are but a span, and the man is like a bubble.

Under the above, on a tablet, " To the Honour and Glorie of God, in the pretious memorie of my deare sonne Nicholas Blake, who fell asleep in Christ, Febr. xij An : Do: mdcxxxiiij, Aetatis suae ix°

" For yeares with many Graces (more by far
Then to such tender age accustomed are)
God lent thee here. but may it be a child
Of such sweet hopes, so vertuous & so mild,
Should pass so soon away, and not partake
That Promise of long Life, wᶜʰ God did make?
Nay, Nay, that Promise holds, for although here
They Pilgrimage was short, thy joys elsewhere
Doe never die, & they whole man shall stand
Crowned ere long with Life i' th' promised Land,
Wᶜʰ Life while God for thee vouchaves to keep
Here he was pleased to lay thy Corps asleep.

Requiesce mi fili! requisce in pace! cupit etiam dissolvi et tecum esse cum Christo pater tuus virinquecoarctacus. Martinis Blake, S.T.B. Hvjvsq, ecclesiœ passtor olim indignus, tempore opportuno etiam reverfurus. – Rest my son! rest in peace! that he too was released, and was with you in Christ, being straitened on every side, is the wish of your father, Martin Blake, S.T.B. formerly the unworthy minister of this Church of Barnstaple, to which at a fitting season he may again return.

Below the tablet, a man in canonicals, apparently earnest in exhortation. On his right is, a glory and angels. – *Quantum ad hoc mihi lacrum est mori.* – For this how much better is it for me to die.

And to the left, an empty pulpit with a crowd of persons pressing round it. – *Quantum ad hos permanere in carne magis necessarium.* –For the sake of these how much more necessary that I should remain in the flesh.

Tradition adds to the other insults offered to Mr. Blake, that *he was dragged from his pulpit during divine service.* I have sought diligently for evidence on this point, but find not the slightest. Is it likely that had such an occurrence taken place, it would not have come to the knowledge of Dr. Walker, and been recorded in his work?

CHAPTER V.

Present State of the Town–Population–Poor's Rate - Archdeaconry,
Deanery, and Vicarage–Church–Independent or Congregational
Dissenters–Methodists–Baptists–Quakers–Sunday Schools–
Grammar School–Appendix.

PRESENT STATE OF THE TOWN*

Barnstaple stands without a rival to her claim to be considered the
Metropolis of North Devon. Thus it was in former times, and thus

---

* I am bound to make a few remarks (which come very properly under this head) on the incorrect statements put forth in modern topographical works.

The following extracts are from "Cook's Topographical and Statistical Description of the County of Devon," 3rd edition, published four or five years since, which I have selected as containing more errors than other similar works I have met with,and because being a small volume, its circulation is greater.

"Fishing nets at Barnstaple are wove in a loom." - p.60.

"The Market [at Hartland] is on a Saturday, and is much frequented by the fishermen of Barnstaple, Bideford, and the adjacent towns, who come in their boats." - p. 119.

There is no market held at Hartland; the nearest landing-place is a mile and half distant, and from thence to Barnstaple a hazardous voyage for boats, of seven or eight leagues.

"The corporation at present consists of a mayor, two bailiffs, two aldermen,twenty two common councilmen, and other officers." -p.128. – This was never the case at any period.

"Barnstaple sends two representatives to Parliament, the number of voters being about 260."- p. 128. – Less than half the actual amount.

"Baize, silk stockings, and waistcoat manufactories, still give life to the place." — *Ibid.* – Indeed!

"The river Taw is of considerable breadth here, but very shallow, owing to the great and continual increase of sand, which, it is greatly to be feared, will in time entirely choak the port." – *Ibid.*

An earthquake *may* arrest the Taw in its course, and open for it another channel to the sea, or form for it a passage to some subterranean gulph; then, without doubt, would the port be choaked by sand, which the tide must deposit; but such occurrences are not "greatly to be feared;" and whilst nature is permitted to hold on her wonted course, there is no fear but that there will always be as great a depth of water here as there has ever been.

These are but a portion of the palpable errors to be found in the above-mentioned volume relative to *one* town. –What of the rest?

Similar inaccuracies, although not to so great an extent, are to be met with in numerous topographical works, all professing to be correct; they certainly furnish correct copies, in many cases literal ones, of the mis-statements foisted on the public in preceding publications.

it is now, whether we look at the extent of her population, her commerce, or her wealth. As a residence, the town is at once healthful, pleasant, and commodious; lying on the margin of a considerable river, and but a few miles from the Bristol Channel, the inhabitants enjoy the invigorating effects of the sea breeze; whilst the influx and reflux of the ever-changing tides, the arrival and departure of shipping, and the consequent commercial activity which prevails, afford a constant and pleasing variety of scene.

The regular but gradual ascent of the different streets from the water, gives the important advantage of excellent drainage, so needful to the health and comfort of the inhabitants, without, what is so much felt in the neighbouring towns, the inconvenience of a steep acclivity.

The principal improvements effected in the town had their rise in an act of parliament, usually termed "The Improvement Act," which, after a lengthened and obstinate struggle between the Corporation and the Parishioners, after being petitioned for and also opposed by petition, was passed 10th June, 1811. It is said to have pleased neither party; but be that as it may, much good has resulted from it, although principally of a negative kind.

Who can think of the multitude of aerial waterspouts pouring their torrents from the house-tops, during a fall of rain, several feet into the street, right and left, the centre being at the same time a flooded kennel! Those unsightly nuisances, the huge overhanging penthouse, and its ground-floor neighbour, the "bulk," projecting from almost every house; both worse than useless, and withal so old that they might almost plead a prescriptive right to the places they occupied. The butchers and their stalls, ranged on each side of the principal street of the town, flanked by massive forms or chopping blocks, over which, maugre the fleshmonger's tallow candle, the unwary passenger has been seen to tumble headlong! The odour exhaled from the contents of a dung-pit or *cloaca* lying on the footways, and carted through the streets at all hours of the day! Who can look back on the existence of these, and a long list of other delectable things, and not speak well of the instrument which has swept them all off, and opened the way for more substantial and visible improvement. Since this act came into operation, a spirit of liberality and emulation has evinced itself amongst the inhabitants, who have vied with each other in removing low antiquated fronts and ill contrived dwellings, and replacing them by tasteful and commodious structures. I may instance in proof of this, that out of sixty-eight houses, forming a portion of High Street, and running in continuous lines on each side, twenty-four have been wholly rebuilt, and twenty-five, either by having been refronted or the old fronts modernized, have become so altered in appearance, as in most instances to have the effect of new houses. But although the improvements have been greatest in High Street, from its being the principal mart and thoroughfare, they are visibly great in every part of the town, even the backmost districts of it.

A considerable number of houses of a superior description have been erected of late, some of them such as Barum's richest sons who lived a century or two ago would have designated palaces. Modern dwellings of a lesser order are fast multiplying, and indeed of every grade down to the cottage of the artisan and labourer, of which class form two to three hundred have been built within the last fifteen years, and in a stile uniting neatness and convenience such as the poor man of the last generation scarcely ever enjoyed. A large proportion of those were erected as a consequence of the establishment of lace manufactories in the vicinity. To that at Stony Bridge in particular, the several streets laid down in the plan of the town, between Vicarage Lawn, and the Factory, owe their origin entirely.* Mention of Ebberly Place must not be omitted. This neat and beautifully-situated row of houses, eight in number, was formed (it is believed at a much greater expense to the owner, than if the whole had been built anew) out of a building previously used as a Horse Barrack.

The property then bounded and inclosed by the same wall as at present, was purchased from government in 1817 by Henry Hole, Esq. of Ebberly House, near Torrington, who converted it to its present purpose. He has recently sold it.

* Only a single house was to be found in this district previous to 1826, more that 120 are now tenanted there. For the erection of these houses, half an acre of land was purchased at seven hundred pounds, and another at one thousand pounds per acre; two acres of the same property had not long before been sold for £360. An adjoining field measuring a borough acre (about three quarters of a statute acre) sold for the same purpose at five hundred pounds.

From a church rate (drawn on a parchment roll) which has fortunately escaped the general wreck which our parish documents have for the most part suffered.*

I am enabled to furnish an accurate statement of the increase of houses during the last 120 years.† I find by this record, that in 1709, Barnstaple contained but five hundred and seventy-six houses; by the population returns in 1821, I discover the number at that time to have been seven hundred and ninety-nine; and the parish rate book for 1830 exhibits a list of upwards of four hundred and twenty since the year 1709.

The desirable objects of lighting and newly paving the streets, have been partially accomplished within the last four years, under the sanction of the improvement act. All the principal streets, and a considerable portion of the outskirts of the town, were lit by oil lamps in 1826, at an expence somewhat exceeding £150; of which more than £138 was raised by subscription. The lamps are not used during the summer months. The carriage way in High Street, which, in common with others, used to have a considerable and in some parts really a dangerous slope from the houses on each side to the centre, was raised in the middle throughout, newly pitched, and excellent foot paths of flag stones laid down in 1827 at the cost of £640, of which £200 was subscribed by the owners and occupiers of houses in that particular street, the Commissioners agreeing to appropriate the whole produce of the rate on property in High Street, towards the payment of the remaining sum, until it should be liquidated. The inhabitants of Cross Street and Joy Street, soon followed in succession, and on the same plan. A similar improvement, but with footpaths paved in the ordinary way, had been previously effected in Bear Street, at the joint expense of Henry Hole, Esq. and the parish of Barnstaple.

---

* This is the oldest official document (with the exception of the registers, and a "survey of seats") to be found in the Parish depository. The dates of the earliest entries are as follow:–Orders of Vestry, October 5, 1729 - churchwarden's accounts, June 1734 - Overseer's accounts, October 23, 1747. Extracts from these will form Appendix [A.] to this chapter.

† Some particular selected from this rate, with a comparison of the value of property here in 1709 and 1830, will be found in Appendix [B].

Much more would have been effected under the immediate influence of the Improvement Act, than has been yet accomplished, but for the trifling rate which the Commissioners are empowered to levy on the property in the parish, which is limited to " six pence in the pound according to the annual value, on all houses, wharfs, buildings, outhouses, yards, and gardens;" and " four pence in the pound according to the annual value, upon the rectorial and vicarial tythes of the parish, the waterworks, the tolls, dues, &c. belonging and payable to the mayor, aldermen, and burgesses, together with all arable, meadow, and pasture lands, situate within the borough and parish." The gross produce of this rate is £480 annually.* The act restricts the sum to be borrowed for general purposes to *six hundred pounds*, (which has been long since raised,) but permits the corporation to take upon the credit of the town dues, &c. to the amount of six thousand pounds, to be laid out in " altering, removing, building, and otherwise improving the markets or market houses."

POPULATION

What the number of inhabitants was in former times as compared with the present, is a proposition not to be easily solved.

According to a parish census in 1803, and official returns made to Parliament in 1811 and 1821, Barnstaple contained in

1803. – Males	1472	Females	2115	Total	3587
1811. – "	1633	"	2386	"	4019
1821. – "	2217	"	2862	"	5079

Being an increase in the first eight years of 432, and in the next ten years of 1,060, making an addition of 1,492 in eighteen years. It will, perhaps, be desirable to note some further particulars of the latest return.

Of the number previously stated, there were of the different ages as follow:-

	Males		Females		Total	
Under 5 – Males	367	Females	341	Total	708
5 to 10 –	"	282	"	280	"	562
10 to 15 –	"	233	"	212	"	445
15 to 20 –	"	218	"	294	"	512
20 to 30 –	"	294	"	582	"	876
30 to 40 –	"	279	"	350	"	629
40 to 50 –	"	240	"	295	"	535
50 to 60 –	"	137	"	200	"	337
60 to 70 –	"	106	"	163	"	269
70 to 80 –	"	44	"	106	"	150
80 to 90 –	"	15	"	35	"	50
90 to 100 –	"	2	"	4	"	6

Total   5079

These formed 1,028 families, of whom there were

Chiefly employed in Agriculture 21
. . . . Trade 856
Independent 105
Nondescript 56

Total 1038*

The earliest mention I find made of the extent of the population of Barnstaple, is with reference to a census taken in the reign of Edward VI, at which period the Town is said to have contained " 2,000 Houselying people," understood to apply to " persons of an age to receive the sacrament, or about sixteen years old and upwards."

* I am conscious of this discrepancy of numbers, but am not chargeable with the error; it is given in an official (printed) copy of the census, and most probably in that sent to the House of Commons.

Supposing this to be correct, (which, however, must be considered as very doubtful,) and the proportion of persons above and below sixteen to have been the same as at present, the whole population cannot be taken at less than 3,500, whilst in 1803 it was but 3,587* an increase of only 87 in two centuries and a half. By official documents it is shewn that the increase of population in the County of Devon, in the 18th century, was upwards of 106,000.† If Barnstaple advanced in similar proportion during this period, as was evidently the case from the increase in the number of houses, how greatly must she have retrogaded during the preceding 150 years, if the correctness of the earliest return referred to be admitted. A word or two on the statement made in an extract from a brief at page 81, relative to the population in 1710; to prove its incorrectness it is only necessary to look at the number of houses which the town contained only a year previous. The inhabitants could have scarcely been more than half as many as they were then stated to be.

POOR'S RATE

Of the weight of this branch of taxation, the inhabitants of Barnstaple have no great reason to complain, seeing it is light in comparison with what is contributed for the same purposes by the greater part of the kingdom.

Annexed is a copy of an official return of the Poor's Rate§ & c. made to the House of Commons in 1817.

From a "List of Poor receiving parochial relief," dated and published Aug. 15, 1820, I have made the following extracts and calculations, which will serve to shew that the parish bounty was

* I am aware that it has been stated in a periodical work, that in the year 1801, the total number of inhabitants returned under the Population Act, was 3,748, of which number 1495 were males, and 2,253 females;" but having no means of ascertaining the correctness of this statement, I have chosen rather to adopt the above, which is extracted from a census now in the parish chest.

† The population of Devon was, in 1700, 248,200; 1750, 272,200; 1801, 354,400; 1811, 396,100; 1821, 447,900.

§ A similar return, but referring more particularly to what is expended in relief of the poor, is, in compliance with an Act of Parliament, made annually; but on making application to the assistant overseer for the particular of the last return, I was informed that *no copies were preserved!*

calculations, which will serve to shew that the parish bounty was not ill-bestowed. The age which a large proportion of these unfortunate persons attained, also speaks well for the longevity of the inhabitants of the town. No document of the kind has been published since.

" Number of poor in the Work-house, 34. — Paid out, 208.

	£	s.	d.
"Average weekly pay for eighteen weeks from 6th April to 3rd August	34	2	8 ¼*
Received for work done by the poor in the workhouse, for the above period	3	8	10 ½

Of the 208 persons or families mentioned, I find there were of the ages of

From	50 to 55	6
"	55 to 60	8
"	60 to 65	17
"	65 to 70	21
"	70 to 75	25
"	75 to 80	9
"	80 to 85	13
"	85 to 90	4
"	90 to 95	3
" Aged "	....	15

Total 121

Of the remaining cases described in the list, it may be truly said that the blind, the halt, and the lame, the paralytic, the bedridden, and the insane, help to " make up the sad account."

* This amount must include all that was expended on the poor, as the sums mentioned as paid to the different individual names, make up but £21 1s. 5d.

	£	s.	d.
The Amount of Rate collected for 1829-30 was something above	2013	0	0
Weekly sum paid to 146 persons or families receiving constant relief.	13	14	10
Ditto, to 46 ditto, receiving occasional relief	3	6	0
Average weekly expenditure in Workhouse (number of inmates, 34)	4	10	0
Lowest weekly sum paid to any individual or family	0	1	0
Highest ditto	0	7	6

The increase of paupers from 1720 to 1735, appears to have been unaccountably great; but from the last mentioned period to the present, very trifling, as will be seen below.

			£	s.	d.
*1720.– Receivers of weekly pay	65	Sum paid	4	0	0
1727.– " "	113	"	5	18	0
1728.– " "	147	"	7	1	0
1729.– " "	125	"	6	12	6
1730.– " "	135	"	6	7	6
1731.– " "	124	"	6	0	6
1732.– " "	147	"	7	9	0
1735.– " "	165	"	7	10	10
1831.– " "	192	"	17	10	10

* Copied from the list of the parish poor, with the sums paid to each, in the hands of a private individual. It is an original document, and (as I fully believe) an authentic one.
The particulars of the remaining years are taken from the parish books.

ARCHDEACONRY, DEANERY, AND VICARAGE

The Archdeaconry of Barnstaple has under its jurisdiction six Deaneries, which contain in all one hundred and thirty-one parishes.* In the "Liber Regis," under the head of "Dignities in the gift of the Lord Bishop of Exeter," we find Archdeaconry of Barnstaple; has the impropriation of Countisbury and Linton." The same work gives the value of the Archdeaconry, in the reign of Henry VIII. as follows:– "King'sBooks, £49. Yearly Tenths, £4 18s."† –The sub-joined list of Archdeacons, with the exception of the two last, is from "Oliver's History of Exeter."

Archdeacons of Barnstaple

Allured (first I have met with) . . .	—
Ralph, (said to have been in)	1143
William de Auco, witnessed a deed of Bishop Robert Warelivast, between 1155 and	1160
Roger, witnessed Bishop Bartholomew's grant to Lepers of Exon, and confirmation of Plympton Priory, by Bishop John	—
Thomas, witnessed a deed 4th of King John	1203
RalphdeWerewell, presented September 30th	1209
John	—
Ralph, witnessed a deed of Bishop Simon .	1219
Isaac died February 8	1227
Walter de Pembroke, exchanged for the Archdeaconry of Totness . .	—

* According to Polwhele, who gives the numbers belonging to the different Deaneries as follow: Barnstaple, 18, Southmolton 29, Torrington, 20, Chumleigh 15, Hartland, 19, and Shirwell, 30. Whether the gross amount be correct or not, I will not presume to say, but as it respects two of the Deaneries, the enumeration is certainly incorrect. Barnstaple, (see page 485,) contains but 14 parishes, and Shirwell only 29; of the others I have not at present the means of procuring accurate information.

† " Liber Regis," p. 203. - I had taken a copy in full of the taxation of this dignity, from " Taxation Ecclesiastica Angliae et Walliae, Auctoritate, P. Nicholai IV. Circa A.D. 1291." (Copy published by Commissioners of Public Records, in 1802,) but from the great length to which this work has extended beyond what was at first announced, I have omitted that, as well as some other documents, not of general interest.

HenrydeBratton, collated . . . January 21, 1263
    resigned for the Chancellorship.
Richard Blund succeeded . . May 25, 1264
    resigned for Totness.
Godfrey Giffard, collated . . . Nov. 6, 1265
John de Bradleigh . . appointed immediately
Thomas de Hertford, collated . . January, 1271
Philip of Exon, collated . . . August 28, 1279
Ralph Germeyn, succeeded, promoted to
    Pre-centorship 1308
William de Melton, collated . . October 13, 1308
John Wele, collated . . . March 30, 1309
Bartholomew de sancto Laurentio, held it until
    his first Confirmation in the Deanery . . —
William Fits-rogo, held it a short time . . —
Walter Giffard, collated . . . . Dec 3, 1314
    when Richard de Morcester was appointed, who
    died in 1318
Richard de Wideslade, collated . . Sept. 22, 1318
    but resigned the following year
William la Zouche, collated . . Dec. 10, 1329
John de Nassington, was appointed . Dec. 17, 1330
John de Derby . . . . February 23, 1355
Henry Whitefield . . . . February 23, 1384
Robert Rugge . . . . Sept. 8, 1399
Richard Aldryngton, alias Colcomb, collated August 17, 1400
John Orum, collated . . . November 1, 1400
    resigned in 1429
John Waryn, collated . . . Aug. 2, 1429
    died in 1442
Richard Helyer, succeeded on the . . Aug. 3, 1442
    resigned
Michael Tregoire, appointed . . June 16, 1445
    resigned
Roger Keys, collated . . . January 25, 1450
William Fulford . . . . July 12, 1462
    at whose death
John Stubbes was collated . . . October 27, 1475
    who resigned, and was succeeded by

Owen Lord, ... December 10, 1477
    he resigned also, and was followed by
Robert Burforth, who was collated . . February 18, 1478
    and died October 8, 1485
William Elyot succeeded; he was living in . February, 1503
John Veysey came next, but resigned for the
    Precentorship
Richard Norton, followed . . . Aug. 3, 1508
John Yong resigned early in 1515, on a pension
    of £30 per annum.
John Tyake, collated . . . August 12, 1515
    on whose death
Richard Tollett, succeeded . . . January 19, 1518
    he died April 26, 1528
Thomas Brerwood, collated . . April 26, 1528
    died in 1544
John Pollard, collated . . . June 16, 1544
Henry Squire, Fellow of Magdalene College,
    collated . . . . . April 20, 1554
    resigned in 1582.
Robert Lawe, M.A. instituted . . January 7, 1582-3
    on the presentation of Hugo Osbourne,
    Registrar of Barnstaple. He became Treasurer.
William Toker, collated . . . April 24, 1585
    on whose registration
William Helliar, was collated . . November 27, 1605
    he died towards the close of 1645.
James Smith, B.D. was installed . . August 31, 1660
Joshua Tucker, he died in the summer of 1679
William Reade, succeeded Aug. 29, in the same year
    on whose death
Robert Burscough, was collated . .September 24, 1703
Thomas Lynford, collated . . . September 9, 1709
    at whose death
Lewis Stephens, D.D. suceeded to the Archdeaconry.
    He was afterward Archdeacon of Chester.
John Grant, collated . . . October 28, 1731
    he died and was succeeded by
William Hole, B.D, collated . . March 16, 1744-5
    died October 26, 1791, Œtat 82.

Rogger Massey, M.A. collated . . .Nov. 3, 1791
    on whose death
John Andrew, M.A. was collated . . March 14, 1798
    died July 3, 1799, aged 49.
Peregrine Ilbert, M.A. collated . . July 25, 1799
Jonathan Parker Fisher, B.D collated . Aug. 16, 1805
    and installed next day; he resigned for the
    Subdeanery.
Thos. Johns, M.A. collated 3rd, installed 7th Nov.   1807
    died in 1826.
John Bull, D.D.   1826
    resigned in 1830
George Barnes, D.D.   1830

Of the Deanery, it need only be stated, that it comprises the following parishes, over which presides the Dean Rural, who is chosen sometimes bienally, and at others trienally, at the Archdeacon's Visitation:– Barnstaple, Pilton, Filleigh, Chittlehampton, Highbickington, Yarnscombe, Atherington, Tawstock, Newton Tracey, Huntshaw, Horwood, Westleigh, Instow, Fremington.

Relative to the Vicarage, the following occurs in the work before quoted, under the head of "Livings Discharged:" — "BARNSTAPLE V. (St. Peter and St. Paul,) Episc. Prox. 2s.2d. Syn. & Cath. 2s.5d. Archidiac. Prox. 3s.4d. Val. per ann. in decim fœn. lan. agn. oblat. decin. prœdial. & al. emolument in lib. pasch. existen. Pri.*

    "Barnstaple Propr.
    Michael Hyde, 1710
    Frances and Sampson Manaton, 1734.
    Earl Gower, and Sir Matthew Lamb, Bart.
        Trustees of Edward Wortley, Esq. 1765
    Clear Yearly Value   47   0   0
    King's Books   15   8   9" †

* Liber Regis, page 248
† Liber Regis, page 248

The next presentation after the above was made by Lady Bute, Relict of Lord Bute, 1809.

The present Patron is Lord Wharncliffe.*

The Vicarage House, which is stated by Walker to have been built anew by Mr. Blake, (the only evidence I have met with of his having done so,) has been considerably improved by the present Vicar.

THE PARISH CHURCH

Or the Church of St. Peter and St. Paul, which, in the days of old, stood nearly close to the eastern wall,† is now, from the extension of houses in that direction, situate just about the center of the Town. There is nothing in the appearance of the building to interest the traveller, or arrest the attention of the antiquarian; it is therefore the less to be regretted that it should be (as it is, with the Church-yard) almost wholly surrounded by houses.§ The recent removal of the old Guildhall has, indeed, caused part of the building to be visible from the High-cross; and although the partial view thus obtained of the Church is wholly uninteresting, an opportunity has afforded of making a decided improvement in the entrance to it from High-street, which has not been lost. This approach, the ancient lichways# to the Church, is now formed into a slated foot-path†† eighteen feet wide, across which is erected a highly ornamental gateway. This structure, which is wholly of iron, consists of

* A curious tale is told of the manner in which this property was obtained by one of its former patrons, but it is not perhaps quite fit to appear on these pages.

† The gate of the Church-yard leading to Boutport Street, is certainly very near, if not immediately on the site of the wall.

§ It was two or three years since in contemplation to lay open the west end of the Church, by taking down the house on either side the Old Guildhall, then about to be removed. One of the houses being the property of the Corporation, an offer was made of its site to the Parishioners, provided they would purchase the other; several meetings took place on the subject, but whilst one portion of the inhabitants were anxious to forward the measure, it was warmly opposed by the other, and it being found that the Improvement Act neither gave authority, nor could furnish the means, for putting the plan in operation, it was necessarily abandoned.

Lich (lic.Sax.) A dead carcase, whence lichwake, the time or act of watching by the dead; lichgate, the gate through which the dead are carried to the grave. – Todd's Johnson's Dict.

†† This commodious footway has also been carried to the full extent of the Church-yard paths, making in all upwards of 4,000 feet of flagging.

a central pair of gates, eight feet two inches in width, and a single one each side, three feet wide, supported by four hollow piers, seven feet six inches high, formed of four stanchions, the spaces being filled with open work; each pier is surmounted by a head composed of five distinct ornaments, so disposed as to give a beautiful effect to the whole; the style is gothic; the piers are fixed into stones of large dimensions, sunk three feet below the surface of the pathway, and well secured underneath by iron stays. The gates, &c. were manufactured at the Barnstaple Iron Foundry; the weight of iron employed was upwards of three tons and the cost 126l. Two lamp-irons are fixed over the side-gates, but it must be confessed that they rather detract from, than add to the effect intended to be produced. It is a defect, however, which could not well have been avoided, without dispensing with lamps entirely. The design is high creditable to the taste and skill of the architect, (a native of the town,) and the execution of the work is such as would hardly have been excelled at any manufactory in the kingdom. It is a display of art of which Barnstaple may be justly proud; but it is much to be desired, that the edifice to which it introduces the stranger, should be somewhat more in accordance with so tasteful an entrance.

Of the interior of the church, little more can be said than that it is spacious and commodious, being for the most part exceedingly well seated; it is altogether void of architectural beauty. There is not known to exist either record or tradition, to direct us to the period of its first erection; but "the Church of Barnstaple" formed part of the grant made to the Priory of St. Mary Magdalene, at it foundation in the time of William the Conqueror (see p. 17).* It was certainly rebuilt about 1318, in which year it is recorded in the Diocesan Register, to have been consecrated by Bishop Stapledon; it has evidently been more than once subsequently enlarged, but at periods unknown. I have the best authority (that of Mr. Oliver) for stating, that no other mention is made of it in the Bishop's Register. The different alterations the Church has undergone, may account, in some measure, for the irregularity of the structure; but

* It is stated in Lyson's Mag. Brit. (on what authority?) "that the tithes of Barnstaple were appropriated to Malmsbury Abbey, to which Monastry *the Church had been given by King Athelstan.*"

the principal deformity which presents itself, the base of the steeple, appears from an archway formed through it, to have originally occupied its present situation. This unsightly mass of masonry, projects its whole dimensions of nearly seventeen feet within the south wall of the edifice.

The ultimate object of the projected improvement in High-street, already noticed, was the erection of a new tower at the western end of the Church, but there is not now the remotest probability that this will be accomplished; and the present ill- contrived and misplaced belfry bids fair to remain to future generations. The length of the Church from the western door to the eastern window (within the walls) is 121 feet, and its greatest width 66 feet. Nearly in the centre, on the north side, is a double row of seats, eighteen in number, divided by an aisle running north and south. In this enclosure, which is known as the Mayor's Aisle, (formerly called the "Maister's," or Corporator's Aisle,) newly elected Corporators,* on paying two guineas to the Parish, are entitled to single sittings for their lives. Two seats are reserved, one for the Mayor, and the other for the use of the Parliamentary Representatives, and the Recorder: the remaining sittings are disposed of on life-leases, or let at a yearly rent by the churchwardens on behalf of the parish. When the last alteration in the Church took

place, two seats were gained by stopping up a passage which went across the

"Mayor's Aisle;" these were sold on life leases for ú61. This part of the Church

was at the same time modernized. Over the western door is a large and fine-toned

organ, on which is the following inscription:- "MDCCLXIV. THE GIFT OF SR GEORGE AMYAND, BART M. PARLIMENT."

---

* A custom which would certainly be "more honored in the breach than in the observance," has long prevailed here, of not commencing the Service of the Church until the Body corporate are present, and of announcing their arrival by a voluntary on the organ, which continues to play until the gentlemen have taken their places. A few years since, the clergyman of an adjoining parish, having to officiate in our church, began the service at the stated time. The Corporation arrived subsequently, the customary salutation was of course omitted, and they passed to their seats without the soothing "concert of sweet sounds."Prayers being ended, and the Reverend Divine about to commence his sermon - as in solemn silence they have been compelled to walk in, so now in proud defiance they resolved to walk out; and, preceded by the beadles and mace-bearers, quitted the Church, leaving the astonished congregation in "dumb amazement all!" A legal proceeding on the part of the clergyman had like to have been the consequence.

tal inscriptions to the memory of numerous individuals; many of these would furnish food for the antiquary. For the information of person who may hereafter look for, and not find, monuments known to have been fixed in our church, it should be stated, that a considerable number were necessarily removed from their places in 1811 and 1823, many of which were not put up again, but have been destroyed.*

The steeple contains six bells, placed there in 1804, previous to which there were only five. The weight of the present peal is 3 tons, 12 cwt. 7 lbs. being from 7 to 8 cwt, more than the old set.† The work was executed by John Briant, of Herefore, under a contract for ú200*l*., exclusive of freight, &c. Up to this time, and probably from an early period,# there was a set of chimes connected with the churchclock; they were necessarily taken down when the bells were remodelled, and have not since been replaced.

Attached to the Church, and over the Vestry, is a parochial library, founded by John Dodderidge, Esq. (see Grammar School) by whom it was originally endowed, with 112 volumes of books, chiefly works on theology. Additions have been made to the collection from time to time by various individuals, by which the number has been increased to 328; of these, more than a sixth part, and amongst them some of the most valuable, were found on examination about ten years since to be wanting. The room in which the

---

* This happens to be the case with two out of three monuments erected to individuals of one family, ancestors of my own, and from whom I count it an honour to have descended. The names of these individuals were John Peard — died December 12th, 1632, aged 73; and Roger Peard — died October 29th, 1643.

† The costs attending this alteration were as follow:-

	£	s.	d.
Recasting old bells, and new metal added	140	12	9
New Framing, &c.	74	0	0
Freight and Insurance to and from London, and wharfage	38	16	7
	253	9	4

November 10th. "In the eighth year of the reigne of our Soveraigne Lady Anne," Joseph Winstanley, of Barnstaple, watchmaker, covenanted to make "a good and sufficient new sett of chimes, which shall go to the same tune the chimes lately belonging to the said Parish and Church of Barnstaple did," for "the sume of nineteen Pounds, and all the materials belonging to the said old sett of Chimes." Estimates were procured for new chimes, and also for "a Clock and Chimes" in 1804, but neither were put up. A new clock has subsequently been supplied(1820); it cost 130*l*.

books are deposited, and also that now used as a vestry, "was begun to be builded by the corporation of Barnstaple, in the year 1665, and finished in 1767, by Richard Crossing, John Lovering, and John Martin, Merchants, Executors of that worthy and pious Benefactor, John Doddridge, Esquire, by whose "bounty it was furnished with many worthy books." The library, which in former years was much neglected, is now kept in excellent order, and a well arranged and correct catalogue has been prepared, agreeable to the provisions of an Act passed in the 7th of Queen Anne.

On Friday, December, 21st, 1810, at six A.M. the most violent "war of elements" recollected or recorded to have taken place in this neighbourhood, pealed forth its sublime artillery immediately over the town.

"The Lord thundered in the Heavens.
The lightnings lightened the world."

The steeple of the Church presenting in its height the nearest point of attraction to the electric fluid, here, most providentially, its furious career was checked, and, in all probability, the loss of life was thus prevented. "The weathercock, (writes T.B.K., who dates his memorandum on the day of the occurrence,) "on the top of the spire was partly melted and the colour greatly changed, and the leaden cap which covers the spire quite bent up; the dial of the clock was thrown down and split in pieces; the east, west, and south windows shattered; and the roof broken in divers places." A tomb-stone fixed at the foot of the wall at the east end of the Church was wrenched from its place, and borne across the pathway into the grave-yard opposite, (which is enclosed by a wall several feet high,) where the fragments to which it was reduced served to shew the force with which it had been propelled. No damage was done in the town except to the Church, save the partial injury to the roofing of houses caused by a tempestuous wind, which added by its howling to the "mingled horrors of the storm."

The mischief done to the church was found to be very great, but as an alteration in the building was considered at this time to be

354

very needful, it was resolved not to be content with merely repairing it, and a contract was accordingly entered into for removing the heavy looking arches which supported the central part of the roof, from the western end to the chancel, and substituting freestone pillars, and also for building a gallery on the north side, and substituting a new one for that on the south side. These alterations were carried into effect at an expense of about 800*l.*

The Church was subsequently much damaged by a storm of wind, in October, 1823. The consequent repairs of the roof amounted to 114*l.*

In 1823-4, the improvements made in the body of the edifice in 1811 were extended to the chancel, by the erection of corresponding pillars, and the formation of two additional galleries; besides which, the area was newly seated and other alterations made, the whole expense of which appears by the churchwardens' accounts, to have been about 1,400*l.*; but of this sum £653 was realized by the sale of seats. A permanent advantage was also gained in a considerable increase of sittings, the whole number of which is about 1,800; upwards of 120 are free. That a certain number of free sittings should be set apart for indigent persons, was one condition on which the faculty obtained for altering the Church was granted.

The accompanying list of Vicars will, I believe, be found correct, and from the period at which it commences complete* it has been compiled principally from the Parish Register.

—Holman, founder of a Chauntry in the Church-yard,
   now the Grammar School, at what date is not known.
Thomas Martin, died December, 1555.
Sir John Claris, (alias Clarys) Knt. died April, 1590.
John Trender, died November, 1628.
Martyn Blake, died September, 1673.

---

* A plain reason why it does not commence sooner, - Having ascertained two things, first, that a list of Vicars was only to be obtained at the office of the Bishop's Secretary, (an attorney) in Exeter; and secondly, that the charges made there were not the most moderate, I took the precaution of enquiring beforehand, what a list of Vicars would cost? (It was understood that it was only to extend as far back as the "Index" went.) After many applications, the *minimum* was fixed at *two guineas.* Two guineas, perhaps three, for the supply of twenty-five or thirty names and dates, for a literary purpose!

Michael Ogilby, inducted   January 20, 1763*
John Boyse, died October, 1686.
George Bowring, died November, 1702.
John Reed, died April, 1704.
Daniel Hyde, died December 24, 1709.
Samuel Thomson, inducted   October 5, 1710
died April 23, 1734, aged 56.
Thomas Steed, A.M. inducted   September 14, 1734
died November, 1764.
William Marshall, inducted June 9, 1765
 died February 9, 1809, aged 83.
John Mitchell Wade, inducted   1809
(non-resident), died May, 1820.
Henry Luxmoore, A.M. inducted   July, 1820

The Burial-ground, in the north-west corner of which the Church
stands, presents a melancholy and humiliating picture of man's
mortality, being raised by the accumulation of bodies, the greater
part of it, seven feet above the pathways which cross it, and which
are also considerably higher than the adjoining streets.

> "Methinks this dust yet heaves with breath;
> Ten thousand pulses beat;
> Tell me, — in this small hill of death,
> How many mortals meet?"

James Montgomery.

A small addition was made to the Church-yard in 1759, by the
purchase of a portion of that part of it which lies to the east of the
Grammar School. [See Appendix B.] If it was needful to extend
the ground sixty years ago, how desirable must such a measure be
at this time, the population having so greatly increased since that
period. There is, however, now no way left of enlarging the
Church-yard, but by demolishing buildings for the purpose. The old
Priory ground is a spot every way adapted for the formation of a

---

* It must be borne in mind, that the year at this period, (and up to the middle of the succeeding century,)
did not commence until the 25th of March.

new burial place; a measure which must at no very distant period be resorted to.

The Parochial Registers, of which it may be expected that some notice should be taken, commence with the earliest period at which such registers were instituted, 30th Henry VIII., and much earlier than is the case with many parishes. Below are copies of the first entries that occur in the record of births, marriages, and deaths, and a statement of the number of each that occur in the two earliest volumes of the registers.

"Here followeth all the names of such as hath byn Chrystned w'in the p'is of Bar'* from the x Day of October, in the yerre of o' lord god, a thousand ffyve hundred xxxviij, untyll the Anun'cacon of or lady next following, accordying to the kyngs . . . . . and his vice gerent the lord Parom't Cromwell, lord p'vy seale, & knyght of the garter."

"Margaret, the dafter of John Geddon, was crystyned; vij. day of nov^r.

November, 1538.

Walter cowyn and Johan Hooper† maryed the xvjth Daye.

December 1538.

Thomsin Clowtman was bured xiijth Daye."

The oldest volumes (there are duplicates of the first) are for the most part in excellent preservation, as far as it respects the ravages of time; but have suffered considerably from spoliation. Numerous leaves have been abstracted, and also a great many scraps; these last, doubtless, contained interesting anecdotes, or noticed occurrences relative to the Town, which would now form valuable matter for history. A few trivial records have been left, which will be interspersed under their proper dates in Chapter 7.

Number of Baptisms, Marriages, and Burials, registered from 1538 to 1620.

* The contractions are differently formed, but cannot be copied.

† This name, which is quite distinct in one of the duplicates, is so differently written in the other, that more than four letters cannot possibly be traced in it, it is totally unlike what it was intended for. I should judge one of the registers to have been kept by the Minister, the other by the Clerk. Some of the oldest writing is very beautiful, and as fresh as if penned but yesterday.

	BAPTISMS	BARRIAGES	BURIALS
1st period of 10 years	644	163	568*
2nd ditto	553	181	416
3rd ditto	743	153	477
4th ditto	920	242	616
5th ditto	1045	292	690
6th ditto	1037	315	851
7th period of 10 years	1060	325	717
*8th (8 years)	764	312	504#

A Terrier was drawn up in 1726, of which a copy was printed and circulated in 1804. A transcript of it will be found at Appendix [C].

CROSS-STREET CHAPEL ; OR, MEETING HOUSE FOR CONGREGATIONAL PROTESTANT DISSENTERS.

The dissenting interest in Barnstaple, like that of many other towns, had its origin in that cruel and impolitic statute, known as the Act of Uniformity, which was passed in 1662, and took effect on

* The mortality in one of those years, (1546), appears to have been very great, amounting to 142, being 102 above the average of the seven preceding, and 96 more than the seven succeeding years. There is no data by which this calamity is to be accounted for, but it was evidently sudden, as the deaths which had been but six from 1st July up to 6th September, were twenty in the remaining part of the month. The deaths form the commencement to the close of the year were as follows;-

April 6	August 4	December 11
May 2	September 20	January, no entry
June 6	1st to 19 Oct. 43	February 4
July 2	10th to 30th Nov. . 42	March 12

No entry was made (the register is here quite perfect) from October 19th to November 10th. the mortality was evidently greatest in these months, and the number which must have died in the three weeks during which the registry was omitted, would greatly augment the number of burials first stated. Those in January were probably but few. It is remarkable that this should have occurred precisely a century anterior to the period when the town and neighbourhood were devastated by the plague, which is well known to have been the case in 1646. It unfortunately happened, (although perhaps it is not much to be wondered at) that the register is silent on the subject. I find in it the following memorandum in the same hand writing as the entries subsequently made. "The register of ye town of Barnestaple, was not kept from the yeare of o Lord, Anno Dom. 1642, until the year Anno 1647;" an interesting period, including the time of the Civil War, with the pestilence which followed in its train.

† This makes up 78 years, instead of 82 as stated above. The entries for the remaining four years are wanting, partly from their not having been made, and partly owing to leaves having been torn out.

It was my intention to have continued the statement to the present time, with the view of ascertaining the progress of the population, but I was compelled to relinquish the task.

Bartholomew's day in that year,* which at once thrust from the pale of the Church of England, upwards of *two thousand* of her best Ministers, the vital blood of the Hierarchy, of whom says the great Mr. Locke, "that Bartholomew day was *fatal to our church and religion,* by throwing out a very great number of worthy, learned, pious, and orthodox divines.

What a triumph for the powers of darkness! I see "in my mind's eye," the demon of persecution forgetting awhile, in his unholy exultation at the success of his mission, his own irremediable doom, "hie back to his dark confine," eager to receive the plaudits of his prince, and the congratulations of his compeers, who welcome with blasphemous joy the news of such a conquest. But what was the issue? the effects of this deadly blow have been slowly and silently but surely working to the present hour; the seed sown on "that Bartholomew Day," "grew and waxed a "great tree," which is striking its roots deeper and deeper into the nations of the earth; "but the end is not yet."

Jonathan Hanmer, and Oliver Peard, two of the "noble army" of ejected ministers who patiently suffered the loss of all things for conscience sake, were the founders of the first congregation of dissenters in this town.

Mr. Hanmer has been so unfairly dealt with by Doctor Walker, in his "Sufferings of the Clergy," that it would not be doing justice to the memory of so worthy a man, to suffer a memorial of his native town to go forth to the world, without a vindication of his character from the unjust aspersions cast upon it.

Dr. Walker says, in reference to Mr. Blake's recall, that he was obliged to bear with "the cumbrance of a factious lecturer, one Hanmer," who was "thrust upon him lest he should be a second time dispossessed of his living."

So far from Mr. Blake's objecting to Mr. Hanmer as a colleague, these two amiable men lived on terms of the greatest harmony; and after Mr. Hanmer was driven from the Church, Mr. Blake continues his intercourse with him,, and was accustomed to say to him and several other expelled ministers who resided here, "My heart bleeds whenever I see you, to think that such worthy persons should be silenced and cast out, and your places filled up by such as are sadly ignorant and scandalous."

That in early life Mr. Hanmer's character stood high with his Diocesan, is sufficiently shewn by his having been selected to preach the Bishop's visitation previous had a similar appointment from the Archdeacon.

"*Salutem in Christo.*

"I have appointed my triennial visitation, and intend (God willing) to visit in person. I have made choice of you to preach at Barnstable, on Wednesday the Thirtieth day of March. I pray therefore prepare yourself to do it. In expectation whereof I sign myself

Your loving friend and diocesan,
Jos. Exon.

From my Palace in Exon,
Feb. 13, 1635"

In his reply to his Lordship, which conveyed a respectful but earnest request to be excused preaching, he says – "I shall entreat your Lordship to consider (omitting my present weakness and indisposition of body) how many of my worthy brethren in the ministry there are, whose shoulders are more fit for this burden; at whose feet it would become me to sit. And withall it is no longer since than the Archdeacon's last visitation, that I *(sed quam impar!)* was this way employed."

That he was held in esteem by the Bishop of the Diocese, in the decline off his years, and *subsequent to his ejectment*, is evidenced by the following document found among Mr. Hanmer's papers, dated 1665, and addressed to the parishioners of Bishop's Tawton.

"We desire you forthwith to make satisfaction to Mr. Jonathan Hanmer, in his past demands. As also to admonish you, that if you shall delay to do it, such a course will speedily be taken against you as will be very much to your prejudice. Withal adding, as your performance of your duty in doing right to Mr. Hanmer upon this my brotherly desire and admonition, shall be now taken by me as an act of kindness and respect; so if this entreaty shall be despis'd, and you shall persist (contrary to the laws of God and of this kingdom) to detain his dues from him, I shall think myself obliged in all just and legal ways to discountenance you, by taking care (within the compass of my jurisdiction) that the laws be strictly executed upon you, when you shall be required, &c." Signed, "SETH EXON."

It will be admitted that *"a factious"* Clergyman was not a person *likely* to be in favour with the dignitaries of the church.

Mr. Hanmer was well qualified by his learning, talents, and piety, for the promulgation of the gospel of which he was both a popular and a useful preacher. "His lectures in Barnstaple," (which were kept up by a free and generous subscription or contribution of such as attended) says Doctor Calamy, "were greatly thronged, vast numbers repairing to them from all parts round the town, some who lived many miles distant, and among the rest, divers persons of character and distinction; and he was endeared to the people, both of the higher and lower ranks in life."

This excellent man was born in Barnstaple, "in or about 1605;" he studied at Emanuel College, Cambridge, where he took the degree of M.A. He was ordained priest in St. Margaret's church, Westminster, 1632. He became possessed of the living of Instow, and subsequently of the Vicarage of Bishop's Tawton, which he enjoyed at the same time with the Lectureship of Barnstaple, up to the memorable period of the passing of the act of uniformity.*

Mr. Hanmer's connection with his people continued until his decease; "he came to his grave in full age," Dec. 16, 1687†

* I am indebted for many of the above particulars to "A Cursory View of the lives of the Rev. Jonathan Hanmer, A.M. and the Rev. John Hanmer, A.M. &c. by H.W. Gardiner;" which contains among other interesting particulars relative to Mr. Hanmer and the dissenting interest at Barnstaple, a number of rules for the regulation of the Church, under the following heads:– "The manner of forming the society or Church of Christ, in Barnstaple, by the Rev. Jonathan Hanmer. – The qualifications requisite in those that visit – The pastor's duty to the people. – The duty of people to their pastors. – Their duty towards each other and to all mankind. – some additional general directions."

† In May, 1827, as the parish sexton was digging a grave in the S.E. quarter of the churchyard, he met with an impediment which proved by the following inscription, cut on a small white marble slab, to be the tomb of Mr. Hanmer's family, close adjoining to which was that of Judge Dodderidge;– "Prope abhinc orientem versus jacent Reliquae CATHARINAE uxoris Mr. JONATHAE HANMER, hujus villae praelectoris quae obiit A.D. MDCLXVI Nec non liberorum eorundem, SARE obiit A.D. MDCLI ELIZABETHAE A.D. MDCLVI. JONATHAE et SARAE MDCLXIII Resurgent." - The slab was found fixed in the centre of the end wall of the two sepulchres, the top stones of which were about three feet below the surface of the ground. The inscription was taken from its subterranean depositary, and affixed to the sepulchre of the Rev. John Hanmer, son of Jonathan Hanmer. Mr. Hanmer's remains were probably interred in the Castle Meeting, where there were several vaults; but this cannot now be ascertained.

We come now to the history of the Congregational or Independent Dissenters of Barnstaple; this was furnished up to the year 1777 by one of its ministers, the Rev. Samuel Badcock, who left in manuscript the following account:–

"The dissenting congregation in this place was originally gathered by Mr. Jonathan Hanmer, (grandfather of the poet Gay,) and Mr. Oliver Peard. the former was a lecturer at the church in the protectorship of Cromwell. He was a man of very considerable abilities and great application. he wrote a treatise on Christian Confirmation, recommended by Mr. Baxter," (and various other pieces.) "Both he and Mr. Peard were ejected by the Act of Uniformity in 1662. Dr. Calamy has given an account of both. When Charles II. granted an indulgence in 1672,* the congregation built a meeting-house near the castle, and formed themselves into a regular church on the congregational plan, under the pastorship of Mr. Oliver Peard, who (by the approbation of the people) chose for his assistant Mr. John Hanmer, the son of his former colleague, who, though not ejected from any living by the Act of Sequestration, yet refusing to take the oaths, and comply with the other requisites of conformity, was silenced for some years, and being obliged to quit the college,ministers, and spoken of with peculiar honour in the continuation of his account. In May, 17692, Mr. Hanmer (by the consent of Mr. Peard(was chosen co-pastor, and after the death of Mr. Peard September 9, 1696,† Mr. Hanmer

* This "Indulgence" brought only a temporary suspension of the unjust and cruel laws then in force against the Nonconformists. Besides the well-known and never to be forgotten Five-mile Act, which forbade Ministers to appear within five miles of any market town. The Conventicle Act was also in operation, which provided, "That every person above sixteen years of age, present at any meeting, under pretence of any exercise of religion, in other manner than is the practice of the Church of England, where there are five persons more than the household, shall for the first offence, by a Justice of Peace, be recorded and sent to gaol three months, till he pay 5*l.*; and for the second offence, six months till he pay 10*l.*; and the third time, being convicted by a Jury, shall be banished to some of the American Plantations, except New England or Virginia." We who are Dissenters should look at what the Nonconformists suffered from the restoration of Charles II until the acession of William; we should "think on these things," and be thankful for the privileges we enjoy; not that we enjoy more than we have a right to, but let us be grateful that our right is not wrested from us by the might of oppression as was the case with our forefathers. *We* worship openly and without fear or molestation; *they* could only meet secretly and in dread, not merely of detection, but of the punishment which would be sure to follow. they did not however "forsake the assembling themselves together," although obliged to meeting in obscure places, and where there was more than one way of egress, to place persons on the watch whilst they were assembled, and to forbear singing.

† 1696, Sept. "Oliver Peard, Non. Con. buried 12th day."— *Parish Register.*

362

"was desired to take upon himself the whole of the pastoral office, which he complied with. As the congregation was very large, Mr. Hanmer was prevailed on to choose an assistant. The person fixed on was Mr. William Peard, (son of Mr. O. Peard, the former pastor,) who, at that time, was settled over a congregation at Appledore, near Bideford. This was about the year 1700. Mr. Hanmer soon after this was rendered almost incapable of ministerial work, and some disputes arising in the congregation, respecting the choice of an assistant, a considerable part of the congregation seceded in 1705, (leaving the congregation at the castle entirely under the care of Mr. Peard.) For some time the seceders worshipped in a private house, till a very commodious chapel was built for them in Cross Street. The first candidate for the separate congregation was a Mr. Birne, or Bearne. A blunder he made in the pulpit was the only cause of his being rejected. He was to preach a funeral sermon for an old gentleman well known, which drew a large audience. The poor man had forgotten to note down where his text was to be found. He told them (with a most disconcerted air) that he believed his test was in the Proverbs, but he was not certain, but the words were so and so. This unlucky blunder was the parent of a thousand more; his sermon was a very chaos of crude divinity. Some were chagrined, others disgusted, and a third sort gratified with something to make a jest of. The preacher was too much mortified to make a second attempt, and the people that invited him too much mortified to desire it. This Mr. Birne afterwards settled at Hammersmith, and in his latter days made a worse blunder than at first. He conformed to the Establishment, and became so enamoured of his canonicals that he wore them all day long!! But, poor man, he was near seventy! When the Cross Street Chapel was completed, the congregation invited Mr. George Boucher, in the year 1706, to settle among them. He was at that time with the people at Bovey – had been a student at old Mr. Hallett's academy at Exeter, and was ordained in 1701. Mr. Hanmer did not long survive the separation. The time of his death is specified in Dr. Calamy's Continuation and some account of his character from his funeral sermon by Mr Boucher. Mr. Peard, of the castle meeting, dying, he was succeeded by Mr. John Powell, who before that had "been settled with a congregation at Blandford. The name of this gentleman, (and also Mr. Boucher's) is among the subscribing ministers at the Exeter assembly in 1719. About a year before his death, he became totally incapacitated for ministerial work, on which account the congregation invited Mr. Thomas Bishop to be their pastor. He had been a chaplain in the family of Sir John Davey, Bart, and preached at Shobrook, near Crediton. He settled at Barnstaple, January 1, 1720. Mr. Bishop was succeeded by Mr. John Walrond in the year 1738. He was nephew of that Mr. Walrond, of Exeter, who was a principal opposer of Arianism and Mr. Pierce, in 1719. Mr. Boucher, at the Cross Street Meeting was growing exceedingly infirm, it was proposed to Mr. Walrond in the year 1753, (as he had always lived in the greatest harmony with Mr. Boucher and his people,) to unite both congregations under his own ministry, and for the satisfaction of both, it was judged most eligible to preach at each meeting alternately.* Through Mr. Waldron's prudence and moderation, this scheme was effected to the "satisfaction of Mr. Boucher and both societies." (Mr. Walrond published an excellent Discours on Ejaculatory Prayer, 8vo. 1747.) " Mr. Walrond dying in the year 1769, the united congregations

---

* The following is a copy of an agreement drawn up on this occasion, (dated four years earlier than the time mentioned by Mr. Badcock) entitled, "Articles for uniting the two dissenting congregations in Barum, delivered to Mr. Walrond, Jan. 1749.

"First. That the Rev. John Walrond, be chosen joint Pastor, with our Rev. George Boucher, and that he preach once every Lord's day at the Meeting in Cross Street, and that the Sacrament of the Lord's Supper be administered in that place alternately.

"Secondly. That the said Mr. John Walrond shall have the money arising by subscription, which the said Mr. George Boucher now hath, or is usually paid to him, by us who are his constant hearers, except where change of circumstance in worldly affairs make an alteration; and also that the said Mr. John Walrond shall have all such money as now doth or may hereafter arise from the seats in our said Meeting House, after deducting the charge for necessary repairs and taxes of all kinds for the said house.

"Thirdly. That in case the said Mr. John Walrond do survive our said Mr. George Boucher, he shall become sole Pastor of the united congregations.

" — — Hooper	John Skinner	John Besley
Edward Gribble	Robert Gribble	Wm. Gribble
Lewis Langdon	George Rawle	Henry Cowell
John Coats	Richard Symons	Wm. Besley "
William Peard	John Hollamore	
Samuel Joce	Matthew Reeder	

The service was continued at each place alternately, until 1800. The Castle Meeting was sold in 1806, and has since been occupied as a warehouse for timber.

invited Mr. Samuel Badcock to settle among them. He accordingly removed from Wimborne, in Dorsetshire, and preached his first sermon at Barnstaple, April 1, 1770. The number of communicants from the first institution of the society to the present time :

1777, — 80 to 100; — stated hearers, about 500."

Mr. Badcock ranked high as a literary character; he wrote a considerable portion of White's Bampton Lectures, and greatly distinguished himself by his talents as a reviewer, particularly by his severe strictures on Priestly and Madan.

Notwithstanding his bold censure of the " poor man " Mr. Birne, he also " conformed to the Establishment," and was " ordained by Bishop Ross, on the title of the Curacy of Broadclist."

We naturally ask, what could induce a man so firmly attached to the cause of dissent as Mr. Badcock appeared to have been, to turn his back upon it so abruptly? His going over to the Episcopalians was with him, in all probability, as his resigning his charge of the congregation here certainly was, an act of expediency rather than choice; he was accused, and after some time acknowledged himself guilty, of gross immorality, and had thus no alternative but that of retiring from his office or losing his hearers. It may be truly said, that when his indiscretion drove him from among dissenters, his talents opened a way for him into the church.

Mr. Badcock was succeeded by the Rev. Benjamin Seaward, who was ordained here 20th August, 1777; he filled the pastoral office until his death, in 1799. Religion was at this period at a very low ebb in the congregation. In the same year, the Rev. Richard Taprell, then of Southmolton, accepted a call from the church, and remained until January, 1804, when he became minister of a dissenting church at Braunton. The Rev. Henry William Gardiner, A.M. (a descendant of Colonel James Gardiner, so well remembered as a brave soldier and an exemplary Christian,) next became pastor; he removed to Barnstaple from Southwold, Sufolk, in 1804, and continued to minister here for twenty-three years.

Mr. Gardiner had been for some years one of the secretaries to the Hibernian Society, but being desirous to devote himself more particularly to the interests of tha valuable institution, he retired from Cross Street Chapel, at Lady-day, 1827, and was succeeded

by the present Minister, the Rev. Benjamin Kent, who settled here
July 1, in the same year, having for the preceding fourteen years,
presided over the congregation at the Tabernacle, Trowbridge. The
present number of hearers is about 600, and of communicants, 94.

This society supports, besides a sabbath school, (for which see
"Sunday Schools,") an institution called the Sick Man's Friend,
established in 1809, which has for its object the relief of the sick
poor, without regard to sect or denomination.

In 1826, an Auxiliary Religious Tract Society was formed in
conjunction with the Baptist Friends, which under the auspices of
both congregations, is still in operation.

The Chapel is not a very commodious one, but has been rendered
by several recent alterations, as much so as the stile of the present
building and its confined site will admit it. It was newly seated,
and a gallery was erected on one side in 1806 ; an addition was
made to the gallery in 1821, which was again extended in 1824.
These improvements were effected at an expense of from 500*l.* to
600*l.* the whole of which was borne by the congregation.

The Meeting House is vested in the five undermentioned persons
as Trustees — John Gribble, William Gribble, John Pitt, Timothy
Harding Willis, and John Bowen.

The undermentioned donations and bequests have been made to
this, or the Castle Meeting :–

	£	s.	d.
1711 – Joseph Baller, by will, dated March 3rd. in that year, an annuity of . . .	100	0	0
1714 – Martin Westacot, a rent charge arising out of a house in the Square, now occupied by Mr. Woollacot, of . .	1	10	0
1726 – Mary Carder, a house in Holland Street, now in the occupation of James Petter, let at Christmas, 1783, on lease for 99 years, at a yearly rent of	1	1	0
1736 – John Langdon	10	0	0
1739 – Mary Bagilhole, a house in the Cattle Market, for the use of the Minister, held under the corporation of Barum, at a rent of 5s. per annum .			

					£	s.	d.
1746 – Rachael Moll	.	.	.	.	100	0	0
Jeffery Bagilhole	.	.	.	.	100	0	0
Sarah Parminter	.	.	.	.	10	0	0
1753 – Elizabeth Frost	.	.	.	.	20	0	0
1756 – Samuel Joce	.	.	.	.	20	0	0
1765 – Oliver Pike	.	.	.	.	100	0	0
1766 – John Besley, Surgeon	.	.	.	.	50	0	0
1767 – Alice Peard	.	.	.	.	20	0	0
1770 – Wm. Trisstram, a rent charge payable from a house in High Street, now inhabited by Anthony Huxtable	.	.	.		3	0	0
1776 – Sophia Sloly	.	.	.	.	20	0	0
Hannah Peard	.	.	.	.	20	0	0

The income realized by the above gifts is as follows, independent of the minster's house :–

	£	s.	d.
Interest of 750l. 18s. 11d. 3per cents red. into which the money, bequests, and Mr. Baller's annuity, have been converted	22	8	0
Interest of 20l. given by Mrs. Badcock, 1798	1	0	0
Rent of House in Holland Street*	1	1	0
Rent Charge on House in Square	1	10	0
Rent Charge on House in High Street	3	10	0
	£29	9	0
Interest of 100l. received from Hon. Mrs. Welman	5	0	0
	£34	9	0

In 1812, Thomas Stiff, Esq. of London, gave to the Trustees of this Chapel, a garden to be appropriated as a burial ground. It is situate but a short distance from the church-yard, but the way to it is rather circuitous, (see plan of the town.) The first corpse interred here, was that of Elizabeth Herapath, in June 1813.

* This property, which is much underlet, the trustees had no right whatever to lease for so long a term, the present trustees have not however sought to disturb the title.

THE METHODIST CHAPEL, OR MEETING HOUSE
OF WESLEYAN METHODISTS.

It does not appear that the venerable John Wesley, whose name is associated with so large a portion of the christian world, and whose " praise is in all the churches," every preached in this town, although he did repeatedly in Bideford, and other places in the neighbourhood. The first preachers who erected the standard of Methodism here, were Richard Drew and John Sandoe, who about the year 1788, visited this town as Missionaries from the Methodist Conference; their piety and zeal were their chief recommendations, but the tide of prejudice ran so strong against them that their ministry was attended by only a few of the lower class of the inhabitants; they preached in an obscure room in Boutport Street, and sometimes in the public Streets and in the Square; where, when on one occasion Mr. Sandoe was addressing a numerous assemblage, the Mayor sent two of his Constables to silence him, and disperse his congregation; in consequence of this interruption, the preacher removed to the farther extremity of the Bridge, which is out of the jurisdiction of the local authorities of the town, whither he was followed by the greater part of his auditor, and there concluded his discourse. Undaunted by persecution, these zealous ministers pursued their course, and were after a while joined by a few of the inhabitants who embraced their doctrines, and thus a small community was formed. It is worthy of being recorded to the honor of his liberality and christian benevolence, that when no other person was found with an ability and disposition to render the preachers any support, a pious man of another denomination* persuaded of the purity of their motives sought an interview with them, and welcomed them to his house.

About the year 1790, a person engaged as a clerk in the manufactory at Rawleigh, who was a member of the Methodist body, and has been a local preacher in Bristol, became leader of the little society, (now about half a dozen members,) and ministered to them

* Mr. William Drewett, for more than half a century a member of the Independent Church.

in the absence of the itinerant preachers, who visited Barnstaple but once in a fortnight, on a week-day evening. Under his instrumentality the infant church increased, and a more commodious place for conducting their religious services was found to be requisite. A subscription was soon raised, and a small chapel, which accommodated about an hundred persons, was erected in Holland Street. Here the society grew and flourished, but their prosperity was but of short duration; the breaking up of the establishment at Rawleigh in 1795, caused the removal of the individual by whose services the Methodists had been so materially benefitted, the cause again languished, and was at a very low ebb, until 1798. In this year the 58th regiment of foot was stationed here, belonging to which was a serjeant Davis, a man of excellent character, and an accredited local preacher in the Methodist connexion, an avocation which his commanding officer permitted him to pursue in the intervals of his military duties. This individual zealously devoted himself to the service of the society, preaching not only on sabbath days, but frequently on the week nights; the novelty of a person in soldier's uniform occupying the pulpit attracted a numerous auditory, and many persons in consequence united themselves to the church. On his removal after a few weeks' sojourn here, the society was again deprived of a resident preacher, and the cause once more retrograded.

Until 1810, the society in this town had been considered a part of what was then called the Cullompton Circuit, and was visited by the preachers stationed there; but in that year the Conference appointed a preacher to confine his labours to this and the neighbouring towns. The result of this arrangement was that the cause increased, and the congregation becoming much larger than the chapel would accommodate, the present commodious meeting-house was in 1814 erected in Boutport Street, and vested in twenty-one trustees. The stated number of hearers is about 400, and of members upwards of 100.

BAPTIST OR EBENEZER CHAPEL

The Baptist interest in this town is but of recent origin, no society in that connexion having, as far as is known, ever congregated here for public worship until 1814. In this year a room in High Street was opened for divine service, which at first could only be performed every third sabbath, there being no stated minister.

In November 1817, a church consisting of eleven members was formed at the Castle Inn, the room usually occupied by the congregation not being large enough for the service. On the same day, three persons were baptized by immersion in the river near the North Walk. In 1818, the chapel in Holland Street, already mentioned as having been occupied by the Methodists, was obtained, and held until the opening of the present meeting house, on 29th September, 1824. The chapel which is neat and roomy, is furnished with a baptistry and vestry, and has a small burying-ground.

It is vested in the under-named Trustees : –

William Prance, Charles Ferris, Robert Dyer, Robert Fearon, David Best, —— Taylor, Charles Veysey.

The erection, and purchase of the site cost about 800*l*. The situation is ineligible, but a more convenient one could not be obtained. The congregation has been supplied by the following ministers :–

Mr. Glanville, from December, 1817 to April, 1818.
Mr. Rogers, from April, 1818, to September, 1820.
Mr. Mitchell, from October, 1820, to March, 1823.
Rev. Mr. Johns, who was ordained here September 29, 1829, from January, 1824, to April, 1825.
Mr. Aveline, who was much beloved by his people, and quitted them only on account of continued ill health, from May, 1825, to August, 1829.
Rev. Isaac Orchard, from January, 1830, to the end of the year.

During the intervals between March 1823, and January 1824, the congregation was, as is the case at present, destitute of a minister, and served by occasional supplies.

QUAKERS' MEETING

I am not aware, that up to the year 1829, there were ever any members of the Society of Friends resident in Barnstaple; there are now four of this respected denomination carrying on business here. They have not as yet a Meeting House, but they assemble for worship, with a few individuals of the same persuasion living in a parish not far distant, at a room in Joy Street, which was first set apart for this purpose in September 1829.

SUNDAY SCHOOLS

Five of these very excellent institutions, all maintained by voluntary contributions, are in operation here. They will be best noticed in the order in which they were established.

Cross Street, 1805.—Superintendant and Teachers, all gratuitous, Number of Children, 160. —Expenditure for the past year, 7*l*.

Methodist, 1811.—Superintendant and Teachers, all gratuitous, Number of Children, 130.—Annual cost, 8*l*. 8*s*.

Baptist, 1819.— Superintendant and Teachers, all gratuitous, Number of Children, 94. — Annual cost, not ascertained.

Church, 1823.— Secretary 20*l*. per annum, two other Assistants, 7*l*. 16*s*. — Number of Children, 230.— Expenditure for the year ending Midsummer, 1830, (as per printed statement) 31*l*. 9*s*. 3*d*.

Back Lane, (in connexion with Cross Street,) 1830. — Number of Children, 45.

THE GRAMMAR OR HIGH SCHOOL

Is of great antiquity; " when it was founded is not known, but it may boast of a remote origin."* It is said, and with great probability, to have been anciently conducted by the Priests of Saint Mary, and Saint Nicholas's Chapel, but appears not to have

* Carlisle

been endowed until the year 1646, (for the endowments and other particulars, of which a repetition here is unnecessary, see Chapter 2.) The annexed list of Masters of this seminary is the most perfect I have been able to obtain. It is partly extracted from "Carlisle's endowed Grammar Schools," but principally from Parochial Records.

1597. – ——Symmons, " put out " in this year, and was
    succeeded by Richard Symmons, A.M.
1600. – Samuel Butler, " inhibited from teaching 'till he "shews
    by what authority he teaches;" Dec. 1601.
1601. – —— Mansfield, appointed by the Bishop of Exeter,
    on the removal of Mr. Butler.
1630. – Thomas Branker.
    John Roshier, died Oct. 1669.
1669. – George Hume, " died 1693, aged 80; buryed in Pilton."*
    Edward Allison, died Dec. 1679.
    Nathaniel Viner, died Sep. 1680.
    William Raynor, removed to Tiverton.
    Robert Luck, A.M. "a poet of no mean rank, and
    who probablyinspired Gay with a taste "for poetry."†
1740. – John Wright, A.M.
1742. – William Cooke, A.M.
1792. – William Dyer
1795. – Henry Nickolls, A.M.

The last mentioned gentleman still holds the appointment, having established and maintained his reputation as an able tutor, and good disciplinarian during the long period of thirty-five years.

* Carlisle

† *Ibid.* - That this was the case may be considered as more than probable. In a volume of poems published by Mr. Luck after Gay's death, and dedicated to the Duke of Queensbury, the following lines occur:-

" O Queensbury! could happy *Gay*
    This offering to thee bring,
'Tis his, my Lord, (he'd smiling say,)
    Who taught your *Gay* to sing."

To have been instrumental in adding to the reputation which this divine appears to have enjoyed, would have been a pleasing task; – the reverse is a repulsive one. Most sincerely do I regret that he should have "tarnished his fair fame" by imbibing and nourishing such a spirit as is evinced in the concluding part of the subjoined letter. Some men can think and act rationally on every subject but one, and on that their imaginations or their passions " run riot," and lead them into acts of extravagance at which human nature, in the exercise of sober reason, must blush.

That Mr. Luck's disposition was merciful in the main, this very letter sufficiently testifies; but he had his weak side, and the spirit of bigotry was ever at hand to take advantage of it; thus did he, who was usually

The usual number of pupils is about forty, one only is educated on the foundation, but one or two others are generally received gratuitously.

Some distinguished literary characters received their education at this school, among whom may be noticed :-

Doctor Harding, born at Combmartin, in 1512

Bishop Jewell, born at Berrynarbor, an
adjoining village,1522.

Gay, the celebrated Poet.

Samuel Musgrave, M.D. the learned editor of Euripides.

Judge Dodderidge, the eminent lawyer and
antiquary, who was a native of the town, is supposed to have been educated here, as was probably his nephew John Dodderidge, also a native, the author of a work on the Antiquity of Parliament.

humane and forgiving, become to a poor unfortunate puritan,* cruel and revengeful. Persecution on account of religious opinions, is at best hateful; but the infliction by a dispenser of law of a heavy penalty on a " very poor man," not for the offence, for which alone the law has prescribed the penalty, but only because the individual has "greatly dared" to act up to the dignity of a rational being, by thinking and acting for himself in matters of religion - *thus* to persecute betrays a latent principle of intolerance which in other times might have followed the sufferer to a prison or a stake.

Copy (*printed from the original*) of a letter written by "the Rev. Robert Luck, Surrogate of the Archdeaconry Court [of Barnstaple,] and Master of Barum Grammar School, to Mr. Jos. Tucker, of Tawstock, Registrar of the Archdeaconry :" —

" Dear Sr. - I was out of town last Tuesday, and so cou'd not answer your kind letter then; I assure you Ihave only wanted an opportunity to visit you, which this Lent will give, and I shall take. I have not forgot nor forborn Randall; he has repeated his assurances of paying the 40s. I doubt not but to have the money or paper speedily. If he gives me a note, I will so far give it credit, as to send you forthwith upon it 20s.

"One Henry Merrick, of W. Down, has had a little one sworn agst him; he pleads innocence in words and face, so far as to incline a man to believe him; however to avoyd trouble the poor fellow has left a pound in my hands, which George brings you; and will raise the like sum by next Fryday, if you will take care to send a dismission to me, which I will signe and seal. It is too little, but he is very poor. The w— is Anne Norman, of W. Down, widow, of whom I shall take care. Here's but a small appearance to-day.

I am, your faithfull humble svt.

R. LUCK.

" Feb. 9th, 1710

My wife salutes you.

"Just now I am well assur'd Merrick is a rank Anabaptist. He lodg'd the mony upon condition you and I shou'd both agree to the commutation. Pray write me word that you do not accept of the terms propos'd, which will give me an opportunity to treat him as his character deserves. I wish we cou'd force him to do pennance. A citation shall be provided for him next Fryday, instead of a dismission."

* The proscribed individual was no doubt a dissenter, but the term Anabaptist was in all probability merely used opprobriously.

The two first named individuals are said to have been school fellows, but the difference in their ages makes this doubtful, but whether or no they were engaged at the same time, as well as in the same place, in storing their minds with the elements of literary warfare, they engaged warmly in after life in the field of controversy. Let history speak of their respective merits.

" Thomas Harding, D.D., one of those time serving priests, whose versatile conduct reflects no honour on any profession, was born in Devonshire in 1512. He was appointed Professor of Hebrew by King Henry VIII, whose *half-reforming* principles he adopted."

" He became subsequently " a complete Protestant," and lastly a " confirmed Papist." After the accession of Queen Elizabeth, he went to Louvaine, where he began his famous controversy against Bishop Jewell, against whom we wrote seven tracts in favour of Popery. His works shew him to have been a man of learning and ability."

" John Jewell, a learned English writer and Bishop. Upon the accession of Mary, in 1553, he was one of the first who felt the rage of the storm then raised against the reformation. He was called upon to subscribe to some of the Popish doctrines under the severest penalties, which he submitted to. He fled to Franckfort in the second year of Queen Mary's reign, where he made a public recantation of his subscription to the Popish doctrines. He returned to England in 1558. He is stiled " one of the greatest champions of the reformed religion." His defence of it against Harding and other Popish divines was in such esteem, that Queen Elizabeth, King James I, King Charles I., and four successive Archbishops, ordered it to be kept chained in all parish churches for public use."

I should be held inexcusable, were I not to devote a page or two of this work to the narration of some particulars relative to that sweet singer amongst our British poets, who was here first " taught to sing."

A brief but interesting memoir of Gay, penned by his *nephew* the Rev. Joseph Baller, was published in 1820, by Mr. Henry Lee, in a duodecimo volume, entitled, "Gay's Chair." The following extracts from Mr. Baller's narrative, embrace all that has any bearing on the long disputed question of the poet's birth place.

" The county of Devon has been rendered famous by giving birth to many eminent characters, particularly to the celebrated poet Mr. JOHN GAY, a gentleman of great wit and humour, whose writings are read by all lovers of true taste and genius, and which, in all probability, will continue to entertain the world, and hand down his name to the latest posterity.

" He was born in *Barnstaple*, in the year 1688, and was the youngest child of Mr WILLIAM GAY, the second son of JOHN GAY, Esq. of Frithelstock, near Great Torrington, of an ancient and worthy family, who had been resident in this county several centuries. He, (the subject of this memoir,) with his elder brother JONATHAN, and two sisters, were left orphans very early in life; their father and mother both dying in or about the year 1694. The elder brother JONATHAN inheriting the paternal estate, the youngest children were possessed of but moderate fortunes.

" While a boy he resided with his mother at a house the corner of Joy-street, facing Holland-street in Barnstaple, and became a pupil to Mr. RAYNER, master of the Grammar School, who shortly after removed to Tiverton, and his place was supplied by MR. ROBERT LUCK, under whose tuition GAY continued some time, and made considerable progress."

" When he left school, he was, by the advice of his relatives, bound apprentice to a mercer in London. Young GAY, not being able to bear the confinement of a shop, soon felt a remarkable depression of spirits, and consequent decline of health; he was therefore oblig-ed to quit that situation, and retire to Barnstaple, in the hope of receiving benefit from his native air. Here he was kindly received at the house of his uncle, his mother's brother, the Reverend JOHN HANMER, the nonconformist minister of that town.

" After continuing some months in Barnstaple, his health became reinstated, upon which he returned to London, where he lived for some time as a private gentleman."

" In the autumn of 1732, he retired with the DUKE OF QUEENSBURY of Amesbury, Wiltshire, in the hope off effectually removing the severe disorder which has so long afflicted him.

" At this crisis it was his intention to pass some months in Devonshire, and apartments were accordingly prepared for him at a house near Landkey, in the vicinity of Barnstaple; but his friends were disappointed in their expectations of seeing him. By his going to London in the latter part of November, for the purpose of introducing on the stage his opera of Achilles, his disorder returned with double violence, and baffling the skill of the most eminent physicians, it put a period to life, December the 4th, 1732, in the 44th year of his age. Dying a bachelor, and without a will, his sisters, KATHERINE BALLER and JOANNA FORTESCUE, became entitled to his effects, and soon after they obtained letters of administration to confirm their claim." The property amounted to about 6000*l.*

" Mr. Baller's manuscript" (says Mr. Lee) " concludes with these words :– ' I, the elder son of Mr. Gay's oldest sister, Katherine Baller, have drawn up this memoir, both from my own knowledge, and from what I have at different times heard from my beloved mother. J.B.' "

Upon this evidence, furnished by a son of the poet's sister, it will hardly be any longer questioned that Barnstaple has a just claim to the honor of having been Gay's birth place. His name certainly does not appear in our Parish Register,* but omissions have doubtless been made, and the embryo poet was as likely to be amongst them as any other infant. Nothing certainly can invalidate Mr. Baller's testimony but actual proof of the registry of Mr. Gay's birth in some other parish.

Gay's Chair. — About twelve years since, there was sold by auction, along with other effects of a Mr. Clark then recently deceased, an ingeniously-formed chair which on subsequent examination was found to contain a secret drawer, " full of manuscript papers."

The annexed description, accompanied by a wood engraving, is given in the work already referred to.

"Under the arms of the chair are drawers, with the necessary implements for writing, each drawer turns on a pivot, and has

---

* The name of Gay, or Gaye, however, appears frequently, and in a way which shews the family which bore it to have been both numerous and respectable.

In 1544-5, three burials of persons so called are recorded on one page of the register; namely, Mr. Richard Gaye, Mr. John Gaye, "gontill man," and Johano Gaye. The appellation Mr. is not very rarely bestowed, but that of gentleman I do not recollect to have seen applied in more than one or two instances besides the above.

" attached to it a brass candlestick. The wooden leaf for reading or writing upon may be raised or depressed at the student's pleasure. Under the seat is a drawer for books or paper, and behind it is the concealed drawer in which were found the manuscripts; it is curiously fastened by a small bolt not perceivable, till the larger drawer is removed. The chair is made of a very fine grained dark coloured mahogany; the seat, back, and arms stuffed, and covered with brown leather, ornamented with brass nails; the whole, considering its antiquity, in pretty good repair, is admirably constructed for meditative ease and literary application."

The chair, which a few years previous had been purchased at a sale of some of the effects of the late Mrs. Williams, niece of the Rev. Joseph Baller, was proved beyond all reasonable doubt to have been Gay's. Mr. Lee purchased both it and the M.S.S. some if not all of which latter he gave to the world in his publication.

APPENDIX TO CHAPTER V

[A.]

"Barum, Anno 1709." —Extracts from "a rate made upon all lands & tenements within the town and parish of Barnstaple aforesaid, for and towards the reparation of the Parish Church there, and for provision, necessary utensils and ornaments, and defraying the incident charges belonging to the said church;" and a comparative statement of the value of property in Barnstaple in 1709 and 1830. *

	£ s. d.	£ s. d.
"Swan Inn,"		
(now Messrs. Trix and Ware's) . .	13 13 0	24 0 0
"Thomas Harris's house,"		
(now Mr. George Hartree's) . .	5 0 0	17 0 0
"Three Tuns"	6 13 0	19 0 0
"Jacob Monier, for his house,"		
(Mr. E. Harris's) . . .	5 6 0	22 0 0
"Mr. Joseph Baller, for his own		
house," (Messrs. Vernon's) . . .	12 0 0	30 0 0
"Zack, Chapple, for the Broadgate,"		
(Hearson's Court) . . .	10 0 0	50 0 9
"Mr. Serjeant Hooper, for his house,"		
(now the Golden Lion) . . .	12 0 0	54 0 0
"James Herson, for his house and		
kilns," (Square Lime Kilns, and		
house adjoining)	8 0 0	64 0 0

*It may, perhaps, be taken for granted that houses and lands were at the former period, as at present, rated below their actual value. The difference between the rate and the net rental is now usually about one half.

	£	s	d	£	s	d
"Elizabeth Halls, for the Angel" . .	8	0	0	24	0	0
"John Parminter, for ye New Work" (Quay Place) . . .	16	0	0	70	0	0
"House, late Mr. Jeffry Bagilhole's," (John Gribble's, Esq.). . . .	10	13	0	46	0	0
"The owners of the Sheep Market," . .	10	13	0	24	0	0
"Mrs. Standish, for the Castle House, 5*l.*– James Gibbs, for ye Castle, [Hill, &c.] 4*l.*" . . .	9	0	0	50	0	0
"The Occupier of Maudlyn Rack-close," .	16	0	0	*138	0	0
"Occupiers of the houses in Ramally, "qy. Ram Alley," (the ground on which Mr. Thomas Harris's house and premises now stand,) . .	4	0	0	32	0	0
"The occupier of ye house and ground, late Mr. E. Ridge's, in Vickaridge Lane," (Vicarage Lawn,) .	12	13	0	30	0	0
"The Occupier of the house called ye Broadgate," (Lovering's Court,) .	10	0	0	46	0	0
"Amos Cardew, for ye Falcon Inn," . .	3	6	0	16	0	0
"The Occupier of Sarum, [Salem] House and Gardens," (The property of Mrs. Tinson, wholly rebuilt, and comprising three houses.) . .	8	0	0	24	0	0
"Joan Gill, for ground at Cooney Causey," (Port Marsh) . . .	2	10	0	35	0	0
"Occupier of Gooslees" . . .	2	0	0	11	0	0
"Occupier of Maidenford . . .	26	13	0	48	0	0
"Mr. Joseph Baller, for Dawking's Park"	10	0	0	22	0	0
"Mr. Serjt. Hooper, for Frankmarsh," . .	58	0	0	140	0	0
Ditto, Holl Ground," . .	24	0	0	50	0	0
Ditto, Holsford Marsh," . .	12	0	0	45	0	0
Ditto, The Mill on Holsford Marsh," .	5	0	0	8	0	0
"The undertakers or receivers of ye Waterworks,"	10	0	0	36	0	0

* The Land is rated at 30*l.* A tan yard, fourteen cottages, and a genteel dwelling house, make up the remaining increase.

	No. of Houses	Lowest Rate	Highest Rate	Whole Amount	Amount to 1830	Total Increase
High Street ...	110	1 0	17 0	751 7	2416	1664 13
Boutport	127	0 13	12 0	563 0	2169	1606 0
Bear Street ...	42	1 0	5 6	111 4	454	342 16
Joy Street	24	1 13	10 13	97 9	380	282 11
Holland Street .	14	1 6	5 6	46 11	221	174 9
Castle, Quay, & Cross Street	86	1 0	12 0	468 15	1053	584 5
Paige Lane	6	1 0	4 0	12 18	73	60 2
Potter's Lane	7	1 13	4 13	25 11	28	2 9
Tuly Lane	5	1 0	3 16	15 9	46	30 11
Green Lane	8	1 0	2 0	16 5	131	114 15
Anchor Lane	15	1 6	4 0	35 3	135	99 17
Alms Lane	5	1 6	2 13	13 8	11	0 0
Back Lane	95	1 0	3 16	161 5	896	734 15
Litchdon Causey and Litchdon*	32	1 0	8 0	75 4	445	369 16
Lands, (Number of parcels)	76	1 10	58 0	835 8	1746	910 12
					£10204	£6977 11

	£	s.	d.
Increase of Rate	6977	11	0
Deduct Decrease on Alms Lane	2	18	0
	£6974	13	0

To the above increase must be added –

	£	s.	d.
Fort Hill House, rated at	34	0	0
Ebberly Place, deducting 7l. the probable rate of the land on which it is built	140	0	0
Derby Factory and Houses, deducting what the property was previously rated at . . .	400	0	0
Gammon's Lane	16	0	0
Vicarial Tythes	145	0	0
Great Farm	90	0	0
Penny Halfpenny	50	0	0
Mill End and Prideaux's Quays	17	0	0
Total increase on the rate	£7866	13	0

* I anticipate the question, where was Litchdon Causey? On the S.E. side of what is now the Square, which was not laid out until 1730, previous to this, the road to Litchdon was by a raised way, which might be correctly termed *Litchdon Causey.*

The actual improvement in the annual value of rateable property in the Parish for the period referred to in the foregoing statements, may be fairly set own at 20,000*l.*

*Extracts from oldest Parish Books ; viz.—Orders of Vestry,
Churchwarden's Accounts, and Overseer's ditto.*

1729, Oct. 5. " Ordered that the parish of Barnstaple do join with the other parishes in the hundred of Braunton, in defending a prosecution instituted by James Parkin, of Ilfordcombe, for a pretended robbery of 60*l.* from his person, within the limits of the said hundred."

" Paid for 47 hedghogs, and 1 sparrow hawk, at 2*d.* – 8*s.*

" Paid the Paritor for his a Tendance on Mary Priscoat,
          her pennance,–1*s.*

" And for the use of the sheet,– 1s.

" Charges at visitation,– 2*s* 6*d.*
   Whole expenditure this year, by the Churchwardens,– 42*l.* 2*s.* 9*d.*
   1735-6. Expenditure this year by the Churchwardens. – 200*l.* 5*s.* 4*d.*
   1738-9. Expenses for dinners, – 5*s.*

" Treating the Dean Rural,– 5*s.*
   1739-40. " Numbering and taking a catalogue of the Books in
          the library, - 4*s.*
   1741-2.   " Paid for Tobacco and Frankincense burnt
          in the Church,– 2*s.* 6*d.*
   1746, April 27. " Ordered that Richard Thomas, sexton of this Parish
          be removed from his office, for suffering (he having the custody of
          the keys of the church) the bells of the church to ring two long
          peaks at 5 o'clock and 8 o'clock in the morning, on Wednesday
          last, in triumph and for joy that the mobb and populace of this
          town and neighbourhood in great multitudes in the night before,
          in the night time, feloniously did break open the dwelling house of
          Mrs. Mary Parminter, and carried away from thence 500 bushels
          of wheat and upwards, under pretence of preventing the
          exportation thereof."

1746-7. " Paid for a forme of prayer to be used on the thanks giving day
for the *suppression of the rebellion*,– 1s.

1747. Prices of provisions, Wheat, 3s.6d. bushel; Beef, 2d. lb; Butter, 5d.

" To Mr. Thos. Rowland, for returning the warrant of the state of the
horned cattle, by the Mayor's order,– 2s. 6d.

1748. Rent of Workhouse,– 5l.

Parish Surgeon, Edwd. Houndle, for physic and surgery, and
Midwifery, in Workhouse,– 10l. per annum.

1749, April. Wheat, 3s. 1d.; Beef, 2½d.; Butter, 4½d.
October. Wheat, 3s. 6d.; Beef, 2d.; Butter, 4d.

1751. Parish Surgeon's salary,– 5l.
April. Wheat, 3s.; Beef, 2d.; Butter, 4d.

1752, April. Wheat, 4s. 8d.; Beef, 2½d.; Butter, 6d.
July 10. " Paid for frankincence, senemon, and charcole,– 3½d.

1755, April 1. Ordered that *a new watter engine for
extinguishing fire* be bought.

1756, Nov. 10. " Ordered that the person or persons who pulled
down the window in north isle, do forthwith repair
and put up such window, or they will be prosecuted at
the expense of the parish." – Signed by Mary Parminter
and Mary Bagilholl.

1757, April. Wheat, 9s.; Beef, 2 ½d.; Butter, 5d.
October, Wheat, 4s. 6d.; Beef, 2½d.; Butter, 4¾d.

1758, April. Wheat, 4s. 7d.; Beef, 3d.; Butter, 5½d.
" Extraordinaries.– June 30, Ale in two days, about getting
Charles Short and May married,– 1s."
" July 7. Paid for marrying Charles Griffey to
Mary May (Griffey belongs to Clovelley,)– 2l. 2s. "
March 1. " Ordered that all woollen manufacturers
paying their men in goods or by way of truck, bill,
or note, or in any other manner than money, be prosecuted
by the parish."
October. Wheat, 3s. 11d.; Beef, 3d.; Butter, 5d.; half a gill
of Wine, 1¼d.

1759, Jan, 26. " Ordered that a suitable entertainment be prepared
at the cost of the Parish for the Rt. Rev. the Bishop of Ferns
and Leighlie and his attendants, who is expected at this town
about 20th February next, to consecrate a plot of ground for
an additional burying place." (" A piece of waste ground at
the east end of the free school," purchased in June, 1758, for 21l.)
April. Wheat, 4s., Beef, 3d.; Butter, 4¾d.

October. Wheat, 3s.5d.; Beef, 2³/₄d.; Butter, 4³/₄d.

1760 April. Wheat, 4s. 6d.; Beef, 3d.; Butter, 5¹/₂d.

October. Wheat 4s. 6d.; Beef, 2¹/₂d.; Butter, 5d.

1762-3. "To Journeys Cᵗ. in Acct. of Memorial,– 1l.1s."

" The Sexton's Bill, and for taking the Havannah, 2l. 5s. 10d.

1764-5.– " Paid for a Bottle of Madeira for the Bishop,– 2s. 6d.

Paid Mr. Crang, for the Angells,– 6l. 6s.

1773, May 4. " To so much expenses with the Dean Ruler,– 6s.

1778, March 25.–" Expences on Account of the Poor this year so greatly excessively great, that 85 rates will be hardly sufficient to defray them. A Committee appointed to examine into the Overseer's proceedings.

Dec. 16. " Ordered that a Faculty be applied for, to remove the Pay Table from where it now stands in the Church into the South Aisle."

1782, April 20. Thomas Heath appointed sole Overseer of the poor at 20l. per annum, and the benefit of the labour of the poor in the workhouse.

[C.]

EXON DIOCESE, BARNSTAPLE DEANRY.—A Terrier* of the Mansion House, Outhouses, and Gardens, and of such Tythes and Profits as belong unto the Vicarage of Barnstaple, made and drawn according to the directions of the Right Reverend Father in God, Stephen Lord, Bishop of Exon, delivered at his Primary Visitation holden at Barnstaple, September 2nd, 1726.

VICARAGE HOUSE, OUTHOUSES, AND GARDENS.— The VicarageHouse, whereof one half is double roofed and two stories in height, containing eight bays of building, is built with stone and mud walls rough casted, excepting the porch in the front which is built with brick; the whole house is covered with Cornish slates; the number of rooms above and below are thirteen; the kitchen, pantry, and hall are floored with lime ashes, the parlour and chambers with deal; and the two cellars are pitched with small stones. All the rooms above and below are ceiled, and none wain-

---

* Teriar or Terrier, a Land Roll or Survey of Lands, &c. In the Exchequer, there is a Terrier of all the Glebe Lands in England, made about 11 Edw. III.– *Tomlin's Law Dictionary.*

scoated, except one side of the Hall, kitchen and pantry.

OUTHOUSES.– The Outhouses are a brewhouse, linny, and stable with reed, containing four bays of building all pitches with small stones, but the brewhouse and linny are covered with Cornish slates.

GARDENS.– Before the Vicarage towards the south are two gardens containing nine perches and half; behind the house towards the north are two courts pitched with small stones, containing five perches; on the outside of the courts is a garden planted with fruit trees, bounded on the east and north by a rack field, and fenced with elm hedges, and a large ditch on the outside, belonging to the garden; on the west it is bounded with the brewhouse and a mud wall commonly called a cob wall, and on the south with a brick and mud wall which parts the two courts from the garden; the garden, exclusive of the hedge and ditch, contains half an acre and nine perches; there is no other glebe besides the church yard, in which there are nine elm trees.

GIFTS OR BEQESTS, AND PENSIONS.– Mistris Martin, of Barnstaple, widow, gave in her last will in these words :– " I give and bequeath to the Minister of the parish of Barnstaple the sum of five pounds yearly, the better to encourage him to use and exercise of the necessary duty of catechizing of youth in his parish." Mr. John Symons, of Barnstaple, merchant, gave by will a brass sconce to the Church of Barnstaple.

PENSION.– The Incumbent pays five pounds yearly to the Patron of the Vicarage.

SURPLICE FEES.– The Surplice Fees by custom immemorial are as follow, vis. For a marriage with banns, two shillings and sixpence; with a licence, five shillings; for churching a woman, one shilling; for a funeral, one shilling; and for reading the service in the Church before the interment of the corpse, five shillings; for a common grave in the chancel, ten shillings; for a walled one, commonly called a sepulchre, three pounds, and every time it is opened for the interment of a corpse, ten shillings; and for a sepulchre in the church yard, twenty shillings. Two pence becomes due at Easter for an offering from every person who is above sixteen years of age.

TITHES.– All manner of tithes (corn only excepted) are due to the Vicar in kind, no prescriptions either real or intended.

FURNITURE OF THE CHURCH.– In the steeple are five bells, a clock and chimes; in the church a font of stone with a carved wooden cover, a pulpit of carved and painted wood, with a crimson velvet cushion, and a reading pew with a desk, covered with green plush; two bibles, of the largest volume and last translation, one bound in two volumes, in red turkey leather; in the body of the church is a large brass sconce, and two brass-candlesticks, one at each end of the reading desk; in the chancel, is a communion table, covered with a crimson velvet carpet, and upon it a common prayer book bound in red turkey leather; the communion plate consists of two silver flaggons, weighing ninety one ounces and a quarter, with this inscription on each of them : " The purchase of the town and parish 1684, John Boyse, vicar, James Kimpland, jun. Christoper Hunt churchwardens;" two silver chalices, with covers gilt, weighing forty six ounces, and two silver pattins, weighing fifteen ounces and eight pennyweights.

REPAIRS OF THE CHURCH AND CHANCEL – The church, and the north and south parts of the chancel, are repaired at the sole charge of the parish. The parishioners out of respect and regard for their minister, have been pleased for a course of many years to repair likewise his part of the chancel. The church yard fence is repaired by the owners of the houses and garden walls, which make the fence of the church yard.

CLERK AND SEXTONS.– The customary salary of the clerk is five pounds per ann.; the head sextons, four pounds per ann.; and the under sextons, forty shillings per ann.; their salaries are paid by the churchwardens; the clerk is appointed by the incumbent, and the sextons by the churchwardens.

Signed by the vicar, churchwardens, and other substantial inhabitants, the fifteen day of May, ann.dom. 1727.

SAMUEAL THOMSON, Vicar,
RICHARD NEWELL ⎫
JOHN GAYDON, Mayor ⎬ Churchwardens
JOHN WEBBER, Alderman
PHILIP BOWDEN, Clerk
ROBERT TRISTRAM,
J. PARMINTER,
BENJA. BALLER, JUN.
CHARLES WRIGHT,
WILLM. FAIRCHILD,
PETER L'OISEAU

MEMORANDUM.– That in the year 1736 some of the elm trees in the church yard were blown down by a violent storm, the rest were rooted up, and ten young ones planted in their room, by

THOMAS STEED, Vicar

Barnstaple, 4th April, 1804,
Compared with the original Terrier.

HENRY GRIBBLE, Churchwarden

CHAPTER VI.

Manufactures and Commerce– Markets and Fairs– River and Quays– Queen Anne's Walk– Bridges– Infirmary– Guildhall– Prison and Bridewell– Theatre– Assembly Rooms– Freemasons– Mechanic's Institute–Annuitant Societies– Benefit Clubs – Friendly Institution and Savings' Bank– Roads and Walks– Water Works– Inns, Coaches, Waggons, and Vans– Appendix.

MANUFACTURES AND COMMERCE

Statistical writers who have noticed Barnstaple, almost universally concur in describing it as having been a considerable manufacturing town for woollens, at a very early period; but I have not been able to obtain any records by which to fix the time when our ancestors first engaged in the trade, or to what extent they carried it in ancient days.

I find however a reference to the time of Edward II. of a nature which warrants the conclusion that this branch of manufacture then flourished here. " 2nd Edward II. [1308] Mayor and Burgesses petitioned the Lord Treasurer, to have the custom on narrow cloth, imposed 28 Edward I., taken off." This effort to have the duty removed would hardly have been made, had not the impost immediately, and in some considerable degree, affected the interests of the town. The appeal was successful, the " custom" having been taken off in the same year.

Passing by the many historical notices alluded to, which, whilst they afford fair presumptive evidence that the woollen trade was a staple here for several centuries, to go no farther, and merely remarking by the way that weavers and tuckers appear to have been numerous here about 1630, we descend at once from the commencement of the fourteenth to the beginning of the eighteenth century, at which time the manufacture was certainly carried on to a very considerable extent, so as to furnish employment to many hundreds of person in the town and neighbourhood.

The quantity of wool imported from Ireland, amounting in 1727-8, to upwards of three hundred tons, (see Appendix [A] to this chapter) added to the produce of the extensive home-district, of which Barnstaple was the only mart, is of itself sufficient to shew that the trade was then very flourishing. The earliest period respecting which I am enabled to enter most fully into detail, is that from 1760 to the decline of the trade, which commenced according to the best information I have been able to procure, about the year 1771. The descriptions of goods then manufactured were termed duroys, tammies, serges, shaloons, baizes, Barnstaple stuffs, (an article similar to what are now termed merinos,) flannels, plushes, webbs, (wove in coloured stripes, and used for waistcoats, &c.) and everlastings. I am informed by an individual who had the best means of forming an estimate, that there were in the town only at this time a hundred combers; these in their ordinary work would "double-comb" about two tons of wool weekly. Almost every poor person's house had a loom in it, notwithstanding which, manufacturers being unable to get sufficient work done at home, had what was termed spinning houses, many of them twelve miles form the town, where they at stated times or by an agent on the spot gave and received work from person engaged by them in that neighbourhood. Three dye houses were kept at work. Considerable quantities of the different sorts of goods, were exported to America, and other foreign parts. Large sales were also made at home, particularly in Bristol and Exeter, both at the fairs, and by orders received from these cities. An idea may be formed of the extent of business transacted at Bristol, by mention of the fact, that on one occasion a manufacturer considered he had had " a good fair " when he had a hundred pieces (about 5,000 yards) of baize left on hand. What remained unsold was always left in the hands of the factor.

Independent however of the extensive trade that was carried on in piece goods, considerable business was done, in what was technically termed chains, (the warp or longitudinal threads of the cloth prepared for being wove,) large quantities of which were sent to Exeter, and many other places. The check which this then lucrative trade experienced in 1771, arose out of causes not now to be easily defined, but the American war had doubtless a very injurious effect upon it subsequently.

In 1774, a bold and for a time successful attempt was made to revive the woollen business, and also to introduce the manufacture of cotton goods. Two extensive mills were erected about half a mile from the town, and brought into operation on a scale sufficiently large to furnish employ to a thousand persons, including ninety wool-combers. The demand for our country wool became so great, (as I have been informed by a gentleman who was a partner in the concern at the time of its being given up,) that it advanced from 6*d* to 10*d*. per pound. A great part of the business done here, was in the fabric of chains; woollen cloths, calicoes, and " Rawleigh flannels," were made to a great extent; the last named article was formed of a cotton chain with a weft of woollen. A number of cotton spinning machines were also employed. Things (as I learn from the authority above alluded to) went on very briskly here until after the breaking out of the war, which succeeded the French revolution (1793), when it declined very materially. In 1795, a fire, supposed to have been the work of an incendiary, consumed the cotton mill, with its machinery, and the concern was abandoned.

Subsequent to 1760, some considerable quantities of flannels and serges were sold to the East India Company, but this is no longer the case, and the woollen trade formerly so extensive, is now confined to a single manufacturer, who makes the following description of goods, principally for exportation,– blankets, blanketings, swanskins, plains, coal pits, and serges.

A manufactory of cotton hose was commenced in 1796, but it ceased on the demise of the projector, in about twenty years. It has since been revived, and continues at present, but on a very small scale.

In 1821, the building which remained uninjured at Rawleigh, was taken by some gentlemen from Nottingham and Derby, and converted into a manufactory for bobbin net, which has since been carried on in an extensive way.

A dissolution of partnership took place amongst the proprietors of this concern in about four years from its commencement, which led to the establishment of a new one in Vicarage Lane, (see plan of town.) The whole of the machinery is here propelled by steam, for which purpose an engine of sixteen horse power is employed.

The individual who set this manufactory on foot having also one at Derby, this, and the little town which has sprung up around it has received that appellation.

In 1825, an enterprising and ingenious person, who was employed at Rawleigh and had a principal share in the superintendance of the machinery there, erected a mill adjoining the London road, less than a quarter of a mile from the town. This is also worked by a steam engine, of eight horse power.

Thus were three lace manufactories, a branch of trade wholly new to the town, set at work here in the short period of five years;* they now furnish employment to upwards of one thousand persons.

One of the proprietors of that last noticed, has an establishment in the town, where worked-lace dresses, veils, &c. are prepared, and may be had at prices far below what is commonly paid for articles of a similar fabric.

In 1822, partly as a consequence of the lace trade having commenced here, the " Barnstaple Iron Foundry " was established (by the writer, but passed into other hands in 1827); it has proved a great accommodation to the town and neighbourhood, there being no other within thirty miles of this place, and not one nearer than Bristol, from whence goods can be procured otherwise than by land carriage.

---

* I should perhaps state, that the first and last mentioned of these are both without the parish, (each on the margin of a stream which separates this from the adjoining one,) but being so near the town, and benefitting as they do very materially its trade, they may, I conceive, with strict propriety be designated Barnstaple Manufactories.

I am here reminded of my having omitted to state the extent of the parish; it being now too late to do this in its proper place, I crave leave to do it here. The parochial boundaries are, – on the south, the Taw; north and north west, the Yeo, dividing Barnstaple from Pilton at the bridges which connect the parishes; eastward, by a stone on the road to Goodleigh, near Yeotown Lodge, distant about 1 1/2 mile; and to Maidenford Bridge, about the same distance; south east, by "Cooney Gut," a quarter of a mile on the London road, and which runs between Barnstaple and the pleasant village of Newport.

The manufacturer of a coarse but very useful description of earthenware has long been in operation, (one of the Corporation Bye Laws framed in 1689, has reference to potters;) the clay from which it is made is dug in the parish of Fremington, about three miles from hence. Numerous potteries in the neighbourhood are supplied from this "clay-pit," the only one hereabout, and considerable quantities of the wares manufactured form it are exported coastwise.

The testimony of historians (two of them at least) as it respects the COMMERCE of Barnstaple in former times, comes in such a tangible shape, that it may fairly be allowed to have some weight in the scale of evidence respecting it.

Risdon, who resided but a few miles distant, must be presumed to have made himself well acquainted with the state of things here; and Camden, whose work was the result of an actual survey, has a just claim to be considered as having made a true report. We may however glance at a period long antecedent to that spoken of by either of these venerable chroniclers. We have seen that Barnstaple was a port of some note in the reign of Edward III., from which, and the fair proof afforded us that the woollen manufacture was in operation here in the reign of Edward II., we may reasonably infer, that this was not only a maritime but a commercial port, in the fourteenth century. The Custom House records (to which I have been indulged with free access) have not, unfortunately, been preserved from an earlier date than 1727, and that only of the imports;* of these the statement given at appendix [A], embraces the account for the first two years, 1727-8. The duties then

---

* The exports, the earliest statement of which refers to 1742, were principally to Newfoundland, but occasionally to New England, Portugal, Spain, &c. The following may be taken as a sample of a consignment to Newfoundland. Feb. 1742. —

" 26 Trusses Narrow German Linen.
15 Pieces British made Sail Cloth.
5 Packs containing Barum Bayes, [Baize] Kerseys, and Coarse Cloth..
1 Puncheon, containing Manchester Linens, and Men's Woollen Stockings.
10 Pieces coloured Broad Cloths.
10 Packs contianing Rugs.
2 Casks Pewter, wrought.
1 Pack Woollen Caps.
60 Dozen Cod Lines, in a cask.
And provisions as per Vict. Bill."

payable on these goods, tobacco only excepted, were comparatively trifling. The imposts accruing to importations in 1728, (the first year for which the amount can be ascertained) reached to 27,923*l.* 1*s.* 7*d.* of which 26,244*l.* 5*s.* 2*d.* was for tobacco; in the following year, the gross sum was 30,507*l.* 18*s.* 5*d,* that for tobacco being 28,525*l.* 12*s.* 11*d.* We must not however suppose that the enormous quantity of this narcotic was all manufactured here for consumption; bonds were given for by far the larger part of the duties, and the great bulk of the article as appears from the small proportions subsequently paid on the different bonds, was exported; much of it probably for the purpose of being landed on different parts of the coast, as contraband.* From some now unassignable cause, the importation of tobacco did not continue long after this period, and the receipts of the port for 1734, were but 935*l.* 3*s.* 6½*d.*; and for 1739, 972*l.* 17*s.* 1¼*d.* The duty on coals has of late years amounted to nearly 3000*l.* per annum, but up to 1822 scarcely any other dues were received but for this article and timber.

The year last mentioned introduces us to an important era in the commercial history of Barnstaple, being the first of the establishment of warehouses, usually termed Bonded Warehouses,† for the reception of foreign produce, on which duties are payable. This important advantage, which has greatly contributed to the increase of our trade, was obtained at the different periods, and for the various descriptions of merchandize specified below :–

Wine and Spirits, . . .	. June 3, 1822
Rum	. Dec. 30,1822
Sugar, Molasses, Mahogany, &c. &c. .	. Sept. 24 1823
All other goods, except Tobacco,	
East India goods, &c. . .	February,1828

* Smuggling was certainly carried on to a great extent in this article, and in many ways. I find "further entries" (of goods contained in the vessel over and above what the master had sworn on making his first report to be the whole contents of the cargo) made in one quarter, by (" G. Buck and Sons") of parcels of tobacco from three cargoes, amounting in all to " 96,000 lbs." the whole of which was no doubt intended to have been smuggled ashore, had opportunities offered for the purpose.

† Previous to 27th George III., Merchants on giving bonds to government for the payment of duties accruing from such goods as they might import, were allowed to take the articles into their own warehouses, but by an act passed in that year, this system was superseded by the present one of placing goods in cellars or buildings set apart for the purpose, on which the owner and the King's officers each place a lock. Up to 1825 the Customs and Excise had both a share in the management of such establishments, it is now vested in the Customs only.

(See copies of the several warrants under their respective dates in appendix [B] to this chapter.)

No time was lost in making a practical use of the benefits thus obtained;* a building was speedily erected, agreeable to the required regulations, for the joint benefit of all the houses then carrying on the wine and spirit trade, and was first used in November, 1822. Two years subsequent to this, Messrs. Cotton and Sons, (who, it is but fair to say, were the first to propose an application to government for the extension of the bonding system to this port,) built a warehouse for their own separate use; since which, a third, and the most extensive, has been fitted up by Messrs. Nickols and Company, but this is, in conformity with the stipulation expressed in warrant No. 4, open to all who may choose to avail themselves of the accommodation it offers.

The beneficial effects of this trade-encouraging system being extended to Barnstaple, are fully apparent; we have again a foreign trade, and one which though as yet but small, bids fair to increase.

We import goods from the Baltic, France, Spain, Portugal, the Azores, and North America.

The following comparative statement from the latest official return of the amount of customs received at the different ports, reports favourably of ours :–

Year ending January 5th, 1830.— Barnstaple, 12,963*l*.; Bideford, (also a bonded port), 5,925*l*.; Ilfracombe, 940*l*.

By the accounts just made up at our Custom House, I find the receipts up to January 5th, 1831, to have been 13,557*l*. 0*s*. 4*d*. shewing an increase in the past year of 594*l*. Appendix [C] enumerates the quantities of the different articles on which duties have been paid during the year.

The Custom House, which until lately was inconvenient and altogether unsuitable for the transaction of public business, became by purchase the property of the present collector, E.R. Roberts, Esq. who in 1825 rebuilt and fitted it up in a manner every way appropriate.

---

* With an exception as it respects Timber, no description of which has yet been placed under bond, although a good deal is imported yearly from our North American Colonies.

The Customs establishment comprises eight officers, and is conducted at an expense of about 900*l.* per annum.

The limits of the Port of Barnstaple were laid down and clearly defined by a commission appointed 29th Charles II. and remained undisturbed until about twenty years since, when on the petition of the inhabitants of Appledore to the Lords of the Treasury, stating the inconvenience arising from that creek being attached to the Port of Barnstaple, and praying redress, it was annexed to that of Bideford, and the boundaries of the respective harbours underwent a material alteration. Extracts from official documents relative to this Port at both the above periods are inserted in Appendix [D], as are also some statements relative to the port, shipping, &c. extracted from Macpherson's "Annals of Commerce."

Newspapers stand so intimately connected with the subject of commerce, and lend such powerful and efficient aid to its operations, that I may very properly notice under this head the establishment of THE NORTH DEVON JOURNAL, the first number of which appeared on Friday, July 2nd, 1824. In about twelve months from its commencement, it was followed by a second paper, THE BARNSTAPLE HERALD, set up for the express purpose of opposing the first, but which soon met with the fate it deserved, in being discontinued after a publication of fifty-two numbers; it had never any chance of success. THE JOURNAL successfully, though silently, combated the opposition, and established itself on a firm basis. It is now published on Thursday mornings, early enough for dispatch by that day's mail, and is consequently received in London by Friday's post. The paper is, and has always been, conducted in a spirited manner, and does not rank among the least advantages of which Barnstaple has to boast.

RIVER AND QUAYS

The River Taw, which adds so greatly to the appearance, wealth, and salubrity of our town, has its source on the lofty and desolate region of Dartmoor; from whence it runs northward in the direction of Chulmleigh; then, changing its course, it winds its devious track westward, towards the lovely vale of Tawton, in passing through which it comes close in view of the elegant and sweetly-situate mansion of Sir Bourchier Palk Wrey, Bart. and thence flows on to Barnstaple. Here, in constant and beautiful exemplification of the power and wisdom of the Creator, it is seen "ever and anon" to rise and swell, bearing on its bosom many a goodly bark, which, before motionless, we now behold, as if endowed with animation, gliding swiftly onward toward the "Severn Sea,"— but I am digressing.

The river which at New Bridge, three miles distant, is crossed by a bridge of three arches, widens considerably as it approaches the town, and still more so after passing it. The flow of water at the highest tide of an ordinary spring, is ten feet, but it frequently rises to thirteen feet; and when it happens that a high spring is accompanied by a south west wind, it reaches to sixteen or eighteen feet; when this occurs, most of the houses on the Quay and in the Cattle Market are inundated; but as the inhabitants are generally aware of what is to take place, but little inconvenience is felt, particularly as the unwelcome visitant so soon retires.*

The bed of the river is composed chiefly of sand, which prevails to a great depth,† and is constantly varying its position according as what is termed the *fresh* (the land water) is high or low. When the former is the case, the river deepens on the south side, when the contrary happens, the greater depth is on the north side.

---

*I am not aware of more than one instance having been recorded in which any serious damage has happened from he overflow of the river, this occurred upwards of two centuries ago, a tempestuous wind was its powerful auxiliary in accomplishing the havoc that was made.

" The 20th daye of Janiarij, 1606, there was suche a mightie storme and tempeste from the river of Barnistaple, wh the comminge of the tyde, that yt caused much lose of goods and howses to the vallow of some thousand pounds, besyde the death of one James ffrost, a toaker, and some of his children, ye which his howses fell down upon them & killed them, this storme begane at 3 of Clocke in the morninge, and continewed tyll 12 of Clock of the same daye." – *Parish Register*

Wyot, who gives a long account of the same occurrence, (but under an uncertain date,) says, the water was " by report higher by v of vi foote than ever remembered by those now lyvinge," that it " cast down divers walls in Litchdon, hurted all the walls on the Kay next the river, &c.

† The remains of a vessel, supposed to have been about 100 tons, lies imbedded in a part of the river called Black Hedge; her timbers may sometimes be seen at low water, but all knowledge as to how or when the wreck took place is "beyond the memory of man."

There is sufficient water at the Quays on spring tides for vessels of 100 tons burden, and four miles down for ships carrying 200 tons. In the " Pool " formed by the confluence of the Taw and Torridge, a ship of war may lie afloat at low water.

On the Bar, which lies three miles from the mouth of the former river, the tide rises thirty feet and upwards.

This immense accumulation of sand, on which at times the surf breaks with irresistible violence, has proved fatal to many a gallant vessel, but the danger which used to attend the passage by persons unaquainted with the direction of the channel through it, has been of late materially lessened by the erection of two light houses, on Braunton Sands.

The Yeo.— " the little *Yeaw*"* must not be wholly passed over. This stream, which rises about eight miles northward of the town, forms one of the most prominent objects of attraction from the late splendid but now desolate and forsaken mansion of *Yeotown*. It answers however a far more beneficial purpose; several water wheels are put in motion by it, among which may be mentioned that which propels the powerful machinery at Rawleigh. The last service of this kind which it performs, is that of setting at work Port Mill, which, by the way, is, without doubt, the same as is mentioned in Domesday, as having belonged to the Bishop of Constance.

Quays.— We look in vain for the " wharff or key, conteynynge in length fyve hundred yardes and more," alledged in 1555 to have been built;† The present quays, as will be seen, occupy but a small portion of this space.

The legal quays were recognized by the Commission already alluded to, to be " that open place commonly called the Key of Barnstaple," (now known as the *Great Quay*,) " to which there belongeth two slips containing from north to south, from the merchant's walk unto the north wall of the house called the New Work, in length towards the river Tawe, two hundred and seven foot, or thereabouts; and in breadth from the key head where the crane

* Risdon.

†Where was it built? It could only have been from the Bridge westward, but the utmost extent in that direction, namely, to the extremity of the Castle Quay, is less that 1,100 feet.

" standeth near the merchant's walk aforesaid, unto the walk [wall] of the Key hall, ninety-three foot or thereabouts; and from the bottom of the slip adjoining to the north wall of the New Work aforesaid, in breadth ninety-three foot, or thereabouts; and from the middle of the key to the Custom House, four foot, or thereabouts. Also, one other open place or Key [*Little Quay*] at Barnstaple aforesaid, betwixt the south wall of the New Work aforesaid, and the north wall of the house called the Royal Oak, whereunto belongeth one slip, containing in length from one wall to the other towards the river Tawe aforesaid, one hundred and five foot; and from the bottom of the slip, in breadth ninety-three foot; and from the middle of the key and north end thereof, in breadth each forty-five foot, or thereabouts."*

Besides these, there are two others, namely, the *Castle* or *Prideaux's Quay*, and *Mill-end* originally termed *Union Quay*, situate at opposite extremities of the North Walk, both of which the corporation claim and use as private property.

The lineal extent of the two authorised quays as described above, is 312 feet, being all that is available to the public† out of the 1,500 feet quay *said* to have been erected in the reign of Philip and Mary, the remaining space from the bridge to the North Walk being all covered by buildings, principally if not wholly the property of the corporation.

In illustration of the remark made earlier, as to the insufficiency of the accommodation for shipping at the quays, I may instance that vessels are not unfrequently obliged to lie three abrest, and to discharge in that situation. The centre slip formed at the Great Quay a few years since, was certainly a great improvement, but did not supply the want of room to a sufficient extent. How far the corporation have a right to appropriate either of the quays as private property, is a question that has long been agitated, and which is now likely to be at no distant period set at rest, as may be seen from what follows.

---

*Instow Quay is also by the same authority declared to be a legal or licensedQuay, and to belong to the Port of Barnstaple.

†A few feet of each of the others only excepted, which can only be used by sufferance, and which are scarcely ever resorted to by vessels.

Subsequent to the erection of the Bridge which connects Mill-end Quay with the new Braunton Road, a demand was made by the Corporation on the Trustees of that turnpike of 80*l*. for such part of the quay and North Walk as would be required for the purposes of the road, which was agreed to be paid them. The trustees offered this money under an impression that it was to be applied towards the removal of a part of the Mermaid Inn, so as to render the approach from the Braunton road to High Street uninterrupted, and therefore made this a condition of the payment. Some misunderstanding took place, which caused the corporation to rescind their proposal of receiving 80*l*. at the same time hinting that the Braunton trustees were at their mercy, having no power to enter the town without their permission.

This caused the trustees to pass a vote " that the solicitor to this trust do state a case for the opinion of counsel, respecting the right claimed by the corporation to Mill- end Quay."

The counsel consulted, (Mr. Bayly,) says, " I am of opinion, that the corporation have not the exclusive right to the Mill-end Quay into the North Walk, but as Lords of the Manor the soil is their's, subject to the right of the public to pass over it as they have been accustomed."

The learned gentleman advised some recompence to be made for the land that might be required; but before the suggestion was acted on, the turnpike trust procured a second opinion from Mr. Bayly, who says, " when I recommended to the trustees to tender a sufficient compensation for the land that would be required, I of course only meant such a compensation as the owners of the land so circumstanced would be entitled to, for such their interest in it so subject; not the full value which the land would be of to a person who held the entire property in it, unaffected by any such rights, might have made of it by selling it for building, or keeping it for that purpose; *but only the value of land which the proprietor could not inclose, or build upon, but when the buildings he might erect would be liable to be pulled down the next moment.*"

The trustees now made an offer of 10*l*. to the corporation, which they rejected, but proposed to settle the matter in an amicable manner by arbitration. Attempts have been made to accomplish this, which have hitherto failed, and the matter is still at issue.

Previous to this affair taking place, the corporation had leased the greater part of the quay, on which to the great detriment of the North Walk, the lessee had erected a dwelling house, to which probably Mr. Bayly alluded in his opinion. A question seems naturally to arise out of this subject,— can we believe that the corporation, on learning what Mr. Bayly thought of their claim to the property in question, did not also consult counsel? If they did, they have never promulgatedthe result; what is the inference?

Quay Dues.— I am in possession of copies of three different tables of these; the oldest was drawn up in 1679; a transcript of this is given at Appendix [E]. It will be found to differ but little from the list at present acted upon. These dues appear to have been originally a prescriptive right, but since confirmed by charter, though notparticularly specified.*

There are not wanting persons to complain of the payment of impost as a hardship, but certainly on very weak grounds. That the conservators of the town property should be empowered to demand and receive such a toll, is certainly most reasonable, and that the scale at which they are fixed is moderate, must be acknowledged.

On the west side of the principal quay stands

QUEEN ANNE'S WALK

of which a representation is given with the plan of the town. It is said to have been built in that Queen's reign for an exchange, but it was certainly a " Merchant's Walk " at least as early as the time of Charles II. (see page 395;) it might have been a walk only, and was probably inclossed and covered at the period above alluded to; it is

---

* I ought perhaps to notice that the term *Lathstedes* has been understood by some persons to mean Quay Dues; it is however far more probable that *lastage* was intended by it.* These dues must have been by far too valuable to have been included either in the purchase of the manor from Mr. Marrow by Sir John Chichester, or in the sale by that gentleman to the Corporation.

* Lastage, customs in some markets and fairs for carrying things; also a duty paid for wares sold by the last; also the ballast of a ship.

in length 67 feet, and nearly12 in breadth. It is ornamented with various heraldic designs, said to be the armorial bearings of individuals who contributed to its erection. Under the royal statue is inscribed :

ANNA
Intemeratae Fidei Testimonium
Roberti Rolle, de Stevenstone,
In agro Devoniensi Armigeri

And on two tablets at the end of the piazza, as follows :

Haec Porticus Corporis Politici de Barum
Sumptibus restaurator est.
Opus tam decorum et utile munificentia
promoverunt idemq; suis insigniis
Ornarunt viri ipsi ornatissimi
et nohorabiles.

Efficiendum curavit
Robertus Incledon generosus
Oppidi Praefectus
Anno Christo
MDCCXIII.

The walk was " rebuilt by the corporation, 1798."

BRIDGES

Barnstaple, or *The Long Bridge*.— As it was not known three centuries ago who " made the right great and sumeptus bridge at Berstaple," it will be vain now to enquire who was its founder; it is, however, but of little importance for us to know whether we are indepted for the accommodation the structure affords us, to " one of the Tracys," to " one Stamford, a citizen of London," to " the bounty of the Maids," to each of which its origin has been attributed; or, what perhaps is more probable than either, to the united efforts and contributions of persons who resided in the town and neighbourhood, among whom " one of the Tracys," as Lord of

Barnstaple, might have been a principal. The period of its erection was probably in the twelfth or thirteenth century, but there is no certain evidence respecting it.

The subjoined document will be regarded as curious in the present day, to those at least who may not have seen similar ones. The practice of obtaining benefaction in this way was not then uncommon.

"John Holland, Maior of the towne of Barstaple, and others Maisters of the said towne of Barstaple, and others Maisters of the said towne, their letters testimonial to John Gerway, to collect alms in Dorsetshire, for maintenance of the Longbridge and Cawseys of Barstaple, Jany. xx. xxxvi. H. viii.

" To all trew christian people to whom this p'sent writtings of testimoniall shall come, to be seen or herd, John Holland, Maior of the towne of Barstaple, Philippe Comer, John Mannynge, Richard Skyn, Henry Webber, Thoms Jeffry, JohnGoddesland, and Willm Cameford, maisters of the said towne, and also Roger Worth, towneclarke, & John Sequence, & Richd Wythyrydge, wardens of the bridge, of the said towne of Barstaple, send gretting in God everlastinge.

" For as moche as we pftly know that there is a great hugy mighty perylous and dreadfull water, named Taw, ronynge & beinge between the towne of Barstaple, aforesaid, & the Pshe of Tawstock, w^thin the countie of Devon, over the wch the King's subjects and many other daily and yerly ride and dryve to and from many and sondry townes of the said shyre, and other sondry pshes, with all man^r of disstresses, catall & other bests, and also do cary and recary all man^r carrags & thyngs necessary for thelpe of man, upon a bridge of lyme & stone, named the longe Bridge of Barstaple, whereas salte water doth ebbe and flowe foure tymes in the day & the night; and the bridge is in length xiii goodly arches, and is walled on ev'y side fyve fote of hythe, and at the one end thereof is a goodly cawsy* lying over a marshe a quart^r of a mile in length, and is rayled on the syde wher as any time is for the savegard of

* This causey, then not wider than the footpath now is, was much lower than the present turnpike road. When the paved way was broken up a few years ago, the date, as it was supposed to be, of the formation of the causey was not displaced; four stones are so disposed as to form certainly a rude resemblance to the figures 1601, which may perhaps mark the year in which the ground was raised.

"the King's lovynge subjects that thereupon shall passe, and at the other end of the said bridge is another cawsey* as long as the other is, with longe stones sett an end on every syde thereof, to thentent that evy person, that is to say, manne, woman & child shall have p'ft knowledge how to kipe ther way wthout damag. And at evy springe, bothe marshes & cawsies ben over heled and ov'flow wth salte water. In consyderation whereof, for the reparaton and upholdynge of the said bridge, yerly to be hadd & done, to thentent that all such the King's liege people, wch daily & yerely do and shall resorte from all pshes of the shyre & elsewhere, wch in this realm may in savegard wthout any damag or jepdy, go, come, ride, dryve, cary, recary, & passe, as well in tsher owne pp'r persons, as wth ther distress and cariages, over, through, & upon the foresaid violente, daungerous, & jep'dous streme & water aforsaid.

" We the aforenamed John Holland, Mayor of the said towne of Barstable, Philippe Comer and other abovenamed, do desyer & hertily pray you, in and for the honor & love of God, and of your cherite, to departe wth some portions of yr goods after yr powers, towards the repara'con, mayn'tence, and edfiinge of the said bridge & cawsies, for the wch we donte dout but that you shall get made of almyghty God for yr so doing, and of us harty thanks. And also ons in the yeare, we have a gentle dirge and masse solemly songe with all the prists & clarks in the church for all the bretherne, sisterne, and well doers to the said bridge & cawsie, and over all these we hartily pray you to p'mitte and suffer one John Gorway, his assigns and deputies, the wch is now appoynted by us, for the collection of yor charitable almes and gifts, of, and for thaccomplishynge of the p'rmiss's, peasabully to go, come, and pass amonge you, within the shyre of Dorsett, during the tyme of foure yeres next comynge, after the date of these p'esents, without any manr of lette interruption, vexation or troble by any of you, but to be susteyned as ye entend hereaftr to have us to do you like plesr, if any such nede should happen to you, or any of yours. In Witness whereof for the more credence of the p'rmiss's to be trew we above specifyed John

---

*Strange as this may seem now, there was without doubt a causey leading from the Bridge to High Street, (though certainly not so long as is here represented) and so low as to be constantly overflowed to a considerable depth. What did not our forefathers put up with?

"Holland, Maior, Philippe Comer, John Mannynge, Richd Skynn, Henry Webber, Thos Jeffry, John Godesland, & Willm Cameford, with our hole asssents & conssents to this o^r p'sente writtine testimonial, have put to or towne seale, in o^r yeld haulle, in Barstaple aforesaied, yeven the twenty day of January, in the xxxvi yere of the reigne of o^r Sovargne Lord King Henry the viiith by the grave of God of England, Fraunce, & Irland, King, defender of the faiith, and in imediately under God sup'me hedd of the church of England & of Ireland."

The bridge is here described as having but thirteen arches; Leland, seven years after, speaks of it as having sixteen; it is likely therefore that the three additional ones were erected out of the proceeds of John Gorway's begging expedition. This edifice underwent another improvement in 1580.

" North peere," says Philip Wyot, " of the great bridge built on wood, taken down and rebuilt in three weeks on an arch, cost xxvi pounds, called Maiden Arches."

The inscription which follows, copied from a stone fixed in a parapet wall over the first arch, has reference to the same alteration.

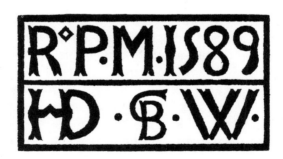

(Robert Prowse, Mayor, 1589, Henry Downe Senior Bridgewarden.)

The following, also transcribed from tablets on the bridge walls, mark the dates of subsequent alterations. " This [the second] arch was widened 18782 " . " This bridge was widened in 1796" . Over the first arch, " Six of these arches were widened in 1807 ".

In 1829, a very great improvement was effected by the removal of two small dwelling houses from the entrance to the bridge on the west side, by which the approach to it has been widened to twenty six feet, and the corner rounded to a convenient sweep;* but a more important one is in contemplation, that of widening the roadway throughout four feet, which added to its present dimensions, will make it about 20 feet wide. The bridge is in length, including the approaches, 700 feet and upwards, and from the inside of the extreme arches more than 500 feet; height from the parapet wall to the low-water line, 26 feet. The capacity of the arches may be judged of by the fact, that vessels exceeding 100 tons register are built at Lichdon, which of course must be taken through the bridge. The foundation of the structure is formed wholly or in part of wood, the timber on which the piers rest may be sometimes seen, when the water is unusually low. The affairs of the bridge are managed by the corporation as trustees, two of whom are annually chosen bridgewardens,† an office to which the bye laws assign a salary of

---

* I have called this a very great improvement, and so it is; but a greater might and ought to have been made, by taking off a portion of the house on the east side; this would have made the entrance uniform in appearance, and have been a valuable accommodation, as well to pedestrians as for carriages, of which it may be safely asserted, that of twenty coming over the bridge, nineteen are driven into the Square. The building in question is one for the removal of which or a part of it provision is made in the Improvement Act; the commissioners perhaps could not readily furnish the purchase money, but the bridge funds could, and 500l. (or more if necessary) would have been well laid out in making the alteration. As the town cannot be entered from the bridge in a direct line, it is the bounden duty of the trustees to remove the obstruction presented by the house in question to a commodious curve. Why is this not done? We know the means for effecting it are ample! Can there by any private interests in the way? Let us hope that as the projected improvements are as yet not fully made known, this very essential one is intended to form one of them.

†In Wood's continuation of Philip Wyot's register, occurs the following, under the date of 1643 :–
    "1588 - Henry Down, George Baker, Bridgewardens. – Neither of them being of the counsel
    at that time, it being 27 years from the tyme of Mr. Baker's (one of the individuals chosen)
    being Maior to the time that he was bridgwarden. So that if he had been of the common council,
    he must have been Maior long before, and therefore cannot plead antiquity, that the
    bridgwardens were always of the comon counsel."

6s. 8d. per annum. In the same code provision is also made for the due election of these officers, the manner in which their accounts are to be settled, &c. (see bye laws.)

Pilton Bridge or *Causey*, for either term may with equal propriety be applied to it, is about a furlong and half in length, and unites Barnstaple with Pilton.* It has at the northern extremity, two arches over the Yeo, and one at the southern endacross the Mill Leat, (a branch of the Yeo.) Tradition assigns the erection to a gentleman named Stowford, who coming to Barnstaple from his residence at West Down, saw a woman and child washed off from the causey and drowned, and in consequence resolved on building a bridge, at his own expense. Another account adds, that Mr. Stowford resided in London, and left money in the hands of the authorities here for the accomplishment of his design. In Frayne's continuation of Wyot, it is said " 1678. Mr. Richard Salisbury, Maior, began the building of Pilton Bridge." I find it recorded however, that in 1581, it was " repaired by corporation," and in 1656, " Wardens of long bridge ordered to repair pillar at the N. end of Pilton bridge, and walls on top thereof." The best way in which we can reconcile these statements, is by supposing what is not improbable) that there might have been no arch over the leat, but a footway for passengers only, until 1678, and in that year one was built. Both causey and arches were, as was common in former times, narrow, and irregularly built, but " this causey and the bridges were widened ten feet, in the year 1821." This was effected by public subscription.

The road is very good, and has a carriage way of 21 feet, with a footpath of six feet in width; the thoroughfare over it is very considerable. It has lately been made turnpike, as part of the new Ilfracombe road.

Union Bridge.— I have chosen this appellation, so peculiarly appropriate for bridges in general, in preference to the harsh term of Mill-end, which is not in fact the original name of the

---

* This is now a large and very respectable village; it can boast of some antiquity, the parish contains about two thousand inhabitants. There was formerly a Priory here, the foundation of which was anterior to that of our own. A list of its Priors may be seen in Oliver's Monastries of Devon. There exists still an ancient charity termed Saint Margaret's Hospital.

Quay* adjoining to which the bridge is built, and after which it has been called. The purpose for which this bridge was erected has already been explained. The facility with which the Yeo can now be crossed at this point is an acquisition to Barnstaple, offering many a pleasant summer's walk, and a most delightful level drive of four miles and three quarters to Braunton, with the river for a great part of the distance close in view.

MARKETS AND FAIRS

" When markets were first established," says a learned author, " is unknown." This may well be the case, as such institutions must in the very nature of things be of a very remote antiquity; coeval at least with the invention of money, the want of which would of course be felt wherever a community was formed, as being a superior mode of exchange to that of barter.

The Saxons, for the prevention of fraud, instituted some strict and severe laws for the regulation of buyers and sellers; they were doubtless rendered necessary by the half civilized state of society in those days.† Barnstaple had the privilege of a regular market at a very early period, as is evidenced by one of the inquisitions before

---

* I should have noticed under the head "Quays" that this was built in 1701, and cost as stated in the corporation accounts, 56*l.* 4*s.* 7½*d.* A stone (now removed to the leaping stock at the end of the long bridge) was placed on it, with this inscription –

This is the *Union Quay*, Thomas Harris, Mayor, 1701."

It was lengthened in 1799.

† In the laws of Ida it is expressly said,— "Si mercator inter vulgus mercetur, faciat hoc coram testibus. Si furto ablatum illud emptum inveniatur, et ipse non emerit id coram bonis testibus, confirmat poenae loco, quod nec furte conscius, uecfuratus sit, vel compenset poenae loco tirgenta sex solidos."–

Wilkin's Leg. Ang. Sax. p. 18, L. L. Inæ 25. – If a merchant purchase anything among the common people, he shall do it in the presence of witnesses. If he cannot prove that he bought before good witnesses, but is found to have bought and carried it away secretly, he shall be held guilty as if he had stolen it, and shall pay a fine of thirty six shillings.– In those of Athelstan, it is enacted, " that no one shall make a purchase beyond 20 pennies *extra portam*, [without the gate] but that such bargains should take place within the town, in the presence of the portreve, or some other person of veracity, or of the reeves in the Felc-mote." –*Ibid p. 58, L. L. Athels.* 12.

" Markets were held on Sundays, but were forbidden by the laws of the Northumbrian priests, about 930, but not abolished until 27 Hy VI., when it was enacted 'that all manner of fairs and markets in the principal feasts, on *Sundays* and *Goodfridays*, shall clearly cease upon pain and forfeiture of all goods,&c. &c.'" – *Appendix to Com. Rep. of Public Records.*

referred to. It was at this time held on " Wednesday and Friday in every week." It continued by prescription to the time of Queen Mary, when it became a chartered right, the day for holding it being fixed for Friday; and King James appointed a clerk of the market,* with extensive powers (see the respective charters). In 1672, there appeared to have been four regularly appointed market days, weekly. Friday is now the principal day for holding the market, and the only one in the week on which cattle, grain, poultry, or beef of a choice quality, is to be purchased. Tuesday is considered as a sort of second market day, and generally produces as good, though a less abundant supply of vegetables and fruit as the Friday. There is however seldom a lack on any week-day† of fresh meat (beef excepted), or vegetables. Our friday's market sustains a good name for the quantity, quality, and cheapness of its wares;§ fish, for which there is no particular market day, is generally plenty, and the price very moderate, with the exception of salmon, which is both scarce and (whilst in season) dear; a considerable quantity is caught in the neighbourhood, but the greater part is sent off to Bristol and other places by coach.

* It was clearly never intended that the Mayor should, as is customary, fill this office; can he do it legally? If so, he may also fill that of Town Clerk.

† Nor is this all, each succeeding week presents the "God-dishonoring" spectacle of a SUNDAY market, a practice in favor of which not one solid argument can be advanced, and for the prevention of which the law has devised two separate modes of proceeding; but it is nevertheless publicly carried on in the centre of this populous town, and beneath the very court where four times in the year " His Majesty's royal proclamation for the encouragement of piety and virtue" in which the observance of the sabbath is particularly enjoined, is read. Lest it should be urged that workmen do not receive their wages in time to make their purchases on Saturday nights, (which, were it the case, could not warrant such a breach of the sabbath,) be it known that those at the lace manufactories, much to the credit of their employers, are paid on Thursdays, and that if there are any labourers who do not get their pay until eleven o'clock on Saturday night, the market is then open to them. The existence of the abuses has, I have the best reason to know, been *repeatedly* represented to " the powers that be;" had I an hundred tongues, I would raise them against it. One word more; upwards of two hundred children (the Church School) assemble in a room over the butchers' market, where they are taught to " keep holy the sabbath day," with the example of the buyers and sellers breaking it constantly in view! — What an anomaly!!

§ The vegetable market is held in the open street, as was that for the sale of meat until since the passing of the Improvement Act, in which provision is also made for purchasing a site and laying out a pannier market; but this could only be done by destroying houses, and that at a cost too great to warrant an expectation of its present accomplishment.

A very commodious meat market was opened in 1812. It has thirty-four shops, and extends in a double line from High Street into Anchor Lane.* There is a covered footway on each side, six feet wide, and an ample cart road in the centre. Over the butcher's stalls, is the corn market.

Fairs.– There are five annually appointed marts, properly coming under this appellation, which are held as follows; Friday before third Saturday in March; Friday before April 21; Friday before last Saturday in July; Sept. 19; and the second Friday in December; but four of these being exclusively for the sale of sheep and cattle, and perhaps also from being always held on Fridays, are better known as *Great Markets*; two of them are of long standing, but the others have been but lately set on foot, they are however found very convenient, and the whole are usually well supplied with live stock.

The principal fair, or what is commonly termed *Barnstaple Fair*, is that in September, and is the only one held by grant from the crown; it rests on the same foundation, both as a prescriptive and chartered right, as the Friday's market. It commenced anciently on the 9th July (21st N.S.). I do not find when or why the time for holding it was changed, but it was probably done on the granting of Queen Mary's charter, September being considered perhaps a more convenient time than July. What may be denominated the pleasure fair, or that department appropriated for the sale of trinkets, sweetmeats, &c. now " incident to all fairs," at present held in Cross Street, was " before 34 Eliz. [1591] kept on Quay, corporation found standings."" The ancient privileges* belonging to Saint Mary Magdalen's fair at Barum," are described as follow :–

---

*Traditionally but most ignorantly said to have been so named from *ships having been formerly anchored* there (at nearly the highest point of a walled town). I am indebted for the following very probable definition of the term, to the polite attention of a gentleman residing at a remote part of the county, who, having observed "Anchor Lane" on the plane of the town, writes – " It may possibly have taken its appellation from the cell of an anchorite or hermit near it, perhaps at the corner of the churchyard. Such a spot was often selected for the habitation of a recluse, and the abodes of these idle devotees were generally called *Anchor*-holds."

†These regulations are evidently of ancient date, both by the time specified for the fair to commence, and from the mention of the mayor and commonalty.

" 1st. It shall continue for four days, viz. on the eve and the day of the blessed Mary Magdalen, and the two next days following.

" 2d. The whole soil of Boutport Street, and the other streets within the said Borough, belongs to the Mayor and Comonaltie of the said Borough during the fair, and until 12 o'clock at noon on the day afterwards.

" 3rd. The said Mayor and Comonaltie may set and demise the said soil one day before the eve of the said fair, and have the whole profits of the said fair, and the Bailiffs of the said Borough shall collect and receive the same.

" 4th. Also that they shall there have the 'cognizance of Pleas, and a court of Pie Pondre,* as incident to all fairs."

The usual regulations observed with respect to the continuance of the fair are these, if the 19th† of Sept. be on a Monday, Tuesday, or Wednesday, it finishes on the Saturday night, but if on either of the three subsequent days, it is commonly allowed to continue until Friday in the second week. The first and second days only are devoted to the purpose for which fairs were originally designed, which I scarcely need say was the sale and purchase of staple commodities.

The morning of the first day is well occupied by farmers, graziers, and salesmen, in bargaining for droves of the superior breed of horned cattle, for the production of which the North of Devon is so justly celebrated, and which are driven into Boutport Street§ from the country in every direction, from day break to ten o'clock, by

---

* *Court Pie Poudre,* (*pedis pulverisati,* because fairs being held mostly during the summer, the suitors have dusty feet; or, as others say, because justice is done so speedily, that the dust cannot be wiped from the feet before the decision is given; or, as Barrington says {Anc. Stat, 337} from Pied-pouldreaux, a pedlar,) an ancient court, noticed in several of the statutes, held in fairs, for rendering justice to buyers and sellers, and the redress of grievances arising out of them.– *En. Met. Art. Court.*

†"1588. The fair this year was kept on Monday the ix September, [O.S.] because there should be no buying and selling Sunday."– *Wyot.*

§ So great is the number of cattle frequently exhibited, that this spacious area will not contain them, and they often extend into the adjoining streets, sometimes even into High Street. The following is the only estimate I recollect to have seen of the quantum of business done at this fair:– "Some idea may be formed of the immense number and the proportionate sale, from this circumstance, that of 1,440 bullocks which came into the fair by the northern entrance of the town (over Pilton Bridge), not 300 were driven out by that road, and of those, perhaps more than half were sold. And by a calculation we have just seen, more than 20,000l. was expended in the purchase of cattle." – *North Devon Journal, September 24th,* 1824.

noon or soon after, the business here is usually completed. A considerable quantity of sheep is also penned. In the afternoon a goodly shew of horses and colts is exhibited in an open space at the south end of the North Walk, as is also the case on the following day. The remainder of the fair (as in fact is the whole of it by far the greater part of those who attend it) is spent at best in idle amusement, by too many in rioting and drunkenness. A large portion of the money expended is borne off by the conductors of various travelling exhibitions, which by attracting the gaze of the fair-going-folk, usually succeed in obtaining some of their cash.

It is generally regretted that a clause was not inserted in the Act passed in 1811, for improving the town, &c. to have fixed the commencement of the fair on the Wednesday before or after the 19th of September, and limiting its continuance to the Saturday following; but whilst those to whom it belongs to keep it within its prescribed limits, and who have not in fact the power to extend it beyond the charter-days, join in this complaint, the fair is notwithstanding suffered to extend in some instances over twice the period of time allotted for it.

BANKING HOUSES.*

There are two of these valuable auxiliaries to commerce in Barnstaple.

The Barnstaple Bank takes precedence in order to time. It was established in 1791, under the firm of Cutcliffe, Roch, and Gribble; now Drake, Gribble and Marshal.—London agents, Sir James Esdaile and Company, Lombard Street.

The North Devon Bank was set on foot in 1807; the orginal firm was Bury, Nott, Pyke, Scott, Law, and Tardrew; since altered to Pyke, Law, and Bencraft.—London agents, Barclay, Tritton, and Company, Lombard Street.

---

* This article should have followed that of "Commerce" and was so intended, but inadvertently omitted.

Both these establishments have proved themselves worthy of the public confidence. Amidst the many shocks that within the past twenty years have so rudely assailed the whole commercial world, and laid prostrate many of the most extensive banking concerns in the three kingdoms, the Barnstaple Banks have remained unmoved. They have been tried indeed, but never found wanting, and each succeeding trial has but rendered them more stable in the estimation of all within the sphere of their influence.

NORTH DEVON INFIRMARY.

An edifice
By mercy and benevolence upreared,
To lessen human misery. Here disease
Meets with a timely check, and rosy health
Again revisits the late pallid cheek.
Or if, spite of all human aid, stern death
Demand his victim; pity watches o'er
The humble sufferer, calms his agony,
And smooths the rugged passage to the tomb.

All that is necessary to be said relative to the first establishment of this truly benevolent institution, is comprised in the following copy of an inscription which was written on parchment, and inclosed in a glass bottle, which, after being hermeticaly sealed, was deposited along with various gold, silver, and copper coins of the reign of George IV, beneath the foundation stone of the building.

" NORTH DEVON INFIRMARY, BARNSTAPLE. This Institution was established in the year 1824, by voluntary contributions, and the foundation stone laid on the 5th day of January, 1825, by HUGH EARL FORTESCUE projector and principal contributor.—John Shapland, of Barnstaple, architect.

" —When the donations amounted to 2,000*l*. and the annual subscriptions to 400*l*. the subscribers considered that the surest means of perpetuating so laudable an undertaking, would be the "erection of a small building, containing 20 beds, but capable of future additions and improvements; the present building 68 feet in length, and 30 in breadth, with a basement and two upper stories, was thereforedetermined upon; but previous to its erection, Sir John Davie, Bart., bequeathed a legacy of 500*l*., in consequence of which, an additional or attic story was directed to be built, for the purpose of being furnished when the increased funds of the establishment may permit, which, from the liberal means already afforded, may be expected soon to be accomplished. And it is hoped, that an institution calculated to be so eminently beneficial to society, may meet from succeeding generations, the same fostering care with which it has been so promptly and humanely established. The land on which the building is erected, containing three-quarters of an acre, was purchased of George Acland Barbor, Esq. and conveyed to the Right Honorable Earl Fortescue and his heirs, in trust for the use and benefit of the institution." The following abbreviations of the report made at the last annual meeting of the governors and subscribers, held August 31, 1830, exhibits a statement of the number of persons who have participated in the benefits dispensed form this fountain of benevolence to the suffering sons of humanity, from its commencement, as well as of the receipts and expenditure of the institution

		In patients	Out Patients
Admitted during the past year	. .	201	134
From commencement of the Institution	.	724	514
of whom were			
Discharged, cured . . .	.	418	306
" relieved . .	.	208	170
" incurable . .	.	29	3
" at their own request .	.	10	
" for misconduct . .	.	9	
" Left clandestinely .	.	2	
" Died . . .	.	9	
" Remain on the books .	.	30	24

The receipts for the past year were 698*l*.; and the expenditure 742*l*. 11*s*. 6*d*. The present stock consists of

	£	s.	d.
New 4 per cents . . .	856	12	9
Poll Deeds	650	0	0
Two Ditto received as donations .	50	0	0
	£1556	12	9

DR.

	£	s.	d.
Benefactions and Subscriptions . .	6784	7	6
Proceeds of Bazaars . . .	421	17	1
Dividents and Interest . . .	131	5	0
Balance due to the Treasurers . .	124	5	11
	£7461	15	6

CR.

	£	s.	d.
Ground, Enclosure, and Building . .	2607	17	6
Furniture	546	19	11
Invested in Poll Deeds . . .	650	0	0
In the New 4 per cts. 856*l*. 12*s*. 6*d*. cost .	887	11	10
Expenses of the general establishment for four years	2770	6	3
	£7461	15	6

Two noble and eminently successful attempts have been made to assist the funds of the institution by means of bazaars. The first was held at the Rooms on the 4th of January, 1828, and produced, including what was received for admittance, 345*l*. 19*s*. 6*d*., which, with the proceeds of one at Bideford, made up the above sum.

The lst took place January 12th, 1831, when the sale alone realized 577*l*. 10*s* 7*d*.— A *petit* theatrical exhibition in a room adjoining the bazaar, 40*l*. 7*s*. 6*d*.— Admission money, 31*l*. 1*s*.— Two donations, 15*l*.— making a grand total of 663*l*. 19*s*. 1*d*

A sermon is preached annually in January, for the benefit of the charity, which usually produces 50*l.* or 60*l.* Discourses are also occasionally delivered for the same benevolent purpose at the Independent and Methodist Chapels.

A wing erected at the west end of the building has just been completed. It has a frontage of 25½ feet, and is 39½ feet in depth; it contains, besides the basement story, three wards, each having room for 14 beds, which with the original building renders the infirmary sufficiently capacious for the accommodation of nearly eighty patients. A second wing will, no doubt, be erected as soon as the funds may render such a measure practicable.

The first patient who died in the infirmary, was William Zachary, a foreigner; who was, in compliance with his own request, interred in the burial ground belonging to the Baptist Chapel, in September, 1826.

GUILDHALL

Few towns probably possess a building worse adapted for the transacting of judicial business than our late Guildhall,* or one better suited for the purpose than the present; it is erected over the entrance to the butcher's market. The Court or Hall, into which there are three separate doors of entrance, is 49 feet in length, by 28½ feet in width, and 19½ high. In front of the bench (which is at a good elevation from the floor) is a capacious table for the town-clerk, solicitors, and others having business to transact; beyond which are boxes for the prisoners and witnesses, and between these another for the petty jury; at the end of the room are rising seats for the accommodation of persons without the inclosed space, of which the jury box is the boundary. Within the barrier there are seats on each side, and immediately over head two galleries, one appropriated to ladies, and the other for the use of the grand jury. On the same floor with the hall is the council room, 23 feet by 18, and over this two jury rooms.

* Pulled down and the materials sold by auction in April 1827.

The Guildhall was first used at the election of 1826, at which time it was in an unfinished state. The first court held in it, was that of the michaelmas sessions following, on which occasion the important measure of holding the sessions for the future four times in the year instead of twice, was finally determined.

The front, which is in the grecian stile, is handsome, but the effect which it ought to have is almost wholly lost, from, the building having been erected in a line with the adjoining ones. Had it been set back 10 or 15 feets from the street, it would have been a great ornament to the town; situate as it is, it may be passed by strangers without anything more being seen that the market gates; or, should an eye perchance be turned upwards, it will be rather wearied than gratified; the building being lofty, and the street comparatively narrow.

PRISON AND BRIDEWELL

The following extracts from the letter mentioned in the preface as having led to the publication of this work, will shew what the *old prison* was.

" The rooms or cells constituting the jail, are two; one facing the street, which measures 14 feet-8 inches, by 9 feet-9 inches, and is 7 feet-4 inches high; the other (the entrance to which is through the first) looking into a small courtlage, and measuring 11 feet-8 inches, by 10 feet-8 inches, and 7 feet-2 inches high. In these rooms must all who are committed for criminal offences be confined, and eight persons have been placed in them at one time, (four in each room) there to eat, drink, and sleep, and perform the offices of nature. Should one prisoner prove refractory, here he must be left to corrupt the rest by his example; or another be diseased, he must remain to spread contagion among his fellows. Both these cases have occurred.

" The bridewell, as it is termed, consists of one under-room at the back of the felon's prison, and two rooms over.

" The only accommodation for debtors, is an upstair room, with one bed. In this three persons have been confined together.

" So totally unfit are these premises for the purposes of a jail, that prisoners, how much soever they may require it, cannot, consistent with their safe custody, be permitted to breathe the fresh air unless strictly watched.

" Whenever the jailor has occasion to enter the inner cell, as he has sometimes been obliged to do at night, when there have been eight in confinement, what security (locked up as he must necessarily be with such a number of felons) has he, either for his own life or for the safe custody of his prisoners, in the event (not a very improbable one) of their being determined to escape?

" The present jailor has, twice since his appointment, journied to London, in charge of insolvent debtors. Who, it will be asked, was intrusted with the care of the prison and its inmates during his absence? — a female! Being unable at one and the same time to discharge two such important but opposite parts of his duty, as that of being abroad with one prisoner and at home with the rest, and having no assistant allowed him, he was obliged on these occasions to leave the prison, prisoners, and all, in the hands of a sister."

It was now no longer a question whether or not a new prison must be provided, but there was a very important thing to be determined, namely, who should build it, the corporation or the parish. It was generally believed that the point couldonly be decided by an appeal to the law; but whilst both parties were apparently preparing for the contest, the corporation proposed referring the matter to the recorder, which the parishioners, bearing in mind that even a victory gained by law is sometimes dearly purchased, agreed to, and the sum of 500*l.* was awarded to be paid by them to the corporate body, who on their parts were to give the parish, as was understood, a release *from all liability to any future charge on account of the prison.* The bond being executed and the money paid, the parishioners considered they had done all that was required of them; but not so; no sooner was the building erected than they were called upon to provide furniture for it, and which, no provision having been made to the contrary in the deed executed by the corporation, they w ere obliged to do.

The *present prison* is certainly an excellent one; it was

commenced in February, 1828, and completed in September, 1829. The front is of wrought stone. Towards the street are separate and convenient apartments for the prison keeper and an under jailor; behind these is a courtlage in which, besides domestic offices, is the constables' prison. A long passage opening into this court, leads to the different apartments. There are seven cells on the ground floor, appropriated as the jail, varying in dimensions from 8 by 9, to 9 by 10 feet square, and seven of similar proportions immediately over them, used as a *bridewell*; there are two excellent day rooms to each department of about 12 feet by 19 feet. There is also a debtor's day room. 11 feet by 17 feet, and night room somewhat larger. The prison yard, across which there is a division, is as airy as the site would admit of, and bounded (in those directions in which it is not enclosed by buildings) by a wall 20 feet high.

THEATRE

This building, although situate almost close to High Street, is completely shut out from public view. It was built about fifty or sixty years since, and is calculated to contain about 350 spectators. The house is always opened at the commencement of the fair, during which there is a performance nightly, and afterwards three times a week, until christmas, when it closes. Even in this short season, the theatre not unfrequently exhibits " a beggarly account of empty benches;" the concern must be far from a profitable one. Kean, since so celebrated in histrionic annals, performed here not long before he made his boo to a London audience.

THE ASSEMBLY ROOMS

Were erected in 1800, by subscription of thirty-five shares, at 30*l*. afterwards increased to 35*l*., and now worth about 40*l*. each; no return has ever been made to the proprietors on account of their shares, but whatever profit has accrued, has been expended in improvements. The building was newly fronted and otherwise altered in 1827.

The establishment comprises a lofty and handsomely decorated ball room, 27 feet by 47 feet, lighted by three cut glass chandeliers, two card rooms, billiard room, news room, supplied with two London daily papers, and three provincial journals, army and navy list; dressing and cloak rooms. There is a monthly winter assembly from September to March. A ball is also regularly held during the fair, which is fully and very respectably attended, and by far the gayest for the year; and one usually at Christmas. I have already stated that it is customary to have an election ball.* There are three card clubs held here weekly; one on Mondays, and another on Fridays, for gentlemen; and one on Thursdays for ladies. Here also public concerts, exhibitions of art, &c. are usually held.

FREEMASONS.

A lodge belonging to this fraternity, and termed *The Loyal Lodge*, No. 469, was established here in September,1783. Up to Christmas, 1828, it was held at the King's Arms Inn, but was then removed to a room in Cross Street, now denominated Freemason's Hall. In April, 1829, the first "Provincial Grand Lodge" was held here, on which occasion Viscount Ebrington, as "Provincial Grand Master," presided. The lodge had at this time thirty members. There is a considerable number of freemasons in the town and neighbourhood, who have not joined the lodge.

BARNSTAPLE MECHANICS' INSTITUTE, FOR THE DIFFUSION OF USEFUL KNOWLEDGE

" The schoolmaster is abroad," said the present highly-gifted Lord Chancellor (Brougham) some time since in the House of Commons; he is indeed, and is making progress too! British mechanics are now almost with one accord pressing forward for admission into the temple of Minerva, and are not only themselves drinking at the

*I am truly happy in having to record that "the ephemera of an evening" was not at the last election, (Aug. 1830) preferred to a more substantial good; there was no "election ball," but 200*l*. was given in lieu of it, to be expended in improving the town.

fountain of knowledge, but are opening new channels for the fructifying streams which issue from it.

The above society was formed October 19th, 1830, and now consists of 163 members; it has already a library of 148 volumes, and supports a reading room, which is supplied with two daily London papers, one weekly provincial journal, and four periodicals; others will doubtless soon be added, but it must be remembered that as yet the institution is an infant but of four months' growth. Both the terms of admission and the weekly subscription are very moderate; the former 2*s*. 6*d*., the latter 2*d*. Lectures are generally given weekly, on Tuesday evenings, and many very acceptable ones have been delivered, some of them by individuals who, but for the calling forth of their latent energies through the medium of this institution, might have never risen higher than calculators of pounds, shillings, and pence.—*Hail! to the Mechanic's Institute of Barnstaple!*

ANNUITANT SOCIETIES

for the benefit of widows. Of these there are two in the town. The first in order of time is The Barnstaple Annuitant Society, the affairs of which at the last annual meeting in May, 1830, stood thus –: 53 members paying 2*l*. 2*s*. per annum each.– 32 annuitants receiving 8*l*. each.– 3 ditto, 6*l*. each.– Stock in funds, new 4 per cents., 5,339*l*. 15*s*. 2*d*.– Cash, 68*l*. 5*s*.

The Barnstaple Second Annuitant Society, had at its last annual meeting in May, 1830,– 121 members paying 2*l*. 2*s*. per annum each.– 9 annuitants receiving 20*l*. each.– 5 ditto, 15*l*. each.– 2 ditto, 10*l*. each.– Money on mortgage at 4 per cent., 6,200*l*.– Stock in new 4 per cents., 550–.– Cash, 231*l*. 17*s*. 10*d*.

BENEFIT CLUBS

There are said to be ten or a dozen of those laudable associations in the town, but I am only furnished with particulars of the six which follows :–

Loyal Union Society, established about 1780; funds, 1400*l.*; number of members,74; contributions, 1*s.* 1*d.* monthly, and 1*s.* 3*d.* on the death of a member; benefit, 5*s.* per week walking pay, 10*s.* per week bed pay; 8*l.* 8*s.* per annum at 70 years of age; 10*l.* at 75; and 3*l.* 10*s.* to be received by surviving relatives after death, in addition to the 1*s.* 3*d.* each member.*

New and Civil Society, established 1814; fund, 300*l.*; number of members, 104; monthly contributions, 1*s.*; benefit, 4*s.* per week walking pay, 8*s.* per week bed pay.

Laudable and Humane Society, established 1817; number of members, 205; contributions, 1*s.* each on the decease of a member.

New Friendly Society, established 1818; funds 600*l.*; number of members 70; monthly contribution, 1*s.* 2*d.*; benefit, 5*s.* per week walking pay, 10*s.* per week bed pay; at 65 years of age, 8*l.* 8*s.*, and at 75, 10*l.* 0*s.* per annum.

New Union and Friendly Society, established 1824; fund, 180*l.*; number of members, 44; monthly contributions, 1*s.* 2*d.*; benefit 5*s.* per week walking pay, 10*s.* per week bed pay.

Friend of Old Age Society, established 1826; fund, 98*l.*; number of members, 56; contributions, 1*s.* monthly, and 1*s.* on the death of a member; benefit, 4*s* per week walking pay, 8*s.* per week bed pay; 2*l.* 10*s.* from the stock, to be paid to representatives after death, in addition to the 1*s.* from each member.

FRIENDLY INSTITUTION AND SAVINGS' BANK

I am unable to furnish any statement of the number of persons who have availed themselves of the benefits offered by either of these institutions, or of the amount contributed to the one, or deposited in the other. By a printed prospectus of the :

" *North Devon Friendly Institution*, for the benefit of the working classes," I find that it was established at Barnstaple April 15th, 1825, and extends to persons male and female being of good character and sound health, between the ages of 10 and 50, and living

---

*This society having existed upwards of fifty years, and being, after paying all demands upon it, in possession of a fund of 1,400*l.*, it may not be amiss to compare the contributions made by its members, and the benefits to be received, with those in class 6 of the Friendly Institution.

within the hundreds of Braunton, Sherwell, Fremington, South-Molton, Hartland, Shebbear, North Tawton, Witheridge, Winkleigh, and Black Torrington," who may, according to their contributions, receive pecuniary benefits, varying in degree from " 2s. per week bed-lying pay, 1s. per week walking pay, a weekly allowance of 1s. after the age of 65, and 2l. on death;" (class 1;) to " 20s. per week bed-lying pay, 10s. per week walking pay, an allowance of 10s. per per week after 65, and 20l. on death." (Class 10.) Office in one of the wings of Litchdon almshouse. Attendance on Fridays from 12 to 2 o'clock.

The Savings' Bank, is a branch of that established at Exeter, December, 1814, under the name of " The Devon and Exeter Savings' Bank." * Attendance is given at the same office as that where the business of the Friendly Institution is conducted, every Wednesday and Friday.

ROADS AND WALKS

Loud and just were the complaints made only a few years back of Devonshire hills and Devonshire roads; but this reproach is no longer cast upon us, or at least is not any longer deserved. Our *hills*, it is true, still retain their places, and we would not have it be otherwise if we could; they are the pride of our county, the boast of its inhabitants, and the admiration of travellers; but our *roads* no longer top them as they did, and the verdant mountains with which Devonshire abounds, may now be surveyed without the labour of climbing, or the risk of descending " frightful precipieces." It is not of course meant to be asserted that this is the case throughout the North of Devon, but it may with propriety be said, as it respects the neighbourhood of Barnstaple. Our roads were first made *turnpike* by Act 3, Geo. III. chap. 35, the which no doubt caused a great alteration for the better; but nearly all the principal improvements that have taken place, have been effected during the last twelve years.

* By the last report of this institution, it appears that in 14 years the number of accounts opened has been 31,285, and of deposits made 114,513l. Whole amount deposited 1,262,996l. 15s. 7d.

It is foreign to my purpose to go over these in detail, but we shall presently have practical evidence of what our roads now are, under the article " Coaches."

The new roads lately made require of course to be noticed. That to Ilfracombe, completed in 1829, distance 10 miles 6 furlongs 21 poles, though perhaps scarcely a mile of it is perfectly level, the inclination throughout is so trifling, as to be scarcely perceptible to a pedestrian. The prospect for the greater part of the way is very confined, but the road is on the whole picturesque, and the scenery for the last two or three miles is enchanting. The Exeter road just completed, the line of which is wholly new from Fishley to Crediton, is said to be nearly an entire level for the whole of that distance, so that we have now in lieu of a road composed almost wholly of steep hills, scarcely one worth noticing betwixt Barnstaple and Exeter, excepting those beyond Crediton. The road is under the trustees of the Barnstaple turnpike as far as Eggesford, the remainder belongs to the Exeter trust.

The formation of these roads, the Ilfracombe and the Eggesford, but particularly the first, has caused an enormous outlay, and including about 7,000*l*. previously due to poll deeds, placed a millstone about the neck of the trust, in the shape of debt (up to October 1830) of 36,880*l*. 15*s*. 4*d*.* The extent of road under their direction is 85 miles.

The Braunton road has already been alluded to, it is an acquisition to Barnstaple,† as well as to numerous parishes to the west of the town.

Walks, and charming ones too, may be found in almost every direction, as may be naturally looked for about a town " pleasantly and sweetly situate as it is, upon a river amidst verdant hills."

* On upwards of 27,000*l*. of this sum, five per cent. interest is stipulated to be paid. Ought such an engagement to have been entered into? and can it, even with the tolls, as is the case at present, at the maximum, be fulfilled?

† The road is convenient, and the entrance to it might have been ornamental, but from the bridge having been injudiciously placed in a situation different from that at first determined on, and owing to the crabbedness of an individual in erecting a building so as directly to interfere both with the view of the bridge and the approach to it, the fine effect which the road and bridge would have had from High Street is completely spoiled; thus sometimes do persons under the influence of petty private feeling, with a ruthless hand mar public improvement. It is to be hoped that this encroachment at least will be removed, if the other be allowed to stand; possibly the removal of one may be the preservation of the other.

The North Walk, a sketch of which is given in the plan of the town, is a promenade which "take it for all in all," with its lofty and umbrageous trees, the river rippling around it, sometimes to its very edge, and forming when at the full an extensive lake; the exhilarating breeze from the tide, and the convenient access to it from the different streets of the town, "we shall not look upon its like again" throughout the kingdom.

It was commenced in 1759, when four or at most six trees were planted, since which additions have been made to it at various times, until it has reached its present extent of two furlongs; the last alteration was effected in 1812.

Four of the first-planted and finest trees were felled about twelve months since, by the corporation, for the purpose of facilitating the approach to the Braunton road. They were, however, scarcely cut down, before the building just now alluded to was erected, by which the removal of two of them at least was rendered nugatory.

The Banks present in fine weather a tempting walk of more than two miles in length, the whole extent of which is by the river side. The scenery they afford is pleasingly varied; the one commanding the windings of the Taw through the rich vale of Tawton, disclosing fresh beauties every step we advance, and leading to the finely wooded grounds of Tawstock Court; the other coming full on the river, with the broad sweep which it takes just below the town, and its course for some miles onward, affording a prospect at once delightful, and which never palls upon the eye. A flowing tide is one of the few objects in nature which, though we saw it yesterday, we can watch to-day, and could gaze upon to-morrow, without satiety. Attractive land scenery is, however, not wanting; the eye in search of the picturesque will find many an inviting spot on which to repose, (amongst which Upcot House is beautifully prominent,) scattered over the side of the bold ridge that with a majestic curve appears to enclose the river.

WATER WORKS.

Barnstaple, as I have observed elsewhere, is abundantly supplied with hard water, and soft water is furnished from a branch of the Yeo, which is taken in near Rawleigh mills, and conveyed to the town in pipes, originally of wood, but which as they decay have their places supplied by leaden ones. The first grant made for this purpose, was by " the Mayor, Aldermen, and Burgesses, of the borough and parish of Barnstaple, to Ambrose Crowley, Edward Dyson, Daniel Dennell, and Richard Loubridge," by which they were empowered, in consideration of a nominal rent of one shilling per annum, to erect engines, lay down pipes, &c. &c. for the purpose of supplying the town with water. A lease for 300 years was subsequently obtained by the company, from the proprietor of the land at Rawleigh, of a right to take water from the stream above-mentioned, at a yearly rent of 4*l.* (or thereabout). The water works are now in the hands of five proprietors; any individual may have the water brought to their houses, on payment of a yearly rent, varying in amount according to the circumstances, but averaging about 18*s.* per annum. A reservoir, erected most probably when the company was first set on foot, stood in Boutport Street, facing Joy Street, until about forty years ago.

INNS, COACHES, WAGGONS AND VANS

The principal Inns are the Golden Lion and Fortescue Arms; both are comparatively of modern date, the former having been established about seventy, and the latter about fifty years. What were formerly the chief houses of accommodation for travellers, have had their day, and long since become private dwellings; the present inns no doubt owe the patronage they have obtained to the advantageous situations they occupy, being near the entrance to the town from the London road and close to the principal street. It singularly happens that these houses are situated close to each other. To draw any comparison between them would be invidious, they are both good, and highly respectable. The Golden Lion is mentioned by some (modern) writers to have been a "town house of the Earl of Bath," but there is no evidence in proof of such a supposition. Wyot, who often speaks of this nobleman, alludes to no residence but that of Tawstock House, which being but two miles distant, it certainly does not seem probable that his lordship kept a house here.

Coaches.– Twenty-six years ago (and I believe long since, but I speak of 1805 from my own knowledge) the stage coach which then ran three times a week, was fourteen hours on the journey from hence to Taunton, where passengers either for London or Bristol had to stay the night; those for the latter city arrived at their destination at eight o'clock on the following evening, thus occupying thirty-eight hours in the journey; and those for the former at five o'clock on the third day, having been fifty-nine hours on the road.

A coach goes from hence still on the same establishment, (but, like the roads, under a somewhat *improved* system,) which reaches Taunton in eight hours, and London in thirty. This is, however, far outdone by the mail coach, which runs to Taunton (on the new road through Bampton and Wiveliscombe) in five hours, to Bristol in eleven, and to London (via Bristol, a distance of nearly 220 miles) in twenty-four hours, stoppages included.

Royal Mail to Taunton, Bristol, Bath, and London every morning at 6; and

Royal Mail to Ilfracombe, every morning at 7;– from Fortescue Arms.

North Devon Telegraph to Tiverton, (with a branch coach to Exeter,) Taunton, Salisbury, and London, every morning, sunday excepted, at half-past 7; and

North Devon Telegraph to Plymouth, Monday, Wednesday, and Friday mornings, at half-past 7;– from Golden Lion.

Waggons and Vans.– Taunton, Bristol, Oxford, and London Fly Waggon, Wednesday and Saturday mornings, at 9;

Van, to the same places and on the same days, at 4 in the morning;

A Light Waggon to Exeter, (Rice's) Monday and Thursday, at 3 in the afternoon;

A Light Waggon to Plymouth, Tuesday morning at eight, and Saturday evening at 4;– from Bell Inn.

A Light Waggon to Stratton and Bude, Tuesday at 12 o'clock;– from Angel Inn.

A Fly Waggon to Exeter, every afternoon, Sunday excepted, at 2 o'clock,– from Seldon's Warehouse, Joy Street.

Besides the above, there are conveyances daily to Bideford, Ilfracombe, Southmolton, and Braunton; three times a week to Torrington and Linton; and twice a week to Chulmleigh.

I must not however, omit, as I had nearly done, mention of the facilities offered for *Water Carriage*. There are to and from this port and London, four regular traders, one of which sails from Griffin's Wharf, London, every 21 days. On the Bristol trade there are five constant traders, of which one sails from the Barnstaple Slip, Broad Quay, every 14 days. There is also considerable mercantile intercourse with Liverpool, but there are no regularly appointed vessels.

There are stated freights for goods from each of these ports, those from London being double the Bristol rate, and from Liverpool one half more than Bristol.

Vessels are constantly trading from hence to different parts of Wales, but without any fixed rule, or period for sailing.

On looking round I find I have yet an omission* to supply, and one too of some importance.

---

* Gentle reader! I crave pardon for this and what others you may discover ; (for you will doubtless find more, and so perhaps shall I, when too late.) afford credence to my plea, — that it is no light thing to prepare and carry through the press a work of this multifarious nature.

POST OFFICE†

Arrival and Departure of the Mails.— Eastern, embracing the whole kingdom, Cornwall, and the greater part of Devon excepted, arrives at half-past 8 evening, and leaves at 6 morning.— Western, including Bideford, Torrington, Exeter, Plymouth, and Cornwall, comes in at 10 morning, and goes out at quarter past 3 afternoon.— Bideford, with bags for eastern mail, comes in at half-past 12 morning, and departs immediately after arrival of London mail.— Ilfracombe, arrives at quarter before eight evening, leaves at 7 morning.— Linton, comes in Tuesday, Thursday, and Saturday, at 10 morning, goes out same days at 3 afternoon.

Delivery of Letters.— Office open in winter from 8, and in summer from 7 morning, until 11 at night, except Sunday, when it is closed during divine service from 11 to 1 and from 3 to 5.— Eastern delivery commences within forty-minutes of the arrival of the mail, *at the office only.*—Letter carrier goes out at 7 morning in summer, and at 8 in winter.— Western delivery commences at half-past 10 morning.

Time by which letters must be put in.— Eastern and Ilfracombe before 10 at night, or on payment of 2*d.* until 11, when the bags are made up.— Western, at a quarter before 3 afternoon, or until quarter past 3 by paying 1*d.*

---

† Fifty years ago, Barnstaple had a post only every other day, and but twenty-five years since letters were dispatched to Ilfracombe only thrice a week.

So late as 1819 (I state this on the best authority) the letters and newspapers received at our office were in number only *one half what the papers now amount to alone.* Which of the three following causes has the largest share in producing this effect — the increase of population, improvement incommerce, or the march of knowledge? We have heard a good deal of late respecting sinecures, but it is plain the appointment of Postmistress of Barnstaple is not one. The office delivery extends to 37 parishes.

APPENDIX TO CHAPTER VI.

[A.]

Statement of Goods imported into Barnstaple, in 1727-8

IRELAND.— *Cork, Waterford, Dublin, Ross, Bantry.*—
1.101 bags, or 24,473 "great stones" wool. 11 hhds., 25 casks tallow. 4
packs, 2 bundles, 12 pieces linen, Irish manufacture. 2,497 bars iron
(Spanish). 21 cwt. ditto. 9 bundles rod ditto. 49 bags glue. 200 Norway
deals. 3 casks runnet. Various quantities of provisions for exportation to
America and Newfoundland.

SPAIN.— *St. Luca, Cadiz, Bilboa.*— 84 pipes, 18 hhds. wine, 49 pipes
olive oil. 3 hhds., 65 barrels, raisins. 19 chests, 12 half chests, oranges and
lemons. 2,300 bushels, 8 lasts, salt. 26 jars olives. 224 bundles canes. 1030
bars, 1,318 double ditto iron. 2 "parcels" liquorice stick. 13 bags walnuts.
1 parcel chesnuts in bulk. 23 cakes rozin. 60 doz. wisps.

FRANCE.— *Alaronde de Berge, Crozick, Brest, Poulliguen, Miskey,
Roan, Alloon de Bardges.*— 9½ charges, 99 mews, 2,840 bushels, salt. 29
hhds. wine. 7 hhds. brandy. 8 casks vinegar. 2 pieces dowlas. 200 burrs.
376 cwt. plaister paris. 1⅔ mount of ditto.

PORTUGAL.— *Lisbon, Oporto, Viana.* — 56 butts, 41½ hhds. wine. 2
m——, 693 moy, 685 bushels, salt. 32 baskets broadfigs. 93 ditto raisins.
115 chests, 77 half chests, 48 boxes, lemons and oranges, and sundry
parcels ditto, in bulk. 18 baskets sugar. 298 bundles "canes (vocal reeds)."
21 cwt., 6 bundles, 1 parcel, cork. 67 pipes oliv oil. 133 bags shomack. 17
chests tallow. 1 bag chesnuts.

ITALY.– *Leghorn.*– 8 tons brimstone, 14 pipes, 1 hhd., olive oil. 10½ jars
sallad ditto. 4 hhds. capers. 1 hhd. almonds. 1 chest, 19 half chests,
Florence wine. 10 barrels anchovies. 2 chests alabaster flower pots. 20
marble figures.

NORWAY.—*Ester Risey.*—2,019 deals. 30 middle balks. 52 spars. 3 dozen
trays. 13½ dozen handspikes. 36 oak boards. 117 spruce deals. 12 white
boards. 12 doz. boat scoops.

NEWFOUNDLAND.—7 pipes, 25 puncheons, 199 hhds., 78 barrels, train
oil. 11 barrels corr fish. Sundry "parcels" dry fish. 3 caggs sounds. 6,000
feet pine board. 922 feet ditto plank. 4,700 barrel staves. 800 hogshead
ditto.

AMERICA.— *South Potomack, Pistaque, Charlestown, Maryland, Boston.* —297 hhds. tobacco. 18 great masts. 18 small and middle ditto. 3,324 pine boards. 90 oaken planks. 20,825 barrel staves. 6,500 hogshead ditto. 5150 pipe staves. 410 barrels pitch. 293 ditto tar. 161 ditto train oil. 2 ditto turpentine. 109 ditto rice. 3 ditto deer skins. Sundry spars, oar rafters, &c.

[B.]

Copies of Treasury Warrants for the Bonding of Goods in the Port of Barnstaple.

" After our hearty commendations.— Having considered your report of the 21st February, 1822, on the memorial of sundry merchants of the port of Barnstaple, praying that port may be approved for the bonding of goods in tables B.C. and E. of the warehouseing act of 43 Geo. III., cap. 132. These are, by virtue of the powers vested in us by the said act, to approve of the port of Barnstaple as a bonding port for wine and spirits, enumerated in table B. of the general warehouseing act, whenever it shall be certified by the proper officers, that warehouses and premises have been provided in all respects fit for the reception thereof, in conformity with the established regulations of the said act; for which this shall be your warrant.

" Whitehall Treasury Chambers, the 3rd day of June, 1822.

" Signed   B Paget
G.H. Somerset,
E.A.M. Maughten "

" After our hearty commendations.— Having considered your report of 10th December, 1822, on a letter from Mr. Nolan, requesting that the port of Barnstaple may be approved, for the bonding of rum in table A. of the warehouseing act. These are to approve of the port of Barnstaple, as a warehouseing port for West India rum, in table A. of the warehouseing act, 43 Geo. III., cap. 132; for which this shall be your warrant.

" Whitehall Treasury Chambers, the 30th day of December, 1822.
         Signed   N. VANSITTART,
                         B. PAGET,
                         G.H. SOMERSET.
         " To the Commissioners of His Majesty's Customs."

" After our hearty commendations.— Having considered your report of the 27th August, 1823, on the petition of John Jerrett, praying that the privilege of warehouseing sugars, molasses, and mahogany, in table A., and timber, wood, hemp, and tallow, in table C., of the warehouseing act of the 43rd Geo. III., cap. 132, may be extended to the port of Barnstaple. These are to authorize and require you to approve of the port of Barnstaple, as a warehouseing port for the goods above enumerated, as soon as proper warehouses and yards shall be provided and made fit and secure for the deposit of such goods, in conformity to the established regulations.
         "Whitehall Treasury Chambers, 24th September, 1824.
                 Signed   B. PAGET,
                                 LOWTHER
                         G.H. SOMERSET
                 Commrs. Customs, &c. &c."

" After our hearty commendations. — Having considered your report of the 2nd Instant, on a petition of Messrs. Nickolls and Co., merchants of Barnstaple, praying that the privilege of bonding at that port may be extended to goods in general, except Tobacco; we do hereby approve under the powers vested in us by the 2nd section of the act 6, Geo. IV., cap. 112, of the port of Barnstaple as a warehouseing port, *for all goods except tobacco,** East India goods, and goods enumerated † in table A. of the act* 4, Geo. IV., *cap*.24 (other than sugar,) upon the warehouses being fitted up in all respects according to the established regulations, and under the express condition that *they shall be open to the general accommodation of the trade of the port.*

---

* The importation of this article is by 29 Geo. IV. limited to a few of the large ports, doubtless on account of the high duty it pays. The lst entry in the custom House accounts relative to tobacco is as follows, under the date of April, 1779;- "One hogshead of American tobacco being part of the cargo of the Betsey, Hugh Sherwood, master, a prize taken from the rebellious Americans by Thomas Fillicull, commander of a private ship of war called the Revenge, together with other privateers belonging to the island of Jersey."

†Chiefly drugs and spices.

Whitehall Treasury Chambers, the * day of February, 1828.

Signed   WELLINGTON
                 HENRY GOULBURN
                 ELIOT

Commrs. of Customs.''

[C.]

Specification of merchandize on which duties were paid in the port of Barnstaple, from January 5th, 1830, to January 5th, 1831[†]

Brandy, 1,815 gal.— Wine, 7,050 gal.— Rum, 8,202 gal.— Sugar, 1,301 cwt. 3 qrs. 18 lbs.— Molasses, 29cwt. 1 qr. 25 lbs.— Coffee, 7,850 lbs.— Pimento, 243 lbs.—Raisins, 327 cwt. 2 qrs. 8 lbs.— Currants, 149 cwt. 1 qr. 22 lbs.— Figs, 10cwt. 1 qr. 19 lbs.— Tallow, 379 cwt. 1 qr. 24 lbs.— Wheat, 250 qrs.— Peas, 4 qrs. 1 bush.— Beans, 42 qrs. 2 bush.— Tares, 67 qrs.— Peas, 4 qrs. 1 bush.— Beans, 42qrs. 2 bush.— Tares, 67 qrs.— Rice, 26 cwt. 3 qrs. 16 lbs.— Almonds, 3 cwt. 1 qr. 12 lbs.— Oil, 802 gal.— Grapes, 30 jars.— Oranges and Lemons, 1,418 boxes.— Timber, 1,126 loads, 7 feet.— Coals, 8,297 chaldrons.— Culm, 4,967 chaldrons.

[D.]

Limits of the Port of Barnstaple, and extracts from official documents relative to it from 1739 to 1800.

The port of Barnstaple was, by commission returned into the Court of Exchequer, in Easter Term, 29 Charles II., declared to extend '' from a rock in the sea called Mort Stone, adjoining to the parish of Morthoe, and so westward on the coast to the south end of the bar of Barnstaple, and from thence on the west side of the river to the creek of Appledore, and

---

* Date left blank in the original warrant.

† It must not be understood with respect to groceries, that no more has been imported than is here mentioned. bonding of these articles is as yet done but on a small scale; by far the larger part of the business hitherto transacted in this way has been done in duty-paid goods.

"unto a rock called Whipple Stone or Hubba Stone, in the parish of Northam; and from the north end of the said bar to the pill called Jewill's Pill, beyond the key commonly called the New Key, in the parish of Instow; and likewise from the said bar to the long bridge of Barnstaple, with all the strands, shores, pills, and creeks, on the north and south sides of the river of Barnstaple, and within the said limits."

The last commission from the court of Exchequer took from this port and added to that of Bideford, " that part of the sea coast which adjoins the bounds and limits of the member port of Bideford or Northam Burrows, in an eastern and southern direction, by Northam Burrows, Graysand Hill, and Skirn, to the village of Appledore, on the west side of the river Torridge, including the whole of the said village, with its appendages, and proceeding in a southern course to a large stone lying on the beach on the west side of the river Torridge, called Hubba Stone, where it again adjoins the bounds and limits of the said member port of Bideford; and from Hubba Stone aforesaid to a certain mill house or water mill, situated in Jewill's pill, in the parish of Instow, on the east side of the said river Torridge, being the boundary of the said member port of Bideford, on the east side of the said river; and from thence in a supposed direct line towards the middle of a certain weir in the parish of Braunton, called Ballamy's Weir, (such supposed line being in the direction north north west, according to compass, or thereabouts,) unto the north east end of the anchoring pool, called Appledore Pool; and from the said north east end of the said pool in a direct line towards Graysand Hill, (such line bearing by compass about west ;) and from thence in a winding direction about north west and by west, along the middle of the channel commonly called the North Gut, into the bay called [Barnstaple or] Bideford Bay, including the middle ridge, and all on the west side of the said channel, together with all bays, channels, &c."

1739. No wool or woollen goods to be imported from Ireland, " to any other port of Britain, but to Biddiford, BARNSTAPLE, Minehead, Bridgewater, Bristol, Milford-haven, Chester, and Liverpool."— 12 *Geo.* II., c. 21.

1778. A new act was passed permitting the exportation of limited quantities of corn, &c. for the use of the fisheries at Newfoundland, Nova Scotia, and Labrador, from the following ports, viz. -

	Wheat Flour	Peas.	Biscuit.
	qrs.	*qrs.*	*tuns.*
London . . .	1400	900	850
Bristol . . .	900	800	800
Poole . . .	3200	1300	1400
Topsham and Teignmouth	2400	1200	1100
Dartmouth . .	2450	950	1000
BARNSTAPLE . .	400	150	150
Liverpool . .	300	150	150
Chester . . .	300	120	100
Weymouth . .	200	120	60

1795, May 5. An embargo laid on all British shipping in all the ports of Great Britain, and the owners of all vessels were required " to furnish able bodied men for the navy; one able seaman being accepted as equivalent to two able bodied men, in the following proportions from each port." BARNSTAPLE, 74.—Bideford, 48.— Dartmouth, 394.— Exeter, 186.— Ilfracombe, 49.— Plymouth, 96.— Falmouth, 21.— Fowey, 70.— Gweek, 7.— Padstow, 19.— Penryn, 11.— Penzance, 35.— Saint Ives, 31.— Truro, 11.— &c. &c.

1796. The ports of BARNSTAPLE and Bideford (no others in Devon) were added to the ports previously appointed in the same session, (1795,) for the entry of foreign wheat and other grain, imported for the bounties.

1800, Sept. 30. Number of vessels, with their tunnage, and the men usually employed in navigating them, which belonged to the following ports in Devonshire.

	Vessels.	Tuns.	Men.
	---	---	---
Exeter . .	148	12,372	772
Dartmouth .	209	11,215	1,048
BARNSTAPLE .	73	5,387	326
Bideford .	67	4,659	256
Ilfracombe .	57	2,851	224

" A Table of Dutyes belonging unto the towne of Barnestaple, for Kayage, Hallage, and other Dutyes for Goods exported and imported there, as followeth. "

---

	d.
Wools, the stone cont. 16 lb. sold here is	1
Wools of Ireland, Walles, or Spaine, not sold here but transported to any porte, the bagge is	iiij
Wools viz. Spannish wools, the packet is	ij
Frize of Ireland or Wales, the hundred yards is	ij
Flacks, the stone cont. 16 lb. is	06
Salt hides, the dicker is	iiij
Tanned hides, the dicker is	ij
Lamb folls, the hundred is	ij
Sheeps folls, the hundred is	iiij
Goat skins, the dozen is	1
Hakes wet or drie, the hundred is	1
Newfoundland ffishe, drie, the hundred is	06
Newfoundland ffishe, wett, the hundred is	1
Calf skins, tanned, a dozen is	1
Kersies, the pack is	iiij
Dunsters, the pack is	iiij
Exbourne, every piece is	06
Bridgewater, every piece is	06
Canvass, every ballott is	1
Red or blue cloth, every piece is	06
Broad cloth, every piece is	1
White wares, every pack is	ij
Figgs and reysons, every tonne is	viij
Prunds, every tonne is	viij
Iron, every tonne is	viij
Lead, every tonne is	viij
Oils, vinegar, trayne, honey, syder, pilshards, herrings, gunger, barrel fish and beiff, per tonne	viij
Tallowe, the stone, in great or smalle casske or cake is	q3[3/4]
Candles, the stone cont 16 lb. is	q3
Kayage of eve3ry pack of cloth is	iiij
Kayage of every tonne of liquid comodityes is	viiij
Keellage of every barque is	iiij
Molton whites, every pack is	iiij
Hempe comb'd or uncomb'd, every stone is	05

" Helling stones, the thousand is 06
Hops, the bagg cont. the hundred is 1
Millstones, per piece is . . . . . . viiij
Tobacco, the hundred weight is 1
Ashes, the tonne is . . . . iiij
Weeds, viz. Welsh weeds, the hundred stone cont.16 lb. the stone is . xii
Mader the balls, viz. greate balls, is xii
Sugar, the cheste is vi
Woade, the tonne is . . . . iiij
Salte, the tonne is . . . . iiij
Corne, the tonne is . . . . iiij
Sythe, the dozen is 1
Brazall wood of all sorts by sea or land, &C. is . . . 06
Butter, the kilterkynne, except sold in the markett by retayle is . 1
Butter, the barroll, except as aforesaid, is ii
Hogshead staves, the thousand is . . . . viij
Barrol stages, the thousand is xii
Deal borads, the hundred cont. 120 boards is . . . vi
Millstones, kayage and cranage is viii
Tarr, the barrell is 1
Battery, brasse pottes, and belle mettell, the cwt is . . 1
Steel, the faggott is 1
Cable yarne, the tonne is viii
Pitch, in casks or barrols is 1
Feathers, the hundred wt. is . . . . . . ij
Grinding stones, flat stones, and free stones, pr tonne . . iiij
Paper, every balle is . . . . ij
Glass, every case is 1
White leather, the hundred is . . . . . ij
Lead oare, the tonne is . . . . iiij
Card boards, the pack is . . . . iiij
All other goods not mentioned in this table are
     to pay tonnage, 8d. per tonne . . . . viij
All goods of high value, as silks of all sorts, and
     spinces of all sorts, for every 20s. worth is . . . 1
Indico, for every xx worth is 1
All little small parsells or small drafts of wool, to pay
     after 2d. the score is 2

" HENRY DRAKE, Maior,
JOHN FAIRCHILD, Alderman,
WM. WESTCOMBE, Alderman."

[F.]

Rental of Lands belonging to the Feoffees of the Long Bridge, commonly called Bridge Lands.*

LESSEE OR TENANT	PROPERTY	RENT		TERM ENDS.	
		l.	*s.*		
Grace Shapcott	House at Bridge end				
E.R. Roberts	Small house on Bridge	2	0		
Corporation	Ground whereon a house stood†	4	0		
E. Harris	House in High Street	46	0		
William Thorn	House in High Street	3	8	Michs.	1841
John Gill	House in High Street	12	12	Lady-day.	1847
Francis Berry	House and Garden Boutport Street				1886
C.E. Palmer	House ditto	40	40	Terms of	
N. Glass, jun	House ditto	30	0	7, 11 or 14	
Geo. Kingson	House ditto	30	0	yrs from	1825
Corporation	House ditto	4	4	Lady-day.	1845
Thomas Lewis	Part of Fortescue Arms	20	0	Lady-day.	1884
—— Thorne	House in Bear Street	1	15	Lady-day.	1801
John Martin	Ditto	2	2	Lady-day,	1860
Wm. Howard	Ditto	5	0	Yearly Tenant	
William Harris	House	6	0	Ditto	
John Pyke	Stable and Garden	1	0	Michs.	1847
J.M. Hardin	House in Holland Street	2	10	Michs.	1846
Wm. Galliford	House and Garden, Holland Street			Yearly Tenant	

* This document was drawn out, up to 1815, by an individual now deceased, who, from the situation he filled, possessed the means of doing it correctly. Holding, as I do, all such statements of *public property to be the property of the public*, I resolved that they should have it. It was of course, necessary to make alterations where leases had run out and been granted anew; but this I could not fully accomplish without assistance from the managers of the bridge affairs. Two of these gentlemen, a feoffee and one of the wardens, gave their full sanction to my having the blanks filled up by the collector of the rents. This individual, very properly perhaps, wished to have the consent of some other of the feoffees; he made application, but I soon learnt that *he was interdicted from supplying the required information*. Were I not quite satisfied that the bridge accounts are now correctly kept, and the fund not misappropriated, this very circum would have raised my suspicions; what can make any one individual feoffee wish to keep *the amount of the bridge rental a secret*, I am wholly at a loss to imagine, but some reason there must of course be. Whichever of the trustees objected, he acted *upon principle* doubtless! I had previously obtained many of the requisite particulars, and have since procured more; I am thus enabled, in spite of the prohibition, to furnish a *correct* though somewhat incomplete statement of one portion of the town property.

† This house was pulled down for the purpose of building the meat market, but the rent is still paid

LESSEE OR TENANT.	PROPERTY	RENT.		TERM ENDS	
		l.	*s.*		
John Pyke	Back House and Garden	1	0	Michs.	1847
C.E. Palmer	Garden in Cross Street				
Wm. Mullins	2 Houses and Garden				
	in Joy Street	8	8	Michs.	1839
George Tyte	House in Joy Street	6	12	Christmas	1858
Jane Blake	House in Tuly Lane	7	0	Yearly Tenant	
J. Rattenbury	Ditto	6	0	Ditto	
George Roue	Ditto	3	0	Ditto	
John Marshall	Garden and Stable	1	10	Michs.	1850
John Dennis	House and 2 Gardens	3	0	Lady-day.	1839
William Reed ⎱					
J. Fairchild ⎰	House in Tuly Lane	12	0	Yearly Tenants	
John Roue	Ditto	8	0	Ditto	
J. Dennis, jun.	House and Garden				
	in Litchdon	3	13	Michas.	1850
Robert Jewell	House in Diamond St.	5	0	Lady-day.	1847
G. Hill	House in Maiden Street	2	2	Lady-day.	1837
——Jordan	House in Well Street	10	0	Death of lessee	
J. Greenslade	House in Anchor Lane				
John Isaac	House at Newport	4	0	25th Oct.,	1849
Wm. Marquiss	2 Fields at Rumsum				
James Whyte	Ground whereon a				
	house stood, Pilton*	0	18	Lady-day.	1881
James Ford	Barnstaple Parks,				
	Burrington	3	0	Lady-day.	1875
H. Saunders	House and Garden				
	Combmartin	2	0	Yearly Tenant	
	7 Houses in Boutport†			In hand	
	Rent Char. (v. charities)	0	10		

---

* This property has long been incorporated with the Lawn attached to Pilton House, and cannot now be traced; in consequence of which a new lease was granted in 1821, at the old rent.

†Seven small tenements, called in the rental "Bridge Row," but popularly known as the "Seven Drunkards." Two or three of the houses are let, but as the whole are shortly to be pulled down and rebuilt, I have not included the property in the rental.

CHAPTER VII.

Chronological Record of Events relative to Barnstaple

Notwithstanding the considerable portion of matter already given, which comes properly under this head, this chapter might have been made much longer than it is. I had materials for many sheets more prepared for the press, but the extent to which the work has already reached, (originally intended to comprise six sheets, but swollen to nearly forty,) forbids my printing it. It may well be supposed that during the long period this work has been going through the press, some occurrences have transpired which it is desirable should be recorded, these with some other additions and corrections will be given, headed by the articles to which they refer.

878. The Danes effect a landing at the mouth of the Taw.*

* The following is the account I have met with of this interesting event :– " Ubbo, who, with his brothers Inguar and Halfden, had conducted the fatal fleet to England, to avenge the death of their father, and who had distinguished himself in the massacre at Peterborough, and who was now the only survivor of those children of Regnar Lodgrog, who had afflicted England, had been harrassing the Britons in South Wales, where he had wintered. After much of that slaughter, which always attended their invasions, he returned with twenty-three ships to the English Channel. Sailing by the North of Devonshire, the Castle of Kynwith attracted his notice, where many of the King's Thegns had embraced the protection of the Earl of Devon. The place was unprovided with subsistences. It had no stronger fortification than a Saxon wall: but Ubbo found that its rocky situation made it impregnable against all assault except at the eastern point. He also remarked that no water was near it, and consequently that a short siege would reduce the inhabitants to every misery of thirst and famine. He preferred, therefore, the certain victory of a blockade to a bloody attack, and surrounded it with his followers. Odun saw the extent of his distress, and the inevitable certainty on which the Pagans calculated, and determined on a vigorous sally. It was bravely executed. While the dawn was mingling with the darkness, Odun pierced at once to the tent of Ubbo, slew him and his attendants, and turning on the affrighted host, destroyed the largest part; a few reached their vessels and escaped. An immense booty rewarded the victors, among which, the capture of their magical standard, the famous Reafan, was to the eye of ignorant superstition, a more fatal disaster than even Ubbo's death and their own defeat."

(Note.) " The Saxon Chronicle makes the number of the slain 840. Flor. Wig. 1,200, p. 316. Asser

437

1167. "A collection made here [impost] of 2*d*. in the pound, towards the succour of the east christians, against the Turks."

1281. For writ of quo warranto referred to from page 12, see No. 1, appendix A, to chapter 3.

Pilton Bridge.†– "3rd Jany., 1451. Bishop Lacey "granted forty days' indulgence to those penitents who should contribute to the bridge and causeway between Pilton and Barnstaple."

1537 "Quindesima. [Quintadecima, pars understood.] Memorandn, [made by 'Jonas Baker, marchant,' in 1634,] that it appears by an ancient quittance bearing date the 13th of Octr., in the 29 yeare of the raigne of King Henry the 8th, that Edward fford, then the Kinges collector of tenthes & ffifteens, did recieve of John Goddisland, then one of the constables of the towne of Barnest, the some of 13*ld*. 14*s*. for one fifteenth & tenth, as by the acquittance of the said collector under his hand & seale appeereth."

Priory.— 1490 "The accumpte of svch monish has hathe byne

"describes the raven as a banner woven by Ubbo's three sisters, the daughters of Ragnar Lodgrog, in one noon-tide. It was believed that the bird appeared as if flying when the Danes were to conquer, but was motionless when they were to be defeated."— *Turner's History of the Ang. Saxons,*
Vol. 2, page 79-80.

The important consequences which resulted from this victory are well known. A rough slab of rock, lying on the Beach at Appledore, still marks the spot where Ubbo was said to have been buried. It is called Hubbastone or Hubblestone.

Thomas Hogg, Esq. of Appledore, has placed in the corridor of his house, (which he denominates Odun Hall,) a Tablet with the following Inscription, in reference to this event:– "This Tablet is to perpetuate the Memory of the victory over the Danes, who in the reign of King Alfred, the Saxon Monarch, landed with thirty-three sail of ships at Appledore, in this County, and were valiantly repulsed by Odun and the Men of Devon, with the loss of their chieftain Huba, and of their invincible standard the Reafan. The Reader, whose imagination kindles at the recital of such scenes as have been dignified by heroic actions cannot but be gratified at the contemplation of this decisive triumph and bold achievement of a small but determined band of heroes, which memorable event led immediately to the expulsion of a ferocious host of invaders, the restoration of the immortal Alfred to his Throne, the establishment of trial by Jury, that polity and those institutions which laid the foundation of the Liberty, the Greatness, and the Glory of our Country."

†This memorandum, (which I had mislaid when the article "Bridges" was written,) was kindly furnished by the individual who extracted it from theBishop's Register.Was not this the first formation of the Bridge and Causeway?

The following notices relative to Pilton (from the same source) may not be unacceptable:-

" Bishop Bronscombe dedicated Pilton Church, October 1259."

" A Recluse within St. Agnes Chapel, Pilton Churchyard, is mentioned by Bishop Grandison, see 2 Reg. fol. 152."

" A Fair was granted to Pilton, 18 Edw. 3rd."

" Charity of St. Leonard, Pilton, 1374, is mentioned, fol. 31 vol. 2. Bp. Brantyngham's Register."

"payde bye the conuent of St. Mary Magdelene, of Barnestaple, for the funerale of . . . . . . .Pryor of the sayde conuent as vpon . . . . remayneth thysse xij dey of Seypt. 1490. "

"Imps. Wee have payede ovt the sume of xiv. viiij. vj. fore byldynge hys seypultvre, & fore markin yse tumb.   yse xiv. vii. vj.

"Item. Mure wee have payede toe the pryorey of Pyltone, and to the munckes ther to prey for hys sole.   yse v^{ld}.

"Item. Mure wee have payede fore hys cuffyn &c. the sume of ivld. & to they chauntrye of Synt Anne, viij. viijd.   yse iv viij.

"Item. Mure we have gyven away thee pure of the Paroche of Barnstapoll, yn the churche of synte Petrus ther on Svndey last.
      yse ij.iiij.iiij.

1555, Feby. 2, "Robt Thorn, late Prior, certified that the tenants of the house of Magdalene paid the Quindecim [Quintadecima]."

1586, Feby. 7. "My Lord of Bath & Mr. H. Acland, justices, sat here at this towne, for the direction of corne to be brought to this market, and for the maintenance of the poor within their own pshes, and none to go abroad, so that somme of ev'y psh appointed to view barnes and mows, and to take a note what store of corn their was, and what people were in such houses as had corne to spare, and allowing ev'y pson a peck a weke, to certify the overplus to the said justices, but what good this order will do the comon . . . . . . buyers of corne, many stand in doubt, because now corne being deare, viz. wheate at viij^s. the bushel, the feare this order may make it dearer, as it did last yere."

Chapels and Chantries.— "A house at the High Cross, late the Jolly Butcher, is described in a deed 39 Eliz. as being " bounded on the north by *the chanterie of Saint George the Martyr*."

1587. "Corne is very deare, wheate sold for viij^s. rye for vi$s$., barly for iiij per bshel."

" About this time [whitsuntide] commandmt given that the beacons sh^d be recdified & diligently watched day and night, and that posthorses sh^d be p'vided in ev'y town, and that ev'y p'son should p'vide in rediness his armour.

" Very high fflood in September, wind at W."

" On St. Luke's day this yere, there was a trental of sermons at Pylton, so that divers, as well men as women, rode and went

" thither; they called it an exercise of holy faste, and there some offered, as they did when they went on pilgrimage. And the like was kept at Sherwill, to the admira'con [admiration] of all p'testants."

" Little or no raine hath fallen for vi or viij weeks, whereby more dearthe & scarcity is to be lookt for."

" May. cccc bushels of rye arrived, not above lxxx b^{ls} sold; wheate rose next market day to ix^s., girts vi viij, barley vi viij."

" June. cccccc b^{ls} of rye at the pcurement of some of this town were brought here, whereby wheat fell from x^s a bushel to viij^s vi^d., which rye was sold for vi^s a bushel."

" August. Wheat sold for ... , rye ij^s. viij, barley i^s. ii^d., by reason of the plenty of new corne."

" Lord Bath & the Countess his wyfe dyned at the new Mr. Maior; the women this yeare were not bidden, wherefore there was *much chatteringe among them.*"

" Mr. Hugh Fortescue and Mr. Robert Dillon kept their christmas here, belike for saving of charges, &c."

" Wheat sold for iij^s. vi^d., barley ij. ij, oats xiij."

1588. "Fine weather in March; wheat sold for ij viij, barley xx^d., rye xxii, oats xi, a xii gallons."

" 110 fat oxen in the market one day, the like never seen before, on friday before easter."

" Victuals & grayne very plenty, best beef 1^d. per pound, wheat iij^s., rye and barley xviij^d. per bl."

" Wheate sold for ij^s. iv^d., rye xx^d, oats xi^d., barley xvi^d."

" Much afraid of a Spanish invasion."

" Octr. Continual rayne, wheate rose to iiij^s. v^d."

1589. "Order from L^d. Bath to the Conbles of Braunton Hundred to p'vide vc bushels of wheate, & so much butter and cheese conveniently to be got in H. of Braunton, to be sent after Sr. F. Drake's ffleet."

March. "Great pvision making for holding the Assizes in this towne."

" The places for the Judges to sit in, one against the Keyhall, and the other by the North end of Mr. Collibear's house, both covered with reede."

" There come hither but 1 judge, L^d. Anderson; he came to town the monday in the afternoon, to the keyhall place there, (where he sat all the assizes,) read the commission, charged the grand jury, & adjourned."

" The tuesday the Judge, L^d. Bath, & other Gent., dined with Mr. Maior."

" Martyne, the goaler, kept some of his prison^rs in house late Bailiffs in this towne, and others in Castle Green, under tyltes with sayles."

" Judge lodged at Mr. Dodderidge's.— Sheriff, at Mawdlene,— Serjt Drue, at Gill. Harris.— Serjt Glandyl at Roger Cade's.— Serjt Harrys, at Mr. W. Collibear's.— Mr. Heale, at Mr. Welche's house."

" Rest of the lawyers well accomodated elsewhere."

" Tuesday, sat on nisi prius."

" Wednesday by 5 o'clock, the judge tried ii or iii causes of nisi prius, and then upon the goal, continued the wednesday and gave judgement upon those who were to be executed."

" Friday and saturday sat on nisi prius & ended."

" The gibbet was set up on the Castle Green, and xviii prisoners hanged, whereof iiij of Plymouth, for a murder.*

" Wheat vis. viijd. victuals dearer."

" A pickard laden with barley malt from the fforeste arrived, to sell for iij^s. the bl."

" July. 8 ships sailed over our bar for Rochelle."

" Divers have cut corn before St. James's day."

" Harvest ended in many places before midst of August."

" March. Victuals about this time very dear."

---

* "The execution is corroborated by the Parish Register.
" Here ffolloweth the names of them Prysoners wch were Buryed in the Church yearde of Barnistaple ye syce [assize] week :–   March, 1590.
"John Parrett, Buryed the xv^th of marche [dyed]
George Strongewithe, Buryed the xx^th daye.
Thomas Stone, Buryed the xx^th daye.
Robart Preidyox, Buryed the xx daye.
Vlalya Payge, Buryed at Byshope tawton ye xx^th daye.
John Bante, of Chagfoorde, the same daye.
John Starkeye, of exon, the same daye.
Edwarde Langdon, of Hunshew, the same daye.
Willyam Goalde, a Prysoner, Buryed ye xix^th daye [dyed]."

" About whitsontide, xix nobles [6*l*. 6*s*. 8*d*.] was given for a heifer that had new calf."

" Plague of pestilence at South Molton and Torrington."

" Watchmen continually to prevent suspected folks of the plague, from coming into town."

" Mr. Maior hath taken great pains and travayle to p'serve this towne from infection of the plague."

" Great store of sider this yere, wch maketh caske deare, a hoxede is sold for iij^s. & a pipe for vi^s."

" Corn is somewhat reasonable; I bought wheat for ij^s. viij^d."

1593. "iiij subsidies and vi fifteenths granted by parliament to be paid her Majty with [query, within] iij yeares."

" Rain and violent winds every day in March; the shyppyng co^d not go to Newfoudland or Rochelle, or those at Rochelle come home."

" Because of the long drieth this yeare, people from Hartland came to Rayleigh [Rawleigh, distant from Hartland 22 miles] and Bideford mills with griests."

" Sir John St. Leger, & other Justices of this north division, met about rating the subsidy."

" I subsidy & ii quindecims to be paid out of hand."

Church.— 1593. "The first set of chimes appear to have been put up in November this year."

" The chayms now going, wch coste besides the bell that was had before xxv*l*., a great charge to small effect."

1594. "Price of corne near at one price. Wheat about v^s.; barley & rye iij^s. ij the bushel; ots xviij."

" Pclamation publishd forbydding the wearing of daggs or pistolles."

" All the brewsters and tiplers of ale within the H. of Braunton & Sherwell app^d at Barn before Mr. Dyllon & Mr. Ackland, justices, & bound by recogn to keep good rule, &c."

" Francis Hawkins was hung in chains at Highbickington, for the murder of a Cornishman, a sailor."

" Wheat a vii^s. vi."

1595. " By reason of rayn and foul weather, wheat is ix^s. a b^l.

" xxx of August. L^d. Bpp came to town, was met in Southgate

442

"Street by the Maior and Maisters in their scarlet gowns; a skoler made a speech; afterwards the Bp dined with Mr. Maior; he confirmed divs children at the Castle Green; on the 2d day such a multitude came in from the country that he co$d$ scarce pass the street; on a sudden he turned up Crock Street [Cross Street] & went to his lodgings, and went out of towne almost for thence; the people lamented they had lost a fine harvest day."

" 28 Novr. E. of Bath, Mr. Pollard, Mr. Carey, Mr. Abbot, justices, sat at the Guildhall, where they had calld all the Con$bles$ of the Nth Division, to give notice to those that were sett to arms, to be in readyness, and that the billes sh$d$ be changed into pykes, and the bows and arryws into muskitts and calyvers."

1596. " 3 May. A sessions held at the Guildhall, the first after the new charter, & the first ever kept in the town."

" In the beginning of this month, May, divers salt petre makers with commission to enter into houses & places to dig and delve up the earth to make the peter, and do make salt peter thereof, and clear salt, they take the earth dug up, and cast water thereunto, and so standeth a certain tyme; then they let the water out of the tubb, and by a certain tyme after boyl the same in a great furnace a long tyme; then they take it out, and put in small vessels to cowle, and thereof cometh the salt petre and salt." *

" All this May hath not been a dry day and night."

" Wheat at xs., rye at vii, barley at vi, ots a ij iiij."

" June. Continual rains. Wheat a xi$s$., barley vii$s$. iiij."

" August. By reason of the continual rain there is great leare of all sorts of corn, but little comes to market."

" Wheat xi$s$, rye & barley viii, oats ii$s$. iiii$d$., whereupon letters sent from the Counsel, to Earl of Bath, he with other justices came to town, viewed the market, and sat the price upon corn there,

---

* This was an odd practice enough, but in 1627, "A proclamation by King Charles stated the practice of making saltpetre in England, by digging up the floors of dwelling houses, dove houses, stables, &c. tended too much to the grievance of his subjects," and that, a patent having been granted to two individuals for making saltpetre by a new process, "the King therefore commands all his subjects of London, Westminster, &c. near to the place where the said patentees have already erected a work for the making of saltpetre, that after notice given them respectively, they carefully keep in proper vessels all human urine, throughout the year, and also as much of that of beasts as can be saved, for the patentees to carry away from time to time." – Fæd. Vol. 18, p. 813.

" (to wit) wheat ix^s., rye vi^s., Barley v^d., oats ij^s, threatening the seller with dures, [imprisonment] if he sold for above that price."

" Same day pclamation made wch did concerne the rats [rates] and taxations of servants waigs, made by the justices of peace for this borough of Barnestaple, &c."

" Small quantite of corn brought to market; townsmen cannot have corn for money."

" Upon letters to Mr. Maior of this town from Mr. Norrys & Mr. Martyn, in London, mentioning the dearth and scarcity of rye & price thereof, that noless than a whole shipp's quantity was to be had, conteyning vij hundred quarters. Mr. Maior & his brethren had a meeting thereon, who debated, but upon the wyllyngness of Mr. Nicholas Downe & John Delbridge, they were all wylling to pcure a whole shipp's lading, (would cost xiij hundred pounds,) divers consented to lend x^{lb}. wch extended to xii hundred pounds. George Stanbury of this towne was appointed to travayl to London to assist Mr. Norrys in obtaining this corne; God speed him well that he may p'cure some corne for the inhabitants of this towne in this time of scarcity; that there is but little cometh to the market, and such snatching and catchying for that little, and such a cry that the like was never heard. People which do want seede do pay xii shilling for a bushel of wheat, and much ado to geate it."

" Not a dry day in November."

" Only barley brought to towne, and snatched up presently."

" 300 soldiers in the town to go to Ireland."

" Many of the gentlemen shed their light horses and petronnels [a small gun used by horsemen] in this town, before the Earl of Bath and Mr. Lewes Pollard, their captayne."

" Intelligence from Norrys and Stanbury, that they had bought a quantity of rye, and that the justices of peace having set a price upon corne now gave leave to the country to sell at large, hoping the market w^d be thereupon supplied; but there cometh less & less, & they aske xv^s. a b^l. for wheat, & commonly sell for xii & vi, & viii for barley."

" Continual rain day and night."

1597, 8 April. "Wheat sold xviij a b^l, barley xiij, rye xiiij, ots iiij."

" 10 June. Wheat sold for xviij, barley for xiij, rye for xv^s. p b^l."

" Arrived three shipes that were sent from hence to Dantsick for rye."

" Now in July by reason of continual raine, wheate sold last fryday for xxs. a bushel.

" Richd. Symons, Mr of Arts, was admytted skolemr [schoolmaster] & the other Symons was put out."

" Corn is fallen, wheat viij, rye vis, barley 5, ots xxiid."

" In innocents week, the Maior with many of his brethn went to Youlston, to visit Mr. Robart Chichester, and carryed unto him some good hansel, they did the same to Mr. Basset's , and also to Tawstock."

1599, "2 April. Mr. Robart Chichester, Lord of this town, beying advertysed of some injuries done him by this town, came hither with Mr. Hugh Wyott, Lawyer & counseller, and the counsel of this town compromised the varyance."

1599. "xxix May. One John Symons, a petie skolemaster of this towne, not very hardly witted, but one of the anabaptistical and precise brethren, had a child brought to the church to be christend, & called it Dorwell; the vicar dislyking it calld it John, which caused a great murmuring among the brethren, who said it came from the Hebrew word Abdeel."*

" A better harvest never heard of than this."

" Wheat iijs, barley ijs. vid."

" Earl of Bath, Mr. Fortescue, & Mr. Hugh Ackland, sat concerning rating of the subsidy."

" Wheat iij iijd., rye ij viid., barley ij iiijd."

1600. "Monday the xix day of Maye, the new kaye upon the Strand, almost in the midst of the other kay, was begun to be buylded."

" This yere, at the request of Sir Robert Bassett, one Sharland, a musician was retaind by Mr. Mayor & his brethren to go about the town about iiij o'clock in the morning with his waits, & is promis'd viijl., began on All Saints Day and to continue till Candlemas."

---

* Philip Wyet here exemplifies in his own person the close connexion betwixt bigotry and ignorance. An anabaptist having his infant child baptised!!!
This was no doubt " the other Symons who was put out" for being a dissenter!

" Mr. Richard Smyth, the hired preacher of this towne, & J^o Smyth, preacher of Pylton, were inhibited to preach in this Diocess, by reason they w^d not wear the surplice."

1601. "Wheat v iiij, rye iiij iiij, barley iiij viiij."

" xix day of December, at night, some of the castle wall was blown down and blown into the castle, and did no harme savyng some ij ravens were found dead, *and belike it sat withinside the wall.*"

" Smyth allow^d to preach again and did preach & adminyster the communion in his surplus as he was commanded."

" Corne continued this yeare nere one rate."

1602. "Assizes at Exeter hold in March. The Lord Chief Baron sent to the common goal Mr. Giles Risdon and Mr. William Burgoyne, being recusants, there to remayne at his pleasure; if they had rather go to gaol than to church, much good might it doe them, I am not of theyr mynde."

" Wheat holdeth up at viij^s. viij^d. a bushel, rye at vi^s. iij^d., barley v^s., ots xxij^d."

1603. 23 Feby. Pclamation published concerning election of Knyghts of the Shire and Burgesses of Parliament, that they should be *grave men*, of good worth and fit for the place."

1604. "This October the deputy of his Majesty's Clerk of the Market came about this county, and made lesse all bushels, pecks, and half-pecks, by the third part after Winchester bushel, countenanced by the Justice of the Peace, to the great admiration of many & is thought to be a great grief."

" The plague entered into this countye."

" And so now our Clerk of the Market, being Henry Downe, followeth the like fashion within this Towne."

1605. "About the middle of this month of August, the Earl of Bath or Sir. Ro. Chichester, Sir Henry Rolle, & Mr. Hugh Ackland, sat in the Guildhall, by virtue of certain orders from the Councell, to meet about alehouses, drunkers, recustants, &c.— *a great cry and little wool.*"

" In ye yere of o^r Lord God 1607, in Janiarij, the ryver of Barnistaple was so frozen*, that manye hundred people did

*Wyot mentions this frost, and says it continued five weeks.

446

walke over hande in hand, and from the Bridge unto the Castell Rock wth staves in their hands, as safe as they could goe on the drye grounde. — Robt. Langdon, clarke, at Barum."

" Wheat ix iij, rye vij, barley vi; by reason of sharp cold winter hay sold for viij & ixs. a truss, many cattle died for want of fodder."

" 20th April. The spire on the Key hal was finished."

" 25 May. Mr. Maior recd letter by a pursuivant from the counsell, for appoynting a stage post from this town to Chumleigh, and a poste barke to carry any packet sent hether from my Lord Treasurer into the province of Munster in Ireland."

1609. "Itm. more it appears by a nother acquittance, bearing date the 24th daye of August, in the 7th yeare of the raigne of King James, was received for his Maties ayde, by the rolle of compossicon in the countie of Devon, of the feoffees of the towne of Barnestaple, the some of 20s."— [Jonas Baker, 1634.]

1628. "12th July. A rate agreed on for defraying cost of trained bands."

1631. "6 Decr. Plague at Bordeaux; ordered that all ships coming from thence to this port land no goods for 14 days, penalty 8 days imprisonment."

1633. "Agreed that 20l. be raised toward charges of suppressing Turkish pyrates."

" Composition made for hanging out candles at every man's door."

" There was collected in this towne in the tyme of Mr. Ricd. Ferris his maioraltie, by vertue of a commission from the Lordes of his Maties Privie Counsell, for the repairing of Paul's Church in London, the some of viild. wch was paid vnto Mr. James Welsh one of the Commissioners, 7ld."

1634. "Itm. more there was collected in the year 1634, by the like Comission from the Lordes, for the repairing of Paul's church, and in the maioralty of Mr. John Delbridge, the some of viijld. vs. vd. which was delivered unto Mr. James Welsh, by Mr. Henry Mason, cunstable, as per acquittance appeereth, 8ld. 05s. 05d."

1646. "April. The great plague."

" The great sickness begun in May; 1500 dyed; Mr. John Downe, then Mayor.

"Dyed at Pilton, of the plague, 269." *

1647. "—— Harris took the vane from the Chapple at Litchdon Almshouse, & placd it on the Keyhal."

1650. "10th Oct. Great fear of the plague; the 3 houses at the Fort to be fitted up as a pest house."

1654. "5th Jan. A sum of money raised to free inhabitants from charge of keeping Col. Games company of horse at free quarters."

1658. "Thomas Davy, a tallow chandler, made Towne Clerke."

1676 "In December, the frost was so great that the ouldest man then living did never knowe the like, for it was so hard frozen that many were faine for to rost there meate for to eat it, because the could not gitt watter for to boyle the pot.— John Sloly, Clarke of Barnestaple."

* These brief notices, with the information that the writer of the first and his "family went to remayn at Rookebear in July," and retornd into his own habitation, at Barnestaple, in December, and that the Mayor was elected in the open air without the town," is the sum total of all that I find recorded respecting the effects of this awful visitation in Barnstaple; the Parochial Register, as I have already observed, is quite silent on the subject. There is, however, an interesting account given of the effects of the distemper in four brothers, who lived at a very short distance from the town, and which was perpetuated to a period within my own recollection, by a monumental inscription :—

" To the memory of our foure sweete Sonnes, John, Josh, Thos, & Richd, who were
immaturely taken from us altogether by Divine Providence, are here interred,
the seventeenth day of Augvst, 1646.

" Good and greate God, to thee we do resigne
Our four deare sonnes, for they were chiefly thine,
And, Lord we were not worthy of the name
to be the sonnes of faithful Abrahame,
Hade we not learnt for they just pleasure's sake,
To yield our all as he his Isaacke.
Reader, perhaps thou knewest this field, but ah!
Tis now become another Machphelahe.
What, then this honour it doth crave the more,
Never such seeds were sowne therein before!
Which shall revive, and Christ his angels warne,
To bear this triumph to his heavenly Barne.
In hac spe acquiscunt parentes mutissimi, Joseph & Agne Ley."

Tradition says that the four brothers were fishing on the Banks of the Taw, from whence they drew some rugs which had floated up the river, and thus became infected with the plague, the pestilence having been brought to Bideford from the Levant, and thence spread over the neighbourhood.

Seven elm trees mark the hallowed spot of the sepulture of the brethren, (hallowed it should have been, but the materials were removed during the life time of the late proprietor of the estate on which it stands, and, it is said, used in forming a drain!). There is little doubt but that the trees were planted by the parents of the children about the time of their interment; they are but a short distance from the upper Bank, which, by the way, goes by the name of "The *Seven* Brethren Bank."

1677. "February. Mrs. Richord Roshit, widdow, was buried the 19th day; and she gave me 20th shillings upon her will for a legasay, and I have receavd it. And I would wish that all good Christians that are to be buried in Barnestaple, that the would doe the same to mee as this woman did, if the be abell.— John Sloly, Clarke of the Parish."

1706. September. Eight persons, five males and three females, recorded in the register of burials to have been drowned.

1727. From this year (the first in which I find any mention made of transports) to 1757, 19 persons were transported, viz. in 1727, 1. —1728, 1. —1730, 2. —1738, 2 (1 for 14 years) —1740, 3. —1748. 1. —1750, 3. —1751, 1. —1752, 1. —1754, 1. —1757, 4. This last year there were 15 indictments.

1746. "April. A mob of persons assembled together & broke open three granaries, viz. at the North Gate, Mrs. Parminter's house on the Strand, & the New Works, & took therefrom great quantities of corn. The principal persons concerned in this riot were Mrs. Andrews, a breeches maker, (stiled Captain, who headed the mob and beat up a frying pan with a poker round the town,) David Toms, (stiled her Lieut.) Wm. Bale, Wells Metherell." (See appendix [B.] of Chapter V .)

1757. "June 7. Swarm of bees on Queen Ann's statute, shook into a hive for the use of the Mayor."

1768. "In the centre of Joy Street, Barnstaple, grew a large elm tree,* which was felled on the 7th day of June, by order of the Mayor, Richard Thorne, Esq."

Walks.— 1795, 14th June. Henry Gardiner Tippets, of Barnstaple, Surgeon, by will of this date, gave " to the Mayor, Aldermen, and Capital Burgesses, of the Borough of Barnstaple, and their successors, yearly, so long as the Mayor, Aldermen, and Capital Burgesses, shall permit the Walk, known by the name of the North Walk, or North Parade, within the said borough, to be used as a public walk and no longer, the sum of three pounds, to be applied towards the finishing and keeping in repair the said Walk." The amount is left as a rent-charge on *Hole Ground*, in this parish, now the property of the Rev. Henry Nicholls.

* The corn market is said to have been formerly held here, the bags being pitched under the tree.

1795. "Thursday Oct. 29. Tide flowed over "Tawstock Bank, Cooney Causeway, Square Wall, & in the kitchen of the Golden Lion, and there rose so high as to put out the fire."

1799. "Feby. 10. In the evening sailed from this port the Weazle, sloop of war, Hon Captn. Grey; she had been for a considerable time stationed at Appledore. After her getting over the bar, a tempest gathered rapidly, and the devoted ship perished that night, and with her a crew of 105 persons, and a woman. One of the ship's company had been providentially for him left on shore when she sailed. The event left an impression beyond the ordinary tone of remembrance in cases of shipwreck."

> " The tale is briefly told :– the gallant bark
> Embayed, and by the tempest overtaken,
> When midnight heavens were glooming pitchy dark
> And wave and shore by the loud storm were shaken,
> Drove upon *Baggy's rocky leap* – and hark!
> The seaman's cry, that never more shall waken
> Echo for mirth or woe;– down– down she goes,
> And for her fate a long lament arose."
>
> *Log of the sea-Minstrel*

1800. "In May and June, wheat sold for 1l 3s. and 1l. 4s. per bushel, by John Budd, Esquire, of Willsley, in Landkey; barley at 14s., by Mr. W. Chappell, of Penhill; beef 10d.; mutton, from 7$\frac{1}{2}d$. to 8d. per pound; potatoes, at 1s. 6d. the peck. In August, oats at 5s. 3d. per bushel; butter, 1s. per pound."

1810–11. "A new road made thro' the Long Closes, and the Vicarage road stopped up."

1814. "Peace proclaimed, 30th June. On the thanksgiving day, an illumination. A public dinner for tradesmen, in Boutport Street, and for the poor on the Square. One Nicholas Purchase went to the top of the church steeple in a state of intoxication, threw off his waistcoat which was picked up on High Street, and came down unhurt."

Markets.— Meat market opened at Christmas, 1814, instead of 1812. The foundation laid 29th September, 1813.

1815. Bell's School opened at Midsummer. Now (1831) contains 55 boys, 52 girls. Supported by voluntary contribution.

1817.   "At the Devon Easter Sessions, an indictment preferred against the parish of Barnstaple, by Mr. S. Bremridge, woolstapler, for not repairing certain parts of Barbican and Sowden Lanes," was tried, and a verdict found for defendants, thereby fixing the liability of the repairs on the occupiers of the adjoining lands.   This indictment cost the parish upwards of 100*l*. *

Free Burgesses.— 1824. Sept. 24. F. Hodgson, Esq. presented to the freemen three elegant Wedgewood china jugs, one containing three, and the others two gallons.   On each side of the jugs appears the town arms, with the inscription " Sigillum ad arma pro maiore et corporacione ville Barum," and in front,   " From Frederick Hodgson, M.P. to his brother freemen, as a small token of grateful regard."

1825.   Tuesday, July 19.   Hottest day ever remembered here; thermometer at 99.   Several large fish, supposed grampusses, came up with the evening tide as far as the bridge.   They were seen in the river below Penhill on the following morning, in considerable numbers ploughing their rapid way towards the channel.

1827.   April 30.   "Ordered that the general sessions for this borough and parish, be held four times in the year." †

Sunday, July 22.   Her present most gracious Majesty Queen Adelaide, then Duchess of Clarence, and suite, arrived at Barnstaple, at 6 p.m. on her way to Ilfracombe, to embark for Milford Haven.

Same evening came in from Bristol, the Lady Rodney Steam Packet, the first steam vessel that ever came over the bar.   Sailed on the following morning for Lundy Island, with a party.

Sept. 23.   First mail coach arrived in Barnstaple; letter-bags first brought by mail Sept. 24.

1829.   January 12.   Appledore passage boat upset in a squall off Strand Houses, all who were in her, the owner, Oatway, his son, and three other persons drowned.   A similar accident is not known ever to have occurred.

* The then opening talent of the late Master of the Rolls, Baron Gifford, was displayed on this trial, he having been retained for the defendants. He received *four guineas* with his brief.   A few years afterwards he was a peer of England, and a presiding judge of the highest tribunal in the realm.

† I was in error in stating, previously, that this measure was decided on in October, 1826.

Representative History.— 1830. August. Stephen Lyne Stephens, and George Tudor, Esquire, elected Members of Parliament for Barnstaple; there was another candidate, Sir Colin Campbell. The numbers at the close of the poll were, Stephens 370; Tudor 332; Campbell 246. Many voters did not come forward; the number polled was 522.*

Charities. †— 1830. John Roberts, Esq. who died in November this year, left by will, invested in trustees, 500*l.* four per cent. annuities, upon trust, to distribute the dividends thereof among the inhabitants of the various almshouses in this town; and 60*l.* to the Blue Coat Charity School.

Municipal Body.— Two members of the Common Council, John Roberts, and Charles Besly Gribble, Esquires, have, since the list of Corporators was printed paid the debt of nature. Their successors are not yet appointed.

Up to this time (March 17th, 1831) nothing more has transpired relative to the point at issue betwixt the capital and common burgesses, alluded to previously.

---

* This election was a remakable – nay an extraordinary – one in many respects. To notice one or two particulars;— the " Third Man " was procured, brought forward, and supported by the Body Corporate!! A military band paraded the streets of the town during the poll, with a card in their hats on which was printed " Campbell, the Third Man," and playing " the Campbells are coming." In the ardour of oppositon a considerable sum of money was expended on account of the third man, before it was ascertained who was to stand in the gap, and certain individuals of a certain body are said to " have paid too dear for their whistles," by a thousand pounds or so.

† I have been charged by Philip Bremridge, Esq. with "a false, scandalous, and atrocious libel," alleged to be contained in the first part of this work, (see Appendix to Chapter 11 [H] *Appley's Gift* page 129). To avoid a prosecution, I was called upon to make "a suitable" (which on enquiry I found meant a *public*) apology; strong in my own integrity, I disdained any such compromise, but made the following proposal through Mr. Bremridge's professional agent, which I place on record here, lest the charge should be revived when I am, as I expect shortly to be, locally, (as I certainly feel I now am *legally*,) beyond the reach of British jurisdiction. " Barnstaple, May 8, 1830. If it can be shewn that I have in the first part of the Memorials of Barnstaple, inadvertently made an incorrect statement respecting the charity termed Appley's gift, *I shall most willingly correct such error in the second part of the work, which is shortly to appear.*" Ten months have now elapsed, but no means have been afforded me of fulfilling this pledge! The correspondence that took place on this subject, elicited from Mr. Bremridge the acknowledgement that the corporation had "NO RIGHT WHATEVER TO GRANT A LEASE AT ALL!!" — *The date 1663 at p.130 should have been 1633.*

CONCLUDING ADDRESS

The wisest of men said in his day, that there was "no new thing under the sun;" but it is, perhaps, something new for an individual to complete a history of his native town, in the full prospect of quitting it and his country for ever; yet such is my case. Ere another month has elapsed, I shall have bidden farewell to England, and the winds, if providence permit, will be wafting me across the wide Atlantic. I go, however, with the proud consciousness that I have not compromised my character, either by leaving my task unfinished, as some few of my subscribers allowed themselves after the publication of the first part of the volume to believe would be the case, or by failing to redeem the pledge given in the prefatory address, fearlessly to pursue the historian's only legitimate course — the highway of impartiality.

Some apology is due to my subscribers for a delay of some months beyond the time stipulated for the completion of the work; the great additional quantity of letter-press in the second part will be taken as some excuse, and for the rest it belongs rather to the printer than to the author to cry *peccavi*; I will, however, be content to bear a portion of the blame, and crave pardon for both.

I have now first ventured to assume for my humble work the title of a history, which looking at the extent to which it has reached and the topics it embraces, I may perhaps do, without subjecting myself to the charge of egotism; not however that I am satisfied with what I have done, far, very far from it; on the contrary, I see in it numberless imperfections; they however are of less importance than inaccuracies, which last I hope, and venture to believe, are comparatively few. That I should have escaped them altogether is hardly to be expected, notwithstanding the pains I have taken to avoid them; but this much I can say, my anxiety after correct information has been unceasing, and my exertions to obtain it unwearied.

I feel very reluctant to close this address without naming the individuals to whose kindness I have become indebted during the progress of the work; but so multifarious have been my enquiries, and so numerous the persons who have either rendered me assistance or assayed to do it with courtesy and good will, that from a conviction of the almost impossibility of my calling to mind all who have rendered me service in this way, I must content myself with tendering to each and every one, to whom I am thus a debtor, my best thanks. One service of a particular kind must not pass without a special acknowledgement, namely the gratuitous presentation of a draught of the plan of the town, by Mr. Robert Mortimer. I now bid subscribers, friends, and contributors, a respectful farewell!

Barum, March 18*th*, 1831

INDEX

TO

MEMORIALS
OF
BARNSTAPLE

This index created © 1994 Lazarus Publishing Co. (EDWARD GASKELL)
6 Grenville Street
BIDEFORD
DEVON

Index

2

4

14

William Rufus, 8
William the Conqueror, 6, 8, 17, 351
William the Third, 173
Williams, John, 213
Willis, Brown, 33
Willis, Timothy Harding, 366
Willow Plot, 97
Willsley, 450
Wilson, Richard, 174, 176, 177
Wimborne, 365
Winchester, 30
Wineauldon, John, 169
Winkleigh, 420
Winnock, Ralph, 168
Winstanley, Joseph, 353
Witheridge, 420
Withy Close, 87, 88
Wiveliscombe, 424
Wode, Richard, 170
Wolley Down, 66
Wolston, John, 170
Wonston, Alured, 170
Wood, William, 332
Woodford Thellusson, G., 174
Woodrooffe, James, 155
Woodrough, James, 215
Woollacot, Mr, 366
Woollacott, William, 145
Woolston, John, 170

Worcester, 30
Workhouse, 239
Worth, Paul, 106, 155, 288
Worth, Roger, 154, 303, 400
Worthe, Robert, 171
Wortley, Edward, 349
Wrey, Sir Bourchier, 174, 186
Wright, Charles, 63, 157, 229, 385
Wright, John, 110, 372
Wrothe, Roger, 278
Wyat, Nicholas, 215
Wyatt, Adam, 106, 107
Wychalls, Nicholas, 278
Wydesdale, John, 170
Wylemer, Ralph, 168
Wynemere, Ralph, 168
Wynemor, Ralph, 151
Wynnomere, Ralph, 168
Wyot, 31, 36, 38
Wyot's Register, 205
Wyot, George, 312
Wyot, Peter, 314
Wyot, Philip, 222, 394, 402, 403, 424, 445
Wyott, Hugh, 445
Wyott, Philip, 221
Wyott, Phillip, 14
Wythyrydge, Richard, 400

Y

Yabbeton, Thomas, 168
Yarnscombe, 349
Yarum, 1
Yelland, 73, 74
Yeo, 395, 404
Yeo, of Clifton, 90
Yeo, Walter, 151
Yeolands, 99
Yeotown, 395
Yeotown Lodge, 389
Yong, John, 348
York, 30
Youlston, 176, 445
Youlstone, 124

Z

Zachary, William, 413

READER'S NOTES